Medicine of the Highest Order

The University of Rochester at its Centennial

Medicine of the Highest Order

The University of Rochester at its Centennial

Advancing Health, Enriching Lives

Mark B. Taubman, MD
with Leo Brideau and Teri D'Agostino

Meliora Press
An imprint of the University of Rochester Press

First published 2026

Meliora Press is an imprint of the University of Rochester Press
www.urpress.com
and Boydell & Brewer Limited
www.boydellandbrewer.com

Our Authorised Representative for product safety in the EU is
Easy Access System Europe – Mustamäe tee 50, 10621 Tallinn, Estonia,
gpsr.requests@easproject.com

ISBN-13: 978-1-64825-173-3 (hardback)
ISBN-13: 978-1-64825-174-0 (paperback)

Library of Congress Cataloging-in-Publication Data

Cataloging-in-publication data available from the Library of Congress

Typeset by BBR Design, UK

CONTENTS

E. Primary Care and the Community

F. Building State-of-the-Art Specialties

II. MAINTAINING URMC'S LEADERSHIP IN EDUCATION

G. School of Medicine and Dentistry Divisions

III. BUILDING MULTIDISCIPLINARY PROGRAMS OF EXCELLENCE

H. Enhancing Collaborative Research

I. Cancer

J. Neurosciences and the Del Monte Neuroscience Institute

K. Immunology and Infectious Diseases

V. MODERNIZING OPERATIONS TO SUPPORT GROWTH

VI. CONFRONTING THE COVID-19 PANDEMIC

VII. EPILOGUE

VIII. NOTES ON CONTRIBUTORS

ACKNOWLEDGEMENT

In 2003, I was recruited to Rochester by Bradford Berk to serve as chief of the Cardiology division at the University of Rochester. Thus began an unanticipated journey that ultimately led me to become dean of the School of Medicine and Dentistry and chief executive officer (CEO) of the University of Rochester Medical Center (URMC). Over my twenty-three years at the Medical Center, I have been privileged to help further the story of an academic medical center founded 100 years ago on a bold new idea. I have been blessed to work in an unusually open and collaborative environment with wonderful faculty, staff, and learners who very much live the University's motto, *Meliora!*

I thank my editors and co-authors, Teri D'Agostino and Leo Brideau, who helped make this ambitious undertaking a reality. Both played important roles in the history of URMC and were invaluable to the writing of this book. I would particularly like to acknowledge the critical role Teri played as my chief of staff while I served as both dean and CEO. I would also like to acknowledge Ellen Caruso, who served for fifteen years as my executive assistant and whose warmth and friendliness set the perfect tone.

I am grateful to the leaders of the University and Medical Center for their support of my career and for having had faith in my ability to rise to each challenge presented. In particular, I acknowledge fellow vascular biologist and close friend, Brad Berk, the only person who could have persuaded an inveterate "downstate" New Yorker to move to Rochester. Brad's journey from chief of Cardiology to URMC CEO was similar to mine, but his courage and resilience in overcoming a life-altering bicycling accident inspired the entire community. I owe a great debt to URMC CEO Jay Stein, not only for having played a role in my recruitment, but for his audacious vision of what a great academic medical center should look like in the twenty-first century. The story this book relates is of the remarkable growth in URMC, in size, stature, and importance to NY State over the past twenty-five years, which would likely have been very different without Jay Stein.

I would like to thank University President Joel Seligman for his faith in appointing me as dean of the School of Medicine and Dentistry and URMC CEO and for his collegiality and support during the many years we worked together. I appreciate University President Sarah Mangelsdorf for her support and her willingness, as a newcomer to the University, to undertake two of the most ambitious construction projects in the University's history. I would also like to extend my thanks to University Board of Trustee members and Medical School alumni, Philip Pizzo and Edward Miller, and to Arthur Rubenstein, who served as personal advisors during my tenures as dean and CEO and whose support was critical to the success of the Medical Center's strategic plans.

This book chronicles URMC's achievements during the first quarter of the 21st century and will serve as a snapshot of the Medical Center on its one hundredth anniversary. These achievements were the work of the extraordinary faculty, staff, learners, and the Board volunteers who drove us. In particular, the institution has been blessed with many wonderful deans, department chairs, center directors, researchers, educators, and clinicians whose accomplishments are described in detail in the book. The growth and development of the UR Medicine network also owes much thanks to a number of skilled and foresighted administrators who shepherded the institution over the quarter century. Together, these leaders are the reason we remain a leader in education, research, and clinical medicine.

Many people contributed information and critical reviews of the chapters in this book, including current and former chairs and center directors, deans, and hospital administrators. The following is a list of all of the contributors. Although I have attempted to be comprehensive, I apologize to any whose contributions have been inadvertently unacknowledged.

Sincerely,

Mark B. Taubman, MD

Adams, Jamie L.
Alfieris, George M.
Anolik, Adam P.
Anolik, Jennifer H.
Apostolakos, Michael J.
Baumhauer, Judith F.
Beckerman, Jackie
Benesch, Curtis G.
Bennett, Nancy M.
Berk, Bradford C.
Berliant, Marc N.
Bohjanen, Paul R.
Boyce, Irena
Burke, Christine
Burton, Richard I.
Bushinsky, David A.
Bushnell, Timothy P.
Caine, Eric D.
Campbell, Thomas L.
Carpizo, Darren R.
Chen, Leway
Chen, Stacie B.
Chen, Yuhchyau
Clinton, Morrison
Constine, Louis S. (Sandy)
Conwell, Yeates
DeFranco, Micheline
Denney-Koelsch, Erin M.
Dewey, Cynthia
Dewhurst, Steve

DiLoreto, David A.
Dirksen, Robert T.
Dozier, Ann M.
Eaton, Michael P.
Eliav, Eli
Evarts, C. McCollister
Fahy, Michael P.
Feldon, Steven E.
Fogarty, Colleen T.
Fong, Chin-To
Forrester, James
Friedberg, Jonathan W.
Gallucci, Kathleen
George, Amy
Gestring, Mark L.
Goldstein, Steven I.
Haas, Curtis E.
Halterman, Jill S.
Hammes, Stephen R.
Harvey, Jennifer A.
Hasselberg, Michael
Hayes, Jeffrey J.
Hazard, Michael
Heatwole, Chad R.
Hernandez-Alejandro, Roberto
Hines, Victoria
Holloway, Robert G.
Hopkin, Justin L.
Ilan, Goldenberg
Johnson, Joseph A.
Johnson, Wallace E.
Joseph, Jean V.
Józefowicz, Ralph F.
Kamali, Michael F.
Kitko, Lisa A.
Knight, Peter A.
Lambert, David R.
Land, Hartmut K.
Lang, Valerie J.
Lawrence, B. Paige
Lee, Hochang B. (Ben)
Levin, Alex V.
Levstik, Mark A.
Levy, Paul C.
Libby, Richard T.
Linehan, David C.
Ling, Frederick S.
Looney, R. John
Lyness, Jeffrey M.
Maniocci, Lorrie
Maquat, Lynne E.
McAleavey, Stephen
McAnarney, Elizabeth R.
McCann, Robert M.
McCormick, Gaelen
McCullough, Sharon
Medina-Walpole, Annette
Messing, Edward M.
Metzler, Nancy
Meyerowitz, Cyril
Mikols, Gerard
Mitten, David J.
Morgan, Adrienne
Morrell, Craig
Mossman, Tim R.
Nelson, Lisa
Newlands, Shawn D.
O'Banion, M. Kerry
Ockenden, Mary I.
O'Regan, Ruth M.
Panzer, Robert J.
Parrinello, Kathleen
Patel, Rajeev K.
Pentland, Alice P.
Peyre, Sarah E.
Pilcher, Webster H.
Powell, Jerry
Pressman, Eva K.
Raynor, Jennifer P.
Ritchlin, Christopher T.
Rivera, M. Patricia
Robbins, Brett W.

Robert, Jacques
Robinson, Peter G.
Rooney, S. Craig
Rosero, Spencer Z.
Ross, Lainie Friedman
Rotondo, Michael F.
Rubery, Paul T.
Schwarz, Edward M.
Scofield, Steven M.
Shinaman, Aileen
Singh, Renu
Smoller, Bruce
Stein, Jay H.
Stoner, Michael C.
Strawderman, Robert L.
Tarolli, Christopher G.
Temple, Larissa
Utell, Mark J.
Van Wijngaarden, Edwin
Waldman, David L.
Walton, Mary Pat
Waugh, Richard E.
Whitney-Miller, Christa L.
Williams, Edith M.
Williamson, Nora
Wilson, Karen M.
Wolfanger, Lorie
Wyatt, Jeffrey

ABBREVIATIONS

AAAS	American Association for the Advancement of Science
AAMC	Association of American Medical Colleges
ACGME	Accreditation Council for Graduate Medical Education
AHP	Accountable Health Partners
AI	Artificial Intelligence
APPs	Advanced Practice Provider
CDC	Centers for Disease Control and Prevention
CEO	Chief Executive Officer
CFO	Chief Financial Officer
CMO	Chief Medical Officer
CNS	Central Nervous System
COO	Chief Operating Officer
COPD	Chronic Obstructive Pulmonary Disease
CPEP	Comprehensive Psychiatric Emergency Program
CT	Computed Tomography
CTSA	Clinical and Translational Science Award
CTSI	Clinical and Translational Science Institute
CVRI	Cardiovascular Research Institute
DOM	Department of Medicine
ED	Emergency Department
EEG	Electroencephalogram
EIOH	Eastman Institute of Oral Health
FDA	Food and Drug Administration
FLH	Finger Lakes Health
FTE	Full-Time Equivalent
GCH	Golisano Children's Hospital
HH	Highland Hospital
HIV	Human Immunodeficiency Virus
HRSA	Health Resources and Services Administration
ICU	Intensive Care Unit
IDD	Intellectual and Developmental Disabilities
IT	Information Technology
KMRB	Kornberg Medical Research Building
MIT	Massachusetts Institute of Technology

MRI	Magnetic Resonance Imaging
MSKCC	Memorial Sloan-Kettering Cancer Center
MSTP	Medical Scientist Training Program
NCI	National Cancer Institute
NIH	National Institutes of Health
NP	Nurse Practitioner
NSF	National Science Foundation
NYU	New York University
Ob/Gyn	Obstetrics and Gynecology
OR	Operating Room
PA	Physician Assistant
PCN	Primary Care Network
PCORI	Patient Centered Outcomes Research Institute
PCP	Primary Care Provider
PGY	Postgraduate Year
PI	Principal Investigator
RGH	Rochester General Hospital
RIT	Rochester Institute of Technology
RRH	Rochester Regional Health
SAD	Senior Associate Dean
SJFU	St. John Fisher University
SMD	School of Medicine and Dentistry
SMH	Strong Memorial Hospital
SON	School of Nursing
SUNY	State University of New York
UCLA	University of California, Los Angeles
UCSF	University of California, San Francisco
URMC	University of Rochester Medical Center
URMFG	University of Rochester Medical Faculty Group
WCC	Wilmot Cancer Center
WCI	Wilmot Cancer Institute
VP	Vice President

Chapter 1

INTRODUCTION

This academic year (2025–2026), the University of Rochester Medical Center (URMC) will experience its one hundredth anniversary, over which time it has established itself as one of the premier research-intensive academic medical centers in the country and one of the largest private employers in NY State. There has been much to celebrate throughout its illustrious history as a pathfinder in health education, a leader in clinical and basic research, and an innovator in medical therapeutics and diagnostics.

The focus of this book is on the last twenty-five years of the Medical Center, a period of substantial growth in all of its missions. The clinical enterprise grew from a single hospital with a small ambulatory program and a budget of approximately $400 million to a regional powerhouse with eight hospitals and a large outpatient footprint and a budget of $6.7 billion. The research enterprise experienced extraordinary growth, which included substantial increases in extramural funding, the establishment of many nationally prominent research centers, and the construction of three new research buildings. The educational enterprise also expanded, with the development of new programs and new facilities. It is hard to do justice to all of these accomplishments and to the people responsible for them, even limiting the book to the last twenty-five to thirty years. Fortunately, the birth and early history of URMC have been beautifully chronicled in a number of publications.[1]

Although every era in the history of URMC has been marked by changing external forces, the past twenty-five years have witnessed exceptionally rapid and accelerating changes that required a rethinking of how best to preserve and strengthen the Medical Center's three-part mission of education, research, and patient care. Through the successful implementation of creative

1 Corner, George W. *George Hoyt Whipple and His Friends: The Life-story of a Nobel Prize Pathologist.* Philadelphia, Pennsylvania: J. B. Lippincott Company, 1963; Whipple, ed. *The First Decade: 1926–1936*; Fenn, Wallace, ed. *The First Quarter Century: 1925–1950*; Romano, John, ed. *To Each His Farthest Star*; Cohen, Jules and Joynt, Robert J., eds. *The University of Rochester Medical Center: Teaching, Discovering, Caring.* University of Rochester Press, 2000.

responses to these challenges, URMC has strengthened its long-term viability and appears well positioned to face the challenges of the next quarter century.

In 1950, as URMC celebrated its first twenty-five years, the cost of health care was not a great concern. Health care spending comprised only four percent of the nation's gross domestic product (GDP). By the time of its seventy-fifth anniversary, health care spending had markedly increased, exceeding thirteen percent of GDP, and there were dire predictions that unless one could "bend the curve," it would rapidly exceed twenty percent, limiting the ability of the country to support other programs. By URMC's one hundredth anniversary, health care had grown from a small cottage industry to the nation's largest employer and spending was already at eighteen percent of GDP, its single largest component.

As with every health system in the US, URMC was faced with the challenge of controlling the cost of health care while improving quality and access to care. This was best articulated in the concept of the Triple Aim, introduced in 2007 by the Institute for Healthcare Improvement (IHI). The three components of the Triple Aim were: to improve the patient experience, through measures such as patient satisfaction, access to care and quality of care; to improve the health of the population, by reducing chronic disease rates, improving life expectancy, and increasing preventive care; and to reduce the per capita cost of health care.

Governmental pressure was brought to bear through Medicare and Medicaid payments that fell increasingly short of covering the actual cost of care. In addition, both government and employers (through insurance companies) began the implementation of "value-based" purchasing programs that shifted some of the financial risk to health care providers by establishing rewards and penalties based on quality and efficiency. The institution of value-based purchasing was thought to be the beginning of what many envisioned would be a complete shift from fee-for-service reimbursement to one in which health care systems were paid to care for a population through *per capita* reimbursement. This shift in reimbursement would not only place a "cap" on health care reimbursement but would incentivize programs to focus on prevention and optimal treatment of chronic diseases rather than on high-cost procedures, the "profit centers" of a fee-for-service environment.

The prospect of a capitated system would also drive the development of large and competitive health care systems that could manage a large cadre of basically healthy people at relatively low cost, ensuring that these systems had the funds to continue to provide expensive, state-of-the-art procedures for those in need. These large health systems would also have the scale to provide high-end specialty services, the hallmark of major academic medical centers, whereas smaller systems had neither the volume nor the financial resources to continue to support such services. In Rochester, these factors led in 1997 to the merger of Park Ridge and St. Mary's Hospitals to form the Unity Health System, resulting in the closing of acute hospital services at St. Mary's. Also in 1997, Highland Hospital (HH) became the first affiliate of URMC. In 2001, Genesee Hospital closed its doors after merging with Rochester General Hospital (RGH) and in 2014, Unity merged with RGH to become Rochester Regional Health (RRH). The upshot was that Rochester went from five independent acute hospitals to two hospital systems, both of which developed additional affiliations throughout Western NY. The development of two competitive health care systems also had a significant effect on the educational environment in Rochester, with most medical student and residency training being phased out of RRH affiliates and being shifted to HH and more recently to FF Thompson Hospital.

Key to the development of large systems capable of managing more than one million lives was the development of robust ambulatory practices involving physicians and advanced patient providers (APPs) who were employed by or tightly affiliated with the system. Changes in technology vastly increased the numbers of patients that could be treated in outpatient settings, further driving the development of ambulatory programs.

Although URMC, like most academic medical centers, had always prided itself on the quality of care it provided, national data showed that the American health system had great room for improvement. As patients became more consumer oriented, they also increasingly challenged health care providers to improve both the quality of care and the patient experience. Twenty-five years ago, twenty percent of Americans lacked any health insurance coverage. Through the Affordable Care Act, which went into effect in 2014, that figure has been cut nearly in half to approximately eleven percent. But the lack of health insurance is not the only barrier to adequate access to needed care. Rural communities face severe shortages of health care services. In addition, many rural residents lack access to private transportation and public transportation is often spotty. Language and cultural barriers also impede appropriate access to care.

In response to these challenges, the Medical Center launched a number of major initiatives. These will be discussed in detail in subsequent chapters.

1. URMC moved beyond being principally a provider of highly specialized acute care to building the full continuum of health services, enabling better coordination of care and reducing fragmentation. This initiative included the establishment of a large, robust primary care network (PCN) within the faculty practice, acquiring nursing homes and an assisted living facility, and by the development

of a robust Urgent Care program, which now includes fifteen centers throughout the region.

2. Addressing the overall shift towards ambulatory care, URMC established ambulatory facilities throughout the region, including major outpatient campuses in Brighton and Brockport, and constructed new buildings for ambulatory surgery, imaging, and orthopaedics.
3. URMC strengthened the quality of and access to health care in rural communities by incorporating six rural hospitals into its health care system and recruiting scores of highly qualified doctors and APPs to these communities and linking them to their respective departments at the Medical Center. This not only enhanced the scope and quality of health care in these communities, but in several instances, saved these hospitals from closing. To better reflect its complexity and extent throughout Western NY, the health care system was rebranded as UR Medicine.
4. Concomitant with the development of the PCN, URMC greatly expanded its involvement in the community with the growth of the Family Medicine Program, the development of a variety of specialized programs, the establishment of the Center for Community Health and Prevention, and the opening of behavioral health and complex care buildings in the inner city.
5. To respond best to the growth of value-based purchasing, the University of Rochester Medical Faculty Group (URMFG) was established as an integrated group practice with a robust shared governance committee structure that would lead numerous initiatives, including the development of a uniform compensation plan, the growth of ambulatory and digital services, and drive changes in quality and access. This allowed for the creation of joint operating committees involving URMFG and Strong Memorial Hospital (SMH) to oversee clinical services lines. It also enabled the development of a fully integrated URMC budget, allowing for better fiscal management of all three URMC missions.
6. URMC led the creation of Accountable Health Partners (AHP), a care management and contracting entity that now includes thirteen hospitals and more than 2,400 physicians, including community hospitals, SMH, URMFG and community physicians. AHP's $2 billion worth of contracts cover more than 500,000 patients.
7. URMC adopted modern technology to improve the coordination of care and access to its specialized services. As of November 2026, all hospitals and providers will be on eRecord, the state-of-the-art information system that allows all UR Medicine providers and sites

to access patient records. It also gives patients full access to their medical records, allowing them to see test results, send messages to their providers and book appointments online. Patients' access to providers was greatly enhanced through the ready availability of telemedicine visits. Highly specialized care was made more readily available to rural hospitals through telemedicine consults and services such as telestroke.

8. To reduce overhead costs, URMC exploited the expanded the scale of its health system to centralize administrative and support services. By 2025, laboratory services, pharmacy, materials management, engineering, and information technology had largely been centralized, saving considerable cost and upgrading the quality and safety of these services.
9. SMH was a pioneer in the mid-1980s in applying to health care the principles of continuous quality improvement, a concept previously used only in manufacturing. SMH was one of eight hospitals nationwide that participated in a proof-of-concept demonstration project funded by the Robert Wood Johnson Foundation and led by Donald Berwick, MD. That project launched SMH's journey in continuous quality improvement and evolved into the IHI, of which SMH was a founding member. During the past twenty-five years these efforts have blossomed, ultimately leading to the development of the Quality Institute at URMC.

Chapter 2

MEDICAL CENTER LEADERSHIP

To best deal with the changing landscape of academic medicine, the Medical Center evolved to a more integrated leadership structure, taking advantage of its ownership by the University of Rochester. This chapter provides brief biographies of those who led the transformation. The biography of David C. Linehan, MD, who transformed the department of Surgery and who became URMC chief executive officer (CEO) and dean of the School of Medicine and Dentistry (SMD) in 2024, is presented in the chapter on Surgery (p. 139).

Jay H. Stein, MD, senior VP and provost of the University of Oklahoma Health Sciences Center, Oklahoma City since 1992, became VP and vice provost for health affairs at the University of Rochester and CEO of URMC in August 1995. In a new model for the university, the medical and nursing school deans reported to him, as well as the hospital's general director/CEO and the director of the medical faculty group. Stein reported directly to the University president and to the University Provost for academic matters. Stein received his MD from the University of Tennessee (Memphis), did a residency in internal medicine at the State University of Iowa Hospital, Iowa City, and a fellowship in nephrology at the University of Texas Southwestern Medical School. From 1975 to 1992, Stein had been at the University of Texas Health Science Center at San Antonio, where he had served as chief of the division of Renal Diseases and for fifteen years as chair of the department of Medicine (DOM). There, he developed an international reputation for his work on disorders of sodium and potassium balance, and the pathophysiology of acute renal failure. He was the editor-in-chief of *Internal Medicine*; editor of the textbook series *Contemporary Issues in Nephrology*; and editor-in-chief of the journal *Focus & Opinion: Internal Medicine.*

Figure 2.1. Jay Stein

Stein served as a change agent for URMC, whose status as a major research institution was declining and needed agility in a rapidly changing health care environment. Upon arriving in Rochester, he undertook a comprehensive strategic planning process that addressed the impediments to the growth of the research, education, and patient care missions. Among his most lasting accomplishments were a major expansion of the research programs, including construction of two new research buildings and recruitment of dozens of leading scientists; initiation of a regional health care system, including a PCN and the incorporation of HH. Equally consequential was the movement towards an integrated medical center with the creation of URMFG, the development of a central billing office, and the establishment of centralized services, including the position of URMC chief financial officer (CFO). Stein also recruited many talented individuals who would go on to shape the three missions of the Medical Center over the next two decades.

Figure 2.2. C. McCollister Evarts

C. McCollister Evarts, MD, succeeded Stein as senior VP and vice provost for health affairs and CEO of URMC in June 2003. Evarts received his MD from the University of Rochester, where he remained for a residency in general surgery. After serving as a medical officer in the US Navy for two years, Evarts returned to Rochester for his residency and chief residency in Orthopaedic Surgery. Upon completion of his residency, he moved to the Cleveland Clinic, where he joined the Orthopaedic faculty, rising to department chair. Evarts returned to URMC in 1974 to become chair of Orthopaedics, a position he held until 1987, when he became CEO of the Milton S. Hershey Medical Center and dean of the College of Medicine at Pennsylvania State University. Evarts had a transforming effect as chair of Orthopaedics at URMC, establishing an academic component and building a research enterprise that brought the department to national prominence. Although he retired from Pennsylvania State in 2000, Evarts came out of retirement in the summer of 2003 to lead URMC.

Evarts continued the aggressive research agenda set by Stein, purchasing a facility on Bailey Road to house the Aab Cardiovascular Research Institute, supporting SMD's application for a Clinical Translational Science Award, and initiating the construction of a new research building to house the Clinical and Translational Science Institute (CTSI). Evarts also oversaw expansion of the outpatient services at Clinton Crossings; the growth of SMH, including the Kessler Burn and Trauma unit and additional observation beds; and the launch and growth of the Flaum Eye Institute. Importantly, he drove philanthropy and construction of the Wilmot Cancer Center (WCC). His tenure was also marked by growth at the School of Nursing (SON), with the addition of the Loretta Ford wing. Evarts was succeeded in 2007 by Bradford C. Berk, MD, PhD.

Figure 2.3. Bradford Berk

Berk, a Rochester native, is a graduate of the MD/PhD program at the University of Rochester, where he worked on microtubules in the laboratory of Patricia Hinkle (Physiology). He did a residency in internal medicine and a fellowship in cardiovascular diseases at the Brigham and Women's Hospital, where he remained as a faculty member, developing a program in vascular biology in the laboratory of R. Wayne Alexander, MD, PhD, who subsequently recruited him to Emory University. From Emory, Berk moved to the University of Washington, where he established a well-funded research program studying signal transduction in the vasculature, particularly in response to shear stress and oxidative stress. He was recruited back to Rochester by Jay Stein in 1998 to become Paul N. Yu Professor and chief of Cardiology and was then quickly promoted to Charles E. Dewey Professor and Chair of DOM, a position he held until 2006, when he became senior VP for Health Sciences and CEO of URMC. He also served as the founding director of the Aab Cardiovascular Research Institute (CVRI). Berk's accomplishments within Cardiology and Medicine are discussed elsewhere. In May 2009, Berk sustained a serious spinal cord injury as a result of a bicycle accident. Fortunately, he was able to return to full-time status in March 2010 and remained as URMC CEO and VP for Health Sciences until the end of 2014.

Berk initiated a comprehensive strategy to expand URMC's regional presence under the UR Medicine brand. This included affiliation with FF Thompson Health in Canandaigua, the establishment of Strong West in Brockport, and the initiation of plans to affiliate with hospitals in NY's southern tier. He oversaw the construction of the Ambulatory Surgical Center at Sawgrass, the Saunder's Research Building, and the addition of three floors to the WCI. He also oversaw the planning, philanthropy, and construction of Golisano Children's Hospital (GCH). Drawing from his experiences as a patient, Berk emphasized patient- and family-centered care as a guiding principle for the clinical programs throughout the UR Medicine network. He also expanded Stein's research strategic plan, creating Integrated Disease Programs that aligned the research with clinical and teaching missions and establishing the RNA Biology Center and Del Monte Neuroscience Institute.

Berk stepped down as CEO at the end of 2014 but has continued to work at the Aab CVRI as a cardiovascular investigator and to develop the University of Rochester Neurorestoration Institute. His experience recovering from spinal cord injury also prompted Berk to publish a book, *Getting Your Brain & Body Back: Everything You Need to Know after Spinal Cord Injury, Stroke, or Traumatic Injury* (Bradford C. Berk, MD, PhD. The Experiment, 2021), a comprehensive guide from injury to recovery for those who have experienced similar life-changing neurologic events.

Figure 2.4. Mark Taubman

Berk was succeeded as URMC CEO and senior VP for Health Sciences by Mark B. Taubman, MD. Taubman received his MD from NYU, where he was part of the Medical Scientist Training Program (MSTP). Like Berk, he did his residency in internal medicine and a fellowship in Cardiovascular Diseases at the Brigham and Women's Hospital, Boston, remaining as faculty in the Cardiology division. There, he developed a research program in vascular biology in the laboratory of Bernardo Nadal, Cardiology chair at Boston Children's Hospital. During their time at the Brigham and Women's Hospital, Taubman and Berk developed a collaborative program in vascular biology that continued to thrive after both investigators left Boston. Taubman subsequently joined the faculty at Mount Sinai School of Medicine, where he developed a well-funded internationally prominent research program focused on thrombosis and vascular inflammation. He directed the Cardiovascular Diseases fellowship and the MSTP. Taubman was recruited to the University of Rochester in 2003 by Berk to serve as Paul N. Yu Professor and chief of Cardiology and to join Berk in establishing the Aab CVRI. In 2007, he was appointed Charles E. Dewey Professor and Chair of DOM.

In May 2009, after Berk suffered his spinal cord injury, President Joel Seligman named Taubman as interim CEO of URMC, and upon Berk's return in March 2010, Taubman was appointed as dean of SMD. For the next five years, Berk and Taubman worked closely to restructure URMFG, expand the research strategic plan, and better integrate URMC finances in order to support the research mission. In succeeding Berk as CEO, Taubman continued in the role of dean, thereby consolidating both positions. This enabled Taubman to complete the financial integration of URMC and to markedly enhance the support of the academic missions. Taubman expanded on themes established during Berk's tenure, including further growing UR Medicine and promoting integrated research and clinical programs of excellence. He strengthened the relationship between SON and SMD, supporting the development of the Institute for Innovative Education and the expansion of Helen Wood Hall, and also supported the growth of Eastman Institute for Oral Health (EIOH). He completed the incorporation of three southern tier hospitals and oversaw the planning and construction of the Saunders Orthopaedics and Physical Performance Center and the planning of the new Emergency Department and Hospital

Tower. He also shepherded the Medical Center through the COVID-19 pandemic. In 2024, Taubman stepped down after fourteen years as dean and nine years as URMC CEO and has subsequently focused on writing this one hundredth anniversary book.

Part I

BUILDING A HEALTH CARE SYSTEM

A. *Creating a World Class Hospital Network*

Chapter 3

HISTORY OF STRONG MEMORIAL HOSPITAL AND THE SCHOOL OF MEDICINE AND DENTISTRY (SMD)

In 1910, Abraham Flexner, under the auspices of the Carnegie Foundation for the Advancement of Teaching, published a report on medical schools entitled *Medical Education in the United States and Canada* that led to a revolution in how medicine was taught across the country. The report made a series of recommendations based upon the experience of the Johns Hopkins medical school to improve the quality of physicians, which included: reducing the number of medical schools (from 155 to 31), increasing the prerequisites to enter medical school, training physicians to practice in a scientific manner and engage medical faculty in research, give medical schools control of clinical instruction in hospitals, hire trained, full-time staff for medical education, increase funding to medical schools, and strengthen state regulation of medical licensure.

In 1920, Flexner approached Rev. Benjamin Rush Rhees, president of the University, with the idea of establishing a medical school that would be based upon his ideals. Flexner and Rhees then approached George Eastman, founder of Eastman Kodak Company, to help support the building of a university, medical school, and hospital on land located on the southern boundaries of Rochester near the Genesee River. With $5 million from Eastman, $5 million from the General Education Board of the Rockefeller Foundation, and $1 million from the daughters of the late Henry Alvah Strong, former business partner to Eastman, the University was able to build a medical center on the site which was purchased between 1922 and 1923. That site also provided sufficient space to move the University of Rochester College for Men from its Prince Street location. The purchase of additional property in 1926 enabled the University to fully develop the River Campus in space adjacent to the new medical center.

The funds also enabled President Rhees to recruit George Hoyt Whipple, MD, from the University of California at San Francisco to become the first dean of SMD. Whipple had been inculcated with the principles of William Osler,

FRS, FRCP and the Johns Hopkins Medical School, where he had received his medical training and had been a faculty member. Hired in 1921, Dean Whipple helped shape the school from its inception, hiring faculty and staff and supervising the design and construction of the buildings. The plan for Strong Memorial Hospital was put into the hands of Nathaniel Faxon, MD, appointed hospital director by Dean Whipple, and Carl Schmidt, a Rochester architect. Although the overall principle was one of austerity, it was agreed that the entrance to the hospital and lobby should be warm and inviting.

The Medical School opened on September 17, 1925, with a class of twenty men and two women. The sixty-five faculty were hand-picked by Whipple. Many came from Johns Hopkins, earning the moniker "Johns Hopkins Country Club of Rochester" from George W. Corner, FRS, FRSE, the first professor of medicine at the University of Rochester. Faculty members engaged in their own research and were encouraged to include students. SMH opened its doors as a 250-bed facility on January 4, 1926. The first surgery was performed on January 7 and the first baby was delivered on January 14.

In 1923, the University sold part of the property from the proposed SMH site on Crittenden Boulevard to the city of Rochester for the construction of the 250-bed Rochester Municipal Hospital, which was connected to SMH and also opened in 1926. The University agreed to share the cost of operating the municipal hospital and to help staff it. In 1963, the University acquired the Rochester Municipal Hospital, which the city no longer wanted to run. This also provided the University with the necessary space to expand beyond five hundred beds. The "new SMH," which had the capacity for 697 beds,

Figure 3.1. The 1926 Strong Memorial Hospital

Figure 3.2. The 1975 Strong Memorial Hospital

opened on February 24, 1975, after many years of planning, labor disputes, and cost increases. The new building reoriented the entrance from Crittenden Boulevard to Elmwood Avenue. The *Rochester Democrat & Chronicle* commented on how quickly all patients were moved and highlighted the new modern technology in the hospital—the pneumatic tube system!

In 1985, a pre- and post-surgical unit, the ambulatory surgical center (ASC), was constructed next to the basement operating rooms (OR) for patients who would come in for surgery and go home the same day. By 1990, the ASC was working so well that it was expanded to enable virtually all elective surgical cases to be admitted on the morning of surgery, rather than the day before. The new Day of Surgery Admission Unit, adjacent to the ASC in the hospital basement, was considered very innovative and served as a model for many institutions.

SMH continued to grow to accommodate the needs of the community and region. By the early 1990s, SMH had expanded to 739 beds. Prior to 1996, all outpatient services at SMH were located in the 2100 tower on the Crittenden side of the hospital or scattered in a few miscellaneous areas in the old hospital. That year marked the opening of an expanded seven-story, 222,642 square-foot, state-of-the-art Ambulatory Care Facility (ACF) and adjacent parking garage. Tied to the project was a new William and Mildred Levine Lobby and front entrance. Two floors of the former 2100 tower were converted to research units. In 2001, an expanded ED tower was opened. Fourteen additional ORs were added on the basement level of the tower, adjacent to the 1975 OR suite. The old ED was subsequently renovated to

Figure 3.3. URMC in 1996

Figure 3.4. URMC with the addition of ACF, ED, WCC, and GCH

accommodate expanded cardiac catheterization and electrophysiology laboratories, which were becoming busier than ever as angioplasty, coronary artery stenting, and catheter ablations procedures grew. The site was convenient to the cardiac outpatient clinics and to the new ED.

Despite these expansions, demand for SMH services continued to outstrip capacity. This led to the construction of the five-story Wilmot Cancer Center (WCC) on Crittenden Boulevard in 2008 to house outpatient services, radiation oncology, and research, followed by a three-story inpatient extension in 2012. In 2015, the eight-story Golisano Children's Hospital (GCH) was constructed, connected to SMH and adjacent to the WCC. The move of patients to these new buildings—both of which remained under the SMH license—increased SMH bed capacity to 897 inpatients.

The new ED and expansion of inpatient beds have been insufficient to keep pace with the increasing demands brought about by the aging of the population, the growth of the UR Medicine network, the growth in high-end specialty services, many of which are only available at URMC, the closure or reduction of clinical services throughout western New York (e.g. The Genesee Hospital and St. Mary's Hospital), and the reduction of long-term care beds. This has resulted in significant overcrowding in the ED, peaking during the COVID-19 pandemic, and a hospital census that routinely exceeds 100 percent of licensed beds and can reach as high as 120 percent!

On September 8, 2023, the University broke ground on the 650,000 square-foot Strong Expansion project, which upon its completion will more than triple the size of the existing ED and add a nine-story inpatient tower—the most comprehensive modernization project since 1975. Not only will the project increase the number of inpatient beds, but units in the current patient tower will be renovated so that all patients will have modern, private rooms. Cardiovascular services are expected to be consolidated in the new tower to create one of the most advanced treatment facilities in the world for patients with heart disease.

The growth of SMH and its associated clinical enterprise owes much to a group of extraordinary hospital leaders.

Figure 3.5. Architect's rendering of the Strong Expansion project

Paul F. Griner

Figure 3.6. Paul Griner

Paul F. Griner, MD, served as CEO of SMH from 1984 until 1995. A graduate of Harvard College, Griner received his MD with honors from the University of Rochester SMD. After completing his residency in internal medicine at Massachusetts General Hospital, he spent three years in the Air Force at Andrews Air Force Hospital in Washington, DC, receiving the Air Force Commendation Medal upon discharge. He returned to the University of Rochester in 1964 as chief resident in internal medicine and then fellow in hematology, subsequently joining the faculty of the division of Hematology in the department of Medicine, where he was credited with being the first in the country to cure aplastic anemia in an adult with immunotherapy. In 1973, he became the inaugural Samuel E. Durand Professor of Medicine.

Griner became a national leader in health policy, publishing and lecturing extensively on improving the efficiency and effectiveness of clinical practice, the relationship between managerial and clinical decision-making in the hospital, and future directions in medicine. He was among the first physicians to study and report on the unnecessary use of costly medical facilities, tests, and technology and was a pioneer in the application of decision theory to improve the quality of care and reduce health care costs. In 1985, he was PI on a research project, *New Strategies for Cost-Effective Health Care Practices in Teaching Hospitals*; his co-PI was Loretta Ford, dean of SON. Their findings led them to recommend greater integration and partnership in care between physicians and nurses, and more discriminate use of tests and procedures. He was a consultant to the federal government during the Clinton administration, testifying before Congressional committees on universal health insurance. He also served as a consultant to the Institute for Healthcare Improvement in Cambridge, Massachussetts.

In 1984, Griner was named CEO at SMH. During his eleven-year tenure, SMH opened the ASC and earned designation as a NY State bone marrow transplant center. He also formed a task force, directed by chair of Surgery Seymour I. Schwartz, MD, to establish a liver transplant center at the University. The first transplant was performed in 1992. During his more than sixty-year career, Griner was president of three national medical organizations, a member of the NY State Governor's Health Care Advisory Board and was elected to the Institute of Medicine of the National Academy of Sciences. From 2011–15, he served as a member of the University of Rochester Board of Trustees, and subsequently as Trustee Emeritus.

During his multifaceted career at URMC, Griner was known for his principled leadership, his visionary approach to health care modernization, and most of all, for the compassion and careful attention he paid to each patient in his care. Griner died in June 2024 at age ninety-one.

Leo P. Brideau

Figure 3.7. Leo Brideau

Following Paul Griner's retirement in 1994 from his highly successful tenure as CEO of SMH, University President Thomas Jackson appointed Leo P. Brideau, MHA, FACHE, as general director and CEO of SMH. Brideau, a MHA graduate of the Medical College of Virginia, joined the Medical Center in 1980 as the deputy to James Bartlett, MD, Strong's chief medical officer. He served in that role until 1983, when he was appointed interim CEO of Strong upon the departure of Gennaro Vasile, PhD. When Griner was appointed CEO in 1984, he asked Brideau to serve as the chief operating officer of Strong.

In his tenure both as CEO and COO, Brideau oversaw the construction of the Ambulatory Care Facility project. He negotiated the entry of Highland Health System, the Visiting Nurse Service, and the Westfall Nursing Home (now Highlands at Brighton) into the University. In July 1997, Stein appointed him president and CEO of Strong Partners Health System, which included these new affiliates and sought to strengthen URMC's presence in the broader region. He was succeeded by Steven I. Goldstein, who Brideau had recruited to serve as COO of Strong.

During his tenure as CEO of SMH, Brideau oversaw a two-year, post-MBA or MHA administrative fellowship affiliated with Washington University in St. Louis, the University of Iowa and the Medical College of Virginia, which ultimately graduated fifteen fellows—including Kathy Parrinello, the current CEO of SMH and several other current and past leaders at URMC.

Brideau left the University in 2001 to accept a position as regional CEO for Ascension Health. After a thirteen-year stint with Ascension Health, Brideau returned in 2015 on a consulting basis to serve as a senior advisor to URMC leadership, a role he still plays today.

Steven I. Goldstein

Figure 3.8. Steven Goldstein

In 1997, Steven I. Goldstein, MHA, succeeded Brideau as CEO and president of SMH and HH, a role he would hold for twenty-seven years. Goldstein received his MHA from St. Louis University. He subsequently held executive leadership posts at the University of Nebraska's Psychiatric Institute and its hospitals and clinics, and The Children's Medical Center in Dayton where he ultimately served as acting president and CEO. As a seasoned health care administrator, he was recruited to Rochester to Greater Rochester Health System (now RRH), where he served as president and CEO of RGH and senior VP of the full network. He was recruited to SMH in 1996 by Brideau to serve as COO.

During his twenty-seven years as CEO of SMH and HH, Goldstein ensured the growth and success of both hospitals, conceptualized and completed capital improvements, helped to develop the primary care network, drove regional growth including the addition of six affiliate hospitals, managed UR Medicine's nursing homes and home care corporation, and helped to develop AHP. Since stepping away as CEO, Goldstein has continued to direct the strategic integration of UR Medicine and the financial turnaround of the affiliates.

Kathleen Parrinello

Figure 3.9. Kathleen Parrinello

Kathleen Parrinello, RN, PhD, FACHE, is a dual alumna of the University of Rochester, receiving her RN from SON and her PhD from the Warner School of Education. She joined URMC in 1975 as a clinical nurse on the surgical service at SMH, became nurse manager of the Cardiothoracic unit and then held several other nursing director roles at SMH. She subsequently spent a year as a clinician and educator at Rush Presbyterian Medical Center in Chicago, before returning to URMC in 1989 as the clinical chief for Surgical Nursing. In 1996, she was appointed senior director for Clinical Operations at SMH, and in 2000, she became its COO. As senior director and COO, Parrinello oversaw the construction of the 2001 ED tower and the new ICU floors, the WCC tower expansion and the GCH construction. She played a key role in the development and expansion of the urgent care program and in the establishment of the Strong West campus in Batavia. Parrinello was also instrumental in developing many of the offsite clinical programs that greatly expanded services throughout the region and were critical to the growth of UR Medicine. Importantly, she led SMH in developing the not-for-profit company known as the Finger Lakes Performing Provider System in partnership with RRH to manage the NYS Delivery System Reform Incentive Program that began in 2014 and has led to system-wide organization of programs to meet the needs of underserved individuals and promote health equity. In July 2024, Parrinello was appointed to the role of president and CEO of SMH and HH, roles vacated by Goldstein, who had served a remarkable twenty-seven years in that role. As CEO of SMH and HH, Parrinello continues to lead UR Medicine's two Monroe County hospitals.

Chapter 4

SMH NURSING AND THE CHIEF NURSING EXECUTIVE

Nursing at URMC has a storied history. Helen Wood, the first superintendent of SON in 1925, established the role as a joint position overseeing nursing education and research and the clinical nursing service at SMH. This was reinforced by Loretta Ford, the founder of the Unification Model, who was recruited in 1972 to be the first dean of an independent nursing school and the director of Clinical Nursing at SMH.

With the move into the new hospital in 1975, nursing practice became more specialized, with patient units designated as Ob/Gyn, Surgery, Medicine, Pediatrics, Emergency Department, Ambulatory and Psychiatry. Each service had a clinical nursing chief who worked closely with the chairs of the medical departments to manage patient care across the hospital. The complexity of the system required the appointment of a full-time chief nursing officer (CNO), Margaret Sovie, RN, PhD, who oversaw the clinical nursing chiefs and reported primarily to the CEO of SMH. The CNO and clinical nursing chiefs reported secondarily to the dean of SON as faculty in the School. Many of the teaching faculty also served as clinical nurse specialists at SMH.

Sovie, who left to be the CNO at the Hospital of the University of Pennsylvania in 1987, was succeeded by Anne Marie Brooks, who served as CNO for ten years. Brooks received a BS, MS, and PhD in Nursing from The Catholic University of America in Washington, DC and MBA from Loyola College of Maryland in Baltimore. During her tenure, nursing practice continued to grow as the clinical enterprise expanded.

Figure 4.1. Patricia Witzel

Following Brooks' departure in 1997, Patricia Witzel, RN, MS, MBA, was appointed as CNO. Witzel was a graduate of the University of Rochester, where she received her RN from SON and her MBA from the Simon School of Business. Witzel found herself amid a nursing unionization effort and—supported by SMH CEO Leo Brideau, SMH COO Steven Goldstein, and Senior Director for Hospital Operations Kathy Parrinello—immediately instituted measures to provide nursing with a greater voice. Key was the establishment of the Professional Nursing Council (PNC), a shared governance model that gives nursing staff a greater role in deciding how health care is provided at the bedside. Concomitant with the development of the PNC was a change in structure, making the CNO an associate VP of URMC who reported directly to the CEO of SMH. In keeping with the long tradition of partnership with the SON, Witzel was also appointed as assistant dean of clinical practice at the SON and worked closely with Dean Chiverton, providing a powerful force that advanced the SON and enhanced clinical services at SMH.

During Witzel's tenure, ambulatory nursing grew quickly onsite and offsite, beginning in 2001 with the relocation of outpatient Orthopaedics to Clinton Crossings. Nursing currently staffs more than 250 practice sites throughout the community and region. In 2004, SMH earned designation as a Magnet Hospital, identifying it as a hospital that was a "magnet" for nursing recruitment and retention and had achieved high standards in the areas of nursing care quality, safety, and patient experience. The Magnet Recognition Program was established in the 1990s in part based upon the pioneering work of Sovie, whose landmark study for the 1983 American Association of Nursing (AAN) Task Force on Nursing Practice delineated its criteria. In 2024, SMH earned Magnet Hospital designation for a fifth consecutive cycle; only one percent of US hospitals have achieved that designation in five consecutive review cycles.

The first acute care nurse practitioner (NP) to work in an inpatient setting was hired in cardiac surgery in 1978 to assist in surgery and to round on patients while the faculty and residents were busy in the OR. By 2006, more than 350 NPs were working at SMH. That year, under Witzel's leadership, the Margaret D. Sovie Center for Advanced Practice was established, supported by funds donated by Sovie's husband after her death, as a model professional organization to support advanced practice. Today the center, under the leadership of Cheryl A. Lustik, DNP, chief advanced practice officer, contains more than 1,000 NPs and physician assistants (PA)s working in various settings across URMC and its affiliates.

Witzel retired in 2017, after serving for twenty years as CNO and overseeing the remarkable expansion of nursing services. She had previously received the Distinguished Alumni Award from the SON and had been elected as a fellow of the National Academy of Practice.

Witzel was succeeded by Karen K. Davis, RN, MSN, PhD, who was recruited from the Johns Hopkins Health System, where she had served as VP and CNO at Howard County General Hospital, a Hopkins affiliate in Columbia, MD. In keeping with the development of the UR Medicine health system, Davis was given the title of chief nursing executive (CNE) with nursing oversight responsibilities for SMH (with a Nursing Department of more than 3,500 health care professionals), Highland Hospital, and affiliated hospitals. Like her predecessor, Davis, who had received her PhD from Johns Hopkins, also was appointed as assistant dean for clinical practice at the SON and associate VP for URMC.

Figure 4.2. Karen Davis

During her seven-year tenure as CNE, Davis confronted two remarkable challenges: the COVID-19 pandemic and the subsequent nationwide nursing shortage created by widespread retirements and the proliferation of "traveling" nurses. Added to these challenges was the need to enhance nursing services in our affiliates. Nursing played a key role in the successful URMC response to the pandemic, adapting to an inpatient census that reached as high as 120 percent of licensed beds. Davis also partnered with the SON to develop new programs designed to generate more nurses to address the workforce shortages. She skillfully navigated these challenges, while still pursuing the fifth consecutive Magnet Hospital designation for SMH.

Upon Davis's departure in 2024 to become CNO of Vanderbilt University Hospital, E. Katherine Valcin, RN, DNP, served as interim CNE and then in 2025—after a national search led by SON Dean Kitko—was chosen as permanent CNE and assistant dean of clinical practice in the SON. Valcin received a BS in Nursing at Roberts Wesleyan College, an MS in Nursing with a concentration in education at Duke University and a post master's certificate in clinical nurse leadership and a DNP from the University of Rochester. At URMC, she rose to clinical nurse educator and senior nurse manager of the MICU before taking the helm of adult critical care nursing in 2015. In 2023, she received national recognition as a Fellow of the American College of Critical Care Medicine, an honor that is usually reserved for MDs. She currently serves as president of the New York Organization for Nursing Leadership.

Chapter 5

PHARMACY

In chronicling the remarkable growth of URMC over the past twenty-five years, one would be remiss not to highlight the role of the department of Pharmacy under the leadership of Curtis E. Haas, PharmD, FCCP. Haas received his BS from Albany College of Pharmacy and completed his PharmD at the University at Buffalo School of Pharmacy and Pharmaceutical Sciences (UBSPPS). Prior to his recruitment to SMH in 2006 as chief pharmacy officer, Haas was a tenured associate professor at UBSPPS. Haas is an expert in critical care pharmacy and maintained an active teaching, practice and research career with numerous publications and national presentations in critical care therapeutics. He has served as a board member and past president of the American College of Clinical Pharmacy (ACCP) and has served on the Pharmacotherapy Specialty Council of the Board of Pharmacy Specialties.

Figure 5.1. Curtis Haas

At the time of Haas's arrival, URMC Pharmacy was a relatively small program that had little regional or national recognition for excellence. Clinical programs were limited and the few residents that trained at SMH were normally graduates of local schools of pharmacy. One exception was the Emergency Pharmacy program under Daniel Hays, PharmD, who pioneered the role of a clinical pharmacist in the ED and established one of the first two postgraduate education programs in emergency pharmacy in the US.

Under Haas's leadership, URMC's Pharmacy grew from seven clinical pharmacists (all acute care) and 273 employees in 2006 to eighty-four clinical pharmacists and 788 employees in 2025. Over half of these positions are now in the ambulatory environment. During that same period, combined drug spending rose from less than \$100 million to approximately \$800 million in 2025, reflecting the growth of infusion services and specialty pharmacy. In keeping with its remarkable growth, the Pharmacy has gained a national reputation for excellence in all aspects of health system pharmacy. In 2022, the department was recognized by Vizient with a Pharmacy Vision Award for Integrated Transformational Practice for demonstrating organizational excellence and success in driving supply chain improvement, quality and strategic growth.

On arrival, Haas developed a comprehensive strategic plan that has driven Pharmacy growth, excellence and innovation. One goal was to make SMH one of the most automated and technologically advanced acute care pharmacies in the US. This included the introduction of robotics that provide patient-specific, closed-loop packaging, storage, and dispensing of over six million doses per year with essentially no errors. This was accompanied by automated storage and retrieval technology, which revolutionized inventory management. Autonomous IV robotics and an automated workflow management system were introduced for sterile compounding, greatly improving quality and safety.

In September 2012, the New England Compounding Center (NECC), an "outsourcing" pharmacy that supplied hospitals with compounded pharmaceuticals, was responsible for a meningitis outbreak that resulted in the deaths of sixty-four people due to fungal contamination of corticosteroid injections intended for intrathecal use. At the time SMH, like all hospitals, worked with several outsourcing pharmacies (not including NECC) to source sterile compounded products. Spurred by this event, URMC launched a plan to develop its own capabilities, allowing us to control quality and eliminate our dependence on outsourcing pharmacies. In 2015, the department opened the Bailey Road Compounding Center (BRCC) clean room facility in Henrietta. A PhD-trained quality control specialist was hired to manage all aspects of the program, which now distributes sterile compounded products to all UR Medicine affiliates. To our knowledge, URMC is the only large academic medical center that has no dependence on outsourcing pharmacies. In addition to providing the highest-quality products, the BRCC also reduces costs: total savings for FY25 exceeded $9 million.

In 2019, Pharmacy opened a Consolidated Services Center (CSC) in Greece. The CSC, which is licensed as a pharmacy and drug wholesaler/distributor, houses four programs: a Shared Service Center (SSC) that manages inventory and drug distribution to over 300 clinic locations, a home infusion program, a compounding facility for regional infusion centers, and a storage and distribution center for home medical equipment program. The SSC centralizes inventory, reduces waste, allows compliant management of 340B inventory, and avoids mingling of acute care and ambulatory inventory.

Another major aspect of the Pharmacy strategic plan was the development of ambulatory programs. Retail pharmacy access at all hours of the day has been a major issue in Rochester. To address this, in 2018 the Sherwood I. Deutsch outpatient pharmacy in the lobby of SMH became a pharmacy that never closes. It has proven an overwhelming success and remains the only 24-hour pharmacy in Rochester. Of note, RRH and other community providers send their patients to SMH at night and on holidays to get prescriptions filled for urgent needs.

In 2008, an employee pharmacy program was established to provide a personalized source of pharmacy care for University employees. The program, which is used by about forty percent of University employees, provides out-of-pocket discounts on prescriptions and delivers them to all University locations or to employees' homes. Plans are underway to open a site in the outpatient pharmacy at SMH so that it can be accessed at all hours by all employees.

The Specialty Pharmacy program was launched in 2011, initially to provide complex therapies for University employees. Starting with two FTEs working out of a small office at the back of the employee pharmacy, it has grown to more than ninety FTEs and represents one of the largest health system-owned specialty pharmacies in the country. A major objective of the specialty pharmacy is to provide a patient-centered, high-quality clinical program that will lead to better outcomes. To that end, patients have easy access to a clinical pharmacist and a medication access specialist. In addition, we have embedded more than thirty-five specialty trained pharmacists throughout our specialty clinics. The specialty pharmacy team has published more than sixty manuscripts and abstracts demonstrating better patient outcomes, lower rates of adverse events, higher adherence, and less financial toxicity.

By 2020, it had become clear that "brick and mortar" was not the future of pharmacy fulfillment and that the University needed to take the lead in responding to this. In 2022, the department embarked on a "digital pharmacy" strategy, partnering with our primary care network to bring the pharmacy to the patient. This included embedding more pharmacy resources, including fourteen clinical pharmacists, within practices across primary care sites and establishing a call center to support patient outreach, clinical services, data entry management, etc. The success of this program has been striking, with increased capture rates from all practices in which it has been implemented and with volumes doubling to more than 120,000 prescriptions per month. The growth of our specialty pharmacy and digital pharmacy programs ultimately necessitated greater production space. In 2024, a "central fill" pharmacy was opened in Greece, to handle all specialty pharmacy orders.

The Pharmacy launched two programs in home care: home infusion—a collaboration with UR Medicine Home Care—and home medical equipment. The latter program focuses on respiratory care and collaborates with Sleep Medicine and Respiratory Therapy to provide in-home respiratory services, including CPAP, BIPAP, and most recently, home oxygen therapy. Together with Food and Nutrition Services and supported by certified clinical dieticians, the home medical equipment also provides enteral nutrition to 800–900 patients.

Growth in the Pharmacy's clinical programs has been matched by growth in its educational programs, which include pharmacy student clinical/experiential rotations, internship programs, postgraduate residency programs, a leadership fellowship, and formal, accredited pharmacy technician education.

Accreditation of schools and colleges of pharmacy by the Accreditation Council for Pharmacy Education (ACPE) requires Introductory Pharmacy Practice Experience (IPPE) and Advanced Pharmacy Practice Experience (APPE). SMH serves as the premier and largest APPE training site for students at St. John Fisher University's (SJFU) Wegmans School of Pharmacy. Of note is a scholars' program for top-ranked SJFU students that arranges for students to complete more than eighty percent of their APPE experiences at URMC inpatient and ambulatory sites. SMH accepts students from multiple other schools and colleges of pharmacy throughout the northeast on a one-off basis and also offers IPPE experiences.

SMH provides an internship that spans three years for students who have completed the first year of a PharmD program. This internship provides students with a progressive scope of responsibility, with an early focus on operational aspects and a later emphasis on clinical patient care. Over the past twenty years, the program has grown to offer PGY-1 residencies in acute care at SMH and HH, pediatric acute care, and ambulatory care, and PGY-2 residencies in ambulatory care, specialty pharmacy administration and leadership, critical care, infectious diseases, oncology, and emergency medicine. These programs have increasingly matched with students from all over the US, reflecting our Pharmacy's national reputation.

In 2022, the department developed a fellowship in Pharmacy Leadership and Administration. This is an 18- to 24-month program that includes completion of the master's in medical management at the Simon School. This program is open to pharmacists with at least three to five years of practice experience and preferably with at least PGY-1 residency training.

URMC's Pharmacy is the largest provider of continuing education credits for pharmacists and pharmacy technicians in the region, partnering with SJFU Wegmans School of Pharmacy to provide ACPE credits. The University has recently applied to the ACPE to become a certified CPE provider, which will allow us to expand our programming and provide CPE credits for many existing CME programs that are relevant to pharmacy.

The extraordinary growth of URMC's Pharmacy has been largely related to our participation in the federal 340B program. Since 2006, we have gone from minimal involvement in the program to being one of the largest in the country. According to the original legislation, the purpose of the 340B program was to "stretch scarce federal resources as far as possible, reaching more eligible patients and providing more comprehensive services." The recently drafted SUSTAIN 340B Act saw the program as being intended to "help safety net providers maintain, improve, and expand patient access to health care services by requiring drug manufacturers, as a condition of participation in the Medicaid program ... to provide discounts to covered entities that serve a disproportionate share of low income and underserved patients." Plainly speaking, the margin generated by these discounts would be used by the hospitals to offset losses accrued by providing uncompensated or undercompensated care to underserved communities.

Although the pharmaceutical industry agreed to the 340B program as a condition of being included in Medicaid and Medicare coverage, the industry has recently taken steps to severely restrict access to 340B discounted drugs for contract pharmacy accounts. To address this, URMC worked with several contract pharmacy partners to create a pharmaceutical strategy to mitigate the harm. Although this strategy has minimized our losses in the short term, a more durable solution will be to maximize the use of URMC-owned pharmacies.

Chapter 6

QUALITY AND SAFETY AND THE SMH CHIEF MEDICAL OFFICER

The last twenty-five years have seen a substantial shift in the focus in the role of the chief medical officer (CMO), from overseeing hospital appointments and monitoring practice standards to leading the charge for quality, safety, and value. This was in part driven by several high-profile studies suggesting that hospital errors were widespread and responsible for as many as 100,000 deaths per year and by concerns that health care costs were spiraling out of control and would not be sustainable. The inverse relationship between quality and cost drove institutions to focus their efforts particularly on developing programs that would improve quality. At URMC, these efforts were driven by two extraordinary CMOs, working in partnership with the CNOs.

Figure 6.1. Ray Mayewski

Raymond Mayewski, MD, was appointed CMO of SMH and HH in 1998. In 2003, in keeping with the expanded role of the CMO, Mayewski was also named URMC VP. Mayewski received his MD from Temple Medical School in Philadelphia and did his residency in internal medicine and fellowship in pulmonary diseases at URMC. In the 1980s, Mayewski became one of the first physicians to establish a dedicated clinic for patients with AIDS. At URMC, he quickly established a reputation as a skilled administrator, an innovative leader, a superb clinician—a "physician's physician"—and a great communicator. His approach could be summed up by a simple maxim: if you're unsure what to do, ask what would be best for the patients, and do it. A testament to this is the Dr. Raymond J. Mayewski Professorship, currently held by the chief of the General Medicine division, one of many endowed professorships established by his grateful patients. Mayewski often served as the public face of URMC, presenting an image of friendliness and welcoming to the community.

Mayewski had the talent to provide whatever the Medical Center needed, referred to at one time as "Rambo" because of his ability to get things done. His extraordinary career of service at URMC included serving as chief of the

General Medicine division in the department of Medicine, inaugural director of the Medical Faculty Group, associate dean for Clinical Affairs in SMD, and director of the Center for Primary Care. In his role as HH CMO, he worked with Goldstein to develop new programs in orthopaedics, obstetrics and gynecology, and bariatrics, among others, helping to ensure the hospitals' vibrancy. Following his retirement as CMO, Mayewski remained active in the region, serving as medical director at St. James in Hornell from 2017–18, and as interim president of Arnot Medical Services for Arnot-Ogden Medical Center in Elmira from 2018–20.

Mayewski died on July 8, 2025, at age seventy-eight, having left an indelible legacy.

Following Mayewski's retirement in 2017 from the position he held for twenty years, Michael Apostolakos, MD, was named CMO of SMH and HH, and URMC VP. Apostolakos received his MD from the State University of New York's (SUNY) Buffalo's Jacobs School of Medicine & Biomedical Sciences and did his residency in internal medicine and fellowship in pulmonary and critical care medicine at URMC. Prior to becoming CMO, he served as the director of the SMH adult critical care program for twenty years, the director of the Medical ICU, the chair of the Critical Care Quality and Resuscitation councils, and director of the Critical Care Medicine fellowship. As a champion of quality, he led successful efforts to reduce central-line associated bloodstream infections (CLABSI) and ventilator-associated pneumonias, implemented rapid response teams, and championed the Wash-Glove-Wash and I Pledge campaigns to improve hand hygiene. Apostolakos also was known as a consummate teacher, winning the Arthur W. Bauman Teaching Award twice and the Emergency Medicine Resident Teaching Award three times. In 2019, he became the second Georgia & Thomas Gosnell Professor in Quality and Safety.

Figure 6.2. Michael Apostolakos

A key component of the enhanced focus on quality and safety was the appointment in 1995 of Robert Panzer, MD, as the inaugural chief quality officer (CQO) and associate CMO. Panzer received his MD from Albany Medical College and completed a residency in internal medicine and fellowship in general internal medicine at URMC, before joining the faculty. In recognition of the growing importance of quality and safety initiatives and the burgeoning health care system, in 2007 he was made URMC associate VP for Patient Care Quality and

Figure 6.3. Robert Panzer

Safety, responsible for overseeing and supporting quality, patient safety, and clinical improvement activities throughout the system (see below). Panzer, a professor in the departments of Medicine (General Medicine) and Public Health Sciences, was well recognized for his work with national organizations and networks to heighten the practice of quality improvement, and was first author of the article "Increasing Demands for Quality Measurement," published in a special edition of *Journal of the American Medical Association* in 2013.[2]

Even before Panzer became the official CQO, he ensured that SMH was an early adopter of quality best practices, becoming one of thirty health care organizations to participate in the IHI (Institute for Health Improvement) Quality Management Network for the full decade of the 1990s. In 1997, SMH was one of the first health care organizations to initiate a "lean redesign" program coordinated by the IHI using the General Motors "PICOS" model. In subsequent years, URMC continued to participate in IHI initiatives.

Under the leadership of Panzer and Mayewski, SMH developed an intensive Patient Safety certificate course, introduced a weekly Report of Harm, with the goal of "zero preventable harm," and introduced mandatory annual education in quality and safety for all residents leading to a reduction in CLABSIs. SMH was one of fifteen institutions in the High Reliability Organization Collaborative convened by the Agency for Healthcare Research and Quality (AHRQ). In 2012, in recognition of his achievements on behalf of quality and safety, Panzer was appointed as the inaugural Georgia & Thomas Gosnell Professor in Quality and Safety, one of two professorships funded by the Gosnells. Panzer stepped down as CQO in 2024 but continues to serve as a senior quality adviser for URMC.

In 2013, SMH rolled out the Unit-based Performance Program (UPP), a major initiative modeled on the Comprehensive Unit-based Safety Program (CUSP) at Johns Hopkins, which restructures inpatient units to empower staff to improve patient safety, the patient experience (iCARE values), and operational efficiency. Panzer and GCH chief quality and patient safety officer Michael Leonard, MD, teamed up with Johns Hopkins to customize the CUSP model for URMC. UPP teams—led by a faculty medical director and nurse manager and

Figure 6.4. Michael Leonard

2 Panzer, R. J., Gitomer, R. S., Greene, W. H., Webster, P. R., Landry, K. R., and Riccobono, C. A. "Increasing Demands for Quality Measurement." *Journal of the American Medical Association*, November 2013, 310(18): 1971–80. DOI: 10.1001/jama.2013.282047.PMID: 24219953

staffed by key members of each clinical area—were established over several years in forty-two patient units (it took almost ten years for Johns Hopkins to roll this out in fifty-two units). The UPP teams' charge was to develop specific projects that would improve patient outcomes and satisfaction. In 2015, just two years after the program's initiation, nearly half the UPP teams were able to reduce the incidence of three targeted hospital-acquired infections by at least ten percent over the previous year, and twelve teams decreased the incidence of these infections by forty percent or more. Those teams achieved similar improvements in PFCC measures (such as response to patient concerns or communication) and efficiency measures (such as resource use or hospital length-of-stay). The success of the program and the promise to integrate residents into the UPP teams were key factors in URMC being chosen as one of eight institutions by the ACGME for its Pursuing Excellence in Clinical Learning Environments Initiative. To date, about sixty percent of UPP teams have resident involvement and over forty-five resident teams have completed the program.

MCIC (Medical Center Insurance Company) Vermont (https://www.mcic.com) is a reciprocal risk-retention group established in 1978 by Columbia University, Cornell University, Johns Hopkins, Yale School of Medicine, and the University of Rochester to provide medical professional and general liability. What makes MCIC unique is its partnership with the hospitals in developing programs that lead to risk reduction and improved patient safety, thereby enabling lower premiums and providing cost stability. Panzer and colleagues, including Spencer Studwell, Esq., director of Risk Management for URMC, worked closely with MCIC on a variety of safety initiatives, one of the most striking of which recorded a nearly fifty percent decrease in the share of MCIC malpractice payments for obstetrics relative to other specialties.

As the number of quality and safety initiatives grew within the Medical Center, particularly within individual departments, it became critical that the efforts be well coordinated. This led Apostolakos to establish a Quality Institute, whose mission is "to drive equitable, high-value, person-centered outcomes while prioritizing safety and wellbeing." The leadership was expanded to include two new URMC associate VP, Irena Boyce, PhD, chief improvement officer and Leonard as chief health care safety officer.

Figure 6.5.
Irena Boyce

Boyce, a professor of clinical nursing at the SON and a professor of Public Sciences at SMD, received a bachelor's degree in health systems administration from the University of Ben-Gurion, Israel, and a PhD in health services research and policy from the University of Rochester. Her research areas include outcomes-based quality improvement evaluations, the economic impact of clinical interventions, and using patient-reported outcomes and social determinants of health for predictive analytics. Leonard, a professor in the departments of Pediatrics and Public Health Sciences, received his MD from SUNY at Buffalo School of Medicine & Biomedical Sciences and completed his residency in pediatrics at the John R. Oishei Children's Hospital of Buffalo. Like Boyce, Leonard's interests are in the area of improvement science, with a focus on developing strategies to reduce the risk of medical errors and adverse events, improving the quality of patient care, and developing interprofessional educational models that integrate improvement science.

The Quality Institute oversees and coordinates a variety of strategic initiatives based upon six pillars: 1) Clinical Quality and Regulatory Resources; 2) Data and Analytics; 3) Research; 4) Healthcare Safety; 5) Educational Opportunities; and 6) Applied Quality Improvement. These include the Patient-Reported Outcomes Measurement Information System (PROMIS) and the UPP and PEI initiatives described above. Today, URMC is the largest patient-reported outcomes collector in the world, with over 8.4 million surveys completed by over 640,000 unique patients. These are being used for shared clinical decision-making with the patients, incorporating patients' preferences.

A key component of the Quality Institute has been its broad educational initiatives, which in FY2024 involved over 5,000 participants. Many of these, using the MyPath online learning system, are designed to achieve high reliability, which is the foundation of exceptional health care delivery, by focusing on clinical quality, health care safety, patient experience, health care worker wellness, and consistent performance.

The Opioid Safety Office provides a collaborative, multidisciplinary approach to treat pain effectively and improve safe opioid prescribing. Its goals include implementing universal screening for substance use disorders; creating an outpatient e-consult service for patients with pain and substance use disorder; expanding access to medications for substance use disorders; expanding inpatient harm-reduction services; disseminating a post-operative opioid prescribing program developed by Surgery; and developing an opioid safety dashboard to track metrics. The impact of Surgery's work has been remarkable, with a substantial drop in the number of patients who need opioids post-op, the amount of opioid prescribed for those who do need it, and the number of patients requiring a prescription on discharge!

Chapter 7

AFFILIATES

URMC has a long history of providing specialty services typically found only in larger urban areas. Many of the referrals for these services have been a direct result of the reputation of the specialty faculty and their relationship with regional providers. Typically, these referrals have represented a third of admissions to SMH and have been critical for the reputation and financial success of the Medical Center. Today they represent closer to forty percent of admissions.

During the late 1990s, community hospitals experienced significant reductions in inpatient census as advances in technology enabled many acute patients to be treated as outpatients. In addition, insurance companies tightened admission criteria and established observation and short-stay protocols with reduced reimbursement rates for the treatment of many illnesses. In smaller rural hospitals this was compounded by the inability to recruit physicians to replace retiring medical staff or in-demand medical specialists. This led patients to bypass rural hospitals and seek care in urban areas. The resulting decline in revenue drove these rural hospitals to develop clinical program partnerships, specialty service contracts, and eventually institutional affiliations with urban medical centers in an attempt to broaden their service capabilities and retain patients locally.

Not surprisingly, there was competition among urban hospitals to provide these specialty services for both reputational and financial reasons. Large acute care hospitals in Rochester, Buffalo, and Syracuse all vied for these patients, who were critical for the expansion of specialty programs. As this competition intensified, faculty saw an erosion in historic referral patterns. Fearing that this erosion would negatively impact their clinical and educational programs, many departments became interested in developing programs with hospitals throughout the region. In addition, hospitals and insurance companies developed contractual relationships that created narrow networks of hospitals and physicians to better provide care to populations and to integrate value contract goals of optimizing quality and minimizing costs.

At the same time, urban medical centers recognized that as part of multi-hospital systems they could better expand clinical programs and

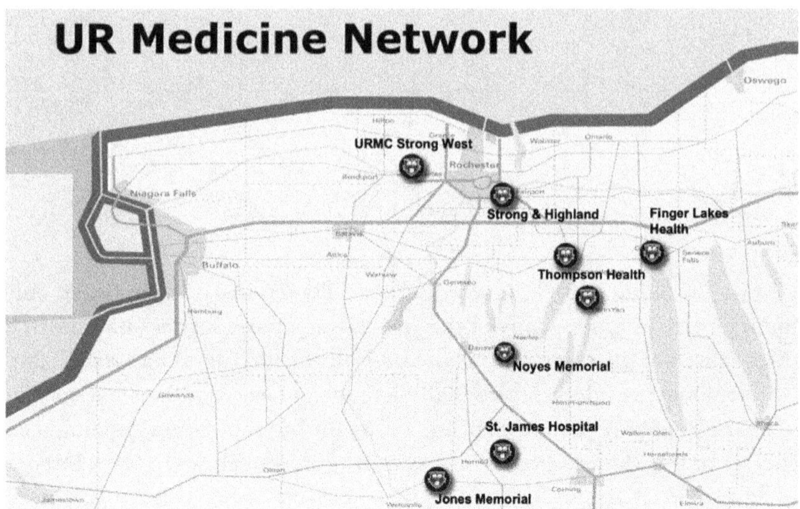

Figure 7.1. Map of UR Medicine affiliates

achieve economies of scale to reduce health care costs. The ever-larger patient populations needed to support the increasing subspecialization of medicine could only be achieved by expanding the geographic reach of medical centers and their providers. These forces virtually mandated the creation of large, fully integrated health systems. Over the past thirty years, URMC has established such a system, which now encompasses seven affiliated hospitals and Strong West, a satellite of SMH.

By the mid 1990s, URMC leadership had already understood the importance of growing beyond its main campus and establishing control over a comprehensive continuum of care. Led by SMH CEO Leo Brideau and URMC CEO Jay Stein, the University entered into the first of many formal hospital affiliations. Highland Hospital (HH) and its subsidiaries—The Highlands at Pittsford and The Highlands Living Center—became part of the University in July 1996. This was followed quickly by the addition of the Visiting Nurse Service and the Westfall Nursing Home, later renamed Highlands at Brighton.

HH is a 261-bed facility located approximately one mile from the Medical Center. At the time HH joined the University, it was experiencing a decline in its admissions, in part because many primary care patients were not being approved for admission by insurers. By the late 1990s, the hospital's very survival was in doubt.

HH was the primary admitting hospital for faculty from URMC's department of Family Medicine and a training ground for family medicine residents. The Family Medicine faculty, together with faculty from URMC's DOM, represented the bulk of primary care practitioners. Stein realized that in order for URMC to be competitive in the future, it was going to have to expand its primary care program dramatically and greatly expand outreach in surrounding counties. Michael Weidner, CEO of HH, was asked to lead the primary care recruitment effort. These are detailed in a later chapter.

SMH and HH CEO Steven Goldstein, in partnership with Raymond Mayewski, MD, CMO of SMH and HH, embarked on an effort to move faculty and, when possible, entire programs from SMH to HH. This effort was very successful and rescued HH. Over the years many medical specialties were added to the hospital, including bariatric surgery, orthopaedic joint surgery, the geriatric fracture program, gynecologic oncology, breast surgery, neurosurgery and neurology. Other programs, such as cardiology, medical oncology, and geriatrics, were significantly expanded. Today, HH is a thriving, financially stable hospital, and has joined SMH as a referral hospital for the health system. The transformation of HH no doubt was aided by the closure of St. Mary's Hospital in 1997 and The Genesee Hospital in 2001.

Later, the closure of Lakeside Hospital in Brockport meant that three of the seven acute hospitals in greater Rochester no longer existed. URMC acquired the Lakeside campus and converted it into Strong West, a remote site of SMH with a free-standing ED, an ambulatory surgery center and multiple specialty services to support the Brockport community. The absence of three hospitals placed great strain on the remaining four, a strain that has only worsened in recent times, resulting in both SMH and HH regularly operating at greater than one hundred percent of capacity.

The transformation of HH required completing a number of major capital projects. Goldstein was ably assisted in this transformation by Cynthia Becker, RN, MS, MBA, FACHE. Becker, who served as chief operating officer of HH, began her career at SMH as a staff nurse and progressed to serve at HH as emergency department manager, then VP for Patient Care Services and CNO before being promoted to the COO position. Under Becker's and Goldstein's guidance, the Ob/Gyn service created six more private rooms to accommodate the addition of a large obstetrics group in 2002. The number of operating rooms grew from nine to seventeen over the past twenty-five years. The ED underwent a major expansion and renovation in 2020 that included the addition of twenty-six observation beds. The largest of these capital projects was the creation of the new southeast bed tower in 2023 that added fifty-eight private rooms. These major capital projects were carried out without utilizing University capital funds, a tribute to the strong leadership of Goldstein, Mayewski, and Becker.

Beginning in the early 2000s, URMC faculty began providing an increasing number of specialty services to FF Thompson Hospital (FFT) in Canandaigua. By 2012, the University operated fourteen clinical programs at FFT. The leadership at Thompson Health, the parent of FFT, recognized the significant value the University could bring to its ability to serve its community. URMC found FFT to be an attractive candidate for affiliation. It was a 113-bed low-cost community hospital with an excellent reputation in a growing community. The mutual value of formalizing an affiliation became clear to both parties and in June 2012, under the leadership of Goldstein and CEO Bradford Berk, Thompson Health was incorporated into the University of Rochester. At the time of the affiliation, Thompson was led by CEO Linda Janczak, RN. She was succeeded in 2012 by Michael Stapleton, MSN, FACHE, who had previously served as Thompson's chief operating officer.

The affiliation enabled Thompson to achieve major expansions. Thompson's urgent care centers increased from one in 2012 to three. A new breast-imaging center opened in 2015 and a 44,000 square-foot facility to house the Canandaigua Medical Group opened in 2018. A new twelve-bed ICU opened in 2020 and a new outpatient rehabilitation facility opened in 2023. Several additional expansion projects are in the planning stage. Thompson has become the largest employer in Ontario County.

The challenges facing rural hospitals proved to be too much for many. From 2010 to 2025, 151 rural hospitals in the US permanently closed their

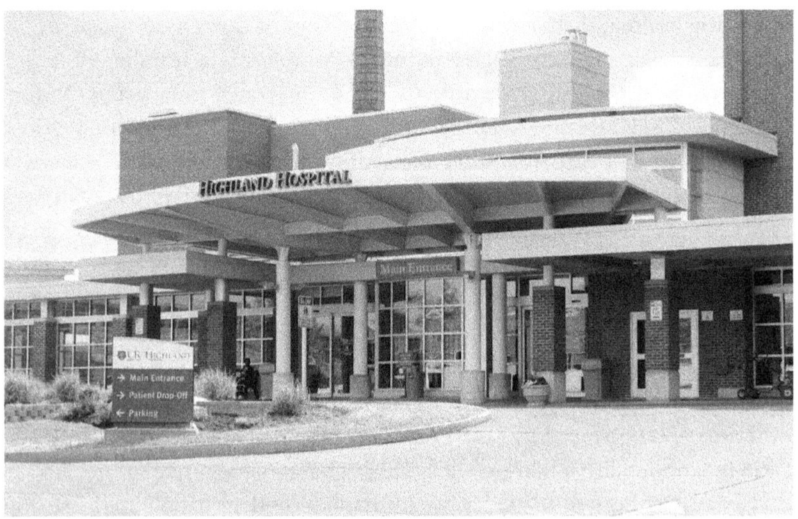

Figure 7.2. Today's Highland Hospital

Figure 7.3. FF Thompson Hospital

doors. Currently a significant number of the remaining rural hospitals in NY State are considered as being in danger of closing. The communities to the south of Monroe County had long been important sources of referrals for URMC. Efforts began in the early 1990s to solidify relationships with doctors and hospitals in a region stretching from Ithaca in the east, to the Pennsylvania border to the south, and to Olean in the west. URMC sponsored cardiac catheterization laboratories at Cayuga Medical Center in Ithaca and at Olean General Hospital, and acquired a number of primary care practices in these communities. In the end, however, it proved difficult to sustain formal relationships at distances greater than two hours from Rochester, and efforts in Ithaca and Olean were abandoned.

Led by Goldstein and Berk, attention then turned to the three hospitals immediately to the south of Rochester: Nicholas H. Noyes Memorial Hospital (Noyes) in Dansville, St. James Hospital in Hornell, and Jones Memorial Hospital in Wellsville. Their leaders recognized that meeting their future capital needs and rejuvenating an aging medical staff would be beyond their ability to achieve alone. All three hospitals therefore sought affiliation with a larger system. Goldstein thought that by linking the efforts of the three southern region hospitals, a more sustainable health system could be created. That strategy was ultimately consummated between 2016 and 2018 under the leadership of Taubman and Goldstein.

Figure 7.4. The Ann and Carl Myers Cancer Center

Noyes was a low-cost, sixty-seven-bed hospital that had been a collaborating partner with URMC in cardiology and neuro-medicine since 2012. It was thought that by shoring up more local services, patients who normally would have to be referred to SMH and HH would be able to remain at Noyes. Therefore, an expansion of the WCI, the Ann and Carl Myers Cancer Center, opened on the Noyes campus in 2017. This model of strengthening services at local hospitals allows patients to receive care closer to home while helping to improve the financial strength of rural hospitals. It also reserves the academic medical center for those patients most in need of interventional care. This thinking stands in stark contrast to the usual "hub and spoke" model in which affiliated hospitals are seen principally as feeders to the specialty hospital.

Noyes joined as a UR Medicine affiliate in January 2016. At the time, it was led by Amy Pollard, RN, who retired in 2021. She was succeeded by John Teeters, MD, a cardiologist who also served as medical director of AHP. Under Teeters's leadership, Noyes has become a successful referral center for complex patients who reside in the southern region.

Jones Memorial, a seventy-bed hospital near the Pennsylvania border, had also been a collaborating hospital since 2012, with URMC programs in anesthesiology, cardiology, endocrinology, otolaryngology, and neuromedicine, and also planned an opening of a WCI medical oncology service for 2015. Its financial situation was more precarious than Noyes's, but URMC leadership was confident in its ability to achieve a financial turnaround. After extensive negotiations, both Jones and Noyes were incorporated into the University in 2016.

Figure 7.5. Nicholas H. Noyes Memorial Hospital

Despite the strong efforts of Jones CEO Eva Benedict, RN, its financial position continued to deteriorate. Through URMC's efforts, Jones was awarded a grant of $32 million in capital and operating funds from NY State that enabled it to execute a three-year strategic plan and complete badly needed modernization. The plan called for the recruitment of a significant number of physicians and APPs, securing fairer insurance rates, growing outpatient programs by establishing rural health clinics, and expanding use of the 340B pharmaceutical program. Today Jones is on sound financial footing and enjoys an upgraded facility. Benedict retired in 2021 and was succeeded by James Helms, MBA, CPA, who previously served as Jones's chief financial officer.

Because of its location between Noyes and Jones, St. James in Hornell was an important piece of the southern region strategy. The hospital was

Figure 7.6. Jones Memorial Hospital

Figure 7.7. St. James Hospital

owned by Trinity Health, based in Michigan. It had a terribly outdated facility that needed to be replaced, suffered from extremely low occupancy, and was severely distressed financially. As a result, Trinity was in the process of closing it. URMC leadership stepped in and worked with the board and administration to secure grants from NY State that stabilized the hospital while a new strategic plan was implemented. A $63 million grant from NY State permitted the construction of a new fifteen-bed hospital and a medical village housing both primary and specialty care services. In addition to the capital funds, NY State provided critically important operating funds for seven years as the strategic plan was successfully implemented. The incorporation of St. James into the University occurred in 2018, providing URMC with the last critical component to develop a robust southern region health system. Upon affiliation, Leo Brideau, who had returned in 2015 as a consultant to URMC, assumed the CEO role of St. James for five months until Brian O'Donovan, MPA, was appointed CEO. O'Donovan was succeeded in 2022 by Wendy Disbrow, MBA, RN.

In 2019, Finger Lakes Health (FLH) in Geneva issued a request for proposals, seeking to affiliate with a larger health system. FLH is comprised of Geneva General Hospital, a 117-bed hospital in Geneva; Soldiers and Sailors Memorial Hospital, a twenty-five-bed critical access hospital in Penn Yan; four skilled nursing facilities; and a number of outpatient facilities, including a dialysis center. Led by Goldstein and Taubman, URMC submitted a response that ultimately was accepted. However, formal affiliation was put on hold until the consequences of the COVID-19 pandemic could be better understood. Instead, a management agreement was entered into in October 2020 that allowed URMC and FLH leadership to begin to develop and implement a strategic plan. Affiliation was further delayed due to a lengthy review by the Federal Trade Commission. In 2022, FLH was finally incorporated into URMC.

FLH has been led by Jose Acevedo, MD, a pulmonary and critical care specialist. He served as director of Hospitalist services at Maimonides Medical Center until his appointment as CMO at FLH in 2004.

As expected, each of the rural hospitals in the UR Medicine network has faced the challenges affecting all rural hospitals in America. At one time or another, each has been in danger of becoming financially unsustainable, but with the combination of management expertise from URMC, effective local leadership and successful recruitment of providers, all affiliates are now financially solvent with dramatically expanded clinical services.

The financial turnaround at the URMC affiliates has been multifactorial. But two initiatives have been most important in stabilizing the financials of the affiliates: the successful recruitment by Karol Marciano of physicians and APPs, and a deliberate strategy—led by the tireless efforts of Bilal Ahmed, MD, the CMO at Noyes and St. James (as well as HH)—to increase the number of patients who are able to remain at their local hospitals.

Before affiliation, each of the limited specialty services at the rural hospitals were medically unstable, relying on one or possibly two providers, and were financially unsustainable because of low patient volumes. After

Figure 7.8. Geneva General Hospital

Figure 7.9. Soldiers and Sailors Hospital

affiliation, these hospitals developed strategic plans to enhance specialty services for their rural communities. An important support to their planning processes was the insightful market data analyses provided regularly by Michele Lawrence, MBA, MHA, senior director of Business Development, and her team.

Karol Marciano, URMFG's associate VP for Provider Network Development, assumed responsibility for recruiting providers into a model that shared specialists across multiple hospitals, thus stabilizing these services and making them financially sustainable. For the regional affiliates alone, over the past nine years, 134 doctors and fifty-seven APPs in primary care in twenty different specialties have been recruited by Karol and her team. The implementation of a detailed retention program that pays close attention to the needs of these providers and their families, has resulted in a retention rate of over eighty percent. This recruitment has enhanced the ability of the rural hospitals to manage patients locally. This proved particularly important during the COVID-19 pandemic and is playing an increasingly important role in mitigating the overcrowding at SMH and HH.

The strengthening of clinical services at all the rural affiliates has paid dividends financially as well. While more than half of rural hospitals in America are threatened with bankruptcy, all the regional affiliates are financially stable with strong balance sheets, enabling them to continue serving their communities for the long term—a remarkable success story.

B. Establishing the Medical Faculty Group

Chapter 8

UNIVERSITY OF ROCHESTER MEDICAL FACULTY GROUP (URMFG)

A critical response of URMC to the changing health care environment was to transform the traditional, decentralized clinical practice configuration of twenty-two separate departments and 120 divisions into a unified multi-specialty group nimble enough to provide high-quality care and efficient access at a sustainable cost. This led CEO Jay Stein to establish URMFG, with Raymond Mayewski, MD, as its founding director. Mayewski's initial focus was to build a centralized framework for physician credentialing, compliance, billing, and contract negotiations.

Mayewski, who was also CMO of SMH and HH, was succeeded in 2004 by Kenneth E. DeHaven, MD, who was appointed senior associate dean (SAD) for Clinical Affairs in addition to director of URMFG. DeHaven, a pioneer in the use of arthroscopy in sports medicine and the founder and director of the division of Sports Medicine in Orthopaedics, had been at the University since 1975. DeHaven was succeeded at the end of 2008 by Mayewski, who helped shepherd the reorganization process. At the time, URMFG activities were limited; billing was still largely decentralized and contract negotiations with commercial payers were separate from those of the hospital.

Understanding the need to empower faculty to play a major role in transforming the health care system, Mayewski and Dean Mark Taubman engaged the Chartis Group between the fall of 2011 and the spring of 2013 to analyze the structure, function, and overall performance of the medical faculty group and to help chart a course for the future. Their recommendations included a shared-governance structure and the development of common centralized resources. Based upon their recommendations, URMC conducted a national search for a full-time leader of URMFG whose task would be to execute the Chartis recommendations.

Figure 8.1. Michael Rotondo

Michael F. Rotondo, MD, a Rochester native, was chosen as the inaugural CEO of URMFG, SAD for Clinical Affairs, and associate VP of SMH. The SMH appointment highlighted the goal of creating a vibrant faculty group that would coordinate with SMH to respond to new technologies and the changing health care environment. Rotondo received his MD from Georgetown University School of Medicine, did his residency in general surgery at Thomas Jefferson University Hospital, and his fellowship in traumatology and surgical critical care at the University of Pennsylvania Medical Center, where he remained as faculty, established a national reputation in trauma surgery, and ultimately became director of its Level One Trauma Center. In 1999, he was recruited to The Brody School of Medicine at East Carolina University as vice chairman of Surgery and chief of Trauma and Surgical Critical Care, and in 2005 became Surgery chair. Two years later, he was tapped to head the Brody School's multispecialty physician practice group, where he oversaw a restructuring and financial turnaround. Rotondo, who has published over 250 articles largely related to trauma and critical care surgery, has been a national leader in the field, serving as president of the American Association for the Surgery of Trauma, the world's leading scientific trauma society; president of the Eastern Association of the Surgery of Trauma; chair of the Committee on Trauma for the American College of Surgeons; and president of the Halsted Society. He currently is a director of the American Board of Surgery.

Upon his arrival in Rochester, Rotondo moved quickly to strengthen the shared governance structure of URMFG and to develop a set of centralized resources that would enable URMFG to act as an integrated multispecialty group. This would be a multistep process, beginning with the transformation of URMFG from a federated model of independent department practices to an integrated model with shared governance and services, and ultimately to a multispecialty model with common governance and centrally controlled policies and finances. The second step would be the transformation of the clinical enterprise from three distinct entities (URMFG, SMH, SMD) to a financially and operationally integrated academic medical center. A key intermediate step would be the establishment of URMFG and SMH Joint Operating Committees to oversee the clinical service lines.

As a start, Rotondo established five activity domains recommended by Chartis, and ECG Consulting (a Boston-based health management consulting firm) was brought in to assist in developing a cohesive approach to financial management and operations control.

The Finance Committee (domain one) was reconfigured to emphasize fiscal discipline and transparency; develop reliability, consistency, and trust in practice-wide accounting methods; and optimize and standardize business operations. The accounting infrastructure was analyzed and reconfigured to match standard business practices, generalized across the departments, and with a new atmosphere of accountability. Results were tracked by the

Finance Committee and the URMFG Executive Committee (comprised of faculty rotating from clinical departments and key URMC leadership), and were reported to the dean and to the CEO of URMC at regular intervals, facilitating the development of department-specific interventions to improve performance.

A Compensation Committee, which had substantial faculty representation and was led by an academic department chair, was tasked with establishing a master compensation plan. A key component of the final plan, adopted in 2016, was to assure that faculty were compensated at market-competitive rates.

Review of national benchmarks showed significant misalignments between faculty productivity and compensation. URMC committed to narrowing the gap between pay and productivity, and ensuring that there were no gender-related differences in compensation, by infusing new dollars to support the faculty group which were supplemented through business improvement plans, aggressive value-based rate negotiations, and more efficient service delivery approaches.

A Clinical Operations Committee (domain two) was established to standardize and streamline clinical operations. The committee identified practice metrics that would create access and value for patients and developed policies that defined how URMFG practices would operate. For example, one key performance standard was that eighty percent of new patient visits would occur within fourteen days of the visit request. Over time, the focus on high-performing clinical operations expanded to include an ambulatory leadership team, Patient-Reported Outcomes Measurement Information System (PROMIS), patient engagement, and telemedicine.

A Regional Development Committee (domain three) was established to develop a tactical primary care practice plan for the UR Medicine network and to promote health system development through the establishment of regional multispecialty groups.

An Information Technology Committee (domain four) was established to collaborate with URMC Information Technology to develop analytics that would drive business development, direct care management, optimize operational performance for enhanced patient experience, and reduce costs through judicious utilization.

The People and Culture Committee (domain five) was designed to help promote the new distributive leadership model, enterprise-wide thinking and positive faculty engagement. It also was designed to address issues like physician burnout and work–life balance. These included identifying technologies to improve workflow, particularly in relation to the electronic medical record. This led to the establishment of an eRecord advisory council, a Health Information Technology group and to the University of Rochester

Health Lab to focus on effectively using Artificial Intelligence to support the mission. URMFG also established a physician wellness program that was a major driver and a key component of the new URMC-wide Office of Wellbeing, discussed later in this book.

Over the past ten years, these committees have been restructured as needed to adapt to new initiatives. These include an APP optimization project designed at standardizing the expectations of patient-facing effort for APPs and allowing them to work at the top of their license; and Digital First, which brings novel approaches to enhance access to care and streamline business functions.

Key to success of the URMFG transformation was the hiring of Victoria Hines, MHA, who served for ten years as COO of URMFG and VP of URMC, and who shepherded many of the initiatives discussed above. Hines received her MHA from the Medical College of Virginia/Virginia Commonwealth University. Prior to joining URMFG, Hines served as the president and CEO of Visiting Nurse Service of Rochester and Monroe County, Inc. and of Finger Lakes Visiting Nurse Service (the home care organizations of URMC). She also served as associate dean for Administration and Finance for the SON, and for much of her career taught foundational leadership principles at the SON and for nursing leaders at URMC. Of particular note was Hines's involvement in the growth and restructuring of URMC's burgeoning ambulatory programs and of the telemedicine initiative, a key part of URMC's response to the COVID-19 pandemic.

Figure 8.2. Victoria Hines

The past dozen years have seen the transition of URMFG into a vibrant organization with shared governance that now includes approximately 2,000 physicians and works with SMH to oversee clinical operations. It has served as a catalyst for a variety of URMC-wide initiatives, including digital medicine, wellness, the Health Lab, and the redesign of ambulatory services. Its transformation proved essential for URMC's success, as will be discussed later in the book, and to the development of AHP.

Chapter 9

ACCOUNTABLE HEALTH PARTNERS (AHP)

Spurred by the Affordable Care Act, new provider and payment models were introduced to help achieve these goals of the "Triple Aim," including Patient Centered Medical Homes, bundled payments, and Accountable Care Organizations (ACOs). ACOs, established initially for Medicare patients, were required to be "accountable" for the overall care of their beneficiaries, have adequate participation of primary care and specialist physicians, define processes to promote evidence-based medicine, report on quality and costs, and coordinate care. Over time the ACOs would need to take on more financial risk, while developing best practices protocols, care management systems, and networks aligned around improving the value (Cost/Quality) of care.

In 2012, URMC contracted with The Chartis Group to work with representatives from the hospitals, faculty, and community physicians to develop an Accountable Care Network (ACN). ACNs were clinically integrated networks that were more flexible than ACOs, in that they could support multiple contracts, including those outside of Medicare. The ACN would help align hospitals and physicians within the growing UR Medicine network around performance improvement and new payment models. The ACN would contract as single entity with insurers and employers, define standards of care and performance targets, and share information to improve care coordination and quality, monitor physician and hospital performance, and reduce costs. The ACN needed to be structured as a for-profit company to be able to contract on behalf of non-for-profit providers and private physicians.

Considerable time was spent developing the ACN governance structure. One concern was balancing the need of the University to have sufficient control over the new organization to protect its missions while giving private physicians and community hospitals a meaningful voice. Another concern was how to unite specialists, who traditionally competed for patients, around common goals to improve the quality and cost of care. To achieve this, the ACN Board of Directors would have representatives from four ownership groups: SMH, community hospitals, URMFG, and community physicians. All matters of substance would require approval by the majority of all four groups. Although this protected the interests of each of the groups because each had the power to block any decision, it also set up the potential for gridlock. The success of the network therefore would depend on the ability to communicate and align around common goals to improve patient care.

In 2013, AHP was created as a for-profit Limited Liability Company that housed an Independent Practice Association, allowing it to contract with insurance companies. The initial capital investment of $3 million was split equally among the hospitals. Robert McCann, MD, was chosen as the first CEO. McCann received his MD from SUNY Upstate and did his residency in internal medicine at the University of Rochester. In 1990, he helped develop RGH's Independent Living for Seniors program which prevented older people from unnecessary hospitalizations and nursing home admission. During this time, McCann also obtained board certification in Geriatrics and Palliative Care. In 1999, he was recruited to HH to become chief of Internal Medicine, a position he held until 2021. McCann helped transform HH from a respected local community hospital into a nationally recognized leader in geriatric care, expanding subspecialty services, including palliative care, geriatrics, endocrinology, cardiology, and neurology. McCann quickly developed the necessary infrastructure, hiring Renee Sutton to lead Physician Relations, Mark Cronin as chief operating officer and James Wright as chief financial officer. John "Chad" Teeters, MD, the current CEO of Noyes Memorial Hospital, was subsequently chosen as executive medical director.

Figure 9.1. Robert McCann

Over the past twelve years, AHP has grown to more than 3,500 physicians and thirteen hospitals. It should be noted that AHP extends beyond the boundaries of the UR Medicine network and includes physicians and hospitals affiliated with the Guthrie Healthcare System, Arnot Health, and Wyoming County Community Health System. The providers and participating hospitals are represented in Figure 9.2.

AHP currently has nine contracts with insurers, the University of Rochester Health Plan, HH and FF Thompson, representing over $2 billion in premiums and covering over 500,000 lives. These contracts are value-based, aimed at improving quality and reducing cost of care. The contracts include the potential for gain (upside) or loss (downside), with limits on the amount that can be earned or lost each year. To date, the return on investment for AHP has exceeded $140 million. Over time, it is anticipated that these contracts will assume greater risk, allowing for higher upsides and downsides. In 2016, AHP formed an insurance company to cover potential losses. It should be noted that AHP contracts are in addition to fee for service

AHP Network - 2025

	PCP Adult Physician	PCP Adult APP	PCP Peds Physician	PCP Peds APP	Ob/Gyn Physician	CNMs	Other Specialists (Physician, OD, DPM)	Totals
Community	23	13	84	31	30	1	156	**338**
FQHC	17	43	12	5	1	-	3	**81**
UR-Employed	245	118	17	11	66	28	1,569	**2,054**
Other Hospital Employed	182	133	27	19	24	7	713	**1,105**
Total	**467**	**310**	**140**	**66**	**121**	**36**	**2,441**	**3,581**

Strong
Highland
Thompson
St. James
Noyes
Jones
WCCHS
Finger Lakes
Arnot Health
Guthrie
Accountable Health Partners

Figure 9.2. Current AHP membership

rates negotiated between the hospitals, physicians and third-party payers, which still make up the majority of revenue for UR Medicine.

AHP produces dashboards that improve care by providing information on common health measures and identifying gaps in care that practices can address in real time. AHP employs embedded care managers and pharmacists who work closely with providers and patients to improve outcomes. AHP has proven invaluable in growing the UR Medicine network and has driven a uniform high-quality standard of care throughout the health system.

At the end of 2024, McCann stepped down from his role at the helm of AHP, having established AHP as the pre-eminent clinically integrated network in upstate NY and a national force in developing new care models.

Chapter 10

UNIVERSITY OF ROCHESTER HEALTH LAB AND DIGITAL MEDICINE

A major addition to the research infrastructure over the past ten years has been the University of Rochester Health Lab. The Health Lab was established in 2016 through the efforts of Rotondo and David J. Mitten, MD (departments of Orthopaedics and Biomedical Engineering), as a multidisciplinary collaboration integrating data, education, and engineering to create new technologies that revolutionize health care and provide accessible, better health solutions. Mitten received his BA in chemical engineering and his MD from the University of Rochester, where he remained for residencies in general surgery and orthopaedics. He then did a fellowship in plastic and reconstructive surgery at UCLA, before returning to URMC Orthopaedics, where he developed a prominent program in hand and upper extremity surgery. Throughout his career, Mitten has used his engineering skills to drive innovation in health care and delivery.

Figure 10.1. David Mitten

The Health Lab is structured around three cores. The Data Core, directed by Kathleen Fear, PhD (SON), provides data analysis to help develop novel solutions to problems; data visualization to help communicate findings; advanced analytics to predict future trends and optimize decision-making; and analysis to investigate the impact of the new solution. The Education Core, directed by Wendi Cross, PhD (Psychiatry and Pediatrics), exposes trainees to health care innovation and technology, provides expertise in leading a project team driving change and innovation, and mentors while working with project teams. The Software Engineering Core, directed by Christiano Tapparello, PhD (Electrical and Computer Engineering), aims to create tailored solutions to complex challenges in health care, building on research findings to define easy-to-use interfaces and functionalities, and conducting trials to evaluate and establish minimal viable products.

The Health Lab has been involved in a variety of initiatives. One of these is the development by the Software Engineering Core of a virtual reality application that simulates a serene aquarium setting, allowing patients to venture into an underwater world, reducing anxiety levels and minimizing the need for sedation across a range of medical procedures. Other projects include using eRecord to measure and understand sleep disruptions in the neurology unit, and a study in the Pediatric ICU—where alarms occur at a rate of about eight alarms per patient per hour—to identify nonactionable alarms and use analytics to reduce the alarms.

Spearheaded by Rotondo, the Health Lab has engaged in a partnership with Butterfly Network, Inc. to use point-of-care ultrasound (POCUS) devices in an enterprise-wide initiative that touches all missions. The pocket-sized portable ultrasound device connects to a smartphone or tablet and uses a single probe for whole-body imaging. The device works with enterprise workflow software to provide immediate and accurate diagnostic information. The deployment of point-of-care ultrasound has already led to significant clinical improvements, such as the early diagnosis of cholecystitis, the ability to distinguish abscesses from cellulitis, early detection of bladder masses, identifying foreign bodies, detecting valvular vegetations, screening for abdominal aneurysms, and identifying thyroid nodules.

PROMIS

A great impetus for establishing the Health Lab was the use of patient reported outcomes (PROs) to get a better understanding of how patients are feeling and functioning in response to treatment. In 2015, spearheaded by Judith F. Baumhauer, MD, MPH (Orthopaedics), currently vice dean for Academic Affairs, URMC became one of the first academic centers in the US to collect PROs at the site of service using PROMIS (Patient Reported Outcomes Measurement Information System). PROMIS, initiated as part of the NIH Roadmap and funded by the NIH, is a natural extension of the biopsychosocial model. It uses item response theory and computer adaptive technology to ask questions about symptoms, such as pain, depression, anxiety, and physical function.

Under Mitten's direction, the Health Lab developed an electronic platform called UR VOICE (University of Rochester Validated Outcomes In Clinical Experience) and used iPads to collect data on symptom domains that mattered most to patients being treated by Orthopaedics—physical function, pain interference, and depression. Providers could instantaneously view the results in the electronic record, allowing them to share the results with their patients. After a successful pilot, PROMIS was rolled out to the entire Orthopaedic department (approximately 17,000 visits per month).

Within three months, the WCI began collecting PROMIS data on anxiety, physical function, fatigue, social roles, and isolation, as a replacement for an accreditation-required paper-formatted "stress thermometer" question. The data influenced clinical care and allowed researchers to compare treatments responses. Dermatology began collecting physical function, pain interference, and depression, and worked with PROMIS hosts at Northwestern University to introduce a new domain, "itch." By 2018, sixty percent of URMC departments and divisions were collecting PROMIS data. Pilot grant programs were begun to explore how symptom management impacted care. Our leadership with PROMIS and the large volume of patients who contributed data led the *New England Journal of Medicine* to ask us to write an article on the program.[3]

In late 2023, eRecord incorporated PROMIS into its programming. In 2024, URMC began collecting population health PROMIS domains every six months along with the standard site of service collections. Today, URMC is the largest PRO collector in the world, with over 8.4 million surveys completed by over 640,000 unique patients. These are being used for a shared clinical decision-making with the patients, incorporating patients' preferences.

Digital Transformation

Another major role for the Health Lab has been the digital transformation initiative. Spearheaded in 2019 by Rotondo and URMFG, the initiative sought to prepare URMC for the perceived revolution in digital medicine and artificial intelligence (AI). To establish a vigorous digital medicine infrastructure, Michael J. Hasselberg, PhD, RN, PMHNP-BC, was appointed the first senior director for Digital Health at UR Medicine (and subsequently in 2022 to chief digital health officer). He also became co-director of the Health Lab. Hasselberg, a psychiatric nurse practitioner and professor of Psychiatry, Clinical Nursing and Data Science, received his PhD in health practice research from the University of Rochester SON. Hasselberg founded the UR Medicine telepsychiatry program and Project ECHO® (Extension for Community Healthcare Outcomes). He has served as an expert advisor on digital health innovation to the Department of Health & Human Services, the National Quality

Figure 10.2.
Michael Hasselberg

3 Baumhauer, J. F. "Patient Reported Outcomes: Are They Living Up to Their Potential?" *N Engl J Med.* 2017. PMID: 28679102

Forum, New York State Department of Health, and multiple health systems across the US.

ECHO is a novel model, developed by Sanjeev Arora, MD, at the University of New Mexico, to improve care across the lifespan by teaching community-based clinicians the skills to treat complex patients in their own practices, as opposed to referring the patient to specialists. ECHO has been shown to improve health outcomes while reducing geographic barriers and the cost of care through a multidisciplinary team-based approach that links expert interdisciplinary specialist teams with primary care clinicians through regularly scheduled teleECHO™ clinics using web-based videoconferencing technology. During each session, experts mentor primary care clinicians to help manage their patient cases and share their expertise via mentoring, guidance, feedback, and didactic education. Currently URMC has nine ECHO programs that focus on autism, behavioral health, developmental disabilities, eating disorders, geriatric health, and pediatric allergy.

With the appointments of Hasselberg as senior director for Digital Health, Gregg Nicandri, MD, as chief medical information officer, and Rosemary Ventura, DNP, RN-BC, as chief nursing information officer, an advisory committee was formed to develop a UR Medicine digital transformation strategy. A three-phase "Digital First" strategic plan was developed involving a Digital Front Door to attract patients to the UR Medicine health care system, patient engagement, and the collection of patient and outcome data. One of the earliest accomplishments of the Digital First program was the launch of the ambulatory eConsults program in 2020 to provide patients with access to non-urgent specialty services that could be managed by their primary care provider. Over five years, the program has grown to more than 39,000 eConsults per year by including specialty services and expanding the number of addressable conditions. The eConsults launch proved particularly propitious in that UR Medicine was able to quickly pivot to telehealth at the onset of the COVID-19 pandemic.

As the pandemic began to wane, the Digital First strategy went into high gear. This included a campaign to enhance patient portal access through MyChart, the launch of online scheduling, and the deployment of an AI ChatBot (Hyro) to assist with finding a provider, appointment scheduling and viewing, and MyChart activation. eCheck-in was launched to allow patients to complete the registration process through the MyChart portal or kiosks placed in select ambulatory clinics. eCheck-in also enabled the collection of PROs directly into MyChart. Expanding on the telehealth initiatives established during the COVID-19 pandemic, an on-demand telemedicine service line, offered during and outside of normal business hours, was established within the primary care network using "digital health" APPs to administer virtual care for routine medical issues. This concept was subsequently expanded to provide behavioral health services. Digital care pathways, such as blood pressure monitoring, colorectal cancer screening, and post-stroke discharge, were also developed within eRecord.

Through the efforts of the Health Lab, URMC has become one of the leaders in AI. In 2024, the Medical Center began a pilot program using Dragon Ambient Experience, which acts as a virtual scribe that captures the spoken conversation during patient visits. URMC became a founding partner of the Coalition of Health AI, a federal-level nonprofit organization aimed at establishing best practices and standards for the development and implementation of AI technologies in the health care sector. UR Medicine was also among the first health systems in the country to receive secure access to GPT-4 Generative AI, a type of deep learning model used to generate human-like text. In 2025, UR Medicine became a founding health system of the Qualified Health Public Benefit Corporation, which partners with health systems to provide algorithms for using AI in the clinical setting.

C. Dentistry and the Creation of the Eastman Institute for Oral Health (EIOH)

Chapter 11

CREATING THE EASTMAN INSTITUTE FOR ORAL HEALTH

Since its inception, what is known today as the EIOH has been unique in academic dentistry, combining vigorous community engagement and service, advanced education and training, and leading-edge oral health research. Its roots date to 1901, when members of the Rochester Dental Society established a free dental clinic staffed by volunteers. Although the clinic failed after two years, it was resurrected in 1904 to provide dental care to Rochester city school children. George Eastman made a substantial donation to the clinic in 1909 and committed to developing a more expansive and more securely funded facility. In 1916, the Rochester Dental Dispensary began operation, with Harvey J. Burkhart, DDS, as director. A year later, it moved into a newly constructed building on East Main Street, which included a school for dental hygienists and a tonsil-adenoid clinic. To help secure its solvency, Eastman made a gift of $1 million and 1,000 shares of Eastman Kodak stock to the Dispensary.

When plans were developed to create a school of medicine at the University of Rochester, Eastman requested that it include dental education and that it be known as a school of medicine and dentistry, i.e. SMD. However, an undergraduate dental school was never initiated. The Rochester Dental Dispensary, which had been designated as the clinical site for the education of predoctoral dental students, continued as a separate entity, with its own clinical service, education and research; it was renamed the Eastman Dental Dispensary in 1941 and became the Eastman Dental Center (EDC) in 1965. After Burkhart's death, Basil Bibby, DDS, became director in 1947 and was succeeded in 1969 by William McHugh, LDS, BDS, DDSc.

In the absence of a dental school, an innovative fellows program was established in SMD with funding from the Rockefeller Foundation, providing research opportunities for graduates from dental schools throughout the world. SMD became one of the first US institutions to award a PhD in a basic science to academic dentists, many of whom went on to have stellar academic careers, including five who became dental school deans. In 1951, a MS in oral biology was initiated, administered by a new department, which in 1955

Figure 11.1. Today's Eastman tower

became Dentistry and Dental Research and in 1972 was renamed Dental Research. In 1975, a new department of Clinical Dentistry was to oversee clinical operations and education. In 1978, EDC moved from its inner-city location to a new building on the URMC campus.

The appointment of William H. Bowen, BDS, PhD, as chair of Dental Research in 1982 was accompanied by the recruitment of a number of prominent basic scientists, including Lawrence A. Tabak, DDS, PhD, who later became the director of the National Institute for Dental and Craniofacial Research (NIDCR) and acting director of the NIH. Other prominent recruits included Robert A. Burne, DDS, and Robert G. Quivey, PhD, both oral microbiologists, and James Melvin, DDS, PhD, an internationally recognized expert in salivary physiology. Bowen, together with EDC leadership, was able to secure NIDCR grant funding for a Cariology Center and a combined specialty and PhD program.

Figure 11.2. Cyril Meyerowitz

In 1998, in keeping with URMC CEO Jay Stein's strategic plan, the EDC—with Ron Billings, DDS, as director—became part of the University of Rochester and the department of Dentistry. Chaired by Cyril Meyerowitz, DDS, the department of Dentistry became the academic home for all EDC and SMD dental faculty, replacing the department of Clinical Dentistry. Meyerowitz succeeded Billings as director of EDC in 1999. The department of Dental Research became the Center for Oral Biology (COB), directed by Tabak. The culmination of the strategic plan occurred in 2009 with the integration of the EDC, the department of Dentistry and the COB into the EIOH, under the leadership of Meyerowitz, as a fully unified, integrated entity combining clinical care and community service, postdoctoral residency programs, hospital programs, and educational and research activities. At that time, Quivey, professor of Microbiology and Immunology, became director of the COB, succeeding Melvin, who had taken over as director on Tabak's departure.

Meyerowitz received his DDS from the University of Witwatersrand, South Africa and an MS in oral biology at the University of Rochester, where he also completed a residency in General Dentistry and a clinical and research fellowship before joining the faculty of SMD with a joint appointment in EDC in 1975. Throughout his career, Meyerowitz has been involved in dental education and research, serving nationally on the Commission on Dental Accreditation, the Commission for Change and Innovation of the American Dental Education Association and as chair of the Council of Dental Education and Licensure of the American Dental Association (ADA). His research has focused on salivary dysfunction and its relationship to dental caries and the relationship of systemic diseases to oral health. More recently he has focused on practice-based research (see below). During his tenure as director of EDC and EIOH, the University consistently maintained a top-ten ranking in NIDCR funding, markedly expanded its community service programs, and dramatically improved access to care by growing new clinical programs and establishing sites throughout the region.

William R. Calnon, DDS, president of the EDC Foundation Board, served as acting director of the EIOH in 2012 while a national search was underway to identify Meyerowitz's successor. Calnon received his DDS from SUNY at Buffalo School of Dental Medicine and completed his residency at URMC. A part-time professor of dentistry at the University and a private practitioner in Spencerport, Calnon had served as president of the ADA, the Monroe County Dental Society, the Seventh District Dental Society, and the New York State Dental Association. Calnon served as president of the EDC Foundation Board until 2023, where he was pivotal in assuring that the foundation provided critical resources to the educational, research, and clinical missions of the EIOH.

Figure 11.3. William Calnon

In 2013, Eli Eliav, DMD, PhD, was named director of the EIOH and the first vice dean for Oral Health at SMD. In 2019, recognizing his important clinical leadership role, he was appointed VP for Oral Health at URMC. A nationally recognized expert in oral medicine and orofacial pain, Eliav had been serving as director of the Center for Temporomandibular Disorders and Orofacial Pain and as chair of the department of Diagnostic Sciences at New Jersey Dental School (UMDNJ), which became Rutgers School of Dental Medicine in 2013. Eliav earned his DMD and PhD and completed his residency in Oral Medicine at Hebrew University, Israel. He then completed a research fellowship at the NIDCR, where he studied neurosensory mechanisms related to pain. During his time at UMDNJ, Eliav developed an international reputation for his work on orofacial pain, work that has continued to thrive in Rochester. He also serves as editor-in-chief of *Quintessence International*, which provides vital information and special reports on clinical and research advances related to all dentistry disciplines. Eliav has overseen a remarkable period of growth and transformation for the EIOH.

Figure 11.4. Eli Eliav

Clinical Dentistry

Since its inception, EIOH (note that going forward, this term will be used throughout to represent all iterations of the dental program) has been the safety net provider for the Finger Lakes region and a national leader in community and outreach dentistry, operating specialized programs for city schools, community health centers, nursing homes, and people with IDD. Partnerships with several community-based agencies like the Healthy Baby Network, Urban League, Salvation Army, Refugee Center, and homeless shelters have introduced dental care to those who otherwise would have limited or no access. By 1997, seventy percent of clinical operations were directed towards the underserved, with Medicaid being the largest reimbursor. In fact, Eastman currently is the largest provider to Medicaid patients in the Finger Lakes, and the only source for dental specialty care. EIOH's role as safety net has been challenged by the need to expand rapidly and enhance its clinical delivery system to accommodate surging demands for services. The main campus facility, constructed in 1978 to serve 40–50,000 patient visits per year, had reached 60,000 by 1997, and climbed to 102,000 by 2024! Similarly, outreach volume has grown to about 37,000 patients. Several major initiatives, and several new departments, were introduced to address these issues.

In 1967, EIOH introduced SMILEmobiles, the first mobile vans providing dental care in NY State; over the past twenty-five years, four additional

Figure 11.5. Today's EIOH Department Chairs

SMILEmobiles have been brought into service. The SMILEmobile program serves underinsured and uninsured children in fifteen city schools and three Head Start programs, eliminating the need for parents to miss work to take their children to the dentist. The program has had a significant impact on preventing tooth decay and maintaining oral health for approximately 39,000 children. In 2016, through the generous support of the Lobozzo Family, a new SMILEmobile was built to provide treatment for patients with special needs. This unit, which travels to area nursing homes, refugee centers, college campuses, high schools, group homes, etc., features a wheelchair lift, wider doors, and an air glide chair that allows more maneuverability for the wheelchair-bound patient. It also serves as a unique site for training pediatric and general dentists, dental hygienists, and dental assistants, and in treating patients with special and complex needs, and was central to the EIOH receiving a $3.5 million Health and Human Services grant in 2015. Teledentistry serves as a complement to the SMILEmobile program, providing services for children, patients with IDD, older adults, and those who would otherwise need to travel long distances. EIOH has

Figure 11.6. EIOH SMILEmobile

consolidated its teledentistry initiative into a teledentistry division and was recently highlighted as an example of a successful teledentistry program in a major NIH report.[4]

In 2008, EIOH was awarded a $3.9 million New York State grant to increase access, capacity, and emergency services for the underserved. Aided by an additional large gift in 2011 from Jack W. Howitt, DDS, a University of Rochester and Eastman Dental alumnus and president of Midland Management, EIOH established a first-of-its-kind, dedicated urgent care dental clinic (Howitt Urgent Dental Care), led by Yan-Fang Ren, DDS, PhD, and Linda Rasubala, DDS, PhD, at its main site on the URMC campus, and established urgent care facilities at Eastman Dental Downtown. Anticipating the opioid crisis' impact, Ren launched a pioneering, evidence-based opioid-reduction initiative in 2013—three years ahead of CDC and ADA dental opioid guidelines. Within a year, they achieved an eighty percent reduction in opioid prescriptions, and by early 2020 had fully eliminated opioid prescriptions, setting a new standard for acute pain control in dentistry. In 2024, a new department of Diagnostic Sciences chaired by Ren was established to better meet the increasing needs for dental emergency services in the

4 https://www.nidcr.nih.gov/sites/default/files/2021-12/Oral-Health-in-America-Advances-and-Challenges.pdf#page=723

community and to enhance patient care and resident training by providing advanced diagnostic technologies.

Historically, EIOH had a relatively small full-time faculty, partnering with community dentists for support of teaching and some clinical operations. However, over the past twenty-five years, the full-time faculty has grown to forty-seven. With this growth, state-of-the-art general, specialty, and oral and maxillofacial surgery practice sites were established at Clinton Crossings.

The EIOH also developed a new department of Oral Medicine, chaired by Sharon Elad, DMD, MSc, unique in upstate NY, which serves as the regional hub for a multidisciplinary oral health team that provides comprehensive, non-surgical dental treatment, including oral complications of cancer therapy. The department conducts research and is engaged in numerous extramurally funded national and international research collaborations. Residents from all EIOH training programs benefit from new didactic courses and a clinical rotation in Oral Medicine.

EIOH has made significant strides in the field of special needs dentistry, recognizing the unique oral health challenges faced by individuals with disabilities. This includes specialized training for dental residents, focusing on techniques and strategies for providing care to individuals with various physical, developmental, and cognitive disabilities. The curriculum emphasizes compassionate, patient-centered care, equipping dentists with the skills to handle complex cases and communicate effectively with patients and their families. EIOH also collaborates with community organizations and advocacy

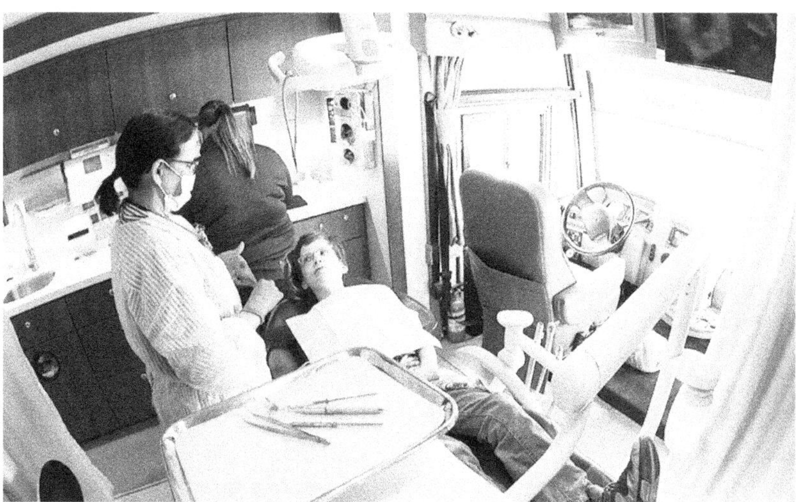

Figure 11.7. A young student receives care in the SMILEmobile.

groups to promote awareness and access to dental services for special needs populations. These efforts reduce barriers to care and improve overall health outcomes. The multidisciplinary Complex Care Center, which opened in 2016, has three clinic rooms equipped with handicap-accessible dental chairs to provide dental care to children and adults. In 2019, aided by a gift from Henry Schein, the program markedly expanded with the opening of a first-of-its-kind Specialty Care Clinic at EIOH's main campus.

Another area in which EIOH has been at the forefront is in partnering with Ob/Gyn to tackle the problem of severe tooth decay among young children, which affects one-third of socioeconomically disadvantaged and racial/ethnic minority preschool children in the US and can have a substantial adverse impact on children and their families. Leading the way has been Jin Xiao, DDS, PhD, director of the Eastman Dental Pregnancy and Infant Oral Health program. Her focus is to educate women on the importance of oral hygiene for themselves and their children and to eliminate barriers to adequate dental care during pregnancy. Among Xiao's projects has been SMARTeeth-Smart Connected Oral Health Community: Using AI and Digital Technologies to Close the Gaps in Oral Health Disparity. While at a routine obstetrician visit, a participating patient has intra-oral photos taken, and her phone is installed with an app, SMARTeeth (developed by Xiao and her team), which can detect signs of tooth decay on the patient or her children. If she has dental pain or concerns, she can secure a virtual dental visit, and if needed, a subsequent appointment for treatment. In 2018, Xiao established a Pregnancy and Infant Dental Clinic, another first of its kind, as part of the specialty care clinic.

Figure 11.8. Jin Xiao

Dental Education

EIOH is unique among academic oral health centers in the US: despite the absence of an undergraduate dental school, it has developed internationally recognized postdoctoral and dental residency programs, capitalizing on its vibrant research and its robust clinical services.

Under Eliav's leadership, the MS program was restructured, with the development of new core and elective courses and the establishment of a Clinical and Translational Science track, emphasizing research. The changes have proven extremely popular, and enrollment has soared from two MS students in 2017 to fifty-six in 2024. EIOH offers a variety of postdoctoral dental education and residency training programs leading to a Certificate of Advanced Study or a Certificate of Completion. Several of these programs offer an additional educational track leading to a master of science degree. EIOH also has tuition-based residency programs in many specialties for dentists who obtained their degrees from dental schools outside of the US and Canada. Preceptor programs are offered in every residency program as well as fellowship programs in urgent care, specialty care, research, and teledentistry.

To further educational opportunities, EIOH has developed partnerships and collaborations with universities around the world. These include sister Eastman Institutions in Paris, Rome, London, and Sweden, which are linked in the Eastman International Alliance (EIA) and provide an Eastman Global Rounds webinar and collaborative platform, and formal partnerships with universities in Italy, Saudi Arabia, Kuwait, Israel, India, Argentina, Poland, Romania and China. Visit the EIA and EIOH websites for all of the educational programs.

The General Dentistry department, led by Hans Malmstrom, DDS, has two general dentistry residency programs: advanced education in general dentistry, one of the largest (sixty residents) in the country; and general practice (six residents) led by Maricelle Abayon, DMD. The department is home to an innovative advanced dental faculty training program where international participants earn a certificate in general dentistry and a graduate degree before returning to academic positions in their home countries.

Recently Alexandra Tsigarida, DDS, was appointed chair of the Periodontology department, succeeding Jack Caton, DDS, who had led the department for thirty-five years. The department is recognized internationally for its rich history of research, with significant contributions in periodontal and dental implant biology and treatment. It has an internationally regarded nine-person periodontology residency program, directed by Elli Anna Kotsailidi, DDS.

The Prosthodontics department, chaired by Carlo Ercoli, DDS, has established collaborative programs within SMD related to the treatment of trauma and cancer patients and has transformed its clinical and laboratory operation to include the full breadth of digital technology. Ercoli also led efforts to fund renovations of the Prosthodontic Clinic, a new, state-of-the-art prosthodontic laboratory, the Gerald N. Graser Endowed Implant Fellowship and the Ronald H. Jarvis Endowed Fund. Under the direction of Konstantinos Chochlidakis, DDS, the number of residents in prosthodontics has increased to nine and all are enrolled in the master's in clinical and translational science.

The Oral and Maxillofacial Surgery (OMFS) department is chaired by John Vorrasi, DDS. Under the supervision of Dina Amin, DDS, residency program director, the department recently initiated a six-year program, using the resources of the undergraduate medical school, leading to an MD and a certificate in OMFS. The program is designed for those who want to pursue fellowship training in craniofacial, head and neck oncology, and microvascular surgery, and who want to join academic departments. OMFS also established a partnership with the Simon School to offer an executive master's in business administration (EMBA) degree to select residents enrolled in the OMFS certificate program.

What started as a temporomandibular joint clinic has evolved into the most extensive CODA-accredited Orofacial Pain residency program in the US. The program, which involves collaborations with other URMC departments and programs, such as the Headache Center, Sleep Clinic, and outpatient physical therapy, is led by Junad Khan, BDS, MSD, and currently has eleven residents who are trained in the treatment of acute and chronic oral pain resulting in particular from cancer, surgery, dental implants, or trauma.

The Orthodontics and Dentofacial Orthopaedics department, chaired by Emile Rossouw, BSc, has a two-year, twelve-person residency program directed by Dimitrios Michelogiannakis, DDS. Residents work alongside a team of highly trained specialists to treat patients with medically complex conditions and also have rich opportunities for research.

Cynthia Wong, DMD, chairs the Pediatric Dentistry department, with Erin Shope, DMD, as associate chair. Its twelve-person residency program, directed by Isamar Rivera-Ramos, DMD, PhD, employs innovative teaching techniques to create pediatric dentists who are advocates for the "whole child." Residents gain extensive hospital-based experiences, including the operating room, emergency department, inpatient floors, craniofacial team, and hemophilia team. The pediatric residency clinic draws patients from across the state and Pennsylvania.

The Community Dentistry and Oral Disease Prevention department, led by interim chair Sangeeta Gajendra, DDS, houses a dental public health residency, which was successfully transferred in 2019 from the NY State Department of Health in Albany. Recently Gajendra received a NIH-funded HIV multidisciplinary research project involving faculty from Public Health Sciences, Psychiatry and Internal Medicine. The department also has established a fluoride varnish program, a NY State-funded sealant program and a Dental Home program.

In 2021, HRSA selected the EIOH to establish a Primary Care Dental Faculty Development Center. Led by Linda Rasubala, DDS, the Center serves as a resource and training hub for junior primary care dental faculty in the US, preparing them to become leaders in primary care dentistry and clinical educators capable of addressing issues of health equity. The curriculum is delivered primarily online through individual and group sessions.

Dental Research

As dentistry approached the end of the 20th century, two programs stood out for their research excellence: the Cariology Center led by Bowen, and the COB led by Tabak, who also served as SMD SAD for Research. Both programs resided within SMD but were closely aligned with translational dental researchers, including Martin Curzon, MD, John Featherstone, PhD, and Domenick Zero, DDS. After the merger, additional research recruitment funding from the EDF helped build a cadre of outstanding scientists within the COB.

Catherine Ovitt, PhD—whose work focused on developing therapeutic strategies for their repair or regeneration of salivary glands after damage from radiation treatment due to head and neck cancers or from autoimmune diseases—was recruited in 2001 to join the COB and the new department of Biomedical Genetics. In 2002, Wei Hsu, PhD, was also recruited to the COB and Biomedical Genetics, where he did groundbreaking work on the role of stem cells in tissue regeneration and reconstructive surgical repair. Appointed as a Dean's Professor of Biomedical Genetics in 2016, he left the University to join Harvard's Forsyth Institute in 2021. Two other scientists who established national reputations during their time in the COB were Rulang Jiang, PhD (now at Cincinnati Children's Hospital), who focused on the developmental mechanisms underlying craniofacial developmental disorders, and Hyun "Michel" Koo, DDS, PhD (now at University of Pennsylvania), who focused on how biofilms form and cause oral diseases.

As indications of its great success, EIOH faculty have published more than 1,500 research papers in peer-reviewed journals in the last ten years, and the University has consistently ranked near the top in federal research funding in oral health.

To more closely integrate oral health-related research within EIOH, in 2022 a department of Oral and Craniofacial Sciences (DOCS) was established, replacing the COB. Thomas Diekwisch, DMD, PhD, PhD, was recruited to serve as the Margaret and Cy Welcher Professor in Dental Research and the founding chair. Previously, he served as director for the Center for Craniofacial Research and Diagnosis and Head of the Department of Periodontics at Texas A&M

Figure 11.9. Thomas Diekwisch

University College of Dentistry. Diekwisch received a PhD in Anatomy from the department of Anatomy and Cell Biology, a PhD in the Philosophy of Science from the Institute for Philosophy and a DMD from the School of Dentistry at Philipps-University of Marburg, Germany. At the time of his recruitment, Diekwisch was the PI of three federally funded grants totaling $4.7 million. His research spans three areas including: epigenetic mechanisms of mitotic cell division, chromatin, heterochromatin, histone variants and modifications; biomineralization of odontogenic tissues; and generating tools for engineering and regeneration of complex periodontal tissues. Among his numerous publications is a manuscript on tooth eruption in a late Cretaceous Mosasaur, an enormous aquatic reptile that was a victim of the mass extinction that occurred sixty-five million years ago. Joining Diekwisch was Xianghong Luan, MD, a professor at Texas A&M College of Dentistry and the PI of two federally funded grants totaling $3.8 million which focus on microRNAs and small molecule microenvironment design for the regeneration of periodontal and craniofacial tissues.

Research in the DOCS highlights the oral cavity as an entryway to the human body and the craniofacial region as a principal organ for sensation, expression, and protection. Currently, the department is home to five major research laboratories, whose programs cover a wide array of areas, including oral infectious diseases, dental caries, salivary diagnosis and therapy, craniofacial development, orofacial and chronic pain, periodontal diagnosis and therapy, implants, materials, laser technology, nerve injury, pain modulation, practice-based research, and community-based disease prevention. More can be found about these individual research programs at the DOCS website.

Clinical and translational research has also remained a major focus of the EIOH, with more than twenty faculty members actively involved in projects. Of particular note are the following programs.

EIOH became an integral part of the NIDCR-funded National Dental Practice-Based Research Network (PBRN), a nationwide community of participating dental professionals and organizations established in 2012 to advance knowledge of dental practices and to discover ways to improve them. At the time, EIOH was chosen to direct the Northeast node, one of six regional nodes throughout the country, with Cyril Meyerowitz serving as the director of the Northeast node until 2024, when he handed over the reins to Dorota Kopycka-Kedzierawski, DDS, MPH. As of January 2024, the PBRN had completed fifty-six studies, published 229 peer-reviewed articles, and engaged over 75,000 patients nationwide, addressing critical gaps in dental knowledge and practice, from

Figure 11.10. Dorota Kopycka-Kedzierawski

exploring opioid prescription practices to advancing treatments for cracked teeth.

Kopycka-Kedzierawski received her DDS from the Medical University of Lublin, Poland, and completed a residency in general practice dentistry and an MPH at the University of Rochester. She has been actively involved with the PBRN since 2012, serving as PI and co-investigator for several pivotal studies in addition to her role as assistant director. She is currently PI of a double-blind placebo-controlled phase II randomized controlled trial entitled *Povidone Iodine Efficacy Study*, which is assessing the efficacy of povidone-iodine in preventing new cavitated caries lesions that require follow-up restorative/surgical intervention. Her research interests include teledentistry, oral epidemiology, and dental practice-based research. Kopycka-Kedzierawski also leads the EIOH Clinical and Translational Research Core, which was established in 2020 to assist faculty and residents in their research undertakings, in applying for government, commercial and foundation grants, in identifying and allocating resources, and in strengthening linkages with the CTSI.

In addition to her work in the Eastman Dental Pregnancy and Infant Oral Health Program (described above), Jin Xiao's research group is involved in a broad range of research projects involved in oral microbiology and salivary research, and perinatal health.

In conclusion, EIOH's successful faculty recruitment has led to significant growth in research, clinical services, and educational programs. EIOH is recognized as an international leader in academic dentistry and research, with many current EIOH faculty and alumni holding leadership positions in their respective national associations. Various reports rank the EIOH among the top dental schools in the nation and most of its dental residency programs were ranked by Universities.com as 2024's *Best in the US.* In 2017, EIOH celebrated a century of education and research innovation and community service by hosting an international scientific and educational symposium and Centennial Gala attended by 700 professionals from twenty-five countries. The institution continues its mission to provide oral health care to the greater Rochester community and to innovate in education and research.

D. Pediatrics and the Creation of the Golisano Children's Hospital

Chapter 12

DEPARTMENT OF PEDIATRICS AND THE CREATION OF THE GOLISANO CHILDREN'S HOSPITAL (GCH)

Since its inception in 1925, Pediatrics has had a national reputation for academic distinction and leadership, starting with its first chair, Samuel W. Clausen, MD, whose studies on Vitamin A were made when undernutrition was a common health problem for children. Three of its nine chairs have been elected to the National Academy of Medicine and all nine have been leaders of their scientific fields. Researchers in the department have been responsible for two of the most important advances in pediatrics in the 20th century—the development of surfactant for the prevention of respiratory distress in premature infants, and the creation of a vaccine against *Hemophilus influenzae*, type B (Hib), a major cause of meningitis in children. In 1996, two former faculty—David H. Smith, MD, and Porter W. Anderson, PhD—shared the Albert Lasker Clinical Medical Research Award and the Pasteur Award from the World Health Organization for their role in developing the Hib vaccine. During the past twelve years, GCH has appeared in the *U.S. News & World Report* top fifty children's hospitals in eight of eleven pediatric subspecialties.

Rochester has always had a distinguished group of community pediatricians, many of whom trained in the University's residency program. As local hospitals began to relinquish inpatient pediatric care, it became clear that the unusual camaraderie among community and academic pediatricians should be preserved and strengthened to ensure that the community has a single standard of care. Although consolidation into two health systems in Rochester has resulted in a highly competitive environment in which most of the programmatic relationships between the two systems have been severed, pediatrics is a notable exception; the pediatricians serving the inpatient and outpatient facilities at RRH have remained faculty members at the University, the department oversees the management of the NICU at RGH, and RGH has remained a training site for students, pediatric residents, and fellows.

During the past twenty-five years, Pediatrics has been fortunate to have had four outstanding chairs who have transformed pediatric care throughout the region. Elizabeth R. McAnarney, MD, received her MD from SUNY Upstate and completed a residency in pediatrics at URMC in 1968. She has remained at the University ever since, serving as director of the division of Adolescent Medicine for twenty-two years, and from 1993 to 2006, as pediatrician-in-chief of GCH and chair of Pediatrics. From 2009–10, she served as acting dean of SMD.

Figure 12.1. Elizabeth McAnarney

McAnarney is a leader in the field of adolescent medicine, due in part to her long advocacy. Her work, which focused on the relationship of young maternal age and perinatal outcomes, changed the way that health care providers cared for pregnant teens and their babies. She was the lead editor of the *Textbook of Adolescent Medicine,* published in 1992. She served as president of the Society for Adolescent Medicine and the American Pediatric Society (APS). She was elected to the National Academy of Medicine and in 2013 was awarded the John Howland Award, the most prestigious award given by the APS. In 2018, McAnarney was named distinguished university professor, becoming the thirteenth recipient and first woman to receive the highest title bestowed on faculty at the University!

McAnarney's thirteen-year tenure as chair saw impressive growth. The full-time pediatric faculty doubled in size, as did national and state grant support. Most significantly, her efforts led to a transformative gift of $14 million in 2002 from B. Thomas Golisano to name GCH, which encompassed the fourth floor of SMH and with the NICU located on the third floor next to obstetrical services. The gift helped recruit outstanding faculty and expand programs, such as cardiovascular services, general surgery, and neurosciences. Although the new GCH was a marked improvement, McAnarney recognized that as a hospital-within-a-hospital, GCH lacked an identity and facilities commensurate with its role as a major referral center for pediatrics in upstate NY and began advocating for a physically separate children's hospital. That mantle was taken up by her successor, Nina F. Schor, MD, PhD, who was recruited from the University of Pittsburgh in 2006 to be chair of Pediatrics and pediatrician-in-chief (later changed to physician-in-chief) of GCH. In 2008, Schor became the inaugural William H. Eilinger Chair of Pediatrics, funded by a generous gift from the estate of William H. Eilinger, a University of Rochester alumnus.

Figure 12.2. Nina Schor

Schor received her MD from Cornell University Medical College and her PhD from Rockefeller

University. She completed a residency in pediatrics at Boston Children's Hospital, a fellowship in child neurology, and a research fellowship in the laboratory of Manfred Karnofsky, PhD, all at Harvard University. Prior to joining URMC, Schor spent twenty years at the University of Pittsburgh Medical Center, where she served as chief of Child Neurology and associate dean for Medical Student Research at the School of Medicine, helping develop the university's pediatric research program into a nationally recognized powerhouse. She led a highly funded, internationally prominent research program in neuroblastoma, aimed at understanding the neurobiology of this tumor and exploiting this to design and test novel strategies for the therapy of chemoresistant neuroblastoma.

Schor further grew the national visibility of the department, promoting translational research and integrating innovative technologies. Pediatrics grew from 110 faculty members to over 170, and new divisions were created in Palliative Care, Sleep Allergy, and Hospitalist Medicine. She developed research centers focused on premature infants, translational molecular programs, and red blood cell development, and secured an institutional training grant that fostered research among URMC clinical fellows and junior faculty physician-scientists. Most importantly, she turned the dream of a physically separate children's hospital into reality, overseeing the planning and development of the GCH tower. The eight-story, $145 million, 245,000 square-foot building, which opened in 2015, included private patient rooms, many family-friendly amenities, advanced medical technologies, and separate pediatric support services (see below). The opening of the new GCH marked a new era for pediatric care and reinforced URMC's position as the leader in pediatric health care in upstate NY.

In 2018, Schor left URMC to become deputy director of the National Institute of Neurological Disorders and Stroke. She was followed as William H. Eilinger Chair of Pediatrics and physician-in-chief at GCH by Patrick Brophy, MD, MHCDS. Brophy received his MD from the University of Saskatchewan College of Medicine, did a residency in pediatrics at the University of Manitoba, and completed clinical and research fellowships in pediatric nephrology at the University of Michigan. Prior to coming to URMC, Brophy developed a nationally recognized program in kidney development *in utero* and had served for a decade as director of Pediatric Nephrology at the University of Iowa, where he founded the Signal Center for Health Innovation and led efforts to use technology, particularly telehealth, to improve patient outreach.

Figure 12.3.
Patrick Brophy

Brophy's initial term as chair was marked by several challenges, including the COVID-19 pandemic as well as a recurrence of mantle cell lymphoma, for which he was one of the first patients to receive CAR T-cell therapy (see p. 311) at URMC. Despite these challenges, his tenure was a period of strategic growth and innovation. Brophy developed a new strategic plan based upon seven pillars: primary care; analytics and digital health; education; population health and partnership; community and advocacy; research; and culture and opportunity. Key to executing the plan was creating an administrative structure to manage the enormous growth in the department and the new GCH. This included establishing vice chairs for academic affairs, behavioral population health, research, clinical and translational research, education, community and government affairs, equity and inclusion, and innovation and integration. The department recruited eighty-three new faculty members and launched several programs, including a regional cardiology partnership between GCH, Upstate Golisano Children's Hospital in Syracuse, and Oishei Hospital in Buffalo, as well as a new division of Breastfeeding and Lactation.

Brophy markedly expanded community outreach efforts, engaging in initiatives with over seventy community partners across the continuum from prenatal to young adulthood. Among the most significant accomplishments were successful, multi-tiered investments to address the pediatric behavioral health crisis. These included a new Behavioral Health & Wellness Center, expansion of the Mobile Crisis Team and school partnerships, and plans for the region's first pediatric walk-in behavioral health center. Brophy stepped down as chair in early 2023 to serve as the provincial head of Child Health and Pediatrics for his native province of Saskatchewan. Sadly, he died later that year from a second recurrence of his lymphoma. He was followed as William H. Eilinger Chair of Pediatrics and physician-in-chief at GCH by Jill S. Halterman, MD, MPH.

Halterman received her MD from the University of Rochester, completed an internship in pediatrics at Children's Hospital of Philadelphia, and then returned to URMC for her pediatric residency, after which she joined the faculty. At the University, she developed a well-funded, nationally recognized clinical research program to understand the multifactorial contributions driving asthma disparities and to improve care for historically marginalized children with this disease. She led multiple large, randomized trials in outpatient settings to improve asthma care and reduce morbidity and established asthma treatment programs that have been nationally recognized and are being

Figure 12.4. Jill Halterman

replicated across the country. In recognition of her achievements, she was awarded the Dr. Elizabeth R. McAnarney Professorship in Pediatrics funded by Roger & Carolyn Friedlander in 2020. She was also named executive vice chair of Pediatrics, as part of the restructuring of the department noted above during Brophy's tenure.

Not surprisingly, Halterman hit the ground running! The department has already made strides in improving access to care, advancing research, and launching new initiatives including a vision for "GCH 2.0." Halterman's focus has been on building a system of comprehensive, equitable, and coordinated care for children across upstate NY.

The department of Pediatrics—which now handles over 100,000 outpatient visits a year and approximately 6,800 admissions to GCH—has grown to more than 200 faculty and over 2,500 employees, in addition to working with over 400 community providers. Currently GCH has fifty-two private pediatric rooms, in addition to one of its crown jewels, the sixty-eight-bed (each in a private room) Level IV NICU, which serves as the perinatal center for the Finger Lakes region and admits 1,200 newborns each year.

The division of Neonatology, which also oversees the fourteen-bed Level II special care nursery at RGH, is led by Carl T. D'Angio, MD, and currently has a faculty of forty-one, including twenty-six neonatologists. Recently GCH was designated as a Level 1 (the highest classification) Pediatric Trauma Center by the American College of Surgeons and NY State. It is beyond the scope of this book to detail the growth of all new programs developed over the past twenty-five years. A few will be highlighted below.

Child and Adolescent Eating Disorder Program

The Child and Adolescent Eating Disorder Program was established a quarter of a century ago within the division of Adolescent Medicine. The program, founded by Richard E. Kreipe, MD, treats individuals with diagnosed eating disorders and those who may be exhibiting signs and symptoms of an eating disorder. Kreipe, professor emeritus of Pediatrics, received his MD from Temple University School of Medicine, completed a residency and chief residency in pediatrics at St. Christopher's Hospital for Children, Philadelphia, and completed a fellowship in general pediatrics and adolescent medicine at URMC. Over his thirty-five years at URMC, he has developed an international reputation for his work on pediatric eating disorders, including co-editing the *Textbook*

Figure 12.5. Richard Kreipe

of Adolescent Health Care, published by the American Academy of Pediatrics. Kreipe is a recipient of the Outstanding Achievement in Adolescent Medicine award from the Society for Adolescent Health and Medicine and the Academy of Eating Disorders Leadership award. In 2012, he was honored as the inaugural Dr. Elizabeth R. McAnarney Professor in Pediatrics funded by Roger & Carolyn Friedlander.

Most patients in the Eating Disorders program are seen in outpatient clinics by a multidisciplinary team that develops a comprehensive plan, including medical treatment and monitoring, education, nutritional counseling, mental health therapy for the individual and family, and outpatient group therapy. The model developed by Kreipe and co-workers helped establish URMC as one of the premier treatment centers for eating disorders and served as a cornerstone of the Western New York Comprehensive Care Center for Eating Disorders, an integrated, coordinated system of care serving children, adolescents, and young adults, of which Kreipe was the founding medical director. In 2017, the University initiated the world's first Project ECHO® tele-education hub specializing in the care of individuals with eating disorders and their families, educating local community providers on identifying and managing eating disorders, and providing them with the interprofessional skills necessary to effectively participate on multidisciplinary eating disorder teams.

University of Rochester Batten Center

One of the jewels of URMC over the last twenty-five years has been the University of Rochester Batten Center (URBC). Batten disease is a fatal, inherited disorder of the nervous system that typically begins in childhood. The University is recognized as one of the world leaders in research on Batten disease and the URBC is one of only five institutions named by the Batten Disease Support, Research, and Advocacy Foundation as a Center of Excellence. The URBC, previously directed by Jonathan Mink, MD, PhD, and currently directed by Jennifer Vermilion, MD, is a comprehensive Batten disease clinical and research center. The center studies the natural history of Batten diseases, identifies biomarkers for early diagnosis, seeks to understand the genetic and molecular mechanisms underpinning the disease, and explores potential gene therapies. Researchers at URBC are also involved in clinical trials testing new therapies to slow or halt disease progression. The URBC is now part of the recently established Golisano IDD Institute.

Center for Food Allergy

The Center for Food Allergy is a multidisciplinary program that provides comprehensive care to families with food allergies. The center, which includes specialists in allergy, gastroenterology, dermatology, and counseling, is part of the FARE® (Food Allergy Research and Education) Clinical Network Center, a coalition of top food allergy centers. As a FARE Center of Excellence, URMC serves as a site for major clinical trials, develops best practices of care for patients with food allergies, and contributes to the development of a national food allergy patient registry and biorepository. The center is led by Kirsi Järvinen-Seppo, MD, PhD, chief of the division of Pediatric Allergy and Immunology. Järvinen-Seppo received her MD and PhD from the University of Helsinki, Finland, and completed her residency in pediatrics and clinical and research fellowships in allergy and immunology at Mount Sinai School of Medicine. Her NIH-funded and nationally recognized translational research program studies the infant immune system and the development of food allergies, atopic dermatitis and the whole atopic march. A particular focus has been on the role of maternal and infant environmental factors and breast milk composition in shaping the early infant immune system. In 2016, she was honored as the inaugural Founders' Distinguished Chair in Pediatric Allergy, funded by Eric M. Dreyfuss, MD, one of the first allergy and immunology fellows trained at the University, who had a distinguished

Figure 12.6. Kirsi Järvinen-Seppo receives the Dean's Medal from Eric Dreyfuss

career as a pediatric allergist at URMC for over fifty years. Before his death in 2021, he established a second professorship, the Dr. Eric M. Dreyfuss Professorship, and a research endowment. He was awarded the SMD Dean's Medal in 2021.

Developmental and Behavioral Pediatrics

Figure 12.7. Susan Hyman

The division of Developmental & Behavioral Pediatrics (led by Dennis Z. Kuo, MD, MHS), the largest in upstate NY, offers comprehensive care to children and adolescents with IDD, such as autism, fetal alcohol spectrum disorders, and cerebral palsy. In 2017, the William and Mildred Levine Autism Clinic, supported by a generous gift from the William and Mildred Levine Foundation, was established on the third floor of the new Imaging Sciences Building on East River Road, under the leadership of Susan L. Hyman, MD, a national authority in autism. As part of her ELAM project (see chapter 72), Hyman had analyzed the breadth of IDD services and research at the University, with an eye towards ultimately obtaining NIH designation as an IDD Research Center. The Levine Autism Clinic serves the unique physical, sensory, and environmental needs of children and adolescents with autism and enables specialists in autism, child and adolescent psychiatry, and neurology to work side by side. It is a key part of the new Golisano IDD Institute. URMC is also the largest provider of ambulatory children's mental health services, has the region's only child and adolescent psychiatry inpatient unit, and the only adolescent partial hospital in western NY. These services represent an outstanding collaboration between Pediatrics and Psychiatry and are discussed in full in chapter 51.

Poison Control and Breastfeeding

Figure 12.8. Ruth Lawrence

Ruth A. Lawrence, MD, received her MD from the University of Rochester in 1949. After completing a residency, chief residency and fellowship (rooming-In project) in pediatrics at Yale University, she was recruited back to URMC to run the well-baby and the preemie nursery. At SMH, she played a critical role in the creation of Rochester's first neonatal and pediatric intensive care units. Lawrence began to write articles on the benefits of breastfeeding, which had been losing favor because of the growing popularity of formula feeding. These articles gained significant traction, leading to a surge of interest in the value of breastfeeding and to the publication of her seminal book, *Breastfeeding: A Guide for the Medical Profession*, first published in 1979 and currently in its ninth edition.[5] Co-authored by her son, Robert M. Lawrence, MD. Beginning with the seventh edition, this textbook remains the definitive reference for clinicians worldwide on breastfeeding and lactation medicine practices. Lawrence was a founder of the Academy of Breastfeeding Medicine and the United States Breastfeeding Coalition.

Lawrence was also an innovator in toxicology. In 1958, she established the Poison Control Center and Drug Information Center, the second such center in the country and the first to provide direct support to the public. This pioneering initiative set a new standard for emergency medical response and patient care. In recognition of her exceptional career, Lawrence received the Lifetime Achievement Award from the American Academy of Clinical Toxicology, was named Distinguished Alumna Professor of Pediatrics and Obstetrics/Gynecology by the University of Rochester, and subsequently became the inaugural Northumberland Trust Professor in Pediatrics. The Ruth A. Lawrence Professor in Pediatrics was established in her name. Lawrence passed away in October 2025 at the age of 101. She made an indelible contribution to the health of women and children worldwide.

In 2022, URMC established the division of Breastfeeding and Lactation Medicine (led by Casey Rosen-Carol, MD, MPH, who was Lawrence's last clinical fellow), a collaboration between Pediatrics and Ob/Gyn. The division, one of the first in the world dedicated to the study of breastfeeding, promotes research in human milk and feeding science, best practice implementation, and breastfeeding education. It includes breastfeeding medicine providers, dentists, toxicologists, family medicine physicians, and researchers. The Ruth A. Lawrence Educational Fund was established in June 2024 to support the educational efforts of the division.

Genetic Counseling

For most of this century, genetic evaluation, diagnosis, and counseling at URMC was overseen by Chin-To Fong, MD, who served as chief of the divisions of Pediatric Genetics and Medical Genetics in a distinguished thirty-five-year career at the University. Fong received his MD from Harvard University and

5 Lawrence, Ruth A. and Lawrence, Robert M. *Breastfeeding: A Guide for the Medical Profession.* Elsevier, 2021.

did a residency in Pediatrics and fellowship in Medical Genetics and Clinical Biochemical Genetics at Washington University, St. Louis. Fong's studies included the genetics of neuroblastoma, experimental gene transfer, and the genetic and environmental factors associated with cleft lip and palate and with preterm delivery. During his tenure as chief, the two divisions grew into a full-spectrum genetic service providing diagnostic dysmorphology, identification and management of inborn metabolic disorders, and cancer and cardiovascular genetic counseling, as well as providing input to multi-disciplinary clinics serving patients with craniofacial and pulmonary genetic disorders. In 2012, Fong received the Arnold P. Gold Foundation Humanism in Medicine Award, nominated by SMD medical students who felt he exemplified the qualities of a caring and compassionate mentor in teaching and advising medical students.

Figure 12.9. Chin-To Fong

In 2020, Alex V. Levin, MD, MHSc, was recruited from the Wills Eye Institute in Philadelphia to become the Adeline Lutz—Steven S. T. Ching, MD, Distinguished Professor in Ophthalmology and chief of Pediatric Ophthalmology and Ocular Genetics at the FEI, as well as chief of Pediatric Genetics at GCH. Levin received his MD from Jefferson Medical College, Pennsylvania and completed residencies in pediatrics at Children's Hospital of Philadelphia and ophthalmology at Wills Eye Hospital. Levin then went to the University of Toronto's Hospital for Sick Children, where he did a fellowship in pediatric ophthalmology and strabismus and received an MHSc in bioethics. He is the only physician worldwide to hold US board certifications in pediatrics, ophthalmology, and child abuse pediatrics simultaneously. Levin's research program has generated hundreds of publications and thirteen books on ocular genetics and gene therapy, children's vision screening, children's eye disorders, ocular manifestations of child abuse and bioethics. Of particular import is Levin's collaboration with Edwin M. Stone, MD, PhD, and Budd Tucker, PhD, of the University of Iowa towards the development of open-access, low-cost, not-for-profit, ocular gene therapy for retinal dystrophies.

Figure 12.10. Alex Levin

A major outcome of Levin's recruitment was the formation of a new division of Clinical Genetics within Pediatrics that established a single administrative entity for four services: pediatric genetics, metabolic genetics, adult/medical genetics, and cancer genetics (including the WCI Hereditary Cancer Screening and Risk Program). The goals of this division are to develop streamlined genetic testing, provide shorter times to genetics consultation, increase availability of genetic counseling services to UR Medicine patients across all specialties, and build a national powerhouse in clinical genetics. One initiative begun by Fong was the creation of a Master of Science in Genetic Counseling (MSGC). With the strong support of Levin, this came to fruition in 2023 under the direction of Audrey L. Schroeder, MS, MSGC. This full-time, two-year program, which prepares students for a career as genetic counselors, includes extensive hands-on training in URMC's Genetics clinics spanning multiple departments as well as completion of a master's research thesis.

Education

Education has been a priority for the department since its inception. Samuel Clausen was a master educator, known widely for his teaching presence on the pediatric inpatient floors where children who had pre-vaccine, often fatal infectious conditions (polio, pertussis, diphtheria, etc.) were hospitalized. True to Clausen's vision, the department has robust training programs for medical students, residents, and fellows, refining its curricula to emphasize evidence-based practices, interprofessional collaboration, and hands-on clinical experiences. The department has also been a national leader in the integration of robust community outreach initiatives, which has added significant value to the educational experience. Patricia Chess, MD, MS, a neonatologist, serves as vice chair for Education and oversees a wide array of programs.

The Pediatric Clerkship is one of SMD's core clerkships. Third-year medical students rotate through pediatrics, in groups of approximately twelve, for five weeks at a time, either at GCH or at RGH. The majority of time is spent as members of an inpatient ward team, with the remainder devoted to either a subspecialty, newborn, or acute ambulatory experience. The four-week pediatric acting internship allows fourth-year students to assume primary responsibility for patients under the direct supervision of second- or third-year residents.

The pediatrics residency has grown over the years and has trained a substantial portion of the pediatricians practicing in the Rochester metro area. Currently the program accepts sixteen residents per year, including two for child neurology. Residents rotate predominantly at SMH, but continue to spend time at RGH. A special feature of the residency program is the Hoekelman Center, which serves as a focal point to link students and residents with the community and has received numerous national awards.

The four-year med-peds residency, established in 1967 as one of the first in the nation, currently takes eight residents per year, who receive rigorous training in both medicine and pediatrics. Pediatric inpatient rotations are predominantly at SMH, with some time at RGH, whereas the medicine inpatient rotations are at SMH and HH. There is also the option of rotating at FF Thompson Hospital, which serves a more rural population.

Over the past twenty-five years there has been remarkable growth in the number of fellowships. The department now has seventeen ACGME-accredited and/or departmental fellowships (see the Pediatrics website for a full list). Of particular note is the NIH T32-sponsored General Pediatrics & Primary Care Fellowship, which offers a primary care research curriculum for fellows with diverse racial/ethnic and educational backgrounds to improve the health of adults and children living in poverty. The fellowship provides experiential learning in health disparities research, population health, and research dissemination, and allows MDs or DOs to earn a master's in public health sciences. The program is also open to PhDs, who develop projects that enable them to learn from clinical fellows and faculty about primary health care challenges.

Pediatrics Research

Building on its legacy of world-class discoveries, there have been increasing efforts to grow and centralize the research activities of the department. This led in 2021 to the establishment of the Center for Children's Health Research (CCHR), which serves to harmonize all research efforts, optimize synergy among research administration and infrastructure, and establish a singular "culture of community" across the pediatrics research enterprise. The CCHR is structured around six key programs of excellence: 1) Neurodevelopment and Behavior (autism, intellectual disabilities, and disease mechanisms); 2) Maternal Child Health (prematurity, health outcomes, nutrition, and environmental exposures); 3) Cancer and Blood Diseases (anemia pathogenesis, treatment and survivorship for hematologic malignancies); 4) Infection, Immunity, and the Environment (host-environment interactions and allergic diseases); 5) Healthcare Delivery and Population Health; and 6) Cardiopulmonary Health and Development (lung function, lung infections, and cardiac development).

The CCHR has been successful in streamlining clinical trials and in facilitating collaborations throughout the University by establishing interdisciplinary research centers. The department has over 350 active research studies and averages $25 million in research funding per year, with approximately sixty percent derived from the NIH. Approximately 150 publications are generated per year. A description of the individual research laboratories and centers can be found on the department website. In recognition of their achievements, a number of department researchers have received endowed professorships, most established within the past twenty-five years. Their work is summarized briefly below.

Laurie A. Steiner, MD, is the Lindsey Distinguished Professorship for Pediatric Research (established in 2006). Steiner is a neonatologist, who serves as the executive vice chair and vice chair for Academic Affairs in Pediatrics. The Steiner lab studies the molecular mechanisms underlying the development of red blood cells in normal and disease states. A particular focus is the role of chromatin structure and chromatin modifiers in this process.

Matthew D. McGraw, MD, holds the George Washington Goler Chair in Pediatrics (established in 1980). McGraw's research focuses on mechanisms of fibrotic lung diseases, particularly bronchiolitis obliterans, a devastating fibrotic lung disease characterized by progressive luminal narrowing and obliteration of the small airways, or bronchioles.

Karen M. Wilson, MD, MPH, was recruited from Mount Sinai School of Medicine to be the Ruth A. Lawrence Professor in Pediatrics (established 2019). Wilson, who received her MD and MPH from the University of Rochester and did her residency and fellowship in pediatrics at GCH, is internationally known for her research on the impact of secondhand tobacco smoke exposure on children, particularly in multi-unit housing, and on developing approaches to help parents quit smoking. Her program has recently evolved to include secondhand marijuana smoke exposure. Wilson serves as the vice-chair for Clinical and Translational Research in Pediatrics and is a co-director of the CTSI.

George A. Porter, MD, PhD, is the Rhea and Raymond White Professor in Pediatric Cardiology (established 2019). Porter's laboratory studies mechanisms that control cardiac development, concentrating on the roles played by mitochondria. He is the site principal investigator at Rochester for the Pediatric Cardiac Genomics Consortium, which has enrolled more than 10,000 patients with congenital heart defects to perform genotype-phenotype correlation using advanced genetic testing.

Thomas J. Mariani, PhD, is the David H. Smith Professor in Pediatrics (established in 2019). Mariani is a leader in the application of genomics to pulmonary biology and lung disease. His laboratory focuses upon defining regulatory networks involved in lung development and maturation, and which may be perturbed in diseased states. Mariani serves as vice chair for research in Pediatrics and as chief scientific officer in the CCHR.

Dennis Z. Kuo, MD, MHS, is the Purcell Family Distinguished Professor (established in 2021) and chief of the division of Developmental and Behavioral Pediatrics. Kuo's clinical and research programs focus on patient- and family-centered care for children with medical complexity, care coordination, early childhood health, and health care system reform for children with disabilities and medical complexity.

Jill M. Cholette, MD, the Medical Director of the PICU, is the inaugural Gordon Family Professor in Pediatrics (established in 2020). As a pediatric cardiologist, Cholette's research focuses on the role of inflammation in the development of thrombosis in children undergoing cardiac surgery, determining the optimal anticoagulation regimen for post-op cardiac surgery patients, and identifying the best use of blood products in critically ill pediatric patients.

James Palis, MD, holds a Northumberland Trust Professorship in Pediatrics (established in 2014). He has devoted his career to understanding the cellular and molecular events underlying the ontogeny of the hematopoietic system. His work has led to a better understanding of the molecular basis for genetic disorders, bone marrow failure syndromes, and leukemias. A particularly exciting focus has been his work on the self-renewal of erythroid precursors to generate blood *ex vivo,* for which he holds seven patents.

Marjorie J. Arca, MD, is the Joseph M. Lobozzo II Professor in Pediatric Surgery (established 2013), chief of the division of Pediatric Surgery, and surgeon-in-chief and director of Surgical Strategy and Operations at GCH. Her work is discussed in detail in chapter 23.

These professorships were the result of the extraordinary philanthropic efforts of the department and GCH. Vital to these efforts has been the GCH Board, whose focus is on fundraising and promoting an increased awareness of GCH, and which is comprised of leading individuals throughout the community. The current board chair is Kim J. McCluski, a resident of Pittsford, whose son was treated at GCH. The Board oversees a variety of fundraising events including: the GCH Stroll for Strong Kids and 5k Run, the Golf Classic, the Fairport Music Festival (which has raised an aggregate of $2.9 million), the GCH Gala, and the Drive for Miracles Radiothon. Due to the efforts of the Board and UR Advancement, over $258 million has been raised in support of Pediatrics and GCH since 2000.

E. Primary Care and the Community

Chapter 13

PRIMARY CARE NETWORK

A critical aim of URMC strategic plans over the past twenty-five years has been the development of a workforce of sufficient size and composition to care for more than one million patients. A major component of this effort was the development of a primary care network. As discussed in the previous chapter, Pediatrics had been instrumental in establishing a long-standing community-wide pediatrics program that involved University-employed and private practitioners and included all the local hospitals. However, like many academic health systems, URMC had traditionally focused on specialty services, leaving adult primary care in the purview of private physicians. Some of these physicians took part in teaching students and residents and thus were given clinical appointments in SMD. It wasn't until 1991 that the Medical Center opened its first satellite adult primary care practice. This was done in response to the community's demand for more primary care physicians who are University of Rochester faculty and in recognition of the growing need to provide more rigorous ambulatory clinical experiences for students and residents.

The development of a more robust primary care presence ramped up at the turn of the century under the leadership of CEO Jay Stein, when URMC acquired three large internal medicine practices with twenty physicians and opened its ambulatory offices at Clinton Crossings. The affiliation with HH led to the further addition of many of Highland's primary care practices. With the growth in hospitalist programs, the focus of primary care shifted from inpatient services to seeing patients and teaching in ambulatory settings throughout the region, and to developing into the current Primary Care Network (PCN).

From 2008 to 2023, PCN expansion became a top priority in order to prepare for a possible shift from fee-for-service to capitated population health. Leading that expansion was Wallace E. Johnson, MD, Ralph W. Prince Professor of Medicine, who served as Medicine's associate chair for Primary Care and director of the PCN. Johnson received his MD from SUNY at Buffalo and then

Figure 13.1. Wallace Johnson

did his residency in internal medicine at the University of Rochester's SMH. He subsequently developed a robust clinical practice at Eastside Internal Medicine in Fairport. During Johnson's tenure, thirty-two community practices joined URMC, adding and consolidating approximately seventy physicians and 200 staff, many who were previously in private practice outside of Monroe County. The acquisition of these practices was instrumental in assuring the success of Strong West in Brockport, in solidifying UR Medicine's presence in Batavia where a large practice was established in 2018, and in facilitating the 2018 affiliation with St. James Hospital in Hornell.

The establishment of the PCN was also instrumental in recruiting and retaining graduating residents. Over 100 graduating residents in Internal Medicine, Family Medicine, and Medicine-Pediatrics joined or initiated local primary care practices in the past three decades. Many residents were particularly interested in working with underserved populations, leading, for example, to the PCN opening its first practice in downtown Rochester at Manhattan Square in 2015.

In 2023, Johnson stepped down from his administrative responsibilities but continued his clinical practice. He was succeeded by Steven R. Judge, MD, as Ralph W. Prince Professor of Medicine, associate chair for Primary Care, and director of the PCN. Judge received his MD from Dartmouth Medical School and then completed his residency and chief residency in internal medicine at the University of Rochester. Known as an outstanding teacher, he had worked closely with Johnson in expanding the PCN and serving as its medical director.

Figure 13.2. Steven Judge

The PCN currently operates as a service line with Family Medicine and the General Medicine division of the DOM. This facilitates academic and research ties between primary care faculty in the various primary care disciplines. The PCN comprises thirty-nine practice sites in five counties with approximately 200 MD/DO faculty members, 100 APPs and 500 staff serving approximately 265,000 patients. PCN physicians also provide upwards of 20,000 hours annually of shoulder-to-shoulder teaching of medical students and residents. PCN NPs also teach extensively in support of the SON, helping cement primary care as the career path for many new NPs.

Chapter 14

GENERAL MEDICINE DIVISION (DEPARTMENT OF MEDICINE)

The General Medicine division (GMD) was established in the department of Medicine (DOM) in the early 1970s, with Paul Griner, MD, as its first chief. Griner was one of the founders of what is now known as the Society for General Internal Medicine. In 1978, he established a fellowship in General Internal Medicine at URMC, funded by the Kaiser Family Foundation. In 1984, Griner stepped away from his role as GMD leader to become the general director (CEO) of SMH. He was succeeded in GMD by Alvin Mushlin, MD, ScM, Raymond Mayewski, MD, Rudolph Napodano, MD, Robert Panzer, MD, and William Hall, MD, all of whom made major contributions to URMC. David Lambert, MD, served as division chief from 2002–8, before becoming SAD for medical education, a position he held until 2025. Lambert was followed briefly as division chief by Ralph Manchester, MD, who stepped down to devote his time to University Health Services, which he had directed since 1994.

In 2009, Marc Berliant, MD, was recruited to become chief of GMD and the Raymond J. Mayewski Professor of Medicine. Berliant received his MD from the University of Illinois and then came to URMC for his residency in internal medicine, subsequently spending over twenty-five years in Rochester as one of the area's most highly regarded private practitioners. Prior to Berliant's appointment as chief, faculty and residents treated patients representing distinctly differently socioeconomic populations in separate internal medicine clinics. Berliant's first order of business was to merge the separate groups so that residents and faculty worked together. It sent a clear message of commitment to health equity and gave residents a more balanced educational experience and a greater appreciation for patient diversity. In 2023, Berliant stepped down as GMD chief to focus on his role as vice chair for clinical programs in the DOM. Catherine Gracey, MD, was named interim chief and a national search is underway for a permanent successor.

Figure 14.1. Marc Berliant

The GMD is comprised of fourteen academic general internists who play major roles in the internal medicine residency educational programs and serve as preceptors and providers in Strong Internal Medicine (SIM). SIM is a faculty-resident safety net practice that provides care to a diverse population of approximately 12,000 patients comprised of approximately fifty-five percent Black and approximately seventeen percent Latinx patients. SIM is recognized by the National Committee on Quality Assurance as the highest-level Patient Centered Medical Home.

SIM employs a team-based care model, involving social workers, pharmacists, dietitians, advanced practice practitioners, care managers, data coordinators, and referral specialists. Funding through the Delivery System Reform Incentive Payment (DSRIP) has also allowed SIM to embed behavioral health providers, such as behavioral health nurse practitioners, licensed clinical social workers, marriage and family therapists and clinical psychologists. In addition, the Farash Foundation funds a unique medical legal partnership (developed by Mahala Schlagman, MD) in which an attorney works in the practice to address patient problems with benefits, housing, immigration status, orders of protection, etc.

Over the past fifteen years, SIM has become a hub for inventive health care delivery models. These include: 1) an addiction recovery program; 2) a pharmacy collaborative drug therapy protocol featuring direct prescribing by pharmacists; 3) a diabetes retinal screening project; 4) a smoking cessation program; 5) a home visit program for homebound patients; and 6) an asthma telemedicine program.

GMD has also been instrumental in developing a patient care dashboard in which each provider's performance on quality metrics can be reviewed. This serves as a powerful educational tool for students and residents, and prepares URMC for value-based reimbursement models. GMD was also the recipient of a Greater Rochester Health Foundation Award to reduce hospital readmissions and a $2.85 million NY State Department of Health Hospital-Medical Home Demonstration Grant. GMD faculty are responsible for the ambulatory education of seventy internal medicine residents at SIM and at a smaller continuity clinic at HH. SIM also serves as a host site for Psychiatry's psychology postdoctoral fellowship in integrated care, the community pharmacy residency program, and for APP student clinical rotations.

GMD faculty were instrumental in the development of the block model of resident scheduling and the primary care track of the residency program. The block model, in which residents spend two out of eight weeks in an ambulatory setting, has resulted in greater emphasis on primary care and preventive medicine and has vastly improved resident satisfaction. An offshoot of this is the rural primary care internal medicine program, which expands the workforce of primary care physicians in underserved rural locations by providing interested residents with outpatient training in different rural communities, ranging from thirty minutes to three hours away from URMC.

Chapter 15

DEPARTMENT OF FAMILY MEDICINE

The department of Family Medicine (FM) has a storied history as one of the oldest and most accomplished departments in the US. The HH family medicine residency program, begun in 1968, was the third program opened in the US and the first in NY State. The Family Medicine Center (FMC) was opened in 1975 at 885 South Avenue. In 1989, FM was formally established as a department of SMD, with John C. Dickinson, MD, as the inaugural chair. When Dickinson stepped down in 2004, he was succeeded as William Rocktaschel Professor and Chair by Thomas L. Campbell, MD, who also took on the role of associate director of UR's Center for Primary Care.

Figure 15.1. Thomas Campbell

Campbell received his MD from Harvard University and then came to the University for his residency and fellowship in FM. Enamored by the biopsychosocial model and family systems, he received additional training in George Engel's psychosomatic medicine fellowship and the Family Therapy Training Program. Campbell has written extensively on the relationship between families and health, including *Families and Health* (with William Doherty, PhD) and *Family-Oriented Primary Care: A Manual for Medical Providers* (with Susan McDaniel PhD and David Seaburn, MS). He was editor of the journal *Families, Systems, & Health,* president of the Association of Departments of Family Medicine, and chair of the Council of Academic Family Medicine.

A year after becoming chair, Campbell orchestrated the move of the practice, along with Strong Behavioral Health, the Highland Apothecary, Cornhill Internal Medicine, and a laboratories collection station, to 777 South Clinton Avenue, a site named the Lovejoy Family Medicine Center. Over time, it was renovated, and additional office space was developed next door. In 2011, the FMC Achieved Level 3 Patient-Centered Medical Home status from the National Committee for Quality Assurance. In 2016, the department opened an NP residency, the only program in the US fully integrated into a FM Residency!

Figure 15.2. Colleen Fogarty

In 2019, Colleen T. Fogarty, MD, was selected as the next William Rocktaschel Professor and chair of FM. Fogarty received an MD from the University of Connecticut School of Medicine and an MS in epidemiology and biostatistics from the Boston University School of Public Health. She came to URMC for her FM residency and received additional training in family systems from the University of Rochester Family Therapy Training Program in Psychiatry. Prior to becoming chair, she served as associate chair of Clinical Practice and Interprofessional Education, medical director at Highland Family Medicine (HFM), and assistant residency director and director of the Faculty Development fellowship. She has been recognized nationally for linking health professions, education, and interprofessional practice to transform care delivery, improve health outcomes, and decrease costs.

The HFM practice at South Clinton Avenue operates under the HH license. This practice cares for a diverse population of 25,000 patients and receives 75,000 visits annually, relatively equally divided among residents and fellows, faculty family physicians, and NPs. The practice provides outpatient and inpatient maternity care, ambulatory care of persons of all ages, and inpatient care.

In 2014, in response to the rising opioid epidemic, Holly Russell, MD, and Elizabeth Loomis, MD, initiated the HFM Buprenorphine group. This group (currently five family physicians and four NPs) provides twice-weekly buprenorphine management for persons coming out of recovery programs who need a community clinician. Half of the patients served by the Suboxone group also get their primary care at HFM; the others have other primary care physicians in the community.

FM has a long-standing relationship with the HH Medicine. FM faculty attend on patients from the HFM practice who are admitted to the FM inpatient service at HH. The department also has a robust relationship with the HH Obstetrics and Gynecology (Ob/Gyn). Since the inception of the department, FM faculty have provided prenatal care and attended births at HH, and FM residents have included maternity and labor/delivery care as core to their overall training.

Over the past twenty-five years, FM has played a pivotal role in the educational activities of URMC, developing signature programs and promoting the biopsychosocial educational model throughout the institution. Over each of the last five years, HFM has been highly sought after as a training site for psychology doctoral interns and postdoctoral fellows, as well as master's trainees in Marriage and Family Therapy.

The HH/URMC FM residency is among the most highly ranked programs in the US. Stephen Schultz, MD, served as its director for twenty years before David C. Holub, MD, took on the role in 2022. The program trains fourteen residents per year, predominantly at HFM, where residents develop a continuity practice on clinical teams working closely with staff, NPs, and family physicians. Two residents per year train at Jordan Health/Brown Square, an urban practice in an underserved area. These six residents receive clinical supervision from FM faculty who have their continuity practices at Jordan, together with Jordan-employed family physicians. Despite the national decline in student interest in FM and primary care, the HH/URMC program continues to be a magnet for high-quality FM residency training, offering in-depth training in psychosocial medicine and providing one of the most robust Ob/Gyn experiences in the northeast.

The residency program has been highly successful in providing outstanding family physicians for the community. In the past five years, fifty-eight graduates have remained in the region, with thirty working in the Rochester area. Recently, FM received a HRSA planning grant to establish a rural training track, in collaboration with UR Medicine regional partners at Tri-County Family Medicine and Noyes Hospital. This training track will add two residents per year at the rural site—with the first two to be recruited in the 2026 residency match—and hopefully will grow faculty for our regional affiliates.

The NP residency is a twelve-month program established in 2017 for master's-prepared nurse practitioners who intend to practice in primary care. The residency incorporates precepted continuity clinical time, specialty rotations, didactic conferences, and on-call training. It has been funded by three consecutive HRSA Advanced Nurse Education-Nurse Practitioner Residency and Fellowship grants, the last of which in August 2023 allowed the residency to expand to six slots per year. In addition to four training slots at the HFM practice, there are training slots at Tri-County Family Medicine. These trainees will help to fill the gaps in primary care access in our rural communities.

In addition to the residency program, the FM oversees several fellowships. The highly collaborative, two-year Faculty Development fellowship trains future academic family physicians.

One of the nation's oldest postgraduate programs, the Maternal-Child Health fellowship program trains family physicians in high-risk and surgical obstetrics, including prenatal care and management of common newborn conditions. With the award of a HRSA grant in 2021, this one-year program was able to expand from two to four fellows per year, with the additional fellows focusing on rural obstetrics.

The Sports Medicine fellowship is for primary care physicians seeking to be part of an academically focused sports medicine program. Fellows receive training and practice in orthopedic clinics with primary care sports medicine physicians and orthopedic surgeons. They perform 500–750 procedures per year, including joint and soft tissue injections, casting and splinting, musculoskeletal ultrasound, compartment pressure testing, orthobiologic administration, osteopathic manipulative treatment, and sports concussion care.

FM has also played an important role in faculty education and development. Susan McDaniel, PhD, is a family psychologist and the Dr. Laurie Sands Distinguished Professor of Families & Health in Psychiatry and FM. She received her PhD in clinical psychology from the University of North Carolina at Chapel Hill and was a postdoctoral fellow in family therapy at the Texas Research Institute for Mental Services in Houston. McDaniel came to the URMC in 1980 and currently directs the Institute for the Family in Psychiatry and is the vice chair of FM. She developed and directs the University of Rochester Physician Communication Coaching Program. She has held leadership positions and served on boards and committees on national medical and mental health associations, as well as serving as president of the American Psychological Association.

Figure 15.3. Susan McDaniel

FM's research program at SMD has a national reputation in the areas of communication in health care, health disparities, and deaf health, all of which are rooted in the biopsychosocial model. Currently there are eight active research faculty, many with ties to other departments, and a number who have attained national and international recognition. University of Rochester FM is among the most highly ranked FM departments in NIH funding and has had 221 publications over the past five years. Several programs that have been nationally prominent over the last twenty-five years are summarized below.

Kevin Fiscella, MD, associate director of Research for FM, received his MD from the Medical College of Virginia and his MPH from the University of Rochester. He completed a faculty development fellowship in FM, trained in family therapy in Psychiatry and joined the faculty in 1996. He works as a family physician, HIV physician, and addiction medicine physician at Jordan Health. His research and policy work includes more than 200 peer-reviewed publications primarily focused

Figure 15.4. Kevin Fiscella

on pragmatic strategies to improve equity within primary care related to cancer, cardiovascular disease prevention and HIV. A recipient of the Curtis G. Hames Research Award from the Society of Teachers of Family Medicine, Fiscella has been one of the Medical Center's best-funded investigators and is currently principal investigator on two large NIH grants: *Translating the ABCs into HIV Care* and *Team Based Home Blood Pressure Monitoring in Primary Care.*

Figure 15.5. Ronald Epstein

Ronald M. Epstein, MD, co-director of the Center for Communication and Disparities Research and Mindful Practice Programs, received his MD from Harvard Medical School and did his residency in family medicine at the University of Rochester. Epstein was the first George Engel and John Romano Dean's Teaching Scholar at SMD. Epstein is an internationally recognized physician, educator, researcher, and writer who has done groundbreaking research into communication in medical settings. He has developed educational programs to optimize communication between health professionals and people who are seriously ill, and promote professional self-awareness, mindfulness, and wellbeing. In addition to his book, *Attending: Medicine, Mindfulness and Humanity*,[6] Epstein has published more than 300 scholarly articles. He has been a Fulbright Scholar at the Institute for Health Studies in Barcelona, Spain and is a frequent keynote speaker at major national and international conferences on medical education, communication, and mindfulness in health care. He received the Lynn Payer Award from the Academy of Communication in Healthcare for lifetime achievement in research on communication and health, the Humanism in Medicine Award from the NY Academy of Medicine and the American Cancer Society's highest award, the Clinical Research Professorship.

6 Epstein, Ronald. *Attending: Medicine, Mindfulness, and Humanity*. New York, Simon & Schuster, Inc., 2017.

Chapter 16

CENTER FOR COMMUNITY HEALTH AND PREVENTION

In 2006, CEO Evarts established the Center for Community Health and Prevention (CCHP) under the leadership of Nancy M. Bennett, MD, MS. Bennett received her MD from New York University (NYU) School of Medicine and did her residency and chief residency in internal medicine at Bellevue Hospital. She completed a fellowship in general internal medicine at Columbia-Presbyterian Hospital, where she also earned an MS in epidemiology. In 1988, she came to the University of Rochester as faculty in the DOM and four years later became deputy director of the Monroe County Department of Public Health (DOPH), a position she held until 2006, when she returned full-time to URMC to launch the CCHP. During her time in Rochester, Bennett has been viewed as one of this region's most influential community health leaders and as a pioneer in studying and striving for health equity, with more than 150 peer-reviewed publications. Her efforts have been acknowledged by the Charles C. Shepard Science Award for Scientific Excellence from the CDC, an Innovation in Prevention Award from the US Department of Health and Human Services, and the Dr. Albert David Kaiser Medal: Physician Lifetime Achievement Award.

Figure 16.1. Nancy Bennett

The CCHP is a public health improvement collaboration between the County and SMD, established by Dean Lowell Goldsmith and inspired by George Eastman's charge when he endowed the Medical School, that "the skills and talents be used to make Rochester the healthiest community in the world." The goal of the center was to apply the resources of URMC to improving public health through service and research. The establishment of the center captured significant national attention[7] because most academic

---

7 Cohen, J. J. "Rochester throws down the Gauntlet." *Academic Medicine* 74(12) (December 1999): 1311.

medical centers had done little to engage with their communities to improve public health.

At its onset, the center was supported by several grants from the CDC, including the Emerging Infections Program (EIP), the most prominent source of infectious disease epidemiologic data for the US and the foundation for a variety of vaccine-effectiveness studies. In addition, the center had a variety of grants from NY State and foundations addressing the prevention and early detection of chronic diseases.

The CCHP also became the community engagement core of URMC's CTSI, developing strong partnerships with many community organizations and leaders through the Community Advisory Council (an active, ongoing council for almost twenty years). Bennett served as the director of Community Engagement for the CTSI until 2014, when she became CTSI co-director and co-principal investigator of the Clinical and Translational Science Award (CTSA). Bennett also served as chair of the national CTSA community engagement workgroup.

By 2008, the center had grown to have almost $3 million per year in extramural funding and moved to the Eastman Building on the old campus of the University in downtown Rochester. The building, originally the science building donated to the University of Rochester by George Eastman, included CCHP offices and a library and meeting rooms open to the community. Bennett and Geoffrey C. Williams, an MD who had received a PhD in health psychology at the University of Rochester and had developed a research program on the treatment of tobacco dependence and other difficult-to-change habits, proposed the development of the Healthy Living Center (HLC). The HLC combined clinical prevention services for individuals and groups with research into motivation and behavior change (tobacco, diet, physical activity, stress management) and provided an umbrella and scientific basis for the CCHP's community chronic disease prevention efforts. The HLC was funded in 2009 by a $1.2 million NIH supplement to the CTSA. The services were offered to employees across the University. The center also partnered with the SON to develop a comprehensive disease prevention program for employees.

By 2010, the community health mission of the CCHP was firmly established: to join forces with the community to promote health equity and improve health through research, education, services, and policy, and to establish local and national models for prevention and community engagement.

In 2011, the CCHP and its community partners were awarded a $3.6 million Community Transformation Grant by the CDC that enabled the CCHP to work with several community organizations to increase capacity for

Figure 16.2. The Center for Community Health on Prince Street

chronic disease prevention through community-wide implementation of the Diabetes Prevention Program, expansion of the HLC, and development and implementation of the Blood Pressure Advocate Program. The Teen Health and Success Partnership was started in collaboration with the Hillside Work Scholarship Program, supported by Wegmans Foods Market, and eventually transitioned to full University of Rochester sponsorship. By 2013, it was supporting seventy-five disadvantaged teens a year in part-time employment and mentoring with a hundred percent high school graduation rates.

The CCHP remains the home of the Rochester EIP, which has been continuously funded for almost thirty years. Ghinwa Dumyati, MD, succeeded Bennett as principal investigator and, in addition to her national work, led a community coalition in the development and implementation of a city-wide program to reduce health care-associated infections. In 2015, Bennett assumed the chair of the CDC's Advisory Committee on Immunization Practices, a testimony to the CCHP's great success in increasing rates and reducing disparities in immunization across the Rochester community.

With the start of the COVID-19 pandemic, the CCHP communicable disease group took on major roles in local surveillance, working at the health department to assist in data collection, performing and reporting all local analyses, and providing extensive community education. The group also continued reporting in-depth data to the national EIP, which had the most extensive and important data for the early national response to COVID.

The CCHP received an additional $2.7 million per year from the CDC to perform local COVID-19 surveillance and several connected studies, bringing the yearly CDC grant to over $5 million.

When vaccines became available, Bennett and the CCHP led the Finger Lakes COVID-19 Vaccine Hub and Task Force to implement COVID vaccination across the Finger Lakes region. Bennett established a University-wide team that created a broad-based coalition across ten counties, including public health, all hospitals and large clinics, government, pharmacies, businesses, and schools. As a result of their efforts, the Finger Lakes region had one of the highest immunization rates in the US and the CCHP was recognized with the "Outstanding Leadership in Public Health in NYS" award from NYS, the URMC Board Excellence Award, and the Greater Rochester Quality Council gold team excellence award.

In 2020, Bennett and colleagues in the CTSI proposed the establishment of the Office of Health Equity Research (OHER) within the CTSI. When Bennett retired at the end of 2023, Edith Williams, PhD, was chosen to direct the newly combined CCHP and OHER.

Chapter 17

TRANSITIONAL CARE MEDICINE DIVISION (DEPARTMENT OF MEDICINE)

A collaborative effort between DOM and Pediatrics led to the creation of the division of Transitional Care Medicine (DTCM), one of the few such divisions in the US. A relatively new discipline, transitional care focuses on actions that ensure the coordination and continuity of care received by patients as they transfer between different locations or levels of care.

The program began as the vision of Tiffany Pulcino, MD, MPH. After completing her Med/Peds residency in 2008 at the University of Rochester, Pulcino joined the departments of Pediatrics and Medicine, where she focused on developing a novel care model for adolescents and young adults with childhood-onset conditions, such as cystic fibrosis (CF), sickle cell anemia, childhood cancers, autism, and IDD. This interdisciplinary model included medical providers, nursing, respiratory therapy, nutrition support, physical therapy, applied behavioral analysis, embedded behavioral health, pharmacology, social work, embedded care management, and dental care.

Figure 17.1. Tiffany Pulcino

The culmination of Pulcino's efforts was the opening in 2016 of the University of Rochester Complex Care Center (CCC) on Culver Road in downtown Rochester. This 2,500 square-foot center was one of the first primary care practices in the nation specifically designed to care for adults with chronic childhood-onset conditions and the only primary care practice caring for this unique population of patients with medical, dental, and Applied Behavioral Analysis (ABA) services at a single site. The ABA team includes board-certified behavioral analysts who use a proven scientific approach to assess behaviors, teach new skills, plan for long-term success, and train and support caregivers.

Figure 17.2. Steve Scofield

With the opening of the CCC, the accredited CF program, directed by Steven M. Scofield, MD, a graduate of the University of Rochester Med/Peds residency, was expanded to include children and adults and moved from Scofield's long-standing practice at the Culver Medical Group to the CCC. Recently, the program, now directed by Francis Coyne, MD, obtained recognition from the National Alliance of Sickle Cell Centers. In addition, three clinic rooms were equipped with handicap-accessible dental chairs to provide dental care to adult and pediatric patients. EIOH established the CCC as a dental residency training site to ensure that future generations of oral health specialists gain experience in treating patients with complex conditions.

In addition to CCC at Culver Road, the inpatient and outpatient transitional care model was expanded throughout UR Medicine, with the ABA team actively involved in providing hospital-based care on medical floors, GCH and at CPEP (Comprehensive Psychiatric Emergency Program). A two-bed infusion center was also developed for acute sickle cell and other diseases, and work is ongoing to expand transfusion/apheresis services for sickle cell disease in collaboration with adult Hematology.

In 2018, a dedicated hospitalist program was opened at HH to care for CCC patients needing admission and the DTCM was formalized within Pediatrics, under the directorship of Pulcino. In 2023, the DTCM was shifted to the DOM, with Scofield retiring from the Culver Medical Group to serve as its interim director. The DTCM currently serves approximately 1,300 patients per year in the CCC and oversees over 500 admissions per year at HH. DTCM continues to be at the forefront of new care delivery systems. They have recently developed a combined pulmonary-primary care clinic for neuromuscular and ventilator patients; are working towards an interdisciplinary clinic with neurology for patients with muscular dystrophy and spinal muscular atrophy; and are developing a novel home care delivery model.

On the educational front, a fellowship in transitional care medicine was recently established, a transitional care rotation was developed for Med/Peds residents, and electives were developed in pulmonary and sickle cell disease. The division also provides education to adult pulmonary fellows in CF clinic. DTCM is an active participant in research through the CF foundation's research infrastructure and is involved in a variety of quality improvement projects addressing CF, sickle cell and initiatives for those with IDD, including a large NYS grant aimed at improving nursing knowledge, skills, and attitudes towards the IDD population. These programs are likely to be expanded with the growth of the Golisano IDD Institute.

Chapter 18

HOSPITALIST DIVISION (DEPARTMENT OF MEDICINE)

One of the most striking changes in inpatient medical care, and critical to the growth in the primary care programs at URMC, has been the rise of the "hospitalist," a term defined in an essay[8] in the *New England Journal of Medicine* published in 1996 by Robert Wachter, MD, of UCSF. That same year Andrew Rudmann, MD, became URMC's first hospitalist, attending on patients who did not have a primary care provider (PCP) or whose PCPs did not have admitting privileges at SMH. In 2000, Alec O'Connor, MD, and Valerie Lang, MD, joined the faculty as part of a new hospitalist group led by Rudmann in GMD, with an average daily caseload of thirty patients. As PCPs saw the value of the service in providing high-quality standardized inpatient care and in allowing them to focus on the burgeoning outpatient demands, the hospitalist group (physicians and APPs) continued to grow in number and began attending on resident teams. In 2005, Hospital Medicine became a separate division (HMD) of the DOM, with Rudmann as chief. By 2012, the average daily caseload of patients in its care had grown to 121 patients.

Figure 18.1. Andrew Rudmann

After Rudmann stepped down, Lang served as acting chief in 2015 before Berliant, director of GMD, also served as acting chief from 2016–17. Justin L. Hopkin, MD, became division chief in 2018 and continued to expand the program. Hopkin received his MD from the University of Washington and did his residency and chief residency in internal medicine at the University of Colorado, where he trained in primary care. He went on to practice in rural Wyoming for eight years before joining the HMD at URMC.

Figure 18.2. Justin Hopkin

8 Wachter, R. and Goldman, L. "The Emerging Role of 'hospitalists' in the American Health Care System." *New Eng. J. of Med.* 335(7) (1996): 514–17.

The opening of the Medical Observation Unit in 2016 enabled hospitalist-led teams to handle more complex patients than those cared for in the ED observation unit. Two years later, hospitalist ED teams were established in response to the increasing numbers of admitted patients boarding in the ED due to the high inpatient census.

In 2017, HMD initiated a bedside procedure team to expedite procedures such as paracentesis, thoracentesis, lumbar punctures, central lines, and hemodialysis lines. This resulted in better outcomes by providing standardized protocols and by employing ultrasound guidance, and was extended to other teams, including outpatient hepatology and the Wilmot Cancer Institute (WCI). HMD was also involved in developing the multidisciplinary Adult Inpatient Eating Disorder Program, unique in upstate NY, which stabilizes adult inpatients with severe eating disorders.

With the onset of the COVID-19 pandemic, DHM took on an even greater role in the management of inpatients; community-based PCPs no longer admitted patients to SMH and all general medicine patients were covered by the division. The program ultimately expanded to provide seven-day coverage. Daily census grew from 218 to 310 patients during January 2021's COVID-19 pandemic surge. Post-pandemic, the daily census has continued to increase and in 2024 average daily census reached approximately 335 patients.

HMD currently includes over seventy physician hospitalists and fifty APPs. Another ten APPs from other departments/divisions also serve as hospitalists. Hospitalists serve as medical directors for eight patient units at SMH. In partnership with the unit nurse managers, they lead interdisciplinary unit-based teams, comprised of physicians, APPs, nurses, care coordinators, social workers, physical therapists, mobility assistants, and others. A nocturnist team was started in 2019 to provide the first in-house overnight attending coverage of HMD patients; currently, two evening admitters plus a nocturnist manage up to forty-five admissions nightly with APPs and residents. The high level of oversight and teaching of residents and APPs by this team has recently been shown to improve education and safety.

The extraordinary success of HMD in managing general medicine patients has led to formal collaborations with a variety of specialty services. The Geriatric Fracture Center, formed in 2016, became the first such program, collaborating with Orthopaedics, Anesthesiology, Pharmacy, Emergency Medicine, Physical Medicine, and Nursing. A hepatology co-management team was developed in 2019 in collaboration with hepatologists and the liver transplant team. An advanced heart failure co-management service was launched in 2022 in collaboration with Nursing, Infectious Diseases, and Cardiology. In the same year, the WCI Hospitalist Program was brought under the umbrella of the division. More recently, HMD has developed co-management programs designed specifically to oversee general medical care and perioperative risk mitigation for older patients undergoing trauma and emergency general surgery, thoracic surgery, colorectal surgery, and urologic surgery, and has collaborated with Surgery, Anesthesia, Geriatrics, and Nursing to pursue recognition by the American College of Surgeons' General Surgical Verification Program as an "Age Friendly Health System."

HMD plays a major role in educating medical students, residents, practicing physicians, and interprofessional teams in the general medical care of adult inpatients. Each resident team is aligned with a teaching hospitalist, who conducts daily attending rounds. Hospitalists precept and mentor medical students, direct educational programs for the residency program and Medical School, and conduct research on innovative approaches to medical education. In addition, HMD faculty have taken the lead in administering key DOM teaching programs, with Valerie Lang serving as Internal Medicine clerkship director (2002–15) and subsequently as associate chair for medical education research and scholarship; Amy Blatt, MD, serving as internal medicine residency program director; Jennifer M. Pascoe, MD, as internal medicine clerkship director, and Amit S. Dhamoon, MD, PhD, as the primary care clerkship director. Faculty scholarship has revolved largely around medical and residency education, quality improvement and health delivery. Ashley Jenkins, MD, the first dedicated researcher in the division, focuses primarily on the care of patients with childhood illness, such as sickle cell disease, who are transitioning to adulthood.

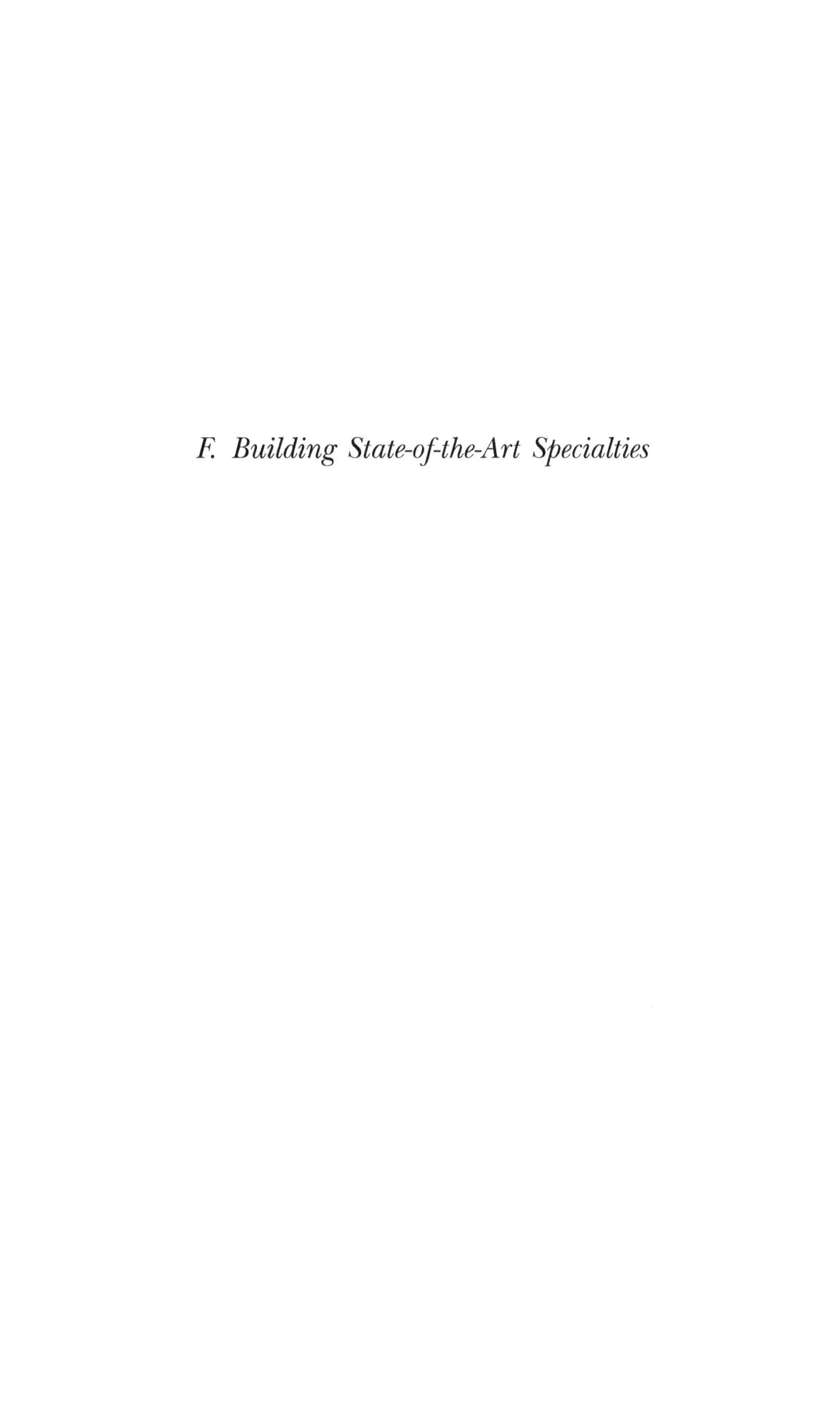

F. Building State-of-the-Art Specialties

The preceding chapters outlined the development of a large health network that provides primary health care to a substantial portion of the region. Concomitant with the growth of primary care services was a similar expansion in specialty programs, needed not only to provide patients in the growing network with sufficient access to critical specialists, but to allow URMC, as a quaternary academic health care system, to offer leading-edge programs in every discipline. This would ensure that patients would never have to leave the region to get state-of-the-art care while solidifying URMC's reputation as a regional and national referral center. It would also further drive the growth and quality of the research and educational programs.

The following chapters detail the evolution over the past twenty-five years of clinical specialties, along with their research and educational programs. Obstetrics and gynecology is a fitting transition into this section of the book, because it is also a key component of the PCN, serving as a primary health care provider for many women.

Chapter 19

DEPARTMENT OF OBSTETRICS AND GYNECOLOGY

The department of Ob/Gyn was established in 1923 by George Corner, MD, an embryologist who played a critical role in the discovery of progesterone. In 1925, he appointed Karl Wilson, MD, who trained at Johns Hopkins under the founders of gynecology, Howard Kelly, MD, and of obstetrics, John Williams, MD, to become the first chair of Ob/Gyn, making URMC one of the first academic medical centers to combine obstetrics and gynecology into a single department. Over the next twenty-seven years, Wilson grew the faculty and initiated the residency program. He was succeeded in 1952 by Curtis Lund, MD, who continued to attract renowned faculty, such as Mortimer Rosen, MD, who researched fetal brain development, and William Creasman, MD, a prominent gynecologic oncologist.

Lund served until 1974, when Henry Thiede, MD, a former faculty member and Rochester native, was recruited back as chair. Under Thiede, the department grew exponentially. He launched an academic midwifery service that remains in place today, developed the fields of urogynecology and reproductive endocrinology, and established a fellowship in maternal fetal medicine (MFM) in 1975. The Henry A. Thiede Chair in Ob/Gyn was created in 1991 through a generous gift from the Gosnell family.

David Guzick, MD, PhD, became Henry A. Thiede Chair in Ob/Gyn in 1995. A nationally renowned clinical investigator, he markedly expanded the research profile of the department, before being appointed as dean of SMD in 2003. Guzick was succeeded as Ob/Gyn chair by James Woods, MD. Woods received his MD from Wake Forest University, completed a residency in Ob/Gyn at the Tripler Army Medical Center in Honolulu, HI, and a fellowship in maternal and fetal medicine at Mattel Children's Hospital of UCLA. He joined URMC in 1986 as chief of Maternal Medicine. Woods developed a national reputation for his work on communication in obstetrics and menopause management, on which he authored four books. He was the founder of *Peri-FACTS*, an online multimedia journal

Figure 19.1. James Woods

on critical issues in obstetrics and gynecology that was used by 600 hospitals and 230 nursing schools, with 30,000 subscribers around the world before it closed in 2023. In 1996, the James R. Woods, Jr. Professorship in Ob/Gyn was established at the University in his honor.

As chair, Woods fostered continued growth in the department, with full-time faculty increasing to forty-five, and the construction of new outpatient centers for Ob/Gyn care at 400 Red Creek Drive and subsequently at 125 Lattimore Road. These new locations allowed expansion of all the Ob/Gyn subspecialties. The department also added fellowships in urogynecology and reconstructive pelvic surgery, and in minimally invasive gynecologic surgery.

Figure 19.2. Eva Pressman

In 2013, Eva Pressman, MD, succeeded Woods as the Henry A. Thiede Chair in Ob/Gyn. Pressman received her MD from Duke University School of Medicine and did a residency in Ob/Gyn and a fellowship in maternal fetal medicine at Johns Hopkins. Prior to coming to Rochester in 1999, she was on the faculty at Johns Hopkins, serving as associate director of the Ob/Gyn residency program. Pressman's clinical practice and research has focused on medical complications of pregnancy and preterm birth. During her tenure, the Ob/Gyn faculty has more than doubled to 117 to keep pace with the growth in services now offered at all UR Medicine affiliates.

HH has been a community resource for Ob/Gyn care for over 100 years and, since the closure of Genesee Hospital in May 2001, has been the busiest obstetric service in the region, with more than 3,000 deliveries annually. Since 1999, HH has been a center for gynecologic oncology and at the forefront of research into gynecologic malignancies, aided by the introduction of robotic surgery in 2005 and by robust involvement in clinical trials.

By the early 2000s, Urogynecology was well established clinically, but lacked the academic base. In 2001, Gunhilde Buchsbaum, MD, the sole urogynecologist at URMC, initiated the landmark Sister Study. This NIH-funded research examined pelvic floor disorders in nulliparous and parous sister pairs, establishing the genetic predisposition to urinary incontinence and pelvic organ prolapse post-menopause. In 2003, Buchsbaum became the first division director and founded the urogynecology fellowship. Upon Buchsbaum's retirement in 2018, Erin Duecy, MD, the program's first fellow, became division director. Under her leadership, the program has continued to grow, with focus on vaginal and robotic surgery, adoption of neuromodulation, and intravesical botulinum toxin procedures. Collaborative care models were established with Gynecologic Oncology to enhance quality of life during and after cancer treatment, and with Colorectal Surgery to provide combined urogynecology and colorectal procedures for pelvic floor disorders.

In 2020, the Urogynecology division transitioned into the division of Urogynecology & Minimally Invasive Gynecology (MIGS), integrating MIGS faculty members who had previously worked within the division of General Ob/Gyn, under the leadership of Fred Howard, MD, an internationally recognized surgeon who played a pivotal role in the development of MIGS and the management of chronic pelvic pain. His textbook, *Pelvic Pain: Diagnosis & Management*, published in 2000, set the standard for clinical practice in this field. In 2024, the program established a medical student MIGS elective.

The division of Reproductive Endocrinology and Infertility (REI), established by Thiede in 1982, offered the first *in-vitro* fertilization program in NY State, and in 1991, under the leadership of Vivian Lewis, MD, established the region's first donor oocyte program, and in 2005, its first program offering preimplantation genetic diagnosis. In 2007, Kathleen Hoeger, MD, became director of REI and oversaw the move into its new location at Red Creek. Hoeger subsequently initiated an oocyte cryopreservation program and established the Fertility Preservation and CARE (childbearing after recovery) programs, which since 2012 have been directed and expanded by Wendy Vitek, MD. In 2021, Vitek established the first reproductive endocrinology fellowship in upstate NY. To accommodate the growth of REI programs, a new center is scheduled for completion in 2026.

General Ob/Gyn became an academic division in 1996 under David Foster, MD, who was recruited from Johns Hopkins. Areas of focus include vulvar disorders, family planning, and integrated behavioral health. The current era of General Ob/Gyn began in 2012 with the opening of the URMC Women's Health Center at Lattimore Road, which contains General Ob/Gyn practices, the Gender Wellness Ob/Gyn program, Complex Family Planning, Maternal Fetal Medicine clinics, Ob/Gyn ultrasound, UR Midwifery, and Gynecologic Oncology practices.

MFM became a division in 1986, initially led by Woods. In 2003, Pressman was appointed division director, followed in 2014 by Loralei L. Thornburg, MD. Both also held the title of James R. Woods, Jr. Professorship in Ob/Gyn. Over the last twenty-five years, the MFM division has grown from five faculty and two genetics counselors, with occasional fellows in 2001, to twelve faculty, five genetic counselors and six fellows. The largest MFM group outside of NY City, it performs more than 25,000 ultrasounds and 8,000 consultations annually, as well as complex procedures such as fetal transfusions and fetal shunt placements.

Figure 19.3. Loralei Thornburg

Under Thornburg's guidance, specialty clinics have been developed focusing on patients with prior pregnancy loss, those with diabetes before and during pregnancy, and those with complex and adult congenital heart diseases. In addition to a "complex delivery team," the program includes a prenatal supportive care clinic in conjunction with Neonatology and Palliative Care. An initiative with the NICU for excellence in "small baby care" has enabled URMC to offer neonatal support and care as early as twenty-two weeks' gestation. Because patients with preeclampsia, pregnancy loss and prior infertility have increased risk for stroke, heart disease, and diabetes, an MFM/Cardiology preeclampsia follow-up clinic was also established in collaboration with Cardiology to help at-risk patients adopt healthy lifestyle management and blood pressure control.

The Midwifery Division, established by Elizabeth M. Cooper, CNM, EdD, in 1995 and currently led by Tracy Webber, DNP, MPA, has grown to a vibrant practice of fifteen midwives. The largest midwifery practice in the region, it provides optimal patient outcomes with the lowest cesarean delivery rates in the state.

Ob/Gyn has a rich history of collaboration. As discussed in chapter 12, Ob/Gyn and Pediatrics worked together to establish the division of Breastfeeding Medicine in 2016. Ob/Gyn has collaborated with Psychiatry on several well-funded projects, including a PCORI project on patient navigation for management of depression in OB/Gyn clinics and a Project ECHO® program on the effects of pre- and postnatal exposure on child neurodevelopmental outcomes. As previously discussed, the department has recently joined forces with the EIOH, as well as faculty in Computer Sciences and Family Medicine, to develop a program to use Ob/Gyn offices to tackle disparities in dental care and to expand dental outreach.

The residency in Ob/Gyn (currently directed by Courtney Olson-Chen, MD) is a four-year program that admits eight residents each year. Residents rotate at SMH and HH, and the program features a robust research curriculum that includes didactic sessions in statistics, study design, scientific writing, and literature interpretation, and enables residents to initiate a research project during the first year. With the addition of three fellowships during Pressman's tenure, the department now runs three-year fellowships in urogynecology and reconstructive pelvic surgery, maternal fetal medicine, reproductive endocrinology, and gynecologic oncology, as well as a two-year fellowship in complex family planning that enables fellows to get an advanced degree, such as an MA in clinical investigation. It also runs the Ob/Gyn clerkship for medical students and several fourth-year electives and acting internships.

Research has seen similar growth, encompassing prenatal and early childhood, reproduction, maternal-fetal medicine, and menopause and later life. Timothy D. Dye, PhD, was recruited to head the Research division in 2014. A medical anthropologist and social epidemiologist who specializes in applied public health, particularly within marginalized, isolated, and global populations, Dye's work focuses on biomedical informatics and data science, particularly at the intersection of social science and health. Also noteworthy was the recruitment of Richard G. Moore, MD, in 2015 to head the division of Gynecologic Oncology. An expert in the treatment and early diagnosis of endometrial and ovarian cancer, he has created important ties to the WCI. Aided by these and other recruits, research funding has risen to $11.3 million administered through Ob/Gyn and $25.9 million in grants where Ob/Gyn faculty serve as co-PIs or on multi-PI studies. More detail about individual research programs is available on the department's website.

Chapter 20

DEPARTMENT OF EMERGENCY MEDICINE

Emergency Medicine (EM) became a recognized specialty in 1979; prior to that, patients were seen by general surgeons, internists, family physicians, and a variety of specialists based upon their presenting symptoms. The department of EM (DEM) was established at SMD in 1993, with Sandra Schneider, MD, as its founding chair. Schneider received her MD and completed her residency in EM at the University of Pittsburgh. Soon after becoming chair, she initiated an EM residency and developed fellowships in pediatric EM and international EM. An early proponent of making EM an academic specialty, she developed a national reputation as a researcher and educator, leading to her becoming a member of the board of directors, and, in 2011, president of the American College of Emergency Physicians (ACEP).

Figure 20.1.
Sandra Schneider

A defining moment for DEM was the opening of the 55,000 square-foot Frank and Caroline Gannett Emergency Center in 2001. The new facility, roughly three times larger than the previous ED, included a pediatric unit, a community psychiatric emergency program (CPEP), a sophisticated trauma/critical care unit, and an observation unit. Two additional floors were added in 2004 to house the Pediatric Intensive Care Unit, in-hospital Ronald McDonald House and the Kessler Burn & Trauma Center. Although the new ED was designed for a daily census of 200 patients per day, the closing of The Genesee Hospital in 2001 saw the census balloon to approximately 300 patients per day, necessitating the addition of a second bed to each room.

Schneider remained as chair until 2007, until stepping down to focus on research and her work with ACEP. She subsequently became senior research director for the North Shore/Long Island Jewish department of EM. Schneider was followed briefly as chair by Latha G. Stead, MD, a former undergraduate of the University of Rochester who had previously served as chair of EM at the Mayo Clinic, where she had developed a national reputation for her research on stroke. She was succeeded in 2009 by Michael F. Kamali, MD. Kamali received his MD from New York Medical College and did his residency in EM at URMC. He subsequently joined the faculty, becoming assistant medical director and director of quality assurance. As chair, Kamali has overseen a remarkable transformation of emergency services.

Figure 20.2. Michael Kamali

In 2013, Lakeside Memorial Hospital closed, ending twenty-four-hour emergency care in the Brockport area. To ensure high-quality care in the region, URMC purchased most of the assets of Lakeside to create Strong West, an outpatient medical village operating under the SMH license that would be a hub for UR Medicine providers. In 2014, Strong West received NY State approval for an off-campus ED, the first in upstate NY and only the second in the state. Unlike urgent care centers, this ED—which has an isolation treatment room, enhanced lab and imaging capabilities, a pharmacy, and three observation beds—would be able to care for patients arriving by ambulance with around-the-clock staffing by DEM faculty. Patients who required more intensive care and hospitalization would be stabilized and then transferred to other hospitals. The urgent care center in Spencerport, part of the Lakeside acquisition, was kept open and run by DEM. Over time, Strong West has expanded to include a fifteen-bed observation unit, an urgent care center, an ambulatory surgical suite with three ORs and two procedure rooms, and offices for

Figure 20.3. The Emergency Department in 2001

primary care and a variety of specialties. In 2024, Strong West treated 24,767 ED patients, performed 2,407 surgeries, and transferred 2,273 patients to regional hospitals for admission. In 2017, Strong West earned Press Ganey's Guardian of Excellence Award, ranking in the top five percent (out of 26,000 facilities) for patient experience in care delivery.

One of the most striking developments in the past ten years has been the urgent care program. Working with Chartis health care consulting, Kamali and URMC administration developed a comprehensive plan for urgent care that identified key sites throughout the region to be developed in stages either through the purchase of property, some with existing urgent care facilities, or through new construction. The centers would be managed by DEM and would be staffed by RNs and staff physicians. Each center would be tied into the electronic medical record and have the equivalent of a hotline to the SMH ED, providing immediate consultation when necessary, and assuring that URMC centers would provide the highest level of urgent care throughout the region. The program, which currently has fifteen locations including eight managed by URMC's regional hospitals, has proven incredibly successful. Monroe County locations alone saw close to 150,000 visits in 2024.

In 2009, the Wolk ED was opened at HH, supported by a generous gift from the Louis S. and Molly B. Wolk Foundation, and replacing a facility that had been last renovated in 1975! Highland's new ED, prompted by

Figure 20.4. Strong West

Figure 20.5. Urgent Care Center

a sixty-seven percent increase in patient visits in the five years preceding its groundbreaking, more than doubled in area and raised the number of acute-care beds to twenty-six. A more recent expansion converted all twenty-six beds into private rooms, including specialized rooms for geriatric patients that reduce the risk of falls or delirium, and specialized rooms for obstetrical patients. Currently, the HH ED sees over 50,000 patients a year. The ED is staffed by DEM faculty, some of whom rotate through SMH and other sites, in keeping with our goal of developing a uniform and comprehensive patient care system.

With the expansion of the regional program, DEM has worked to provide staffing and management of the regional EDs. Most hospitals, if not fully staffed by the department, have a majority presence that helps ensure a common approach to patient care. This has resulted in increases in ED volumes at URMC's regional affiliates. The development of the urgent care program and the regional affiliations have increased the need for additional faculty. Between 2010 and 2025, DEM grew from approximately forty faculty to 120.

From its inception, URMC's department has been an exemplar of an academic DEM. Its residency is a nationally recognized, three-year program that has grown over time to accept fifteen residents per year. The program, which is predominantly at SMH, offers substantial flexibility, including specialized tracks in emergency medical services, pediatric EM, ultrasound, wilderness medicine (an intensive, two-year curriculum incorporating survival skills to prepare trainees for careers as expedition leaders, medics, medical directors, and researchers), toxicology, research and education. A tribute to the program is the continuing success at attracting graduates to the faculty; approximately fifty percent of DEM faculty are graduates of its residency program, yielding an excellent balance of internally and externally trained physicians.

DEM also oversees five fellowships: pediatric emergency medicine (three years), emergency ultrasound (one year, focusing on bedside ultrasound), medical education (one or two years), medical toxicology (two years), and international emergency medicine (two years). Fellows in most programs have the option to receive a master's degree in public health, clinical investigation, medical education, or medical management, or to concentrate specifically on becoming a clinical educator. The medical education fellowship, established in 2022, is a partnership with the Warner School of Education and leads to a Master of Health Professions Education degree. The department also offers three fellowships for APPs, including emergency medicine, critical care medicine, and urgent care medicine.

Figure 20.6. Jeffrey Bazarian

Research in DEM runs the gamut from basic to translational to clinical research, and more can be found on the department website. One notable program has been concussion research, led by Jeffrey J. Bazarian, MD, MPH. Bazarian received his MD and MPH and did a residency in EM at URMC, before joining the faculty. Bazarian's traumatic brain injury research program, part of the multidisciplinary UR Medicine Concussion Care program, aims to develop neuroimaging and blood-based biomarkers of axonal injury after concussion and repetitive head hits, and to understand the pathophysiologic mechanisms of recovery. Studies involve subjects seen in UR Medicine EDs, as well as contact athletes at the University and RIT. Since 2009, over 700 collegiate athletes and over 100 non-athletes have been studied using a wide array of biomarkers, imaging, cognitive, electroencephalogram, and functional assessments. Bazarian has served on several traumatic brain injury-related task forces and panels for the CDC, the NIH, the NSF, and the Institute of Medicine. In 2008, he worked with the Defense and Veterans Brain Injury Center to develop mild traumatic brain injury management guidelines for returning troops.

DEM has developed several programs to facilitate clinical research. The Emergency Department Research Associate (EDRA) program, begun in 1996, is available to investigators who wish to study patients seen in the

EDs at SMH and HH. The program, which has enrolled tens of thousands of patients, has a robust quality-assurance process that ensures research protocols are followed and provides regular feedback on study enrollment, successes, and challenges to investigators. Research associates are trained in fundamental concepts of clinical research, confidentiality, consent, and procedural skills, and then progress to a hands-on learning model that provides them with ongoing research education, study-specific training, and quality-improvement-driven learning. The *Emergency Medicine Research Experience/Internship: PH394e* course, which was developed as required training for undergraduate students to function as an EDRA, exposes students to clinical research in the ED setting and teaches them to think critically about research protocols and study execution. Students who successfully complete this course are eligible to apply for a paid position as an ED enroller.

The Industry-Sponsored Research program has established itself as a reliable and high-enrolling site for clinical trials in EM. The program, which has its own dedicated, state-of-the-art Biosafety Level 2 clinical research laboratory and staff, works with industry partners to conduct studies whose funding is outside the scope of state and federal agencies. DEM also supports a two-year research fellowship for physicians who have completed their residency in EM. The program provides an MS in clinical investigation and an option to track into a PhD.

Volumes for all ED services have continued to increase, as has inpatient occupancy at SMH, which routinely exceeds a hundred percent and makes it difficult to quickly transfer admitted patients out of the ED. The Strong

Figure 20.7. Architect's Rendering of the New ED

Expansion Project will more than triple the size of the ED and CPEP to 120,000 square feet and will add more than 200 examination/treatment and patient observation stations (all private). The project also doubles the observation unit to forty-eight beds and increases the footprint of the pediatric ED. The new space addresses UR Medicine's growing role in providing emergency services, particularly those requiring the highest levels of care, throughout western NY. Set to go live in 2028, the project is one of the largest in the history of the University and furthers its commitment to provide the region with world-class patient care.

Chapter 21

DEPARTMENT OF PATHOLOGY AND LABORATORY MEDICINE (DPLM)

The growth and regionalization of the clinical programs placed extraordinary demands on pathology and laboratory services that required heavy recruitment of faculty and staff, and ultimately the centralization of services.

DPLM can trace its origins to the founding of URMC: George H. Whipple, the first SMD dean and 1934 Nobel Prize winner in Physiology and Medicine, was also the first chair of the department. Under his leadership, and that of Lowell Orbison, MD, Roger Terry, MD, Stanley Patten, MD, PhD, Thomas Bonfiglio, MD, and Steven Spitalnik, MD, the department grew into a multi-faceted enterprise of basic science and clinical work.

Figure 21.1. Daniel Ryan

Daniel H. Ryan, MD, became the sixth chair of DPLM in 2004, following the two-year interim chairmanship of Dean Arvan, MD. During his brief tenure, Arvan helped establish a productivity-based funding model that would be key to DPLM's future. A graduate of Johns Hopkins, Ryan received his pathology training at URMC and then joined the faculty in 1980 as director of the Hematology Lab. In 1997, he became director of Clinical Laboratories. As chair, Ryan appointed Neil Blumberg, MD, director of Clinical Laboratories, and Brendan Boyce, MBChB, vice chair for Anatomic Pathology. In assuming DPLM's leadership, Ryan articulated two goals: to enhance national research stature (building on strong basic science programs in cellular metabolism related to bone and joint disease, lipid metabolism and insulin related pathways; androgen receptor biology; and clinical research in blood product transfusion immunology) and to become the regional patient care and customer service leader in clinical laboratory testing.

Ryan spearheaded an aggressive recruitment campaign that included in his first five years as chair twenty-one full-time primary faculty members, including three basic scientists. Notable senior recruitments included Richard Burack, MD, PhD (hematopathology), David Hicks, MD (surgical pathology), Bruce Goldman, MD (autopsy), Mahlon Johnson, MD, PhD (neuropathology), and Archibald Perkins MD, PhD (hematopathology). Notable junior faculty recruitments included Jiaoti Huang (GU Pathology, now chair of Pathology at Duke), Christa Whitney-Miller (Surgical Pathology, now chair of Pathology at URMC), Lianping Xing, BMed, PhD (bone research), Majed Refaai, MD (transfusion medicine), Jim Corsetti, MD, PhD (clinical chemistry), and Myra Coppage, PhD (tissue typing). These recruitments, along with investigators from other departments, allowed DPLM to develop a well-funded collaborative research program. The recruitment of Hicks also accelerated the department's transition into a fully realized subspecialty surgical pathology model.

As director of Clinical Laboratories and interim chair, Arvan had established a strong outpatient laboratory business model. With the leadership of program administrators Jay Marchwinski and Bob Johnson, Ryan completed the transition from a largely inpatient service to a highly competitive customer service-driven outpatient model. One of the seminal achievements of Ryan's administration was the development of the URMC Clinical Trials Central Laboratory (CTCL), the only full-service national CTCL based in an academic pathology department. The CTCL, led by Johnson, Judy Sterry, and Kris Kuryla, began to earn positive margins in 2014, some of which helped support the academic missions of the DPLM. The Cytogenetics and Microarray Laboratories, led by Nancy Wang, PhD, and Anwar Iqbal, MD, also developed a successful reference laboratory business.

As planned, Ryan stepped down as chair after eight years. Retirement was not yet in the cards, however, as his successor, John Krolewski, MD, PhD, proved not a good fit for DPLM. Accordingly, after an eight-month breather, Ryan returned as chair for two additional years. Ryan decided after retirement to explore with curiosity and self-kindness the strong but unfocused feelings about gender that had been hidden for sixty years. She soon understood that she is a transgender woman, Eileen Amy Ryan, and once embarked on her journey of transition, never looked back. Eileen has reconnected with the DPLM, and is active in the Association of Academic Pathology, where she presents her perspective on emotional wellness and LGBTQ+ issues in pathology as a chair emerita. To be consistent with how she identified as department chair, this narrative uses he/him pronouns and her former name Daniel to refer to those years.

Bruce Smoller, MD, began his tenure as chair of the DPLM in 2014. Smoller earned his MD from the University of Cincinnati, completed an anatomic and clinical pathology residency at Beth Israel Hospital, Boston, and completed a fellowship in dermatopathology

Figure 21.2. Bruce Smoller

at New York Hospital/Cornell University Medical Center. Prior to joining URMC, he had served for seven years as chair of Pathology at the University of Arkansas, and subsequently as executive VP and secretary-treasurer for the United States and Canadian Academy of Pathology. Smoller also spent five years as editor-in-chief of the *Journal of Cutaneous Pathology*. He has authored more than 200 peer-reviewed articles and thirteen textbooks. His primary research interests revolve around cutaneous T cell lymphoma and the role of immunopathology as a diagnostic tool.

Smoller's tenure was characterized by a transformation from what was largely a "generalist" model to one of subspecialization, enabling faculty members to dedicate their service work entirely to their fields of fellowship-trained expertise, increasing the quality of diagnostic reports, educational experiences for trainees, and interactions with subspecialists throughout URMC. The advances in science and technology and the growth of UR Medicine resulted in a marked increase in laboratory testing. To accommodate this growth and ensure high-quality service throughout the system, Smoller and URMC administration developed a multiphased plan to create a central laboratory by moving clinical operations to an off-site location at Bailey Road. The first phase, housing all non-urgent clinical pathology laboratory testing across 130,000 square feet, opened in 2019 under the medical direction of Tamera Paczos, MD. This centralized facility allowed for a near doubling of clinical tests and resulted in enterprise savings. A division of Outreach Pathology, comprised of pathologists responsible for diagnostic services at affiliated hospitals, was developed to ensure high-quality services throughout the region. To accomplish the transformation to a subspecialist model and the expansion of clinical testing, the departmental faculty almost doubled.

Figure 21.3. Christa Whitney-Miller

In 2022, Smoller stepped back from his role as department chair. He was succeeded by Christa Whitney-Miller, MD, who became the ninth chair of DPLM and the inaugural Frieda Robscheit-Robbins Professor. Whitney-Miller, a native of Rochester, received her MD from SUNY Upstate and completed an anatomic and clinical pathology residency and a surgical pathology fellowship at the University of Pennsylvania. She had faculty appointments at the University of Pennsylvania and The Ohio State University before coming to URMC in 2009, where she subsequently served as director of the GI Pathology Service, director of Surgical Pathology, and vice chair of Anatomic Pathology. She also founded the GI/hepatobiliary pathology fellowship. A specialist in gastrointestinal pathology, she has established a clinical research program on HER2 overexpression in GI malignancies. Whitney-Miller oversaw the completion of the next phase of the Bailey Road central laboratory—a 20,000 square-foot, second-floor addition housing histology and portions of the cytopathology preparatory laboratory. This enabled the full consolidation of surgical pathology and cytopathology services among all URMC affiliates. Xiaolan Ou, MD, PhD, became the new medical director of the facility.

The evolving paradigm of precision medicine, particularly related to cancer treatment, requires increasingly complex diagnostic testing and is fundamentally changing the practice of pathology. DPLM has been at the forefront in utilizing new technologies and implanting strategies to address these growing demands. A few examples are highlighted below.

DPLM developed a rapid tissue acquisition program in which technical staff from surgical pathology are stationed in the ORs and can immediately retrieve all tissue specimens as soon as they are available for rapid transport to the pathology laboratory. This safeguards the molecular quality of patient specimens, enabling the laboratory to generate analytic data on which to base valid diagnostic decisions. At the start of the millennium, the Molecular Diagnostics laboratory offered single gene mutational analysis for high-frequency oncologic mutations via Sanger sequencing under the tutelage of Paul G. Rothberg, PhD. In 2018, with help from new faculty member Yi Ding, MD, PhD, the laboratory began offering a next-generation sequencing-based panel for detection of oncologic mutations. Shortly thereafter, Zoltan N. Oltvai, MD, was recruited to take over the directorship of the Molecular Diagnostics laboratory, which continues to expand the number and types of oncologic mutations it can detect.

DPLM developed a subspecialty-based surgical pathology system, combining disease-specific diagnostic expertise with translational research based on organ systems and disease categories to meet the demands for precision cancer care. For example, the breast pathology subspecialty service has worked closely with the multidiscipline breast center to modify a risk stratification model using semi-quantitative information from immunohistochemistry to help identify patients at low, moderate or high risk of breast cancer relapse following endocrine therapy.

Figure 21.4. Neil Blumberg

Transfusion Medicine, directed for many years by Neil Blumberg, MD, has been a national leader in transfusion immunomodulation research to improve the efficacy and reduce the toxicity of blood transfusions. DPLM-led blood transfusion research has involved investigators from Pediatrics, Medicine, Microbiology

& Immunology, Surgery, and Anesthesiology, as well as the WCI and the American Red Cross. Based upon this research, SMH was the first hospital in the country to adopt universal leukoreduction, minimizing post-operative infections, organ failure, alloimmunization, and inflammation. DPLM also took the lead in demonstrating that ABO blood type matching is critical for platelets, plasma and cryoprecipitate, not only red cells. By avoiding ABO mismatching, URMC has almost completely abrogated platelet transfusion refractoriness, which can impair the ability to cure hematologic malignancies. These approaches minimize bleeding, inflammation, and mortality in medical and surgical patients.

DPLM has a vigorous research program, buoyed by key recruitments over the past twenty-five years and rich interdepartmental collaboration. More than half of the faculty currently receive extramural research funding. Major areas of interest include cancer, cell biology and genetics, hematology and immunology, and musculoskeletal diseases. DPLM also provides major support for the Electron Microscopy Core. The reader is referred to the website for details of each program.

Figure 21.5. Brendan Boyce

One program that has received particular attention was that of Brendan F. Boyce, MBChB. Boyce received his MBChB from the University of Glasgow, Scotland and trained as a surgical pathologist in Glasgow Royal Infirmary. He subsequently spent a two-year sabbatical doing basic research in Greg Mundy's laboratory at the University of Texas, San Antonio, where he developed a supra-calvarial injection model that enabled him to study bone resorption *in vivo* in mice. He was the first to demonstrate that osteoclasts undergo apoptosis in response to bisphosphonates and estrogen as part of their anti-resorptive actions. He moved to URMC in 1999 as director of Surgical Pathology (and later vice chair for Anatomic Pathology) with his postdoctoral fellow, Lianping Xing, PhD, who subsequently was promoted to professor in recognition of her seminal contributions to cytokine- and senescence-mediated bone loss. Boyce recruited Zhenqiang Yao, PhD, in 2003, who also developed nationally recognized programs in age-related bone loss and metastatic bone disease. Recent research findings include elucidation of the role of NF-kB[9] signaling in bone resorption and formation; identifying novel populations of neutrophils that promote age-related osteoporosis in mice and B cells that promote bone destruction during aging; and demonstrating that the

9 Nuclear factor kappa-light-chain-enhancer of activated B cells.

FDA-approved drug, maraviroc, might be repurposed to treat age-related osteoporosis by reducing specific populations of neutrophils in the bone marrow. The metabolic bone disease program has trained over forty students and postdoctoral fellows, many now with positions in academia and industry. The prominence of Boyce's program is underscored by his roles in leading several international societies, including presidency of the International Society of Bone Morphometry, and as senior associate editor of the *Journal of Bone and Mineral Research.*

The DPLM has expanded and transformed its educational portfolio, adapting to the rapidly changing landscape of medicine and technology. Smoller created the position of vice chair of Education to oversee all educational programming, a post first held by Scott Kirkley, MD, and upon his retirement in 2020 by Jennifer Findeis-Hosey, MD. During Smoller's tenure, the number of residency positions increased to twenty per year. Changes made to the curriculum included: use of digital/virtual microscopy, adapting to the development of the subspecialty practice model, addition of a lab management rotation, incorporating pathology informatics, implementing leadership development and formal resident mentoring. Residents receive personalized training tailored to their career goals and have ample opportunity to participate in research programs. The department recently began to offer specific anatomic pathology only and clinical pathology only tracts.

To address concerns that DPLM was not attracting top candidates because most residents were opting for subspecialty training, fellowships were established in dermatopathology, transfusion medicine, pediatric pathology, and general surgical pathology. Also of note was the development of a combined training program in Laboratory Management in conjunction with an MBA from the Simon School. To our knowledge, the University is the first institution in the country to offer fellowship training in laboratory management and medical directorship, where fellows receive hands-on experience by taking on the role of laboratory medical director at one or more of the UR Medicine acute care laboratories. Because of these changes, DPLM has experienced great improvement in attracting the best candidates, ninety-five percent of whom enter fellowships and one-third of whom remain in academics (more than two-thirds in the past five years).

The PhD program in pathology, one of thirteen multidisciplinary graduate tracks in SMD, involves over sixty laboratories. Students concentrate in either cell biology of disease, cancer biology or bioinformatics. Under the direction of Robert Mooney, PhD, who retired in 2016, Richard Libby, PhD, who became SAD for Graduate Education in 2018, and now Helene McMurray, PhD, the program has had substantial growth and currently has thirty-nine students.

In 2006, NY State passed the "Clinical Laboratory Technology Practice" act, requiring clinical laboratory practitioners to be licensed. The new law required candidates for licensure to complete several credits of didactic instruction and 750 hours of clinical training at a degree-granting institution. To address this, DPLM developed a new two-semester, nine-month certificate program in Clinical/Medical Technology that prepares graduates for state licensure, national certification, and entrance into the profession. Since its inception in 2017, ninety students have completed the program, with nearly eighty percent taking positions at SMH or at other laboratories within UR Medicine. Based upon the successes of this program, similar ones have been initiated in phlebotomy services, histology technology, and cytopathology.

The department has also made concerted efforts to foster an inclusive and equitable culture. Bradley Turner, MD, MPH, MHA, the department's first diversity officer, was a founding board member of the Black Physician Network, a community organization with a mission to decrease disparities of underrepresented physicians in medicine through collaborative networking and mentorship. Turner was also a founding board member of the Academy of Health Science Charter School in Rochester, a free public charter school offering grades 5–8 and focused on health sciences whose goal is to expose underrepresented minorities to the health science job industry.

Figure 21.6. Bradley Turner

Chapter 22

DEPARTMENT OF IMAGING SCIENCES

The department of Imaging Sciences (DIS) experienced remarkable increases in the number of studies and procedures resulting from the growth of UR Medicine. This, coupled with rapid changes in technology, necessitated substantial growth in faculty and staff, along with new imaging space outside the Medical Center.

DIS was established in 1925, originally as the department of Medical Photography, under the leadership of Stafford Warren, MD, a pioneer in nuclear medicine, the inventor of the mammogram, and the medical director of the Manhattan Project. The department was renamed Radiology in 1939. Warren left in 1947 to become the first dean of the School of Medicine at UCLA. He was succeeded by several distinguished chairs: Andrew H. Dowdy, MD (1947–8), George H. Ramsey, MD (1948–60), Louis H. Hempelmann, Jr., MD (1960–71), Harry W. Fischer, MD (1971–85), and Robert O'Mara, MD (1988–91). Many of these leaders had connections to the Manhattan Project and contributed significantly to radiobiology and radiation effects. Fischer was a pioneer in contrast media development, and in the design of imaging departments. During his tenure, URMC installed its first CT and MRI scanners.

Arvin E. Robinson, MD, was recruited from Tulane University to chair Radiology in 1993. He played a key role in consolidating services within SMH, expanding fellowship training programs, and promoting research in functional MRI (fMRI), ultrasound tissue characterization, and CT scanning. In 2003, he left to become chair of Radiology at Texas Tech, and was succeeded at URMC by David Waldman, MD, PhD.

Waldman received his MD and PhD from the University of Rochester, where he also did his internship in internal medicine and residency in radiology. After a fellowship in vascular/interventional radiology at Rhode Island Hospital/Brown University, Waldman returned to URMC in 1994 to become the first director of the new division of Angiography and Interventional Radiology. Under his leadership, Radiology expanded significantly as the clinical faculty grew from thirty-five

Figure 22.1.
David Waldman

to over seventy full-time members, and research faculty were recruited to develop programs in photodynamic therapy and MRI coil design. He fostered strong relationships with other departments, leading to new initiatives in endovascular therapies and ultrasound technologies.

During Waldman's tenure, a major emphasis was placed on IT. A next-generation data aggregation system was developed, enabling all radiologists in the network to work within the same PACS (Picture Archiving and Communication System). This allowed for efficient data transfer among facilities. The expansion of imaging IT also necessitated centralization: URMC was one of the first to implement an enterprise-wide archive for all imaging, Vendor Neutral Archive, giving providers a consolidated view of the patient.

These innovations laid the foundation for the development of AI in imaging. Clinical researchers were hired and collaborations established with Computer Science and the Hajim School of Engineering & Applied Sciences. As a result, URMC became one of the first to use AI for clinical image interpretation. Today, DIS runs over fifteen clinical AI modules, supporting image interpretation, stroke management, and transplant and endograft planning. Recently, the department was recognized by the American College of Radiology as one of the first Centers for Healthcare-AI (ARCH-AI), the first national quality assurance program for AI in radiology.

In 2006, the department changed its name from Radiology to Imaging Sciences to better reflect the technology and breadth of imaging modalities. Over the past twenty-five years, it has been a national leader in introducing several advanced imaging technologies, including 3T MRI, 256-slice CT, fixed positron emission tomography (PET), first-time-of-flight PET, PET/MRI, and dual-energy CT. DIS is currently planning the implementation of a 7T MRI and a radiopharmaceutical development program, including the installation of an on-site cyclotron.

Under Waldman's leadership, DIS played a pivotal role in developing the UR Medicine network by establishing more than a dozen imaging sites throughout the region and covering off-hour shifts at regional hospitals. In 2021, the E. Michael Saunders Medical Imaging Center opened in Dansville with a PET/CT, 1.5T MRI, an advanced interventional radiology suite, and a modern nuclear medicine camera. This center was made possible by a generous gift from the Saunders Foundation.

A strategic plan was developed that included expanding imaging services on the ground floor of SMH, with separate areas for adult imaging, pediatric imaging (in the new GCH), and breast imaging at the WCI. The plan also featured an eight-room angio/interventional radiology area, complete with two dedicated CT scanners and six angiography suites, and a twenty-five-bed preparation/recovery area, making it one of the largest in the US.

Figure 22.2. The Imaging Center at East River Road

In 2017, URMC relocated outpatient imaging services to a new 90,000 square-foot, three-story Outpatient Imaging Center on East River Road. The center, which included the region's first dedicated interventional radiology clinic, provided a full range of imaging modalities and allowed for renovation and expansion of inpatient imaging at SMH. Further expansion of outpatient services occurred in 2020 with the acquisition of University Medical Imaging (UMI), a locally owned outpatient imaging center founded in 1990. UMI, which employed ninety staff members, was the only private practice in the region with a diagnostic medical staff comprised entirely of fellowship-trained radiologists, seventy-five percent of whom were trained at URMC.

In 2020, Waldman stepped down as chair, becoming associate VP and chief medical technology development officer. He was succeeded as chair by Jennifer Harvey, MD, who was recruited from the University of Virginia, where she had served as chief of Breast Imaging and vice chair for Education and Faculty Development. Harvey received her MD and completed her residency in radiology from the University of Arizona College of Medicine. An international expert in women's imaging, her research has focused on methods for measuring changes in breast density to detect breast cancer earlier. She is also the founding editor of the *Journal of Breast Imaging*. Harvey became the inaugural

Figure 22.3. Jennifer Harvey

Stanley M. Rogoff, MD, and Raymond Gramiak, MD, Professor in Radiology, established with an anonymous gift in honor of Stanley Rogoff, graduate of SMD and former chief of Diagnostic Radiology at URMC, and Raymond Gramiak, also a graduate of SMD and URMC faculty member and pioneer in ultrasonography.

During Harvey's tenure, DIS has continued to grow and now has 114 clinical faculty and ten full-time research faculty. In 2024, the department interpreted 1,100,000 studies (compared to 300,000 in 2002) and brought in over 150,000 studies from outside facilities. Most mammography units were upgraded to 3-D, a dedicated mammography information system was installed that allows risk-based screening, and a research program was developed using whole breast ultrasound imaging. Dual energy CT scanners were installed in key areas, resulting in improved image quality, better tissue characterization, reduced radiation exposure, and the ability to create virtual non-enhanced images. MRI technology was also overhauled to create faster scan times, improved image quality, and integration of AI for enhanced image analysis and processing, leading to more efficient and accurate diagnoses.

DIS offers a comprehensive educational program, including a four-year diagnostic radiology residency program (currently, thirty-six residents) and a five-year interventional radiology residency (currently, ten residents). DIS sponsors fellowships in various specialties, including Musculoskeletal Imaging, Neuroradiology, Pediatric Radiology, Abdomen/Body, Breast Imaging, Cardiothoracic Imaging, and MRI, with dedicated time for research. DIS also offers a two-week elective for medical students, providing exposure to general radiology and subspecialties. DIS also offers a multidisciplinary MS in diagnostic imaging, a one-year program for residents, medical, and engineering students interested in careers in medical imaging.

Faculty in DIS are involved in a wide range of research activities. Of particular note is the extent of collaboration between investigators in DIS and those in River Campus departments. Nebojsa Durik, PhD, who is vice chair for research in DIS and is also appointed in Biomedical Engineering, has established the Ultrasound Tomography Center, a multidisciplinary clinical and research unit with physicians and scientists throughout the University. Timothy M. Baran, who received his PhD in Optics from the University and has appointments in DIS, Biomedical Engineering, and Optics, focuses on photodynamic therapy, a technique that uses photosensitive drugs to selectively destroy tumors and infections, such as abscesses. Mohammad Mehrmohammadi, PhD, who also is appointed in Biomedical Engineering, has established the Photoacoustic and Ultrasonic Research & Engineering (PURE) laboratory to develop novel ultrasound-based methods to detect, diagnose, and treat various pathologies.

Vikram S. Dogra, MBBS, is employing ultrasound and photoacoustic imaging, a technology that uses laser and ultrasound to differentiate cancer from normal tissue, to develop new diagnostic approaches to detect cancer. Wing-Chi E. Kwok, PhD, focuses on improving MRI imaging to better diagnose arthritic diseases and evaluate drug treatment. Axel W. E. Wismueller, MD, PhD, a pioneer in using AI in radiology, is developing robust and adaptive systems for computer-aided analysis and visualization. Applications range from brain mapping, multiple sclerosis and Alzheimer's disease to breast cancer.

DIS participates in the Rochester Center for Biomedical Ultrasound (RCBU) and plays a critical role in the leadership of the Rochester Center for Advanced Brain Imaging and Neurophysiology center (CABIN), where Madalina Tivarus, PhD, serves as director and Jianhui Zhong, PhD, serves as associate director. The Tivarus laboratory uses advanced neuroimaging techniques to study patients with brain tumors, epilepsy, Alzheimer's disease, HIV-associated neurocognitive impairment, and multiple sclerosis. Similarly, the Zhong laboratory employs advanced MRI techniques for quantitative analysis of brain structural and functional networks. CABIN also houses Wismueller's research program. DIS supports over a hundred clinical trials through its comprehensive imaging support services. More detailed descriptions of the individual research programs are available on each investigator's website.

The research efforts have also led to two important start-up companies, in which the University has an equity stake. VirtualScopics, founded by Saara Totterman, MD, specializes in three-dimensional image processing and has evolved into a global imaging core lab supporting clinical trials. Koning Health was founded by Roula Ning, PhD, who, together with Avice O'Connell, MD, then-director of Women's Imaging at URMC, developed a dedicated low-dose cone beam breast CT unit, which received FDA approval in 2017. Since that time, the company has grown significantly.

Chapter 23

DEPARTMENT OF SURGERY

The department of Surgery has a distinguished history of surgical leadership, beginning in 1923, when John J. Morton, MD, was recruited from Yale University by George Whipple to become its first chair. Morton devoted his initial focus to planning for the outpatient clinics, emergency ward, and operating rooms at SMH and recruiting staff for the clinical, educational, and research missions. The first surgery, a resection of a mixed tumor of the parotid, was performed on January 7, 1926. Morton continued as chair until 1953.

Morton was succeeded as chair by W. J. Merle Scott, MD, who was recruited to URMC as a surgical faculty member shortly after Morton's arrival. During Scott's tenure, several general surgical residents joined the faculty, including John H. Morton, MD, J. Raymond Hinshaw, MD, James A. DeWeese, MD, and Seymour I. Schwartz, MD. In addition, there was a marked increase in research. Charles Rob, MD, a distinguished vascular surgeon and professor of surgery at St. Mary's Hospital, London, became chair in 1960. Rob was responsible for amalgamating the residency program on a citywide basis, including The Genesee Hospital, RGH, HH, and St. Mary's Hospital. William R. Drucker, MD, former chair of surgery at the University of Toronto and dean of the University of Virginia Medical School, became Surgery chair at URMC in 1977. A more integrated residency program was developed, with most of the time spent at SMH and block rotations through the other hospitals.

Drucker was succeeded by Seymour Schwartz in 1987. Schwartz, who had served for twenty years as director of Surgical Research, continued to grow the faculty, with key recruitments in many areas and the appointment of many new division chiefs. Upon his retirement in 1998, Schwartz was appointed distinguished alumni professor of Surgery and the Seymour I. Schwartz Chair of Surgery was endowed. Schwartz, who retired from the operating room at age seventy-two, remained active at the Medical Center until his death at the age of ninety-two in 2020.

Figure 23.1. Seymour Schwartz

Seymour Schwartz's storied career began at the University in 1950, when he arrived for surgical residency. He finished residency in 1957 after a twenty-month leave to serve in the US Navy during the Korean War and then joined the surgical faculty. For the next sixty years he cultivated expertise in hepatobiliary surgery and other complex operations and rose through the ranks of academic medicine, both inside and outside of Rochester.

Most notably, Schwartz edited and co-authored the standard textbook for the profession, *Schwartz's Principles of Surgery*, during the years that his own career was advancing. The first edition of the book became known as "the surgeon's bible" and was unique for being rooted in basic science. McGraw-Hill first published it in 1969, and it is now in its 11th edition, which was issued in 2019 to mark its fiftieth anniversary. It has been translated into many languages and is known by virtually every surgical trainee in the world. Schwartz served as president of the country's three most important surgical societies: the Society of Clinical Surgery, the American Surgical Association, and the American College of Surgeons (ACS). He was editor-in-chief of *Contemporary Surgery* for twenty-eight years, the *Yearbook of Surgery* for twenty-two years, and the *Journal of the American College of Surgeons* for ten years. The ACS honored Schwartz as an "Icon of Surgery" in 2017.

Schwartz was also an avid historian who published six books on American history. He was a collector of rare maps, some of which now reside in the Dr. Ruth W. Schwartz and Dr. Seymour I. Schwartz Collection in the department of Rare Books, Special Collections, and Preservation on the River Campus. An international expert on the mapping of the New World, Schwartz wrote four books on the subject, served on the Board of Trustees of the Museum of American History and the Smithsonian Institution, and was a member of the Advisory Board of the Geography and Map Division of the Library of Congress. He became an accordion player after winning the instrument in a poker game while in the Navy, wrote lyrics for the SMD's annual student musical production, and composed special limericks for each graduate of the surgical residency program.

In his later years, Schwartz became fascinated by physicians who had become literary figures, and he profiled some of the nation's finest in a book called *From Medicine to Manuscript*, published in 2018. It features essays and biographies on exceptional talents such as Oliver Sacks, Khaled Hosseini, Atul Gawande, Tess Gerritsen, and Abraham Verghese.

Schwartz was quite simply a giant in both his field and in the life of URMC, where he was an approachable, gracious, and insightful guide to generations of physicians who drew on the deep experience and knowledge that he so willingly shared.

James V. Sitzmann, MD, a nationally prominent colorectal surgeon, was recruited in 1999 to become the department's next chair. Sitzmann received his MD from the University of Minnesota and did his residency in surgery at Johns Hopkins, where he remained as faculty. Prior to joining URMC, Sitzmann served as chair of Surgery at Georgetown Medical Center. Just two years after his arrival, Sitzmann had a devastating bicycle accident and was unable to continue as chair. Although his tenure was brief, Sitzmann expanded the programs in trauma and transplantation.

As he had prior to the appointment of Schwartz, Arthur Hengerer, MD, served as interim chair until 2004, when Jeffrey H. Peters, MD, a nationally regarded esophageal surgeon and researcher, was recruited from the University of Southern California to be the Seymour I. Schwartz Chair of Surgery and surgeon-in-chief at SMH.

Figure 23.2. Jeffrey Peters

Peters received an MD from Ohio State University, did a residency in surgery and a postdoctoral research fellowship in immunology at Johns Hopkins, and did a clinical esophageal fellowship at Creighton University School of Medicine. During his tenure, Peters restructured the department, creating eleven divisions: Cardiac Surgery, Colorectal Surgery, Gastrointestinal & Bariatric Surgery, Pediatric Surgery, Plastic Surgery, Research, Surgical Oncology, Thoracic & Foregut Surgery, Transplant & Hepatobiliary Surgery, Trauma/Emergency Surgery, and Vascular Surgery. This was accompanied by faculty recruitment, the expansion of surgical services at SMH, and the opening of the new Ambulatory Surgical Center at Sawgrass. Peters established a new division (Supportive Care in Cancer) to serve as the home for one of SMD's and WCI's signature research programs, Cancer Prevention and Control, led by Gary Morrow, PhD. He also oversaw the introduction of the Surgical Health Outcomes Research Enterprise (SHORE), a program that identifies the most effective ways to deliver high-quality care, reduce medical errors, control costs, and improve patient safety. Peters left URMC in 2014 to become the COO of University Hospitals of Cleveland.

In 2014, David C. Linehan, MD, was recruited to be the Seymour I. Schwartz Chair of Surgery and surgeon-in-chief at SMH. Linehan received his MD from the University of Massachusetts, did a residency in surgery at the Beth Israel Deaconess Medical Center and a research fellowship at the Brigham and Women's Hospital, Boston. He was the Kristin Ann Carr Fellow in Surgical Oncology at MSKCC. Prior to coming to Rochester, Linehan had

Figure 23.3. David Linehan

spent fifteen years at Washington University in St. Louis serving as chief of Hepatobiliary, Pancreatic and Gastrointestinal Surgery and directing the fellowship training program. A nationally prominent pancreatic and gastrointestinal surgeon, Linehan developed a well-funded research program studying tumor microenvironment to develop novel approaches to treat pancreatic cancer and related tumors. His particular focus is on using immunotherapy to eliminate immune cells that promote cancer progression and to stimulate immune cells that fight cancer.

Under Linehan's leadership, the surgical faculty flourished with the recruitment of more than fifty surgeons who brought new talent and specialty services to Rochester. He attracted many scientists, particularly in the areas of tumor biology and immunology, and promoted the growth of surgeon-scientists. During his tenure, annual research funding increased from $4.9 million in FY15 to $11.3 million in FY23, with over eighty-five percent coming from the NIH. The department now ranks in the top fifteen in NIH funding. The growth in clinical and research expertise has enabled the department to attract the best and brightest trainees, continuing URMC's legacy as having a top-tier surgical training program.

Figure 23.4. Theodor Kaufman

Linehan also established the division of Regional General Surgery to provide a coordinated approach to surgical care throughout the growing UR Medicine network, particularly in the Finger Lakes and Southern Tier regions. Theodor I. Kaufman, MD, was recruited in 2020 from Bassett Healthcare in Cooperstown, NY to serve as chief of the division, which has grown to include seven faculty. Kaufman received his MD from SUNY Health Science Center at Brooklyn and did his residency in general surgery at the Bassett Medical Center. Based at FF Thompson Hospital, Kaufman is working with surgeons from URMC affiliates to create a regional strategy that provides coverage and assures that their constituencies are provided with a full range of local general surgery options. While at Bassett, Kaufman developed a training program to educate surgeons interested in practicing in a rural setting. He hopes to establish a similar program for UR Medicine. Kaufman's recruitment enabled UR Medicine to launch the ACS National Surgical Quality Improvement Program (NSQIP) at FF Thompson, Jones Memorial, Noyes Memorial, and St. James hospitals. A "UR Med Small/Rural Collaborative" was established within NSQIP to look at results across the system, the first such collaborative.

During Linehan's tenure the department took on a major role in the WCI, providing leadership for the Genetics, Epigenetics and Metabolism Program (Darren Carpizo, MD, PhD), the Cancer Prevention and Control

Program (Gary Morrow, PhD, and Karen Mustian, PhD) and the Cancer Control and Psychoneuroimmunology Laboratory (Michelle Janelsins-Benton, PhD, MPH). In 2022, he recruited AnaPaula Cupertino, PhD, into the department following completion of her tenure as the first associate director of Community Outreach and Engagement at WCI. A social behavioral scientist who received her PhD in Human Development from the University of California, Davis, Cupertino's work has focused on health disparities in underserved and minority communities, primarily among Latinos and immigrants. Much of her work has been in tobacco control, improving smoking cessation and access to cessation treatments using novel community-based approaches, including Decídetext, an innovative, mobile smoking cessation intervention. Cupertino also took over as the leader of SHORE, which oversees departmental health outcomes research and community engagement.

Figure 23.5. AnaPaula Cupertino

When Linehan was chosen to serve as URMC CEO and dean of SMD, succeeding Mark Taubman in 2024, Ryan C. Fields, MD, was recruited from Washington University, St. Louis, to serve as the Seymour I. Schwartz Chair of Surgery, surgeon-in-chief at SMH, and director of Translational Research of the WCI. Fields is a surgical oncologist and translational scientist who served as chief of Surgical Oncology, the leader of the Solid Tumor Therapeutics Program at the Alvin J. Siteman Comprehensive Cancer Center, and director of resident research in the department of Surgery at Washington University. Fields received his MD from Duke University, did his general surgery residency at Barnes-Jewish Hospital at Washington University, and a fellowship in surgical oncology at MSKCC. Fields's clinical focus is on the multidisciplinary treatment of solid tumors. A well-funded investigator with more than 350 peer-reviewed publications, Fields's research is centered on the biology and genetics of how cancer spreads.

Surgery Education

The department of Surgery has always been at the forefront of education at URMC. The General Surgery residency program, previously directed for over ten years by Rabih M. Salloum, MD, and currently by Yanjie Qi, MD, is a five-year program that accepts seven categorical residents per year. In addition, the department oversees residency programs in Plastic Surgery, Cardiothoracic Surgery, and Vascular Surgery, and fellowship programs in Bariatric and GI Surgery, Breast Oncology, Cardiothoracic Surgery, Colon & Rectal Surgery, and Surgical Critical Care. The department is heavily involved in teaching medical students, including overseeing a required five-week surgical clerkship in the third year, a fourth-year subinternship, and a variety of electives in all divisions of the department.

The department has also played an increasing role in the training of APPs. The Surgical APP fellowship is a one-year postgraduate program that prepares NPs and PAs to work with complex patients, such as those typically seen in pre-operative, intra-operative, and post-operative surgical settings. The APP fellowship in cardiac critical care is a one-year postgraduate program for NPs and PAs that includes hands-on training in all aspects of mechanical circulatory support, cardiac catheterization and electrophysiology laboratories, echocardiography, and advanced heart failure. The department also collaborates with the Pulmonary and Critical Care Division in DOM to administer the APP fellowship in critical care medicine.

One of the most striking educational developments in the department has been the Cancer Control Research training program. Funded by an NCI T32 since 2004, this program has had fifty fellows, including Michelle Janelsins-Benton, who is now PI of the training grant. Thirty-eight are currently in tenure-track faculty positions in twenty-one academic institutions and four are in industry (the remainder are still completing the program). Graduates have received more than $100 million as principal investigators on NIH grants.

Divisions

The following sections outline the clinical, educational, and research programs of the individual divisions of Surgery. The division of Cardiac Surgery is discussed in a later chapter.

Acute Care Surgery and Trauma

In 1961, John H. Morton, MD, was designated by chair of Surgery Rob as coordinator of trauma surgery and was placed in charge of surgical care in the SMH ED. Trauma became a section of Surgery in 1989, under the leadership of David V. Feliciano, MD. Upon Feliciano's departure in 1994 to become chair of Surgery at Grady Memorial Hospital in Atlanta, Palmer Q. Bessey, MD, became section chief. The management of trauma changed significantly with the recruitment in 2001 of Paul Bankey, MD, PhD, as section chief. Bankey got his MD from the University of Minnesota and remained there for his residency in general surgery and fellowship in

Figure 23.6. Paul Bankey

surgical critical care. He also received a PhD in nutrition sciences from the University of Minnesota-Twin Cities. In 2005, a new division of Acute Care Surgery and Trauma was created, with Bankey serving as division chief. Mark Gestring, MD, was selected to succeed Bankey as division chief in 2018 and continues to serve in that role. Gestring got his MD from New Jersey Medical School, did his residency in general surgery at SUNY at Stony Brook and Brown University, and did his fellowship in trauma surgical critical care at the University of Pennsylvania.

Figure 23.7. Mark Gestring

A major step forward for the division and the region was the establishment in 2011 of The Kessler Burn and Trauma Center at SMH, made possible through the generous philanthropic support of Laurence and Dennis Kessler. Since 2014, The Kessler Burn and Trauma Center has been designated by the American College of Surgeons as the highest level (Level 1) trauma center and the only such center in the Finger Lakes region, serving a population of 1.5 million spanning thirteen counties. Throughout the COVID pandemic, when other Level 1 trauma centers in upstate NY were shut down for periods of time, the Kessler Burn and Trauma Center was always open and available for transfers.

The division, which currently has eight full-time surgeons, offers a one-year fellowship in trauma and surgical critical care. The Trauma Skills laboratory was developed to provide hands-on training in a variety of trauma-specific skills, such as complex vascular access, application of tourniquets and pelvic binders, the use of resuscitation balloon occlusion of the aorta, chest tube insertion, and ultrasound. A Mobile Trauma Skills Lab was developed to provide the same kind of training throughout UR Medicine. The division offers a variety of continuing education and training programs for health care professionals: Rural Trauma Team Development (RTTDC®); Advanced Trauma Life Support (ATLS®); Advanced Trauma Care for Nursing (ATCN®); Prehospital Trauma Life Support (PHTLS®); Disaster Management and Emergency Preparedness (DMEP®); and Trauma Simulation. It is also involved in programs geared to the lay public, including Stop the Bleed (STB®), fall prevention, pedestrian safety, and distracted driving.

The division has been at the forefront of URMC efforts to partner with the community to address violence and injury. The Rochester Youth Violence Partnership (RYVP) is a hospital-based intervention program that targets trauma victims under the age of eighteen who present with a knife or gun injury. Established in 2006, RYVP is headed by the Kessler Burn and Trauma Center and supported by twenty-eight local nonprofit, government, and service-based organizations. The hospital serves as the first responder by recognizing the problem, identifying at-risk patients, and treating injuries. Once the patient is stabilized and the psychosocial issues identified, a coordinated series of law enforcement- and community partner-led interventions are initiated. The RYVP was recently honored with the American Hospital Association's prestigious NOVA Award for its commitment to improving community health.

The Firearm Injury Prevention Program was recently established to find ways to prevent firearm-related suicide, unintentional injury and death, assaults, and homicides through education, resource-sharing, research, and open dialogue. Headed by Corey Nichols-Hadeed, JD, and Jennifer West, PhD, it is a collaboration among faculty and staff from several URMC departments (Psychiatry, Emergency Medicine, Pediatrics, and Surgery), and health care providers, community agencies, and community members throughout the Finger Lakes.

Plastic Surgery

The division of Plastic Surgery can trace its roots to 1934, when Forrest Young, MD, completed a surgical residency at SMH. After an additional six months of training at Barnes Hospital, St. Louis, he returned to URMC as its plastic and reconstructive surgeon, contributing significantly to the literature on cleft lip and palate surgery, as well as the treatment of third-degree burns. Plastic Surgery became a division of Surgery in 1946, and in 1950, Robert M. McCormack, MD, who had been a resident at SMH under Young, was recruited back to URMC to succeed him as division chief. In 1959, Lester Cramer, MD, in collaboration with the Eastman Dental Center, established a program for treating cleft lip and palate. In 1975, a combined fellowship in hand surgery was established in collaboration with Orthopaedics. McCormack served as chief for thirty-three years. In 1984, he was succeeded by R. Christie Wray, Jr., MD, who was recruited from Washington University, St. Louis.

Wray, whose clinical expertise was in hand and upper extremity surgery, was particularly regarded for his excellence in teaching. Under his direction, the division established a coordinated residency, with the first three years in general surgery and the last two committed to plastic surgery. In 1990, he recruited Joseph Serletti, MD, who led the residency program and upon Wray's departure in 1998 became the next division chief. Serletti received his MD from the University of Rochester, where he remained for his general surgery and plastic surgery training. Before joining the SMD faculty, he completed a craniofacial fellowship at Johns

Figure 23.8. Joseph Serletti

Hopkins. Serletti is internationally known for his work in free flap breast augmentation and for reconstructive microsurgery of the head, neck, and extremities. He has published over 300 articles and authored six book chapters.

Serletti, and his wife Bonnie, also a graduate of SMD and of the residency program in Ob/Gyn at SMH, recently made a $1.5 million gift to endow the Serletti Family Cleft and Craniofacial Humanitarian Outreach Initiative at URMC. The gift will initially support local and international outreach efforts of the Pediatric Cleft and Craniofacial Center at GCH. In the future, this endowment will fund the Serletti Family Professorship, which will help attract, retain, and honor exemplary faculty in the plastic surgery division.

Figure 23.9. Howard Langstein

In 2005, Howard N. Langstein, MD, an expert in microvascular reconstruction, was recruited from M. D. Anderson Hospital in Houston to succeed Serletti, who had left to become head of plastic surgery at the University of Pennsylvania. Langstein received his MD and did residencies in general surgery and plastic surgery at NYU. In 2012, Langstein, who also served as vice chair of Academic Affairs and Faculty Development in Surgery, established a partnership with Healogics, the world's largest wound care management company, to establish a hyperbaric oxygen therapy facility, the Strong Wound Healing Center.

During Langstein's tenure, the division, which currently has seven faculty, continued to grow and to expand clinical services and research. The recruitment in 2009 of Derek Bell, MD, was followed by marked expansion of the burn program and the development of a robust quality assurance program that helped establish it as having among the lowest mortality rates in the country. In 2016, in recognition of this, the Kessler Burn Center became one of sixty-five sites and only the second in NY State to be designated as an American Burn Association certified burn program. Also of note was the recruitment in 2018 of Jonathan I. Leckenby, MBBS, PhD, a microsurgeon with expertise in facial paralysis, who established an NIH-funded laboratory investigating peripheral and spinal nerve regeneration, focusing on preventing and/or reversing symptoms of peripheral neuropathy induced by cancer treatment.

Figure 23.10. Clinton Morrison

Upon Langstein's retirement in 2023, Clinton Morrison, MD, was appointed as interim chief. Under Morrison's early tenure the faculty has grown to nine surgeons, including further expansion in hand and extremity surgery and gender-affirming care. Morrison received his MD from the University of Louisville, did a combined residency program in general surgery and plastic surgery at Brown University, and did a fellowship in craniofacial plastic surgery and pediatrics at Seattle Children's Hospital. He was recruited by Langstein to URMC in 2014 to become the plastic surgery team director of the Pediatric Cleft and Craniofacial Center at GCH. He also serves as director of the residency program in Plastic Surgery.

Abdominal Transplant and Liver Surgery

URMC has a rich history of providing transplant services to patients in the region and remains a pioneer in liver transplantation. The solid organ transplantation program has involved long-standing collaborations between the departments of Surgery and Medicine.

The first living-donor kidney transplant was done in 1966 by Allyn May, MD (General Surgery), and Charles A. Linke, MD (Urology), followed two years later by the first deceased-donor kidney transplant. As chair of Surgery, Seymour Schwartz had a vision to expand transplantation to other organs and as a first step recruited a pre-eminent transplant trained surgeon and researcher, James V. Cerilli, MD. By 1998, 1,000 kidney transplants had been completed. In 2004, URMC did its first simultaneous liver/kidney transplant. Transplantation continued to develop, with several surgeons heading the discipline. The first paired donor exchange kidney transplant was performed in 2013. By 2014, 2,000 kidney transplants had been completed and by 2018, yearly volumes had exceeded 100. In 2022, URMC performed its first simultaneous kidney/heart transplant.

In 2019, URMC became the first in the northeast to remove living donor kidneys robotically, providing donors with an easier and shorter recovery period. Led by Randeep S. Kashyap, MD, MPH, the program subsequently began robotic kidney implantation, expanding access to transplantation for patients with high body mass index and those who might otherwise suffer from delayed healing. The kidney transplant program has continued to rapidly expand. In 2025, the program's three thousandth kidney transplant was performed.

The first kidney/pancreas transplants and liver transplants at URMC were performed in 1992 by Alan I. Reed, MD, who was recruited by Schwartz to initiate the program, but left after two years to become surgical director of liver transplantation at the University of Florida. Under the direction of Oscar L. Bronsther, MD, the liver transplant program continued to develop and in 1999 Amadeo Marcos, MD, was recruited to start the living donor liver transplant program. This program became the busiest living donor program in the country by the time Marcos left two years later to direct transplantation at the University of Pittsburgh. He was succeeded as division chief by Adel Bozorgzadeh, MD, who recruited additional transplant surgeons. While initially experiencing significant growth, volumes began to decline, in part due to changes in the rules governing organ procurement and allocation.

Figure 23.11. Mark Orloff

Following Bozorgzadeh's departure in 2008, Mark Orloff, MD, became chief of the division of Solid Organ Transplantation. Orloff received his MD and completed his residency in general surgery at UCLA. He subsequently undertook fellowship training in hepatobiliary surgery at the Royal Postgraduate Medical School, University of London and in liver transplantation at UCLA. In 1991, Orloff was recruited from UCLA to URMC, where he developed a national reputation for his work in liver transplantation and hepatobiliary surgery. During Orloff's tenure he developed the concept of a multidisciplinary, co-located service line with Jeremy Taylor, MD, a transplant nephrologist. In 2016, Orloff stepped down as division chief to become vice chair for Clinical Operations and Regional Development in Surgery.

Figure 23.12. Roberto Hernandez-Alejandro

Roberto Hernandez-Alejandro, MD, was recruited as the new chief of Solid Organ Transplantation from Western University in Ontario, Canada in 2016. Hernandez-Alejandro received his MD from the Universidad de La Salle, Mexico. He did his residency in general surgery in Mexico, followed by fellowships in kidney and pancreas transplantation at the University of Calgary and in liver transplantation and hepato-pancreato-biliary surgery at Western University, London, Ontario. He spent four months each at the University of Toronto and at the University of Kyoto in Japan, furthering his knowledge and expertise in living donor liver transplantation. During his time in Canada, Hernandez-Alejandro developed an international reputation for novel research using hepato-pancreato-biliary surgery for treatment of cancer, resulting in over 200 peer-reviewed publications. He was the first surgeon in North America to perform ALPPS (Associating Liver Partition and Portal Vein Ligation for Staged Hepatectomy), a two-step surgical technique that separates cancerous liver tissue from healthy tissue and promotes the rapid growth of the latter. In 2019, he was elected to the editorial board of *Annals of Surgery*, was elected as a member of the American Surgical Association in 2022 and became a Council Member of the International Liver Transplant Society in 2025.

During Hernandez-Alejandro's tenure, the liver transplant program—the only one in upstate NY—has regained national prominence, spurred by the recruitment of leading faculty from around the world. URMC restarted its live donor liver transplant program, performing more than eighty operations over the past seven and a half years. Hernandez-Alejandro also expanded opportunities for transplant through increased use of organs procured after cardiac death. Hernandez-Alejandro pioneered a program using liver transplantation for unresectable colorectal cancer liver metastases (CRLM), which he and colleagues have recently shown to extend life without cancer progression for carefully selected patients. As of July 2024, the University had performed more liver transplants for patients with CRLM than any other center in North America. As an indication of the University's leadership in this field, the division was given the responsibility for managing the American Society of Transplant Surgeons Research Registry for patients with CRLM. In 2023, URMC completed its 2,000th liver transplant.

Transplant Institute

In keeping with the URMC strategic approach of creating multidisciplinary, multidepartmental centers, a Transplant Institute (TI) was established in 2023, under the leadership of Hernandez-Alejandro and Nancy Metzler, executive director of Transplant Services. The TI co-locates transplant surgeons, hepatologists, nephrologists, infectious disease physicians, psychiatrists/psychologists, and staff working together as a single administrative and financial entity with common goals.

Figure 23.13. Nancy Metzler

At the center of the TI model are six pillars: 1) Quality and Safety; 2) Patient & Family Centered Care; 3) People; 4) Growth & Infrastructure; 5) Finance; and 6) System Integration. One of the goals of the TI is to expand the growing body of research at the University and through collaborations with other national and international transplant centers. Another goal is to serve as a center for training the next generation of transplant surgeons, with a particular focus on living donation for both liver and kidney, robotic surgery for living kidney donors and kidney recipients, and expansion into hepatobiliary surgery. Recently, the TI received accreditation by the American Society of Transplant Surgeons to restart a transplant surgery fellowship program.

Although solid organ transplantation has seen many iterations and many directors over the past twenty-five years, a constant and stabilizing force has been Metzler. In 2024, Metzler received the annual Heckenkemper Leader in Transplant Administration/Quality Award given by UNOS (United Network for Organ Sharing) to an individual who has made significant contributions to organ donation and transplantation. During her tenure as executive director of Transplant Services, Metzler has been a constant figure on local, state, and national committees and boards, focusing on improving the transplant and procurement system.

Colorectal Surgery

With the advent of advanced surgical techniques for managing colorectal diseases, it became evident that a dedicated colorectal surgical division was necessary. Recognizing this need, Peters recruited John R. T. Monson, MD, in 2008 to serve as the inaugural chief of the Colorectal Division. At the time, the department already had a strong foundation with colorectal surgeons Jenny R. Speranza, MD, and Samantha K. Hendren, MD, MPH, and surgical oncologist Rabih M. Salloum, MD. Under Monson's leadership, the division expanded with the recruitment of Christina Cellini, MD, who continues to oversee the surgical endoscopy program, Todd Francone, MD, and Fergal Fleming, MBBCh.

Monson also served as director of SHORE and as vice chair for Health Services Research in Surgery. Monson was a leader in multidisciplinary care of rectal cancer and supported the growth of minimally invasive colorectal surgery approaches. He played a key role in the move of the outpatient colorectal surgical program to Sawgrass. Under the direction of Jenny Speranza, the Colorectal Physiology Center was created, providing the region with state-of-the-art diagnostics and therapies available for bowel incontinence and pelvic floor disorders. In 2011, Speranza became the first surgeon in the nation to implant a sacral nerve stimulator, a pacemaker-like device for the treatment of bowel incontinence. The pelvic floor program continues to thrive and has developed a national reputation under Speranza's leadership.

The first anal dysplasia program in the state, outside of NY City, was launched to prevent anal cancer by screening and treating pre-cancerous lesions. Fergal Fleming played a pivotal role in launching several quality initiatives, including the first endoscopic retrograde pancreatography, a comprehensive, multidisciplinary approach that aims to optimize recovery from surgery. In 2012, the division became an integral part of the Upstate NY Surgical Quality Initiative to improve the quality of care for surgical patients through data-driven, evidence-based best practice.

In 2016, Larissa Temple, MD, was recruited from MSKCC to be chief of Colorectal Surgery, director of SHORE, and, beginning in 2020, as vice chair for Care Transformation. Temple received her MD from the University of Calgary, did a residency in General Surgery at the University of Toronto, and completed fellowships in Surgical Oncology at MSKCC and colorectal surgery at St. Luke's-Roosevelt Hospital Center. While on faculty at MSKCC, she became the director of the Colorectal Survivorship Program and the vice deputy physician-in-chief for Quality and Safety. A specialist in colorectal cancers and minimally invasive procedures, Temple came to Rochester with a national reputation as a leader in patient reported outcomes and surgical quality improvement. She served as chair of the Quality Assessment Committee for the American Society of Colon and Rectal Surgery (ASCRS), president of the Research Foundation of the ASCRS, and was a member of the ACS's Board of Governors.

Figure 23.14. Larissa Temple

During Temple's tenure, the division has grown to eight surgeons with the recruitment of Gabriela C. Poles, MD, MPH, who is leading URMC efforts to improve geriatric surgical outcomes through implementation of the ACS's geriatric surgical verification program; Lisa M. Cannon, MD, who brought new state-of-the-art surgical approaches to the treatment of complex inflammatory bowel disease as part of a multidisciplinary program with Gastroenterology; and Zhaomin (Tim) Xu, MD, MPH, who integrated the anal cancer screening program into the clinic and expanded its access to community health partners. Innovation has continued to be a cornerstone of the division, with faculty introducing novel anastomotic techniques, procedures for rectal prolapse, expanded minimally invasive options for recurrent pelvic disease and single port options for luminal disease. Faculty received extramural funding to support research in patient reported outcomes, disparities in health care delivery and care optimization in the elderly.

Fleming has helped establish the division as a national leader in the evolution of colorectal cancer management, ranging from total mesorectal excision, involving the complete removal of the rectum, surrounding mesorectum, and a margin of healthy tissue; transanal endoscopic microsurgery; robotics for complex sphincter-preserving therapy; to non-operative management. The division has been and continues to be active in a variety of paradigm-shifting clinical trials. As a testament to its national prominence in the field, URMC became one of six institutions in the US to receive accreditation in 2017 from the National Accreditation Program for Rectal Cancer, administered by the ACS's Commission on Cancer.

With the expansion of our health system, colorectal surgical volumes have substantially increased. To accommodate the expansion, in 2022 Cannon and Poles established a full-time division presence at HH, including outpatient and endoscopy programs. Inpatient care, which includes APPs dedicated to the colorectal service, now occurs primarily at the WCI and in the new surgical wing at HH. In 2024, the division moved into a newly renovated outpatient facility, which was three times the size of its original space and included endoscopic capabilities. Under Christina Cellini's leadership, the colorectal division initiated a colorectal surgical training program, which in 2017 obtained ACGME accreditation. As the program has matured, it has received increased national attention, commensurate with the growing stature of the division.

Surgical Oncology

Although the department of Surgery has had many noted oncologic surgeons, including Seymour Schwartz, the last twenty-five years have been remarkable for the growth of the surgical oncology program. When Chair Jeffrey Peters restructured the department of Surgery, he created the division of Surgical Oncology, with Luke O. Schoeniger, MD, PhD, as its first chief. At the time, the division was composed of only four faculty. Schoeniger received his MD and a PhD in molecular biology from the NYU School of Medicine, then completed his residency in general surgery and fellowship in surgical oncology at Johns Hopkins. A specialist in hepatobiliary, pancreatic and gastrointestinal surgery, Schoeniger's areas of interest included diseases of the liver and pancreas, as well as laparoscopic and robotic surgery.

Figure 23.15. Luke Schoeniger

Kristin Skinner, MD, was recruited in 2006 to serve as chief of Surgical Oncology and to develop a Comprehensive Breast Care Center (CBCC) as part of WCI. Skinner, a University of Rochester undergraduate, received her MD from Johns Hopkins, and completed her training in general surgery and fellowship in surgical oncology at UCLA. Prior to coming to URMC, Skinner had served as chief of Surgical Oncology and director of the Multidisciplinary Breast Cancer Program at NYU. An accomplished breast cancer surgeon, Skinner was also involved in research evaluating molecular markers of breast cancer and breast cancer risk, and on the application of intraductal approaches to breast cancer diagnosis and treatment.

Under Skinner's leadership, in 2009 WCI became one of only eight cancer centers (out of 430) in the US to receive a New Program Outstanding Achievement Award from the Commission on Cancer of the ACS. Two years later, the CBCC received full accreditation designation by the National Accreditation Program for Breast

Figure 23.16. Kristin Skinner

Centers, a program administered by the ACS, one of only twelve such accredited institutions in NY State and the only one in Western NY. In 2014, Skinner oversaw the expansion and the move of the CBCC from URMC to its current location in Henrietta.

In 2008, Jacob Moalem, MD, was hired as the first endocrine surgeon in the division, following a fellowship at UCSF. At the time, surgical residents were not meeting the minimum criteria for thyroid and parathyroid surgeries. With Moalem's arrival, the program has grown substantially and now has three surgeons who perform over 600 operations annually. It also has established a national reputation as a quaternary referral center for complex endocrine cases serving all of western NY and northern Pennsylvania. Endocrine surgery has developed a diverse research program with basic science, health services, and outcomes components.

Figure 23.17. Jacob Moalem

In 2022, Anna Weiss, MD, was recruited from the Dana-Farber Cancer Institute, Boston, to lead the Breast Cancer Service Line and the Pluta CBCC, named in recognition of a generous gift from the Pluta Cancer Foundation. Since Weiss's arrival, URMC's breast surgery team has grown substantially (it now includes six breast-only surgeons) and surgical volumes have doubled. Weiss initiated two notable programs: the Breast Health Program, which manages all benign breast disease and patients at an elevated risk of breast cancer, and the Breast Survivorship Program, which manages patients after their breast cancer treatment. Although the Henrietta facility remains the primary location, breast surgeons now conduct clinics throughout the region. In 2025, Weiss became the inaugural Pluta Professor of Breast Care.

Figure 23.18. Anna Weiss

A further boost to the division occurred in 2020, with the recruitment of Darren Carpizo, MD, PhD, as the new chief of Surgical Oncology. Carpizo received his MD from the University of Illinois at Chicago and did his surgical residency at UCLA. As a resident, he was part of a special program for training physician scientists which culminated in a PhD in molecular, cell and developmental biology. He subsequently completed a surgical oncology fellowship at MSKCC focusing on hepatobiliary and pancreatic cancers, and then joined the faculty at Rutgers-Cancer Institute of New Jersey where he served as the section

Figure 23.19. Darren Carpizo

chief of gastrointestinal surgical oncology and leader of the hepatobiliary oncology program. Carpizo is an NIH-funded surgeon-scientist whose research involves cancer biology and ranges from early drug discovery projects to translational studies of novel therapies. A major focus of his work has been on understanding the molecular mechanisms that control cancer dormancy, particularly in pancreatic cancer, and to devise therapies that either maintain the dormant state or drive the cells into senescence. Carpizo is a leader in the development of regional therapies for cancer, including hepatic artery infusion pumps and heated intraperitoneal chemotherapy. He serves as vice chair of Basic/Translational Research in Surgery and as the co-leader of the Genetics, Epigenetics and Metabolism research program at WCI. Under Carpizo, Surgical Oncology has grown to eleven full-time clinical and four research faculty members.

One of the strengths of the division has been its diverse body of research productivity, resulting in substantial federal funding, high-impact publications and the creation of novel therapeutic clinical trials. Since David Linehan's recruitment as chair of Surgery, tumor immunology has become a central focal point for research within the department. This includes the establishment of the Center for Tumor Immunology Research, directed by Linehan and co-directed by Scott Gerber, PhD, who received his doctorate in Microbiology & Immunology from SMD. The Center, which includes tumor immunobiologists from the departments of Surgery, Microbiology & Immunology, Electrical & Computer Engineering, and Radiation Oncology, focuses on better understanding the complexities of the tumor microenvironment to design more effective immunotherapeutic approaches to treat cancer. Specific research themes include: targeting myeloid cells to treat pancreatic cancer; stimulating the immune system to enhance radiotherapy; genetic alterations of melanoma to improve treatment efficacy; T cell engineering for cancer immunotherapy; the microbiome and cancer; and predicting treatment efficacy using shear wave elastography. The Center also plays an important role in education, serving as fertile ground for PhD and MD/PhD candidates (currently the division is involved in training fifteen graduate students), for undergraduates, and for residents.

Another strength of the division has been its role in URMC's post-operative opioid stewardship program—a comprehensive program, overseen by Jacob Moalem, that involves an extensive collaboration among Surgery, the Quality Institute, and the Recovery Center of Excellence. This work involves a holistic approach to eliminating opioid over-prescription through patient, family and provider education, as well as innovative modifications to the medical records that allow prescriptions to be matched to patient needs. Surgical teams establish evidence-based prescription targets and dashboards, allowing them to monitor variations in prescribing behavior by any clinical or demographic factor, so that significant outliers and opportunities for improvement can be identified. The project has led to a dramatic reduction in opioid use across the department and an increase in the proportion of opioid-free discharges.

Thoracic and Foregut Surgery

The modern era of thoracic surgery at URMC can trace its roots back to 1987, with the arrival of Richard Feins, MD, a graduate of the general surgery and cardio-thoracic surgery residency program at URMC, who developed a non-cardiac thoracic surgical service providing care for patients referred from five hospitals within the area. Feins subsequently recruited David Johnstone, MD, whose main interest was bullous disease of the lung, and Thomas J. Watson, MD, who had expertise in foregut manometry testing and surgery, along with pulmonary surgery.

Figure 23.20. Thomas Watson

In 2004, Surgery Chair Jeffrey Peters split the division of Cardiothoracic surgery into two, creating a new division of Thoracic and Foregut Surgery. With Fein's departure to become chief of Thoracic Surgery at University of North Carolina in 2005, Watson assumed the role of division chief. Watson received his MD and did his residency in general surgery and cardiothoracic surgery and fellowship in esophageal surgery at the University of Southern California, before joining URMC in 1996. He established a robust research program in esophageal disease and developed a unique manometry laboratory that has grown exponentially and now conducts approximately 2,500 to 3,000 procedures per year. He also recruited several new faculty members, including Carolyn E. Jones, MD, Christian Peyre, MD, and Joseph Wizorek, MD. When Watson left in 2015 to become chairman of Surgery for the Medstar Hospital Group in Washington, DC, Jones became division chief.

Jones received her MD from George Washington University School of Medicine and completed her residency and fellowship training in cardiothoracic surgery at URMC. Under her leadership, the division has continued to expand, recruiting Michael J. Lada, MD, an expert in minimally invasive thoracic surgery, lung cancer, and esophageal diseases, and Ryan Campagna, MD, an expert in thoracic robotic surgery and esophageal diseases. The division now includes six full-time clinical faculty members and has become a major referral center

Figure 23.21. Carolyn Jones

in upstate NY, offering state-of-the-art procedures and therapies that include curative *en bloc* esophagectomy for esophageal cancer, vagal sparing removal of the esophagus, laparoscopic Nissen fundoplication and esophageal myotomy and endoluminal therapies for gastroesophageal reflux disease.

The traditional fellowship in thoracic surgery, a two-year program for physicians who have completed a general surgery residency, has a long-standing history at URMC. As discussed further in the chapter on Cardiovascular Diseases, the University was an early adopter of the integrated six-year cardiothoracic residency model for medical school graduates that incorporates general surgical training within its curriculum. Peyre serves as program director for both the traditional fellowship and the integrated residency.

Bariatric and Gastrointestinal (GI) Surgery

A key component of the success of HH after its acquisition by URMC was the development and growth of specialized programs that helped establish it as an important regional referral center. The division of Bariatric and GI Surgery, under the leadership of Joseph A. Johnson, MD, epitomizes this.

Figure 23.22. Joseph Johnson

The origins of the division stem from 1995, when Rene B. Menguy, MD, moved his bariatric surgery practice from The Genesee Hospital to HH. William E. O'Malley, MD, joined Menguy in 1996 after completing his residency in general surgery at URMC and took over the bariatric surgery program after Menguy's retirement in 1998. On July 7, 2000, O'Malley performed a laparoscopic gastric bypass, the first minimally invasive gastric bypass procedure in upstate New York. The division of Bariatric & GI Surgery was established in 1998, with Johnson as the division chief (a title he still holds), and O'Malley as director of Bariatric Surgery. In 2001, Johnson was also appointed as chief of Surgery at HH, a position he held until his retirement from the role in 2022. Johnson received his MD from New York Medical College, completed his residency training in general surgery at URMC in 1993, and was then hired by Seymour Schwartz to perform general and minimally invasive surgery at HH, joining Tulsi Dass, MBBS, and Robert L. Caldwell, MD. Caldwell performed the first laparoscopic cholecystectomy (1991) and Johnson performed the first laparoscopic splenectomy (1994) in Rochester.

Figure 23.23. William O'Malley

Johnson and O'Malley established the Bariatric Surgery Center at HH as one of the top programs in

NY State for minimally invasive weight loss surgery. This Bariatric Surgery Center was designated as a Metabolic and Bariatric Surgery Accreditation and Quality Improvement Program (MBSAQIP) Comprehensive Center, a joint program of the ACS and the American Society for Metabolic and Bariatric Surgery that recognizes a commitment to high-quality, safe bariatric surgical care. In 2009, O'Malley and Johnson established a bariatric surgery fellowship, which has now trained fifteen bariatric surgeons. O'Malley left the University in 2025 to join the US Navy as a general surgeon.

Currently the Bariatric Surgery Center performs over 500 bariatric procedures per year, making it one of the busiest programs in NY State. An increasing percentage of the surgeries are performed robotically. Additional faculty have been recruited to support the growth of the bariatric and minimally invasive surgical program at HH. These include Thad J. Boss, MD, who passed away at a young age of colon cancer, and Lael E. Forbes, MD, who subsequently left Rochester, and more recently David E. Burns, MD, a graduate of SMD and of the residency program in general surgery at URMC, and Maria Durdach, MD, and Kaci L. Schiavone, MD, also graduates of the residency program in general surgery at URMC. In addition to bariatric surgery, the division performs general surgery and serves as the emergency general surgery service for HH. The practice has also expanded to include endoscopy.

Vascular Surgery

Vascular Surgery has had an illustrious history and has been at the forefront of training leaders in the field. Charles Rob, a pioneer in carotid, aortic and vein bypass grafting, brought modern vascular surgery to upstate NY during his tenure as Surgery chair, and together with James DeWeese, created the division of Vascular Surgery. In 1966, DeWeese partnered with James Adams, MD, to develop the DeWeese–Adams clip, which replaced caval ligation as treatment for recurrent pulmonary embolism and for a period was the most utilized device for treatment of patients with thromboembolic disease. When Richard M. Green, MD, an alumnus of the University of Rochester medical school and residency programs, became division chief in 1991, he created an innovative environment that yielded many leaders in American vascular surgery. Timothy Chuter MD, and Roy K. Greenberg, MD, were instrumental in the development of modern bifurcated endovascular aortic repair grafts, revolutionizing the treatment of aortic surgery. Kenneth Ouriel, MD, led multiple national trials that established the safety and efficacy of thrombolytic therapy for arterial occlusive disease.

Karl Illig, MD, another alumnus of URMC's vascular surgery program, became chief of the division in 2008, replacing Green, who left to become chief of Vascular Surgery at Columbia Presbyterian Medical Center. Illig ran a robust clinical trials program that led to the development of several innovative devices. He played an important role in promoting endovascular aortic care and was a thought leader in dialysis access and thoracic outlet syndrome. Upon Illig's departure in 2010 to become chief of Vascular Surgery at the University of South Florida, David L. Gillespie, MD, became division chief. Prior to joining URMC, Gillespie had a twenty-three-year career as chief of Vascular Surgery at Walter Reed Army Medical Center, Washington, DC, and at the Uniformed Services University of the Health Sciences' F. Edward Hebert School of Medicine in Bethesda, Maryland.

Figure 23.24. Karl Illig

A new era for the division began in 2013 with the recruitment of Michael Stoner, MD, who had been the chief of Vascular Surgery at East Carolina University. Stoner received his MD from the University of Buffalo, did his residency in general surgery at the Medical College of Virginia, and his fellowship in vascular surgery at MGH. His clinical research has focused on comparative effectiveness and value for cardiovascular care. Upon Stoner's arrival, URMC became an early adopter of the national Vascular Quality Initiative (VQI). Overseen by the Society for Vascular Surgery, the VQI is designed to improve the quality, safety, effectiveness, and cost of vascular health care. Rochester has become a nationally recognized leader in the VQI and has been ranked at the highest level longer than any program in the state. Stoner serves as the NY State medical director and is supported by a nursing-based quality and research team.

Figure 23.25. Michael Stoner

Stoner's tenure as chief has also been marked by substantial growth in the division. In 2017, the UR Medicine Vein Center became the region's first vascular surgeon-led team to earn Intersocietal Accreditation Commission accreditation for comprehensive vein care. This site remains the only faculty-led vein center in the region, providing referral and second-opinion care for a diverse population. That same year, URMC opened a new 11,700-square-foot suite at 140 Canal Boulevard, which has become one of the premier outpatient cardiovascular care locations in upstate NY, housing vascular surgery, the vein center, and one of URMC's major cardiology groups. Roan J. Glocker, MD, MPH, an alumnus of the URMC general surgery residency, was recruited to develop practices at HH and FF Thompson, and to expand the training program and clinical research to these sites. By 2023, there were eight full-time faculty, with a volume of 3,000 cases per year at five sites (SMH, HH, FF Thompson, Sawgrass, and Canal View). Endovascular procedures or hybrid open/endovascular cases represent eighty percent of cases.

URMC has become a regional hub for TransCarotid Artery Revascularization, a minimally invasive procedure developed to treat carotid artery disease and prevent stroke. This program, started in 2015, remains the largest vascular surgeon-led minimal-access carotid program in the northeast. URMC surgeons were instrumental in the development and optimization of the technique, and in establishing the safety of nominal-sized pre-stent angioplasty, which has become the standard. Currently surgeons and anesthesiologists are working to codify protocols around the use of local anesthesia to improve patient experience while maintaining excellent outcomes.

The University has played an important role in the evolution of vascular surgery education, going back to the 1980s when DeWeese headed a commission that resulted in the creation of formal accredited vascular fellowships. In 2006, the University became one of the first institutions to embrace an integrated five-year residency program in vascular surgery, which includes core rotations in general surgery and vascular disease. There is also an option for an additional dedicated research year.

The Cardiovascular Engineering Lab is a cross-disciplinary (vascular surgery, cardiology, and biomedical engineering), multi-institutional (RIT, Cleveland Clinic, The Ohio State University) team, headed by Stoner and Doran S. Mix, MD, to create novel diagnostic, therapeutic, and predictive devices and tools for cardiovascular care. The lab is currently working on abdominal aortic aneurysmal disease and is conducting fundamental research and clinical trials focused on aortic elastography. The aim is to develop novel ultrasound and MRI-based techniques to better predict the risk of aortic rupture and dissection. The lab is also studying the role of microbiome and microplastics in aortic aneurysm disease.

In 2022, the Ouriels established the Kenneth and Joy Ouriel Family Professorship in the division of Vascular Surgery. Kenneth Ouriel, a University of Rochester undergraduate, received his MD from the University of Chicago. He returned to URMC for his general surgery residency and vascular surgery fellowship, and remained as faculty until 1998, when he became chief of Vascular Surgery, and subsequently served as chief of surgery at the Cleveland Clinic. In 2010, Ken founded Syntactx, a medical device development solution company. Ouriel is the author of five textbooks and more than 350 scientific articles. He recently joined the University of Rochester Board of Trustees.

Figure 23.26.
Ken Ouriel

Pediatric Surgery

Pediatric Surgery is one of the newest divisions of the Department of Surgery, beginning in 1997 with the recruitment of Walter Pegoli, MD, to serve as its first chief. In 2006, Pegoli was also appointed surgeon-in-chief of GCH. Pegoli received his MD from New York Medical College, did a residency in General Surgery at the University of Maryland and a fellowship in Pediatric Surgery at Johns Hopkins. Pegoli's expertise included neonatal surgery, non-cardiac thoracic surgery, complex gastrointestinal surgery and surgical oncology. Prior to Pegoli's arrival, URMC had no full-time pediatric surgeons, but instead relied on community physicians to provide surgical services. Under Pegoli's leadership, the division began to recruit full-time surgeons. Of particular note was Derek S. Wakeman, MD, who currently directs our pediatric trauma service. In 2014, Pegoli became the inaugural Joseph M. Lobozzo II Professor in pediatric surgery, supported by a generous gift from Joseph Lobozzo, the founder and former chairman of JML Optical Industries, Inc, and a longstanding member of the URMC board. During his tenure, URMC became the leader in pediatric surgery in Upstate NY and the only center for some specialties, including complex pediatric cardiovascular surgery, neurology and electrophysiology. Pegoli was instrumental in shepherding the move to the new GCH, ensuring the development of state-of-the-art operating rooms and post-operative facilities that would enable URMC to perform minimally invasive and hybrid procedures and the addition of critically needed pediatric ICU beds.

Figure 23.27. Dr. Walter Pegoli

Marjorie Arca, MD, was recruited from the University of Wisconsin-Madison to be the Joseph M. Lobozzo II Professor in Pediatric Surgery and Surgeon-in-Chief of GCH. Arca received her MD from the University of California, Los Angeles, did a residency in General Surgery and a fellowship in Pediatric Surgery at the University of Michigan, and a fellowship in Laparoscopic Surgery at the Cleveland Clinic. Arca was nationally known for her work in treating congenital abnormalities, short bowel syndrome, biliary atresia, and pediatric tumors and held leadership positions in the American Pediatric Surgical Association. Under her leadership, the Division has continued to expand, with the recruitment of Nicole Wilson, MD, PhD, and Abdelhafeez Adbelhaffez, MD, and David Darcy MD. As of 2025 contains six faculty, four APP's and

Figure 23.28. Dr. Marjorie Arca

one RN, who see approximately 1,100 ambulatory visits and perform over 2,000 operative procedures a year. The growth of pediatric surgical services under the leadership of Pegoli and Arca, together with the development of a dedicated quality improvement team, enabled GCH to achieve designation in 2022 as a Level 1 Pediatric Trauma Center by the American College of Surgeons and NY State, the highest possible classification for trauma care. In 2024, Arca was named Director of Surgical Strategy and Operations.

Chapter 24

DEPARTMENT OF UROLOGY

Urology began in 1928 as a division of Surgery with the recruitment of David M. Davis, MD, from Johns Hopkins as its first chief. Two years later, he was succeeded by Winfield W. Scott, MD, also from Johns Hopkins, who directed the division for thirty years, recruiting several other nationally prominent urologists and establishing the residency program. Scott was also responsible for the acquisition of the Buswell Fund, which remains the largest single endowment in any URMC department. He was succeeded as chief by Donald McDonald, MD, a leader in prostate cancer research recruited from the University of Washington. Upon McDonald's departure in 1967, Irwin Frank, MD, who was born at SMH and received his education (BA, MD, residency in Urology) at the University of Rochester, served for two years as interim chief. Frank passed away in 2020, having been at URMC for his entire career and serving as medical director of SMH and SAD for Clinical Affairs in SMD. He had a national presence, serving as president of the American Urological Association (AUA), and was a founding member and past president of the NY State Urological Society.

Figure 24.1. Irwin Frank

In 1969, Abraham T. K. Crockett, MD, was recruited from UCLA to serve as chief of Urology, and in 1973 oversaw its transition to independent department status. Crockett was best known for his work with the National Aeronautics and Space Administration on the effects of weightlessness on the kidney and on kidney stone formation. He was instrumental in the department obtaining one of the five original extra corporeal shock wave lithotripters in the US, which revolutionized the surgical management of stone disease. He was also responsible for recruiting and/or training Jean Joseph, MD, Ronald Rabinowitz, MD, and Erdal Erturk, MD, the region's premier stone surgeon for more than thirty years.

The last quarter century has seen extraordinary growth in Urology under the leadership of Edward M. Messing, MD, who was recruited to be the Winfield W. Scott Chair of Urology in 1995 and remained in that position for twenty-two years. Prior to coming to Rochester, he served on the faculty at the University of Wisconsin for thirteen years. Messing received his MD from NYU, did his internship and residency in general surgery at NYU-Bellevue, and did a residency in urology at Stanford University. Messing is internationally respected for his work on bladder cancer and as a pioneer in screening for hematuria for early detection of prostate cancer, which led to the first at-home urine test. He led important trials on the use of androgen deprivation therapy for prostate cancer and the use of Gemcitabine to treat and prevent recurrences of bladder cancer, changing the standard of care of these malignancies. Messing received the Ramon Guiteras Award, the highest honor given to an academic urologist, and the Presidential Citation from the AUA for his work in bladder cancer research and urologic education.

Figure 24.2. Edward Messing

Messing's tenure was marked by the recruitment of clinical faculty (the adult faculty grew from five to seventeen) into specialized areas, including oncology, reproductive urology, stone disease, neurology, male sexual medicine, urinary tract reconstruction, and general urology. In addition, he expanded practice locations to include HH and Unity Hospital, Geneva General Hospital and FF Thompson.

Messing was a great supporter of pediatric urology. The division of Pediatric Urology was established by Ronald Rabinowitz, one of Crockett's recruits. Rabinowitz earned his MD and did his urology residency at the University of Pittsburgh, followed by a fellowship in pediatric urology at the Hospital for Sick Children, Toronto. Rabinowitz is an internationally renowned expert in pediatric urology and urologic history, and currently serves as historian for the AUA, from which he has received the Distinguished Service Award, the Lifetime Achievement Award, and in 2023, the William P. Didusch Art and History Award. With Messing's support and encouragement, Rabinowitz established the largest pediatric urology practice in upstate NY and the only pediatric urology practice in the region.

Figure 24.3. Ronald Rabinowitz

Messing's tenure was particularly noteworthy for the growth of the research program, marked by recruitment of the first basic science faculty, including Yi Fen Lee, PhD, who studies the role of extracellular vesicles in cancer development and progression, and Shu Yuan Yeh, PhD, whose research focuses on the roles of estrogen and androgen receptors in prostate cancer, bladder cancer, benign prostatic hyperplasia, and male fertility. He also fostered collaborations with scientists in other departments, such as Edward Schwarz, PhD (Center for Musculoskeletal Research), and Ronald Wood, PhD (Ob/Gyn). Since stepping down as chair, Messing has remained active in the department, and in 2022 assumed the AUA presidency.

Jean Joseph, MD, succeeded Messing in 2018 as the Winfield W. Scott Chair of Urology. Joseph received his MD and did his residency training at URMC. He subsequently undertook fellowship training in reconstructive urologic surgery at University College London and studied laparoscopic prostatectomy at the Institute Mutualiste Montsouris in Paris, France, before joining the URMC faculty. With Messing's encouragement, Joseph became a national leader in urologic robotic surgery. In 2001, he was one of only a handful of surgeons in the US to perform laparoscopic radical prostatectomy and has now performed over 5,000 robotic procedures. Prior to becoming chair, he was director of the section of Urologic Laparoscopy and Robotic Surgery, and director of the Center for Robotic Surgery and Innovation. He also directed the fellowships in endourology, laparoscopy, and robotic surgery. Joseph's research has focused on developing new ways to diagnose and treat prostate, bladder, and kidney cancers. He has had leadership positions in the Society of Urologic Robotic Surgery, the Endourological Society, and the AUA.

Figure 24.4. Jean Joseph

Joseph has continued to grow the department, which now consists of thirty-three faculty, including four pediatric urologists. Urologic services expanded to eleven sites throughout the region, with new practices added in Brockport, Geneseo, Dansville, Hornell, and Wellsville. Three Rochester-based urology offices and the clinical trials office were consolidated at Sawgrass, better integrating the faculty and strengthening their participation in clinical trials.

Joseph has also continued to recruit faculty engaged in research, including Colin Dinney, MD, the former chair of Urology at M. D. Anderson Cancer Center and an expert in cancer therapeutics, and David McConkey, PhD, who will serve as vice chair of research. McConkey is an expert in the use of genomics to study the molecular mechanisms involved in bladder cancer progression and the inaugural director of the Johns Hopkins Greenberg Bladder Cancer Institute. The department conducts clinical trials in prostate cancer, bladder cancer, and renal cancer. Other areas of research include kidney stones, erectile dysfunction, interstitial cystitis, and incontinence. As noted above, Urology continues to pioneer new techniques in robotic and laparoscopic surgery for the treatment of a wide array of conditions.

More information about the individual research programs is available on the Urology website.

Joseph has also seen the establishment of several endowed professorships, including the Susan and Edward M. Messing, MD, Professorship in Urologic Oncology, which was critical to the recruitment of McConkey, and the Sally and Ronald Rabinowitz Endowed Professorship in Pediatric Urology. In addition, two Henry C. Buswell, MD, professorships were established using resources from the original Buswell Fund.

One of the most striking innovations led by Messing and Joseph has been the Surgical Research and Genitourinary Engineering Laboratory, currently directed by Thomas L. Osinski, MD, which specializes in the development of anatomical models to train surgical skills in a low-risk environment. Patient-specific models are created from either CT or MRI scans by 3-D printing using multi-material resins that can create a model with multiple materials or colors. The models react similarly to tissues, allowing realistic simulation of complex surgical procedures, and enable surgeons to familiarize themselves with the anatomy of a challenging case prior to the actual procedure, and to educate patients on the nature of the procedure they'll be undergoing. The use of such models has also markedly enhanced the training of residents and fellows, and increased the national prestige of the Urology training programs.

Under Joseph's leadership, the residency program underwent significant changes in curriculum, allowing it to expand to three residents per year and to add a full year of research to the five years of clinical training, funded in part by an AUA award. The program has also taken advantage of the department's position as a leader in simulation and is one of only a few programs in the US that has a dedicated Xi robot housed in a mock operating room specifically for resident training. These changes have spurred Urology residents to pursue academic careers. In addition to its highly regarded two-year fellowship in endourology, departmental fellowships were introduced in minimally invasive surgery and in oncology. Research and clinical opportunities, including a subinternship, are also available for medical students.

Chapter 25

DEPARTMENT OF OPHTHALMOLOGY AND THE FLAUM EYE INSTITUTE

Ophthalmology was established in 1931 at URMC as a division of Surgery, headed by John Gipner, MD, who initiated a small clinical practice and a residency training program. Only two years earlier, the Institute of Optics had been established by the University as the first academic optical center in the world. Gipner was followed as chief in 1961 by Albert Conrad Snell, Jr., MD. In 1964, the Center for Visual Science (CVS) was created at the University as an inter-departmental research and teaching program. It has grown into one of the most prominent visual science institutions in the world.

Upon Snell's retirement in 1978, Henry Metz, MD, became chair of the new department of Ophthalmology. Metz recruited the first full-time research faculty and secured NIH funds to create new laboratory space. George Bresnick, MD, followed as chair in 1994 and continued to grow the research program, including the groundbreaking work of Manuel del Cerro, MD, on retinal cell transplantation. Bresnick also initiated Project Eye Care, expanding the department's efforts to provide eye care to the disadvantaged. After Bresnick's departure in 1997, Barrett Katz, MD, became interim chair, followed as interim chair by Steven Ching, MD, in 1999.

At the start of the new millennium, the department had five separate clinical practices and two tenure-track basic scientists. Most of the didactic teaching and staffing of the resident clinic was performed by community physicians. Laying the groundwork for change was the newly formed Alliance for Excellence in Ophthalmology between the CVS and Bausch & Lomb. David R. Williams, PhD, the director of CVS, had recently discovered that the adaptive optics used primarily for improving resolution of astronomical telescopes could be applied to the human visual system both for imaging of the retina and the correction of refractive error. He was joined in 2001 by Scott M. MacRae, MD, a leader in the nascent field of laser-assisted surgery to correct refractive error. These changes, along with the research initiatives developed by CEO Jay Stein, formed the basis for the successful recruitment of Steven Feldon, MD, as chair in 2001.

Feldon received his MD from Einstein College of Medicine, completed an internship in internal medicine at UCLA, and a residency in ophthalmology at Massachusetts Eye and Ear Infirmary, Boston. He subsequently received an MBA from the University of Southern California (USC). At the time of his recruitment to URMC, Feldon was a professor of ophthalmology, neurology, and neurosurgery at USC's Doheny Eye Institute, served as chief of staff of the Doheny Eye Hospital, chief of service at the USC University Hospital, and medical director for the ophthalmology faculty at Doheny. In addition to his clinical skills as a neuro-ophthalmologist and orbital surgeon, Feldon was a serial inventor of ophthalmological devices and was experienced in starting medical device companies. Feldon was optimistic that Ophthalmology could evolve into a first-tier academic center by leveraging the assets already available at the University and the unique academic–industry relationship with Bausch & Lomb.

Figure 25.1. Steven Feldon

During the next eighteen years, Feldon transformed the department. In 2005, he helped establish the Eye Institute, which became the David and Ilene Flaum Eye Institute (FEI) in 2009, in recognition of the philanthropy of the Flaum family. David Flaum was the founder of Flaum Management Company, Inc. of Rochester, which offers development, management, brokerage, and consulting services. He was also a member of the University of Rochester Board of Trustees, as well as the URMC board. Flaum's commitment to the Institute's mission was driven not only by his own struggle with vision problems, but also by his conviction that under Feldon's leadership, the Institute could become a world-renowned facility and an engine for economic development

Figure 25.2. David and Ilene Flaum

and job creation. Also in 2009, the department received a $7 million gift from the estate of Adeline Lutz and her late husband Walter "Jack" Lutz. Adeline was a piano teacher, Jack an engineer at Kodak. Adeline had thirteen procedures at URMC, including two corneal transplants and the repair of two macular holes. To honor the entire staff and her corneal surgeon Ching, Adeline and Jack gave back to the Eye Institute to help it become a major national center for eye care, ophthalmic research, and education.

Aided by this philanthropy and a NIH construction grant, the Institute undertook a complete renovation of 20,000 square feet of space devoted exclusively to eye research. The research space was purposefully co-located with new ophthalmology clinical space to maximize interactions among scientists and clinicians. The first-floor wet lab space, which was committed to eye-related stem cells, molecular biology, and immunology studies, was completed in 2007. The ground-floor space, completed in 2009, was primarily dedicated to advanced optical imaging in humans and animal models. Other programs in the space (named the Adeline P. Lutz Pavilion) were built around visual rehabilitation, refractive, and ocular surface disease, including the construction of a one-of-a-kind, climate-controlled dry eye lab.

A great example of the expanding relationship between URMC and the River Campus was the partnership between the FEI and the CVS. In 2012,

Figure 25.3. Adeline Lutz (center) is joined by Diane and Steve Feldon, along with former University President Joel Seligman.

Figure 25.4. Flaum Eye Institute

under the leadership of Williams, the CVS relocated its laboratories from the River Campus to the Medical Center, where they could be adjacent to FEI research and clinical facilities.

Under Feldon's leadership, the FEI grew to national prominence across all missions. Spurred by the purchase of several large community ophthalmology and optometry practices, the faculty expanded from seven to forty-five physicians and scientists. The strategy employed by Feldon presaged the regionalization that subsequently transformed the entire health care system. Clinical volumes grew from 12,000 patient visits and 500 surgeries to 80,000 visits and 4,000 surgeries per year. The residency grew in prestige, expanding to four residents per year, and fellowships were initiated in vitreoretinal surgery and cornea and external disease. NIH research funding increased from $200,000 per year in 2002 to $3.8 million per year in 2018.

Figure 25.5. David DiLoreto

In December 2019, David DiLoreto, MD, was selected as the new chair of the department and director of the FEI. DiLoreto received his MD and his PhD in neuroanatomy at the University of Rochester. He completed residency in ophthalmology at USC's Doheny Eye Institute and a fellowship in retina at the Wilmer Eye Institute of Johns Hopkins. He then joined the faculty of FEI as a retina specialist and clinical researcher. His current research interests focus on stem cell transplantation to restore vision.

As chair, DiLoreto accelerated the momentum established by Feldon, recruiting thirty-seven new faculty members. Of note are three internationally prominent faculty, including Alex Levin, MD, to serve as chief of Pediatric Ophthalmology and to start an ocular genetics program; Susana Marcos, PhD, who was co-recruited with the Institute of Optics in 2021 to succeed Williams as the director of CVS; and Vikas Khetan, MD, an ocular oncologist and retina surgeon, who initiated the first treatments for ocular melanoma and retinoblastoma in upstate NY.

On the educational front, an optometric residency program was initiated, as were fellowships in ocular genetics, glaucoma, neuro-ophthalmology, and pediatric ophthalmology. In 2020, the ophthalmology residency was integrated with an internal medicine internship. The FEI is involved in several medical school courses and offers in-depth clinical teaching beyond the one-week basic ophthalmology rotation, including immersion experience from two to four weeks in general ophthalmology, pediatric ophthalmology, and ocular genetics.

Over the past four years, the regional program has expanded from six to eleven satellites, and the clinical program has grown to 140,000 patient visits and 7,000 ophthalmologic surgeries per year. In 2023, the department ranked fourteenth nationwide in total NIH dollars received for vision research. The FEI is now divided into nine collaborative service lines: Comprehensive (cataract surgery); Cornea; Glaucoma; Neuro-ophthalmology; Oculoplastics; Optometry; Pediatric Ophthalmology; Retina; and Uveitis.

The FEI has a separate service devoted to community outreach and population health, and to assuring that all have access to high-quality eye care. Rajeev Ramchandran, MD, the director of population health, is developing a vision health system for western NY that incorporates public education and care based on a vertically integrated community engagement model pioneered by the LV Prasad Eye Institute (LVPEI). The FEI opened a practice in downtown Rochester and has established satellite offices throughout the region, working closely with community agencies, religious organizations, and other groups to make eye care accessible. The FEI addresses the pediatric population through "Vision Van" screenings (6,000 screened; 600 examined per year), examinations in schools, and the distribution of free eyeglasses. The Institute has also embedded teleophthalmology in eight primary care offices across the region to screen for glaucoma and diabetic retinopathy in patients who do not routinely receive eye care, and added a

Figure 25.6. Downtown Rochester Ophthalmology Practice

telemedicine camera in the SMH ED to improve treatment of central retinal artery occlusions by facilitating the use of tissue plasminogen activator within six hours of onset. In July 2022, the FEI opened the region's only urgent eyecare clinic.

The recruitment of Alex Levin, MD, enabled the development of an ocular genetics program, which involves new curriculum for the residents, an ocular genetics fellowship, a genetics counselor training program, ocular genetics medical school rotations, and the ability for a medical student to take a year out to perform as a pediatric and genetics clinical trials coordinator. The FEI has also developed an ocular gene therapy program that includes ongoing trials to treat retinopathy from Batten's disease as well as a form of retinitis pigmentosa, MAK.

FEI has a long and unique relationship with the LVPEI. Founded in 1987 by Gullipalli N. Rao, MD, a former corneal/external disease fellow of James Aquavella, MD, and URMC faculty member, the LVPEI has developed into India's premier and world-renowned academic ophthalmic institution. This relationship has seen the development of: 1) rotations for FEI and LVPEI residents at each other's institutions; 2) a formalized certificate-granting ophthalmic nurse assistant training program with the SON; 3) a medical student and undergraduate research externship at LVPEI; 4) collaboration in public and population health research and capacity building, in collaboration with Public Health Sciences; 5) numerous scientific collaborations; and 6) sharing of educational resources, and clinical and research faculty lectures.

The reputation of the research faculty at FEI has enabled it to develop important collaborations throughout the US (more than sixty individual collaborations with prominent scientists at other institutions) and the world (more than forty individual international collaborators). Many of these involve large research initiatives based in Rochester. For example, faculty are working with investigators at the University of Wisconsin and Harvard to create a new adaptive optics imaging platform to accelerate the development of stem cell therapy and optogenetics for vision restoration, and are collaborating with investigators in Geneva, Switzerland and Paris, France on the transfection of retinal ganglion cells with light-gated channels to restore vision in animal models of retinal degeneration. Other collaborations involve investigations in Murcia, Spain optimizing development and design of refractive correctors; in Oxford, UK optimizing training-induced vision recovery after stroke; and in Bristol, UK tracking immune responses in mouse and human retinas.

James Aquavella, an internationally known author and researcher on corneal diseases, was the first fellowship-trained corneal surgeon in the US. He has been a cornerstone of ophthalmology in the Rochester community since the mid-1960s. He was a founder and past president of the Cornea Society, a director of the Eye Bank Association of America, and a recipient of the American Academy of Ophthalmology Honor and Senior Honor Awards. A president of the Contact Lens Association of Ophthalmology, he is well known for his work in the development of the therapeutic contact lens and the collagen shield. A critical catalyst for research, Aquavella and his wife Catherine have created two endowed professorships in FEI.

Figure 25.7.
James Aquavella

The FEI research enterprise is extensive. Details of specific projects and investigators can be found on the FEI website. This chapter will highlight some of the many great accomplishments of the FEI investigators and collaborators.

Figure 25.8.
Krystal Huxlin

Krystal Huxlin, MD, the James V. Aquavella professor of ophthalmology, directed the research efforts from 2012 to 2024. Huxlin, who is also the associate director of the CVS and co-director of the CVS training program, received her PhD in neuroscience at the University of Sydney, Australia before joining URMC. Huxlin is internationally known for her work on visual restoration, for which she holds twelve patents. She was the founder and inaugural president of the Rochester Chapter of the Society for Neuroscience, is an elected fellow of Optica, and a Fellow of the Association for Research in Vision and Ophthalmology. She is also a member of the Board of Directors of the Vision Sciences Society, serving as president in 2024.

Vision Restoration and Rehabilitation

William Merigan, MD's group has achieved optogenetic vision restoration in blind regions of macaque retina by transfecting optogenetic agents into retinal ganglion cells. As part of the National Eye Institute Audacious Goals Initiative, Juliette E. McGregor, MD, DiLoreto, and collaborators have used adaptive optics microscopy to visualize and determine the fate of transplanted photoreceptor stem cells in the living eye and are now implanting scaffolds seeded with stem cells for use in human trials. Huxlin continues to develop novel methods to optimize vision restoration approaches in patients with stroke and other visual processing disorders.

Ocular Surface Disorders

Susana Marcos, MD's laboratory has perfected techniques that image the cornea and sclera with high resolution, allow for three-dimensional quantification of corneal topography, and enable measurement of corneal biomechanics. The FEI has continued to be a world leader in Dry Eye Syndrome and has developed new technologies to measure tear thickness, coverage, and composition that enable better evaluation of the efficacy of pharmaceutical and other interventions. Investigators have identified critical molecular pathways that can aid in new pharmacological therapies to promote corneal nerve regeneration and treat corneal fibrosis, a leading cause of blindness. FEI investigators have used large-scale genomic data, molecular biology, and bacterial genetics to identify and prioritize drivers of ocular infection and to validate trials of novel antimicrobial therapies, which are beginning at LVPEI.

Refractive Error Correction

Investigators are developing methods for measuring corneal biomechanics as biomarkers for keratoconus and to monitor the efficacy of treatments aimed at stiffening the cornea. Laser Induced Refractive Index Change (LIRIC) is a process invented at the University by a team led by Huxlin, Wayne Knox, PhD (Optics), and Jonathan Ellis, PhD (Optics, Mechanical Engineering), that may be transformative for refractive error correction. Based on animal testing performed in Huxlin's laboratory, LIRIC underwent its first human trial successfully in 2018, with a second trial planned for 2024. Marcos's team is studying age-related lens changes and is employing adaptive optics and vision simulators to test the efficacy of new intraocular lenses, contact lenses, or corneal profile designs to treat presbyopia and myopia. Marcos is also developing new methods for halting myopia progression.

Adaptive Optics Imaging

The FEI is a world leader in the use of adaptive optics imaging to study a wide variety of diseases. Jesse Schallek, MD's lab has employed Adaptive Optics Scanning Light Ophthalmoscopy to study single neurons, glia and blood cells. His team has provided the first detailed images of single immune cell behavior in the living, inflamed retina. The team is also using advanced imaging to examine the vascular consequences of changes in intraocular pressure and to understand retinal remodeling and inflammation in the setting of glaucoma.

Cell Biology of Ocular Diseases

Collynn Woeller, PhD, and Feldon have made progress in understanding thyroid eye disease, enabling better, more cost-effective treatments that ultimately may lead to preventing it. Amy Kiernan, MD's research focuses on anterior segment development and disorders that affect the front of the eye and lead to risk for glaucoma. She and Richard Libby, PhD, are developing new models to understand the pathways controlling cellular viability in glaucoma and the defects underlying pediatric glaucoma risk. Investigators are also employing adaptive optics and stem cell approaches to study inherited retinal dystrophies. Ruchira Singh, PhD, is using patient-derived human-induced pluripotent stem cells to study the molecular mechanism underlying macular degenerative diseases.

Chapter 26

DEPARTMENT OF OTOLARYNGOLOGY

During the past twenty-five years, two divisions of the department of Surgery (Otolaryngology and Neurosurgery) became independent departments, following the lead of Urology, Orthopaedics, and Ophthalmology, which became independent in the 1960s and 1970s. This chapter will outline the establishment and growth of Otolaryngology. Neurosurgery will be discussed later under the umbrella of the Neurosciences program of excellence.

Otolaryngology began as a division in Surgery in 1928, with the recruitment of Clyde Heatly, MD, as its first chief. With no space available within the Medical Center, he established an office within the city and began a residency program. One of his initial residents, Gertrude Bales, MD, became the first full-time otolaryngology faculty member to practice solely at SMH. John P. Frazer, MD, became the first full-time chief of Otolaryngology in 1962. During his tenure, the division grew in faculty and the residency expanded from three to six trainees.

Figure 26.1. Arthur Hengerer

Arthur S. Hengerer, MD, a specialist in pediatric otology, became division chief in 1981. Hengerer received his MD from Albany Medical College and served his residency in otolaryngology at Upstate Medical Center in Syracuse, before completing a fellowship in pediatric otolaryngology at Boston Children's Hospital and Beth Israel Hospital in Boston. Hengerer developed a robust clinical program, recruiting fellowship-trained faculty in many subspecialty areas, including adult and pediatric otolaryngology; allergies, sinus, and ear problems; facial plastic, reconstructive, and cosmetic surgery; head and neck surgery; laryngology; and neurotology. He also spearheaded the expansion and relocation of outpatient programs to a 20,000 square-foot facility at Clinton Woods in Brighton.

A focus for Hengerer was the development of a research program. This included the appointment of Robert Frisina, PhD, as director of otolaryngology research. Frisina was instrumental in the establishment of the Rochester International Center for Hearing and Speech Research (ICHSR), a collaboration between the University and the National Technical Institute for the Deaf at RIT. Over the ensuing years, the ICHSR has received approximately $15 million from the National Institute of Aging. As a result, the department became one of the top twenty otolaryngology programs in NIH funding. Hengerer also oversaw the transition of otolaryngology into an independent department in 2004. Although he stepped down as chair at the end of 2007, he remained active on the faculty until his retirement in 2018, and also involved himself with physician wellness, acting as a co-lead at the National Academy of Medicine Action Collaborative on Clinician Well-Being and Resilience.

Hengerer was followed as chair by Shawn D. Newlands, MD, PhD, MBA. Newlands received his MD and PhD in Neurosciences in 1990 from the University of Texas Medical Branch and then completed a residency in otolaryngology at the University of Washington. Newlands's primary research interest is in the physiology of the vestibular system, particularly in recovery from injuries to the inner ear. During residency, he studied under Albert Fuchs, MD, at the University of Washington and later was mentored by Michael King, MD, David Dickman, MD, and Dora Angelaki, MD, at the University of Mississippi Medical Center. He returned to the University of Texas in 1999, where he established an NIH-funded research program and became the department chair in 2004. Newlands's clinical interests are in head and neck surgical oncology. Recently, he helped lead a clinical trial to study the use of a statin to reduce hearing loss from people taking Cisplatin for cancer chemotherapy. Newlands also served institutional roles, including leading outpatient clinical services as associate CMO for ambulatory care since 2017 and serving as interim chief medical information officer from 2018 to 2019.

Figure 26.2. Shawn Newlands

Under Newlands's leadership, Otolaryngology has grown to thirty faculty, fifteen APPs, twenty-four audiologists, and twenty-two certified speech pathologists. The department added its first fellowship-trained rhinologists (Li Xing-Man, MD, and Issac L. Schmale, MD) and laryngologists (John Ingle, MD, G. Todd Schneider, MD, and Ellen L. Ferraro, MD). The sleep surgery program was expanded, under the direction of Sveta Karelsky, MD. With department growth, directors were named in the subspecialty areas of otology (Ben Crane, MD, PhD), rhinology (Li Xing-Man, MD), facial plastic and reconstructive surgery (Timothy Doerr, MD) and pediatric otolaryngology (Margo McKenna, MD). The number of outpatient sites also grew, and now includes Clinton Woods, Lattimore Road (pediatric otolaryngology), SMH, HH, Geneva, Greece, Geneseo, and Batavia. The department is now the chief provider of tertiary services in laryngology, rhinology, otology, pediatric otolaryngology, and sleep surgery in western NY.

The growth and scope of the Speech Pathology program is particularly noteworthy. Staff has quadrupled to more than thirty speech language pathologists. A large SMH inpatient team provides care for acute rehabilitation patients, acute care patients, and for patients who participate in the Integrative Cognitive Rehabilitation program. Outpatient speech pathology services are provided at the WCC, as well as at Clinton Crossings, Clinton Woods, Batavia, and Geneseo. Outpatient therapy focuses on voice and neurologic disorders, patients treated for head and neck cancers, and swallowing evaluation and treatment. Specialty services have been added to include a gender-aligning voice program, a facial rehabilitation program, and singing voice therapy. Speech language pathologists have been integrated into the Amyotrophic Lateral Sclerosis and Huntington's disease clinics and have worked closely with the Movement Disorders Clinic on multidisciplinary team training in Parkinson's disease.

The UR Medicine Voice Center's multidisciplinary approach involves audiologists, speech pathologists, and physicians who are fellowship-trained in voice disorders, mental health providers, nutritional support specialists, rehabilitation specialists, and singing specialists, to evaluate and treat children and adults who have voice, speech, language, cognition, and/or swallowing problems. As part of the Eastman Performing Arts in Medicine program, the Center provides care for all vocal performers, from elite professionals who need immediate voice care services to those who sing for enjoyment. The program also offers SPEAK OUT!®, a therapy designed to improve voice and swallowing in patients with Parkinson's disease.

Audiology has also grown immensely and now includes over twenty-four audiologists, three hearing-aid technicians, and many other support staff. In the 1990s, URMC audiology staff was an integral part of testing the efficacy of Universal Newborn Hearing Screening in NY State, which led to the passing of a law requiring hearing screening of all infants born in NY State. Today the URMC program screens over 6,000 infants yearly at SMH and HH, and provides outpatient screening and diagnostic testing for many infants born at regional hospitals. Staff continues to be involved as consultants to the NY State Early Hearing Detection and Intervention advisory panel, and the program serves as a model for screening the hearing of infants across the state. In 2018, audiology opened an office decorated in a child-friendly theme on Lattimore Road. This office, which sees over 7,000 infants and children a year, is the only audiologic testing facility in western NY providing services exclusively to children.

In 2003, with the move of audiology to Clinton Woods, a hearing aid dispensing program was added to what had previously been largely diagnostic services. The hearing aid program now has offices in Greece, Batavia, Geneseo, and the Southern Tier, in keeping with the regional expansion of Otolaryngology. In recent years, audiology has continued to expand its programs, including care for implantable bone-anchored hearing aids, balance testing, and tinnitus care. The cochlear implant program treats nearly fifty new patients each year.

The residency in otolaryngology has evolved from a two-year general surgery residency, followed by a three-year otolaryngology residency, to a five-year program completely overseen by the department. There is dedicated time in the second and third years to develop a research project. The program expanded to fifteen residents (three per year) in 2018. The department is also involved in teaching medical students, providing a variety of clinical and research opportunities. Educational opportunities in speech pathology and audiology have expanded under the leadership of speech and audiology directors Christy Monczynski Hopson, AuD, and Mark Orlando, PhD. Fellowship training is now offered to speech pathologists and includes Acute Care at SMH, Head & Neck Cancer at the WCI, Acute Rehabilitation at SMH, and Voice & Swallowing Center at Clinton Woods.

Newlands's tenure has been marked by the recruitment of MDs and PhDs involved in research and by the development of collaborative programs with other departments, such as Neurosciences and Biomedical Engineering, resulting in the University being among the top twenty institutions for National Institute for Deafness and Communication Disorders funding. The primary strength of the research program has been in hearing and balance research. More information about these research programs can be found on the URMC website. Recent NIH-sponsored research programs include *The Development of Vestibular-Perceptual Adaptation Paradigms For Treating Persistent Vertigo & Perceived Disequilibrium* (Eric Anson, PhD), *Multi-modal Vestibular Perception* (Benjamin T. Crane, MD, PhD), *Behavioral and Physiological Consequences of Auditory Nerve Loss* (Kenneth S. Henry, PhD), and *Synaptic Mechanisms of Mammalian Vestibular Efferent Responses* (J. Christopher Holt, PhD). The department also hosts an NIH-funded national otolaryngologist-scientists network (PI, Newlands) for the Triological Society that brings together the majority of NIH-funded otolaryngologists from around the country to mentor younger otolaryngologists interested in a clinician-scientist career.

Chapter 27

DEPARTMENT OF ANESTHESIOLOGY AND PERIOPERATIVE MEDICINE

The enormous growth in surgical and procedural volumes necessitated substantial growth in anesthesia and perioperative services, and a restructuring of how these services are delivered throughout the health care system.

The first anesthetic was administered at SMH shortly after its opening in 1926. At the time, anesthesia was administered by nurse anesthetists under surgical supervision. In 1950, Robert Sweet, MD, was recruited as the first head of a newly formed division of Anesthesiology, consisting of himself and thirteen nurse anesthetists, within the department of Surgery. Three years later, Sweet established an anesthesiology residency program. Anesthesiology formally became a department in 1969, under the chairmanship of Alastair J. Gillies, MD, who expanded the faculty, enhanced the scope of cases, and established research programs. Ronald A. Gabel, MD, was recruited from the Brigham and Women's Hospital, Boston in 1983 as the department's second chair. During Gabel's tenure, the department developed the first computerized operating room database, formed several subspecialty divisions, and established a multidisciplinary Pain Treatment Center. Gabel also formed an OR management committee with representatives from Anesthesiology, Surgery, Nursing, and hospital administration.

In 1992, Denham S. Ward, MD, PhD, was recruited from UCLA to become chair and to take a leadership role in managing the ORs at SMH. The department became a national leader in simulation, purchasing one of the nation's first anesthesia human patient simulators and hosting the first international conference on medical simulation. Ward also initiated several innovative education programs, such as TAPS (Training Anesthesiologists as Physician Scientists) and the Anesthesiology MBA. Clinical services expanded to include the liver transplant program and the preadmission evaluation clinic. The department also merged with the HH Anesthesiology Group, forming a clinical practice track. After stepping down as chair, Ward became associate dean for Faculty Development-Medical

Figure 27.1. Denham Ward

Education, with responsibility for creating a variety of faculty development programs for SMD.

In 2001, James L. Robotham, MD, succeeded Ward as chair. He oversaw the expansion of the ORs and worked with Shey-Shing Sheu, PhD, of Pharmacology and Physiology to establish the Mitochondrial Research & Innovation Group, one of the leading groups in the country. In 2008, Ward returned as chair, overseeing the opening of the Ambulatory Surgical Center at Sawgrass and new Pain Treatment facilities. In keeping with the increase in faculty size, he further expanded the residency program.

Figure 27.2. Michael Eaton

In 2011, Michael P. Eaton, MD, became chair of a department renamed Anesthesia and Perioperative Medicine. Eaton received his MD from Michigan State University. He joined URMC in 1995, where he became director of cardiac anesthesia. He recently completed thirteen years as chair, the longest in that role. Eaton's tenure was particularly distinctive for growing the anesthesia residency program and establishing an integrated four-year continuum of education, including innovative tracks offering master's degrees in clinical investigation, medical management, and health professions education. He established the multidisciplinary Difficult Airway Response Team to reduce mortality due to airway loss in patients with complex anatomy; established the University of Rochester Center for Perioperative Medicine, a nationally recognized center integrating care designed to improve outcomes after surgery; oversaw design of operating rooms in the new GCH; and integrated anesthesia care across UR Medicine affiliates. Eaton's research focuses on the interaction of cardiopulmonary bypass with human blood, and approaches to minimize the adverse effects of this interaction.

In October 2024, Michael James Scott, MB, ChB, became chair. Scott's work in quality improvement has led to worldwide acceptance of a new standard of care for surgical patients, called Enhanced Recovery after Surgery (ERAS), which focuses on preoperative counselling and screening, optimization of nutrition, standardized analgesic and anesthetic regimens, and early mobilization post-surgery.

Anesthesiology and Perioperative Medicine currently has eighty-two faculty, thirty-seven anesthesia technicians, forty-four Certified Registered Nurse Anesthetists (cRNAs), forty-five nurses, thirty-four support staff, and sixty-seven residents/fellows that work in five distinct clinical services: 1) The Academic Anesthesiology practice, which covers all surgical cases at SMH, GCH, Sawgrass, obstetrical anesthesia/analgesia, Strong West, and eighteen non-OR anesthetizing locations; 2) The Clinical Anesthesia

Practice, which covers HH and FF Thompson; 3) The Pain Treatment Center; 4) Critical Care intensivists, who cover the Burn and Trauma, Surgical, Neuro and Cardiac ICUs, and 5) The Center for Perioperative Medicine. In 2024, these services provided 90,965 procedures in seventy-eight ORs and sixteen non-operating locations. The department now has fifteen divisions which span periprocedural care, pain medicine, and critical care.

The outpatient Pain Treatment Center at Sawgrass is the only multidisciplinary pain center in western NY staffed by anesthesiologists, physiatrists, neurologists, psychologists, and acupuncturists. Its comprehensive services address the full spectrum of painful conditions, and faculty partner with referring physicians and patients to craft multi-modal plans to help restore function and improve quality of life. The regional Anesthesiology/Acute Pain Service performs peripheral blocks and neuraxial anesthesia, chiefly at Sawgrass (where it performs about 3,000 blocks per year). Using advanced techniques and ultrasound guidance, the Center has shown a high success rate, shortened Post-Anesthesia Care Unit stays, reduced opioid-related side-effects, and improved patient satisfaction.

The Center for Perioperative Medicine, developed in 2012, is responsible for the preparation of patients having surgery or invasive procedures with anesthesia and for the longitudinal coordination of care for complex patients across the surgical encounter. Over the past decade, the center has shifted from simple evaluation to the adoption of the ERAS standard of care for surgical. Treatment of coexisting disease is optimized to ensure good surgical outcomes and minimize perioperative morbidity.

The Difficult Airway Response Team (DART) was created in September 2015 to reduce harm and adverse outcomes during difficult airway management outside of the operating room. DART consists of providers from Anesthesiology, Otolaryngology and Head and Neck Surgery, Trauma Surgery, Critical Care Medicine and Emergency Medicine, and can be activated at all times in the event of difficult airway-related emergencies at SMH.

The department is involved in medical student teaching, even during the first year, and sponsors a summer externship program for a select group of post-first year students. The residency program currently has eighteen postgraduate year (PGY) 1 slots and has been critical in supplying anesthesiologists for the region's health care systems. Sixty-five percent of anesthesiologists working in Rochester but not at the University were trained by the department. An important change in the residency program was the introduction in 2011 of a four-year, integrated (Categorical) program in anesthesiology and perioperative medicine. Traditionally, residents completed an internship in either medicine or surgery before starting anesthesiology training as PGY2s. Now, residents join the department as PGY1s. Scheduling is coordinated with other departments and juxtaposes "floor" rotations. For example, residents complete a month of cardiology before the cardiac anesthesia rotation. Similar rotations are paired with the pediatric, obstetric, and neurologic anesthesia subspecialties. The program also offers unique non-clinical residency tracks that allow residents to develop expertise in medical education, administration, and/or research through graduate-level course work and departmental projects. In addition, the department now has four fellowship programs: pain medicine, cardiac anesthesiology, critical care medicine, and pediatric anesthesiology.

Peter Papadakos, MD, has been a mainstay of the department for over twenty-five years. He received his MD from Mount Sinai School of Medicine in NY, where he also completed an anesthesiology residency and a fellowship in surgical critical care. Papadakos is internationally recognized for his work in critical care, acute respiratory distress syndrome and mechanical ventilation. He is one of the founders of surgical critical care in Rochester and serves as the associate director of the Strong Regional Trauma Center. In 2011, he was recognized by the *New York Times* and the international media for identifying a major patient safety issue—that of electronic distraction in health care—and coined the term "Distracted Doctoring." He has worked to develop electronic etiquette guidelines to prevent electronic distraction for hospitals and national agencies. Papadakos co-edited with Stephen Bertman, MD, the textbook *Distracted Doctoring: Returning to Patient-Centered Care in the Digital Age.* He has become a regular contributor to *Time Magazine, Forbes,* and *Medscape* in the field of health care policy.

Figure 27.3.
Peter Papadakos

The department has vibrant research programs, with projects in mitochondrial disease, neurodegenerative disease, ischemia-reperfusion, the treatment and prevention of chronic pain, coagulation, quality measurement and the impact of report cards on quality of care, and respiratory physiology. The department's website includes details of each of these programs and investigators. A few programs are highlighted below.

Basic science research is centered on the study of mitochondrial function and is housed within the Mitochondrial Research and Innovation Group. The Group brings together laboratories throughout the University to better understand mitochondrial function from all angles, bridging biophysics and biochemistry to integrative physiology and clinical outcomes.

Laurent Glance, the vice chair for Research, heads a vibrant outcomes group that includes a broad range of research programs, all dedicated to improving outcomes and quality in patients who require anesthesia services.

Glance's own research focuses on the limitations of risk adjustments for measuring quality of care, optimizing injury severity scoring, the impact of non-public reporting on trauma outcomes, and quality reporting in obstetrics.

A centerpiece of the department's research, led by Robert Dworkin, has been the Analgesic, Anesthetic, and Addiction Clinical Trial Translations, Innovations, Opportunities, and Networks, and Pediatric Anesthesia Safety Initiative (ACTTION/PASI). ACTTION is a public–private partnership with the FDA designed to develop novel analgesic, anesthetic, addiction, and peripheral neuropathy interventions that improve efficacy and safety. The ACTTION partnership conducts evidence-based consensus meetings and reviews, performs methodological research studies, and develops novel clinical outcome assessments and sensitive biomarkers to improve clinical trial. ACTTION has published 139 articles in peer-reviewed journals and has received approximately $6 million in FDA funding and over $13 million in private (primarily industry) funding.

Figure 27.4.
Robert Dworkin

Chapter 28

DEPARTMENT OF MEDICINE (DOM)

Medicine was one of the original departments of SMD and it has been a leader in academic medicine since. William S. McCann, MD, was appointed as first chair of DOM in 1923, selecting Lawrence A. Kohn, MD, as the first internal medicine (IM) resident in 1925. McCann was involved in research related to disorders of the heart and lungs, and was instrumental in the establishment of URMC Cardiology. In 1957, he was succeeded as chair of DOM by Lawrence E. Young, MD, who served for seventeen years. Following Young, DOM went through a period of multiple leadership changes, with no fewer than nine physicians serving as either chair or acting chair over a twenty-five-year period. Of note was Richard B. Hornick, MD, who did groundbreaking work on typhoid fever and infectious diarrhea, who served as chair from 1979 until 1985, and who helped grow the Medical Center's reputation in infectious diseases. Also of note was Raphael Dolin, MD, who was recruited by Hornick to be chief of Infectious Diseases and who served as chair from 1991 until 1998.

The twenty-first century began with Bradford Berk as Charles A. Dewey Professor and Chair of DOM, and physician-in-chief at SMH. During his tenure as chair, Berk initiated impactful clinical and research agendas. The department added eighty-four new faculty members, helping to drive an annual fifteen percent increase in research revenues and a doubling of patient care revenues. He established new divisions of Hospital Medicine and Geriatric Medicine, and recruited several new division chiefs, including Mark Taubman, MD (Cardiology), Steve Georas, MD (Pulmonary), and Uma Sundaram, MD, and Richard Farmer, MD (Gastroenterology). Berk established a new DOM compensation plan and a centralized billing service. He also launched the Aab Cardiovascular Research Institute and, with the support of CEO "Mac" Evarts and Taubman, shepherded its move to a facility in Henrietta. Berk was appointed URMC CEO in 2006.

In 2008, Taubman, chief of Cardiology, succeeded Berk as Charles A. Dewey Professor and Chair of DOM, and physician-in-chief at SMH. In June 2009, he was tapped to serve as interim URMC CEO following Berk's unfortunate accident. During his short tenure as chair, Taubman oversaw the recruitment of new division chiefs, including Steve Hammes, MD (Endocrinology), Marc Berliant, MD (General Medicine), John Treanor, MD (Infectious Diseases), and Charles Lowenstein, MD (Cardiology). He also leveraged royalties received from the human papillomavirus (HPV) vaccine to create endowed professorships and to provide funding for interdivisional research under the direction of Patricia Sime, MD, who was appointed vice chair for research. He also incorporated Palliative Care as a new division.

In 2010, Paul C. Levy, MD, the Ralph W. Prince Professor of Medicine, was chosen as the Charles A. Dewey Professor and Chair of DOM, and physician-in-chief at SMH. Levy received his MD from The Ohio State University, and then came to the University of Rochester, where he completed residency and chief residency in IM and a fellowship in pulmonary critical care. He joined the faculty of Pulmonary and Critical Care in 1989, and three years later was appointed as director of the division's Clinical Services. Levy's early career included collaborative research with Mark Utell, MD, and John Looney, MD, studying Fc-receptor subtypes on monocytes and alveolar macrophages. In 1996, Raphael Dolin, chair of DOM, appointed Levy as associate chair for Clinical Affairs; in 2003, he was promoted to vice chair. Prior to being named DOM chair, Levy had twice served as acting chair, following the appointments of Berk and Taubman as URMC CEO and interim CEO, respectively.

Figure 28.1. Paul Levy

As associate chair and vice chair, Levy developed and implemented new programs within the department. The inpatient medical service more than doubled in size, and key initiatives were launched to enhance quality and patient safety. He also provided invaluable expertise to UMRC over several decades through his work as medical director in the Office of Compliance, a unique position fostered by Edward ("Ted") Case, Esq., who directed the Office.

As chair of DOM, Levy appointed seven new division chiefs, and supported philanthropy efforts that resulted in seven new endowed professorships, bringing the total to eighteen in the department. He guided his faculty through the rollout of eRecord, the implementation of a new compensation plan, and the growth of UR Medicine. He oversaw the expansion of the Hospital Medicine division and enhanced physician coverage across all medicine inpatient specialties at SMH and HH. Levy maintained emphasis on the department's research and education missions, fostering program growth in strategic areas, and promoting in-depth faculty mentoring and career development programs, such as the initiation of an annual pilot grant program that supports research, educational, and clinical innovation projects.

Levy stepped down after two terms as chair but has remained active within Pulmonary and Critical Care Medicine.

In 2021, Ruth O'Regan, MD, was recruited from the University of Wisconsin to become the Charles A. Dewey Professor and Chair of DOM, physician-in-chief at SMH and the associate director for education and mentoring at the WCI. A native of Galway, Ireland, O'Regan earned her MD at University College, Dublin, and completed a residency in IM at Mater Hospital, Dublin. She did residencies in IM at the Medical College of Wisconsin and Northwestern University, and a fellowship in hematology/oncology at Northwestern University. O'Regan subsequently joined the faculty of Emory University, where she focused on developing novel therapeutic approaches for treatment-resistant breast cancers, such as triple negative and endocrine-resistant metastatic breast cancers, for which she was recognized with the Louisa and Rand Glenn Family Chair in Breast Cancer Research. At Emory she led the Translational Breast Cancer Research Program, was medical director of the Emory Breast Center, chief of Hematology and Medical Oncology at the Georgia Cancer Center for Excellence at Grady Memorial Hospital, and director of the hematology/oncology fellowship. O'Regan was recruited to the University of Wisconsin School of Medicine and Public Health in 2015, where she served as chief of Hematology, Medical Oncology and Palliative Care and deputy director of the Carbone Cancer Center. She also served as chief scientific officer of the Big Ten Cancer Research Consortium and vice chair of the National Comprehensive Cancer Network's Board of Directors. At the time of her URMC appointment, O'Regan had written more than 100 peer-reviewed publications in leading oncology, radiology, molecular biology, surgery, and pathology journals, and serves as editor-in-chief of *Clinical Breast Cancer* and Breast Section Editor for *Cancer*.

Figure 28.2. Ruth O'Regan

Currently, DOM has approximately 550 faculty across fourteen divisions, more than 200 APPs, and more than 800 additional staff, making it URMC's largest clinical and academic department. As of 2024, the department had eighty fellows, 114 residents, and $41.3 million of annual research funding. It conducted approximately 125,000 outpatient visits per year, as well as 16,000 inpatient discharges. The following sections describe most of the historical divisions in DOM. Other divisions are highlighted elsewhere in the book: Infectious Diseases as part of Immunology and Infection; Cardiology as part of Cardiovascular Diseases; Hematology and Oncology as part of Cancer; General Medicine, Transitional Care, and Hospitalists as part of Primary Care and the Community.

Education in Medicine

Residency Training

The IM residency program, the largest at URMC, dates to the Medical Center's origins, with William McCann serving as program director from 1926 until 1957, followed by Larry Young. William L. Morgan, MD, became program director in 1962. Young created two additional residency programs—the Medicine-Pediatrics (Med-Peds) program and the Associated Hospitals Program, a city-wide residency for internal medicine which involved six hospitals and selected community health centers and private practices. The latter program—which became the Primary Care Program in Internal Medicine in 1985—closed in 2001. Morgan continued as IM residency director, before handing the reins over to Robert F. Betts, MD, in 1989.

Figure 28.3. Donald Bordley

Donald Bordley, MD, William L. Morgan professor of medicine and associate department chair for education, became program director in 1997. Bordley, a native of Cooperstown, NY who did his residency in IM and a general medicine fellowship at URMC, started out as IM residency program director at RGH. In 1994, he was recruited to URMC, initially to direct the IM clerkship. Like Morgan, Bordley was one of a relatively small group of residency program directors who approached it as a calling, rather than one rung on the academic ladder; as a result, he helped transform residency education around the country. Bordley played a major role in the Association of Program Directors of Internal Medicine (APDIM), serving on numerous committees and as president. In 2017, he received the 2017 Dema C. Daley Founders Award from the APDIM for his years of service on behalf of residency education.

To diversify residents' clinical training experience, Bordley, with the strong support of CEO Jay Stein, expanded the residency to HH. It remains a popular site for residents and medical students. Bordley also developed a required Palliative Care rotation and expanded the number of outpatient electives. He took advantage of the expanding hospitalist services at SMH and HH to create a new teaching model in which each resident team was paired with a single hospitalist attending, replacing the system in which each patient had a different community-based PCP or specialist.

Alec O'Connor, MD, MPH, succeeded Bordley as program director in 2012. O'Connor, a member of the Hospitalist division, who did his IM residency and chief residency at URMC, continued to emphasize ambulatory training, overseeing the transition from a traditional required half day per week of continuity clinic structure into a "6+2" block structure that better

Figure 28.4.
Alec O'Connor

emphasized ambulatory education and training. The curriculum was also extensively modernized, and new track opportunities were established in community advocacy and medicine-psychiatry. These changes generated a new appeal for the practice of general IM and resulted in more residents choosing primary care as a career option. A new research pathway was initiated in 2012. O'Connor also worked with Berliant to develop a primary care residency program. At SMH, twenty-four-hour call shifts were eliminated and a nocturnist program was initiated to improve supervision, support, and education of residents overnight. Amy E. Blatt, MD, William L. Morgan, Jr. Professor of Medicine, succeeded O'Connor as program director in 2022. Blatt, who did her Med-Peds residency and chief residency at URMC, had previously served as director for the IM third-year clerkship and as associate program director for the IM and Med-Peds residencies.

The initiation of duty hour limits, increase in inpatient acuity, and shift of services to outpatient settings, resulted in a substantial increase in the number of IM residents. In 1999, the program consisted of twenty-four interns, three of whom were preliminary interns, and sixty-eight total residents. By 2024, the program had increased to forty interns, twelve of whom were preliminary interns (including eight neurology interns) and ninety-three total residents. In 2022, the residency was expanded to FF Thompson, concomitant with the shifting of the medicine clerkship from RRH to FF Thompson.

Figure 28.5.
Brett Robbins

Brett Robbins, MD, took over the Med-Peds program from Barbara Schuster, MD, in 1999 and remained at the helm until 2024, when he became SAD for Graduate Medical Education. Robbins, who did his Med-Peds residency training at URMC, has special interests in medical education, the transition of youth with chronic illness to adulthood, and diversity/equity/inclusion. Under his leadership, the residency thrived, adding faculty and moving the IM portion of training from RGH to SMH and HH. It also established a new continuity clinic and added educational tracks for global health, lifestyle medicine, research, and community advocacy. In addition to running the Med-Peds program, Robbins served as vice chair for education in DOM, where he oversaw the administrative consolidation of the fifteen fellowships into a core group of seven administrators.

Divisions

Allergy, Immunology, and Rheumatology (AIR)

AIR began in the late 1950s as two separate units. The Clinical Immunology division, founded by John H. Vaughn, MD, focused on translational research across a broad range of immunological diseases, including systemic rheumatologic diseases such as rheumatoid arthritis and lupus as well as allergic diseases. The Rheumatology division, founded by Ralph Jacox, MD, was noted for its outstanding clinician-teachers who were instrumental in developing the diagnostic criteria for rheumatoid arthritis (Jacox) and diagnostic classification criteria for juvenile inflammatory arthritis (John Baum, MD). In 1984, under John Leddy, MD, the two divisions were combined to form AIR, enabling better integration of the clinical, research, and education missions. During Leddy's tenure, AIR had some extraordinary research successes, including: the first description and functional characterization of human C5 and C6 deficiencies and the characterization of defective complement regulation by erythrocytes in paroxysmal nocturnal hemoglobinuria (Leddy and Stephen I. Rosenfeld, MD), the initial description and characterization of the human Fcγ receptors, FcγRI and FcγRII, and the development of the first monoclonal antibodies against these receptors (Rosenfeld, Leddy, Clark L. Anderson, MD, Richard J. Looney, MD, and George N. Abraham, MD).

In 1996, Leddy was followed as chief by Ignacio Sãnz, MD. Sãnz received his MD from the University of Santander Medical School in Spain and did his residency in IM at the National Center for Medical Research in Madrid. He then did a postdoctoral fellowship at Southwestern Medical School in Dallas and a fellowship in rheumatology at the University of Texas Health Sciences Center in San Antonio. Under Sãnz's leadership, AIR became an international leader in B-cell research. Among its many major contributions was developing multiparameter flow cytometry to characterize human B cells subsets and identify abnormalities in patients with lupus, rheumatoid arthritis, and Sjögren's syndrome (Sãnz and Jennifer H. Anolik, MD, PhD). It also led to one of the first clinical trials of B cell depletion therapy, using rituximab, to treat autoimmune disease (Looney and Anolik). AIR developed collaborations with investigators in the Center for Vaccine Biology & Immunology, such as Tim R. Mosmann, PhD, and Deborah J. Fowell, PhD, that bolstered the University's pre-eminence in B cell research and earned an NIH Autoimmunity Center of Excellence (2002–14) award.

Figure 28.6. Ignacio Sãnz

A second major area of investigation was the program in osteoimmunology, led by Christopher T. Ritchlin, MD, in collaboration with Eddie Schwarz, PhD, director of the Center for Musculoskeletal Research. These investigators identified a marked expansion of osteoclast precursors in psoriatic arthritis and produced the first monoclonal antibody against human DC-STAMP, a critical regulator of osteoclast development. The program oversaw the first trial of a biologic (etanercept) for prosthetic hip loosening and established 3-D-CT scanning to quantify peri-prosthetic osteolysis (Looney and Schwarz).

Figure 28.7. Christopher Ritchlin

Having spearheaded the osteoimmunology program, Ritchlin was chosen to succeed Sãnz as chief of AIR in 2014. Ritchlin received his MD and did an internship in IM at Albany Medical College, followed by a residency in IM at Mount Sinai Hospital, NY, a fellowship in rheumatology at NYU Langone Medical Center, and an MPH in clinical investigation at the University of Rochester. Ritchlin had a worldwide reputation for his work on psoriatic arthritis and was a lead investigator in several international clinical trials testing the efficacy and safety of biologic agents in psoriatic arthritis. He teamed with Francisco Tausk, MD (Dermatology), to establish the first Psoriasis and Psoriatic Arthritis Clinic, in which patients were evaluated jointly by both physicians to manage complex psoriatic disease.

Under Ritchlin's leadership, the clinical and research programs in B cell biology and osteoimmunology continued to thrive. AIR recruited four allergists and five rheumatologists, including Benjamin Korman, MD, a leading young translational investigator in scleroderma. In addition, AIR undertook a marked expansion of its research and clinical programs in allergy, spurred by Looney, whose research was focused on the role of the modern lifestyle in promoting allergic diseases. Establishing that members of the Old Order Mennonites (OOM) in Penn Yan had fewer than ten percent of the allergic disease seen in the rest of upstate NY, Looney initiated studies on how the microbiome and the immune system developed during the first two years of life in infants growing up in OOM families in Penn Yan compared with those growing up in Rochester. These studies were instrumental in the recruitment of Kirsi Järvinen-Seppo, MD, PhD, to re-establish the division of Pediatric Allergy and Immunology and direct a Center for Food Allergy. Under the leadership of Looney and Järvinen-Seppo, the allergy program grew within AIR and Pediatrics, and developed strong collaborations with physician scientists in Dermatology, Otolaryngology, Gastroenterology, and Pulmonary & Critical Care Medicine. This culminated in 2019 in the University's selection as a World Allergy Organization Center of Excellence.

Since 2014, the number of allergists at URMC has increased from one to eight in Medicine and six in Pediatrics.

The twenty-first century has experienced a revolution treating rheumatic and immunologic diseases with targeted biologics. Beginning with the anti-TNF (Tumor Necrosis Factor) agents in the early 2000s, there are now more than forty FDA-approved biologics for a diverse array of immune-mediated diseases and dozens more in the pipeline. The high cost and complexity of administration of these infusion therapies required new operational and financial models to be developed. Among these models was the URMC Specialty Pharmacy, which has greatly improved patient education and service for the home delivery of biologic agents. To accommodate the growth of AIR services, additional outpatient offices were opened locally on Lattimore Road, and in Canandaigua, Batavia, Brockport, and Geneseo. Infusion clinics were initiated in 2007 and expanded over the next eighteen years to include fourteen infusion chairs for rheumatology and allergy at the Red Creek and Lattimore Road sites.

To further support clinical and research programs, musculoskeletal ultrasound (MSK-US) was established within AIR by Ralf G. Thiele, MD, who helped develop the criteria for national accreditation of MSK-US. MSK-US has emerged as a pivotal point of care service in rheumatology, and through Thiele's efforts, the MSK-US service at URMC has been the national leader. Norman C. Madsen, BMBS, MSc, also an expert in MSK-US, serves as the course director of the training program for Ultrasound School of North American Rheumatologists, a society that trains health professionals in rheumatologic ultrasonography, establishes guidelines for image acquisition and interpretation, and promotes research relevant to ultrasonography of rheumatic disease. In addition, Darren A. Tabechian, MD, established ultrasound guided synovial biopsies, enhancing clinical capabilities and allowing a major expansion of the research efforts led by Jennifer Anolik.

Anolik has served as division chief since Ritchlin's retirement in 2021. Anolik graduated from the MD-PhD program at the University, remained for her residency in IM and fellowship in rheumatology, and then joined the faculty. Like Sãnz, she has established an international reputation for her work on B cells, particularly as targets for the treatment of lupus and rheumatoid arthritis. Through her efforts, in 2014 the University was one of eleven institutions chosen to join the NIH Accelerating Medicines Partnership in Rheumatoid Arthritis and Lupus Network to develop new treatments for patients with autoimmune diseases using state-of-the-art single cell and spatial transcriptomic

Figure 28.8. Jennifer Anolik

analytic approaches. The URMC program was extended in 2022 to include psoriatic arthritis and Sjögren's disease (Anolik serves as the PI of the Rheumatoid Arthritis Research Team and Ritchlin as the PI of the Psoriatic Disease Team). In 2015, Anolik's accomplishments earned her election to the American Society for Clinical Investigation, one of the nation's oldest and most respected medical honor societies.

During Anolik's tenure as chief, research has continued to grow in breadth and impact, with total annual funding growing from $9.6 million to $16.2 million, predominantly from the NIH. New faculty have been recruited in Allergy and Rheumatology, bringing the total numbers to ten and fifteen respectively, and the number of APPs has significantly expanded. In addition, several new outpatient facilities opened, increasing outpatient services to seven clinics and two infusion centers. The RA-CHAMP and IQ-LUPUS programs were developed by Allen P. Anandarajah, MBBS, to help people with rheumatoid arthritis and lupus and their families navigate barriers to health care.

AIR oversees two long-standing fellowships that have been responsible for training more than half the allergists and rheumatologists in the region. The Allergy/Immunology fellowship was started by John Condemi, MD, in 1961; the rheumatology fellowship by Leddy in 1985. The division also offers a unique three-year combined training program in allergy/immunology and rheumatology that leads to board eligibility in both disciplines. AIR also collaborates with the department of Pediatrics to offer a four-year combined Adult and Pediatric Rheumatology program whose curriculum has a special focus on the transition from adolescent to adult care and prepares fellows for board eligibility in both disciplines. All fellowship programs provide ample opportunity for research.

AIR is also actively involved in training medical students, residents, and physician scientists across the spectrum. The Physician Scientist Training Program in DOM, established and directed by Anolik, provides a fast track from residency to fellowship and assures protected research mentorship. Anolik and Järvinen-Seppo recently spearheaded a collaboration among DOM, Pediatrics, and Dermatology that received an NIH ROChester Stimulating Access to Research during Residency (ROCStARR) Health and Immune Function Across the Lifespan grant. This grant enables residents to pursue an additional year of training focused on mentored research to study immune-related diseases.

Over the past twenty-five years, AIR has benefitted remarkably from the philanthropy of several of its distinguished faculty. Stephen Rosenfeld, MD, received his BA and MD from the University of Rochester and joined the faculty in 1972, where he went on to have a distinguished career as a

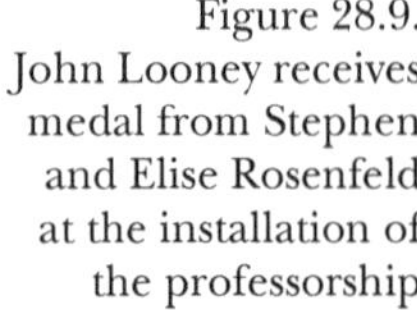
Figure 28.9. John Looney receives medal from Stephen and Elise Rosenfeld at the installation of the professorship

physician, researcher, and teacher. In 2011, he established the Dr. Stephen I. Rosenfeld and Elise A. Rosenfeld Distinguished Professorship in Allergy and Clinical Immunology (Looney was the inaugural Rosenfeld Professor). Rosenfeld received the first Dean's Medal awarded by SMD in 2008. He passed away in 2019. Other philanthropic funds established by AIR faculty include the Rosenfeld-Condemi-Dreyfus Fellowship Fund and the Condemi Educational Fund.

Endocrinology, Diabetes, and Metabolism (EDM)

The last twenty-five years have seen remarkable growth in EDM. However, it began with a major disappointment for URMC related to the groundbreaking work of endocrinologist Donald Young, MD who, in the 1990s, discovered the gene for the enzyme cox-2 and demonstrated its role in causing inflammation. The discovery led to the development of a new class of anti-inflammatory agents that inhibited cox-2 (cyclooxygenase-2), and it was hoped that his research efforts would enable the University to be the beneficiary of significant royalties derived from such agents. When Pfizer developed the cox-2 inhibitor Celebrex without offering royalties, the University filed a patent-infringement lawsuit. After years of litigation, including an appeal to the US Supreme Court, the lawsuit was rejected in a landmark decision. Although the University's role in the discovery of the gene and the biologic significance of the discovery was uncontested, as was the fact that it enabled companies to create new drugs, the courts ruled that the University's patent was invalid because it did not include the precise chemical formula for a cox-2 inhibitor or explain how such an inhibitor would be developed.

With the departure in 2001 of division chief Robert W. Harrison III, MD, David Bushinsky, MD, the chief of Nephrology, was appointed as acting division chief. Bushinsky remained in that position for nine years while multiple searches were conducted to identify a new division chief. Although several outstanding candidates were identified, they were lured away by other institutions offering endowed professorships to their chiefs. Fortunately, through the efforts of Alvin Ureles, MD, and the Wolk Foundation, in 2008 DOM was able to establish the Louis S. Wolk Distinguished Professorship, and shortly thereafter were able to recruit Stephen Hammes, MD, PhD, an outstanding physician-scientist.

Figure 28.10. Alvin Ureles

Alvin L. Ureles, emeritus professor of Medicine, received his MD from the University of Rochester in 1945. He did his residency in IM at Beth Israel Hospital, Boston, and an endocrinology fellowship at MGH, where he helped to pioneer nuclear and ultrasound medicine as it related to thyroid disease, including the use of radioactive iodine in the treatment of thyroid cancer. Ureles returned to Rochester, serving as chief of IM at The Genesee Hospital for over twenty years. He then moved to URMC, where he established the Wolk Thyroid Center and continued his work on thyroid diseases.

Figure 28.11. Stephen Hammes

Stephen Hammes, the first Louis S. Wolk Distinguished Professor in Medicine, received his MD and PhD at Duke University, after which he completed his IM residency and endocrinology fellowship at UCSF. In 1999, Hammes became faculty at the University of Texas, Southwestern Medical Center in Dallas, where he pioneered research related to rapid, extranuclear, or "nongenomic," steroid effects. He was also one of the first to use genetic mouse models to elucidate the role of androgen signaling in female fertility, demonstrating a critical role for androgens in normal ovarian function. Hammes has overseen a remarkable growth of the division. This includes expanding the outpatient clinical and procedural services to Clinton Crossings and Sawgrass, in addition to previous sites at SMH and HH. The number of faculty increased from four in 2009 to fifteen in 2023, and the number of APPs, nurses, and educators grew to twenty-one. In 2023, EDM had more than 30,000 outpatient visits (approximately 5,300 referrals), roughly four times the volumes of 2009. The division also developed several signature programs. This includes a diabetes program started in the 1990s by Steven D. Wittlin, MD, and currently led by Susanne Miedlich, MD, and Sara R. MacLeod, DO, MPH. This program serves tens of thousands of patients, offering services such as nutrition expertise, diabetes education, gestational diabetes care, mental health counseling, and the most up-to-date diabetes technology.

The creation of specialized programs for endocrine-based disorders serves as an excellent example of the multidepartmental approach that has characterized the past twenty-five years. The division has developed collaborations with the division of Hematology/Oncology and departments, including Surgery, Neurosurgery, Radiation Oncology, Orthopaedics and Otolaryngology, to develop premier multidisciplinary clinics in the care of thyroid cancer, pituitary disease, adrenal pathophysiology, and metabolic bone disease. The transgender clinic, the first and only dedicated transgender program in the region that is run by endocrinologists with expertise in steroid hormone biology, takes a multidisciplinary approach with therapists, gynecologists, plastic surgeons, and others. The program follows established guidelines on the medical treatment of transgender patients to ensure safe and successful options for patients with gender dysphoria.

The crown jewel in the division has always been its fellowship program, which over the past fifteen years has expanded from a total of two to nine fellows. This includes the addition of an optional third-year research track. With this academic approach, approximately half of graduating fellows have remained in academic medicine. Nearly all faculty participate in medical student education, from teaching formal coursework to volunteering at the inner-city St. Joseph's Medical Student Clinic.

Figure 28.12. Laura Calvi

EDM research activities have increased by more than fourfold. Laura M. Calvi, MD, the SKAWA Foundation Endowed Professor in Endocrinology and Metabolism, is an international leader in the field of bone microenvironment and hematopoiesis and has served as president of the American Society for Bone and Mineral Research. Calvi's research program studies cellular and molecular interactions between the bone marrow microenvironment and hematopoietic stem cells to identify therapies that can expand stem cells, accelerate hematopoietic recovery after injury or aid in targeting malignant stem cells. A seminal discovery was the identification of a niche component regulating hematopoietic stem cells that is modulated by malignancy and can be therapeutically targeted. Calvi has also contributed to the understanding of how aging impacts the bone marrow microenvironment, on how skeletal stem cells affect the bone marrow microenvironment, and on the effects of radiation injury on hematopoietic and marrow microenvironmental cells. She leads the Cancer Microenvironment program of the WCI. Recent additions to the division include Olga I. Astapova, MD, PhD, whose lab focuses on mechanisms of androgen actions in the ovary, and Carlos Diaz-Balzac, MD, PhD, whose lab studies neural reproductive development. The reader is referred to the division website for full details of the division's research activities.

Gastroenterology and Hepatology

The division of Gastroenterology and Hepatology got off to a rocky start at the beginning of the twenty-first century, with the resignation of several division chiefs. In 2004, to stabilize the situation, Bradford Berk, the chair of DOM, turned to Richard G. Farmer, MD, an internationally prominent gastroenterologist based in Washington, DC. Farmer had been chief of Gastroenterology at the Cleveland Clinic Foundation for ten years and had then served sixteen years as its chair of Medicine. He subsequently moved to Washington, DC, where he was a consultant for the US State Department and served on the faculty of Georgetown University. Farmer had been a member of a national commission that ultimately developed the Digestive Disease Institute at the NIH and was also instrumental in developing continuing medical education programs in Russia and Eastern Europe. He was president of the American College of Gastroenterology and subsequently received the honor of Mastership. He was elected to the Institute of Medicine of the National Academy of Sciences in 1983. While chief of the division of Gastroenterology and Hepatology at URMC, Farmer continued to work for the State Department, splitting his time between Rochester and Washington, DC.

Figure 28.13. Richard Farmer

Under Farmer's guidance, ambulatory visits and endoscopic procedures increased by more than thirty percent. He developed programs in quality assurance and established the "Gut Club," a community-wide outreach to area gastroenterologists hosting more than forty prominent national speakers. In 2008, Farmer recruited Vivek Kaul, MD, from SUNY Upstate Medical University to further develop advanced endoscopic services and to establish new programs in interventional endoscopy. In 2009, Kaul was appointed director of clinical operations for the division and soon thereafter was named division chief and Segal-Watson Professor of Medicine, providing the division with full-time leadership.

Figure 28.14. Vivek Kaul

After earning his MD from Delhi University, Kaul did his IM residency at SUNY-Downstate Medical Center, then completed his gastroenterology fellowship training at Albert Einstein Medical Center in Philadelphia. He also completed an advanced endoscopy fellowship at the Milwaukee Pancreatico-Biliary Center. Kaul's clinical, research, and medical education interests focused on therapeutic endoscopy and endosurgery, interventional endoscopic ultrasound, and advanced endoscopic retrograde cholangiopancreatography, particularly related to Barrett's esophagus and esophageal and pancreatic cancers.

As chief, Kaul helped design and open the Gastroenterology, Hepatology and Endoscopy Center at Sawgrass, and continued to expand clinical and advanced endoscopy services. The division also added an interventional endoscopy suite in the Center for Advanced Therapeutic Endoscopy at SMH that provided state-of-the-art capabilities, such as a confocal laser endomicroscopy system, endoluminal cryoablation therapy, endoscopic ultrasound equipment, and an array of endoscopic technologies to enable advanced pancreatic-biliary endoscopy and care for patients with gastrointestinal cancers. Kaul also bolstered the division by recruiting new faculty members and a skilled group of physician assistants and nurse practitioners, improving access and case management for patients.

Figure 28.15. Mark Levstik

Mark A. Levstik, MD, has served as division chief since 2019, and in 2024 was named as Segal-Watson Professor of Medicine. Levstik obtained his MD from the Royal College of Surgeons in Ireland. He completed a residency in IM, including serving as chief resident at Michigan State University in Grand Rapids, a fellowship in gastroenterology and hepatology at the University of Iowa, and a fellowship in transplant hepatology at the University of Western Ontario in London, Ontario. After several years on the faculty at the University of Tennessee, he was recruited back to the University of Western Ontario's Multi-Organ Transplant Unit, where he served as the president of its Clinical Teachers Association. In 2016, he was recruited to the URMC as professor of both Medicine and Surgery, and as chief of the Comprehensive Liver Center. Levstik has served on numerous national committees and has spoken widely on his work in liver transplantation, with a specific interest in live-donor liver transplantation. His research interests also involve liver transplant quality and non-invasive Liver Fibrosis Measurement (FibroScan). After helping to re-establish transplant hepatology and partnering in the live-donor program development, he turned his attention to building the division, aggressively recruiting faculty and expanding the inflammatory bowel disease (IBD), general gastroenterology, and general hepatology subdivisions.

The division currently has twenty-four faculty and nineteen APPs who run four multidisciplinary care clinics: the Center for Advanced Therapeutic Endoscopy, the Bariatric Endoscopy Program, the Konar Center for Digestive and Liver Disease, and the Center for Inflammatory Bowel Disease. Asad Ullah, MD, has been part of the division for over twenty-five years, where he served as chief of Endoscopy at SMH. Ullah's special interests include advanced endoscopic procedures, pancreaticobiliary diseases, and GI malignancies. Ashok N. Shah, MD, was also a mainstay of the division for over thirty years, recognized for his teaching, clinical acumen, and compassionate patient care. In 2007, he was made a Master of the American College of Gastroenterology (MACG), a rare honor that recognized his stature and achievements in clinical gastroenterology. He retired from clinical practice in 2018 and sadly passed away in 2023 at the age of eighty-four.

The faculty has continually been involved in ongoing research. Lawrence J. Saubermann, MD's work focuses on the intestinal mucosal immune system and how it is involved in IBD, such as Crohn's disease, ulcerative colitis, microscopic/lymphocytic colitis, and celiac sprue. His projects include trials testing new biologic agents and novel serologic markers of disease activity for IBD, and examining the effects of environmental toxins on the mucosal immune system. He is a co-investigator on a longitudinal countywide database study of inflammatory bowel disease subjects. Jonathan Huang, DO, serves as director of the Digestive and Liver Disease Center for Research. His research interests include viral hepatitis, hepatic encephalopathy, autoimmune hepatitis, and hepatobiliary malignancies. In addition, faculty is actively involved in evaluating new endoscopic technologies for a variety of diseases, including fistula closure and per oral endoscopy myotomy (Truptesh H. Kothari, MD), Barrett's esophagus, biliary, and pancreatic diseases (Shivangi T. Kothari, MD).

The clinical research program has grown significantly over the last fifteen years and has enabled URMC to participate in high-profile, federally funded national trials. These include trials in Barrett's and esophageal neoplasia and pancreatic disease (NIH-SHARP). Enrollment is also about to start on a very high-profile Barrett's trial in collaboration with the University of Colorado, funded by a $14 million grant from the National Institute of Diabetes and Digestive and Kidney Diseases.

The division has a long-standing, nationally regarded three-year fellowship in Gastroenterology, which currently accepts four residents per year. The program was pioneered by Arthur J. DeCross, MD, a graduate of the URMC IM residency program. DeCross has also been very involved with educational programs for medical students and medical residents, and serves on several education-related committees of the American Gastroenterological Association. He has received many awards at URMC related to teaching. His primary areas of clinical expertise are in inflammatory bowel diseases, celiac disease, and specialized nutritional support of gastrointestinal disorders. Danielle Marino, MD, a graduate of the division's fellowship in gastroenterology, now oversees the fellowship program.

Geriatrics and Aging

Established as a division in DOM in 2008, Geriatrics and Aging has had a strong national presence for over fifty years. The division asserts that "all roads in geriatrics lead to Rochester," because it has trained or supported the development of so many of the nation's leaders in geriatrics. T. Franklin Williams, MD, was a founding father of geriatric medicine and a mentor for generations of geriatricians and academic leaders. Williams came to Rochester in 1968 as a faculty in DOM and medical director of Monroe Community Hospital (MCH) under a new affiliation agreement between the University and the county. He subsequently became the director of the National Institute on Aging (NIA), serving from 1983 to 1991 before returning to URMC.

Figure 28.16. William Hall

William Hall, MD, came to Rochester in 1971 as a fellow in the Pulmonary Disease unit. He was the founding director of the Center for Healthy Aging, chief of Medicine at RGH, vice chair of DOM and associate dean at SMD. Hall was responsible for developing a comprehensive plan of medical education in geriatrics involving students, residents, fellows, and community physicians. He led the John A. Hartford Center of Excellence, which supports fellows and junior faculty developing careers in academic geriatrics, for over two decades, as well as serving as PI on an NIA-funded T32 training grant. Hall served as president of the American College of Physicians and served on the Board of Directors of AARP. In April 2024, he received the Nascher/Manning Award, the highest honor and lifetime achievement award from the American Geriatrics Society (AGS).

Paul Katz, MD, joined URMC in 1991, serving as medical director at MCH and as chief of Geriatrics at SMD. Katz energized fellowship training in geriatrics and served as director of the region's first federally funded Geriatric Education Center. In 2010, Katz was elected president of the American Medical Directors Association, the premier organization representing long-term care professionals. He left the University in 2010 to become VP of medical services at Baycrest Geriatric Health Care System in Toronto, one of the premier academic health sciences centers focused on aging.

Robert McCann, MD, was chief of Medicine at HH from 1999 to 2022. Under his leadership, HH became regionally and nationally distinguished as a geriatrics center of excellence and an "Age-Friendly Health System." Programs initiated during his tenure include an Acute Care for Elders Unit, a Hospital Elder Life Program (delirium prevention) and the Geriatric Fracture Center at HH and SMH. This innovative program, a co-management model that uses patient-centered, protocol-driven care to standardize the care of older adults with fragility fractures, has been shown to improve outcomes and has been replicated worldwide. McCann also served as the inaugural CEO of AHP.

For many years, geriatric medicine consisted of three distinct divisions (SMD Geriatrics, Highland Geriatrics, MCH), each with its own leader and budget. In keeping with the theme of integration and recognizing the central role geriatrics would play as the health care system developed, it was critical that the divisions be finally united under one roof. That task was given in 2016 to Annette Medina-Walpole, MD, the Paul H. Fine Professor of Medicine. Medina-Walpole came to the University in 1998 after completing her MD at the University of Chicago, a residency and chief residency in IM at the University of North Carolina, and a fellowship in geriatric medicine at the University of Washington. From 2008–14, she served as medical director for the Living Center at Highlands at Pittsford, and from 2014–21 as medical director of MCH. Medina-Walpole, who has served as president and board chair of AGS and led a multi-year initiative for diversity, equity, and inclusion in geriatrics, was the 2016 recipient of the AGS Dennis W. Jahnigen Memorial Public Service Award for her work in furthering geriatric education and in addressing workforce shortages among geriatric health professionals.

Figure 28.17. Annette Medina-Walpole

Today, the integrated division of Geriatrics and Aging serves as the academic home to more than twenty-five core faculty members. Main sites of service include HH, SMH, and MCH; as well as ten skilled nursing and thirty-three senior living facilities. MCH is the largest skilled nursing facility in Rochester with 566 beds, including a twenty-eight-bed rehabilitation unit. Through the University's long-standing affiliation with MCH, the division of Geriatrics has provided medical care to a diverse population with unique and complex care needs, including memory care, respiratory care, and ventilators, and has maintained MCH as a premier teaching nursing home. MCH is home to the division's administrative offices, fellowship program, and the Finger Lakes Geriatric Education Center.

Figure 28.18. Yeates Conwell

Yeates Conwell, MD, is professor of Psychiatry, where he has served as vice chair and director of the division of Geriatric Mental Health and Memory Care, and co-founder of the Center for the Study and Prevention of Suicide. The primary focus of Conwell's research program has been identifying risk factors for suicide in the second half of life, with particular emphasis on the design and implementation of preventive interventions in community settings and their linkage to health care services. Conwell's work established the basis for Psychiatry's tele-mental health program that, under the subsequent leadership of Michael Hasselberg, NP, MS, PhD, has become a national model for provision of statewide geriatric health care delivery. Conwell has lectured and written extensively on suicide and depression in later life, drawing on research that has been continuously funded by the NIH, CDC, and foundations for the past thirty-five years. He has served as president of the American Foundation for Suicide Prevention, and as a consultant to international agencies and centers dedicated to suicide prevention research. In 2012, he was selected as an Innovation Advisor for the Center for Medicare and Medicaid Innovation.

URMC is known for its work in geriatric education. Since 1999, HRSA-funded Geriatric Academic Career Awards (K awards) in interprofessional geriatrics education have been given to nine faculty (Medina-Walpole was one of the inaugural awardees), seven of whom are current division members. Division faculty currently direct and teach in the Foundations in Biopsychosocial Practice course, provide a geriatrics elective, serve as a home institution for the Medical Student Training in Aging Research summer research program, and work with AGS-sponsored Aging Interest Groups. The comprehensive aging theme woven through all four years of the undergraduate medical school curriculum has served as a national model.

The division boasts one of the oldest and most recognized fellowship programs in the country. Most graduates choose academic careers and many have become leaders in the field. The division also plays an important role in training palliative care and geriatric psychiatry fellows, and internal medicine, med-peds, and family medicine residents.

The Finger Lakes Geriatric Education Center (FLGEC) is the largest regional educational initiative at URMC, reaching over 15,000 health professionals and over 5,000 caregivers annually across a thirty-county region of upstate NY. Headed by Thomas Caprio, MD, MPH, and funded by HRSA for decades, its programs range from activities for health professionals and medical students in the initial phases of training, to seasoned professionals pursuing continuing education activities, and to family caregivers. The FLGEC supports distance learning and online training opportunities and has strong partnerships with other academic institutions and community-based organizations and with educational partners across central and western NY. It is now integral to the University of Rochester Aging Institute (see below), assisting in the dissemination of the Age-Friendly Health System initiative.

Research in aging is an excellent example of collaboration throughout the University. One example is Rochester Aging Research (RoAR), which brings together investigators engaged in basic and translational sciences at the University to promote novel research into the mechanisms that promote longevity and extend life and health span by modifying the aging process. The Center is directed by Vera Gorbunova, PhD, Doris Johns Cherry, Professor of Biology, and Andrei Seluanov, PhD (Biology), whose research focuses on the mechanisms of longevity and cancer resistance. Both investigators play a major role in the research programs of the WCI. Other areas of research within the center include regeneration and stem cells, immune responses and vaccination in older adults, oxidative stress in aging and disease, metabolism and aging, and Alzheimer's disease and related dementias.

Another example of collaboration is the Office for Aging Research and Health Service (OARHS). Established by Conwell and colleagues in 2012, OARHS integrates academic, clinical, educational, and community resources to improve health outcomes and patient experience at lower cost for older adults and caregivers. In 2003, OARHS established a unique partnership with Eldersource Care Management Services, Lifespan, and Catholic Family Center. With support from the NIH, CDC, and foundations, this partnership has remained vibrant and has led to improvements that include training community-based agency care managers to detect and do basic management of late-life mental illness, adopting screening for mental disorders in agency clients, and revising the agencies' data management systems to support research. OARHS has developed and tested care models that link lonely and socially disconnected seniors with other caring older adult volunteers in order to reduce the risk of suicide. It also incorporated an integrated care management model into the Memory Care Program to bring the strengths of community aging services into the clinic to address social factors in the care of patients with memory concerns.

The division has also collaborated with investigators in Public Health Sciences to examine how organizational factors and health care policies impact the outcomes of nursing home residents, long-term services and supports recipients, and veterans. They have created a comprehensive database in partnership with the Centers for Medicare & Medicaid Services that allows them to track patients' progress through the disablement process from independent community living, through dependence on community-based long-term services and supports to institutional and end-of-life care.

University of Rochester Aging Institute (URAI)

In recognition of the growing needs of our region's older adult population and the distributed strengths of the institution in geriatric research, training, and clinical care, a comprehensive needs assessment was conducted in 2017 targeting all potential stakeholders in aging and geriatrics throughout the University and the Rochester community. This led to the formation in 2019 of the URAI.

The URAI integrates all existing aging-related strengths and expertise in research, patient care, education and community outreach to empower older adults with knowledge to defy their genetic limits and achieve healthful longevity.

The URAI brings together OARHS and RoAR using a framework for collaboration comprised of three pillars of strength: Vital Discovery (research), Vital Care (patient care and workforce education), and Vital Living (community collaboration and engagement).

Vital Discovery builds an enabling research infrastructure to develop international renown as a leader in aging research; expand federal and foundation funding to promote team science, data science, and multidisciplinary aging studies; discover novel approaches to increase longevity and health span; and translate scientific discovery into innovative approaches to improving patient care and clinical outcomes.

Vital Care increases access to high-quality geriatrics care throughout our region; disseminates geriatrics best practices and models of care across UR Medicine; enhances aging population management; expands regional geriatrics outreach via technology and telehealth; leads the nation in geriatrics workforce development; and transforms UR Medicine into an Age-Friendly Health System.

Vital Living offers evidence-based evaluations and lifestyle interventions that promote vitality in aging; creates new community partnerships that optimize quality of life, engagement, and health; engages older adults as both teachers and learners at the University of Rochester; and empowers older adults to achieve healthful longevity and establish Rochester as a model Age-Friendly Community.

Nephrology

Nephrology has experienced remarkable growth since 1989, when David Bushinsky, MD, was recruited to head a division that consisted of three clinicians, a visiting research fellow, no external grant support, and no chronic dialysis patients. Bushinsky received his MD and completed his residency in IM and fellowship in nephrology at Tufts University. He then went to the University of Chicago, where he initiated studies on the mechanism by which metabolic acids induce physicochemical bone dissolution and cell-mediated bone resorption. He also developed a strain of rodents that exhibit genetic hypercalciuria, the most common metabolic abnormality in humans with nephrolithiasis, and who spontaneously form kidney stones. This internationally recognized research has continued to this day at URMC, where it has been consistently funded by the NIH and has led to more than 350 publications. A member of the American Society for Clinical Investigation and the Association of American Physicians, Bushinsky was named the inaugural John J. Kuiper Distinguished Professor of Medicine, established in 2012 by a generous gift from John Kuiper, MD, in appreciation of residency and fellowship training he received at the University.

Figure 28.19. David Bushinsky

During Bushinsky's tenure, the division increased its faculty to twenty-three. Among them were several outstanding researchers, including Michael Flessner, MD, PhD, who did groundbreaking studies on intestinal ion transport to better understand peritoneal dialysis before leaving to head the Nephrology division at the University of Mississippi; Martin Zand, MD, PhD, who led the clinical nephrology transplant service and developed a nationally recognized research program on B cell vaccine responses and immune desensitization in renal transplantation and who currently directs the CTSI; Keith Nehrke, PhD, who studies mitochondrial regulation of calcium signaling, mitochondrial potassium channels, and cardio-protection; Nancy Krieger, PhD, who studies how kidney disease affects bone cells and bone mineral; and Fahad Saeed, MB, BS, who investigates how patients with chronic kidney disease choose dialysis modality and the ethics of choosing not to be dialyzed. Bushinsky was also instrumental in recruiting George Schwartz, MD, a well-funded clinician scientist who studies proton transport in the kidney, to direct pediatric nephrology. As a result, federal research funding grew from zero to $2.6 million per year.

The clinical operation also welcomed new faculty and APPs. The number of daily nephrology consultations grew to involve approximately ten percent of all inpatients at SMH. Bushinsky also developed collaborations with Fresenius Corporation to build eleven chronic dialysis centers, and with Medina Memorial Hospital to open additional centers throughout the region, making dialysis more convenient for patients with chronic kidney failure.

SMH nephrologists serve as medical directors at each of these centers. As a result, the number of chronic dialysis patients overseen by the division grew to approximately 600 (previously all chronic dialysis patients were referred to nephrologists outside of URMC). Bushinsky also initiated a peritoneal dialysis program that has now grown to over 120 patients.

In keeping with the regional strategy, the division incorporated the HH nephrologists, formerly an independent private practice, under the leadership of Melissa J. Schiff, MD. In addition, URMC nephrologists expanded their practices to cover FF Thompson Hospital and established regional outpatient clinics at several locations. Nephrologists have also been an integral part of URMC's kidney transplant program since its inception, playing a particularly critical role in pre-transplant evaluation and post-transplant care. Over the past twenty-five years, Rufino C. Pabico, MD, Martin Zand, MD, and Jeremy C. Taylor, MD, have served as Transplant directors of Nephrology.

One of Bushinsky's most important accomplishments was the rejuvenation of the nephrology fellowship, which had been on probation at the time he arrived. Since then, the two-year fellowship has grown to three fellows per year and attracts outstanding candidates. Several subsequently joined the faculty, including Rebeca D. Monk, MD, currently chief of IM at HH; Sai S. Reddy, MD, clinical director and currently interim chief of Nephrology; and Richard E. Wing, MD, who heads the division's APP services.

In October 2018, after almost thirty years of heading the Nephrology division, Bushinsky stepped down as chief, remaining at URMC as an active clinician/scientist. Thu Le, MD, was recruited from the University of Virginia as the next John J. Kuiper Distinguished Professor of Medicine and chief of Nephrology. Le received her MD from George Washington University School of Medicine and did her residency in IM and fellowship in nephrology at Duke University. At Virginia, Le developed a prominent research program investigating renal mechanisms and genetic determinants of hypertension and kidney disease progression.

Figure 28.20. Thu Le

Under Le's leadership, the division continued to prosper. It grew to thirty-three faculty, with thirty-six percent female, and the number of APPs grew to fifteen. Le recruited several outstanding scientists, including Dean Johnson, PhD, who has been involved in developing a novel sheet-membrane dialyzer for wearable dialysis; Jing (Jason) Wu, PhD, who focuses on renal hemodynamic mechanisms in hypertension and chronic kidney disease; Yumei Feng Earley, PhD, who studies neural and molecular mechanisms regulating blood pressure and metabolism; and most recently, Rebecca

Levy, MD, who investigates risk factors for inequities in health outcomes in adolescents and young adults with kidney disease. As a result of these recruitments, total grant funding for the division had grown to $4.1 million at the end of 2024. Please see the division website for the details on each of the individual research programs.

Nephrology also assumed medical directorship for three additional dialysis units in the region, thereby increasing outpatient dialysis volume to 750 patients. Most recently, a dialysis unit was established at St. John's Nursing Home to provide hemodialysis for end-stage renal disease patients in need of skilled nursing care. In April 2025, Le left to become chair of DOM at the University of California, Davis, a testament to her extraordinary achievements as chief of Nephrology at URMC. Sai Reddy, a former URMC IM resident and nephrology fellow, was chosen as interim chief of Nephrology.

Palliative Care

One of the medical hallmarks of the past twenty-five years has been the emergence of palliative care. Outpatient, home-based, and inpatient palliative care services began at SMH and HH in 2001. The Palliative Care Service at SMH resided in the Center for Ethics, Humanities, and Palliative Care, a division of SMD. In 2009, palliative care was recognized as a subspecialty by the American Board of Medical Specialties and shortly thereafter, palliative care became a new division in DOM. At the time, the division had more than twenty palliative care specialists conducting more than 1,000 inpatient consultations per year and several hundred outpatient consultations. That same year, SMH opened the Albert and Phyllis Sussman Palliative Care Unit, which included twelve private rooms able to accommodate a family member overnight.

Leading the palliative efforts at SMH was Timothy E. Quill, MD. Quill earned his MD, did his residency in primary care IM, and also a fellowship

Figure 28.21. Albert and Phyllis Sussman Palliative Care Unit

in advanced biopsychosocial studies at URMC. As a member of the faculty in Medicine, Psychiatry, Medical Humanities, and Nursing, he developed an international reputation as a pioneer in palliative care and end-of-life decision-making. Quill was founding director of the SMH Palliative Care Service, the first chief of Palliative Care, and a president of the American Academy of Hospice and Palliative Medicine, which in 2013 included him in their list of "Hospice and Palliative Medicine Visionaries", and honored him in 2018 with their Lifetime Achievement Award. Quill is author of over 200 publications and five books, including *Voluntarily Stopping Eating and Drinking: A Compassionate, Widely Available Option for Hastening Death* released in 2021 by Oxford University Press. In 2012, he became the inaugural recipient of the Georgia and Thomas Gosnell Distinguished Professorship in Palliative Care. Through his efforts, the SMH program was the first to receive Advanced Certification in Palliative Care from the Joint Commission in 2011.

Figure 28.22. Timothy Quill

Upon stepping down in 2015 as the leader of the palliative care program, Quill was succeeded as chief and Georgia and Thomas Gosnell Distinguished Professor in Palliative Care by Robert Horowitz, MD. Horowitz received his MD and did his residency in IM at URMC. Horowitz's initial endeavors were in the areas of health services, emergency medicine, and cystic fibrosis, serving as medical director of Rochester's Adult Cystic Fibrosis Program from 1999 until 2015. He joined the Palliative Care Program in 2010, serving as its clinical director. A valued educator and respected mentor, he also directed SMD's comprehensive assessments of communication skills, medical knowledge, and professionalism.

Figure 28.23. Robert Horowitz

Horowitz continued to grow the palliative care program at SMH, which now sees 2,000 inpatients and 1,000 outpatients each year. He also helped establish the multidisciplinary Palliative Care Research Center, directed by Benzi M. Kluger, MD. Horowitz also created the first palliative care-based ketamine-assisted psychotherapy program, which provides psychotherapy around serious illness anxieties and existential distress.

Horowitz established the first palliative care team at FF Thompson under the direction of Cheryl Williams, MD, PhD. In 2016, he helped transition the pediatric palliative care program, which had been growing within the DOM's Palliative Care division, to a separate division within Pediatrics, with David N. Korones, MD, as its chief. Pediatric Palliative Care continues to grow, with the formation of the Perinatal Supportive Care program, under the direction of Erin M. Denney-Koelsch, MD, and the GCH bereavement program.

The Palliative Care Service at HH, which received its Advanced Certification in Palliative Care in 2013, was established as a distinct program headed by Daniel A. Mendelson, MD. Mendelson received his MD, did his residency in IM, and his fellowship in geriatrics at URMC. In 2016, he became the inaugural William and Sheila Konar Family Professor in Geriatrics and Palliative Care. He was succeeded as head of Palliative Care Services at HH in 2018 by Chin-Lin Ching, MD, who also received her MD and did her residency in IM at URMC. Under her tenure, HH established a six-bed palliative care unit, a pain service, and a telehealth-based inpatient consultation service for the affiliated regional hospitals in the Southern Tier. For her contributions, Ching received HH's Physician of the Year Award in 2024.

Figure 28.24. Daniel Mendelson

When Horowitz stepped down as division chief in 2023, Erin Denney-Koelsch became interim chief. Denney-Koelsch received her MD at the University of Rochester and remained there as a resident in medicine/pediatrics and as one of the first fellows in hospice and palliative care, before joining the division as faculty. In 2024, Denney-Koelsch oversaw the integration of the SMH, FF Thompson, and HH palliative care programs. This has led to a remarkable increase in collaboration in clinical, educational, research, and quality improvement programs, and has significantly strengthened the telehealth palliative care services being provided to URMC's Southern Tier affiliates. The division is currently working to expand services to Geneva General and to provide in-person presence in the Southern Tier.

The division has been a national leader in palliative care education. Shortly after joining the DOM, the division initiated a one-year fellowship in hospice and palliative medicine, which now accepts four fellows per year. The fellowship offers a pediatric track for pediatricians, Med-Peds, or family physicians; a geriatric track for those doing both geriatrics and palliative care fellowships; and a neuropalliative track for those completing a neurology residency.

The division also oversees a two-week clinical palliative care rotation that emphasizes care of hospitalized seriously ill patients and is mandatory for IM and Med-Peds residents. A similar two-week immersive rotation is available as an elective to third- and fourth-year medical students, who receive palliative care education throughout all four years of training. The SON also offers a hospice and palliative care elective and has integrated palliative care and end-of-life content into the undergraduate and graduate nursing curricula. In addition, Horowitz and Thomas Carroll, MD, have established the advanced communication training program, a popular, interactive workshop on serious illness conversations that has trained over 550 interdisciplinary clinicians across the institution.

Pulmonary and Critical Care Medicine (PCCM)

PCCM can trace its origins to 1968 with the recruitment of Richard W. Hyde, MD, from the University of Pennsylvania to establish and serve as medical director of what was initially known as the Respiratory Therapy department. Hyde fostered a strong foundation of excellence in teaching, research, and patient care, which continues to this day. Over the past five decades, the division has grown to include forty-one faculty members and twenty-eight nurse practitioners, and has expanded to include Critical Care Medicine. Shepherding the remarkable growth of PCCM over the past twenty-five years has been a series of outstanding clinician scientists.

Mark Utell, MD, became chief of PCCM in 1984. Utell received his MD and did his residency in IM at Tufts University and his fellowship in pulmonary medicine at URMC prior to joining the faculty. At the University, he and his colleagues established a nationally recognized program examining the effects of inhaled occupational and environmental toxicants on the human respiratory system. From 1988–2020, Utell served as founding director of the Occupational and Environmental Medicine program. He also served as acting chair of DOM from 1998–9. He is a fellow of the AAAS and a recipient of the Thomas T. Mercer Award from the International Society for Aerosols in Medicine. Under Utell's direction, the division took over responsibility for the Medical ICU, such that all patients were managed by full-time intensivists rather than their PCPs. Accordingly, the name of the division was changed to Pulmonary and Critical Care. He also developed a division of PCCM at HH, established the University of Rochester Sleep Center, which now has locations in Rochester, Brockport, and Canandaigua, and inaugurated the Mary M. Parkes Center for Asthma, Allergy, and Pulmonary Care.

Figure 28.25. Mark Utell

Steve N. Georas, MD, received his MD from Brown University and did his residency in IM and fellowship in pulmonary and critical care medicine at Johns Hopkins, where he subsequently joined the faculty. At Johns Hopkins, he established a well-funded, nationally

Figure 28.26. Steve Georas

recognized program in mechanisms of immune cell activation in the lung, leading to his recruitment as chief of PCCM in 2006 to succeed Utell, who had held the position for twenty-two years. Georas stepped down as chief in 2010 to devote full-time to his highly productive research efforts. In 2017, he became the inaugural Walter & Carmina Mary Parkes Family Distinguished Professor, another example of the Parkes family's philanthropy (see below).

Patricia J. Sime, MD, FRCP, received her MD from the University of Edinburgh, Scotland, where she remained for her residency and fellowship before traveling to McMaster University, Ontario, Canada, to do postdoctoral training in inflammatory and scarring lung diseases. In 1999, she was recruited to URMC, where she established an internationally recognized research program focused on lung inflammation and fibrosis, leading to her election as a fellow of the College of Physicians, a fellow of the Royal College of Physicians (one of the youngest ever), and of the American Society of Clinical Investigation. Prior to her being appointed as chief, Sime had served as vice chair for research for DOM. In 2012, she became the inaugural C. Jane Davis & C. Robert Davis Distinguished Professor in Pulmonary Medicine, funded by a generous gift from Jane Davis, MD, in memory of her late brother, Bob Davis. In 2019, Sime became chair of DOM at Virginia Commonwealth University in Richmond, Virginia.

Figure 28.27. Patricia Sime

In 2022, Patricia Rivera, MD, was recruited from the University of North Carolina (UNC), Chapel Hill to be the C. Jane Davis & C. Robert Davis Distinguished Professor in Pulmonary Medicine, chief of PCCM, and associate director of DEI for WCI. Rivera received her MD from SUNY at Stony Brook, did her residency in IM at North Shore University Hospital-Manhasset, NY, and her fellowship in pulmonary diseases at MSKCC. Prior to joining URMC, she was a professor of medicine at UNC, where she served as co-director of the fellowship program, and director of the Pulmonary Function Test and Bronchoscopy Labs. At UNC, Rivera had developed a prominent research program focused on lung cancer screening. Rivera recently served as president of the American Thoracic Society. She was instrumental in the WCI's successful NCI designation.

Figure 28.28. Patricia Rivera

PCCM oversees inpatient and outpatient services at SMH, HH, and FF Thompson. In recent years, the division has developed specialty programs to address patient care and optimize clinical research. The Mary M. Parkes

Center for Asthma, Allergy, and Pulmonary Care was established in 1995 by Walter Parkes in honor of his daughter Mary, an intensive care nurse whose long battle with asthma ended with her death in 1991. Since its inception, the Center's mission has been to promote the diagnosis, treatment, and research of asthma, allergies, and other pulmonary diseases, and to serve as the region's most comprehensive site for asthma care. Currently led by Sandhya Khurana, MD, and Georas, the center takes a holistic approach to patients and their families, and offers a wide array of services and numerous clinical trials of new therapeutics, including biologics. The center also houses the outpatient allergy clinic of URMC and the Pulmonary Hypertension Center.

The Pulmonary Hypertension program has expanded significantly over the past twenty-five years, driven by a deeper understanding of pathophysiology, enhanced clinical testing, and the advent of new therapeutic options. Under the leadership of R. James White, MD, PhD, the program has examined the role of tissue factor and thrombin signaling in the onset of pulmonary hypertension and has been a center for clinical trials of new therapies, the use of pulmonary rehabilitation, and the use of wearable digital devices for remote monitoring. White played an important role in multicenter clinical trials of tadalafil and oral Treprostinil, which helped pave the way for FDA drug approval.

In 2015, the University became the only institution in upstate NY to receive the distinction as a Pulmonary Fibrosis Foundation's Care Center Network (PFF-CCN) site. This multidisciplinary center, led by Robert M. Kottman, MD, includes faculty in pulmonary, radiology, and pathology, and offers a variety of clinical and therapeutic trials for people with scarring/fibrotic lung disease. As an added distinction, the URMC sarcoidosis program recently received designation as a comprehensive center of excellence by the World Association for Sarcoidosis and Other Granulomatous Disorders. Kottman and David J. Nagel, MD, PhD, are conducting fundamental research on the role of dysregulated cellular metabolism in lung fibroblasts and epithelial cells in pulmonary fibrosis.

In 2025, through the efforts of Alexandra C. Adams, MD, and Sonal S. Munsiff, MD (Infectious Diseases), the URMC Bronchiectasis Program was selected as one of thirty-three centers in the US as part of a Clinical Associate Bronchiectasis and Non-tuberculous Mycobacteria network, which is creating a national registry of patients and developing standards of care that can reduce diagnosis time, ensure state-of-the-art treatment, and improve outcomes.

The division offers a three-year, combined fellowship program in pulmonary and critical care medicine, which has expanded over the years to six fellows per year. Clinical rotations include the ICUs at SMH, HH, and FF Thompson. The division also offers a two-year fellowship in Critical Care for those who intend to practice critical care apart from pulmonary medicine. The division has one of the University's most long-standing (continuously funded for approximately fifty years) training grants, the NIH-funded T32 *Multidisciplinary Training in Lung Biology and Pulmonary Medicine* (directed by Georas and Michael O'Reilly, PhD). This T32 supports four predoctoral graduate students and three postdoctoral fellows annually, allowing pulmonary fellows the opportunity for additional research years mentored by a multidisciplinary faculty from departments throughout the Medical Center. More than half of the pulmonary fellows remain in academic medicine. The division also plays an important role in teaching residents and medical students who rotate through the medical ICU and medical and intensive progressive care unit at SMH, as well as in the ICUs at HH and FF Thompson.

In keeping with the marked growth of APPs within the Medical Center, the division also offers an APP fellowship program in critical care medicine at SMH. This twelve-month, postgraduate specialty training program for Nurse Practitioners and Physician Assistants includes side-by-side education with the critical care fellowship and specialty rotations in the cardiovascular, burn and trauma, surgical, neuromedicine, and medical ICUs.

PCCM has been a leader in basic, translational, and clinical research since its inception and enjoys a long history of fruitful collaborations with other departments and centers that has led to substantial extramural funding from federal and other sources. Some of the major programs are outlined in the following paragraphs. Full details about these research programs are available on the division's website.

The effects of airborne toxicants on human health have been a focus of research at the University dating to the 1940s, leading to a long-standing collaboration between investigators in PCCM and Environmental Sciences that has enabled URMC to maintain a state-of-the-art Inhalation Exposure Facility and to receive a Particulate Matter Center Grant from the Environmental Protection Agency that has supported research on how airborne agents, such as ultrafine particles and gaseous pollutants, contribute to potential human health risks. Studies led by Mark Utell, Günter Oberdörster, DVM, PhD, and Mark W. Frampton, MD, have influenced national ambient air quality standards, shaped our understanding of the effects of changes in these regulations on human health, and illuminated the relationship between specific pollutants and the mechanisms of lung disease.

Rivera's recruitment has also placed URMC in the forefront of lung cancer screening (LCS). Using a comprehensive NIH/NCI-funded North Carolina lung screening registry, Rivera collaborates with colleagues at UNC to examine LCS implementation and quantify outcomes. Their work also focuses on identifying the downstream consequences of screening and evaluating the cumulative risk and multilevel impacts of false positive findings on LCS exams. Rivera has also developed a URMC LCS registry that harmonizes with the North Carolina registry and is working with the WCI Technology & Innovation Group to develop and test an automated technology workflow to abstract data to the URMC registry. Michael A. Nead, MD, PhD, is leading clinical trials to develop and validate new screening and diagnostic tools, including a multianalyte assay for lung cancer prediction, a cancer screening assay, and a proteomic classifier, which aim to enhance the management of pulmonary nodules and early lung cancer detection. He has developed a comprehensive Interventional Pulmonary program designed to improve diagnostic yield and to treat lesions previously thought inaccessible.

Steve Georas has conducted NIH-funded asthma research for more than thirty years, studying airway epithelial barrier dysfunction caused by respiratory viruses and environmental pollutants. Since 2018, he has chaired the Steering Committee of the NIH-funded PrecISE Network, which investigates novel interventions in individuals with severe and exacerbation-prone asthma. Georas also directs the Study of Asthma in Rochester (SOAR2), which enrolls adult asthma patients who have frequent exacerbations in a prospective registry, with the goal of identifying new treatments. Sandhya Khurana conducts clinical trials of new biologics targeting immune mechanisms linked to asthma and other airway diseases.

Twenty years ago, Anthony P. Pietropaoli, MD, launched a cohort study as the clinical arm of team-based translational research into the mechanisms of sepsis, acute lung injury, and other critical illnesses. The cohort, which now contains over 750 research subjects, has fueled numerous collaborations at the University and has enabled PCCM to play an important role in the Critical Illness Outcomes Study, a nationwide cohort study involving over 6,000 patients in sixty-nine ICUs that examines the long-term effects of critical illness, focusing on health care utilization, mortality, and the impact on various aspects of life after discharge.

Chapter 29

DEPARTMENT OF DERMATOLOGY

Dermatology was first established as a division of DOM in 1981, driven in large part by community dermatologists who lobbied SMD to establish an academic division that could provide educational programs. Lowell Goldsmith, MD, an international leader in the genetics and biochemistry of skin diseases, was recruited from Duke University to become the founding chief. At the time, Goldsmith was working on a landmark two-volume set, *Biochemistry and Physiology of the Skin*. When published in 1983, a review in *The New England Journal of Medicine* called it an "astonishing book ... a comprehensive, up-to-date, multi-authored yet consistent review of all of experimental dermatology ..."

Figure 29.1. Lowell Goldsmith

Goldsmith's initial goals were to establish a division large enough to train residents in dermatology and provide the full range of dermatologic subspecialties. The residency program started with three residents. To support their training, Goldsmith hired community dermatologists as part-time faculty and recruited many outstanding faculty from other institutions. Glynis A. Scott, MD, joined as the first dermatopathologist, and Marc D. Brown, MD, as the first Mohs surgeon. Goldsmith's stature allowed him to hire talented faculty who would later become chairs of dermatology: Alfred Lane, MD, a pediatric dermatologist, later became chair at Stanford; Janet A. Fairley, MD, a general dermatologist and researcher, became chair at the University of Iowa; Anthony A. Gaspari, MD, a dermatologist nationally recognized for his work in allergic contact dermatitis, became chair at the University of Maryland.

For decades, dermatology was taught using Kodachrome slides. With digital projection becoming the medium of choice, Goldsmith and Art Papier, MD, supported by the NIH, worked with the creators of the larger and best-characterized Kodachrome collections to create a complete digital image database. They collaborated with dermatologists across the nation to develop a consensus lexicon, which enabled the database to be readily searched and greatly improved its utility for diagnosis, teaching, and skin disease management. Today, the collection is available throughout the country and sets the standard for digital representation and education about skin diseases. Papier and Goldsmith started the company VisualDx to ensure the success of this project.

When the chair of DOM left in 1994, Goldsmith was invited to serve as interim chair. He consented, contingent on SMD promising to elevate Dermatology to an independent department. Goldsmith was named the first chair of Dermatology, retroactive to 1987. In 1996, Goldsmith relinquished his chairmanship to become dean of SMD, a position he held until 2000. Following his deanship, Goldsmith earned an MPH at the University of Rochester and then became clinical professor of Dermatology at the University of North Carolina School of Medicine, Chapel Hill. In 2019, Goldsmith and his wife, Carol, established the Carol A. & Lowell A. Goldsmith Professorship in Dermatology at the University of Rochester. He passed away in North Carolina in 2024 at the age of eighty-six.

Figure 29.2. Alice Pentland

Alice P. Pentland, MD, succeeded Goldsmith as the second Dermatology chair in 1996 and continues in that role. Pentland received her MD from the University of Michigan. After completing an internship in internal medicine at the University of North Carolina, she returned to the University of Michigan for a dermatology residency and fellowship. She subsequently did a fellowship in clinical pharmacology at Washington University School of Medicine, St. Louis. Pentland specializes in the treatment of bullous diseases, such as pemphigus and bullous pemphigoid. She has served as president of the Society for Investigative Dermatology, as secretary-treasurer of the International Society of Investigative Dermatology, and as president of the American Professors of Dermatology. She received a Lifetime Achievement Award in 2005 from the Medical Dermatology Society.

When Pentland became chair, all medical records were on paper, and business was conducted by fixed location phones. Pentland was determined to bring dermatology into the digital age. With Dean Goldsmith's support, she and Philippe Fauchet, PhD, chair of Electrical Engineering, founded the Center for Future Health (CFH), in collaboration with MIT's Media Lab and Georgia Institute of Technology. Modeled after the Media Lab, the CFH focused on integrating the internet, digital imaging and wireless communication to support access to health care across the entire spectrum and to create affordable, easy-to-use "smart health tools" for use by consumers in their homes. The CFH, which was housed in Dermatology, was organized into four multidisciplinary consortia: Aging Well, Healthy Skin, Pathogen

Detection, and Developing Nations and Underserved Communities. Its major accomplishments included the Smart Medical Home, biosensors (smart bandage), a medication advisor prototype, an object location system (memory aid), and a skin cancer detection system. An exhibit at Epcot Center demonstrated the smart home concept. The CFH stopped operation once the concepts became commonplace.

The CFH left a legacy of interdisciplinary research teams, with strong ties to faculty in the departments of Chemistry, Optics, and the Hajim School of Engineering, and with a focus on improving sensing and detection. Benjamin L. Miller, PhD, joined the department in 2002. Miller received a PhD in organic chemistry at Stanford University and did a postdoctoral fellowship with Stuart L. Schreiber, PhD, in the department of Chemistry at Harvard University, where he worked on the design, synthesis, and evaluation of structure-based, nonpeptide combinatorial libraries for binding to SRC Homology 3 domains. Miller's interests in combinatorial chemistry, photonic sensors, and dermatology led him to build tissues on a chip, which can directionally sense cytokine secretion in a microfluidic apparatus from multi-cell type tissue *in vitro.* A prolific researcher, he has been inducted as a fellow of the National Academy of Inventors, Optical Society of America, American Institute of Medical and Biomedical Engineering, and AAAS. A Dean's Professor of Dermatology, he also has appointments in Optics, Biomedical Engineering, and Biochemistry and Biophysics, and is cherished by his students as an outstanding mentor.

Figure 29.3. Benjamin Miller

When Pentland became chair, the department consisted of four clinical dermatology faculty—two PhD researchers and one MD splitting research and clinical work. Over the next ten years, the faculty grew to fourteen, including five conducting research. To address this growth and to increase patient access, new clinical sites were added in Batavia and at Red Creek, in Henrietta. The Red Creek clinic accommodated a second Mohs surgeon, Sherrif F. Ibrahim, MD, PhD, and a state-of-the-art phototherapy unit. It also facilitated collaboration with Rheumatology, which was located at the same facility. Francisco Tausk, MD, worked with Chris Ritchlin, MD (Allergy, Immunology, and Rheumatology), to establish a nationally unique Psoriasis Center, which focuses on in-person management of psoriasis and psoriatic arthritis, and assures that treatment decisions affecting the skin and joints are fully coordinated. The Center has also facilitated NIH-funded research.

Lisa A. Beck, MD, was recruited from Johns Hopkins in 2006. Beck received her MD from SUNY at Stony Brook, completed a residency in internal medicine at URMC, a residency in dermatology at Duke University, and an immunology research fellowship at Johns Hopkins. Beck's major clinical and research interest has been ectopic dermatitis, or eczema. Through her efforts, in 2012, the University became one of four major ADRN (Atopic Dermatitis Research Network) centers in the US supported by NIH, and the home of the sample biorepository. The ADRN was established in 2004 as a consortium of academic medical centers that conduct clinical research studies to learn more about ectopic dermatitis. A key component of the ADRN is the Dermatology Clinical Trials Unit, which has completed more than fifteen clinical atopic dermatitis registry, mechanistic, and interventional trials. Beck's research was instrumental in developing dupilumab (Dupixent®), the first biologic drug for the treatment of adults with moderate to severe eczema. She was the lead author of a 2014 *New England Journal of Medicine* article that set the stage for the FDA approval of dupilumab in March 2017. She is co-director of the URMC Center for Allergic Disease Research, which was recently chosen as one of four US centers designated as World Allergy Organization Centers of Excellence. In 2019, she became the inaugural Lowell Goldsmith Professor of Dermatology.

Figure 29.4. Lisa Beck

The reputation of its specialty programs and the development of the UR Medicine network has necessitated continued growth (the faculty has expanded to twenty-four), new clinic sites, and novel approaches to providing dermatology services throughout the region. In 2019, the department opened an 18,000 square-foot clinic at College Town, custom-built to enable five dermatology/dermatologic surgery clinics to run simultaneously, and to house cosmetic dermatology, dermatopathology, and the clinical research center. Its location proximal to SMH enables faculty, residents, and fellows to see inpatients for consultation, and facilitates processing specimens from clinical research activities. The department has also increased its presence in the VA clinic, expanding from a half-day per week to three days per week.

At the turn of the century, there were seven dermatology residents. The growth in faculty and space has enabled the program to expand to fifteen residents and to develop fellowships in Mohs surgery and dermatopathology. Most residents go on for subspecialty training. In 2019, the department launched a two-year NP training program based heavily on the existing residency curriculum; it includes joint conferences and morning rounds with the residents and provides NPs with extraordinary expertise in dermatology.

The catchment area for dermatologic services has continued to grow, extending to Oswego in the east and down to the Pennsylvania border. To facilitate care for this large, underserved area, the department has instituted an eConsult program, a natural outgrowth of the former CFH. When patients present skin concerns to their PCP, relevant photographs and important background information are sent to a dermatologist, who develops a treatment plan and discusses it with the PCP. In eighty percent of cases, the PCP can handle the case without the patient seeing a dermatologist. If something appears urgent, the patients are referred immediately for biopsy, initiation of aggressive therapy, or admission. The referring PCPs have called eConsults a "game-changer," enabling them to provide quality care to patients in areas that do not have practicing dermatologists and teaching them more about dermatology. This program is expected to grow in the coming years, enabling patients throughout western NY to receive state-of-the-art dermatologic services.

Part II

MAINTAINING URMC'S LEADERSHIP IN EDUCATION

Chapter 30

CREATING A COMPREHENSIVE LEARNING ENVIRONMENT

Although always identified as an innovative educational institution, URMC has felt mounting pressure to substantially transform health professions education in response to the changing landscape of health care delivery. This has required a reimagining of what it means to be a learning organization and, more importantly, ensuring that the Medical Center provides a comprehensive learning environment for health professions students, trainees, the general workforce, patients and their families, and other learners and stakeholders across the region.

URMC, like most academic medical centers, evolved organically with distinct educational entities that had curricula that were appropriate and often innovative for each entity, but with little integration or cross-pollination. The past twenty-five years have been characterized by the evolution of collaborative care delivery models and approaches to team science. Technology, as a disruptor, has changed practice flow and connectivity. Accountability metrics have been increasingly imposed on health care providers. These changes led to a shift towards competency-based education and measurement and have challenged academic institutions to rethink the way they teach and communicate within teams. By aligning educational development and delivery with the transformative changes in health care, it could be possible to close the gap between education and practice, leveraging work as learning and learning as inseparable from operations. This required structural reorganization, an evolution in the definition of learning environment, and the evaluation of education as a mechanism for and strategic partner in better patient care.

As URMC began the metamorphosis of its education systems, several institutional features helped steer how it responded to these issues. URMC's organizational structure integrated its educational entities, research programs, and clinical care delivery system under a single chief executive, who in 2015 also assumed the role of SMD dean. This integration was enabled by the fact that all URMC entities were divisions of the University and strengthened by the physical connection with the River Campus.

SMD and the SON boasted distinguished histories of curricular innovation, as had some of the residency programs. The "biopsychosocial model," developed by George Engel, MD, and John Romano, MD, centered on the interrelationships of biological, behavioral, psychological, and social forces in human health and illness. The model has informed generations of URMC-trained physicians and had a profound impact on SMD's Double Helix Curriculum (see chapter 33). The SON's "unification model" integrated nursing education, clinical practice, and applied research, and was an important step in the development of the NP model. These innovations heralded a paradigm shift, facilitating more interdisciplinary collaboration and respect between medicine and nursing, and elevating the stature of health professions. The patient- and family-centered care (PFCC) initiative established in 2010 served as a further stimulus to developing broad, interprofessional educational initiatives.

Building on these elements and history, URMC moved to further align the health care and education missions. Initial discussions around learning environments in 2011 led to a centralized education infrastructure to support a Medical Center-wide simulation center. Until then, URMC's simulation-based facilities and training had been scattered among twenty-two different departments and schools—duplicating the administrative resources needed to develop programs and maintain equipment. Additionally, there was limited sharing of resources or knowledge, resulting in minimal interprofessional practice as well as low utilization rates of space, equipment, and staff.

The move to centralize simulation inspired novel conversations among clinical departments, the SON, and SMD. These interprofessional discussions around shared simulation needs spurred broader conversations around the learning environment. A guiding vision was established of URMC as a dynamic learning organization, built with a systems thinking approach, team learning, and a shared commitment to personal mastery. Emerging from this education strategic planning process was the creation of two key infrastructures that redefined the learning environment: the Institute for Innovative Education (IIE) and Center for Experiential Learning (CEL).

The IIE was developed initially as a board of URMC's educational leaders, who were charged with addressing the following challenges for all educational programs across the system: 1) broadly incorporating new technology in practice and in educational delivery; 2) implementing team training for collaborative practice; 3) developing new curricula that address quality and safety, health economics, and systems training; 4) fostering expertise in informatics, educating the next generation on how to use "big data;" 5) developing and implementing translational research; and 6) extending the biopsychosocial model to teach all URMC providers the art and science of this hallmark philosophy. The IIE board implemented the first "global" strategic plan focused on learning across URMC and designed to advance the science and delivery of health care (specifically focused on quality and safety), emphasize the training and delivery of exceptional patient- and family-centered care, promote excellence in innovation, and help attract and develop a diverse workforce.

The CEL was created to implement the IIE's strategic vision and support SMD, the SON, postgraduate training, and continuing professional development. The offices of Educational Resources and Continuing Professional Education were merged, allowing capital and human resources to be pooled towards this new vision. Within the first two years, the CEL also absorbed hospital media services and grew the simulation program with dedicated central staff.

Sarah E. Peyre, EdD, has been the driving force behind the CEL and an educational innovation leader at URMC. Peyre received her EdD in educational psychology from the University of Southern California. She was recruited in 2011 from Brigham and Women's Hospital, Boston, where she served as the director of education and research for the STRATUS Center for Medical Simulation. Although Peyre's initial role was to develop programs within Surgery, she was quickly recruited by Dean Taubman to develop the CEL and serve as the executive director of the IIE, and subsequently appointed as associate dean for Innovative Education at SMD and the SON. In 2014, she was named a Macy Faculty Scholar, a prestigious award given to promising educators in medicine and nursing. Her project focused on identifying, developing, and teaching best practices for integrating electronic medical records into PFCC. In 2020, Peyre became the dean of the University's Warner School of Education and Human Development, although she remained actively involved in health education at URMC. After serving as interim University provost from April 2021 to July 2022, she returned to the deanship of the Warner School, where she helped develop the Warner 2030 Strategic Plan, launched the Office of Research and the Office of Student Success, established the Warner Council for Equity, Diversity, and Inclusion, and developed several new academic programs. In July 2024, she returned to URMC as COO and vice dean for Education at SMD.

Figure 30.1. Sarah Peyre

The CEL has grown beyond simulation to include continuing medical education (CME), symposium and event planning, media support, online learning support, and classroom technology support. The Miner Library, which was undergoing its own digital transformation and evolving its role in the learning environment, was also brought under the umbrella of the CEL. Annually, the CEL provides resources for more than 40,000 educational events and programs throughout URMC. The CEL's educational resources have proven essential for accommodating shifts in instructional delivery and learning, e.g. providing technical and/or instructional support to help faculty evolve their teaching styles, which was critical as the University responded to the COVID-19 pandemic.

In 2013, the CME office, which had previously been part of the Office of Academic Affairs, joined the CEL so that its activities could be facilitated in conjunction with broader educational initiatives. This included the integration of national curricula such as TeamSTEPPS and the Institute for Health Improvement education platform to drive URMC's evolving faculty development curriculum.

The educational activities sponsored by the IIE and CEL have been supported and validated by several grant and award agencies such as the Macy Faculty Scholar Program, the National Center for Interprofessional Practice and Education (Incubator site, Nexus Award, Accelerating Interprofessional Community Based Education and Practice Grant), ACGME Pursuing Excellence Innovator Grant, and curriculum recognition through the AAMC.

In the CEL, education specialists drive decisions around infrastructure and programming, while investments in staff development changed the conversation around space and services. This helped create a culture that embraces a broad definition of the learning environment within a complex academic medical center and a stable foundation and mechanism for collaborative curriculum development that brings innovation in education throughout URMC.

The learning environment is, at its core, comprised of people who must be supported in their educational endeavors and be provided with opportunities, laterally and longitudinally. The past twenty-five years has been marked by an evolution in understanding who our learners are and identifying faculty or facilitators to match their learning needs. Further, it has shifted to a broader emphasis on interprofessional practice and co-involvement in the clinics and the community to foster patient and family involvement, fully engaged care, and cultivation of health. Each of URMC's "traditional" educational entities has been involved in this process, fostering innovation, harnessing learning theory into curriculum design, and creating educational service models designed to bring about impactful change.

Chapter 31

THE EDWARD G. MINER LIBRARY

The Edward G. Miner Library occupies a central place in the history of the Medical Center. The first medical library was opened in the Research Laboratory in 1922 and moved to the new SMD in 1925. On December 19, 1952, it was named after Edward G. Miner, who had served for more than forty years as a member of the University of Rochester's Board of Trustees, had been chair of the University Library Committee since 1931, and had been instrumental in the acquisition of many important collections and rare books.

Miner has always served as a hub for academic activities at URMC, particularly for students, who use it not only as a source for information, but as a gathering place for study and discussion. Like most other major medical libraries, Miner has undergone a substantial transformation, beginning with the transition of research literature citation searches from print to electronic in the late 1990s, followed by a similar transition of textbooks and full text of journal articles in the first decade of the 2000s. In 2000, the library had exhausted space to shelve its ever-growing collection of print books and journals, necessitating the transfer of older materials to offsite storage; by 2010, this trend had reversed, as print journal subscriptions were canceled in favor of their electronic counterparts. Priorities in physical library spaces transitioned from book storage to study and collaboration space. Bookshelves were gradually removed from the main floor to make way for computer workstations, classrooms, group study rooms, and general collaboration space. Table 31.1 illustrates the remarkable changes in volumes.

The transition from print to electronic collections drove a shift in the way people conceptualized the library: in addition to being a place for information, the library became a suite of services that could be engaged directly from the clinic, laboratory, or office. A new librarian service model focusing on outreach, The Liaison Librarian program, was launched in 2003, which included a "housecalls" service. Librarians were assigned to specific departments to build relationships and share information about specific resources, tools, and services most relevant to each department. Today, Miner librarians are integrated across educational, clinical, and research

Table 31.1

	2000	2024
In-house print collections storage	Insufficient space	Empty shelves
Offsite storage	Yes	No
Print books	58,784	18,575
e-Books	61	>94,000
Currently subscribed print journals	1,754	0
Currently subscribed electronic journals	69	10,120
Annual Collections budget spent on print (%)	19	286
Databases	19	286
Annual visitors	304,163	118,496

missions, facilitating digital access to thousands of biomedical journals, textbooks, evidence summaries, and other instructional materials. They guide learners and practitioners in the development of literature search and appraisal skills to enable them to navigate the ever-growing body of biomedical literature effectively and efficiently in support of evidence-based practice. They advise researchers on best practices and tools for organizing and managing citations, research data, and scholarly identity, as well as play a pivotal role in the development of comprehensive and complex literature searches for systematic review research teams.

The transformation of the Miner Library owes much to three people. Julia F. Sollenberger received her MLS from Indiana University, Bloomington. She subsequently completed a postgraduate fellowship in biomedical information systems management at the National Library of Medicine (NLM), Bethesda, Maryland, where she remained for several years as systems librarian in the Technical Services division, with responsibility for designing, implementing, and evaluating computer systems, as well as project officer for the conversion of NLM's cataloging records into machine-readable format. In 1980, Sollenberger came to URMC to head information services for the Miner. In 1994, she was appointed assistant director of Miner, and in 1998 was made director of Health Science Libraries & Technologies. In 2009, in recognition of her increasing responsibilities, she was promoted to associate VP and director of Medical Center Libraries & Technologies.

Figure 31.1.
Julia Sollenberger

Figure 31.2. Miner Library post-renovations

In addition to shepherding URMC libraries through the transformation, Sollenberger was influential nationally in the implementation of information and bibliographic databases in academic medical libraries, and in the training of health science librarians in the understanding and use of these resources. Her commitment to making medical information accessible extended beyond URMC to include other health science libraries in the MiracleNet network, and through such programs as CLIC-on-Health, a resource for making consumer health information available to underserved populations.

Christopher Hoolihan received his MLS from the School of Information & Library Science, SUNY at Buffalo, and then served as rare books librarian at Washington University School of Medicine Library in St. Louis, before joining Miner in 1985. During his thirty-four-year career as rare books and manuscripts librarian at Miner, Hoolihan distinguished himself as a bibliographer, archivist, medical historian, art historian, and print historian. He transformed the library's rare book and manuscript collection from a modestly sized collection of 6,500 titles into an outstanding, nationally recognized collection of nearly 25,000 titles encompassing over 55,000 volumes. Now ranked among the top three history of medicine collections in the US, it includes an outstanding collection of early printed anatomical books and atlases. It is especially strong in 17th- through 19th-century obstetrics and gynecology, is the repository for one of the nation's finest collections on yellow fever, and is the home of the Atwater Collection of American Popular Medicine, one of the finest of its kind in North America. Hoolihan also established a faculty manuscript collection, thus preserving and making accessible the history of SMD, the SON, and SMH.

Figure 31.3. Jennifer Raynor

Upon her retirement in 2017, Sollenberger was succeeded by Jennifer Raynor, MLIS, who was appointed associate dean, Miner Libraries. Raynor received her MLIS from the University of Pittsburgh. During the first two decades of her career, she worked in public libraries, holding various positions in technical and public services, including serving as a celebrated local children's librarian. Raynor joined URMC in 2016 to develop clinical and family-centered library services at the GCH Family Resource Library, which had recently opened. As associate dean, Raynor has maintained Miner's commitment to curate collections of high-quality, evidence-based information resources, teach best practices for efficient discovery and use of the biomedical literature, and adopt new skills and technologies to support innovation in education, research, and clinical practice. She successfully steered Miner through the COVID-19 pandemic, staff and leadership transitions, and space renovations to best position Miner for the future and to help preserve its stature as one of the leading academic medical libraries in the country.

Chapter 32

THE SCHOOL OF NURSING

Academic nursing was an integral part of URMC when it was established in 1925—indicative of the founders' understanding of the interreliance of nursing and medicine in the delivery of care. In fact, the University of Rochester was among the first in the nation to offer nursing education under the auspices of a university. Helen Wood, RN, AB, an early advocate for the integration of nursing education, clinical practice, and scientific research, was the first superintendent of the School of Nursing (SON), overseeing nursing education and research, and the clinical nursing service at SMH. To complement robust baccalaureate-level education, an MS in nursing program was added in 1951, laying the groundwork for the clinical specialty programs for which it has become nationally known.

The recruitment of Dean Loretta Ford, RN, EdD, in 1972 was a watershed moment, coinciding with the establishment of the SON as a fully independent school within the University. Previously, the SON operated under the auspices of SMH or, starting in 1960, as a department within SMD. Dean Ford, co-developer and pioneer of the nurse practitioner model, developed the School's signature "Unification Model," a philosophic approach and organizational structure that operationalized the interdependence of education, research, and practice—much as the Flexnerian model did within Medicine.

Figure 32.1. Loretta Ford

Under Ford's guidance, the SON emerged as a national leader, adding highly ranked degree programs informed by evidence-based research, much of which was conducted within the School. Prior to her death in 2025, Ford was inducted into the National Women's Hall of Fame and named a Living Legend by the American Academy of Nursing. The School that she launched, and was built upon by five subsequent deans, is respected today for rigorous curricula that prepare outstanding nurses for leadership, academic, administrative, and bedside nursing roles. It has consistently adapted to meet the needs of an evolving health care delivery system, balancing academic and clinical preparation and preparing graduates for team-based, knowledge-based clinical and academic careers. Although Ford retired in 1986, she continued to consult and lecture on the historical development of nursing nationally and remain involved with the SON as a trusted advisor up until her death in 2025 at the age of 104!

Ford was succeeded in 1986 by Sheila A. Ryan, PhD, RN, FAAN, who, like her predecessor, also served as director of nursing at URMC. During her tenure, Dean Ryan was responsible for the development of a new strategic plan, modification of the Unification Model, reorganization of faculty governance, and expansion of faculty tracks for promotion. In 1995, she established a partnership with the Rochester City School District to operate the East High School-Based Health Center (SBHC), providing free and comprehensive physical and mental health services to nearly 800 students. Staffed by pediatric and family nurse practitioners, licensed social workers, and ambulatory technicians, the center includes an on-site laboratory and medication dispensary and currently provides services such as preventative care and screening, care for chronic health conditions, support in coordinating health care and school collaboration, addressing social determinants of health, mental health, and reproductive/family planning. Subsequently, an SBHC was opened at Monroe High School.

Figure 32.2. Patricia Chiverton

Patricia Chiverton, EdD, RN, FNAP, became the third dean of the SON in 1999. Dean Chiverton received her master's degree in psychiatric mental health nursing from the SON and her EdD from the Warner School of Education before joining the faculty of the SON in 1984. Like most nursing schools, the SON is financially dependent on tuition. At the end of the 20th century, the SON experienced stiff regional competition, as local colleges added nursing programs, often at lower tuition rates. Faced with rising competition for students and faculty, fewer research grants, and a mounting deficit, Chiverton led a transformational strategic plan that would reinvigorate its investment in academics, focus on SON programs that could be most competitive, aggressively fundraise, and launch specialty and entrepreneurial programs that would diversify its revenues. Goals included fiscal sustainability, providing a regional health care workforce, and seeking opportunities to redefine nursing as a solution to health care's emerging needs.

A bold decision was made to close the traditional baccalaureate program, which was struggling to compete with lower-cost tuition programs at local colleges, suffering a decline in licensure exam pass rates, and facing stiff competition for clinical placements. Instead, the SON partnered with Monroe Community College to provide a bachelor's completion program.

This offered an opportunity to build community partnerships and freed the faculty to refocus its mission on research and the development of novel degree programs. These included master's programs in Leadership in Health Care Systems, designed for leadership positions in health care systems, and in Nursing Leadership, designed for leadership roles in the nascent areas of health promotion and disaster management.

In 2002, the SON became among the first in the nation to introduce Accelerated Bachelor's (ABSN) and Master's degree programs for Non-Nurses (AMSN). By crediting students for baccalaureate coursework earned in another field, the rigorous program enabled eligible college graduates to qualify for nursing licensing in one year, creating a rapid source of well-educated nurses at the height of a major nursing shortage. The program has become a popular portal into the nursing profession for displaced employees from Rochester's shrinking manufacturing base.

The PhD in Health Practice Research (whose name changed in 2016 to PhD in Nursing and Health Science) transitioned to a multidisciplinary program, providing opportunities to work with researchers across many disciplines. One of the oldest programs of its kind in the country, this program admitted its first students in 1979 and its curriculum has served as a model for other universities. The Doctor of Nursing Practice (DNP) program was established in 2007, providing the highest level of academic preparation and training designed to prepare advanced nurse practitioners to lead the delivery and evaluation of evidence-based, patient-centered care. Together with a new MS/PhD in Nursing & Health Science, the new educational programs fueled a surge in enrollment during Chiverton's tenure from 303 to 400 students.

One of the most exciting elements of the SON strategic plan was the creation of the Center for Nursing Entrepreneurship—the first of its kind in the nation—to generate funds for education and research by starting up nurse-led businesses. Early efforts included the addition of an SBHC location at what was then Douglas High School, which offered physical and mental health care to Rochester City School students. In subsequent years, the Center incorporated two more lines of business: Passport Health, which provides travel physicals, vaccinations, and other travel-related services to the Rochester community and in 2006 opened a second site in Syracuse; and the Center for Employee Wellness (see below). These programs contribute significantly to the SON's non-tuition revenues.

Key to Chiverton's research plan was the appointment in 2004 of Harriet Kitzman, RN, PhD, FAAN, as associate dean for research. Kitzman received her nursing diploma at the Genesee Hospital and her bachelor's degree in nursing from Lycoming College in Williamsport, Pennsylvania,

Figure 32.3. Harriet Kitzman

before returning to Rochester to complete her master's education. She worked as a supervisor and instructor at RGH and The Genesee Hospital, before joining the University as a project nurse in pediatric primary care and developing a partnership between the department of Pediatrics and the SON that led to the establishment of the pediatric nurse practitioner program. In 1972, she became the school's first clinical chief of Pediatric Nursing. She continued her education, receiving a PhD from the SON, and developed a nationally prominent research program, for which she was recognized as the Loretta C. Ford Professor of Nursing. Under Kitzman's guidance, the SON recruited new cross-disciplinary faculty, encouraged existing faculty to engage in research, and provided pilot support to junior faculty to prepare for major grants. She also spearheaded the development of a center to provide timely and individualized research services, such as methods and statistical consults, health project coordination, and data management and analysis, and a pre- and post-award grant management. Kitzman received the Charles Force Hutchison and Marjorie Hutchison Medal, the University's highest recognition of personal achievement, and the Dean's Medal, the SON's highest honor. She died in 2020 at the age of eighty-two.

Figure 32.4. The School of Nursing today

Although Chiverton also served as VP of Clinical Nursing, her responsibilities did not include direct oversight of the health system's clinical nursing department. Instead, she partnered with SMH Chief Nursing Officer Patricia Witzel, RN, MS, MBA, to assure that the SON's curriculum addressed the needs of the delivery system while using the clinical workforce to assist in training SON students. With common goals and vision, the two nursing leaders were a creative force that markedly advanced the SON and enhanced clinical services at SMH.

To accommodate the many changes described above, SON faculty grew from fifty-four to ninety-four during Chiverton's tenure. She also had a powerful ally in URMC CEO C. McCollister Evarts, who enthusiastically supported the SON's need for incremental space to house its growing programs. This support was brought to fruition in 2006, with the opening of the Loretta C. Ford Education Wing of Helen Wood Hall, which provided increased space and enhanced technology for research and education, and accommodated the growth in student enrollment. The project, aided by a successful $20 million capital campaign, also saw the addition of a large monument sign on Crittenden Boulevard acknowledging the SON, heralding a new chapter in its history.

When Chiverton stepped down in 2008, Kathy Parker, PhD, RN, FAAN, was recruited from Emory University to serve as the fourth dean of the SON. Parker earned her undergraduate degree in nursing from Columbia University, a master's in nursing from Emory, and a doctorate in nursing from Georgia State University. With more than thirty years of clinical practice experience, she was certified as an adult nurse practitioner and a medical/surgical clinical nurse specialist. She was nationally recognized for her research in sleep disorders and one of only five nurses in the US certified in clinical sleep disorders by the American Board of Sleep Medicine.

Figure 32.5. Kathy Parker

Like her predecessor, Parker focused on increasing enrollment in all educational programs, providing flexible study options and providing scholarships and stipends to attract students. In recognition of the role that advanced degree programs played in generating more nurse educators, a necessity for expanding nursing education, the SON opened its PhD program to health professionals other than nurses.

Parker also continued to support the SON's research efforts, promoting Kitzman to SAD for research and expanding the SON's role in research on patient outcomes and health care costs. The SON was tapped to serve as the home of the Center for Research Implementation (CRIT), a key component of the CTSI. In collaboration with Psychiatry and Public Health Sciences, the SON led the CTSI's comparative-effectiveness research function, monitoring the risks and benefits of various interventions and strategies in real-world settings to identify approaches that would be most effective in improving outcomes and lowering costs. These efforts provided a national model for how a nursing school can have a leadership role in a CTSA program and helped to maintain the SON's status among the top funded schools of nursing.

When Parker stepped down in 2012, Kathy H. Rideout, EdD, PPCNP-BC, FNAP, was appointed first as interim dean and a year later as the fifth dean of the SON. Dean Rideout earned her BS in nursing from Indiana University of Pennsylvania and her MS in Nursing (Care of Children) from the University of Pittsburgh. She came to Rochester in 1986 as a member of the SON faculty and as an advanced pediatric nurse at SMH, and subsequently earned her EdD in Curriculum and Teaching Specialization from the Warner School of Education in 1995. A highly respected educator and accomplished clinician, Rideout had served since 2005 as SAD for academic affairs at the SON, overseeing the establishment of the Robert Wood Johnson Foundation New Careers in Nursing Scholarship Program.

Figure 32.6. Kathy Rideout

Rideout's tenure was associated with record enrollment, facilities expansion, and unprecedented diversification in faculty and staff. It was also characterized by a strengthening of the relationship between the SON and SMD and by a growing role for the SON within URMC, exemplified by Rideout becoming the first SON dean to be named a VP of URMC. Dean Rideout worked closely with SMD Dean Mark Taubman to strengthen the partnership between nursing education and medical training programs, and served on the board of the Institute for Innovative Education. Her participation enabled SON to play an integral role in better integrating curricula across the educational continuum at URMC and led to SMD and the SON being named by the American Association of Colleges of Nursing (AACN) as a national exemplar of an ideal relationship between nursing and medical schools.

Driven in large part by broad-based recruitment, the inherent popularity of the ABSN and the growing list of advanced degree programs, such as the master's in nursing education launched in 2015, the SON's enrollment reached its all-time high of 742 students in 2021. Its reputation for advanced practice education continued to soar, with *US News & World Report* ranking the SON master's nursing programs twenty-first out of 683 schools in 2023.

The growth in enrollment caused the SON to accelerate its transition to technology-based and distance learning, which proved fortuitous in maintaining educational programs during the COVID-19 pandemic. In 2021, the SON was one of only five nursing schools recognized as an Apple Distinguished School for its innovations in digital learning. This three-year distinction was renewed in 2024. These digital programs have also been critical in helping to develop nursing workforce for UR Medicine's regional partners.

The growth of the student body and the demand for new technologies necessitated further facility expansion. In May 2022, the ribbon was cut on a $15 million, 26,000 square-foot addition to Helen Wood Hall. The expansion included a twenty-bed skills lab, four simulation labs with high-fidelity mannequins, augmented and virtual reality spaces, and combined clinical and experiential learning to advance nursing education. The growth of programs was also supported by aggressive fundraising, which drew more than $9.6 million in new gifts, and a more than doubling of the endowment to nearly $49.4 million.

Under Rideout's direction, diversity and inclusivity became an integral part of the School's operation and ethos. She created the SON's diversity council, called attention to events recognizing LGBTQI communities, and even ensured that the mannequins in the simulation labs featured a variety of skin tones and genders. Rideout's efforts were recognized nationally; the

Figure 32.7. Expanded School of Nursing

Figure 32.8. Inside the expanded School

SON was honored five consecutive years with the Health Professions Higher Education Excellence in Diversity (HEED) Award, one of only six nursing schools nationwide to have been honored five times or more. The SON also became one of the few nursing schools nationwide to receive funding all seven years of the Robert Wood Johnson Foundation's New Careers in Nursing Scholarship program for underrepresented students.

One of the capstones of Rideout's tenure was the establishment in 2012 of the Center for Employee Wellness, which packages nurse-led wellness coaching and condition management services for eighty-five individual organizations, ranging from school districts to manufacturers and including the University of Rochester, and covering nearly 70,000 community members. This highly successful program, which is covered by local insurers at participating organizations, has set industry standards for outcomes, including: significant improvement in symptoms in seventy-five percent of patients with depression; a reduction in pain and pain interference scores in patients with chronic low back pain; a significant reduction in weight in sixty-five percent of patients in the Healthy Weight Program; an increase in fruit and vegetable consumption in the vast majority of patients in the nutrition program; and a significant increase in aerobic minutes in patients in the exercise program.

Renu Singh, MS, has served as CEO of the Center for Employee Wellness since 2014. Singh, who received her MS in Health Systems Management from RIT, has been a part of the SON leadership for over twenty years, most recently as SAD of Finance and Operations. Although she retired from her dean role in 2023, she has remained at the helm of the Center for Employee Wellness. In 2018, she was named a "Woman of Excellence" by the *Rochester Business Journal* for her career accomplishments, community involvement, leadership, and commitment to mentoring. Singh also conceptualized the SON's Nursing Scholars program (see below).

Figure 32.9. Renu Singh

No chronicle of the recent history of the SON would be complete without acknowledging Madeline "Mattie" Schmitt, RN, PhD, a SON faculty member from 1972 until her retirement in 2005. Schmitt played a major role in the development of the SON as an autonomous school and in establishing and expanding the graduate studies and faculty research programs. She served in many capacities, including assistant dean for Graduate Studies, director of Faculty Research Development, and coordinator of the doctoral program. She became a national leader in research and education related to interprofessional practice and as the SON professor emerita has continued to co-publish seminal articles and conduct collaborative research. She remains sought after as a national consultant and currently serves as an ambassador and community moderator for the National Center for Interprofessional Practice and Education.

Figure 32.10. Madeline Schmitt

Throughout her career, Dean Rideout maintained her clinical practice, working part-time as a pediatric ostomy nurse practitioner at GCH. This commitment to patient care informed her leadership philosophy and kept her, and the SON, grounded in the realities of nursing practice. Rideout stepped down as dean in 2022, continuing her clinical practice at SMH until her untimely death in 2025 at the age of sixty-seven.

In 2022, URMC launched a national search for Rideout's successor, culminating in the recruitment of Lisa A. Kitko, PhD, RN, FAHA FAAN, from the Penn State University College of Nursing as the SON's sixth dean. Kitko received a bachelor's degree in nursing from the University of Pittsburgh and a master's degree as a clinical nurse specialist and PhD in nursing from Penn State University, where she remained as faculty for more than twenty years, most recently as associate dean for graduate education and director of the PhD program.

Figure 32.11. Lisa Kitko

An internationally recognized expert in geriatric nursing, palliative care, and heart failure, Kitko's research, which has been funded by the NIH, NSF, HRSA, and the American Heart Association, has involved the palliative care needs of persons living with life-limiting illnesses and their family members, with a focus on serious illness conversations.

The COVID-19 pandemic exposed inequities in our health systems, and exacerbated workforce shortages that made it exceptionally challenging to work in the health profession. Throughout the country, as many as one in four nurses working prior to the pandemic were leaving the field, and others were choosing to travel from one institution to another. In meeting this challenge, Kitko defined four compass points: equity, inclusion, innovation, and interprofessional collaboration. The SON introduced new curricula that were responsive to workforce realities and met the changing needs of learners. These included a twenty-four-month hybrid online ABSN program to prepare nurses while balancing work or other commitments, a sixteen-month Master's Direct Entry into Nursing Practice Program, and a redesigned NP program that offered more flexible learning formats for working nurses. The SON also became the first school in NY State to offer a new entry point for its DNP program, allowing master's-prepared nurses from diverse specialties to pursue a terminal practice degree in nursing.

One of the most important innovations, taking advantage of the close relationship between the SON and SMH, was the Nursing Scholars Program. This program covers full tuition costs for approximately 100 students per year who commit to work at participating UR Medicine facilities for three years after graduation. This rigorous, twelve-month ABSN program includes 700 hours of clinical training in medical/surgical, obstetrics, pediatrics, psychiatry, and other specialties. It offers a unique opportunity for bachelor's-prepared college graduates to pursue a second career in nursing and has already attracted students from across the US with diverse backgrounds and experiences.

Kitko's efforts have already captured national attention. The SON recently received a ten-year Commission on Collegiate Nursing Education reaccreditation. The SON was endorsed by the International Nursing Association for Clinical Simulation and Learning for implementing rigorous, evidence-based educational practices. In 2023, the School received the AACN 2023 Innovations in Professional Nursing Education award in the academic health center category, and in 2024 was also named a National League for Nursing Center of Excellence in Nursing Education for creating environments that enhance student learning and professional development.

Lydia Rotondo, DNP, RN, CNS, FNAP, FAAN, has played a key role in overseeing the SON educational programs since her arrival at the

University in 2014, when she became director of the DNP program. Since her appointment as associate dean for Education and Student Affairs in 2015 and subsequently as SAD for Graduate Education and Innovation, Rotondo has been responsible for developing several new educational programs and for creating an academic innovation infrastructure that has transformed nursing education through the implementation of educational technology and experiential learning. Rotondo was part of an academic nursing leadership team that advised the NY State Education Department in crafting successful legislation to integrate simulation in clinical nursing education, enabling students to utilize simulation for up to a third of their clinical hours.

Figure 32.12. Lydia Rotondo

Nursing Research

In 2024, the SON received $5.5 million in research funding, approximately half from the NIH. Overseeing the research effort was Sally Norton, PhD, RN, FNAP, FPCN, FAAN, who replaced Harriet Kitzman as associate dean for research in 2019 and became SAD in 2024. Norton, who holds the Independence Foundation Chair in Nursing and Palliative Care, joined the SON in 2001, where she established a national reputation for groundbreaking research on improving communication and care delivery for patients with advanced illness, particularly in palliative and end-of-life care. Norton has been a principal or co-investigator in dozens of funded research studies on palliative care and has authored or co-authored more than 100 papers. She is a fellow of the Hospice and Palliative Care Nurses Association (HPNA), which recognized her as its Distinguished Researcher in 2017, and of AAN. Norton also serves as a co-director of research for the division of Palliative Care in the DOM at SMD.

Figure 32.13. Sally Norton

The SON's research portfolio spans the translational science continuum from laboratories to clinics, community, and health care systems. Major research areas include: Interdisciplinary Sexual Health & HIV Research group; the Rochester Oncology Nursing Research group; Equity for Parent–Child, Adolescent, and Transgenerational Health Research (EmPATH) group; Elaine C. Hubbard Center for Nursing Research on Aging; and the Heart, Electrophysiology, and Arrhythmia Research Team. The following paragraphs highlight a few of these, and further information is available on the SON website.

Kitzman was inspired by the disparities she encountered as a pediatric nurse working with young, socioeconomically disadvantaged mothers. In collaboration with David Olds, PhD, she designed and tested a nurse-home visitation program in Memphis, Tennessee, which became the basis for the Nurse-Family Partnership. This partnership, which sends specially trained nurses to regularly visit first-time mothers-to-be and follows them from early pregnancy through the child's second birthday, was the first early intervention shown to reduce maternal and child mortality. The community health program grew to become a national federally funded program and now serves more than 54,000 families. Susan Groth, PhD, working with the established Rochester and Memphis teams, furthered Kitzman's research, demonstrating how nurse intervention with disadvantaged women at the vulnerable time of childbearing can alter the life-course of both the mother and her offspring thirty years later.

James McMahon, PhD, endowed chair for Innovation in Health Care, has played a pivotal role in advancing HIV and sexual health research at the SON. In 2014, McMahon co-founded the Interdisciplinary Sexual Health and HIV Research group, establishing a collaborative model that brings together faculty, postdoctoral fellows, and students from diverse disciplines. This approach has expanded and strengthened research on the behavioral, social, and epidemiological factors influencing HIV and Hepatitis C risk among marginalized populations. McMahon's own work spans the development of public health interventions—such as pre-exposure prophylaxis for minority women and couples—and epidemiological studies of Hepatitis C transmission. Through his leadership and mentorship, the Group has fostered a dynamic environment that continues to attract and support talented researchers, including Gamji Abu-Ba'are, PhD, MA, and Natalie Leblanc, PhD, MPH, RN, BSN, who are leading NIH-funded projects on HIV prevention, stigma reduction, and health equity.

Over the past twenty-five years, the SON has built upon its historic foundation, leveraging its unique position within a research-intensive academic medical center to advance nursing education, research, and clinical practice. Guided by the Unification Model and inspired by the vision of its pioneering leaders, the School has responded to regional and national challenges with agility and creativity—expanding academic offerings, integrating emerging technologies, and redefining the profession's role in health care systems and public policy. Through innovations like simulation-based learning and practice-ready curricula, SON graduates are exceptionally prepared for the demands of modern health care.

A hallmark of this era has been the SON's commitment to community partnerships and interdisciplinary collaboration, exemplified by initiatives such as the SBHCs and the Center for Employee Wellness. Supported by robust research infrastructure and cross-disciplinary faculty, the School's nationally recognized programs continue to address key health challenges and advance health equity.

Looking ahead, the SON's 2030 Strategic Plan sets a bold course for the future. In close collaboration with URMC and community partners, the School will continue to drive innovation, foster interdisciplinary scholarship, and translate research into practice. By anticipating workforce needs and investing in flexible, student-centered learning, the SON is poised to remain a force in nursing education, research, and practice—developing the next generation of nurse leaders and improving health for all communities it serves.

G. School of Medicine and Dentistry Divisions

Chapter 33

UNDERGRADUATE MEDICAL EDUCATION

The past twenty-five years have seen transformative changes in the curriculum and offerings of the MD program. The class entering in 1999 was the first to experience the Double Helix Curriculum (DHC), the crowning achievement of Dean Edward Hundert's tenure at SMD.

Figure 33.1. Edward Hundert

Edward M. Hundert, MD, received his MD from Harvard Medical School (HMS) and did his residency training in psychiatry at Harvard's McLean Hospital, where he remained as faculty and director of Postgraduate and Continuing Medical Education. He subsequently became involved in the development of Harvard's New Pathway Curriculum, becoming associate dean for Student Affairs at HMS in 1990. In 1997, he was recruited to Rochester as dean of SMD. Hundert oversaw the development of the innovative DHC, making Rochester one of the first schools to integrate basic science and clinical medicine throughout all four years. The DHC, which was widely emulated throughout the country, enhanced SMD's reputation as a national leader in medical education and still remains the foundation of its medical curriculum. Hundert left Rochester in 2002 to become president of Case Western Reserve University. Four years later, he returned to HMS to lead a new curriculum in medical ethics and professionalism and to be director of the Center for Teaching and Learning. From 2014 to 2023, he served as dean for Medical Education at HMS, where he currently serves as the Daniel D. Federman Professor in Residence of Global Health and Social Medicine and Medical Education.

Figure 33.2. David Guzick

Hundert was succeeded as dean by David S. Guzick, MD, PhD. Guzick received his MD and PhD in economics in the MSTP at NYU, did a residency in obstetrics and gynecology at Johns Hopkins, and a fellowship in reproductive endocrinology at the University of Texas, Southwestern Medical School. In 1986, Guzick joined the University of Pittsburgh as director of Reproductive

Endocrinology in the Ob/Gyn department. In 1995, he was recruited to Rochester as the Henry A. Thiede Chair of Ob/Gyn, and in 2002 he was appointed the ninth dean of SMD. Guzick is internationally known in the field of reproductive medicine for the development of mathematical models of clinical outcomes and for his research in polycystic ovary syndrome, endometriosis, and infertility. In 2008, he was elected to the Institute of Medicine of the National Academy of Sciences (now the National Academy of Medicine). As dean, Guzick was a driving force and the PI of the University's CTSA, one of the initial twelve granted by the NIH. Under his leadership, URMC became the first institution to receive extended (six-year) accreditation from the ACGME for its residency programs. Guzick also received high praise from the Liaison Committee on Medical Education (LCME) for his outstanding leadership and a commitment to medical education and medical students, awarding SMD the maximum eight-year accreditation. Guzick also led a highly successful campaign to raise funds for scholarships and reduce medical student debt. Guzick left Rochester in June 2009 to become senior VP of Health Affairs at the University of Florida, and president of University of Florida Health, a position he held until 2018. He was succeeded by Elizabeth R. McAnarney, MD, chair emerita of Pediatrics, who served as acting dean until March 2010, at which time Mark Taubman was appointed as dean.

The DHC used problem-based learning (PBL) and other small group formats to enhance active learning and solidify clinical reasoning. It included themes such as aging, prevention, ethics and law, medical humanities, and nutrition interwoven throughout the four years. Uniform formative assessments at key points ensured that students achieve the desired curricular outcomes. Basic science classes were multidisciplinary, integrating topics such as anatomy, histology, and physiology or genetics, biochemistry, and nutrition. The second year focused on systems-based courses. Clerkships included an eighteen-month ambulatory clinical experience beginning in January of the first year. Traditional clerkships were shortened, allowing for three basic science blocks in the third year. In addition to elective weeks, the final year included Process of Discovery (a translational research course) and a capstone, Successful Interning.

Over the ensuing years, the curriculum evolved, with changes driven by national trends, accreditation requirements, innovative ideas, and student feedback. Two new courses on women's health and childhood disorders were added. The original ambulatory clinical experience was replaced by Skills in Complete Patient Evaluation (SCOPE) in the first year and a primary care clerkship in the second year. SCOPE was subsequently changed to Foundations of Biopsychosocial Practice, beginning in the second half of the first year and providing advanced physical exam skills with instruction on prevention and counseling.

Content delivery was moved to Apple iPads in 2013, eliminating paper printing and microscopes. Small PBL group rooms were redesigned to resemble an ambulatory office with instruments, supplies, and an exam table. Simulation expanded with mannequin use in pharmacology instruction, procedure/task training, and critical care scenarios. Auditorium renovations provided desk space to support student use of devices and facilitate

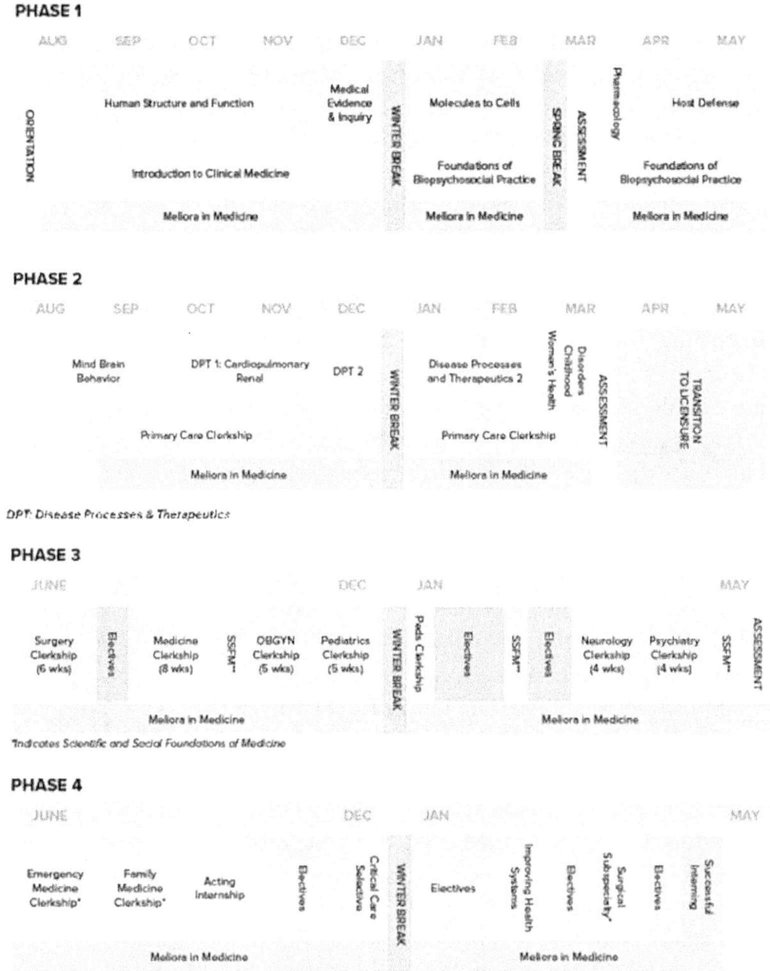

Figure 33.3. The current Medical School curriculum

interactive learning, and all education spaces were upgraded to allow for digital recording and remote conferencing. In 2020, the school began a four-year, longitudinal, point-of-care ultrasound curriculum, with each student receiving a hand-held device.

In 2019, twenty years after the beginning of the DHC, the medical program underwent a full curriculum reform which led to more substantial changes. From a thorough and thoughtful process, which involved a variety of stakeholders, the Double Helix Curriculum-Translations and Transitions (DHC-TT) emerged (see Figure 33.3). Structured in four phases, DHC-TT maintained the core principles of combining the scientific foundations of medicine and early clinical exposure with emphasis on the biopsychosocial model. Instruction in scientific foundations was consolidated, allowing students to begin the clinically intensive phase earlier. A required four-week family medicine clerkship was added, along with a two-week critical care selective. The three basic science blocks were replaced by three week-long Scientific and Social Foundations of Medicine courses in phase three, which include current scientific discovery, bioethics, and other topics. A four-year curricular thread, Meliora in Medicine (MiM), focused on health systems science and bioethics, with topics such as social determinants of health, teamwork, population health, patient safety and quality, and on technology in medicine, such as point-of-care ultrasound, electronic medical record, and information science. Interprofessional education occurred throughout the curriculum. SMD also established elective pathway programs, such as: Deaf Health; Global Health; Medical Education, Health, and Incarceration; Health Equity, and Law; Health Humanities and Bioethics; Latinx; Healthcare Innovation and Economics.

When the first DHC class graduated, Tana Grady-Weliky, MD, held the position of SAD for Medical Education with oversight of all medical school education programs. Grady-Weliky, a psychiatrist who had received her MD from Duke University, had been recruited to Rochester to serve as SAD. She left in 2009 to become associate dean for Medical Education in the Oregon Health and Science University School of Medicine and tragically died of cancer in 2011. An endowed lectureship, the Tana Grady-Weliky, MD, Lecture on Women and Diversity in Medicine was established that year at the University of Rochester in her honor.

Figure 33.4. Tana Grady-Weliky

In 2005, Grady-Weliky's position overseeing all medical education was eliminated and replaced by SADs for each educational area who reported directly to Dean Guzick. David R. Lambert, MD, became the first SAD for

Figure 33.5. David Lambert presides over Match Day

Medical Student Education in 2008 and remains in that role. Lambert received his MD from Dartmouth Medical School and completed a residency in internal medicine at Beth Israel Deaconess Medical Center. He subsequently joined the General Medicine division at URMC, ultimately serving as division chief. During that time, he oversaw the evolution of the DHC into current DHC-TT, introduced the use of iPads for content delivery, and shepherded undergraduate medical education through the COVID-19 pandemic. Most notably, Lambert led SMD through three accreditation cycles (2008, 2016, and 2024), receiving the eight-year maximum each time from the LCME and establishing SMD, in the words of one of the site visitors, as a "medical school to which many of us aspire."

Brenda D. Lee, EdD, served as the assistant dean of Student Services and Medical Education for twenty-three years, before retiring in 2016. Lee is a Rochester native who received her EdD from Antioch College. She was recruited back to Rochester from HMS, where she had served as assistant to the dean. A pioneer in understanding the impact of inequities and developing solutions to combat them, she helped lay the groundwork for a first-of-its-kind, post-baccalaureate program to help prepare promising, historically excluded students towards success in Medical School, and was also instrumental in developing the

Figure 33.6. Brenda Lee

Science and Technology Entry Program. In recognition of her achievements, she received the URMC Gold Medal Award for Excellence in Teaching and was honored as the keynote speaker at the 2022 Medical School commencement. Following Lee's retirement, Kathryn Castle, PhD, took on this role for five years. She was succeeded in 2021 by Flavia Nobay, MD, who became the first associate dean for Student Affairs.

One of Grady-Weliky's major achievements at SMD was the advisory dean program, which was implemented with the DHC. Each entering medical student is assigned one of four faculty advisory deans (ADs), all of whom are practicing clinicians, who guide professional identity formation, career counseling, and access to resources. Career counseling and wellness was also strengthened through a well-designed four-year program that included designated department-based faculty advisors and early intervention efforts. The Office of Student Services houses student affairs (such as career counseling and wellness), financial aid, the registrar, and the Office of Medical Student Enrichment Programs (OMSEP). Paula Smith directed the office through 2017 and was succeeded by Diane Frank, who remains in that role. OMSEP manages an extensive portfolio of community service and volunteer programs, oversees international programs, and supports medical student research efforts.

Philanthropy has been essential to help reduce student debt and recruit the best medical students. Dean Guzick's scholarship campaign from 2003–8 successfully raised $20 million. In 2007, the Levitan Family Endowed Scholarship was established by a generous gift from Alexander Levitan, an oncologist who received his MD from the University of Rochester, and his wife Lucy to provide four years of support for a student who has lived outside of the US. The Levitans have continued to grow the endowment, enabling a new four-year scholarship to be awarded each year. Philanthropy has also supported student research through numerous endowments, including three year-out positions funded by the endowed Levitan Scholars program, Alexander and Lucy Levitan Endowment for Medical Student Research Fellowships, and seven summer positions funded by the SKAWA Foundation. Initially supported by the CTSI, the academic research track was established to foster student research through didactic instruction and structured mentorship. The school continues to work to expand scholarship dollars.

Figure 33.7. John Hansen

John T. Hansen, PhD, formerly the Kilian J. and Caroline F. Schmitt Professor of Neurobiology and Anatomy and currently emeritus professor of Neurosciences, served as associate dean for Admissions for

Figure 33.8. Alexander and Lucy Levitan with student recipients

twenty-one years. Hansen received his PhD in anatomy from Tulane University. Hansen spent more than thirty-five years at SMD as a researcher, studying the role of dopamine neurons in the peripheral and central nervous system; as a teacher, for which he was honored as a Robert Wood Johnson Dean's Senior Teaching Scholar; and as a scholar, publishing over 120 scientific publications, serving as lead editor on five editions of the *Atlas of Human Anatomy*, and authoring several books, including *Netter's Clinical Anatomy* and *TMN Staging Atlas*, which won the 2008 "Book of the Year" award from the British Medical Association. In 2010, he was the first recipient of the University's Presidential Diversity Award for his "advocacy, support, mentoring, planning, and leading URMC's initiatives to increase the recruitment, retention, excellence, and graduation of candidates from diverse backgrounds."

Hansen was succeeded by Flavia Nobay, MD (Emergency Medicine), in 2017, who subsequently became the associate dean for Student Affairs, and in 2021 by Christine M. Hay, MD (Infectious Diseases). Nobay and Hay shared Hansen's commitment to diversity. AAMC data indicate for the five-year period between 2017 and 2023, SMD was at the eighty-second percentile for all medical schools in the percent of graduates who self-identified as Black or African American. For Hispanic, Latinx, or Spanish origin-identifying students,

Figure 33.9. Flavia Nobay

SMD was at the sixty-eighth percentile. Hay expanded the admissions committee membership and, for the class entering in August 2025, there were 5,258 applicants for 104 positions, including six students in the MD-PhD program and two in the MD-MBA program. On average, ten matriculates are from the Rochester Early Medical Scholars program and forty percent of applicants are from NY State. Students are welcomed to the Medical School and to the profession of medicine in August at the Robert and Lillian Brent white coat ceremony.

Figure 33.10. Christine Hay

Rochester's MSTP has been directed by M. Kerry O'Banion, MD, PhD, since 2000. The program matriculates up to eight MD-PhD students each year, an increase from six in 2002. For graduates from 2018 to 2023, SMD is at the eighty-sixth percentile compared with all other medical schools in the percentage of graduates with MD-PhD degrees. As of 2025, the program, one of the oldest in the country, has been supported by the NIH for fifty-one years and been in existence for sixty-six years. MD graduates pursue many specialties and secure residency positions across the country. For graduates from 2018 to 2023, SMD is at the ninetieth percentile for all medical schools for graduates who hold faculty positions. The education program fosters intellectual curiosity and prepares graduates for any residency training.

With the continued expansion of information and technology, medical education is likely to focus more on active learning and the development of critical reasoning and interpretation skills. The role of AI in augmenting the physician's work remains in uncharted territory. Financing of education and the availability of outstanding clinical sites to meet the expanded need of physicians are and will continue to be challenging. The University's MD program is poised to meet the challenges and continue to hold to its foundation of the biopsychosocial model, graduating physicians who are outstanding communicators, humanistic, and ready to lead the profession.

Chapter 34

GRADUATE MEDICAL EDUCATION (GME)

GME has witnessed major changes over the past twenty-five years. In 2003, the ACGME adopted resident duty hour regulations for all accredited medical training institutions in the US, following the lead of NY State, which had established the Libby Zion Law in 1989. The ACGME rules required residents work no more than eighty hours per week with no less than one day off per week. These changes stimulated the development of multiple "night float" rotations for residents, minimizing in-hospital overnight call and leading to an increase in attending presence in many settings, including overnight in the hospital. These efforts also heightened awareness of physician unwellness and burnout, spurring more focus on issues such as resident time off, mistreatment, and discrimination in the learning environment.

While resident duty hours were being reduced, the complexity and volume of inpatients was increasing dramatically, exceeding the number that could be cared for by residents. This led hospitals to develop non-resident care models, including inpatient units managed primarily by APPs. By 2024, approximately seventy percent of the general medicine patients at SMH were cared for by APPs without residents. In many settings, APPs cared for the more straightforward patients, thereby increasing the complexity and acuity of patients on the residency teaching services and reducing resident exposure to more common diagnoses. Technological and treatment advances, changes in reimbursement criteria, and limitations in bed availability resulted in shorter stays, reducing residents' exposure to longitudinal care. Some services (e.g. internal medicine) were significantly affected by hospital overcrowding, resulting in many admitted patients being boarded in the ED, whereas other services (e.g. orthopaedics) experienced pronounced shifts from inpatient to outpatient settings.

A broad range of new topics, such as quality improvement and patient safety, social determinants of health, end-of-life/goals of care discussions, interprofessional collaboration, and point-of-care ultrasound, became essential curricula for all medical trainees. These additional curricular demands further stressed the time available for residents to spend with patients—some studies documented that residents spent just five percent of their time with patients in the inpatient setting—creating challenges to acquiring bedside skills.

Electronic health records (EHR) transformed the storage, sharing, and documentation of patient care, and increased the amount of patient information available to residents. The ease of communication improved markedly, moving from pagers to cell phones to secure text and EHR messaging, but was also accompanied by a substantial increase in the volume of communications. The volume of medical literature also exploded, enabling residents to get the most up-to-date information, but requiring additional training in how to conduct and interpret literature searches.

The above issues necessitated substantial changes in the organization and curricula of most URMC residencies and fellowships, including a reduction in the number of teaching rotations at affiliated institutions. The trend towards subspecialization led to a large increase in the number of fellowships after residency, particularly in surgical subspecialties, and combined training with more than one fellowship became more common (e.g. critical care and infectious diseases, or critical care and cardiology). Also, as a response to many of the above issues, the ACGME implemented the "Next Accreditation System" in July 2013, which included new institution-level Clinical Learning Environment Reviews and specialty-specific milestone reporting by each program twice annually for each trainee.

Figure 34.1. Diane Hartmann

URMC's response to these issues was overseen by Diane Hartmann, MD, currently emeritus professor of Ob/Gyn, who served as SAD for GME and the designated institutional official for URMC's ACGME-accredited residency and fellowship programs. Hartmann received her MD and did her residency in Ob/Gyn at the University of Rochester, before joining the faculty as a general gynecologist with expertise in menopausal and geriatric gynecology. Under Hartmann's watch, the number of ACGME-accredited residencies and fellowships rose from forty-nine to ninety-three and the number of accredited training positions for residents and fellows rose from 598 to 930. Most significantly, she worked seamlessly with residency and fellowship program directors to guide URMC through countless site visits from the ACGME and other regulatory organizations and to ensure that in almost all circumstances, our programs received outstanding reviews. Her constant vigilance enabled URMC to take a proactive approach to dealing with programs that were having difficulties, assuring a good outcome. For many years, Hartmann played a major role in the ACGME, serving as a member of its Board of Directors (as did SMH and HH CEO Steven Goldstein), as Awards Committee chair, and leading many important ACGME initiatives. In 2024, Hartmann, who retired as dean in 2023, was awarded the University's George Eastman Medal in recognition of her leadership of graduate medical education. She was succeeded by Brett Robbins, MD, program director of the Med/Peds residency and vice chair for Education in the DOM.

Among Hartmann's greatest successes was when URMC was chosen as one of the eight national ACGME Pursuing Excellence Innovator sites to improve residency training by improving the clinical learning environment of residency programs. URMC's application proposed embedding residents into its quality teams (UPP: Unit-based Performance Program), where they participate in unit-based quality and safety efforts in every specialty across the hospital. Initially, training was offered to residents in quality and safety principles, and residents would apply those principles in their role on the UPP teams. However, it became clear to program leadership that this intervention needed to be interprofessional to be successful and that learning had to encompass the entire UPP team, as well as the whole unit, and to emphasize teaming skills as much as content expertise. This program has evolved to include dyad leadership training for physician-nurse leaders of the UPP teams and workplace learning for the entire workforce in teaming, quality and safety and improvement processes. The reader is referred to the section on Quality and Safety (p. 30) for more details of this program.

Chapter 35

GRADUATE EDUCATION AND POST-DOCTORAL AFFAIRS (GEPA)

Over the past twenty-five years, SMD's graduate education programs have grown with the expansion of the research enterprise. The number of PhD students has doubled to roughly sixty new students per year and, with the addition of Epidemiology and Translational Biomedical Science, there are now fourteen distinct PhD programs. Master's programs were added in Epidemiology, Genetic Counseling, Health Humanities & Bioethics, Health Services Research & Policy, Immunology, Microbiology & Virology, Medical Pharmacology, and Medical Physics, bringing the total number of programs to fifteen and the total number of students to 500 (360 in doctoral programs, 115 in master's programs, and twenty-five obtaining an advanced certificate). Beginning in 2014, SMD developed advanced certificate programs, which now include Analytic Epidemiology, Clinical Bioethics, Clinical/Medical Technology, Clinical Research Methods (online), Experimental Therapeutics, Health Services Research, Marriage and Family Therapy, and Public Health (online), and are instrumental in cultivating a highly skilled and specialized workforce who are essential for advancing medical and health services.

Figure 35.1. Paul LaCelle

SMD's graduate programs have long been overseen by three outstanding SADs. Paul LaCelle, MD, received his MD from SMD and joined the University of Rochester in 1964 as faculty in Radiation Biology and Biophysics, where he served as chair from 1977 to 1996. He subsequently served as SAD for Graduate Education from 1996 until 2008. After stepping down as dean, LaCelle continued to work in research and mentored scientists until a few months before his death in 2012.

Figure 35.2. Edith Lord

Edith M. Lord, PhD, professor emerita in Microbiology & Immunology (M&I), received her PhD in immunology from the University of California at San Diego and was a postdoctoral fellow at UCSF. She joined the M&I faculty in 1976, where she developed a nationally recognized program in tumor immunology. Prior to serving as SAD for Graduate Education (2008–18), Lord directed the graduate program in M&I. Upon stepping down as SAD, she returned to the laboratory to continue her research on tumor immunology.

Richard T. Libby, PhD, received his PhD from Boston College and then completed postdoctoral fellowships at the Medical Research Council's Institute for Hearing Research in Nottingham, England, and at the Jackson Laboratory in Bar Harbor, Maine. In 2006, he joined the faculty in the departments of Ophthalmology and Biomedical Genetics at the University of Rochester, where he developed a nationally recognized research program focused on cell signaling and glaucoma. In 2018, he was chosen as the first SAD for GEPA, renamed to acknowledge the important role of postdoctoral fellows, and currently remains in that position.

Figure 35.3. Richard Libby

Working closely with Libby is Sharon McCullough, MBA. McCullough has been instrumental in guiding SMD through many of the innovative changes detailed below. She has been with GEPA since 2010, holding progressively responsible positions. She was recognized for her leadership in postdoctoral affairs by being named the inaugural senior assistant dean for GEPA, and as the assistant vice provost for Postdoctoral Affairs.

Figure 35.4. Sharon McCullough

GEPA supports approximately 115 postdoctoral fellows appointed in virtually every basic science and clinical department or center and advised by more than eighty faculty members. A pivotal moment for the institution was 2011, when the Office for Postdoctoral Affairs was established within GEPA. This office formally recognized the unique contributions of postdoctoral fellows and the need for a more structured, supportive environment with the resources for them to thrive. Driven by a partnership between GEPA and the Postdoctoral Association, policies were established setting a minimum stipend, a five-year maximum term limit, annual evaluations, individual development plans, tuition benefits, and life insurance. In addition, postdoctoral fellows were given equal access to health insurance benefits, regardless of their funding source. The formal recognition of postdoctoral fellows as University of Rochester alumni and GEPA's quarterly in-person orientation helped ensure that new postdoctoral fellows were well integrated into the SMD community.

In 2015, GEPA engaged in a major update of the basic science core curriculum, led by Dirk Bohmann, PhD, soon-to-be SAD for Basic Research. The three required introductory courses in biochemistry, molecular biology and genetics, and cell biology were replaced by two entirely new courses that focused on modern methodologies, such as computational biology and genomics, and which employed the literature in addition to textbooks. Weekly sessions were established in which students worked in small groups to address problems faced in modern biological laboratories. The incorporation of contemporary research techniques and emerging scientific knowledge into the curriculum better prepared students for their future careers and enhanced SMD's reputation as a leader in scientific education and research. Another curriculum development was the use of online education (e.g. for the MPH), allowing students to balance their personal and educational commitments, and allowing SMD to reach new student populations.

In 2012, GEPA transitioned from a paper-based system to an online system, Slate, for recruitment and admissions. This resulted in a significant reduction in paper handling, provided access to real-time data, and enabled the quick generation of reports. These changes, together with the initiatives discussed above, led to a marked increase in the number of applicants. University-wide initiatives, such as the Blackboard learning management system; HelioCampus for tasks related to assessment, course evaluations, program evaluation, and accreditation; and Workday's student information system improved the user experience, strengthened our ability to meet accreditation standards, and allowed us to respond better to evolving educational needs.

Over the past fifteen years, GEPA made great strides in diversity, equity, and inclusion. Three new administrative positions were established, and programs were developed to assist incoming PhD students with relocation and transition expenses. An Accountability Panel was created that meets with graduate students from traditionally underrepresented groups to promote bidirectional communication between leadership and students, and ensure that underrepresented voices are heard. Workshops were launched to improve mentorship and communication skills among faculty and students, and a Mosaic Distinguished Alumni Lecture Series was developed, providing an opportunity for alumni from historically underrepresented and underserved groups to share their experiences and career paths.

Students from historically excluded and underrepresented groups are encouraged to explore graduate education in biomedical and health sciences, efforts championed by Elaine Smolock, PhD (M&I). Summer Scholars is a ten-week program that provides undergraduate students with research and educational seminars, career presentations, and research training with faculty mentors. Students can present their research at a final symposium and interact with graduate students and postdoctoral fellows through various social activities. Supported by an NIH grant, the Postbaccalaureate Research Education Program (PREP) is a one-year program that includes a two-week boot camp, hands-on lab experience on NIH-funded projects, and advising from over seventy faculty mentors. The program provides training in scientific writing and communication, and focuses on network-building and preparing participants to be competitive applicants for PhD biomedical graduate programs. Smolock serves as co-director for PREP and Summer Scholars.

Of particular importance to GEPA is myHub. Established in 2014 to enhance learners' scientific education with tailored personal, professional, and career development opportunities, aligning with their individual needs, interests, and skills, myHub integrates eight essential areas: 1) learner life/wellness, 2) writing services, 3) fellowships and grants, 4) career services, 5) internships, 6) graduate student and postdoctoral groups, 7) alumni mentorship, and 8) events. This initiative helps ensure that graduate students and postdoctoral fellows are well rounded and ready for both academic and non-academic careers.

myHub's Career Services (led by Eric Vaughn, MEd) conducts over 225 one-on-one learner meetings and more than twenty-five events annually. Topics include career exploration, cover-letter writing, CV and resume services, individual development plans, interviewing, job search strategies, LinkedIn profile development, negotiation skills, networking strategy, and professional email/communication basics. Career Services also provides internship opportunities, instructs a semester-long Leadership and Management for Scientists course, and engages with alumni through the SMD Alumni Council and the Ambassador Program.

myHub's Writing Services and Training Grant Development (led by Smolock) conducts over 125 one-on-one learner meetings and more than twenty-five events annually. Topics include abstracts, book chapters, dissertation, manuscript preparation, poster composition, protocol review, progress reports, qualifying and preliminary exam preparation, review article and literature review, rotation reports, and fellowship/grant support. Training grant development services support faculty by streamlining institutional support documentation, providing updates about key changes to critical funding mechanisms, and addressing specific funding opportunity language.

myHub's Learner Life and Wellness (established in 2024 and led by Amber Rivera, MSW) is dedicated to enhancing learner retention and success. This program partners with various University resources to offer personalized and group support for personal wellness goals, wellbeing concerns, and interpersonal and communication challenges with colleagues, peers, and faculty. It also facilitates access to supportive services and provides trainee group advising and community-building. The Postdoc Workplace Wellness Series covers essential topics such as aligning expectations with supervisors, mentoring, cultural appreciation and humility, burnout prevention, conflict resolution, and building resiliency.

Chapter 36

OFFICE OF ACADEMIC AFFAIRS (OAA)

Although not traditionally thought of as an "educational" unit, the OAA has played a critical role in facilitating many of the educational endeavors discussed above and has been involved increasingly in the continuing education and professional development of the school's most important resource—its faculty.

At the start of the twenty-first century, the main functions of the OAA were academic promotions and reappointments. The SAD for Academic Affairs (SADAA) had no dedicated space, using existing space in their academic department. Staff support consisted of two administrative assistants who handled the paperwork for appointments, reappointments, and promotions, which was stored in large file cabinets in a room that housed the staff cubicles and a desk for the SADAA to sign paperwork.

Figure 36.1. Richard Burton

In 2002, CEO Jay Stein appointed Richard Burton, MD, as SADAA and provided him and his staff with dedicated space that expanded over the next decade to accommodate separate offices for four staff, the SADAA, and a conference room. Burton received his MD from HMS, completed two years of general surgery residency at SMH and then served two years in the US Air Force. He subsequently completed an orthopaedic residency in the Harvard combined program and a fellowship in hand surgery at The Roosevelt Hospital. He joined the URMC faculty in 1974 as associate chair of Orthopaedics and instituted the hand surgery fellowship program. Among his many clinical achievements was the development of a breakthrough surgery, known widely as the "Burton Procedure," which has become the gold standard for patients with arthritis of the thumb. From 1986 to 2000, Burton was chair and Wehle Professor of Orthopaedics. Under his leadership, the department experienced enormous growth in patient care services, markedly expanded its educational programs and became an international leader in musculoskeletal research. In 2000, Burton was appointed Dean's Professor and for two years served as acting chair of Neurosurgery. Upon stepping down from SADAA in 2012, he served for eight years as a consultant to the new SADAA, and as a mentor for chairs and other leaders. During this time, he wrote *Leading Department Excellence: Achieve the Robust Academic Health Center*, published by Amazon.com. In 2011, he created the Richard and Margaret Burton Distinguished Professorship in Orthopaedics.

Jeffrey M. Lyness, MD, succeeded Burton as SADAA in 2012. Lyness received his MD from the University of Rochester. After an internship in primary care at URMC, he did a residency in psychiatry at Yale University, returning to URMC to do a clinical fellowship and a National Institutes of Mental Health (NIMH)-funded research fellowship in geriatric psychiatry. He then joined the faculty of Psychiatry, where he developed a NIMH-funded research program focused on the relationships between depression and comorbid medical illnesses in older adults. He served as director of the Geriatric Psychiatry program (now a division) and as associate chair for Education. He helped lead the creation of the DHC, including its Mind/Brain/Behavior course, and served as SMD's director of curriculum and as medical director for Continuing Medical Education (CME). He has chaired the AAMC's Group on Faculty Affairs and served as president of the American Association for Geriatric Psychiatry. Lyness remained as SADAA until 2022, when he was named president and CEO of the American Board of Psychiatry and Neurology, an organization that he had served in many capacities over the years. He has received several national awards and honors, including the American Psychiatric Association's Vestermark Psychiatry Educator Award and Apple Distinguished Educator in 2013.

Figure 36.2. Jeffrey Lyness

Judith Baumhauer, MD, MPH, succeeded Lyness as SADAA in 2022 and was subsequently promoted to vice dean for Academic Affairs. Baumhauer received her MD and completed her residency in orthopaedics at the University of Vermont, then a fellowship in foot and ankle surgery at the Medical College of Wisconsin. She joined URMC Orthopaedics in 1995, where she served as associate chair for academic affairs for fifteen years. Baumhauer led multicentered national and international trials to bring new, clinically important orthopaedic products through FDA approval. More recently, she has focused on using patient-reported outcome assessments to measure and manage treatment options for patients and has been the prime mover in URMC's PROMIS initiative (see p. 55). Baumhauer has been president of the American

Figure 36.3. Judith Baumhauer

Board of Orthopaedic Surgery, American Orthopaedic Foot and Ankle Society, and Eastern Orthopaedic Association, PROMIS Health Organization, and a trustee for the *American Journal of Bone and Joint Surgery.* She has won numerous awards, including the 2012 Athena Award in Rochester. She received the 2022 Nicolas Andry Lifetime Achievement award for her work using patient-reported outcome measures, and the 2021 Women's Leadership Career Impact Award by the American Foot and Ankle Society for her contributions to mentoring women in orthopaedic surgery.

Under Burton's leadership, the academic promotion process was streamlined: an ad hoc promotion committee (appointed by the SADAA) submits its report to a Steering Committee of the Medical School Advisory Council (MEDSAC), comprised of the chairs and center directors. If recommended by the Steering Committee, it is presented to MEDSAC for information and then to the SMD dean and University provost for final approval. Several other important modifications were made to the appointment and promotion criteria, some specific to the needs of the Medical Center and others in conjunction with changes throughout the University. One of these allowed for the "tenure clock" to stop moving if a faculty member took a pregnancy, maternity, or medical leave. In 2014, Lyness oversaw a restructuring of the appointment and promotion criteria, based upon feedback from an extensive faculty survey. The new criteria provided more flexibility to the faculty, and in particular provided promotion and tenure pathways recognizing a broader range of types of scholarship, contributions to "team science," and for extraordinary contributions to institutional scholarship or to the URMC mission.

Traditionally, faculty offer letters, generally crafted by chairs or center directors, lacked standardization and often did not clearly delineate what was promised or expected, leading to conflicts between the faculty and chair, and sometimes even legal challenges. Working with the Office of Counsel, Burton initiated a series of important modifications. All offer letters (and reappointment letters as necessary) had two components: a document written by the chair describing the position and the expectations, and a standardized document, developed jointly by the Office of Counsel and the SADAA, that covered or defined tenure, promotions, salary terms, space issues, etc. All letters required approval of the Office of SADAA, Office of Counsel, and human resources if indicated, prior to being sent to the dean. These efforts have helped speed SMD recruitment efforts.

Prior to 2002, the process of dealing with conflict of interest (COI), often unavoidable in biomedical research, was not well organized. Burton took on this challenge, establishing a dialogue with members of the Office of Counsel, including Diane Caselli, currently senior associate general counsel and deputy chief counsel to URMC, and Gunta Liders, associate VP for Research Administration and leader of the Office of Research Project Administration (ORPA). Out of these meetings came the Conflict of Interest Advisory Group (CIAG) comprised of tenured faculty selected by the SADAA and representatives from the Office of Counsel and ORPA and overseen by the OAA. CIAG meets monthly to review possible COIs and to develop management plans and monitor compliance. A reporting form must be completed yearly by all faculty. Failure to complete the COI form or comply with CIAG recommendations could lead to withdrawal of lab space and support. CIAG has proven to be extremely successful in managing COI for our clinicians and researchers.

An ever-increasing role for the OAA has been in faculty development. These have been spearheaded by Janine R. Shapiro, MD. Shapiro received her MD from the University of Montreal and did residencies in internal medicine and anesthesiology at RGH before joining the faculty of Anesthesiology. A William S. McCann Dean's Teaching Fellow from 2007 to 2009, Shapiro was the founding chair of the Medical Education Research Interest Group at SMD. In 2009, she became director of faculty development and subsequently was named associate dean for Faculty Development in the Office of Academic Affairs, succeeding Denham Ward, MD, PhD, who retired as associate dean and chair of Anesthesiology. As associate dean, Shapiro also oversees the Office of CME, which offers a broad array of CME activities and enables URMC-sponsored activities to meet the requirements for CME accreditation.

Figure 36.4. Janine Shapiro

The early-stage faculty boot camp, held twice a year in collaboration with the CTSI, is an all-day, three-day course designed to help senior instructors and new assistant professors identify the skills they need for more successful career advancement. Beginning in 2022, URMC entered into a partnership with VALOR (www.valor-leadership.com) to provide an online, six-month program that offers one-on-one leadership coaching and access to a robust learning platform to established leaders, those who want take a leadership role, and those who want to strengthen existing skills.

Senior Leader Education and Development (SLED) is a two-year program designed to develop senior leaders in academic medicine, addressing topics such as setting direction and vision, leading by developing others, leading by developing and maintaining organizational efficiency, and leading through organizational development. The Dean's Teaching Fellowship program was initially created in the early 1990s by Jules Cohen, MD, former SAD for Medical Education. Initially designed to recognize faculty who made important contributions to medical education, the program was expanded in 2001 to provide a rigorous curriculum in educational research, curricular design, assessment, and teaching methods to eight highly qualified faculty members per year to develop a core group of master educators.

The OAA has played an increasing role in the search for new chairs, center directors, and other senior leaders. Traditionally, the dean would appoint a department chair or senior faculty member to head the search committee. Because the process was often very slow and uneven due to the already extraordinary time demands on senior faculty members, it was decided, during Lyness's term, to bring this function under the OAA and to have the SADAA chair the search committees, aided by the SADs of Clinical Affairs or Research. National search firms were also employed to ensure that the widest net was cast. The outstanding quality of current chairs is a testimony to the success of this strategy. The SADAA also plays a role in chair development, including monthly meetings with new chairs and regular meetings with established chairs. In addition, each new chair is assigned a successful current chair as mentor for at least the first year.

In 2013, Lyness reorganized the Medical Faculty Council as the School of Medicine and Dentistry Faculty Council (SMDFC), which serves in an advisory capacity to the dean. An active SMDFC is in keeping with the theme of faculty development and provides an important mechanism for expression of faculty views and for improving communication between faculty and SMD leadership. Information presented at SMDFC meetings can be brought for discussion to individual departments and centers by their SMDFC representatives. Concerns raised in departmental and center meetings can also be brought directly to SMD leadership.

The SMD Faculty Professionalism Council (FPC) was established by Dean Taubman in 2018 on Lyness's recommendation to promote faculty professionalism, which supports the institution's ICARE values and helps create a positive workplace culture. The FPC is chaired by the SADAA and is advisory to the dean. The FPC articulates expected behaviors, tracks reported concerns from the URMC community, standardizes remediation and disciplinary actions across the SMD, and supports efforts that promote professional behaviors.

Part III

BUILDING MULTIDISCIPLINARY PROGRAMS OF EXCELLENCE

H. Enhancing Collaborative Research

Chapter 37

EVOLVING THE RESEARCH STRATEGIC PLAN

One of the factors that led to Jay Stein's appointment as URMC CEO was the remarkable growth in research during his short tenure heading the Oklahoma Health Sciences Center, with awards increasing by over forty percent. Shortly after taking office, Stein initiated a URMC strategic planning process that included a master facilities plan and recruitment strategy to grow the research, education, and patient care missions. The cornerstone of the $400 million, ten-year strategy was the creation in 1998 of the Aab Institute of Biomedical Sciences,[10] supported by a generous gift from Richard T. Aab, a leader in the field of telecommunications.

Figure 37.1. Richard Aab

The Aab Institute would contain six centers with interdisciplinary research foci: Aging & Developmental Biology, Cancer Biology, Cardiovascular Research, Human Genetics & Molecular Pediatric Disease, Oral Biology, and Vaccine Biology & Immunology. The centers were chosen by a team of scientists from SMD and Arts, Sciences, & Engineering, after considering current institutional strengths, long-term directions of the biomedical sciences, and future disease trends. A major objective was to bring individuals with diverse scientific backgrounds together in contiguous space to work on common themes. To help integrate the centers within the SMD structure, a dual-appointment procedure was established whereby all center members would have academic appointments within a traditional department.

In 1996, plans were unveiled for a new 240,000 square-foot research building to be connected to the Medical Center by a 55,000 square-foot William and Mildred Levine Pavilion. The Pavilion became the main entrance to the Medical School, which now included new medical education facilities, three auditoria, smaller seminar rooms, and an atrium. Named the Arthur

---

10 Goldsmith, L. A., Tabak, L. A. and Stein, J. H. "Aab Institute of Biomedical Sciences." *Molecular Medicine* 5 (1999): 645–53.

Kornberg Medical Research Building (KMRB) after SMD graduate and Nobel laureate Arthur Kornberg, the research building consisted of four floors of wet bench space with an open laboratory design, and one floor of vivarium support. The building opened on September 17, 1999 after three days of celebration, which included the dedication of the Aab Institute, a ribbon-cutting ceremony for the Levine Pavilion, a keynote lecture by Arthur Kornberg, and a Kornberg Symposium, entitled "Basic Research and Invention: The Lifeblood of Medicine and Industry," and featured lectures by four Nobel laureates and two pharmaceutical executives. It should be noted that Stein is particularly proud of his efforts in engaging Kornberg (his Nobel Prize medal is on permanent display in the Flaum Atrium), who had distanced himself from the University because of the antisemitism he had experienced as a medical student in the 1940s.

Howard Federoff, MD, PhD, was chosen as director of the Center for Aging and Developmental Biology, whose goal was to elucidate the function of genes involved in the development, maturation, senescence, and dysfunction of the nervous system. He was succeeded in 2007 by Harris ("Handy") A. Gelbard, MD, PhD, who changed the name to the Center for Neurodevelopment and Disease (CNDD).

Hartmut Land, PhD, recently recruited from the Imperial Cancer Research Fund in London, was chosen as director of the Center for Cancer Biology, whose focus was to explore the molecular architecture, function,

Figure 37.2. Kornberg Medical Research Building

Figure 37.3. The Levine Pavilion at the Medical School's main entrance

and genetics of signaling networks. Under Land's direction, the Center for Cancer Biology ultimately became the new department of Biomedical Genetics, and the newly established WCC became the nexus for cancer research, under the leadership of Richard Fisher, MD.

Bradford Berk, MD, PhD, recruited as chief of the Cardiology division, was chosen as director of the Center for Cardiovascular Research, whose goals were to understand how the cardiovascular system develops and responds to physiological and pathological changes. Following the ascension of Berk to chair of Medicine and the recruitment of Mark Taubman, MD, as the new chief of Cardiology, the Center grew into the Aab Cardiovascular Institute.

Tim Mosmann, PhD, chair of Immunology at the University of Alberta, was recruited to direct the Center for Vaccine Biology and Immunology. The University of Rochester was already a major center for clinical trials of vaccines for HIV, human papillomavirus, influenza, and other respiratory infections, and the site for the successful development of the *Haemophilus influenzae* type b vaccine.

Unlike the others, the Center for Oral Biology, directed by Lawrence Tabak, DDS, PhD, was not new, but rather a restructuring and broadening of the department of Dental Research, which conducted research related to microbial biofilms, cell and molecular physiology of exocrine glands, and development of the craniofacial complex.

In keeping with the new research strategic plan, Shey-Shing Sheu, PhD, SAD for Graduate Studies (1997–2000), restructured the graduate programs, which had largely been departmentally based, into ten interdepartmental research clusters. These clusters dovetailed well with the collaborative structure developed in the new Aab Institute of Biomedical Sciences. The establishment of the research centers was also accompanied by a substantial increase in the recruitment of fundamental and translational scientists, almost tripling the number of faculty with primary research missions. This was supported by funds allocated by URMC's strategic plan and further

Figure 37.4. The Del Monte Neurosciences Institute

spurred by the doubling of the NIH budget. To provide sufficient space and resources, an additional 143,000 square-foot four-story research building, "MRBX," was completed in 2002, connected to KMRB by a glass-enclosed walkway. Like KMRB, MRBX was built with an open laboratory design with longer benches and even greater flexibility. In 2009, MRBX was renamed the Del Monte Research Building in recognition of a generous gift from Rochester entrepreneur Ernest J. Del Monte to develop an additional interdisciplinary center, The Ernest J. Del Monte Neurosciences Institute.

In succeeding Jay Stein as CEO in 2003, C. McCollister Evarts continued to promote an aggressive research agenda, adding musculoskeletal diseases to the other six priority areas and providing support to establish the Center for Musculoskeletal Research. Evarts was instrumental in obtaining philanthropy for and initiating construction of the WCC, which became the focal point for cancer-related research. In 2006, the University became one of twelve institutions to receive the first CTSA from the NIH and plans were begun to develop new space to house the new CTSI. Evarts also established the Center for Community Health and Prevention, under the leadership of Nancy Bennett, which became closely aligned to the CTSI. He also placed an enhanced focus on the SON, overseeing the addition of the Loretta Ford Wing, which houses the Mac Evarts Lounge, named in his honor, as well as expanded education and research space. The expansion of the SON led to new faculty recruitment and a significant increase in NIH funding.

With recruitment rapidly filling the two new research buildings, and virtually no space remaining on the URMC main campus, Evarts saw a need to ensure ample room to expand SMD research programs. In 2004, he bought a vaccine development facility and its surrounding forty-eight acres on Bailey Road in Henrietta from Wyeth Pharmaceuticals Inc. for $4.5 million. The Bailey Road facility was originally built to house Praxis Biologics Inc., a URMC spinoff started by university researchers who developed the vaccine against *Haemophilus influenzae* type b.

The Aab CVRI became the first program to move into the facility; at the time it had grown to fifteen NIH-funded laboratories, housing close to 150 faculty, postdoctoral fellows, students, technicians, and staff. Cardiology billing services were also moved to the new facility. Unfortunately, the economic recession, coupled with the flattening of the NIH budget, substantially limited further growth of the research enterprise, and ultimately the Aab CVRI moved back to the Medical Center. A renovated and expanded facility at Bailey Road has become a central home for UR Medicine pathology and laboratory services.

Upon becoming CEO in 2006, Bradford Berk, an internationally prominent vascular biologist, developed a new strategic plan for the clinical, education, and research missions. A key part of the plan was the completion of the 150,000 square-foot facility (Saunders Research Building) to serve as the academic home of the CTSI. The research plan built upon Stein's "Center" concept but sought to better align the research with clinical and teaching missions by creating Integrated Disease Programs (IDPs) centered on five major disease areas—cancer, cardiovascular disease, immunology and infectious disease, musculoskeletal disease, and neuro-medicine—designed to promote interaction among scientists from different departments and ease the translation of basic discoveries to patient care and novel treatments. Four Innovative Science Programs (ISPs)—stem cell and regenerative medicine, biomedical imaging and biomarkers, nanomedicine, and genomics and systems biology—were identified as key programs that, with further development, could support IDPs. Berk's plan called for the recruitment of 140 new people for the IDPs and ISPs, overseen by executive committees for each area. Unfortunately, recruitment efforts were slowed due to the flattening of the NIH budget, with the resulting drop in NIH pay lines, and the "Great Recession" of 2007–9, both of which put substantial financial pressure on SMD to support its current investigators. Despite the initial financial constraints, several key research centers were established, including the Center for RNA Biology (2007), and the Del Monte Neurosciences Institute (2009).

When Mark Taubman succeeded Berk as CEO in 2015, he developed a new, ten-year research strategic plan which built upon the concepts established during Berk's administration. The plan focused on the establishment of multidisciplinary and multidepartmental programs of excellence that would encompass all Medical Center missions. More than two dozen proposals were submitted, of which sixteen were selected, encompassing approximately ninety-five percent of SMD's funded research. Many of these proposals included investigators on the River Campus. The plan would be fluid, allowing for the establishment of new programs of excellence and the sunsetting of those that no longer made sense. Understanding that SMD did not have the financial resources to markedly expand the research enterprise, the focus was on enhancing existing programs that had or could most easily develop international stature, thus driving the reputation of the University of Rochester. These programs included cancer, neurosciences, immunobiology and infection, musculoskeletal diseases, and RNA biology. The full range of programs is depicted in Figure 37.5. RNA biology and immunobiology are depicted as overriding arches because they impact virtually all fields of research. Two of Berk's original ISPs, bioinformatics and imaging, serve as key technological foundations for all programs. Building on initial successes, the second five years saw the development of two new institutes, the University of Rochester Aging Institute and the Institute for Human Health and the Environment, as high-priority programs. In addition, the Health and Wellness program expanded to encompass the new Office of Health Equity Research.

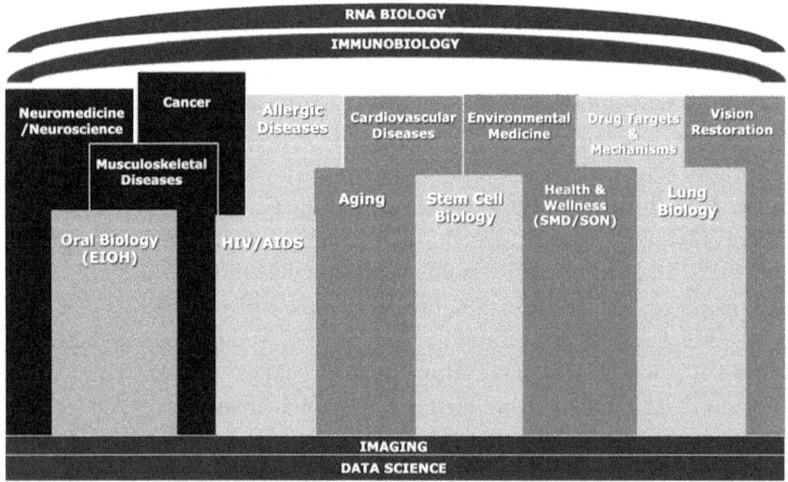

Figure 37.5. Programs of Excellence

To affect their research plans, Berk and Taubman needed to make significant changes in the financial structure of the Medical Center. These changes had begun under Jay Stein, with the appointment of a chief financial officer (CFO) for URMC, Michael Goonan, who would have oversight of all URMC finances. The merging of the dean and CEO positions under Taubman and the appointment of Adam Anolik as URMC CFO allowed for the completion of the financial transition into a single URMC budget, rather than separate budgets for SMH, SMD, and URMFG, overseen by a senior leadership group consisting of the CFO, the URMC CEO/SMD dean, and the CEOs of URMFG and SMH. Medical Center investment in research, which had grown from approximately thirty cents to sixty cents for each dollar of extramural research support (a consequence of the flattening of the NIH budget for over a dozen years), became a top-level URMC expense, rather than a below-the-line negotiated transfer from SMH. This enabled research investment to grow from approximately $35 million in 2010 to approximately $135 million in 2024. As part of this, with the strong support of University Presidents Joel Seligman and Sarah Mangelsdorf, Taubman and Berk established an Academic Reserve Fund, investing a portion of URMC reserves, traditionally held in minimal interest accounts, into the University's endowment pool. Over time, the Academic Reserve Fund has been able to provide approximately $15 million per year to the research effort. A substantial part of these funds was specifically used to support the high-priority programs of excellence.

The change in financial structure enabled Berk and Taubman to recruit key senior faculty for high-priority research programs but also allowed them to focus on the recruitment of outstanding junior faculty throughout URMC. To help oversee the recruitment efforts, Stephen Dewhurst, PhD, the chair of Microbiology and Immunology, was appointed as vice dean for Research with oversight of the SADs for Clinical and Basic Research, as well as the SAD for Graduate Education, a recognition of the vital role that graduate and postgraduate education play in the research enterprise. The increased budget also allowed for the expansion and consolidation of research core facilities under the direction of SADs for Basic Research J. Edward Puzas, PhD, Donald and Mary Clark Professor of Orthopaedics, and Dirk P. Bohmann, PhD, Donald M. Foster, MD, Professor in Biomedical Genetics, as well as the clinical trials office under the direction of Martin S. Zand, MD, PhD, SAD for Clinical Research.

Figure 37.6.
Edward Puzas

Chapter 38

CLINICAL AND TRANSLATIONAL SCIENCE INSTITUTE (CTSI)

A defining moment for URMC research occurred in October 2006, when it became one of twelve institutions to receive one of NIH's inaugural Clinical and Translational Science Awards (CTSA), whose goal was to reduce the time it takes for drugs, medical devices, or therapeutic interventions to reach patients. The five-year, $40 million award, the largest NIH grant ever awarded to SMD, is a comprehensive and integrated set of services and infrastructure to facilitate translational research through establishment of a CTSI. The grant, a collaborative effort involving hundreds of individuals, was spearheaded by Dean David Guzick, who served as the PI for the grant, and Thomas Pearson, MD, MPH, PhD, SAD for Clinical Research, who became the CTSI's first director.

In October 2008, URMC broke ground for the 200,000 square-foot, four-story Clinical and Translational Science Building, the first in the nation. Construction of the $76.4 million building, which occurred during the "Great Recession," was strongly endorsed by NY State, which provided a $50 million grant. The project created over 800 construction jobs and hundreds of permanent jobs at URMC. Completed in April 2011, the building was connected to the SON's Helen Wood Hall, a symbol of the growing partnership between SMD and the SON, which was deemed a strength of the application. It was the first building at the University to receive LEED (Leadership in Energy and Environmental Design) certification for its "Green" design. The new building was named the Saunders Research Building in honor of a $10 million gift from E. Philip Saunders to support clinical and translational research, particularly in neurosciences and cancer.

In addition to housing the CTSI, the building also served as home to the University's National Center for Deaf Health Research, the departments of Public Health Sciences (PHS) and Biostatistics & Computational Biology, and clinical and translational research programs in cancer, cardiovascular disease, neurological disorders, pediatrics, and emergency medicine. The CTSI also served as the nucleus for a coalition of sixteen biomedical research centers in upstate NY, the UNYTE Network.

Figure 38.1. The Saunders Research Building

The CTSA grant was renewed in 2011, by which time the program had expanded to sixty centers. The grant supported a number of new initiatives, including: the Center for Human Experimental Therapeutics (CHET), created to help researchers conceive, plan, and carry out the initial translation of novel interventions from preclinical evaluation into the first human clinical trials; and the Center for Research Implementation and Translation (CRIT), a partnership between the SON, PHS, and Psychiatry to identify new approaches that improve care and lower cost. The new grant placed additional emphasis on the creation of public–private partnerships and on the creation of large teams of researchers focused on complex health problems. One of the strengths of Rochester's CTSI was its focus on population health improvement, embodied in the Center for Community Health and Prevention (CCHP), and in its focus on developing and teaching community-based participatory research methods that would enable investigators to better recruit research participants from the community, thereby enhancing the diversity of participants and the generalizability of the research.

Figure 38.2. Karl Kieburtz

In 2013, Pearson left URMC to become executive VP for Research and Education at the University of Florida Health Sciences Center. He was replaced as CTSI director and SAD for clinical research by Karl Kieburtz,

MD, MPH, an internationally recognized expert in the design and operation of clinical trials for neurodegenerative diseases, such as Parkinson's and Huntington's diseases. Kieburtz, who received his MD and MPH and did his residency in neurology and fellowship in experimental therapeutics at the University of Rochester, was responsible for establishing URMC as a hub for many of the world's largest studies of new treatments for neurological conditions. To accommodate the growth of the CTSI, Kieburtz reorganized the CTSI leadership, adding Martin Zand, MD, PhD, director of the Rochester Center for Health Informatics, and Nancy "Nana" Bennett, MD, director of the CCHP, as co-directors. After overseeing the successful renewal of the CTSA grant in 2016, Kieburtz stepped down from his administrative positions to focus on his personal research interests.

Figure 38.3. Martin Zand

Zand and Bennett succeeded Kieburtz as CTSI co-directors. In 2017, under their leadership, URMC received a $19 million grant from the National Center for Advancing Translational Sciences (NCATS) of the NIH to establish the Center for Leading Innovation and Collaboration (CLIC). The aim of the CLIC was to create virtual and in-person platforms on which all CTSA Program institutions nationwide could share data and educational materials, track their success, communicate with one another, and develop collaborations. The awarding of the CLIC was a testament to the success of the University's CTSI and placed the institution at the forefront of the CTSA program. Zand and Deborah Ossip, PhD (Public Health Sciences), served as co-directors of the CLIC. Ossip, an internationally recognized leader in smoking cessation research, had been the director of the CTSI Population Health Research postdoctoral program. Although the five-year program was not continued by the NIH, the University has continued to play an important role in the national coordination of the CTSA program.

In 2018, Zand was appointed SAD for Clinical Research. Zand received his MD and PhD from Northwestern University, followed by a residency in internal medicine and fellowship in nephrology at Beth Israel Deaconess Medical Center, Boston. An expert in solid organ transplant immunobiology, Zand played a major role in the URMC renal transplant program prior to assuming his CTSI responsibilities.

Zand's focus as SAD and CTSI co-director was on enhancing URMC's capacity for clinical trials. Key was establishing the Office of Clinical Research (OCR), which is currently directed by Ashlee Lang, MPH. The centerpiece of OCR is OnCore, a clinical trial management system that enables researchers to manage protocols, track research participant visits, and manage clinical trial finances, both pre- and post-award. This system has led to marked increases in the number of patients enrolled in clinical trials, has improved clinical trial revenue, and was instrumental in facilitating the WCI's successful application for NCI designation. The OCR provides a variety of services that facilitate clinical research, including a system that stores essential protocol documents, staff credentials, and regulatory tracking documents—a service that helps investigators assess the feasibility of proposed clinical studies and develop meaningful metrics to guide management, manage clinical research finances, and pay subjects immediately after each visit.

In 2020, under the leadership of Zand and Bennett, the CTSA was renewed for the fourth time, resulting in an aggregate of $132 million in NIH funding since its inception. In 2024, Karen Wilson, MD, MPH, the Ruth A. Lawrence Professor in Pediatrics, succeeded Bennett (upon her retirement) as co-director of the CTSI. The CTSI was once again reorganized to best accommodate changes in the national program, which over time has increasingly focused on population health and translational science and away from early translational studies.

Figure 38.4. Karen Wilson

The CTSI now has five operational branches: Informatics and Analytics, Population Health, Research Education and Career Development, Research Services, and Translational Science. Each branch is led by strategic and operational leaders who oversee the execution of the branch's assigned function and programming.

The Informatics team offers a variety of tools, services, and training to help researchers plan, access, analyze, and manage data for their studies. These include the Office of Research IT; the Biostatistics, Epidemiology, and Research Design team; and the Research Data Integration and Analysis group.

The Population Health Branch aims to improve population health and health equity by broadening engagement with community stakeholders, enabling transdisciplinary science, and supporting the integration of special populations into research. This branch coordinates with the CCHP, the Office of Health Equity Research, and the National Center for Deaf Health Research, a CDC-funded Prevention Research Center that is the only research center in the world to work with deaf sign language users and people with hearing loss to promote health and prevent disease using community-based, participatory research.

The Research Education and Career Development Branch oversees educational programs tailored to pre- and postdoctoral students, faculty at all career stages, and research staff. Key programs include a PhD in Translational

Biomedical Science; a BS in Clinical and Translational Sciences for undergraduates, a collaborative between the CTSI and the Colleges of Arts and Sciences and Engineering. The Rochester Early-Stage Investigator Network works across departments and centers to optimize and support training for early-stage investigators from across the translational spectrum. This branch also oversees a range of federally funded training grants, including KL2, K12, and TL1.

The Research Services Branch supports clinical research through consultation and assistance with participant recruitment, navigating FDA regulatory requirements, supporting clinical trials, and training study coordinators. Programs include the Clinical Research Center, which facilitates safe and controlled inpatient and outpatient studies by providing infrastructure and support to clinical research teams; the Office of Regulatory Support, which helps investigators understand and comply with FDA-regulated processes in research involving experimental drugs and devices, and in preclinical laboratory studies; and the OCR.

The Translational Science Branch is the administrative home to internal translational science research efforts and serves as the incubator for strategic initiatives at the institute. It manages the pilot grants program, which has been extraordinarily successful in helping researchers develop translational science projects and in obtaining extramural funding. It is the home of the Continuous Quality Improvement effort, the scientific study of translational barriers and how they can be reduced or removed, and also serves as the home base for examining ways that AI can support clinical and translational research activities.

In summary, the CTSI has transformed the clinical and translational research efforts of URMC, enabling the University to play a leadership role in the nation's clinical research efforts. It has been blessed with a series of extraordinary leaders who have successfully steered the program through four successful renewals and is well positioned for renewal number five.

Chapter 39

DEPARTMENT OF BIOSTATISTICS AND COMPUTATIONAL BIOLOGY (BCB)

Biostatistics was established in 1970 as a free-standing division in the Medical School, led for seventeen years by Charles L. Odoroff, PhD, and then by W. J. ("Jack") Hall, PhD. Martin Tanner, PhD, became division director in 1990 and then chair in 1992, when Biostatistics achieved departmental status. From 1995 to 2002, Biostatistics was led by David Oakes, PhD. Oakes received his PhD from London University and was recruited to URMC in 1983, where he became involved in clinical trials for cardiovascular disease and for treatments of Parkinson's and Huntington's diseases. His research interests have been especially focused on developing models for the effect of explanatory variables on survival and for multivariate survival data. In 2002, a department plan was developed calling for substantial faculty growth and a new division of Computational Biology. This plan was an integral part of URMC efforts to develop national prominence in clinical and translational research. It also presaged the growth of computing and imaging, endeavoring to create a department that provided the University with expertise to handle the expected onslaught of "big data."

Figure 39.1. David Oakes

Andrei Yakovlev, MD, PhD, was recruited as chair of the new department, whose name was changed to Biostatistics and Computational Biology (BCB) to reflect the emphasis on mathematical and computational biology. The goals of BCB were to make major methodological breakthroughs in the analysis of high-throughput biological data and to achieve national prominence in computational biology, enabling URMC to secure more funding for methodological and collaborative research. The Statistical Consulting Center was also expanded and reorganized in 2003 to improve biostatistical support for clinical and translational research.

Figure 39.2. Andrei Yakovlev

Under Yakovlev's leadership, BCB made great strides in recruitment and in achieving its goals, and developed strong ties with the newly developed CTSI.

Figure 39.3. Robert Strawderman

Sadly, Yakovlev died suddenly in 2008. Oakes returned as interim chair, shepherding BCB until 2012, when Robert L. Strawderman III, ScD, was recruited as Dean's Professor and chair of BCB. In 2014, he became the inaugural Donald M. Foster, MD, Distinguished Professor in Biostatistics, one of two professorships established by the estate of Donald M. Foster, a graduate and long-time supporter of SMD. Strawderman received his ScD in Biostatistics from Harvard University. Prior to coming to Rochester, he had been professor of Biological Statistics and Computational Biology and Statistical Science and professor in the Department of Public Health at Weill-Cornell Medical College. Strawderman's primary biomedical research interests include developing and applying new statistical methods for evaluating and predicting patient survival and related outcomes (e.g. recurrent hospitalizations), and new approaches to evaluating quality of life and comparative and cost effectiveness.

Strawderman subsequently spearheaded the development of a new and comprehensive vision for BCB: 1) to be national leader in advancing both methodology and practice in biostatistics and computational biology; 2) to continue its tradition of intellectual leadership through promoting the proper use of rigorous quantitative methods as members of cross-disciplinary research teams; and 3) to continue its evolution as a leader in the education and training of graduate students and postdoctoral scholars in the advanced statistical sciences. He and his colleagues endeavored to create a highly collegial department that could serve as a resource for the entire University and could adapt to the rapid changes in computing technology and data analysis. To achieve national prominence in independent methodological research, Strawderman focused on recruiting faculty with an established profile of independent research and junior faculty that had a clear potential for and interest in the same. This recruitment also focused on hiring faculty with strong interests in collaboration in areas important to URMC research programs. This led to a substantial increase in the number of PI-led extramural grants within BCB and improved the degree of alignment between methodological and collaborative research activities.

BCB currently has twenty-one faculty with research interests spanning traditional biostatistics, stochastic modeling, bioinformatics and computational biology. These interests include analysis of large-scale datasets (e.g. from high-throughput sequencing and imaging applications), Bayesian methods, causal inference, clinical trial design, dynamic treatment regimes, longitudinal data analysis, modeling and analysis of data derived from biological and social networks, nonparametric and semiparametric inference, order-restricted inference, smoothing techniques, statistical computing, stochastic modeling of complex cell systems, and survival analysis.

BCB epitomizes the collaborative nature that developed at the University over the past several decades, being involved in the research efforts of over thirty departments and centers, including the Goergen Institute for Data Science. Of particular note, the Biostatistics and Bioinformatics Shared Resource, co-directed by Derick Peterson, PhD, and Matthew N. McCall, PhD, provides statistical support and collaborative activities for WCI investigators, including study design and conduct; grant, protocol, and manuscript preparation; protocol review; and Data and Safety Monitoring Committee activities. BCB also plays a key role in the CTSI, where Strawderman serves as co-function leader for Biostatistics, Epidemiology and Research Design, and program director for the CTSI's Novel Biostatistical and Epidemiological Methodology pilot program. BCB provides a consulting service for the CTSI, staffed by faculty, research associates and assistants, programmers, and graduate students, that provides researchers with help in study design, data analyses, grant preparation, and programming support for data management. BCB has also been increasingly involved with the URMC Center for Biomedical Informatics (CBI), a central priority of the current SMD Research Strategic Plan.

BCB's role in providing collaborative research support to investigators across URMC was particularly critical in the restructuring of the SMD tenure and promotions criteria. A substantial majority of BCB faculty were co-investigators on numerous grants that required statistical expertise to be competitive for funding—a single BCB faculty member might have facilitated the success of as many as a half dozen grants per year. However, these critical contributions to the research enterprise were insufficiently valued under SMD's existing promotion criteria. This was particularly true for the awarding of tenure, where longitudinal success as a PI on federally funded awards and senior author status on related publications were long considered to be required activities. This structural disadvantage led to the development of an "Institutional" option, where faculty could gain promotion, and in some cases tenure, by providing extraordinary support considered vital to the overall research and/or clinical missions. This proved particularly important in retaining superb collaborative research that has been vital to the success of the CTSI, the WCI, and other programs.

The PhD program in Statistics was instituted in 1969 and originally administered by the Statistics department in the College of Arts and Sciences. Responsibility for all graduate programs in Statistics was transferred to BCB in 1997. Students receive a thorough grounding in statistical theory, providing them with the foundation for conducting research in statistical methodology. Students also gain an appreciation for applied problems in biomedical research and the skills necessary to succeed in collaborative research environments. In 2014, the department introduced a concentration in Bioinformatics and Computational Biology, designed to provide the next generation of biostatisticians with the knowledge required to address critical scientific and public health questions, and to equip them with the skills necessary to develop and use quantitative and computational methodologies and tools to manage, analyze, and integrate massive amounts of complex biomedical data. Over the past six years, the PhD program has averaged five new students per year and currently has twenty-six active students. As of the end of 2024, there had been 128 PhDs awarded in Statistics at the University. Over the past thirty years, Statistics PhD graduates have been one hundred percent successful in obtaining positions in academia, industry, and government, with many achieving distinction in their careers.

BCB also oversees two relatively small master's programs. The MA in Statistics is designed for students seeking preparation for a PhD program or work as a master's-level statistician. The MS in Biostatistics is intended for students who wish to follow careers in health-related professions such as those in the pharmaceutical industry and biomedical or clinical research organizations. The T32 training grant "Training in Environmental Health Biostatistics," funded by the National Institute of Environmental Health Sciences, was awarded and led by David Oakes in 1992, and since 2015 has been led by Sally W. Thurston, PhD. This grant is a collaboration between BCB and Environmental Health Sciences (EHS) and prepares predoctoral and/or postdoctoral trainees for health-related research careers. Trainees are involved in projects related to environmental health and are co-mentored by BCB and EHS faculty.

Chapter 40

DEPARTMENT OF BIOMEDICAL ENGINEERING

One of the best examples of rising collaboration between the Medical Center and the River Campus was the department of Biomedical Engineering (BME). BME was created in 2000, through the efforts of Kevin J. Parker, PhD, dean of the Hajim School of Engineering and Applied Sciences, and SMD Dean Lowell Goldsmith. At the time, there was great interest in translating basic science into useful applications, and biomedical engineering was the fastest growing major on campus, with more than fifty freshmen listing it. Prior to the formal creation of BME, the University had established seven new faculty positions in biomedical engineering, developed four new courses, and built a new research laboratory.

The roots of BME date to 1961, when the University of Rochester became one of the first three institutions nationwide to establish a training program in biomedical engineering. In 1995, a formal graduate program was created, and a new undergraduate program was developed a year later. The programs involved more than three dozen faculty members from departments in engineering and medicine, including: chemical engineers, who developed an artificial bone marrow system that simulated the 3-D scaffolding found within bones; electrical engineers, who patented a new "phantom" to test the accuracy of ultrasound machines; a collaborative team of investigators, who received a $7.8 million NIH grant to study how blood cells attach themselves to blood vessel walls; and mechanical engineers who developed computer models to measure the stresses experienced by a beating embryonic heart and to study pediatric orthopedic biomechanics.

Richard Waugh, PhD, the founding chair of BME, received his PhD in biomedical engineering from Duke University in 1977 and joined the faculty of Biophysics at the University of Rochester in 1980. Waugh is a leader in the study of cell and membrane mechanics and the structural basis for the mechanical behavior of cells and membranes. Although much of his research centers around erythrocytes and the role of cell membrane

Figure 40.1. Richard Waugh

dynamics in hemolytic anemia, he was among the first to examine the mechanical and adhesive properties of leukocytes.

An early success for BME was a $3 million development award from the Whitaker Foundation. This award, one of only six given across the country, enhanced student laboratories and allowed the growth of the BME faculty. Waugh was also the driving force behind the construction of the department's home, Robert B. Goergen Hall. Completed in 2007, this $37.7 million, 101,000 square-foot building includes research facilities, undergraduate and graduate teaching labs, and the University's Integrated Nanosystems Center. In recognition of Waugh's accomplishments in establishing BME, he was appointed associate VP for research in 2013. After stepping down as chair of BME in 2016, he served as interim dean of the Faculty of Arts, Sciences & Engineering and then as vice provost for research. He returned to the laboratory full time in 2021.

One of the signature programs developed during Waugh's tenure was the Center for Medical Technology & Innovation (CMTI), established in 2013. The goals of the CMTI (directed by Greg T. Gdowski, PhD, and Amy L. Lerner, PhD, from BME, and Jonathan J. Stone, MD, from neurosurgery) are to expedite the development of new intellectual property and medical device solutions to address unmet clinical needs; support partnerships between industry and the University to foster the development of new technologies; and establish technology-driven training opportunities.

At the heart of the CMTI is a one-year Medical Technology & Innovation MS in BME focused on medical device product development and commercialization. The objective is to develop new intellectual property for the University and to provide professionals to the medical device industry who can rapidly contribute as members of a research and development group. A unique feature of the program is eight weeks of guided clinical observations in the operating room or other clinical settings. Students identify specific needs in diagnosis and treatment; formulate a focused device solution; assess the feasibility and effectiveness of the potential solution; plan and design the device after a rigorous vetting process; conduct preliminary testing and prototyping of the device; and consider options for further development of intellectual property for the device. The program includes workshops on human factors, observational skills, market research, ethnography and design, as well as computerized drawing, 3-D printing prototypes, machining and electronic fabrication techniques. Students visit companies to study opportunities within the medical device industry and take specialized courses in medical innovation covering entrepreneurship, regulatory processes, and intellectual property pathways.

Figure 40.2.
Diane Dalecki

Waugh was succeeded as chair by Diane Dalecki, PhD (Electrical and Computer Engineering). Dalecki received her PhD in electrical engineering from the University of Rochester. In 2019, she was installed as the first Kevin J. Parker Distinguished Professor in BME, funded with royalties from Blue Noise Mask, a novel half-tone imaging process invented by Dean Parker and his PhD student Theophana Mitsa. Prior to BME becoming a department, Dalecki had written the curriculum for a new undergraduate program in BME. She was one of the department's first faculty members, oversaw its first accreditation visit, and created an introductory BME course that served as a model for similar courses now offered by all Hajim School departments.

Dalecki is an international leader in biomedical ultrasound. Her research focuses on identifying novel ultrasound imaging techniques and in developing new therapeutic applications, particularly related to tissue engineering and regenerative medicine. She directs the Rochester Center for Biomedical Ultrasound (RCBU), a multidisciplinary center that unites over 100 professionals in engineering, medical, and applied sciences at the University of Rochester, RIT, and RGH. The center includes visiting scientists and provides a unique collaborative environment that has helped advance the use of ultrasound in diagnosis and therapeutics. Several technologies developed by RCBU scientists and engineers are now mainstream, including non-linear or tissue-harmonic ultrasound and ultrasound elastography.

Figure 40.3.
Stephen McAleavey

Stephen McAleavey, PhD, became chair of BME in 2023. McAleavey received his PhD in electrical and computer engineering from the University of Rochester and then did a postdoctoral fellowship in biomedical engineering in the laboratory of Gregg Trahey at Duke University, where he contributed to the early development of Acoustic Radiation Force Impulse imaging, a technique that measures tissue stiffness by assessing wave propagation speed. In 2004, he joined the faculty of BME, where he has continued to develop novel advanced ultrasound imaging techniques. Recognizing that the humanities offer an important perspective to biomedical engineers, McAleavey collaborated with Allen Topolski, MFA, Art and Art History chair, to develop a course in *Material Matters,* which explores the similarities between how artists and engineers go about their work, often using the same tools and materials. Building on the strengths of the department, he has broadened collaboration with partners in industry to provide opportunities for students and accelerate research commercialization.

BME has nineteen primary and over sixty-five secondary faculty derived from departments throughout the University, and it enrolls over 200 undergraduates in its BS program in BME. The curriculum centers on fundamental engineering and design principles taught in the context of current problems in medicine and biology, using hands-on engineering training. To ensure in-depth training in engineering, students complete a sequence of four courses in one of four concentrations: Biomechanics; Biosignals & Biosystems; Cell & Tissue Engineering; and Medical Optics. The program culminates in the year-long senior design program in which students collaborate with clinicians and companies to design engineering solutions to real-world problems, like that described above for the MS in Medical Technology & Innovation. Most students supplement their curriculum with research experiences or independent study courses.

In addition to the MS in Medical Technology & Innovation, BME offers two other MS programs: one focusing on an in-depth research project, requiring a thesis, and the other focusing on gaining advanced understanding of the breadth of BME principles and their applications in an area of concentration. The department also oversees the PhD program in BME: more than seventy students study and conduct research in laboratories in both SMD and the Hajim School.

Primary faculty in BME have a broad range of research interests. In addition to its world-class ultrasound and acoustics programs, areas of focus include: 1) Biomechanics: from nano-scale molecular interactions between proteins all the way up to whole body (organism) dynamics; 2) Biomedical Nanotechnology: development of new materials with dimensions on the order of tens to a few hundreds of nanometers; 3) Biomedical Optics: design and application of advanced optical techniques; 4) Cell & Tissue Engineering: generation of living tissue *ex vivo* for replacement or therapeutic applications through materials development, biochemical manipulations, cell culture, and genetic engineering; 5) Medical Imaging: a broad range of hardware and software development projects; and 6) Neuroengineering: combining quantitative methods, the physical sciences, and the biological sciences. The department's website provides further detail on each faculty member's program.

Recently, BME—in partnership with Duke University—received a $7.5 million NIH grant to establish the Translational Center for Barrier Microphysiological Systems. Led by James McGrath, PhD, William R. Kenan Jr. Professor of BME, the Rochester center is one of only four in the country to receive such support. The goal of the center is to develop microphysiological

Figure 40.4. James McGrath (front row, third from left) with the UR Tissue-on-a-Chip Team

tissue chip systems for drug discovery. Small chips with ultrathin membranes that pattern human cells, built using modular, mass-producible µSiM chips pioneered by McGrath, are being designed to mimic human tissue and diseases, including central nervous system disorders, fibrosis, musculoskeletal autoimmune disease, sepsis, and osteomyelitis. These chips will reduce the need for animal models and provide the higher throughput and greater reliability needed by pharmaceutical companies to earn drug approval. The collaborative structure of BME was critical to the awarding of the center, which includes Hani Awad, PhD, the Donald and Mary Clark Distinguished Professor in Orthopaedics, who serves as associate director for development; Benjamin Miller, PhD, Dean's Professor of Dermatology, who crafted photonic biosensors for the chips; and Joan Adamo, PhD, director of the Office of Regulatory Support at the CTSI, who serves as associate director for qualification.

Chapter 41

EXPANDING THE RESEARCH INFRASTRUCTURE

The Division of Comparative Medicine (DCM) and Vivarium

DCM is an academic division of SMD that provides programs of veterinary care, including training, preventive medicine, clinical, and diagnostic professional services. These programs complement the animal care programs in the vivarium, which procures, houses, and cares for laboratory animals. Facilities are available for major surgery, post-operative care, radiology, and necropsy. Specialized resources include a human xenograft facility, a transgenic core facility, and a hazardous substance laboratory. SMD has been continuously accredited by Association for Assessment and Accreditation of Laboratory Animal Care International (AAALAC) since 1966 and was the tenth institution in the US to be so accredited.

Figure 41.1. Jeff Wyatt

Jeffrey Wyatt, DVM, MPH, director of DCM and professor of Environmental Medicine, received his DVM from The Ohio State University in 1982 and then joined the University of Rochester, where he did a residency in comparative medicine and earned an MPH. Wyatt's approach to the DCM has revolved around the "One Health Concept," which emphasizes the interconnectedness of humans, animals, and the environment and was fostered by his long-standing role as chief veterinarian for Rochester's Seneca Park Zoo. From 2005–12, he served as a member of the Monroe County Board of Health, providing a veterinary perspective to public health risk mitigation. Among his ongoing projects has been a collaboration with the US Geological Survey to repatriate extirpated lake sturgeon in the Genesee River as bioindicators of river health; a collaboration in Madagascar, assessing and managing climate change and deforestation risks in twelve species of critically endangered lemurs; and a project in Borneo with URMC physicians that has reduced infant mortality by seventy percent, promoted alternatives to illegal logging, and saved 2,500 critically endangered orangutans. Wyatt's stature as a conservationist has helped establish the University as a national model for animal wellbeing and safety.

The opening of KMRB in 2000, which included 17,713 square feet of vivarium space, was a milestone for the University, in that it represented the first space designed specifically for a vivarium. In 2005, ventilated rack systems were made standard across vivarium space. Surgical facilities were subsequently expanded to accommodate cardiac bypass research. Although additional vivarium space was constructed at the Aab CVRI in Henrietta to accommodate the on-site needs of cardiovascular investigators, it was ultimately closed when the Aab CVRI moved back to the main campus and as changes in technology reduced the need for very large breeding colonies. In 2018, a new URMC core zebrafish facility was opened. It is hoped that new technologies will ultimately replace the need to involve non-human species in research.

Center for Advanced Research Technologies (CART)

Prior to 2009, URMC's core facilities operated independently in departments and centers, often established through institutional investments, instrumentation grants, and programmatic support through NIH center grants. There was no centralized oversight, little communication or coordinated management structure—leading to redundant technology investments and a lack of awareness among faculty and staff about the full range of available resources.

In 2009, SAD Puzas tasked Sally Quataert, PhD (Microbiology & Immunology), with organizing URMC's major core facilities. She began by convening core facility directors and establishing regular meetings to foster communication, collaboration, and problem-solving. In 2012, Timothy P. Bushnell, PhD, was appointed as the first full-time director of the core facilities, known as CART. Bushnell received his PhD from Rensselaer Polytechnic Institute and came to URMC in 1998 as a postdoctoral fellow in DOM (Hematology/Oncology). A Pediatrics faculty member, his main research focus is the development and application of high-end flow cytometric assays. Bushnell's charge was to implement professional management practices and provide centralized oversight for what was then seven major core facilities, laying the foundation for a more strategic, sustainable, and user-focused research support model. Under Bushnell, URMC has strategically invested in its research infrastructure to advance our research capabilities.

Figure 41.2. Timothy Bushnell

As of 2025, CART encompassed ten specialized core facilities, supported by a dedicated team of over sixty professionals. These facilities serve more than 300 active laboratories across the University. CART has an annual budget exceeding $13 million, of which approximately $3 million is provided through direct institutional support. One focus of the cores is training and education initiatives designed to enhance the technical skills of the research community, increase awareness and utilization of CART, and empower investigators to fully leverage cutting-edge technologies in pursuit of their scientific goals.

The Center for Advanced Light Microscopy and Nanoscopy provides access to high-end confocal laser-scanning microscopy, laser microdissection, conventional brightfield, immunofluorescence, and multiphoton microscopy. The center assists with all imaging procedures, aids in customizing staining protocols, and assists in image analysis.

The Electron Microscopy Shared Resource Laboratory supports studies involving electron microscopy from initial project design through imaging interpretation by providing technical expertise and state-of-the-art technology for transmission electron microscopy, scanning electron microscopy and Cryogenic electron microscopy.

The Elemental Analysis facility provides high-sensitivity quantitative analysis of trace elements within biological, chemical, and environmental samples. The facility is equipped with a suite of instruments for inductively coupled plasma mass spectrometry, optical emission spectroscopy, and atomic absorption spectroscopy.

The Flow Cytometry shared resource has sophisticated technologies that place it among the top centers in the world. These include analytical, full spectrum, imaging and mass cytometers, cell sorters, a nanoparticle detection system, a metabolomics instrument, and a suspension array system that permits analysis of up to 100 biomolecules in a single sample.

The Mass Spectrometry (MS) resource laboratory provides instrumentation and technical expertise for MS-based protein or small molecule assays to identify unknown proteins, characterize protein complexes, map post-translational modifications, and quantify peptides and small molecules from complex clinical matrices, tissue extracts, cell lysates, and other samples.

Located in the WCI, the Genomics Research Center has over fifteen scientists who provide RNA/DNA extraction; high-throughput sequencing, single-cell genomics, spatial genomics; next-generation sequencing, real-time polymerase chain reaction, and epigenomics. It also provides bioinformatics support.

The Metabolomics resource uses liquid chromatography-coupled mass spectrometry-based methods to identify and quantify small molecules and can be used to probe the metabolic state of complex biological samples through untargeted and targeted metabolite profiling, lipidomics analysis, and stable isotope tracing.

The Biosafety Level 3 core facility is available for use by investigators whose work requires the manipulation of biological agents that may cause serious or potentially lethal disease from inhalation exposure.

The Biological Supply Center is an in-house distribution center for refrigerated research supplies, such as restriction enzymes, nucleotides, and growth factors. It allows for consolidated shipments that help provide value for all investigators.

The Cold Storage core provides a controlled environment designed for the long-term storage of clinical/research materials in –20°C or –80°C freezers tied into the University's alarm system. The core also has spare –80°C freezers for emergencies.

Priority areas for additional CART investments include: single-cell and spatial proteomics to enable highly resolved molecular profiling; histology and spatial transcriptomics for high-dimensional tissue-based studies; and spectral flow cytometry and advanced imaging modalities to expand phenotyping and visualization capabilities.

Empire Discovery Institute (EDI)

In 2018, the University of Rochester, University at Buffalo, and Roswell Park Comprehensive Cancer Center established the EDI, an independent, nonprofit entity, funded in part through a $35.4 million, five-year grant from Empire State Development aimed at identifying promising drug candidates, examining their efficacy and safety in animal models, and moving them towards clinical trials. These efforts help overcome the "valley of death," the time between the end of funding for the fundamental research and the point where biotech or pharmaceutical companies are willing to fund further development. Another goal is to generate new economic activity in upstate NY through local startup creation. Leading the charge for the creation of the EDI was Peter Robinson, University of Rochester VP for Government and Community Relations, who brought the three institutions together, led the negotiations with Empire State Development, and with CEO Mark Taubman was a founding member of the EDI Board of Directors.

In 2021, the EDI established a research partnership with Deerfield Management Company, a health care investment firm, establishing a new company, Empire-Deerfield Discovery & Development (ED3), with Deerfield committing up to $65 million over a five-year period for projects in high-need areas, such as cancer and Alzheimer's disease, as well as those targeting patients who suffer from hard-to-treat and rare diseases. A partnership, LeapRx, was also established with global pharmaceutical company Novo

Nordisk to accelerate novel drug discovery programs in cardio-metabolic diseases and rare blood disorders.

In addition to receiving financial support, research programs receive pharmaceutical industry expertise in *de novo* drug design, medicinal chemistry, preclinical testing, drug formulation, and pharmacology and safety testing from EDI's world-class scientific advisory board and its extensive network of experienced consultants, contract research organizations, and strategic partners.

The following URMC programs have received EDI support: Denise Hocking, PhD (Pharmacology and Physiology) – wound healing; John Lueck, PhD (Pharmacology and Physiology) – nonsense mutation disease; the Center for RNA Biology's Lynne Maquat, PhD (Biochemistry and Biophysics), Christoph Pröschel, PhD (Biomedical Genetics), Hitomi Sakano, MD (currently at UT, Southwestern Medical Center) – Fragile X Syndrome; Rahesh Singh, PhD (Obstetrics and Gynecology) – cancer and autoimmune disorders; Peng Yao, PhD (Aab Cardiovascular Research Institute; Biochemistry and Biophysics) – RNA platform for heart disease and NASH; and Douglas Anderson, PhD (Aab Cardiovascular Research Institute; Pharmacology and Physiology) – Hemophilia A and COVID-19 variants.

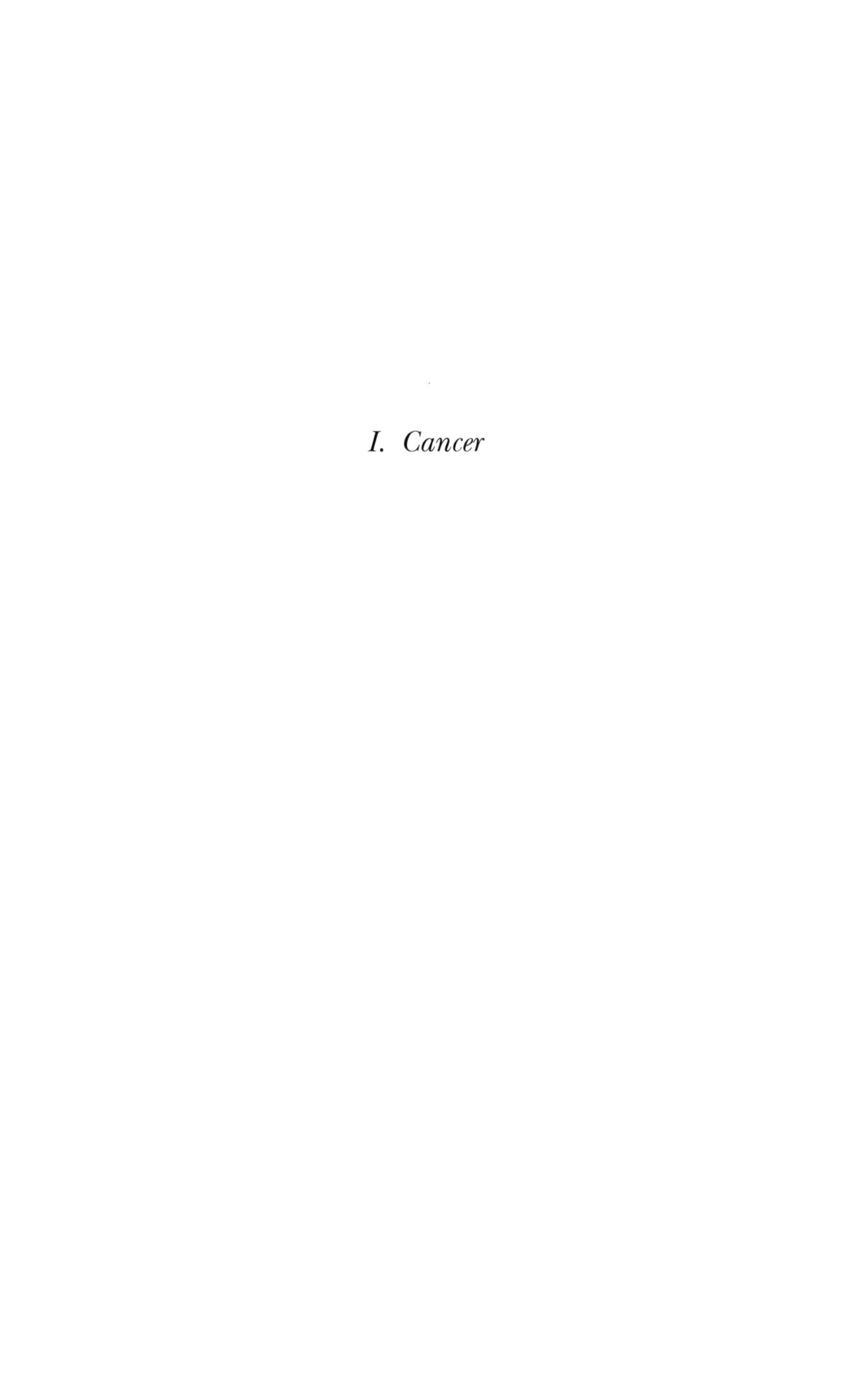

I. Cancer

The last twenty-five years have seen the evolution of research from largely departmental or divisional programs, often separated from the clinical enterprise, to multidisciplinary and multidepartmental programs of excellence that encompass all URMC missions, as depicted in Figure 37.5. The next section of this book highlights some of the major programs of excellence. When possible, departments are discussed in their entirety and attempts have been made to coalesce the research, clinical, and educational aspects of each program.

Chapter 42

WILMOT CANCER INSTITUTE (WCI)

The WCI represents one of the earliest examples of a center that incorporates all missions. The cancer center was chartered by the University Board of Trustees in 1974, and one year later received its first NCI-funded Cancer Center Support Grant (CCSG). Robert A. Cooper Jr., MD, led the center from its founding until his death in 1992. Subsequent directors included Richard Borch, MD, PhD, from 1993–6 and George N. Abraham, MD, from 1997–2001. The cancer center was renamed as the Wilmot Cancer Center (WCC), in tribute to the legacy of philanthropy by the Wilmot Family and the Wilmot Foundation. Richard I. Fisher, MD, was recruited as the new director in 2001 and oversaw plans for the construction of a building dedicated to cancer treatment, research, and education. The 163,000 square-foot, three-story facility opened in 2008. It featured five linear accelerators, comprehensive ambulatory space, an infusion center, clinical research space, and a translational laboratory floor.

Figure 42.1. Richard Fisher

With the marked growth in clinical volumes, a decision was made to increase the number of beds at SMH by moving the inpatient cancer services to the WCC. In 2012, a three-story vertical expansion of WCC was completed, increasing its size to 270,000 square feet, including ninety-two inpatient beds.

Jonathan W. Friedberg, MD, MMSc, succeeded Fisher as WCC director in 2012. Friedberg received his MD from Harvard University, did his residency in internal medicine at MGH, and his fellowship in oncology at the Dana-Farber Cancer Center, Boston. He joined URMC in 2002 and was named chief of Hematology & Oncology in 2009. As WCC director, Friedberg developed the Wilmot Cancer service line and initiated an aggressive regional strategy that made the WCC a major center for cancer treatment. The service line, directed by Daniel L. Mulkerin, MD (Hematology & Oncology), who also serves as WCC chief quality

Figure 42.2. Jonathan Friedberg

officer, is organized into twelve physician-led disease management groups and eight interdisciplinary services that focus on improving quality, patient flow and access, building relationships with internal and external referring providers, strengthening and standardizing tumor boards, and increasing clinical trial accrual on therapeutic studies.

The focus on regionalization began with the acquisition in 2012 of the Pluta Cancer Center in Henrietta, which had forty employees and more than 7,200 annual patient visits. Breast cancer clinical and research services were subsequently consolidated at Pluta, which also became the site of the Integrative Oncology & Wellness Center, providing comprehensive symptom management and survivorship interventions. A year later, the University purchased the assets of Interlakes Oncology and its offices in Greece, Brockport, Canandaigua, and Geneva, and contracted with its staff of fifty physicians, nurses, providers, and administrators, adding 16,500 patient visits per year. Over the years, URMC has continued to establish affiliations throughout upstate NY, and the Wilmot Cancer Institute (WCI, renamed to reflect the breadth of the enterprise) now has thirteen locations throughout central and western NY and sees more than 6,000 analytic cases annually, placing it among the top twenty-five centers in the US.

Figure 42.3. The façade of the Wilmot Cancer Center

Table 42.1. The Wilmot Cancer Service Line

Disease Management Groups
Bone Marrow Transplant/Leukemia
Breast
Gastrointestinal
Genitourinary
Gynecologic Oncology
Head and Neck
Lung Cancer
Lymphoma
Melanoma/Sarcoma
Myeloma
Neuro-Oncology
Pediatric Oncology
Interdisciplinary Services
Cardio-Oncology
Genetics
Geriatric Oncology
Imaging
Palliative Care
Pathology
Psycho-Oncology
Survivorship Program

The WCI has been at the forefront of URMC's changing relationship with the community. A good example of this is the Community Outreach and Engagement (COE) office, established in 2020 by Paula Cupertino, PhD (Surgery and Public Health Sciences), WCI's first associate director of Community Outreach, Engagement, and Disparities. The COE is currently directed by Charles S. Kamen, PhD, MPH (Surgery), and Francisco Cartujano, MD (Public Health Sciences). The COE ensures that the scientific, clinical, education, training, and outreach activities of WCI reflect the priorities and voices of diverse communities within its twenty-seven-county catchment area. The WCI also developed the Cancer Visual Analytic System, a novel, web-based data-mapping tool that includes information on cancer incidence, prevalence, and risk factors, and participation in WCI clinical trials to better inform research, recruitment, and outreach efforts.

A key component of the COE Office is the Cancer Community Action Council (CCAC), which has members from a wide variety of community-centered groups. The CCAC has established four priority working groups: community-driven research, rural outreach, primary prevention, and patient and survivor resources. Since 2020, CCAC partnerships have conducted more

Figure 42.4. The Wilmot Cancer Center atrium

than 700 community events, serving almost 21,000 community members from diverse backgrounds. CACC-sponsored programs have focused particularly on Prevention and Tobacco Cessation. Other programs include: At Home Workout Series; Promote HEALTH, an eight-week virtual program to empower participants to make and maintain lifestyle changes that help lower their risk of cancer and other chronic diseases; lung cancer screening; hereditary cancer screening and risk reduction; and a breast health program that offers evaluation for people with concerns about breast cancer. In addition, the WCI Mammo Van travels throughout the Finger Lakes to provide the same cutting-edge technology and care available to those in Rochester.

A key turning point for the WCI occurred at a 2016 retreat held by Friedberg and attended by approximately 100 faculty throughout the University. The widely endorsed recommendation was to focus on becoming an NCI-designated Cancer Center and regaining the CCSG grant that was lost in 1999. One of the shortcomings noted by the reviewers in 1999 was that key decisions on cancer management and research—as well as most of the resources for faculty recruitment and support—were in individual departments, rather than under the purview of the WCI. To address this, in 2016 new authority was given to the cancer center director, and URMC made a commitment to channel cancer-related funds into the center, rather than departments. This included earmarking $50 million of the academic reserve fund to the director, establishing endowed professorships within the WCI, working with the Wilmot Foundation to develop a $30 million capital campaign, and integrating the budgets of the service line and the research. This led to the strategic recruitment of more than thirty new investigators, including Paula M. Vertino, PhD (SAD for Basic Research), David C. Linehan, MD (chair of Surgery), Jennifer A. Harvey, MD (chair of Imaging Sciences), and Ruth M. O'Regan, MD (chair of DOM), who were attracted by the commitment to create a leading comprehensive cancer center.

By the time of its application to the NCI in 2023, the WCI had grown to 115 members and twelve associate members, representing twenty-six University departments and three schools: SMD, the SON, and the School of Arts, Sciences and Engineering. Cancer-related funding had annual directs of approximately $30 million, including approximately $13 million of NIH directs. Total accruals for clinical trials in 2023 were 1,943, and over five years WCI faculty has produced approximately 1,000 publications, thirty percent in high-impact journals. The application for NCI designation focused on three core research programs.

The Genetics, Epigenetics, and Metabolism (GEM) program, initiated under the guidance of Wilmot Distinguished Professor in Cancer Genomics Paula Vertino, PhD (Biomedical Genetics), is currently led by David McConkey, PhD (vice chair for research, Urology), and Darren Carpizo MD, PhD (Surgery). More can be seen about their individual research interests on the WCI website. The GEM program aims to: 1) provide new insight into the mechanisms that give rise to genetic and epigenetic diversity, and determine their roles in driving cellular plasticity and tumor cell phenotypes; 2) define how cellular and organismal aging exposes new cellular vulnerabilities that enhance cancer risk; and 3) uncover pathways by which oncogenic and oxidative insults converge on cancer cell metabolism to reveal new avenues for therapeutic intervention.

Key achievements of the GEM program have included: 1) a multi-institutional P01 focused on Comparative Genomics of Longevity whose principal investigator is Vera Gorbunova, PhD, Doris Johns Cherry Professor of Biology; 2) the discovery of new mechanisms of RNA quality control and insights into mRNA processing that have enhanced our understanding of the molecular underpinnings of myelodysplastic syndrome and other solid tumors; 3) advances in understanding how mutations in epigenetic regulators impact the trajectory of liver and pancreatic cancers through enhanced plasticity and skewing of cell fate; and 4) identification of novel mechanisms by which microenvironment-derived signals and axon guidance molecules promote cancer cell plasticity. These advances have uncovered new therapeutic possibilities for treating a wide range of cancers.

Figure 42.5. Vera Gorbunova and Andrei Seluanov

Gorbunova, working with Andrei Seluanov, PhD (Biology), has had a long-standing and internationally acclaimed program focusing on longevity and cancer. For many years, their work centered around the naked mole rat, a small rodent that can live up to forty-one years and does not contract age-related illnesses, such as cancer or heart disease. They discovered that the naked mole rat has approximately ten times the amount of high molecular weight hyaluronic acid in its body compared to humans and mice. Significantly, transfer of the naked mole rat hyaluronic acid synthase 2 gene into mice resulted in a lower incidence of spontaneous and induced cancer, extended lifespan and improved health span. In studies evaluating eighteen different rodents, they showed that more robust DNA double-strand break repair correlates with longevity and avoidance of cancer and tied this largely to the capacity of the SIRT6 protein to promote double-strand break repair. Gorbunova and Seluanov have recently extended their work to bowhead whales, who can live up to 200 years, and bats, who can live for thirty-five years and—like the naked mole rat—are resistant to cancer. Their studies suggest that the resistance of bats to cancer is related to a unique interplay between the p53 tumor suppressor gene and the telomerase enzyme.

The Cancer Microenvironment (CM) program is led by SKAWA Foundation Professor in Endocrinology and Metabolism Laura Calvi, MD (Endocrinology), and Scott A. Gerber, PhD (Surgery), who recently succeeded Dean's Professor of Microbiology and Immunology Minsoo Kim, PhD (Microbiology and Immunology, Center for Vaccine Biology and Immunology). The program aims to provide new insights into how tissue microenvironments control cancer initiation and progression. These will drive novel approaches to disrupt cancer stem cell-promoting microenvironments, reprogram tumor-induced microenvironment signals that silence normal cancer immunity, and mitigate dysfunction of normal tissue induced by cancer treatment. Key achievements of the CM program have included: 1) the development of phase I clinical trials to decrease tumor burden and even cure locally advanced pancreatic ductal adenocarcinoma employing multimodal strategies to inhibit myeloid suppressive cell populations and reactivate adaptive immunity; 2) identification of critical immune cell interactions within the cancer microenvironment that are being exploited to improve cell-based immunotherapy; 3) initiation of clinical trials based upon the discovery in hematologic malignancies of targetable interactions in the bone marrow microenvironment that mitigate transformation and improve hematopoietic fitness; 4) upfront checkpoint inhibition in Hodgkin lymphoma to enhance cures and minimize need for morbid radiotherapy; and 5) the establishment of *in vivo* models that have elucidated mechanisms of radiation-induced tissue dysfunction that can be mitigated to enhance treatment efficacy and reduce morbidity in cancer survivors.

Figure 42.6.
Karen Mustian

The Cancer Prevention and Control (CPC) Program is led by Dean's Professor of Surgery Karen Mustian, PhD, MPH, and Philip and Marilyn Wehrheim Professor of Medicine Supriya Mohile, MD, MS (Hematology/Oncology). The program aims to: 1) identify novel, effective interventions to reduce cancer risk for individuals with high probability for a cancer diagnosis; 2) develop innovative, effective supportive care therapies for patients, survivors, and caregivers to mitigate the toxicities and side effects caused by cancer and its treatments; and 3) develop cutting-edge, effective system-level supportive care interventions for oncology practices and health care systems to improve cancer supportive care delivery and outcomes. Recently, the CPC received a Cancer Grand Challenge grant funded by NCI and Cancer Research UK to study cancer cachexia with scientific collaborators from fourteen worldwide institutions.

Figure 42.7.
Supriya Mohile

The CPC represents an outgrowth of the Cancer Control and Supportive Care (CCSC) program, one of the best-funded and most highly acclaimed programs at the Medical Center. For more than thirty-five years, Gary Morrow, PhD (Surgery), mentored dozens of researchers who worked with him to build the CCSC. Morrow, an internationally recognized research leader in the field, has focused on chemotherapy-induced

Figure 42.8.
Gary Morrow

nausea and vomiting, pioneering the concept that when these problems are adequately controlled, patients are more likely to finish a full course of cancer treatment. In 1999, he was part of the nationwide team that set out the first recommendations to doctors on controlling nausea. His work contributed to anti-nausea drugs later being named among the "Top 5 Advances from the Past 50 Years" by the American Society of Clinical Oncology (ASCO). The work of Rose, Bonnez, and Reichman leading to the development of the human papillomavirus (HPV) vaccine, the first to treat cancer, also made the list, giving the University of Rochester two out of the top five!

In 2014, the program received its first National Community Oncology Research Program (NCORP) award for approximately $20 million. At its five-year renewal in 2019, it received an additional $29 million grant from the NCI and was chosen as an NCORP research base, charged with designing and managing clinical studies to be carried out at oncology clinics at more than 1,000 NCORP affiliates. Leading the NCORP program is Karen Mustian, an exercise physiologist, whose work has been instrumental in establishing the value of exercise for cancer patients before, during, and after treatment. She conducted the first-ever exercise studies at WCI and then created two copyrighted and patented intervention programs for patients to use in their homes: YOCAS is a gentle yoga program; EXCAP boosts strength with resistance bands and tracks steps with walking programs. Each has been shown to ease insomnia, fatigue, and anxiety.

A major theme across all three WCI research programs is aging and cancer. This program leverages long-standing basic, translational, and clinical expertise at UR (see p. 200). The WCI had one of the original John Hartford Foundation Grants to train geriatric oncologists and has one of the country's few geriatric oncology clinics. The Specialized Oncology Care and Research for the Elderly clinic, founded by Mohile, is recognized as a national model for providing geriatric oncology specialty care. Mohile's research demonstrated that geriatric assessment in clinical visits in older adults with advanced cancer improved patient-centered and caregiver-centered communication about aging-related concerns. This work led to the awarding in 2021 of a PCORI grant, in collaboration with Lisa Lowenstein of the MD Anderson Cancer Center, studying the impact of disseminating geriatric assessment throughout the WCI catchment area and beyond. Mohile also led a high-impact, randomized trial demonstrating that geriatric assessment summary and plans reduced the risk of serious toxicity in older patients with advanced cancer and aging-related conditions. This finding contributed to her leading a national team to establish practice-changing, evidence-based guidelines for treating older adults with chemotherapy. The geriatric oncology group has published 124 research studies since 2019 and holds research grants exceeding $1.6 million in direct costs per year.

Figure 42.9. Michelle Janelsins-Benton

The work of Michelle C. Janelsins-Benton, PhD, MPH, is closely aligned with the aging group. Janelsins-Benton is the Joan and Gary Morrow Endowed Distinguished Professor of Supportive Care in Cancer and chief of the Supportive Care in Cancer division in Surgery. A graduate of the University of Rochester's T32 Clinical and Translational Cancer Control Research Training Program, Janelsins-Benton leads a nationally acclaimed research team that focuses on understanding clinical, psychological, and biological contributors of cancer-related cognitive decline and on interventions to alleviate this decline involving randomized clinical trials, longitudinal studies, and animal modeling.

To support research efforts, the WCI created four new shared resources and augmented three others. The Biobank Shared Resource has a catalog of more than 10,000 clinically annotated biospecimens from a wide variety of solid and liquid tumors. The Biostatistics and Bioinformatics Shared Resource provides statistical consultation, data analysis, targeted novel methods development, education, training, and mentoring. The Cytometry Shared Resource provides investigators with state-of-the-art instrumentation and technical expertise for both flow cytometry cell analysis and sorting. The Genomics Shared Resource provides high-throughput screening and genomics technologies for studying gene structure and function, including single-cell and spatial genomics, epigenomics, DNA sequencing, transcriptomics, and functional genomics.

The Human Biophysiology Shared Resource provides cutting-edge resources and expertise to integrate human performance and physiology assessment, biospecimen analysis, and clinical and biopsychosocial outcomes to support clinical and translational research studies. It is comprised of the Cancer Control and Psychoneuroimmunology Laboratory, led by Janelsins-Benton, which uses a multidisciplinary approach to elucidate the neurobiologic underpinnings of cognitive decline due to chemotherapy and other cancer treatments; and the PEAK Human Performance Science Clinical Research Lab, led by Mustian, which supports investigators conducting multidisciplinary and translational research related to all forms of human movement.

The Imaging and Radiation Shared Resource provides state-of-the-art tissue imaging and image-targeted irradiation technologies for animal studies modeling targeted cancer treatment methodologies. In July 2023, WCI established the Cancer Metabolomics Shared Resource to identify new biomarkers for cancer and intervention outcomes, investigate the metabolomic landscape inherent to cancer cells to define novel intervention targets, and characterize microenvironmental support of cancer cell survival to identify novel treatment strategies.

On March 18, 2025, the NCI named the WCI as the nation's seventy-third designated cancer center, placing the institute in the top four percent of all cancer centers in the US. The event, the culmination of a ten-year University wide effort led by Jonathan Friedberg and colleagues at the Medical Center, was widely celebrated.

Chapter 43

HEMATOLOGY AND ONCOLOGY DIVISION (DEPARTMENT OF MEDICINE)

Although Hematology & Oncology is a division of DOM, its faculty is so integral to the WCI that it will be discussed as part of this chapter. The Hematology unit, established by DOM chair William S. McCann in the 1920s, has a storied history with the likes of Lemuel W. Diggs, MD, who authored the widely used *Atlas of Morphology of Human Blood Cells* and established the first sickle cell disease unit in the US; John S. Lawrence, MD, who identified the thalassemias; Lawrence E. Young, who did groundbreaking work in immunohematology and spherocytosis; and Robert I. Weed, MD, who, with Biophysics Chair Paul LaCelle, MD, did fundamental studies on red and white cell physical properties and rheology, work that continued under Richard Waugh, PhD.

For most of its history, the Hematology unit was separate from Oncology and focused on non-malignant hematology and hematological malignancies including leukemia, myeloma, and lymphoma. In 1977, Raphael Dolin, DOM chair, recruited Victor J. Marder, MD, to establish a Vascular Medicine unit and to join Marshall A. Lichtman, MD, as co-chiefs of Hematology. Marder, a pioneer in understanding the mechanisms of thrombosis and hemostasis and one of the founders of the International Society on Thrombosis and Hemostasis, was instrumental in developing a large group of clinicians and scientists who became leaders in the field, including Charles W. Francis, MD, Denisa Wagner, PhD, S. Eric Martin, MD, Philip J. Fay, PhD, Tanya Mayadas, PhD, and Patricia J. Simpson-Haidaris, PhD. In 1991, Marder was appointed associate chair for Academic Affairs in DOM, and in 1999 moved to UCLA to be nearer his family. Lichtman, who had been a resident in internal medicine at the University of Rochester, was a leader in the fields of hematopoiesis and leukemogenesis. In 1990, he stepped down as chief of Hematology to become dean of SMD, a position he held for six years.

Figure 43.1. Charles Francis

Marder and Lichtman were succeeded by Charles Francis, who had come to the University in 1976 as a fellow in Hematology and had established an internationally regarded program focusing on the mechanisms of fibrinolysis and on the structure of its products. He oversaw key studies demonstrating the effects of low-intensity ultrasound on fibrinolysis, which formed an important basis for clinical studies on ultrasound as an adjunct to fibrinolytic therapy. Marder and Francis also conducted landmark studies of thrombo-prophylaxis in high-risk patients, particularly those undergoing hip or knee replacement. Francis remained as chief of Hematology until 2001, when Richard Fisher became director of the WCI and chief of a combined division of Hematology & Oncology. Beginning in the 1990s, Francis's interests started to shift towards the relationship between cancer and thrombosis. He, along with Alok Khorana, MD, who had been a fellow in Hematology & Oncology at URMC, and Gary H. Lyman, MD, analyzed risk factors for venous thromboembolism in cancer patients and developed the "Khorana Score" to identify those patients at highest risk. The score is widely used and has formed the basis for successful thrombo-prophylaxis studies. Francis also collaborated with Arthur Moss on identifying markers of thrombosis, such as hypercoagulability and D-dimer, as risk factors for recurrent myocardial infarction.

In 2012, Jonathan Friedberg became director of the WCI and chief of Hematology & Oncology. In 2016, charged with the broad regional expansion of cancer services and the focus on obtaining NCI designation, Friedberg stepped down as chief and was succeeded by Aram F. Hezel, MD. Hezel had been recruited to URMC from MGH, where he had developed a clinical and research program focused on pancreatic and liver cancers. One of the goals of his recruitment was to help develop a multidisciplinary clinic in collaboration with the liver transplant team. Hezel received his MD from SUNY Buffalo School of Medicine, completed his residency in internal medicine at the Beth Israel Deaconess Medical Center, and a fellowship in medical oncology at Dana-Farber Cancer Institute, Boston. In 2016, he became the inaugural John and Ethel Heselden Professor, established in honor of the Heseldens' late daughter, Carol. Since his arrival in Rochester, Hezel has continued to provide new insights into cancer progression, establishing how mutations in several cancer-related genes disable tumor suppressor activity and fuel the growth of pancreatic and bile duct cancer. Although the focus of the division has increasingly moved towards oncology, the division still has seven hematologists studying and treating benign conditions.

Figure 43.2.
Aram Hezel

A key development initiated by Lichtman in 1989 and subsequently advanced by Francis was the establishment of the Bone Marrow Transplant

(BMT) program. In 2000, the program, which was directed for many years by Jane L. Leisveld, MD, and Gordon Phillips, MD, and since 2016 by Patrick M. Reagan, MD, who had been a fellow in Hematology & Oncology at URMC, became one of the first in the country to be accredited by FACT (Foundation for the Accreditation of Cellular Therapy). As of 2025, this very busy program had performed more than 4,400 transplants and currently performs more than 200 per year. Liesveld, who did her residency in internal medicine and fellowships in hematology and medical oncology at URMC, serves as the associate chief of Academic Affairs and Hematology, providing support for education, research mentorship, and faculty mentoring and promotions. Together with Calvi, Liesveld and colleagues have been investigating the role of microenvironmental dysfunction in mediating progression of myelodysplastic syndrome (MDS) to hematologic malignancy, and have initiated trials targeting elements in the microenvironment aimed at inhibiting MDS progression.

Figure 43.3.
Jane Liesveld

In 2016, the BMT program was selected as one of the few national sites to begin clinical trials on CAR (Chimeric Antigen Receptor) T-cell therapy and upon FDA approval became one of the first cancer centers in the US to offer CAR T-cell treatment for eligible patients. The procedure involves removing a cancer patient's T cells, genetically modifying them outside the body to recognize specific antigens on the cancer cells, then infusing them back into the patient to attack the cancer. Patrick Reagan and Jonathan Friedberg collaborated with colleagues at NCI on the initial studies of CAR-T infusions for refractory diffuse large B-cell lymphoma. Now one of the busiest sites in the country, the WCI performs CAR T-cell infusions for a variety of types of hematologic malignancies, including multiple myeloma, some types of non-Hodgkin lymphoma, and adult and pediatric patients with acute lymphocytic leukemia. In 2019, Reagan, Minsoo Kim, PhD (Microbiology and Immunology), and Richard Waugh, PhD (Biomedical Engineering), received a $2.8 million NIH grant to identify approaches to reduce CAR T-cell toxicity by better enabling the T cells to hit their intended targets.

Chunkit Fung, MD, is associate chief of Hematology & Oncology, overseeing Solid Tumor Oncology and Clinical Affairs. Fung, who specializes in genitourinary malignancy, is focusing on behavioral interventions to prevent and manage treatment- and cancer-related toxicities in cancer survivors. He was recently named associate chair for Diversity, Equity, and Inclusion for DOM and has played a key role representing SMD in the University Faculty Senate. Megan Baumgart, MD, directs the three-year fellowship in

Hematology and Medical Oncology. The fellowship, which accepts four residents per year, is one of the largest at URMC and cultivates academic careers by combining outstanding clinical training with a strong emphasis on either basic science or clinical research.

For over forty years, the Wilmot Cancer Research fellowship program has provided support for physicians who have completed their postgraduate training and are interested in research careers. The program has supported more than 100 early career physician scientists, many of whom have gone on to establish important research programs at universities across the country. One of the earliest Wilmot fellows was William Bonnez, MD, who made discoveries that led to the development of the HPV vaccine.

Chapter 44

DEPARTMENT OF BIOMEDICAL GENETICS (BMG)

As part of CEO Jay Stein's strategic plan, Hartmut "Hucky" Land, PhD, was recruited from the Imperial Cancer Research Fund in London, UK, to serve as the director of a new center for cancer biology and as the inaugural Robert and Dorothy Markin Professor, named in honor of Robert Markin, a Rochesterian who founded the Markin Insurance Agency. The new center was ultimately reformulated as BMG. Land received his PhD from the University of Heidelberg and completed his postdoctoral training at MIT. Land's research program focuses on understanding the commonalities among diverse types of cancers, such as their ability to quickly divide and survive despite aggressive treatment, with the goal of discovering new ways to block or interfere with the genetic networks at the core of what makes cells cancerous. In 2015, Land was chosen as an inaugural recipient of the Outstanding Investigator Award from the NCI. Land also serves as the deputy director of the WCI, where he has facilitated the development of collaborative cancer research programs and state-of-the-art infrastructure critical to achieving NCI designation.

Figure 44.1. Hucky Land

As chair of a new department, Land has had the opportunity to shape its vision, mission, and culture, and to recruit outstanding investigators from around the globe to create a highly collaborative, multidisciplinary research environment, employing state-of-the-art approaches in cell biology, genetics, genomics, epigenetics, stem cell biology, and systems and computational biology in the study of genetically tractable human disease models.

The current faculty of twenty is investigating complex biological processes related to stem cell maintenance and differentiation, tissue regeneration and repair, cancer biology, aging, neurological diseases and neurodegeneration, metabolic diseases, and organismal development. A high research priority is elucidating the molecular nature of complex regulatory signaling networks, the mechanisms by which they influence biological processes, and the ways in which malfunctioning signal transduction and epigenetic regulation can cause disease. Another high priority for BMG faculty is the development of "systems approaches," in which predictions derived from theoretical modeling of large data sets are tested experimentally, enabling a deeper understanding of complex processes, such as cell growth, malignant transformation, and development. Topics currently being studied using such systems approaches include regulatory gene networks, genetic, epigenetic and metabolic reprogramming during cell differentiation and disease, circadian rhythms, and neural development and function. The reader is referred to the department website for descriptions of the individual research programs. A few of the programs are highlighted in the paragraphs below.

BMG has several internationally recognized experts in the fields of stem cells, stem cell-based therapies and tissue-specific stem cells. Since receiving his PhD from Stanford University in 1977, Mark D. Noble has emerged as a global leader in stem cell biology. He was part of a team that isolated the first precursor cell from the central nervous system, established the protocol for growing these cells in tissue culture, and was the first to transplant these cells to repair damaged tissue (i.e. demyelinated spinal cord). Noble was recruited to URMC in 2000, where he has continued his groundbreaking work, developing novel approaches to treat spinal cord and peripheral nerve injury, new therapeutic approaches for diseases involving lysosomal dysfunction, and cancer treatments that have less neurotoxicity.

Figure 44.2. Mark Noble

In 2008, Noble became the founder and director of the University of Rochester Stem Cell and Regenerative Medicine Institute, comprising more than forty faculty from fifteen departments, whose research spans a wide range of diseases. This initiative received significant funding through the New York State Stem Cell Science program (2007–22). In 2016, Noble became the inaugural Martha M. Freeman, MD, Professor in Biomedical Genetics, created by the late Martha Mann Freeman, a graduate of the University of Rochester college, the SON, and SMD. In 2023, Margot Mayer-Pröschel, PhD, succeeded Noble as the second Martha M. Freeman, MD, Professor in Biomedical Genetics. Mayer-Pröschel, who received her PhD from the Institute of Virology & Immunology, University of Wurzburg, Germany, and did a postdoctoral fellowship with Noble at the Ludwig Institute for Cancer Research, London, UK, is also nationally recognized for her work identifying stem cells in the central nervous system (CNS). Her laboratory is focused on understanding the

Figure 44.3. Margot Mayer-Pröschel

cellular and molecular targets for a variety of developmental insults to stem and progenitor cell populations in the CNS, and has established several novel animal model systems designed for identifying ideal candidates for therapeutic cell replacement.

Figure 44.4.
Dirk Bohmann

Dirk P. Bohmann received his PhD in biology from the University of Tübingen, Germany, and did a postdoctoral fellowship at the University of California, Berkeley. He joined URMC in 2001 after working as a group leader and senior scientist at the European Molecular Laboratory in Heidelberg, Germany. Bohmann's internationally recognized research program uses fruit fly genetics to study the aging process and how environmental stressors promote age-related diseases such as cancer and degenerative conditions. Bohmann has been instrumental in the development of the University of Rochester Aging Institute (URAI) Center, whose focus has been on the relationship between cancer and aging. He also directed the Biomedical Genetics and Genomics graduate program. In 2016, Bohmann was appointed as SAD for basic research, a position he held until 2023. Also in 2016, he was installed as the inaugural Donald M. Foster, MD, Professor in Biomedical Genetics, created by the late Donald M. Foster, a radiologist who was a graduate and long-time supporter of SMD.

Figure 44.5.
Douglas Portman

In 2023, Douglas S. Portman, PhD, succeeded Bohmann as Donald M. Foster, MD, Professor in Biomedical Genetics. Portman, who received his PhD in Molecular Biology and Genetics from the University of Pennsylvania, has done groundbreaking work, using the genetically tractable roundworm *C. elegans*, to understand how differences in behavior emerge from the activity of neuronal circuits that are genetically programmed in a sex-specific manner. Portman was elected Fellow of the AAAS in 2024. He serves as the current director of the PhD program in Biomedical Genetics and Genomics.

Paula M. Vertino, PhD, was recruited to BMG from Emory University, Atlanta, GA in 2018 as the inaugural Wilmot Distinguished Professor of Cancer Genomics. Vertino received her PhD from SUNY at Buffalo in collaboration with Roswell Park Cancer Institute, Buffalo, and did a postdoctoral fellowship at Johns Hopkins. At Emory, she established an internationally prominent research program in cancer epigenetics and on mechanisms of gene silencing. Vertino and colleagues have combined genome-wide DNA methylation and chromatin analyses with bioinformatics and machine learning to define genomic and epigenomic "signatures" associated with cancer outcomes and environmental exposures. Her work has focused on understanding the epigenetic mechanisms underlying altered gene expression in breast cancer, and exploiting these mechanisms to develop new therapeutic approaches that reprogram the cancer epigenome. Vertino also serves as the associate director of basic and translational sciences of WCI and the co-director of the GEM program. She was appointed as SAD for basic research at SMD in 2023, succeeding Dirk Bohmann.

Figure 44.6.
Paula Vertino

BMG is the home of the PhD program in Biomedical Genetics and Genomics, which involves over fifty faculty from a variety of departments and has over thirty students in training at any given time. The department offers lecture and seminar courses in cell biology, genetics, genomics, systems biology, and biomedicine. In addition, the program has developed concentrations in bioinformatics and cancer biology, the latter in collaboration with WCI.

Chapter 45

RADIATION ONCOLOGY

Radiation Oncology has a storied history associated, in part, with its investigations into radiation effects during the development of the atomic bomb. This was summarized by Henry A. Blair, PhD, in the *Brief History of the UR Atomic Energy Project from 1943–1968.*[11] In 1943, the Atomic Energy Commission chose the University of Rochester as the site for a project (Manhattan Project) to examine the potential adverse human health effects of atomic energy. The project analyzed medical reports from the sites involved with the Manhattan District, the name given to the program to develop the atomic bomb. The fearful atmosphere occasioned by the war led to one of the darker moments in URMC history: from 1943 to 1947, eleven hospital patients were injected with plutonium, uranium salts, and/or polonium to investigate the long-term effects of radiation exposure. In the aftermath of the Manhattan Project, a new preclinical department of Radiation Biology was established in 1947, chaired by Blair. In 1965, the department was renamed Radiation Biology and Biophysics.

Philip Rubin, MD, graduated from SUNY Downstate School of Medicine and did his residency in radiology at the University of Michigan. In 1957, after leading the radiation therapy services program at the NCI, he joined URMC, where he founded a clinical division of Radiation Therapy within the department of Radiology. In 1971, he became the chair of a newly restructured department of Radiation Oncology, a position he held until 1996. Using declassified data from World War II and the Manhattan Project, Rubin became an international expert on radiation tolerance and the long-term effects of radiation exposure, and a powerful catalyst for the evolving specialty of radiation oncology. For over twenty-five years, he was principal investigator of an NCI-funded Clinical Experimental Radiation Research Interface Center grant that investigated the effects of radiation on normal tissue and set the foundation of future

Figure 45.1. Philip Rubin

11 https://www.facilities.rochester.edu/history/MC/1968Blair.pdf

research in cancer survivorship. He contributed to and authored more than thirty-five books, including *Clinical Oncology for Medical Students and Physicians: A Multidisciplinary Approach*, considered the foremost guide on the study of radiation treatment of cancer worldwide. He was among the founders of the Radiation Therapy Oncology Group, a national clinical cooperative group funded by the NCI, was the founder and editor-in-chief of the *International Journal of Radiation Oncology, Biology and Physics*, and served as president of the American Society for Therapeutic Radiology and Oncology, receiving its Gold Medal Award. He died in 2014, having left an indelible mark on the University.

Paul Okunieff, MD, succeeded Rubin as chair and became the inaugural Philip Rubin Professor of Radiation Oncology in 1997. Okunieff received his MD from Harvard Medical School, where he remained for his internal medicine residency at Beth Israel Hospital and his radiation oncology residency at MGH. Prior to joining URMC, he served as branch chief of radiation oncology at the NCI. Okunieff was a pioneer in the use of *in-vivo* nuclear magnetic resonance imaging of tumors. His research led to a novel method to measure radiation-induced DNA fragments in the bloodstream to estimate radiation exposure, and to identify molecules that provide genetically based protection against radiation hazards. Okunieff played a pivotal role in advancing stereotactic radiosurgery. Under his leadership, the department focused on translational research, including work on oligometastases and radiation countermeasures used to improve cancer treatment outcomes and mitigate radiation-induced damage. This work led to a five-year, $21 million NIH award entitled "Risk Management following Irradiation Centers for Biophysical Assessment," which established URMC as one of the first eight centers in the US. The URMC project included investigations of radiation lung injuries, radiation biodosimetry, and radiation bone marrow effects. Okunieff's tenure was also marked by the expansion of clinical services through the acquisition of three regional radiation treatment facilities at HH, FF Thompson, and Unity.

Figure 45.2.
Paul Okunieff

In 2009, Okunieff left to become director of the University of Florida Shands Cancer Center and chair of Radiation Oncology. He was succeeded by Yuhchyau Chen, MD, PhD, as chair and Philip Rubin Professor of Radiation Oncology (she subsequently became the inaugural Richard T. Bell Endowed Professor, established with a gift by Bell, a grateful patient whom she had

Figure 45.3.
Yuhchyau Chen

treated). Chen received an MD and a PhD in experimental pathology from the University of Washington, and did an internship in internal medicine at Virginia Mason Hospital in Seattle before completing a residency and fellowship in radiation oncology at MGH. She joined URMC in 1995. Chen is an accomplished clinical expert in lung and head and neck cancers who studies radiosensitization, radiation biomarkers and radiation effects on normal tissue. She was the first to establish the role of interleukins as indicators of radiation lung injury in post-treatment cancer patients. Chen has held leadership positions on numerous national committees, and in 2012 was a fellow of the Hedwig van Ameringen Executive Leadership in Academic Medicine® Program (ELAM).

Chen presided over marked expansion of clinical services, including the addition of radiation treatment sites at the Pluta Cancer Center, Batavia Radiation Oncology, the Ann and Carl Myers Cancer Center at Noyes Hospital, and Webster Radiation Oncology. The clinical enterprise now includes twelve linear accelerators and eight simulation CT scanners. In 2023, 3,144 new patients began treatment, compared with 168 in 1998. This growth has been accompanied by a doubling in staff to over 160, and a doubling of faculty to forty. Chen also oversaw the acquisition of new cancer treatment technologies, many of which are unique to URMC in upstate NY, enabling the most precise positioning for brain radiosurgery and stereotactic body radiotherapy, and employing high-dose-rate brachytherapy for the treatment of prostate cancer, eye-plaque brachytherapy for choroidal melanoma, and very low-dose anti-inflammatory radiotherapy for osteoarthritis. URMC became the first in the northeastern US to use Ethos adaptive radiotherapy, which integrates AI into real-time radiation planning. Chen also initiated several new educational offerings and enhanced involvement in clinical trials.

Louis "Sandy" Constine, MD, the Philip Rubin Professor of Radiation Oncology and Pediatrics, and vice chair of Radiation Oncology, was recruited by Rubin to the department in 1981. Constine received his MD from Johns Hopkins, did residencies in pediatrics at UCSF and Stanford University, where he also trained in radiation oncology, and completed a fellowship in pediatric hematology-oncology at Seattle Children's Hospital. At URMC, Constine developed a worldwide reputation for his work on the effects of radiation and chemotherapy in children. Author of more than fifty book chapters and more than 300 reports, his book, *Pediatric Radiation Oncology*, is considered the leading text in the field and was a winner of the British Medical Book Award.

Figure 45.4.
Sandy Constine

Constine established and still chairs an international network, known as PENTEC (Pediatric Normal Tissue Effects in Clinic), consisting of over 150 physician-scientists, biostatisticians, physicists, and epidemiologists committed to understanding the differential vulnerability to radiation of all organs in children. Constine was a member of a four-person United Nations task force that released a 240-page document on the adverse effects of radiation on children. He also served as the radiation chair of the Lymphoma Committee of the Southwest Oncology Group and the Hodgkin Lymphoma Committee of the Children's Oncology Group, and as chair of the American Radium Society Appropriateness Criteria Lymphoma Committee.

The residency in Radiation Oncology is one of the oldest in the country, established by Rubin in 1971. The four-year program, directed by Michael Milano, MD, PhD, accepts two residents per year following completion of a year in internal medicine. The MS in medical physics is a two-year program, established in 2024, that prepares students to pursue a medical physics residency, such as the highly competitive program initiated by the department in 2021. This residency is a two-year clinical program that prepares graduates who hold an MS in medical physics or a PhD in physics or a related field to become clinical medical physicists.

The Radiation Oncology Clinical Trials Office was one of the earliest involved in national cooperative group trials through the Radiotherapy Oncology Group (RTOG), which in 2019 merged with two other large national cooperatives to become NRG Oncology, one of four NCI cooperative trial organizations. Chen has served as institutional PI for the RTOG/NRG Oncology program. Studies have focused on identifying drugs that may help to make tumor cells more sensitive to radiation treatments; identifying late effects of radiotherapy to minimize side effects; and identifying more effective ways to reduce nausea, sleeplessness, and excess weight loss associated with radiation treatments. Trial enrollment contributed significantly to URMC achieving NCI designation as a Comprehensive Cancer Center.

An important step in advancing the research program in Radiation Oncology was the 2021 recruitment of Brian Marples, PhD. Marples received his PhD at the CRC Gray Laboratory at Mount Vernon Hospital, Northwood, UK, under the mentorship of Michael Joiner, PhD. He is an internationally renowned radiation biologist and educator who studies how to manipulate the immune system to reduce tissue toxicity after radiation therapy, specifically focused on reducing pulmonary injury in lung cancer patients treated with radiation. On his arrival in Rochester, Marples became the inaugural Dr. Sidney H. and Barbara L. Sobel Professor in Radiation Oncology, established with a generous gift from Sidney Sobel, MD, and his wife, Barbara. Beginning with a fellowship in multidisciplinary oncology at the University of Rochester, Sobel has been a major figure in radiation oncology in the Finger Lakes region, practicing as a radiation oncologist at HH and SMH, serving as chief of radiation oncology, and then building his own treatment facilities in Clifton Springs, Batavia, and Hornell.

J. Neurosciences and the Del Monte Neuroscience Institute

Neurological science has always been a strength at the University of Rochester. Like most institutions, it grew organically, with the establishment of independent departments and centers that often collaborated but also competed for resources. The past twenty-five years have seen remarkable growth in neurosciences at the University, accompanied by enhanced collaboration among these departments and centers, and the recruitment of many outstanding clinicians and scientists.

In 2009, Ernest J. Del Monte, chairman of E. J. Del Monte Corporation, a Rochester-based company that owned and operated seventeen hotels in NY State, and his wife Thelma made a multi-million-dollar commitment to support neurosciences at the University. At the time, it was the second-largest gift in the history of the Medical Center. The gift was in no small part thanks to the efforts of Webster Pilcher, MD, PhD, chair of Neurosurgery, who had been successful in impressing the Del Montes with the excellence and breadth of neuroscience research and clinical services at the Medical Center and the potential for them to provide critical insights leading to new treatments of neurological disease.

The Ernest J. Del Monte Neuromedicine Institute serves as an umbrella for neuroscience-based research centers and clinical departments throughout URMC. The gift enabled the renovation of space in MRBX, renamed after Del Monte, and the coalescence of translational neuroscientists. It also provided funding for several endowed professorships. Pilcher was named as the founding director of the Institute and the first Ernest & Thelma Del Monte Distinguished Professor in Neuromedicine. The following sections describe the major components of the Institute. Although Psychiatry was not formally included as part of the Institute, it is included in this section because of its close research and clinical relationships with many of the Institute's components.

Figure 46.1. Ernest and Thelma Del Monte

Chapter 46

DEPARTMENT OF NEUROLOGY

As in most institutions, Neurology began as a division in the DOM. It became an independent department on July 1, 1966, when Robert J. Joynt, MD, PhD, was recruited from the University of Iowa to become the first chair of a department that included six faculty and trainees.

Joynt, one of the most influential neurologists of the last half century, grew up in the small town of Le Mars, Iowa. After serving as a sergeant in the Signal Corps in India during World War II, he returned to Iowa, where he received his undergraduate degree from Westmar College and his MD from the University of Iowa. He interned in neurology at Royal Victoria Hospital in Montreal, followed by a year as a Fulbright scholar at Cambridge University. He then returned to Iowa City to complete his residency in neurology, subsequently joining the faculty of the University of Iowa. While on the Neurology faculty, he completed a PhD in neuroanatomy.

Figure 46.2. Robert Joynt

Under Joynt's leadership, Neurology achieved national prominence as an academic and clinical center. Joynt was a master diagnostician beloved by his patients and colleagues. He also served as director of the University's original Alzheimer's disease center. Thanks in large part to Joynt's reputation as an educator, Rochester became a top choice for young neurologists in training. Joynt was recognized in 1989 with the Gold Medal Award from the University's Medical Alumni Association for his "integrity, inspiring teaching and devotion to medical students." That same year, he was elected to the National Institute of Medicine. Joynt's encyclopedic knowledge of health and disease ultimately benefitted people around the globe who were treated by the thousands of physicians influenced by him.

Over his career, Joynt headed both leading societies in neurology, the American Academy of Neurology (AAN) and the American Neurological Association (ANA). He also served as president of the American Board of Psychiatry and Neurology. He was a fellow of the AAAS and a member of the Board of Regents of the National Library of Medicine. He served as editor of *Archives of Neurology*, founded *Seminars in Neurology*, and is the author of the field's major textbook, *Baker and Joynt's Clinical Neurology*.

Joynt served as dean of the Medical School from 1985 to 1989, as vice provost for health affairs from 1985 to 1994, and as VP for health affairs from 1989 to 1994, before returning full-time to faculty work. In 1997, the University conferred on him the title of Distinguished University Professor.

Despite his stature as a towering figure in international circles of neurology, he is most remembered for his wit, integrity, and kindness. Honest and generous of spirit, he did his job without fanfare. Balanced with that humor were remarkable insights, such as Joynt's conclusion that the Medical Center could benefit from a more integrated leadership structure. Thus was born a new position—which Joynt was first to hold—that brought the academic and clinical missions of the Medical Center together. Joynt remained an integral part of URMC until his death on April 13, 2012, at SMH at the age of eighty-six.

Figure 46.3. Robert Griggs

Robert "Berch" Griggs, MD, became the Edward A. and Alma Vollertsen Rykenboer Professor of Neurophysiology and chair of Neurology in 1986, building on the foundation laid by Joynt. Griggs received his MD from the University of Pennsylvania. He trained in internal medicine at Case Western Reserve University and URMC, where he was chief resident in internal medicine and a fellow in immunology. He trained in neurology at the National Institute of Neurological Disorders and Stroke (NINDS) and at URMC. Griggs's internationally recognized research program, which generated more than 350 scientific papers and twenty-four texts, focused on the development of new treatments for neuromuscular diseases, including periodic paralyses, non-dystrophic myotonia, Duchenne muscular dystrophy and inflammatory myopathies. He served as president of the Association of University Professors of Neurology and of the AAN, and as editor-in-chief of *Neurology*. He is neurology editor of *Cecil Textbook of Medicine* and an editor of *Cecil Essentials of Medicine*. He was elected to the Institute of Medicine of the National Academy of Sciences in 1998. Since his retirement as chair in 2008, Griggs has continued to play a major role in the clinical, educational, and research activities of the department.

During Griggs's tenure as chair, the number of faculty and staff, outpatient visits, inpatient admissions, and procedures, as well as the number of research grants, increased by at least tenfold, and the clinical, educational, and research programs achieved international prominence. He oversaw the recruitment of world-class faculty in all subspecialties, obtained an

NINDS-sponsored T32 postdoctoral training grant in Experimental Therapeutics of Neurological Diseases, established the Strong Epilepsy Center and three world-class research centers (CHeT, CTN, CNDD; see below), and created the first community-based neurology practice.

Steven A. Goldman, MD, PhD, who was recruited in 2003 as the Dean Zutes Chair in Biology of the Aging Brain and as chief of the division of Cell and Gene Therapy, served as Edward A. and Alma Vollertsen Rykenboer Professor of Neurophysiology and chair of the department of Neurology from 2008 to 2012. Goldman received his MD from Weill Medical College of Cornell University and his PhD with Fernando Nottebohm at Rockefeller University. He remained at Cornell for his internship in internal medicine and residency in neurology, where he subsequently joined the faculty, and where he developed an internationally recognized research program focused on cell genesis and regeneration in the adult brain. During Goldman's tenure as chair, Neurology expanded the reach and scope of its clinical services, with faculty providing services at HH and RGH. Of note was a partnership with Neurosurgery to develop a regional stroke program. The department's clinical programs in neuro-oncology, multiple sclerosis and myelin disease, and pediatric neurology were expanded significantly. He established a training program in neuro-oncology and grew the residency program in neurology. He also continued to grow the research presence, particularly in the Center for Translational Neuromedicine (CTN).

Figure 46.4.
Steven Goldman

Robert G. Holloway, MD, MPH, became the Edward A. and Alma Vollertsen Rykenboer Professor of Neurophysiology and chair of the department of Neurology in 2013 and continues in that role. Holloway received his MD and did an internship in internal medicine at the University of Connecticut. He then came to URMC for his neurology residency and health services research training, and in 1993 joined the faculty. Here, he developed a clinical research program that has helped maintain the University's international reputation as a leader in clinical trials and contributed directly to the approval of over ten FDA-approved therapies and devices. He also became board-certified in Hospice and Palliative Medicine and was instrumental in establishing neuropalliative care as a recognized discipline. Among Holloway's many accomplishments as chair, he established the Neuromedicine ICU, an internationally renowned complex biologic and gene therapy program, a regional

Figure 46.5.
Robert Holloway

telestroke and teleneurology program, a behavioral health integration program, the Headache Center, and expanded neurology practices in the region. He was instrumental in establishing the Del Monte Neuromedicine Institute and in recruiting John Foxe, PhD, as its research director and E. Ray Dorsey, MD, MBA, and Chad Heatwole, MD, as the directors of the Center of Health and Technology (CHeT).

Like his predecessors, Holloway has continued to grow the department and has created five new divisions. By 2024, the size of the department was approximately 400, including more than 100 faculty. Annual volumes tally more than 95,000 cases, 76,000 outpatient visits, 29,000 procedures, and nearly 2,000 inpatient admissions. On the research side, the department has over 150 grants that generate over $30 million of research funding, including $15.2 million from federal sources.

The primary site for inpatient cases is the twenty-four-bed Neurology Unit at SMH, of which eight beds are dedicated to long-term monitoring by the Strong Epilepsy Center. Additional patients are admitted to other units, including the neuromedicine ICU which opened in 2013. In 2014, the department ceased providing inpatient coverage at RGH, at its request. That same year, it formalized a neurohospitalist program, which covers the general inpatient and stroke services. The department started inpatient and consultative services at HH in 2005, under the leadership of Heidi B. Schwarz, MD. HH received NY State Primary Stroke Center designation in 2007 and became a site for residency training. In 2011, a newly remodeled unit opened that focuses on patients with stroke and other neurological conditions. Ambulatory services, which include several sleep centers, cover the region and include a number of local sites as well as those in the region.

The department has played a key role in UR Medicine's growing telemedicine program. The telestroke program, which began in 2018, now covers seventeen sites across the Finger Lakes region and central NY, and provides over 3,000 patient encounters per year. The telestroke team also provides clinical care onboard the Mobile Stroke Unit. A parallel teleneurology service, which provides virtual consultations for patients with acute non-stroke-related neurologic conditions, now includes fourteen sites and has well over 1,000 encounters per year. These programs have enabled countless patients in western and central NY to get high-quality neurologic care at UR Medicine affiliates and other partner hospitals.

The department now encompasses thirteen divisions and two research centers, complete descriptions of which can be found on its website. Several are highlighted below.

In 1975, Ira Shoulson, MD, developed a clinic for movement disorders, with a focus on experimental therapeutics. In 1984, he organized the

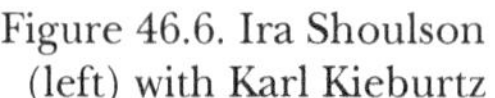

Figure 46.6. Ira Shoulson (left) with Karl Kieburtz

DATATOP (Deprenyl and Tocopherol Anti-Oxidative Therapy of Parkinson's) clinical trial, involving twenty-nine research sites. Two years later, the Parkinson Study Group (PSG) was established and headquartered in Rochester. The Clinical Trials Coordination Center (CTCC) was established in 1989 by Karl Kieburtz, MD, to support the PSG. Since its inception, the CTCC has played a central role in bringing twelve new drugs to market to treat Parkinson's disease, Huntington's disease, and other disorders. Also in 1989, Shoulson and David Oakes, PhD (Biostatistics & Computational Biology), created the Experimental Therapeutics of Neurological Disorders Fellowship program (funded by an NIH T32), which has subsequently trained many of the leaders in movement disorders. Shoulson, who received his MD and did his training in neurology at the University of Rochester, stepped down as division chief in 1999, but continued his clinical research activities at the University as the Louis C. Lasagna Professor of Experimental Therapeutics until 2011. Sadly, he passed away in 2024, having left an indelible legacy at the University. Kieburtz took over as chief of the division in 1999, followed in 2005 by Bernard M. Ravina, MD, and in 2012 by Richard L. Barbano, MD, PhD, who continued to grow the division's clinical and research operations. Karlo Lizarraga, MD, served as chief from 2020–4, expanding the department's global reach through the establishment of the Neurology Peru-Rochester exchange program.

Figure 46.7. Ray Dorsey

Ray Dorsey established an international reputation as a leader in Parkinson's disease treatment and research. Dorsey came to the University in 2005 for an NIH-supported fellowship in movement disorders and experimental therapeutics, and remained here as faculty. In 2007, Dorsey and Kevin Biglan, MD, MPH, launched a telemedicine program for Parkinson's patients in nursing homes. Their studies convincingly demonstrated that telemedicine could provide quality, cost-effective Parkinson's care, and that patients found it preferable to visiting the doctor's office. Dorsey returned to URMC from Johns Hopkins in 2013 to serve as director of the Center for Human Experimental Therapeutics and changed its name to Center for Health + Technology (CHeT, see below). He expanded the scope of the telemedicine program to serve patients with Parkinson's disease throughout NY State. Subsequently, Dorsey received an award from PCORI to conduct a national study of the delivery of telemedicine care to Parkinson's patients in their homes, and was awarded a coveted NIH award to establish a Parkinson's disease University of Rochester-Udall Center aimed at accelerating Parkinson's research through disease modeling, virtual visits, and novel digital health technologies. Dorsey was honored in 2015 at the White House as one of seven "Champions of Change" who are doing extraordinary work to advocate for better treatments and a cure for individuals with Parkinson's disease. He has continued to be a national advocate for Parkinson's disease, and for the role of environmental pollutants in promoting the disease.

Jamie L. Adams, MD, the David M. Levy Professor in Neurology, is currently division chief, as well as associate director of CHeT. A graduate of SMD and the movement disorders fellowship at URMC, her research focuses on the use of technology, such as wearable sensors, smartphone applications, and telemedicine, in individuals with neurodegenerative diseases. She recently was awarded an FDA grant that evaluates how wearable digital sensors can detect early signs of Huntington's disease. The Movement Disorder Program—one of the largest in the country and one of the most prestigious in the world—has been named a Center of Excellence of the Parkinson's Foundation, the Huntington's Disease Society of America, and the Tourette Association of America.

There are few stories as compelling as the productivity of our internationally prominent Neuromuscular Division (NMD), established in 1971 by Robert Griggs. NMD provides multidisciplinary, comprehensive services for patients with more than forty neuromuscular disorders and serves as a hub for numerous clinical trials. With the recruitment in 1974 of Richard T. Moxley, MD, who developed a disease registry for myotonic dystrophy and pioneered mexiletine for myotonic dystrophy (DM) 1, the University became a hot spot for

Figure 46.8.
Richard Moxley

treatment trials and the hub for a Muscular Dystrophy Association (MDA)-funded clinical investigation in Duchenne dystrophy. In recognition of his achievements, Moxley was named in 2011 as the Helen Aresty Fine and Irving Fine Professor of Neurology.

In the 1980s, NY State provided funding to NMD to study facioscapulohumeral muscular dystrophy (FSHD). Denise Figlewicz, PhD, and Al-Rabi N. Tawil, MD, were hired in the 1990s to establish an FSHD genetics laboratory. Tawil, the inaugural Richard Fields Endowed Professor of Neurology, led an international collaborative effort to understand the underlying molecular mechanisms in FSHD and to develop treatments to slow progression and improve strength. His team was instrumental in the discovery of the genetic defects in FSHD types 1 and 2, as well as in Andersen Tawil Syndrome. Griggs's and Tawil's research in periodic paralysis laid the foundation for clinical trials which established that dichlorphenamide was highly effective in preventing the attacks. It received FDA approval in 2015, making it the first drug to treat the condition. Tawil retired in 2024, after spending thirty years at URMC.

Figure 46.9.
Al-Rabi Tawil

Charles Thornton, MD, the Saunders Family Distinguished Professor in Neuromuscular Research, joined the faculty in 1992 after completing fellowships in neurology and neuromuscular medicine at URMC. Together with Moxley and Griggs, he identified DM2. Subsequently, Thornton and colleagues made a significant breakthrough by demonstrating that the genetic defect in DM1 leads to the accumulation of toxic RNA in the cell nuclei. In a 2012 *Nature* study,[12] they showed that antisense oligonucleotides could restore healthy protein functions in cells. In addition, Thornton and colleagues developed an animal model for DM 1 and developed an effective morpholino treatment in this model, and are currently partnering with industry to bring antisense oligonucleotide therapy to human trial. Clinical trials testing new therapies for DM1 are underway worldwide and at URMC.

Figure 46.10.
Charles Thornton

12 Wheeler, T. M., Leger, A. J., Pandey, S. K., MacLeod, A. R., Nakamori, M., Cheng, S. H., Wentworth, B. M., Bennett, C. F. and Thornton, C. A. "Targeting nuclear RNA for in vivo correction of myotonic dystrophy." *Nature*, August 2, 2012, 488(7409): 111–15. DOI: 10.1038/nature11362

Eric Logigian, MD, was recruited in 1998 to become head of the EMG lab; he became NMD division chief in 2001. His research has focused on electrodiagnostic methods for quantitative evaluation of patients with neuromuscular disorders. David Herrmann, MBBCh, became division chief in 2015. Herrmann, the inaugural E. Philip & Carole Saunders Professor in Neuromuscular Research, specializes in the diagnosis and management of peripheral neuropathies. His research focuses on outcome measures and biomarker development in Charcot Marie Tooth (CMT) neuropathies.

Figure 46.11. Eric Logigian

Emma Ciafaloni, MD, was recruited in 2002. At the University of Rochester, she established an international reputation for clinical trials in adult and pediatric neuromuscular diseases, including Duchenne muscular dystrophy, myasthenia gravis, periodic paralyses, nondystrophic myotonias, myotonic dystrophy, and FSHD. In 2017, Ciafaloni became the inaugural Robert C. and Rosalyne H. Griggs Professor in Experimental Therapeutics of Neurological Disease.

Figure 46.12. David Herrmann

Chad Heatwole, who did his residency in neurology and fellowship in clinical neurophysiology at URMC, joined the faculty in 2008. He has pioneered the development of disease-specific, patient-reported clinical trial outcome measures for DM1 and 2, FSHD, congenital myotonic dystrophy, CMT neuropathies and spinal muscular atrophy (SMA). He became director of CHeT in 2022 (see below).

Figure 46.13. Emma Ciafaloni

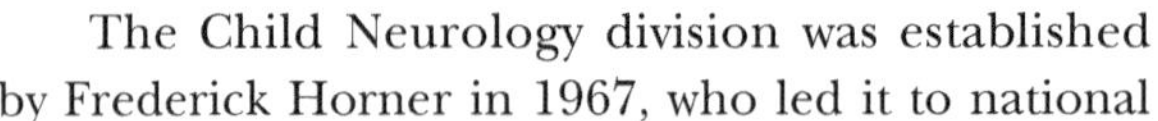

The Child Neurology division was established by Frederick Horner in 1967, who led it to national prominence. In 2001, Jonathan Mink, MD, PhD, was recruited to lead the division. Mink, the inaugural Frederick A. Horner, MD, Endowed Professor in Pediatric Neurology, established the University as a world leader in Batten disease (see p. 82). The division runs the largest child neurology program in NY State and provides national and international care for patients with neurological diseases, including rare diseases. Mink retired in 2023. The division provides multidisciplinary inpatient care at GCH and receives approximately 10,000 outpatient visits annually. The division is home to several clinical programs and centers, including: the Pediatric Multiple Sclerosis and Neuroimmunology Center; the Child Neurology Concussion program; the Leukodystrophy Care Center; and the Pediatric Movement

Disorders program. Current research ranges from fundamental to clinical, and includes neurovirology, neurotoxicology, neurophysiology of motor control and movement disorders, neurodegenerative disorders, clinical trials, and genetics.

The Strong Epilepsy Center (SEC), currently led by Tom Wychowski, MD (adult epilepsy), and Inna Hughes, MD, PhD (child epilepsy), began in 1990 as one of six established that year by NY State, and the only one outside of NY City. It currently manages eight beds at SMH and four pediatric beds at GCH. The SEC and the Pediatric Epilepsy Program comprise the only National Association of Epilepsy Center-certified, level 4 Epilepsy Center in the region. In collaboration with Webster Pilcher and Melissa Lopresti, MD, PhD, of neurosurgery, the SEC has been at the forefront of treatment development for seizure disorders, participating in over twenty-five clinical intervention studies, and has been involved in the evaluation of virtually every anti-epileptic drug approved by the FDA since 1990.

Gretchen L. Birbeck, MD, MPH, Edward A. and Alma Vollertsen Rykenboer Professor in Neurology, was recruited from Michigan State University in 2013, where she served as director of the International Neurologic and Psychiatric Epidemiology Program. Birbeck's research and clinical focus is on the burden of neurological disorders and the effectiveness of health care delivery in sub-Saharan Africa, where she spends six months each year. Over the years, she has developed the resources and created networks necessary to conduct clinical trials in Africa and to create education

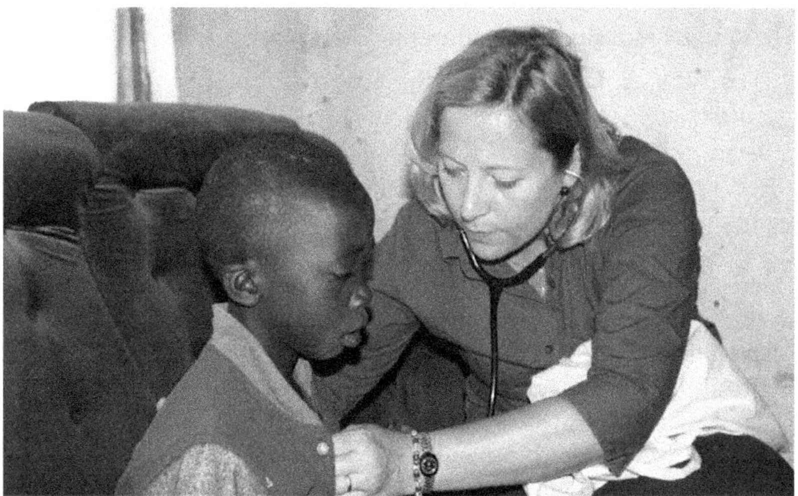

Figure 46.14. Gretchen Birbeck working in Africa

and training programs for African health care providers and researchers. Her specific interest is epilepsy and seizure disorders, which are far more common and constitute a significant health problem in Africa, where they are often associated with cerebral malaria. Birbeck is working to identify low-cost neuroprotective interventions that may help reduce seizures and the resulting neurologic damage, are simple to administer, and inexpensive enough to be of practical use in Africa.

The Neuro-Oncology division was established in 2007 by Nimish A. Mohile, MD (Division Chief), the Ann Aresty Camhi Professor in Neurology, Joohee Sul, MD, and Jennifer Serventi, PAC. In collaboration with the department of Neurosurgery and the WCI, they created the first multidisciplinary neuro-oncology clinic and largest brain tumor clinical trials program in upstate NY, and developed one of the first neuro-oncology fellowships in the country. The multidisciplinary clinic allows patients to receive all their care in one coordinated setting. The program cares for patients with brain and spinal tumors, brain metastases, neurologic complications of cancer, and neurofibromatosis, and offers more than fifteen clinical trials a year encompassing every possible tumor type. It also maintains a prospective database of all patients with primary brain tumors to facilitate research projects.

The Neurology Supportive and Palliative Care division was established in 2020 with the joint recruitment of Benzi M. Kluger, the Julius, Helen, and Robert Fine Distinguished Professor in Neurology. The division, the largest of its kind in the country, improves the quality and availability of palliative care for all people with neurologic illness.

Center for Human Experimental Therapeutics

The Center for Human Experimental Therapeutics (CHeT) was established in 2010, under the direction of Karl Kieburtz, as the first university-based program focused on accelerating the development of novel medical therapies. CHeT, which worked in concert with the CTSI, addressed one of the most significant barriers to developing new treatments: the initial translation of novel interventions from research performed in the lab into the first human clinical trials. CHeT assembles the resources academic and industry scientists need to answer fundamental questions about early-stage research, such as whether the intervention is safe, tolerable, feasible, and targets the intended mechanism. CHeT encompassed the previously established CTCC and the Clinical Materials Services unit, which provided clinical trial supply services.

Ray Dorsey became director of CHeT in 2013. He expanded the Center by creating an Innovation division, which he led, the Outcome Measures division, founded by Chad Heatwole, and an Analytics division led by Charles

Venuto, PharmD. Under Dorsey's leadership, CHeT became a recognized leader and innovator in harnessing digital health technologies such as telemedicine, wearables, remote monitoring, and mobile apps to improve access to care and conduct decentralized clinical trials.

In 2022, Chad Heatwole became the new director of CHeT, previously renamed as the Center for Health + Technology. As director of CHeT and the Center's Outcomes Measures division, Heatwole and his team oversaw the development of more than 250 patient-centered, disease-specific research instruments that focus on measuring changes in health. These instruments have been translated into over thirty-five languages and are used by academic, industry, and government researchers around the globe to measure clinically relevant changes in health in response to therapeutic interventions during clinical trials. Under Heatwole's leadership, CHeT expanded research scope to include non-neurologic diseases, and created CHeT Health, a new unit dedicated to facilitating access to therapeutic research and disseminating CHeT's many discoveries and inventions globally.

Figure 46.15. Chad Heatwole

Center for Neurotherapeutics Discovery

The Center for Neurotherapeutics Discovery (CND) had its roots in the Center for Aging and Developmental Biology, which was initiated by Howard J. Federoff, MD, PhD, as one of the six interdisciplinary research centers that formed the cornerstone of CEO Jay Stein's strategic plan. When Federoff left in 2007, Harris A. ("Handy") Gelbard, MD, PhD, became director and the name was changed to the Center for Neural Development and Disease (CNDD) to better reflect the focus on neurologic disease in the context of development. As the CNDD evolved, the focus expanded to not only understand the development of the nervous system, but to create new therapies to treat or prevent neurologic disease at a molecular level. Accordingly, in 2017, the name was changed to the CND and integrated within the research operation of Neurology. Employing the CND as a base, Gelbard put together an interdisciplinary, international team to develop a new class of small molecule therapeutics. This led to the development of a novel compound, URMC-099, a mixed-lineage kinase 3 inhibitor that inhibits innate immune responses that promote brain inflammation and cognitive impairment in animal models

Figure 46.16. Handy Gelbard

of HIV-1-associated neurocognitive disorders, Alzheimer's disease, and multiple sclerosis. Gelbard and colleagues have continued to study URMC-099, funded by multiple NIH grants, including a program project grant. URMC-099 has engendered twenty-eight national and international composition of matter and method of use patents, which have been licensed to Pioneura, where Gelbard serves as chief science officer.

Neurology Education

Figure 46.17. Ralph Józefowicz

Neurology has built a national and international reputation for excellence across the continuum of neurologic education. This legacy is inseparable from the contributions of Ralph F. Józefowicz, MD, who shaped the department's educational mission for more than thirty years. He came to the University in 1979 for an internship in internal medicine, residency in neurology, and fellowship in neuromuscular medicine, and then joined the faculty. As department chair, Griggs recognized Józefowicz's abilities as a teacher and greatly expanded his role, making him associate chair for education and giving him broad latitude to lead the department's educational endeavors.

Józefowicz has won nearly every teaching award available at SMD, and the residents whom he teaches also receive disproportionately high shares of teaching awards. For six years, Józefowicz led the AAN's education committee, where he promoted the establishment of the Student Interest Group in Neurology, which now has more than 100 chapters in US medical schools. He also developed an ongoing education exchange program between URMC and Jagiellonian University College of Medicine in Krakow, Poland, where he teaches for four weeks each year. He has received the A. B. Baker Award for Lifetime Achievement in Neurologic Education (2010) and the President's Award (2016) from the AAN, who credited him with enhancing the education of neurologists nationwide. He received the Alumni Service Award from SMD in 2018. In 2025, Christopher Tarolli, MD, was appointed associate chair for education, continuing the department's tradition of prioritizing innovation and excellence in teaching across all levels of training.

One of the department's most influential contributions to medical education is the preclinical Mind, Brain, and Behavior (MBB) course, which was launched under Józefowicz's leadership as part of the Double Helix Curriculum. The course has served as a model for medical school neuroscience courses nationally, and since 2000 the American Neurological Association has sponsored junior faculty from across the country to observe and teach in MBB. The course is among the highest-rated by medical students, who have gone into neurology at a rate three or four times the national average.

Józefowicz assumed the directorship of the neurology clerkship in 1994. Under his leadership, it became one of six required clerkships and has consistently been one of the most highly rated by students. The neurology residency program began in 1967, shortly after the arrival of Joynt, and Józefowicz served as program director from 1996 to 2020. During that time, he oversaw the transition to a four-year categorical program while expanding it from four to eight residents per year. Now led by Colleen Tomcik, MD, it remains one of the top programs in the country, with most graduates pursuing a career in academics. In 2003, Józefowicz worked with Jonathan Mink to re-establish the child neurology residency program. Now led by Robert T. Stone, MD, the program, which accepts three residents per year, is among the top in the country.

The department has a wide variety of fellowships, including clinical neurophysiology, epilepsy, neuromuscular medicine, neurocritical care, pediatric neurocritical care, sleep medicine, vascular neurology, neuro-oncology, neonatal critical care, behavioral neurology, and headache medicine. The two-year experimental therapeutics of neurologic disease fellowship has been continuously funded by an NIH T32 for thirty-four years. Graduates have become leading authorities in experimental therapeutics across academia, industry, and government, and have contributed to hundreds of multicenter clinical trials. Currently, the department has twenty-six fellows training in these eleven areas.

Chapter 47

DEPARTMENT OF NEUROSURGERY

Neurosurgical procedures at SMH were initially performed by the first chairman of Surgery, John J. Morton, MD. In 1928, William Perrine Van Wagenen, MD, joined the staff as chief of the neurosurgical service. He was an innovative surgeon, developing the operation of corpus callosotomy for intractable seizures and novel posterior approaches to deep tumors of the cerebrum. In 1939, the neurosurgery residency program became one of eighteen within the US approved for training. Following his retirement, Van Wagenen and his wife Abigail established the Van Wagenen fellowship endowment with a $5 million gift, which allowed a graduating neurosurgery chief resident to spend a research year in a European center prior to embarking on an academic career. The Van Wagenen fellowship has become the most prestigious research fellowship in neurosurgery over the past fifty years and has impacted the careers of many leaders in academic neurosurgery.

Upon Van Wagenen's retirement in 1954, neurosurgery was made a division within Surgery, with Frank Pye Smith, MD, one of Van Wagenen's former residents, as first chief. Smith recruited Joseph V. McDonald, MD, from Johns Hopkins, and for eighteen years the two ran the neurosurgery service. In 1974, following Smith's retirement, McDonald became division chief. In 1980, the Dr. and Mrs. Frank P. Smith Professorship in Neurological Surgery became the first endowed professorship within Surgery, established through a generous gift from Smith and his wife. Over McDonald's tenure, neurosurgical clinical volume expanded, and the training program grew to six total residents. Upon McDonald's retirement in 1990, he was succeeded by Eugene George, MD, and then followed in 1995 by Shige-Hisa Okawara, MD, PhD, as interim chief. In 1999, neurosurgery was made a separate department within SMD, with Robert J. Maciunas, MD, as its first chair.

Figure 47.1. Web Pilcher

Webster H. Pilcher, MD, PhD, received his MD and PhD in neuroscience & anatomy from the University of Rochester, where he remained for his general surgery internship and neurological surgery residency. He did a fellowship in epilepsy surgery and awake brain mapping at Washington University and then returned to URMC to join the faculty, where he developed a nationally recognized epilepsy monitoring and surgery program in collaboration with colleagues in Neurology. Pilcher was appointed the Frank P. Smith Professor and chair of Neurosurgery in 2002, and over the ensuing two decades grew the department from five to eighteen neurosurgeons, transforming a small clinical service department into a nationally recognized clinical and academic enterprise, featuring an array of clinical subspecialty programs, including cerebrovascular disease and stroke, neuro-oncology, epilepsy, peripheral nerve disorders, deep brain stimulation, pediatric neurosurgery, spinal surgery, neuroendocrine tumors, and brain and spine trauma surgery, as well as one of the top neurosurgical fundamental and clinical research programs.

An important accomplishment during Pilcher's tenure was the opening in 2014 of the Neuromedicine ICU, a collaboration between Neurosurgery and Neurology. The unit currently consists of twelve beds staffed by a multidisciplinary team, and serves as a key regional resource for the critical care of patients with neurological and neurosurgical diseases. Pilcher also developed Rochester Neurosurgery Partners, a community-wide neurosurgery initiative that emphasized collaboration rather than competition—at one point providing leadership of neurosurgery to all four Rochester hospitals—and focused upon improving quality outcomes and reducing cost of care for patients with stroke, brain tumors, neurodegenerative diseases, spinal disorders, and other neurological conditions.

During Pilcher's tenure, the department established an ambitious regional footprint with eleven regional outreach clinics. In 2020, as part of URMC's telemedicine initiatives, the department began providing round-the-clock neurosurgery consultations to six hospitals within the Bassett Health System, based in Cooperstown, NY. Faculty were also recruited to provide in-person inpatient and outpatient services for UR Medicine affiliates, as well as in collaborating institutions, such as Arnot Health in Elmira and Cayuga Health in Ithaca. These initiatives ensure that state-of-the-art care for all neurosurgical diseases is available to patients in Rochester and the surrounding region. As of 2024, the volume of neurosurgical procedures at SMH had grown to fifteenth highest in the nation, with over sixty percent coming from patients referred from outside Monroe County.

The growth of clinical programs under Pilcher's tenure has also enhanced the national reputation of the neurosurgery residency program. This seven-year program is based at SMH and uses several of URMC's affiliated hospitals to provide additional clinical experience. The opportunity to engage with outstanding research faculty has added a further dimension to the residency. The residency also uses a new state-of-the-art neurosurgical skills laboratory, opened in 2022, with dedicated cranial and spinal surgical stations, virtual reality and 3-D printed simulation laboratories.

The Translational Brain Mapping program, established in the department by Pilcher and colleagues, combines specialized preoperative functional MRI (fMRI) and structural MRI scanning with electrical stimulation brain mapping during awake brain surgery to create patient-personalized brain maps to promote safe and complete resections of brain tumors or areas of epileptic brain. By having patients engage in activities, such as reading or singing, during these procedures, the team can precisely pinpoint the activated structures of the brain. Using these maps as a guide, surgeons can preserve functions most important to the patient, while simultaneously advancing scientific knowledge of the brain. These awake brain operations rely heavily on real-time intraoperative monitoring of brain functions by neurologists with expertise in clinical neurophysiology and epilepsy monitoring.

This program received national attention when Dan Fabbio, a master's degree student at the Eastman School of Music, was diagnosed with a brain tumor located in a part of the brain known to be active when people listen to and make music. Working with Elizabeth Marvin, PhD, professor of music theory at Eastman, Pilcher and Brad Mahon, a PhD in Neurosurgery, came up with a series of music tests for Fabbio. They asked him to listen to piano

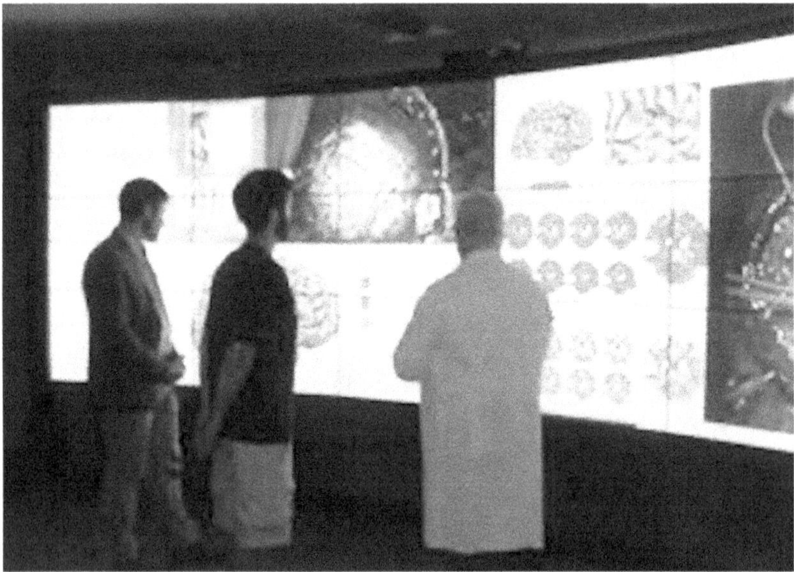

Figure 47.2. Awake brain surgery using patient-personalized brain maps enables the team to safely and fully resect tissue in the brain

melodies and hum them back while he underwent fMRI scans. In between melodies, he listened to and repeated spoken sentences. The scans allowed the researchers to pinpoint the areas of Fabbio's brain that were crucial for music and language processing, and allowed them to produce a 3-D map that served as a guide during surgery. During surgery, Fabbio performed the music and language tests, this time with his brain exposed. In the operating room, once his tumor was removed, Fabbio was given his saxophone and played a song he'd prepared for that moment. The entire operating room erupted in applause (https://youtu.be/95NMmqaFAKE).

Recently this program has expanded with NSF and NIH funding to establish a national consortium of centers to develop protocols for pre- and post-operative neuropsychological testing, fMRI and structural MRI brain imaging, intraoperative image guidance, modalities of brain stimulation, and post-operative evaluation and follow-up that will enhance safety and increase success. Mahon and colleagues have recently developed a standardized intraoperative cart, referred to as "Mind Trace," to be used in all participating centers. The first awake brain operations using Mind Trace were performed at SMH in 2025.

The past twenty-five years has been a period of great collaboration between Neurosurgery and Neurology, one which is discussed in the next chapter. In 2020, in recognition of this, the two departments developed a Joint Oversight Committee, consisting of the administrative leadership of the two departments, which meets monthly with URMC leadership to address all major issues related to neurologic care.

Chapter 48

COMPREHENSIVE STROKE CENTER

The "Stroke Unit," began in 1996 under the leadership of vascular neurologist Curtis G. Benesch, MD, MPH, enabling almost all patients admitted to SMH with stroke to be attended on by neurologists. In 2006, SMH was designated as a Primary Stroke Center by the NY State Department of Health and by The Joint Commission. A year prior to receiving this designation, Babak Jahromi, MD, PhD, was recruited to Neurosurgery as its first dual-trained cerebrovascular neurosurgeon. Jahromi led the development of an active cerebrovascular program at SMH that included surgical procedures for extracranial and intracranial vascular disorders and endovascular therapies for acute stroke. In 2012, supported by Benesch and colleagues, Jahromi established the first "hybrid" endovascular operating room at SMH, providing state-of-the-art endovascular care for patients with acute ischemic stroke, ruptured brain aneurysms, and subarachnoid hemorrhages. A second hybrid room was built in 2018 at SMH to accommodate the increasing number of patients who were candidates for endovascular therapies.

Figure 48.1. Curtis Benesch

In 2012, Neurosurgery and Neurology led a community-wide initiative to decrease the physical, psychosocial, and economic burden of stroke, and to create a model program that could be replicated for other disease processes and in other communities. The Stroke Treatment Alliance of Rochester (STAR), initially funded by a grant from the Greater Rochester Health Foundation, brought together stroke teams from HH, RGH, SMH, and Unity hospitals. The grant, written by Benesch and Jahromi, established a consortium of vascular neurologists and neurosurgeons who provided around-the-clock emergency support and consultation for each hospital. The aim was to increase acute intervention rates for stroke, increase adherence to secondary stroke prevention guidelines, and to create a regional data registry to share outcomes and practices among all member health care facilities. At the time, the Rochester region had one of the highest stroke rates in the state. Although RRH has withdrawn from the program, STAR-NY has expanded to encompass patients and hospitals throughout upstate NY, capitalizing on the department's tele-neurology services that provided around-the-clock emergent stroke consultation. Since 2012, URMC has hosted an annual symposium that brings stroke experts from over twenty hospitals across upstate NY to develop shared protocols and improvements in coordination of care of patients with acute stroke.

In 2014, through collaboration with endovascular neurosurgery, neuromedical critical care, and vascular neurology, URMC received accreditation as a Comprehensive Stroke Center, at the time one of only three such centers in NY State. The center fosters seamless collaboration among various units and departments at URMC, as well as with Emergency Medicine Services (EMS), to provide a comprehensive personalized approach from the time of stroke onset to well beyond hospital discharge. It is currently directed by Benesch and Tarun Bhalla, MD, PhD, who was recruited in 2016 to be chief of Stroke and Cerebrovascular Services in Neurosurgery after Jahromi left for a leadership position at Northwestern University. In 2024, the program admitted 1,300 patients with cerebrovascular disease, including over 900 patients with ischemic stroke, making it one of the largest in the state.

Figure 48.2. Tarun Bhalla

Under Bhalla's leadership, the endovascular and open cerebrovascular program grew from one to four dual-trained neurosurgical faculty, with a commensurate increase in the procedural volumes for stroke and cerebrovascular disease. In 2025, the Comprehensive Stroke Center evaluated 2,792 stroke patients and performed 1,820 cerebrovascular procedures and 185 mechanical thrombectomies, making SMH the second busiest in NY State for performing endovascular thrombectomies for acute stroke. Also in 2025, the Leenhouts family established a $2 million Endowment for Stroke Care and Recovery to support research in stroke care and recovery. A graduate of the University of Rochester College of Arts and Sciences and a former member of the University Board of Trustees, Norman and his wife Arlene had been long-standing supporters of the department, providing seed money for studies on brain mapping and the Leenhouts Family Endowed Visiting Professorship in Stroke Care and Recovery.

In 2018, in partnership with American Medical Response (AMR), URMC initiated operation of a Mobile Stroke Unit (MSU), a high-tech "emergency room on wheels" to provide life-saving care to stroke victims. At the time, it was the thirteenth such unit in the country. The MSU, directed by Bhalla, is equipped with a portable CT scanner, point-of-care laboratory equipment, medications including thrombolytic drugs, telemedicine equipment to allow

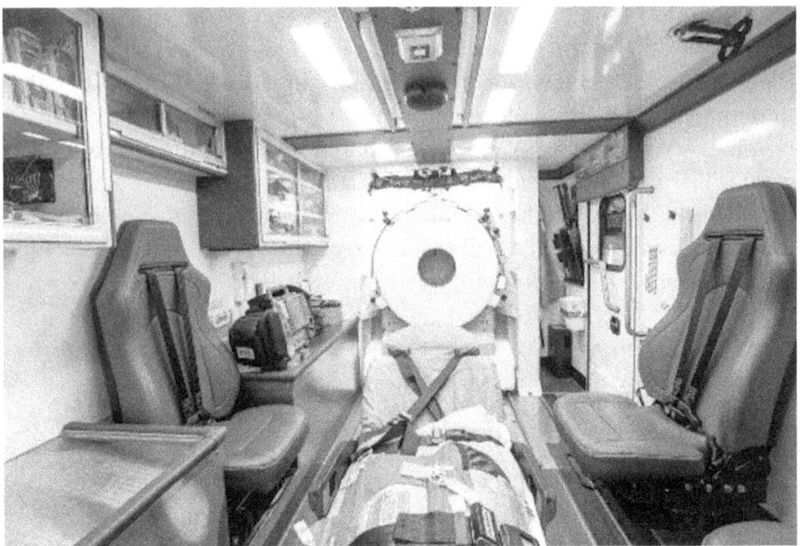

Figure 48.3. Inside the Strokemobile

for virtual neurological examinations, and personnel including a UR Medicine nurse trained in stroke care, a CT technologist, an AMR paramedic, and an EMT. Images are wirelessly transmitted to UR Medicine stroke physicians, who consult with the on-board Emergency Medical Services staff regarding immediate treatment, including administration of tissue plasminogen activator (tPA) to dissolve clots, and continue to remotely monitor the patient while *en route* to the hospital. In 2025, fundraising efforts in the community of Rochester permitted the purchase of a second MSU, which will arrive in 2026.

To date, thirty-two percent of patients treated in the MSU receive thrombolytic drugs within the "golden hour" associated with the best outcomes, whereas only two percent of patients treated in emergency rooms in Rochester receive thrombolytics within that timeframe. Patients treated in the MSU have a shorter hospitalization and are more likely to return home and an independent life rather than to a nursing home or rehabilitation. With the launching of the MSU, it became clear that inner-city Latinx and Black populations not only had double the rate of acute stroke but were more reluctant to call 911 for help. Under Bhalla's leadership, an inner-city health-equity initiative was launched to educate disadvantaged patients and families of the signs and symptoms of stroke and the need to call 911. Since 2019, Bhalla and colleagues have received $1.5 million in funding from the Cabrini Foundation to employ inner-city Spanish-speaking and Black educators to launch an aggressive "health literacy" campaign in Rochester.

Chapter 49

DEPARTMENT OF NEUROSCIENCES

The department of Neuroscience was one of the five original basic science departments of SMD. In 1925, the department—then titled Anatomy and chaired by embryologist and reproductive biologist George W. Corner, MD—was the first to begin instruction of medical students and among the first to offer formalized graduate training leading to advanced degrees. Over time, the focus of the department began a gradual shift towards the neurosciences, prompting a name change in 1985 to "Neurobiology and Anatomy."

Gary D. Paige, MD, PhD, became the Kilian J. and Caroline F. Schmitt Chair of Neurobiology and Anatomy in 1999. Paige received his MD and PhD in neurophysiology from the University of Chicago, and did an internship in anesthesiology at the Michael Reese Hospital in Chicago, followed by a residency in ophthalmology at UCSF. He then joined the department of Otolaryngology at Washington University, St. Louis, where he developed a nationally recognized program in neurosensory physiology, with a particular focus in balance. He was subsequently recruited to URMC Neurology, where he continued his research on neuroplasticity and ran the Balance Disorders and Dizziness Clinic. As chair of Neurobiology and Anatomy, Paige was responsible for promoting widespread collaborations with investigators throughout the institution. He also collaborated with Neurology to develop a unique integrated postgraduate training program in medical neurology for MD-PhD graduates, providing them with a residency in neurology, followed by a research fellowship in neurobiology. After stepping down as chair, Paige continued his clinical work in balance and dizziness as well as his award-winning nature photography.

Figure 49.1.
Gary Paige

Because Neurobiology and Anatomy had a relatively small group of primary research faculty and had many faculty who were largely involved in educational or administrative activities, it was decided to combine the roles of chair of Neurobiology and Anatomy and research director of the Del Monte Neuroscience Institute. The new chair would be provided with an endowment that would allow for the rapid recruitment of ten new scientists, creating a critical mass of new research activity in the department and allow for subsequent growth.

In 2015, John J. Foxe, PhD, was named the Kilian J. and Caroline F. Schmitt Chair of the department of Neurobiology and Anatomy, subsequently renamed the department of Neurosciences, and research director of the Del Monte Neuroscience Institute, renamed the Del Monte Neuroscience Institute (DNI). Foxe had established an internationally recognized translational research program on schizophrenia and developmental disorders, such as autism. A particular focus of his lab was on multisensory integration—how sight, sound, and touch knit together in the brain. Prior to his recruitment, Foxe served as the director of Research for the Rose F. Kennedy Children's Evaluation and Rehabilitation Center at the Albert Einstein College of Medicine in NY. Prior to joining the faculty at Einstein, where he had also received his PhD in Neuroscience, he served for six years as the director of the PhD program in Cognitive Neuroscience at The City College of New York.

Figure 49.2. John Foxe

As research director of the DNI, Foxe was charged with developing a broad strategic plan that would coordinate and expand neuroscience research and education programs throughout the University. Accordingly, Foxe held a retreat that included approximately 100 researchers throughout the University that identified several high-priority research areas for recruitment. Of greatest priority was the creation of a new center focused on autism and other intellectual and developmental disabilities, with a five-year goal of applying for designation as an Intellectual and Developmental Disabilities Research Center (IDDRC) by the National Institute of Child Health and Human Development (NICHD).

In July 2020, the University of Rochester became the first new institution in over a dozen years designated as an IDDRC, a fitting culmination of the remarkable five-year expansion of the DNI and department of Neurosciences under Foxe's leadership. The primary project for the IDDRC is on Batten's disease, in which URMC has been an international leader. In addition, the IDDRC provides grants for pilot projects in other areas. Supporting these projects is an administrative core and four scientific cores: clinical phenotyping and recruitment; translational neuroimaging and neurophysiology; cell and molecular imaging; and animal behavior and neurophysiology. The IDDRC research programs are closely integrated with Developmental and Behavioral Pediatrics, Child and Adult Neurology, Child and Adolescent Behavioral Health and Wellness, and the Complex Care Center clinical programs. Currently, Ania Majewska, PhD, serves as co-director and Sherry M. Mentor, MPH, MS, as administrative director.

Although the IDDCR is new, IDD, which affects 120,000 regionally, has been a priority of URMC for decades. In 1994, the NIH designated URMC as a Leadership Education in Neurodevelopmental Disabilities (LEND) center. This program, directed by Laura Silverman, PhD (Pediatrics), supports the training of virtually all types of health professionals to care for people with IDD. URMC had previously been designated as a University Center of Excellence in Developmental Disabilities (UCEDD). This program, directed by Suzannah Iadarola, PhD, Haggerty-Friedman Professor in Developmental/Behavioral Pediatric Research, develops community partnerships, fosters accessibility and inclusion, and translates research into best practice for people with IDD. By being designated as an IDDRC, the University of Rochester became one of only eight institutions with the "trifecta" of federal awards related to IDD.

On June 13, 2024, philanthropist B. Thomas Golisano announced a $50 million gift, the largest in University history, to build the Golisano IDD Institute. To quote Golisano, "Creating a better world for people with IDD has been a passion of mine for over forty years." The gift will provide state-of-the-art space, which will serve as the home for the IDDRC and coalesce other leading programs in IDD patient care, education, community outreach, and caregiver support. It will also create a second Complex Care Center, which will enable us to care for the growing population of adults living with an IDD and serve as a primary training site for health care providers specializing in IDD. The gift will allow the EIOH to expand its Specialty Clinic and telemedicine services, and allow URMC to expand the integrated care and developmental disabilities training functions provided by LEND and UCEDD.

A key component of the IDDCR and the neuroscience programs throughout the University is the Center for Advanced Brain Imaging and Neurophysiology (CABIN), a facility housed in the Annex building across the street from URMC and 100 yards from the River Campus. Foxe took over the directorship of the facility and oversaw a complete operational restructuring, making it more available to investigators throughout the institution, purchased new equipment, and initiated substantial expansion and renovations. Foxe moved his own laboratory and offices into the facility and revised renovation plans for the Kornberg and Del Monte research buildings to maximize proximity for Medical Center neuroscientists. The facility contains state-of-the-art imaging technologies, including a 3T MRI scanner, a 9.4T animal MRI scanner, high-density electroencephalography, eye tracking, and mobile brain body imaging.

Foxe's involvement in CABIN proved critical to URMC being included as part of the NIH Adolescent Brain Cognitive Development (ABCD) study. The largest long-term study of brain development and child health in the US, the ABCD research consortium includes twenty-one research sites across the country that will follow approximately 10,000 children starting at ages nine and ten for ten years, through the critical period of adolescent development. Researchers track their biological and behavioral development, and use cutting-edge neuroimaging methods to determine how childhood experiences (such as sports, videogames, social media, unhealthy sleep patterns, and smoking) affect brain development and social, behavioral, academic, health, and other outcomes.

The department's research programs are extensive, involving over forty primary and secondary faculty spread throughout the University who are engaged in a broad spectrum of neuroscience research. Major areas of focus include cell signaling and communications; computational neuroscience; learning, memory, and adaptive plasticity; neurobiology of disease; neurodevelopment and aging; and sensory, motor, and integrative systems neuroscience. The department website details individual research programs. The following paragraphs highlight some of the longer-standing programs.

Lizabeth Romanski, PhD, has focused on understanding how social communication information is processed, integrated, and remembered in the brain, and has provided important insight into how the integration of visual and vocal information takes place. Her laboratory established that the ventrolateral prefrontal cortex plays an essential role in audiovisual working memory; when switched off, the ability to remember auditory and visual cues is impaired.

Figure 49.3.
Lizabeth Romanski

Ania Majewska, PhD, is Dean's Professor of Neurosciences and director of the Cell and Molecular Imaging core of the IDDRC. Majewska's research centers on understanding the changes that occur at synapses that mediate how the brain adapts to changes in the environment. A particular interest has been how visual activity shapes the structure and function of connections among neurons in the visual cortex. Other studies have focused on the interactions between immune cells, microglia, and neurons during development and in response to injury. Recent studies in her laboratory have suggested that *in utero* exposure to TCDD (2,3,7,8-tetrachlorodibenzo-*p*-dioxin), a pollutant found in meat, dairy and fish, can alter microglia function and the brain immune system.

Figure 49.4.
Ania Majewska

Figure 49.5.
M. Kerry O'Banion

M. Kerry O'Banion, MD, PhD, the vice chair of Neurosciences, studies the role of neuroinflammation and oxidative stress in Alzheimer's and other neurodegenerative diseases. O'Banion, who came to URMC in 1988 as a Wilmot Foundation Fellow, has directed the MSTP since 2000. In landmark studies, O'Banion and colleagues, including his long-standing collaborator John A. Olschowka, PhD, showed that microglia could be stimulated by cytokines to produce an anti-inflammatory response that would clear amyloid beta, which accumulates in Alzheimer's. Because of O'Banion's work demonstrating that exposure to high-mass, high-charged particles caused biological and cognitive changes in mice that indicated an accelerated risk for the development of Alzheimer's disease, he and colleagues have been funded by the National Aeronautics and Space Administration (NASA) to study the effects of space radiation on brain function.

The department has traditionally served as home for faculty involved in Medical School teaching and administration. John Hansen, PhD, the associate dean for Medical School Admissions from 1996–2016, had his primary appointment in the department and even served as its chair from 1991–5. Diane Piekut, PhD, directs the anatomic gift program for the Medical School. The department remains heavily involved in Medical School curricula design and in teaching and co-directing *Human Structure and Function* and *Mind, Brain, and Behavior*, two major courses taught during the first two years of medical school. The department also offers the Academic Honors Program in Medical Neurobiology, which adds a fifth year of study, research, and teaching experience to the medical curriculum, culminating in an MD, MS.

The department also directs the Neuroscience Graduate Program, which contains a neuroscience track and a neurobiology and anatomy track, which is specifically designed for a medical school setting where teaching comprises an important component of the faculty mission. The program, which involves many departments within SMD, Arts and Sciences, and Engineering, is one of the most popular programs at URMC and currently has more than fifty PhD candidates.

Chapter 50

CENTER FOR TRANSLATIONAL NEUROMEDICINE

The Center for Translational Neuromedicine (CTN) was established in 2007, integrating the research programs of Steven Goldman and Maiken Nedergaard. Since its formation, it has evolved into a flagship program for the University and one of the most productive centers for basic and early-stage translational neuroscience in the world.

Maiken Nedergaard received her MD and DMSc from the University of Copenhagen, Denmark, and did postdoctoral training at the University of Copenhagen and Cornell University Medical School. It was during her time at Cornell that she met, and ultimately married, Goldman. Upon establishing a research laboratory at New York Medical College, Nedergaard quickly developed an international reputation for her work on astrocyte biology. The couple was recruited to URMC in 2003 by Howard Federoff, SAD for Basic Research, who was aided in his efforts by Webster Pilcher.

Figure 50.1. Maiken Nedergaard

For nearly two decades, the CTN has been a world leader in developing new approaches to investigate and treat neurological disease. The center has two divisions. The division of Cell and Gene Therapy, led by Goldman, studies the regulatory control of CNS stem and progenitor cells and uses that knowledge to design novel cell- and gene therapy-based treatments for neurological diseases. One focus has been on glial disorders that are potentially modifiable using strategies based on glial progenitor cell biology. Dysregulated signaling by endogenous glial progenitors plays an important role in a wide array of neuropathologies, including multiple sclerosis and vascular demyelination, hereditary leukodystrophies and storage disorders, glial neoplasms, and even neuropsychiatric disorders. A second focus has been on neuronal disorders that are potentially treatable by stimulating and mobilizing endogenous stem (e.g. Huntington's disease) or progenitor cells (e.g. multiple sclerosis). Goldman has been issued thirty-one patents in the US and is currently involved in several clinical trials using the strategies described above. He also serves as senior VP and head of CNS Therapy at Sana Biotechnology, in Cambridge, Massachusetts.

The division of Glial Disease and Therapeutics, led by Nedergaard, employs a multidisciplinary approach to study brain function in the healthy and diseased nervous system. Research has focused particularly on deciphering the role of neuroglia, cell types that constitute half of the entire cell population of the brain and spinal cord. Work over the past decade has suggested a more substantial role for astrocytes, the most common type of neuroglia, in which they constantly communicate with neurons and regulate their activity, and play a central role in conditions like stroke, Alzheimer's, epilepsy, and spinal cord injury.

One of Nedergaard's seminal discoveries has been the glymphatic system, first described in 2012. This system is a network that runs parallel to blood vessels and pumps cerebral spinal fluid through brain tissue to wash away waste. This system operates primarily during sleep and removes toxic proteins, such as those associated with Alzheimer's disease. Subsequent work has shown that circadian rhythms, specific patterns of neurological activity, and the flow of blood in the brain all play a role in controlling the system. The system deteriorates as we age and can be impaired in sleep disorders. The glymphatic system also can be useful to enhance drug delivery to the central nervous system. These findings have fundamentally changed our understanding of the biological purpose of sleep and opened the door to potential new ways to treat neurological disorders, such as Alzheimer's, Parkinson's, and Huntington's disease, and amyotrophic lateral sclerosis. In 2017, Lauren M. Hablitz, PhD, was recruited to the CTN, where she has been collaborating with Nedergaard to further characterize the glymphatic system.

In 2022, Nedergaard was chosen to lead a new $15 million program funded by the NIH that will bring together teams of researchers from URMC, Penn State University, Boston University, and the University of Copenhagen to accelerate our understanding of the complex mechanics that control the glymphatic system. The new program seeks to develop a detailed, mechanistic understanding of the movement of cerebrospinal fluid across sleep and wakefulness.

In 2014, Nedergaard and Goldman opened a new Center for Basic and Translational Neuroscience at the University of Copenhagen, Denmark. This new center was supported primarily by funding from the Novo Nordisk Foundation. The Copenhagen and Rochester centers are highly collaborative, and many faculty and students have joint appointments at both. In addition, Rigshospitalet, the Copenhagen University Hospital, provides clinical opportunities for faculty and offers experiences for residents and fellows from URMC. The Copenhagen lab now includes over forty faculty, postdoctoral fellows, students, and staff, complementing the seventy at the University of Rochester.

Chapter 51

DEPARTMENT OF PSYCHIATRY

Psychiatry began as a division in DOM shortly after the opening of SMH. The first psychiatric inpatient unit associated with the University opened at the Municipal Hospital in 1927, followed a year later by the establishment of outpatient clinics. The department of Psychiatry—among the first of its kind—was established in 1946 with John Romano, MD, as its first chair. This was followed in 1949 by the completion of "Wing R," one of the first psychiatric facilities in the nation to be built as an integral part of a university hospital.

Romano, who led the department until 1971, is regarded as a founding father of modern American psychiatry and recognized worldwide as a reformer of medical education. Upon becoming chair, Romano invited George L. Engel, MD, to join the University, with dual appointments in Psychiatry and DOM. Engel established a medical psychiatric liaison service and became deeply involved in the incorporation of psychiatric training in the medical school curriculum. He also became one of the leading figures in psychosomatic studies and, under his direction, URMC became a leading center for developing psychosomatic theory and training. The ultimate expression of Engel's ideas came to be termed the "biopsychosocial model," which remains the cornerstone of medical student training at the University of Rochester. For more on Romano and Engel and the biopsychosocial model, read the text *John Romano and George Engel: Their Lives and Work.*[13]

Romano was followed as chair by Lyman C. Wynne, MD, PhD, a pioneer in family-based therapies, which have remained a hallmark of the department's integrative approach. With his wife Adele, also a therapist, Wynne founded the Wynne Center for Family Research, which continues to thrive today. He also underscored the importance of major psychiatric disorders as a departmental focus. Wynne was followed as chair in 1977 by Haroutun M. Babigian, MD, one of Romano's many internationally recruited residents, who added epidemiological and population perspectives, and spearheaded the community

---

13 Cohen, Jules and Brown-Clark, Stephanie. *John Romano and George Engel: Their Lives and Work.* University of Rochester Meliora Press, 2010.

mental health movement in Monroe County. In 1992, Babigian became the inaugural John Romano Professor of Psychiatry.

Following Babigian's untimely death in 1993, Eric D. Caine, MD, became chair of the department and John Romano Professor of Psychiatry, positions that he held until 2017. Caine received his MD from Harvard Medical School and did residencies in psychiatry at Massachusetts Mental Health Center and the Warren Magnuson Clinical Center at the NIH. An internationally recognized leader in suicide prevention, he and his colleagues founded the University of Rochester Center for the Study and Prevention of Suicide in 1998. Caine led three major multidisciplinary research centers at the University of Rochester: the CDC-funded Injury Control Research Center for Suicide Prevention; the National Institute of Mental Health (NIMH)-funded Clinical Research Center for the Study of the Psychopathology of the Elderly; and the NIMH/National Institute of Drug Abuse-funded Center for Public Health and Population Interventions for Preventing Suicide. Caine was also principal investigator of a collaborative consensus process on public health approaches to suicide prevention, supported by a coalition of five NIH institutes, the Substance Abuse and Mental Health Services Administration, and the CDC. Caine also played a significant role in education, serving as the PI of several institutional training grants and as the PI for a series of NIH Fogarty International Center training programs devoted to building collaborative infrastructure and preparing early career Chinese researchers devoted to suicide research and to public health population approaches to suicide prevention.

Figure 51.1.
Eric Caine

Caine stepped down as chair in 2017, but as emeritus professor of psychiatry has continued to be active as a clinician, researcher, and educator. He was followed as chair and John Romano Professor of Psychiatry by Hochang Benjamin Lee, MD, who was recruited from Yale University. Lee received his MD from Jefferson Medical College and did a psychiatry residency and a combined neuropsychiatry/psychiatric epidemiology fellowship at Johns Hopkins. Lee is a national leader in developing innovative models for delivering behavioral health services to medical and surgical patients, and for preventing neuropsychiatric morbidity in elders after major surgery. Prior to joining URMC, he was the founding director and chief of the Psychological Medicine Service and the director of the Psychological Medicine Research Center at Yale. Lee

Figure 51.2.
H. Benjamin Lee

is editor-in-chief for the *Journal of the Academy of Consultation-Liaison Psychiatry* and president of the International College of Psychosomatic Medicine.

Under the leadership of Caine and Lee, Psychiatry experienced remarkable growth. Ambulatory visits grew from 58,000 per year in 1993, to more than 200,000 in 2017, to 500,000 in 2024. Inpatient admissions have grown from 1,700 to 2,600 patients per year, fueled by the addition of twenty-seven child/adolescent beds that more than compensated for a reduction of thirty-seven adult beds. Emergency assessments (including mobile crisis encounters) now exceed 12,000 per year. Concomitant with the growth in volumes has been the growth in faculty, which exceeded 100 by 2017 and stood at over 180 in 2025. Departmental divisions now include Acute and Adult Psychiatry, Addiction Psychiatry, Community Psychiatry, Collaborative Care and Wellness, Geriatric Mental Health and Memory Care, and Medicine in Psychiatry Services. To accommodate the remarkable growth and improve access, the department expanded outside URMC, moving its geriatric and child/adolescent services to Science Parkway; relocating programs related to severe mental disorders, substance-related conditions, and medicine in psychiatry services to the Brighton Business Center on West Henrietta Road; and moving many adult ambulatory programs to a downtown site on North Chestnut Street.

Psychiatry is unique in that it has a division of Medicine in Psychiatry Services (MIPS) that addresses the underrecognized medical needs of psychiatry patients and epitomizes the department's focus on providing comprehensive, integrated care. MIPS division faculty members have expertise in primary care and are trained in family medicine or internal medicine; some have additional training in addiction medicine, mental health, or geriatrics. The MIPS outpatient clinic opened in 1993 to provide primary care for persons suffering severe mental conditions as well as substance use disorders. The enhanced therapeutic and preventive services available to MIPS patients have resulted in substantially fewer medical admissions, reducing health care costs. The MIPS inpatient medical services opened in 2006 and have expanded over time from ten to thirty beds, including the recent addition of a specialized medical-psychiatric unit for persons with substance use disorders.

The past twenty-five years has witnessed the growth of child and adolescent psychiatry, an outstanding example of collaboration between Pediatrics and Psychiatry. The division of Child & Adolescent Psychiatry (CAP) is the largest pediatric provider of outpatient services in the region, and offers the only inpatient and partial hospitalization programs in western NY. CAP oversees a wide range of services, including: the child and adolescent inpatient psychiatric service at GCH; the child and adolescent mobile crisis team; the child and adolescent partial hospitalization program; pediatric behavioral health and wellness ambulatory services; and the pediatric behavioral health consultation and liaison service, which offers evaluation and short-term treatment on the medical inpatient floors and in the primary care and subspecialty clinics.

Figure 51.3. Michael Scharf

Michael A. Scharf, MD, the inaugural Dr. Mark and Maureen Davitt Distinguished Professor in Child and Adolescent Psychiatry, serves as chief of CAP, psychiatrist-in-chief at GCH, and director of Psychiatry graduate medical education. Scharf received his MD from SUNY Buffalo and completed a residency in psychiatry and fellowship in child and adolescent psychiatry at URMC. He then joined the Psychiatry faculty, where he has dedicated his career to ensuring access to quality mental health care for all children and adolescents in the region. He has overseen the extraordinary expansion of pediatric behavioral services, epitomized by growth in ambulatory visits from approximately 4,200 in 1998 to more than 60,000 in 2025.

In 2020, URMC ushered in a new era for pediatric health and wellness with the opening of the Golisano Pediatric Behavioral Health and Wellness Building on the Al Sigl Campus. This two-story, 36,000 square-foot facility, supported by a gift from Tom Golisano, is the largest children's mental health ambulatory service in the region. It has more than doubled the space for pediatric behavioral health and wellness outpatient care, services directed by Linda J. Alpert-Gillis, a graduate of the University's Clinical Psychology PhD program and professor of psychiatry, pediatrics, and clinical nursing. Alpert-Gillis also directs the Laboratory of Innovation in Child Mental Health Care Delivery.

The new building also enabled a marked expansion of URMC's Child and Adolescent Partial Hospitalization Service (CAPHS), the only program of its kind in upstate NY. The program, which opened in 1998, serves as an alternative to psychiatric inpatient admission for adolescents who do not require a secure inpatient unit and for adolescents in need of a step-down from psychiatric hospitalization. This multidisciplinary program is five to seven hours per weekday and includes individual, group, and family therapy, psychiatric evaluation, and psychiatric medication evaluation. A school component is offered during the academic year. In addition to CAPHS, the building provides an intensive outpatient service that enables children to attend their regular school and live at home but receive a higher level of care than that provided by traditional outpatient services. The Partial Hospitalization program now sees more than 10,000 patients per year.

In June 2024, behavioral health services were further enhanced with the opening of the Brighter Days Pediatric Mental Health Urgent Care Center, upstate NY's first walk-in mental health clinic for patients up to the age of eighteen. Supported by a grant from the Brighter Days Foundation, the facility is open from noon to 7 p.m., seven days a week and can see up to 3,000 patients per year. With a staff of over thirty caregivers, including mental health counselors, social workers, nurses, psychologists, and case managers, Brighter Days provides a variety of services, including assessment and evaluation, safety planning, crisis intervention, family-centered support, and linkage to community and educational resources.

Psychiatry has also opened a variety of specialty clinics to provide behavioral health services to patients facing distinct challenges. These include the Deaf Wellness Center, The Memory Care Program (in collaboration with Neurology), Lazos Fuertes for primary Spanish-speaking individuals, and the Heal-Education-and-Law Collaborative, which provides mental health, legal, and social services in one location for victims of intimate partner violence.

CAP has also been an innovator in training providers and staff in preventive behavioral health care. The FairStart program in the Fairport Central School District, one of four school districts that contract with the division for mental health programs, is a three-tiered system that enables districts to manage the behavioral health of their students, providing social and emotional training to teachers and nurses to deal with mental health issues, case-specific consultation and student support workshops, and school-based services for children needing more intervention. Project TEACH (Training and Education for the Advancement of Children's Health) is a NY State program involving seven academic health systems (Scharf serves as the site leader for URMC) that provides education and clinical consultation to pediatricians and primary care doctors. Sources of Strength is a suicide-prevention program that trains secondary school students to strengthen natural coping resources and disseminate the intervention through social networks. Together with the division of Acute Care Surgery and Trauma, CAP has also been heavily involved (Scharf was a founding member) in the Rochester Youth Violence Partnership, a hospital-based violence intervention program.

Befitting its history, the department has a rich portfolio of educational offerings. It plays a central role in bringing the biopsychosocial model to undergraduate medical students through its involvement in the Mind/Brain/Behavior course in Phase 2, and oversees the four-week Psychiatry clerkship in Phase 3. The Laboratory of Behavioral Health Skills is a resource for hands-on learning and competence assessment. Actor-educators engage learners in realistic scenarios to help them in diagnostic interviewing, managing difficult conversations, handling challenging situations with patients, and improving team-based skills.

The four-year psychiatry residency currently accepts eight students per year and provides substantial opportunity for research. The department also has one-year fellowships in Addiction Psychiatry, Consultation-Liaison Psychiatry, Forensic Psychiatry (Charles E. Steinberg Fellowship in Psychiatry and Law), and Geriatric Psychiatry, and a two-year fellowship in Child and Adolescent Psychiatry. Psychiatry offers a one-year psychology internship as a bridge between doctoral study and professional life. It includes an adult track, which offers positions in four specialty areas (Deaf Wellness, Lazos Fuertes, Heath Psychology, and General Psychology), and a child and adolescent track, which has four positions. Postdoctoral fellowships are available in Integrated Care Family Psychology, Child and Adolescent Psychology, and Adult Psychology. Psychiatry also offers practical experiences for social work trainees, including generalist professional practice internships for BSW students and advanced professional practice in an area of concentration for MSW students.

Psychiatry oversees a two-year MS in Marriage and Family Therapy, which includes a master's thesis and practicum training at two sites, and a certificate program in Marriage and Family Therapy, which provides training for those who already have an advanced degree and are interested in specialty training in family therapy theory and clinical practice. In collaboration with the Warner School, a certificate program in Addictions Counseling is available to those with a master's degree in counseling, health professions, or related fields who want substance use training, with the goal of being a Credentialed Alcoholism and Substance Abuse Counselor.

In 2020, the department of Psychiatry was named by HRSA as one of the country's three Rural Centers of Excellence on Substance Use Disorder and awarded a $6.7 million federal grant (PIs, Michele Lawrence, MBA, MPH, and Gloria J. Baciewicz, MD) to identify and adapt evidence-based practices that effectively impact synthetic opioid morbidity and mortality in rural Appalachian communities. This three-year educational dissemination program is designed to connect leaders in substance use disorder and rural medicine from the University's Recovery Center of Excellence with local community leaders and health care providers across twenty-three counties in NY, Ohio, Kentucky, and West Virginia. The department has received additional awards from HRSA, with an aggregate of $12.3 million, to extend the scope of this project.

Psychiatry has had a rich history of groundbreaking research, epitomized by the work of Engel, Romano, Wynne, and Robert Ader, MD, who was instrumental in the development of the new field of psychoneuroimmunology. With the retirement or departure of many key scientists, there were few funded research programs in the department when Caine took the helm. Accordingly, he recruited prominent investigators and sponsored or mentored twenty-four NIH K-awards, setting the foundation for the growth of a new generation of researchers. As chair, Lee has continued the strong support of research, and in addition, has recruited several outstanding senior investigators. As a result, extramural research funding has grown from approximately $1 million in 1999, to $17 million in 2016, to $32 million in 2024. Detailed descriptions of individual research programs can be found on the URMC Psychiatry website. A few are highlighted in the following paragraphs.

Psychiatry has been at the forefront of suicide prevention and research for decades. The Center for the Study and Prevention of Suicide (CSPS), established by Caine and Yeates Conwell, MD, and colleagues, has served as the foundation for research and education in suicide prevention since 1998 and has resulted in the University being awarded three major research centers and being named a Veteran's Administration (VA) Center of Excellence on Suicide Prevention. The CSPS has a NIMH T32 postdoctoral research fellowship in suicide prevention (initiated in 2001 by Conwell) and a VA Advanced Fellowship Program in Veteran Mental Health and Suicide Prevention. The CSPS, currently under the leadership of Kimberly A. Van Orden, PhD, and Peter A. Wyman, PhD, continues to be a world leader in suicide research.

The Strong Ties Community Support Program is a team-based, outpatient mental health clinic developed in the 1990s under Caine that serves adults who are coping with issues related to severe and persistent mental illness, such as schizophrenia, depression, and bipolar disorder. Under the early leadership of Marvin I. Herz, MD, and J. Steven Lamberti, MD, the clinic grew as a primary site for studies examining novel psychopharmacological and psychosocial treatment strategies and conducted several important clinical trials through the national Schizophrenia Trials Network. Research in schizophrenia at URMC was markedly enhanced by the recruitment in 2019 of an internationally recognized schizophrenia group from the Robert Wood Johnson Medical School at Rutgers University headed by Steven M. Silverstein, PhD, and including Judy L. Thompson, PhD, and Brian Keane, PhD. This group established the Schizophrenia Treatment and Research (STAR) laboratory, which has more than ten active research projects. Silverstein, the George L. Engel Professor of Biopsychosocial Medicine and associate chair for Research in Psychiatry, was the director of the division of Schizophrenia Research at Rutgers University Behavioral Health Care and founding co-director of the

Figure 51.4.
Steven Silverstein

Rutgers-Princeton Center for Computational Cognitive Neuropsychiatry. Silverstein's work has demonstrated that changes in the retina are related to neurological or psychiatric disease severity, the stage of disease progression, and cognitive function. He also established the Center for Retina and Brain in collaboration with Ophthalmology and Neurosciences, and the Center for Visual Science.

The Alzheimer's Disease (AD) Care, Research, and Education Program (AD-CARE)—a collaboration with Neurology and Geriatrics—is directed by Anton P. Porsteinsson, MD, the inaugural William B. and Sheila Konar Professor of Psychiatry. Since its inception in 1986, AD-CARE has been a world leader in conducting clinical trials for AD. In the past twenty years, URMC has taken part in virtually every large study of potential AD medications. Currently the group is involved in studies examining the use of new imaging techniques and other technology to better assess and treat patients with memory loss, and in trials testing new compounds designed to better treat slow cognitive decline or prevent AD.

Figure 51.5. Anton Porsteinsson

The Wynne Center for Family Research, directed by Thomas G. O'Connor, PhD, conducts research to understand how family and relationship processes influence behavioral and biological bases of mental and physical health. Conner's research focuses on identifying the mechanisms by which early stress exposures shape children's long-term health and development. The center also supports a two-year postdoctoral fellowship in the areas of family or relationship processes and bio-behavioral development.

One of the most prominent researchers in Psychiatry has been Jan A. Moynihan, PhD, who led the mind-body research program for over twenty years. Moynihan received her PhD in microbiology and immunology from the University of Rochester and subsequently developed an international reputation for her work in psychoneuroimmunology, extending the animal work of Robert Ader to mind-body interactions among humans. In 1998, she was named the second George L. Engel Professor of Biopsychosocial Medicine. She and Kathi Heffner, PhD (SON and Psychiatry), received $5.66 million in NIH funding for two five-year randomized clinical trials examining the effects of mindfulness-based stress reduction and different brain-training activities on the immune system. Moynihan is currently professor emerita in Psychiatry.

Figure 51.6. Jan Moynihan

K. Immunology and Infectious Diseases

The research strategic plan developed by CEO Jay Stein established six centers with interdisciplinary research foci, one of which was Vaccine Biology and Immunology. Subsequent strategic plans by CEOs Brad Berk and Mark Taubman continued to highlight immunology and infection. Under CEO David Linehan, MD, this has culminated in the establishment of a new Institute for Immunological Science. This section will highlight several key components of the program: the department of Microbiology & Immunology, the David H. Smith Center for Vaccine Biology and Immunology, the division of Infectious Diseases of DOM, and the Translational Immunology and Infectious Diseases Institute. A description of the immunology research performed in the division of Allergy, Immunology, and Rheumatology of DOM is discussed in the Medicine section.

Chapter 52

DEPARTMENT OF MICROBIOLOGY AND IMMUNOLOGY

Immunology research at the University of Rochester has a storied history involving faculty in Microbiology as well as in other departments and centers. The research done by Philippa Marrack, PhD, and John Kappler, PhD, in Microbiology ultimately led to the identification of the T cell receptor, and by David Smith, MD, chair of Pediatrics, ultimately led to a successful *Hemophilus influenzae* type B vaccine. In 1983, David W. Scott, PhD, Dean's Professor of Immunology and a pioneer in immune tolerance, recruited four researchers with expertise in T and B cell immunology. In recognition of the growing strength in immunology, the department of Microbiology was renamed Microbiology & Immunology (M&I).

Barbara Iglewski, PhD, became chair of M&I in 1986. The first woman to chair a department at SMD, Iglewski received her PhD in microbiology from Penn State University and developed an international reputation for her work on the bacterial pathogen *Pseudomonas aeruginosa.* This work was critical to the discovery of "quorum sensing," a chemical mechanism by which bacteria communicate to coordinate attacks on cells and initiate disease. Within a year of coming to the University, Iglewski was elected president of the American Society for Microbiology, subsequently chairing its publications board for ten years. In addition to chairing the department, she also served as vice provost for Research and Graduate Education from 1995 to 1998. After stepping down as chair, she continued to do research and teach.

Figure 52.1. Barbara Iglewski

Under Iglewski's leadership, the department's NIH funding rose from thirtieth in 1986 ($1 million in awards) to fourteenth in 2009 ($12.3 million in awards). Among Iglewski's major achievements was her mentorship of postdoctoral trainees, and doctoral students, at least three of whom went on to become deans, at least five academic department chairs or center directors, and at least fourteen full professors. In recognition of her achievements, she received the Arthur Kornberg Research Award, the Lifetime

Mentoring Award, the Susan B. Anthony Lifetime Achievement Award, and the George Eastman Medal. Perhaps Iglewski's greatest legacy was as a trailblazer and a mentor for other women scientists. In 2015, she became the first woman from SMD to be inducted into the US National Women's Hall of Fame (womenofthehall.org). Iglewski passed away in 2023 at age eighty-five.

Stephen Dewhurst, PhD, succeeded Iglewski as chair of M&I in 2009. Dewhurst received his PhD in molecular biology from the University of Nebraska Medical Center and did postdoctoral fellowships at Columbia University and the Harvard School of Public Health. After coming to Rochester in 1990, he developed an international reputation for his research on virology and vaccine development, which advanced understanding of HIV interactions with glial cells, provided fundamental insights into herpes virus HHV-6, and led to improved live attenuated influenza vaccines. His current research focuses on the pathogenesis of HIV infection in the central nervous system. In 2002, Dewhurst became Dean's Professor of M&I, and in 2007 was named SAD for Basic Research, a position he relinquished when he became M&I chair.

Figure 52.2. Stephen Dewhurst

As chair, Dewhurst introduced several critical educational programs, including the HIV-focused NIH T32 predoctoral training program, the NIH Post-baccalaureate Research Education Program (PREP), and the NIH-funded University of Rochester Broadened Experiences in Scientific Training (BEST) program, providing new opportunities for pre- and postdoctoral trainees to prepare for a range of research-related careers. From 2008 to 2020, Dewhurst led the NIH-funded Center for Acquired Immunodeficiency Syndrome (AIDS) Research, and from 2020 to 2024, co-directed the HIV Clinical Trials Unit, which conducts vaccine and treatment trials and engages with communities affected by HIV. In 2014, Dewhurst was appointed vice dean for Research at the SMD, a position he currently holds. In 2021, he stepped down as chair of the department to become interim VP of Research for the University of Rochester, a position made permanent in 2023. In 2020, Dewhurst became the inaugural Albert and Phyllis Ritterson Professor of M&I, made possible by a generous gift from Phyllis Ritterson and other donors.

Jacques Robert, PhD, succeeded Dewhurst as chair and Albert and Phyllis Ritterson Professor of M&I in 2022, having served as vice chair from 2019 to 2020, and as interim chair from 2021 to 2022. Robert received his PhD in developmental biology from the Faculty of Science, University of Geneva, Switzerland, and then

Figure 52.3. Jacques Robert

did a postdoctoral fellowship at the Basel Institute for Immunology before coming to Rochester as a senior postdoctoral fellow in M&I in 1995. At the University of Rochester, Robert established an international reputation for his work on the amphibian model *Xenopus*, which has illuminated developmental and evolutionary aspects of immune responses, tumor immunity, and the impacts of environmental pollutants on the immune system. He has also been a driving force behind the department's educational initiatives, such as the "4+1" program, and his leadership has been key to the continued success of the department's training programs.

In 2025, Tanya N. Mayadas, PhD, was selected as the next chair of M&I and the inaugural director of a new Institute for Immunological Sciences. Mayadas received her PhD in biochemistry from the University of Rochester, followed by a joint postdoctoral fellowship at MIT and Tufts University. From 1993 to 2025, she served on the faculty of Harvard Medical School. Mayadas is internationally recognized for her research on antibody-driven glomerulonephritis, a leading cause of kidney failure, and her lab has identified receptors and signaling pathways in neutrophils that coordinate immune cell entry, activation, and organ damage.

As of 2025, M&I comprises eighteen primary faculty, twenty secondary faculty and three research faculty. Its educational and research programs focus on microbial pathogens (viruses, and prokaryotic and eukaryotic microbes) and the host immune defenses which protect against these organisms. The size and breadth of the faculty allow for a broad range of experiential educational opportunities for undergraduates, graduate students, and medical students.

The department supports a BS in M&I, which is selected by approximately thirty undergraduates in the Biology department. It also offers a "4+1" program that confers a combined BS/MS in M&I, and a stand-alone, two-year MS program in M&I. It serves as the home of the Institute's highly successful PREP program for post-baccalaureate learners; approximately ninety percent of the program graduates have matriculated into PhD programs at universities across the nation. The PhD Program (currently directed by Ruth Serra-Moreno, PhD) has approximately forty students at different stages of their training. The program is enriched by two NIH T32 training grants: *Infection and Immunity: The Pathogenesis of Host-Microbe Interactions*; and *Predoctoral Training Program in Immunology*. The department also plays a critical role in medical education and is principally responsible for the first-year *Host Defense* medical school course. This course includes comprehensive lectures, intensive problem-based learning cases, and independent exercises. In addition, department faculty are active as teachers and mentors in numerous graduate programs, including the MSTP.

Among the many research contributions over the past twenty-five years has been the identification of a key molecule (ST3GAL1)[14] responsible for guiding T cells towards tumors; the development of new experimental models to understand how waterborne microplastics accumulate in the body; the elucidation of how the oral microbiome is altered during pregnancy; the demonstration of the importance of BST2[15] antagonism for COVID-19 virus infectivity and spread; and the identification of prophage disruption of the CRISPR-cas[16] locus as a recurrent mechanism to counteract bacterial immunity.

Currently, M&I has $13.5 million in active research funding, comprising thirty-four awards which cut across many biomedical disciplines, including microbial pathogenesis and anti-infectives; microbial genetics and genomics; the bacterial CRISPR system; respiratory pathogens (most notably, influenza and SARS-CoV-2 virus); HIV; host-microbiome interactions; immune mechanisms, regulation, and autoimmunity; and tumor immunology and immunotherapy. Visit the M&I website for details of the current research programs.

Robert directs a unique, NIH-funded *Xenopus laevis* Research Resource for Immunology, the world's most comprehensive resource specializing in the use of *Xenopus* for immunological research. The facility maintains several genetically defined inbred *Xenopus* strains and clones, as well as research tools such as transgenic animals, monoclonal antibodies, cell lines, and molecular probes. A satellite facility is devoted to studying infectious diseases caused by iridovirus and nontuberculous microbacteria.

Over the past twenty-five years, there have been several faculty members who made important contributions but are no longer in the department, in many cases leaving to take major leadership positions in outstanding institutions. Dennis McCance, PhD (1989–2006), studied molecular mechanisms underlying cancer development, particularly those involving the retinoblastoma tumor suppressor protein, p63 protein signaling in cancer, and tumor microenvironment. He returned to his alma mater, Queen's University Belfast, Northern Ireland, in 2006 to become the director of the Centre for Cancer Research and Cell Biology.

Baek Kim, PhD (1998–2013), advanced our understanding of the role of long-lived myeloid cell reservoirs of HIV and contributed significantly to the development of novel strategies to cure HIV infection. Kim left in

14 ST3GAL1 – ST3 beta-galactoside alpha-2,3-sialyltransferase 1.
15 BST2 – Bone Marrow Stromal Cell Antigen 2.
16 CRISPR – Clustered Regularly Interspaced Short Palindromic Repeats.

2013 to become the inaugural director of Emory's Children's Center for Drug Discovery.

Sanjay B. Maggirwar, PhD, MBA (1997–2019), contributed significantly to research exploring the effects of HIV and its treatments on cardiovascular health. He left in 2019 to become chair of Microbiology, Immunology, and Tropical Medicine at the George Washington University School of Medicine and Health Sciences.

Robert E. Marquis, PhD (1963–2012), was internationally acclaimed for his research on oral streptococci and fluoride effects. He received the 2006 Distinguished Scientist Award from the International Association for Dental Research. He passed away in January 2014 at age eighty.

Nicholas Cohen, PhD (1967–2004), was a leader in evolutionary immunobiology, as well as in psychoneuroimmunology. He served as director of the division of Immunology and director of the M&I graduate program. He retired in 2004.

John Frelinger, PhD (1984–2024), recently retired after a distinguished career marked by the development of innovative immune system-targeted cancer therapies.

Robert Quivey, PhD (1988–2021), Margaret and Cy Welcher Professor of Dental Research, a leading expert in oral microbiology whose research on *Streptococcus mutans* had implications for reducing the global burden of dental caries, served as the director of the Center for Oral Biology from 2009 to 2021.

Edith Lord, PhD (1976–2021), an internationally known tumor immunologist, served as SAD for Graduate Education and Postdoctoral Affairs at SMD from 2008 to 2018. Although she retired in 2021, Lord remains active in the department as an emeritus professor.

Maurice Zauderer, PhD, was on the faculty for twenty-five years prior to founding Vaccinex, Inc., a Rochester-based company which initially licensed novel technologies that he developed in his URMC laboratory. Vaccinex, which went public in 2021, currently focuses on designing novel therapeutics to treat cancer and neurologic diseases such as Alzheimer's and Huntington's diseases by inhibiting the biological effector molecule, semaphoring 4D.

Chapter 53

DAVID H. SMITH CENTER FOR VACCINE BIOLOGY AND IMMUNOLOGY (CVBI)

The CVBI was formed in 1998 as one of CEO Jay Stein's research centers. Tim R. Mosmann, PhD, was recruited to Rochester from the University of Alberta, where he served as chair of Immunology, to be the founding director. Mosmann received his PhD in Microbiology at the University of British Columbia and completed fellowships at the University of Toronto and University of Glasgow. Mosmann has made many important contributions to the field of T cell immunology, and is perhaps best known for his discovery, with his colleague Robert Coffman, PhD, of the subsets of T lymphocytes, which determine whether the host response to infection will be characterized by a predominantly humoral immune response (TH2) or a predominantly cellular immune response (TH1). This discovery changed our understanding of how the host immune response is regulated and had fundamental implications for vaccine design and disease pathogenesis. Mosmann has won many honors and awards for his unique contributions, including the Avery-Landsteiner Prize (German Society for Immunology), the William B. Coley Award (Cancer Research Institute), the Paul Ehrlich/Ludwig Darmstaedter Prize (Paul Ehrlich Foundation), and the Novartis Prize for Basic Immunology.

Figure 53.1. Timothy Mosmann

Research in the center focuses on T cell activation and differentiation, T cell memory and homing, major histocompatibility complex (MHC) class II-restricted antigen presentation, T cell responses to pathogenic organisms, and T cell-mediated autoimmunity. The CVBI faculty plays a key role in the training of graduate students in immunology, microbiology, and virology, and provides a wealth of opportunities for medical students and undergraduates. The CVBI also plays an important role in NYICE and the RPRC (see below).

The CVBI was home to the NIH R24-funded Rochester Human Immunology Center (RHIC) from 2003 to 2012. This project, led by Mosmann, provided centralized support for the development and dissemination of cutting-edge technology and helped to facilitate translational immunology in several clinical and basic research units at URMC. In 2014, the CVBI was awarded a $9 million PO1, Program for Advanced Immune Bioimaging, from the National Institute of Allergy and Infectious Diseases (NIAID) to examine pathways that mediate the immune response in infectious and rheumatologic diseases. Led by Deborah Fowell, PhD, Dean's Professor of M&I, these studies identified potential molecular targets for modulating these responses. The program was renewed for $12 million in 2019. In addition to Fowell and David Topham, PhD, project leaders included Minsoo Kim, PhD, from CVBI, and Patrick Oakes, PhD, from Loyola University in Chicago. The goals of the project are to develop tools and techniques to mark and guide immune system cells into tissues and to use these to explore the movement of immune system cells through inflamed skin tissue and to understand how the immune system responds to flu infection in the airway. Fowell, who came to the University in 2000 and developed a highly recognized program in visualizing the immune system in action, left Rochester in 2020 to chair M&I at Cornell University.

Figure 53.2.
Deborah Fowell

In 2025, the CVBI was subsumed into the new Institute for Immunological Sciences under the leadership of Mayadas and was financially integrated with M&I.

Chapter 54

DIVISION OF INFECTIOUS DISEASES (DEPARTMENT OF MEDICINE)

The last twenty-five years have been a golden age for the University's division of Infectious Diseases (ID), beginning with the approval of a vaccine for the prevention of cervical cancer, approximately eighty percent of which is caused by specific strains of the human papillomavirus (HPV). William Bonnez, MD, Richard Reichman, MD, and Robert Rose, PhD, developed the key technology behind the vaccine at the University in the 1990s. As part of his PhD thesis (1994) in M&I, Rose inserted the gene for the human papillomavirus HPV capsid protein into baculovirus. This noninfectious "empty capsid" assumed the correct folded shape of the infectious virus and provoked the same immune response as infectious particles. This virus-like particle technology, which was awarded several patents, set off a race between the University of Rochester and three other institutions to develop a vaccine against HPV. This proved to be the basis for Merck's Gardasil vaccine for HPV (along with patents issued to the University of Queensland, the NCI, and Georgetown University), which received FDA approval in 2006 for use in girls ages nine to twenty-six. In 2011, the CDC recommended that boys and young men also receive the vaccine to prevent HPV-mediated oral and anal cancers. The impact of the vaccine was described in a 2023 publication, in which it was reported that from 2008 to 2022, rates for precancerous lesions decreased approximately eighty percent among twenty- to twenty-four-year-old women who were screened for cervical cancer.

In recognition of this important breakthrough in the history of cancer treatment, Bonnez, Reichman, and Rose were awarded the George Eastman Medal. In 2014, the American Society for Clinical Oncology asked the oncology community to identify and rank the five most important advances in cancer research and patient care over the past fifty years; the HPV vaccine for cervical cancer was selected as the second most important. The royalties from the University's HPV patents were used to establish several endowed professorships and recruit outstanding physician-scientists, particularly within DOM.

Figure 54.1. William Bonnez, Richard Reichman, and Robert Rose

In addition to his involvement in groundbreaking research, Reichman served as chief of the ID division until 2008, when he was succeeded by John J. Treanor, MD. Treanor received his MD from the University of Rochester and did his residency in internal medicine at the University of Vermont. He returned to Rochester for his fellowship in ID and then joined the division as faculty. Treanor's research interests have focused on control of influenza with vaccines and antivirals, and on the safety and immunogenicity of vaccines for emerging infectious diseases. In 2002, he was chosen to lead the largest study of smallpox vaccine, conducted at seven sites around the US. As described below, he was also the founding director of the New York Influenza Center of Excellence.

Figure 54.2. John Treanor

Treanor was succeeded as chief of ID in 2022 by Paul R. Bohjanen, MD, PhD, who was recruited from the University of Minnesota. Bohjanen graduated from the University of Michigan with an MD, PhD. He then completed an internal medicine residency and an ID fellowship at Duke University, before joining the faculty of the University of Minnesota, ultimately serving as director of the Center for Infectious Diseases and Microbiology Translational Research, director of the ID fellowship, and director of the division of Infectious Diseases and International Research. Bohjanen is internationally recognized for his work on HIV and the global AIDS epidemic. For more than twenty years, he has led a multidisciplinary collaborative program in Uganda that has involved clinical research focused on improving outcomes for patients with AIDS, as well as studies of disease pathogenesis in his laboratory using samples collected from patients in Uganda.[17]

Figure 54.3. Paul Bohjanen

17 https://www.youtube.com/watch?v=RFsoj1tVREo

As of 2024, the ID division was comprised of thirty faculty (including nine hired since 2022), four RNs, fifteen APPs, and a staff of approximately 100. The division supports six consult services, with three devoted to transplant (solid organ, stem cell, and cardiac), and oversees epidemiology/infection prevention at SMH and HH. The general ID clinic, directed by Ted Louie, MD, has approximately 7,500 visits and sees approximately 1,000 new patients per year. The NY State-designated AIDS Center, directed by Peter R. Mariuz, MD, provides primary care for approximately 1,100 patients living with HIV. Since the early 1980s, ID has also operated the Monroe County Sexual Health Clinic, currently directed by Daniela E. DiMarco, MD, MHP, and Marguerite A. Urban, MD, which has approximately 9,000 visits per year. Other key programs overseen by ID include the antibiotic stewardship and outpatient parenteral antibiotic therapy programs, directed by David M. Dobrzynski, MD (who recently passed away) and Alexandra Yamshchikov, MD. The faculty also oversees an outstanding clinical fellowship program, begun in 1970. The two-year program, which provides opportunities for additional years to do research, accepts three residents per year. In addition, faculty serve as mentors for graduate students in a variety of programs throughout URMC.

Figure 54.4. Edward Walsh

Until very recently, ID provided one of the best examples of collaboration with RRH, with URMC faculty providing clinical services and performing extramurally funded research at RGH. Leading this effort were Edward E. Walsh, MD, and Ann Falsey, MD, whose research activities until recently were based primarily at RGH. Walsh joined the ID unit in 1982 and Falsey in 1991, after completing ID fellowships at URMC. Their NIH-funded research has been directed towards respiratory tract infections, primarily those caused by viral pathogens, with a particular focus on Respiratory Syncytial Virus (RSV). Falsey's and Walsh's pioneering studies were the first to firmly establish RSV as second only to influenza virus as a cause of severe respiratory illness in older adults and those with underlying cardiopulmonary disease. Walsh, who until recently served as head of ID at RGH, was national and URMC lead investigator for Pfizer's phase-three clinical trials on their RSV vaccine for older adults. The results of that study, published in the *New England Journal of Medicine*,[18] led to FDA approval of the vaccine. Walsh was also a

18 Walsh, E. E., MD, Marc, G. P. MD, Zareba, A. M., MD, PhD, Falsey, A. R., MD, Jiang, Q., MS, Patton, M., BSc, Polack, F. P., MD, +24, for the RENOIR Clinical Trial Group. "Efficacy and Safety of a Bivalent RSV Prefusion F Vaccine in Older Adults." *N Engl J Med*, April 5, 2023; 388:1465–77. DOI: 10.1056/NEJMoa2213836.

lead investigator on the preliminary trials that preceded the phase three study. Falsey did important preliminary work on the GlaxoSmithKline vaccine, also recently approved by the FDA, including a phase-two clinical trial that resulted in a *New England Journal of Medicine* report on its safety and efficacy.

Figure 54.5. Ann Falsey

The division currently has over $60 million in research funding, including over $40 million in federal and state awards supporting the VTEU, ACTU, and EIP programs (see below). Research in ID focuses on molecular and clinical virology, viral immunology and pathogenesis, and evaluation of viral vaccines and antiviral agents. More can be found about their research on the department's website. The division has long-established collaborations with investigators in M&I, the Human Immunology Center, the CVBI, and the Translational Immunology and Infectious Diseases Institute that have put them in the forefront of research in viral infections and vaccine development, and include several nationally prominent programs supported by the NIH.

Figure 54.6. Michael Keefer

The HIV/AIDS Clinical Trials Unit (CTU), also known as the Rochester Victory Alliance (RVA), has been conducting HIV research since 1987. Directed by Bohjanen, Michael Keefer, MD, and Sonal S. Munsiff, MD, it encompasses the HIV Vaccine Trials Unit and the AIDS Clinical Trials Unit (ACTU), which is a part of a large NIH cooperative whose mission is to reduce the burden of disease due to HIV infection and its complications and ultimately to cure HIV infection. The University's ACTU was one of the first ten sites funded by the NIH in 1986. Since that time, the unit has enrolled over 1,800 participants in more than fifty outpatient studies. The unit's research team includes specialized research nurses, doctors, and support staff who work with research patients and with primary care physicians to coordinate their HIV care. Susan E. Hulse, PAC, serves as site coordinator.

The HIV Vaccine Trials Unit (HVTU) Clinical Research Site—one of the first sites in the US to conduct HIV vaccine studies—is part of a large, multidisciplinary, NIH-funded HIV Vaccine Trials Network (HVTN). Rochester's HVTU's mission is to evaluate the safety, immunogenicity, and efficacy of HIV vaccine candidates, with the goal of developing a safe, effective vaccine for prevention of HIV infections. Keefer, whose laboratory was the first to demonstrate T cell mediated immune responses to a candidate HIV vaccine, has directed the HVTU since 1991. When the HVTN expanded to include international sites in 1999, Keefer assumed the position of associate director of Scientific Administration.

The Vaccine and Treatment Evaluation Unit (VTEU), directed by Falsey and Angela R. Branche, MD, is one of ten NIH-funded sites focused on the development of vaccines and treatments for COVID-19, RSV, and other respiratory viruses; the development of treatments for resistant sexually transmitted diseases; and the development of a universal flu vaccine.

The New York Influenza Center of Excellence (NYICE) is one of six national centers established by the NIAID in 2007 to study influenza. The goals of the overall program were to elucidate the molecular and environmental factors that influence the transmission and evolution of flu viruses; to study the immune system's reaction to infection or vaccination; to identify strains with pandemic potential; to create new vaccine candidates; and to bolster pandemic preparedness. Led by Treanor in partnership with Topham, the $29 million NIH contract was the largest ever awarded to a Medical Center researcher. The goal of NYICE is to understand why immune protection from influenza often fails, even in individuals who have generated an apparently robust immune response following infection or vaccination. A particular focus has been on the impact of infection or vaccination on B cell and antibody specificity and function, including development of memory.

The NYS Emerging Infections Program (EIP), sponsored by the CDC and led by ID faculty member Ghinwa K. Dumyati, MD, is part of a network of twelve state health departments collaborating with academic institutions and federal agencies to provide population-based communicable disease data for surveillance of disease patterns, evaluation of vaccine programs, and to identify populations at risk. The data is used to evaluate public health interventions and inform policy. As a partner with the NY State Department of Health, the University of Rochester is involved in projects covering COVID-19, influenza hospitalization, *Clostidium difficile,* invasive *Staphylococcus aureus,* RSV, HPV vaccine impact, drug-resistant bacteria, and the relationship between health care-associated infections and antimicrobial use.

Chapter 55

TRANSLATIONAL IMMUNOLOGY AND INFECTIOUS DISEASES INSTITUTE (TIIDI)

In 2020, Rochester created a new institute to strengthen and accelerate the study of viral, bacterial, and fungal pathogens. The TIIDI, founded by David Topham and directed by Paul R. Bohjanen since 2022, aims to elucidate the etiology and impact of viral, bacterial, and fungal pathogens and the immune responses to them, and to develop new treatments and strategies to better control the spread of infectious diseases and prevent hospital-acquired infections. The TIIDI consists of ten pillars: Pediatric Diseases and Immunology; Barrier Immunology; HIV/AIDS; Coronavirus, Influenza, and other Respiratory Pathogens; Antibiotic Resistance; Cancer Immunology; Dental/Oral Infections; Vaccines; Computational Biology; and Community and Public Health. In 2025, TIIDI (like the CVBI) was subsumed into the new Immunology Institute, under the leadership of Mayadas.

Figure 55.1. David Topham

Topham is the Marie Curran Wilson and Joseph Chamberlain Wilson Professor in M&I. Topham received his PhD in cellular and molecular biology from the University of Vermont and did postdoctoral training in immunology at St. Jude Children's Research Hospital in Memphis. He joined URMC in 1999, where he developed an internationally recognized program in research related to respiratory viral infections and immunity. In 2009, he was appointed vice provost and executive director of the new Health Sciences Center for Computational Innovation (HSSCI), a partnership between the University and IBM that provided the University with an array of supercomputers to analyze huge amounts of data.

In 2011, the University was named by the NIH as a Respiratory Pathogens Research Center (RPRC), directed by Topham and Ann Falsey. This center was funded by a contract from NIAID. The only such contract awarded by NIAID, it had the potential to last for seven years, with total support ranging between $35–50 million. Key to the award was the availability of the HSCCI, which provided unique computing power. The goal of the RPRC was to help protect against respiratory bacteria and viruses. URMC scientists were essentially "on call" to take on projects related to novel respiratory infections. Although the contract was not renewed by the NIH, the RPRC remains fully active as part of the new Institute for Immunological Sciences.

Figure 55.2. Angela Branche

Angela Branche (Infectious Diseases) serves as the co-director of the TIIDI. Branche received her MD from the American University of the Caribbean, did her residency in internal medicine at NYU Langone Hospital-Brooklyn, NY, and her fellowship in infectious diseases at URMC. She subsequently joined the University's faculty, where she developed a clinical and translational research program exploring the pathogenesis and host response to acute viral respiratory illnesses in adults. She currently serves as the research director for the ID division in the DOM, the co-director of the VTEU, and as an active member of the EIP program. Branche was actively involved in the University's research response to COVID-19, helping to conduct natural history, therapeutic, and vaccine studies.

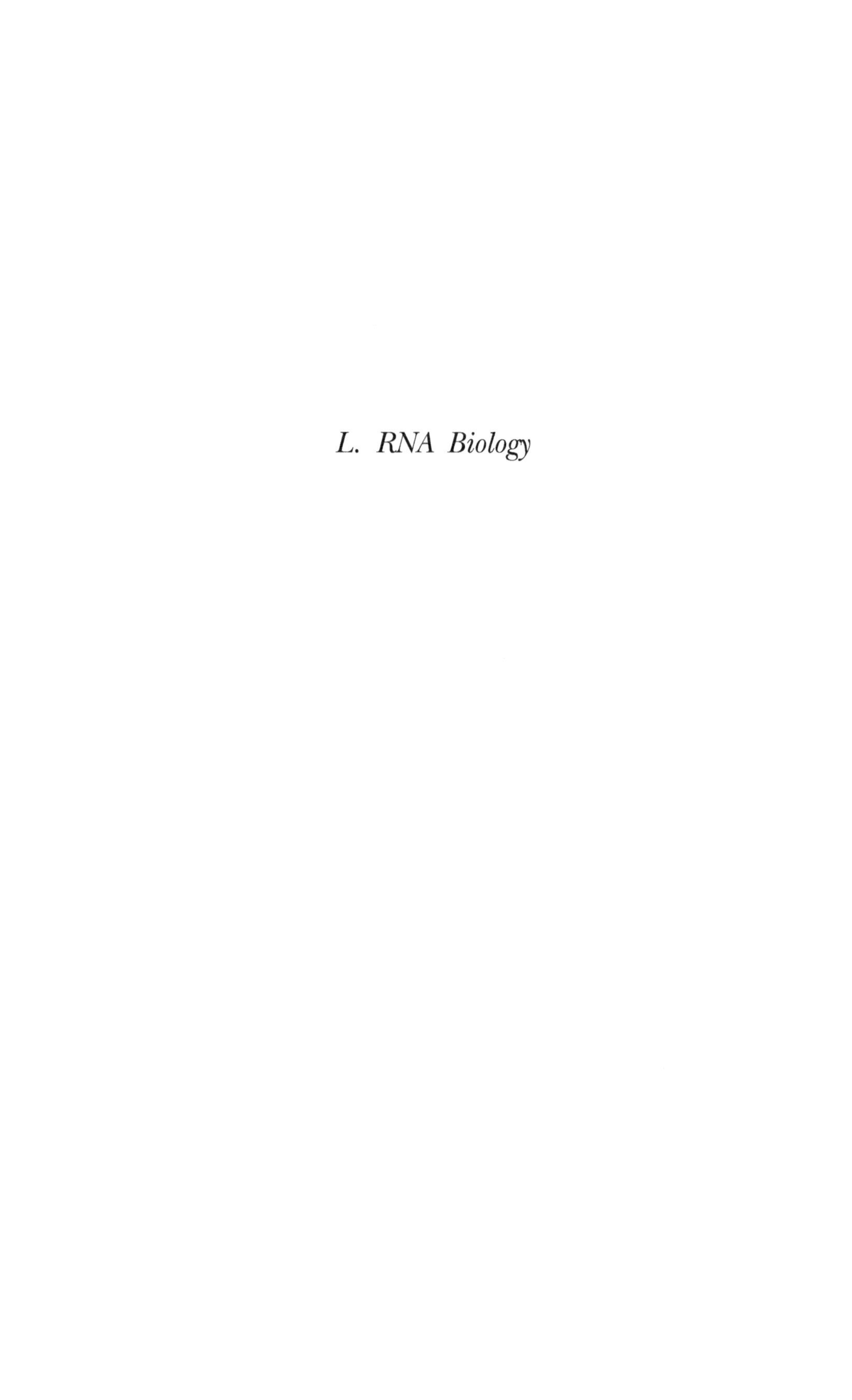

L. RNA Biology

Like immunobiology, RNA biology impacts virtually every disease entity and therefore is depicted in the programs of excellence (Figure 37.5) as an overriding arc. The recent success with the COVID-19 mRNA vaccines highlighted the utility of RNA-based therapeutics. However, it represents the tip of the iceberg, in that RNA-based therapies have the potential to revolutionize the treatment of cancer and neurologic disease, among others. Accordingly, during the last fifteen years, the RNA Biology program of excellence has become a major part of the URMC research strategic plan.

Chapter 56

DEPARTMENT OF BIOCHEMISTRY AND BIOPHYSICS

The department of Biochemistry & Biophysics (DBB) can trace its roots to the formation of SMD, when in 1922 Walter Bloor, PhD, was recruited to be the first chair of Biochemistry. In 1925, Biochemistry awarded the first PhD at the University of Rochester. Two more PhDs were awarded in biochemistry in 1927, one of which was awarded to Vincent duVigneaud, who went on to win a Nobel Prize in chemistry. Bloor served until 1947, when Elmer Stotz, PhD, took over as chair, serving until 1977. The Biophysics department grew out of the University's involvement in the Manhattan Project during World War II, becoming Radiation Biology and Biophysics. As part of the restructuring of the basic sciences at SMD in 1996, the departments of Biochemistry and Biophysics were melded into one department, the DBB, under the leadership of the Biochemistry department's third chair, Fred Sherman, PhD, a member of the National Academy of Sciences. Sherman performed groundbreaking research on the structure of genes and the effects of genetic mutations on proteins in yeast. His use of the yeast system to study genetics had a major impact on the course of biological research throughout the world, and shaped future departmental research. Sherman passed away at age eighty-two in 2012.

Robert A. Bambara, PhD, served as the chair of DBB from 1999 to 2012. Bambara, who received his PhD in molecular biology from Cornell University, orchestrated a transformation in the research focus of the department, in part due to the large number of faculty he recruited during his tenure, many of whom were founding members of the RNA Biology Center (see below). These included Lynne Maquat, PhD, and David H. Mathews, MD, PhD, whose work is described below; Yi-Tao Yu, PhD, post-transcriptional RNA modifications, particularly related to RNA-guided pseudouridylation; Joseph E. Wedekind, PhD, 3-D architecture of non-protein-coding RNAs, with a focus on how they bind to specific small molecules to elicit conformations and alter biological function;

Figure 56.1.
Robert Bambara

Clara L. Kielkopf, PhD, molecular structures and interactions among key pre-mRNA splicing factors in human genetic diseases and hematologic malignancies; Joshua C. Munger, PhD, how human cytomegalovirus and other viruses modulate cellular signaling and metabolism to support viral proliferation; Alan Grossfield, PhD, computer modeling to understand the structure and thermodynamics of biological molecules, particularly related to the biology and physics of lipid-protein interactions; and Dmitri N. Ermolenko, PhD, ribosome function and the mechanics of ribosome movement along mRNA during protein synthesis. Bambara guided the department through the growing pains associated with the merger, and instituted major renovations to the administrative offices and laboratory spaces. He also established the Biophysics and Structural Biology Center (see below). Bambara maintained an active and well-funded research program, publishing over 250 research articles and reviews, many focusing on the biological roles of proteins critical to DNA replication and repair.

Figure 56.2. Jeffrey Hayes

Jeffrey J. Hayes, PhD, has been Shohei Koide Professor and chair of Biochemistry and Biophysics since 2012. Hayes's research employs biochemical and biophysical approaches to define structure and dynamics in model chromatin complexes, and to understand how epigenetic signals alter chromatin to regulate gene expression. His lab also works to elucidate the mechanisms of ATP-dependent and independent chromatin remodeling enzymes. Hayes received his PhD in chemistry from Johns Hopkins, then studied as a postdoctoral fellow in Alan Wolffe's lab at the NIH, before joining the University of Rochester in 1995. Since then, he has maintained continued funding from NIH and has published over 150 research articles. He served on the editorial board of the *Journal of Biological Chemistry* for ten years and has been on the editorial board of *Biochemistry* for over twenty years. In 1997, he received the Arthur Kornberg Faculty Research Award. Hayes's tenure has also been marked by impressive faculty recruitment, many of these recruited jointly with Lynne Maquat for the Center for RNA Biology. These include Paul L. Boutz, PhD, who discovered nuclear "detained" introns, which poise transcripts for rapid gene expression, while working in the laboratory of Nobel laureate Philip Sharp, and while at Rochester has shown that detained introns play a key role in gene mis-regulation in cancers and can result in expression of novel antigens; Jermain Jenkins, PhD, Mitchel O'Connell, PhD, Eric J. Wagner, PhD, and Makaía Papasergi-Scott, PhD.

The DBB currently has approximately 150 personnel, including eighteen primary faculty, research professors, research associates, postdoctoral fellows, technical staff, and approximately sixty graduate students. Graduate students receive PhDs in either biochemistry or biophysics. The department also runs an undergraduate BS program in biochemistry, which graduates approximately thirty students per year. A key element of DBB's educational program is the Cellular and Molecular Biology NIH T32 training grant (PIs, Maquat, and Hayes), which has been in existence since 2005. The grant supports eight students per year (approximately 120 students to date) who are enrolled in one of five PhD programs at the Medical Center. The T32 sponsors two courses designed to enhance student interactions with visiting scholars in the DBB seminar program and to foster critical thinking and presentation skills. An annual retreat brings world-famous scientists, including many Nobel laureates, as keynote speakers, and provides trainees with the opportunity to present their research.

The DBB is also the home of the Graduates Working in Science (GWIS) program, formerly Graduate Women in Science, founded and directed by Maquat, and closely aligned to the T32. GWIS provides mentoring for the professional and personal development of graduate students (inclusive of all genders) at URMC and the College of Arts and Sciences. Meetings are held monthly and feature presentations from experts at the University and outside speakers, including successful scientists in academics, industry, and government, journal editors, and Nobel prize-winners. Topics are wide-ranging and include forensics, grant management, program development, private foundations, science writing, journal editing, patent law, and clinical diagnostics. From 2020–3, the twenty-five GWIS meetings had 403 unique attendees, including graduate students derived from forty different departments and sixteen PhD programs throughout the University. Active GWIS members can receive travel awards to attend a conference, seminar, or other external event that will help them advance their career. In recognition of the importance of GWIS in promoting women in science, Maquat received the University of Rochester Presidential Diversity Award and the 2014 Athena Award, presented annually by the Women's Council of the Rochester Business Alliance to honor the achievements of outstanding female leaders.

The DBB has a long history of world-class research and has had some of the best-funded scientists at the University. Currently, the department has $9.3 million of total and $8.1 million of NIH funding per year. The DBB also serves as the home for two core facilities that support investigators throughout the institution, the Structural Biology and Biophysics facility (see below) and the Metabolomics Program. It also serves as the home of the University's world-renowned RNA Biology Center. Research in the department can be grouped into: 1) Cell cycle and cancer; 2) Cell signaling and metabolic regulation; 3) Chromatin structure, gene regulation, and repair; 4) Genomics and model systems for development; 5) Membrane biology; 6) Molecular biophysics; 7) Protein structure and function; and 8) RNA structure and processing. The reader is directed to the following RNA Biology section and the DBB website for details of the individual research programs. A few of the more long-standing programs are described in the following paragraph.

Eric Phizicky, PhD, who came to the University in 1987, has been one of the leaders in studying tRNA processing, utilizing yeast as a model system. In particular, he has been examining the mechanisms that generate chemical modifications in tRNA, many of which are conserved between yeast and humans, and their effect on tRNA stability and function. In 2013, Phizicky, a Dean's Professor of Biochemistry and Biophysics and founding member of the RNA Biology Center, was honored as a fellow of the American Academy of Microbiology and is a senior editor of the journal *RNA*. Elizabeth Grayhack, PhD, who joined the department in 1994, has made major contributions in defining the rules and mechanisms by which specific arrangements of codons regulate the rate of protein synthesis and mRNA metabolism in yeast. Mark E. Dumont, PhD, who started his tenure at URMC as a postdoctoral fellow in Fred Sherman's laboratory, has devoted his career to studying the structure and function of proteins that play critical roles in cell membranes and which may serve as targets for vaccine development. He has also employed yeast genetics to develop a new class of antibodies for treatment and diagnosis of cystic fibrosis. Harold C. Smith, PhD, emeritus professor of Biochemistry and Biophysics, came to the University in 1986 and did seminal work on the molecular mechanism by which proteins recognize mRNA and form enzyme complexes that regulate cytidine to uridine RNA editing. In 2003, partly supported by seed money from the University of Rochester, he founded OyaGen, Inc., a biopharmaceutical company that develops therapies to fight viral illness, particularly those caused by Human Immunodeficiency Virus, through editing enzymes.

Figure 56.3. Eric Phizicky

The Structural Biology and Biophysics facility is a University of Rochester resource run by the DBB. It provides investigators with access to state-of-the-art biophysical instrumentation that determines macromolecular structures by X-ray crystallography, and quantitatively characterizes biomolecular interactions. Jermaine Jenkins, PhD, a DBB faculty member, manages the facility, trains individuals in the use of core instruments, and assists with experimental design and data interpretation. His primary research interests include X-ray crystallography and cryo-electron microscopy analysis of biomolecular complexes. Operation fees are used to recover costs associated with staff time, routine maintenance, replenishment of expendable supplies, and service contracts. The facility is an excellent example of the expansion of departmental facilities to provide resources to the entire University community, contributing to numerous high-impact publications and extramural grants.

Chapter 57

CENTER FOR RNA BIOLOGY

The Center for RNA Biology (CRB) was founded by Lynne Maquat in 2007 as a means of conducting interdisciplinary research into the function, structure, and processing of RNA. The CRB was a natural outgrowth of the RNA Structure and Function Cluster, established in the 1990s as part of the University Committee for Interdisciplinary Studies, whose mission was to promote interactions among diverse groups of scientists throughout the University. The Center—whose administrative home is within DBB—serves as a hub for RNA biology research across the University and aims to: advance understanding of the function, structure, and processing of RNA; facilitate the discovery of novel RNA targets and RNA tools for pharmaceutical design; provide a platform to launch translational studies with the promise of intellectual property development and licensing; and assure that the University of Rochester is a world leader in RNA biology. Indicative of the collaborative, cross-cutting nature of the Center, the fifteen initial faculty members represented a range of departments and expertise: 1) Bioinformatics – David Mathews; Gaurav Sharma, PhD (Electrical & Computer Engineering); 2) Verification, Mechanism of Action, and Structure – J. Scott Butler, PhD (Microbiology & Immunology); Gloria Culver, PhD (Biology); Clara Kielkopf, PhD; Eric Phizicky; Doug Turner, PhD (Chemistry); Joseph Wedekind; 3) Processing – Lynne Maquat; Fred Sherman; Yi-Tao Yu; and Clinical Importance and Targeting: Lisa Demeter, MD (Medicine); Robert Bambara; Harold Smith, PhD (DBB); Charles Thornton, MD (Neurology).

Lynne E. Maquat, PhD, is the J. Lowell Orbison Endowed Chair and Professor of Biochemistry & Biophysics, director of the Center for RNA Biology, and one of the University's most celebrated scientists. Maquat received her PhD in biochemistry from the University of Wisconsin-Madison. After completing postdoctoral work at the McArdle Laboratory for Cancer Research, she joined Roswell Park Cancer Institute before moving to Rochester. Maquat has been a leader in understanding mRNA degradation, including the discovery of nonsense-mediated mRNA

Figure 57.1.
Lynne Maquat

decay (NMD) in human diseases, Staufen-mediated mRNA decay, and a new mechanism by which microRNAs are degraded. One of her current interests is the development of therapeutics for diseases that she has shown manifest hyperactivated NMD, including the most common single-gene cause of intellectual disability and autism, Fragile X Syndrome. Maquat has been elected to the American Association for the Advancement of Science, the American Academy of Arts and Sciences, the National Academy of Sciences, and the National Academy of Medicine. Among her many honors have been the William C. Rose Award from the American Society for Biochemistry & Molecular Biology, a Canada Gairdner International Award; the Vanderbilt Prize in Biomedical Science; the Wiley Prize in Biomedical Sciences from Rockefeller University, the International Union of Biochemistry and Molecular Biology Medal; the Wolf Prize in Medicine from Israel; the Warren Alpert Foundation Prize from Harvard Medical School; and the Gruber Genetics Prize from the Gruber Foundation and Yale University. Most recently (2024), she received the Dr. Paul Janssen Award for Biochemical Research from Johnson & Johnson; and the Albany Medical Center Prize in Medicine and Biomedical Research.

As of 2024, the CRB consisted of twenty-three active faculty members, spanning thirteen departments within the Medical Center, the College of Arts and Sciences, and the Hajim School of Engineering & Applied Sciences. Among the more recent additions to the CRB are: Mitchell R. O'Connell; John D. Lueck, PhD (Pharmacology & Physiology); Paul L. Boutz; Hitomi Sakano, MD, PhD (Otolaryngology); Eric J. Wagner; Amanda M. Larracuente, PhD (Biology); Laurie A. Steiner, MD (Pediatrics); Christoph Pröschel, PhD (Biomedical Genetics); Doug Anderson (Medicine); Laurie Steiner, MD (Pediatrics); and Jermaine L. Jenkins.

Concomitant with the growth in faculty has been the growth in CRB funding from over thirty-five external sources, including nine different NIH Institutes. As of 2024, CRB faculty had approximately $20 million in yearly funding, and approximately $75 million in total funding. A recent highlight was the awarding of a NY State Center of Excellence in RNA Research and Therapeutics (CERRT) (Maquat, director; Wagner, co-director). The CERRT is a partnership between the CRB and the University at Albany's RNA Institute. The CERRT drives economic development in NY State by fostering collaborations among research companies and academic researchers to ensure that NY businesses have access to cutting-edge RNA research and technologies, and that academic RNA researchers have access to industry capital and resources. The Center develops collaborative training programs with NY State industries that provide their employees with advanced skills training in the latest techniques and next-generation equipment. The Center will also work with NY State biotech, pharmaceutical, and biomedical companies to create internships for talented early-career trainees so that they gain valuable market experience and maximize opportunities for industry recruitment. One focus of the CERRT is to train workers underrepresented in STEM to help expand and diversify the State's biotech workforce.

Research in the CRB is extensive, encompassing studies on RNA metabolism and decay, RNA folding, RNA modification, RNA splicing, RNA "stitching," RNA-protein interactions, the role of non-coding RNAs and tandem repeats, RNA-mediated gene regulation, cancer-related changes in RNA processing, RNA therapeutics and RNA-mediated drug and vaccine discovery, control of transcription and translation, and tRNA biology. It also encompasses a broad range of acquired and inheritable diseases, such as cancer, muscular dystrophy, Fragile X Syndrome, myelodysplastic syndromes, intellectual developmental disorders, diabetes, and obesity. Details of the individual research programs are available on the CRB website. A few are highlighted below.

Figure 57.2. David Matthews

David H. Matthews, MD, PhD, is the Lynne E. Maquat Distinguished Professor and Associate Director of CRB. Matthews received his BA, MD, and PhD from the University of Rochester. As a PhD student in the laboratory of Douglas Turner, PhD, professor of chemistry, he helped develop the Turner Rules—a set of parameters that predict the folding stability of RNA. Research in the Matthews lab uses computational biology and bioinformatics to predict RNA structure and to develop computational tools to target RNAs with pharmaceuticals or to utilize RNAs as therapeutic agents. Recently, Matthews partnered with Liang Huang, PhD, from Oregon State University to develop an algorithm to help find the most stable, efficient mRNA sequences for vaccines and other therapies, such as monoclonal antibodies and anti-cancer drugs. In studies on the SARS-CoV-2 virus, algorithm-derived mRNAs resisted deterioration longer, produced more COVID spike protein, and dramatically increased antibody levels in mice compared to currently used mRNA vaccines.

Figure 57.3. Mitch O'Connell

Mitchell O'Connell, PhD, is the Dean's Associate Professor in Biochemistry and Biophysics. Recruited in 2017 to the University of Rochester from Nobel Laureate Jennifer Doudna's laboratory at University of California, Berkeley, his research focuses on how RNA-targeting CRISPR-Cas systems and their membrane-associated proteins function to enhance anti-viral defense.

O'Connell recently discovered and characterized the first known CRISPR-Cas membrane protein, Csx28. Upon Cas13 activation by viral messenger RNAs, Csx28 assists in protecting against sustained viral infection. The O'Connell laboratory has generated new variants of Cas13 that are more sequence-specific with respect to RNA recognition and shown that these could improve our ability to detect between closely related SARS-CoV-2 strains using a CRISPR-based diagnostic test.

Eric J. Wagner, PhD, is associate director of CRB and co-director of CERRT. Wagner, who was an undergraduate at the University of Rochester, was recruited back to Rochester from the University of Texas Medical Branch-Galveston in 2021. Wagner's laboratory is focused on characterizing transcription termination in eukaryotes, and particularly how the 3' end of RNAs produced from coding and noncoding genes is formed. Wagner has also been widely recognized for his work on the Integrator complex and its regulator, BRAT 1, which promotes the premature termination of RNA synthesis during gene transcription. Wagner's team found that changes to Integrator impact cancer cell growth and neurological development, making it a promising treatment target. His group has also found that the length of RNA is critical to cancer cell division. Long RNAs are easy for cells to regulate, ensuring steady proliferation. Many aggressive cancers actively shorten the length of RNAs to create an unregulated environment where they can spread unchecked. In recognition of his work, Wagner is an elected fellow of the AAAS.

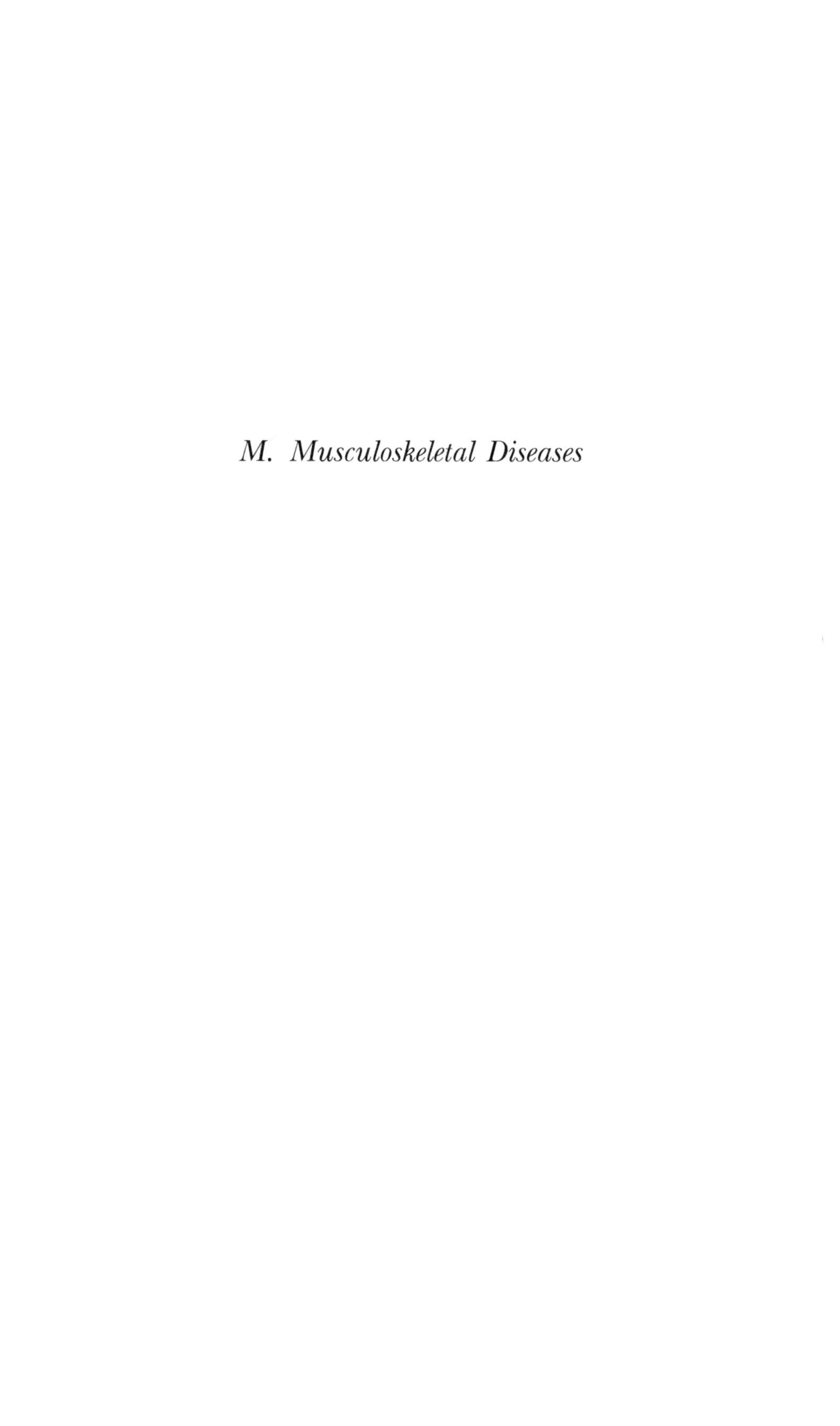

M. Musculoskeletal Diseases

Chapter 58

DEPARTMENT OF ORTHOPAEDICS

The URMC has been a world leader in orthopaedics since its inception as a division of Surgery in 1926. R. Plato Schwartz, MD, the first division chief, opened the "Gait Lab" to study mechanisms of human locomotion. It quickly grew to national prominence and was used by companies throughout the US to design shoes. Schwartz was followed by Robert B. Duthie, MD, in 1959 and Louis Goldstein, MD, in 1969. Orthopaedics became an independent department in 1974, with C. McCollister ("Mac") Evarts, MD, as its first chair.

Evarts developed a robust divisional structure, recruiting outstanding specialists, including Richard Burton, MD (Surgery of the Hand), Kenneth DeHaven, MD (Sports Medicine), Van Jackman, MD (Pediatric Orthopaedics), MD, James Burke, MD (Foot and Ankle Surgery), and Vincent Pellegrini, MD (Reconstructive surgery). The Donald and Mary Clark Musculoskeletal Center in the former ED provided expanded clinical space. J. Edward Puzas, MD, and Randy N. Rosier, MD, PhD, were recruited to develop robust basic, clinical, and translational research programs. Burton became chair when Evarts left to become dean of Penn State College of Medicine, and oversaw the continued expansion of the department and initiated plans to move clinical services to Clinton Crossings. He also oversaw the growth of the research program under Puzas, Rosier, and Regis O'Keefe, MD, PhD.

Figure 58.1.
Randy Rosier

Rosier became Marjorie Strong Wehle Professor and Chair in 2000. Rosier received his MD and PhD from the University of Rochester and did a residency in orthopaedics and a research fellowship at the University of Iowa. As chair, he oversaw the development of the Center for Musculoskeletal Research and the recruitment of Eddie Schwarz, PhD, Hani Awad, PhD, Mike Zuscik, PhD, Xinping Zhang, BMed, PhD, and Hicham Drissi, PhD. Rosier also grew the clinical research infrastructure. Within a few years, the number of clinical trials jumped

Figure 58.2.
Regis O'Keefe

from five to more than eighty, and the department's national NIH funding rank rose to number one. This was also a very active recruitment period, including James O. Sanders, MD (Pediatric Orthopaedics), John Gorczyca, MD (Trauma), Robert Molinari, MD (Spine), Susan Bukata, MD (Oncology), Christopher Drinkwater, MD (Adult Reconstructive Surgery), Sam Flemister, MD (Foot and Ankle), Dave Mitten, MD (Hand), Ilya Voloshin, MD (Shoulder), Rajeev Patel, MD (Physical Medicine & Rehabilitation, PMR), and Clifford Everett, MD (PMR). The Evarts Total Joint Center opened at HH in 2005, and the Ken DeHaven Motor Skills lab opened in 2007.

O'Keefe was named Marjorie Strong Wehle Professor and Chair in 2007. O'Keefe received his MD from Harvard Medical School and completed a surgical internship at New England Deaconess Hospital, Boston, a residency in orthopaedics and a research fellowship at URMC, and a fellowship in orthopaedic oncology at MGH. He then returned to URMC, where he earned a PhD in biochemistry. During O'Keefe's tenure as chair, the Clinton Crossings facility was expanded to ninety-two examination rooms, and by 2014 the number of outpatient visits reached 195,000. Outpatient surgery was consolidated to the Sawgrass Ambulatory Surgery Center; at peak, roughly half of the procedures done at Sawgrass were orthopaedic.

O'Keefe also continued to grow the program at HH, including the recruitment of Steven Kates, MD, who developed a novel care model for geriatric fracture that became an international standard and helped establish HH as a major referral center. Catherine Humphrey, MD, became chief of Orthopaedics at HH and markedly enhanced its trauma services. A Community Care Clinic was initiated with Evarts as director, and Pediatric Orthopaedics was expanded. Brian Giordano, MD, and Christopher Cook, MD, developed a comprehensive and integrated program for hip preservation surgery. Additional recruitments included Wakenda Tyler, MD (Oncology) and Warren Hammert, MD (Plastics and microvascular surgery).

In 2014, when O'Keefe left to become Orthopaedics chair at Washington University, St. Louis he was succeeded by Paul T. Rubery, MD. Rubery received his MD from Weill Medical College of Cornell University, did an internship in general surgery at NY Hospital, and a residency in orthopaedics at the Hospital for Special Surgery. He was recruited to URMC in 1994, where he served as chief of the division of Spine Surgery and associate chair for Clinical Affairs. Rubery has continued to grow the department, particularly in adult reconstruction, hand, sports, pediatrics, spine, and foot and ankle surgery. The spine division developed a very active non-surgical spine group, including five physicians with

Figure 58.3.
Paul Rubery

PMR training. At Dean Taubman's request, this group was merged into the department of PMR in 2018. Orthopaedic services were expanded to include the affiliates, with musculoskeletal clinics in Brockport, Greece, Penfield, Webster, Victor, and Canandaigua. Today, Orthopaedics has nine subspecialty divisions with sixty-nine faculty (up from nineteen in 1995). Patient visits grew from 121,221 in 2004 to 259,327 in 2024; and surgeries from 8,610 in 2004 to 18,169 in 2024.

At the time Rubery was named chair, most orthopaedic procedures were being done in outpatient settings, and the volume had outstripped resources at Clinton Crossings and Sawgrass. With Dean Taubman's encouragement, Rubery put together a task force to assess future musculoskeletal space needs and to examine the possibility of creating an institute that would house clinical, research, and educational activities at one site. After an extensive search, the former Sears store at Marketplace Mall was chosen as the site. The existing Sears was converted into a state-of-the-art ambulatory surgical center with eight operating rooms and shell space for six more. A new four-story clinic tower contained 144 exam rooms, a "procedure space" with four rooms for spinal injections and local anesthesia cases, advanced physical therapy spaces with therapy pools, dedicated athletic performance space for the Center for Human Athleticism and Musculokeletal Performance and Prevention (CHAMPP) program, and advanced imaging

Figure 58.4. The Saunders Center for Orthopaedics and Physical Performance

with multiple CTs and MRIs. The first staff relocated to the new Orthopaedics and Physical Performance Center in September 2021, surgery was begun in February 2023, and the new clinic tower opened in November 2023. The full construction encompassed 330,000 square feet, with a cost of $227 million, making this the largest off-campus construction in the history of the University.

CHAMPP is a multidisciplinary approach to athletic performance, injury prevention, and wellness developed over the past ten years by Michael Maloney, MD, E. Philip Saunders Distinguished Professor of Orthopaedics and the chief of Sports Medicine. In collaboration with Shaun Nelms, East High Educational Partnership Organization superintendent, Maloney established a partnership with the Eastside YMCA, Wegmans, and East and Webster high schools. East and Webster athletes spent the afternoon at the Eastside YMCA three days per week for twelve weeks undergoing athletic performance analysis and training, nutrition counseling, and receiving post-workout meals prepared by Wegmans. An in-person financial wellness program was provided by Canandaigua National Bank as well as tutoring support from students at the Warner School of Education. The program collected health and performance statistics on each athlete before, during, and after the training. Athletes saw dramatic improvement in their sports performance, sleep scores, peer relationships, anxiety, and pain interference, and showed signs of improvement in depression symptoms. The Sports Medicine division now provides medical care for nine local colleges, five professional teams, and most of the high schools in the region. The division also offers UR Medicine Fitness Science, a research-based program designed to optimize performance through strength training, nutrition, sport psychology, and data analysis.

Figure 58.5. Michael Maloney

The five-year orthopaedics residency program is among the most highly regarded in the country. Since its inception in 1934, its graduates include fourteen chairs of academic health center departments (including seven current chairs) and five heads of divisions of Sports Medicine. In 2018, the residency program expanded to eight trainees per year. In addition, fellowship programs have been developed in hand, foot, and ankle, trauma, sports medicine, and spine. A unique feature of training is the Kenneth DeHaven Arthroscopic Surgical Skills Laboratory, directed by Gregg Nicandri, MD, and Ray Kenney, MD, whose primary mission is to facilitate human anatomical education and surgical skills training. This facility has helped make Rochester a national leader in developing surgical simulation tools and novel education programs.

The department has enjoyed tremendous support from the community and Rochester alumni, and has benefitted from year-long fundraising initiatives in 2017 and 2023 that raised $5.6 million and $6.4 million respectively in support of the growth and development of orthopaedic programs. Advancement efforts have established five endowed professorships since 2000, with an additional four to be funded by bequests. Most significantly, the new facility at Marketplace was named the Saunders Center for Orthopaedics and Physical Performance in recognition of a $30 million gift from Phillip and Carole Saunders through the Saunders Foundation.

Chapter 59

CENTER FOR MUSCULOSKELETAL RESEARCH (CMSR)

The efforts of Evarts, Burton, Puzas, and Rosier to expand the research activities of the department came to fruition in 2000, when Rosier was appointed chair of the department and director of the new CMSR. Eddie Schwarz, PhD, the Burton Professor of Orthopaedics and Rehabilitation, received his PhD in immunology from Einstein College of Medicine, and did a postdoctoral fellowship with Inder M. Varma, MD, at the Salk Institute. In 2011, after developing an international reputation for his work on bone infection, Schwarz took over as director of the CMSR, replacing O'Keefe, who had been named as associate dean for Clinical Affairs. The CMSR integrates faculty and trainees from many departments and currently has thirty-one faculty, sixteen new/early-stage investigators, and more than 100 scientists occupying greater than 22,000 square feet of space. NIH funding has grown from $2 million in 2000 to $8.5 million in 2023, and publications have grown from an average of fifteen to ninety per year.

Figure 59.1. Eddie Schwarz

As one of the nation's largest orthopaedics research centers, the scope of research is quite broad and includes: artificial intelligence and machine learning; bone biology and disease; bone cancer biology; cartilage biology and arthritis; drug delivery, fracture repair and bone tissue engineering; muscle biology; musculoskeletal development; musculoskeletal infection; musculoskeletal stem cell biology; population health; and tendon development, repair, and regenerative engineering. Further details of each of these programs can be found on the CMSR website.

Several prominent programs have galvanized the productivity and international reputation of the CMSR. Funds from these programs and those of individual faculty have consistently placed Rochester among the top five NIH-funded orthopaedic research programs. The NIH-funded P50 Center of Research Translation (CORT) was awarded in 2006. The current CORT (Schwarz, Awad, Benjamin Miller, MD) is focused on musculoskeletal infections, the bane of elective total joint replacement surgery. The program focuses on mechanisms that promote *Staphylococcus aureus* colonization of live bone; the development of novel antibiotics that target these mechanisms and can be 3-D-printed into custom spacers; and the development of an assay to elucidate the immune proteome of *Staphylococcus aureus* during orthopaedic infections.

In 2020, the University was awarded $3.8 million as part of a new Clinical Trials on a Chip initiative by the National Center for Advancing Translational Sciences, aimed at developing 3-D platforms engineered to support living human tissues and cells, mimic complex biological functions of organs and systems, and better predict which patients are most likely to benefit from an investigational therapy. The University's Tissue-on-a-Chip program is the first organ-on-a-chip platform designed for modeling scar formation in tendons and represents a collaborative effort among the CMSR (Awad), Dermatology (Miller), and Biomedical Engineering (James McGrath, PhD).

The CMSR recently renewed its National Institute of Arthritis and Musculoskeletal and Skin Diseases (NIAMS)-funded Research Core Center (P30) in musculoskeletal biology and medicine, which it has had since 2012. The Rochester Resource-based Center for Bone, Muscle and Orthopaedic Research (ROCStARR) (Schwarz and Laura Calvi, MD) provides shared facilities and services to groups addressing scientific problems in musculoskeletal biology and medicine. ROCStARR has a unique Enrichment Program designed to expand the musculoskeletal research base by awarding pilot project grants to physician-scientists and research assistant professors who have not received NIH R01 or equivalent grant funding as PIs. It also administers several cores to support investigators: Histology, Biochemistry, and Molecular Imaging; Biomechanics and Multimodal Tissue Imaging; and Muscle and Exercise Biology.

Since 2006, the CMSR has been home to an NIAMS-funded Training in Orthopaedic Research T32 (Awad, Calvi, and Alayna Loiselle, PhD) that provides comprehensive didactic and research education, as well as career development mentoring. Rebranded in 2020 as the Rochester Musculoskeletal (ROCMSK), it recruits postdoctoral fellows and graduate students accepted into six degree-awarding departments.

Chapter 60

DEPARTMENT OF PHYSICAL MEDICINE AND REHABILITATION (PMR)

One of the highlights of the past twenty-five years has been the establishment and growth of PMR. PMR began in the 1960s by internists Roger J. Boulay, MD, and Robert Jones, MD, as part of Preventive Medicine. A PMR residency was established in 1973. In the 1980s, under the leadership of Charles J. Gibson, MD, PMR became a division in the department of Orthopaedics and URMC became one of sixteen NIDRR (National Institute on Disability and Rehabilitation Research)-funded, MSKTC (Model Systems Knowledge Translation Center)-designated Spinal Cord Injury Model Systems, with Gibson and orthopaedic spine surgeon Donald Chan, MD, serving as PIs. In 1990, when the NIDRR reduced the number of centers and eliminated Rochester because of its small population, PMR became a stand-alone department. With Gibson's retirement in 1998, PMR again became a division of Orthopaedics, under the leadership of Stephen F. Levinson, MD, PhD, and then in 2004 of K. Rao Poduri, MD.

Figure 60.1. K. Rao Poduri

Poduri received her MD from Karnatak Medical College in Hubli, India. She completed a residency in PMR and a fellowship in geriatric rehabilitation at URMC, becoming board-certified in PMR, pain medicine, and spinal cord injury medicine. In 2008, prompted by CEO Bradford Berk's feeling that it had the "credibility to stand on its own in providing patient care, with its sound educational, financial and scholarly activity," PMR once again became a stand-alone department, with Poduri at the helm. During Poduri's tenure, the department remained relatively small—relying on strong collaborations with Orthopaedics, whose physiatrists had secondary appointments in PMR, and with the inpatient rehabilitation services at Unity Hospital—but was recognized for its high quality of care and excellent patient evaluations.

Towards the end of Poduri's tenure, it became clear that PMR needed further restructuring. One of the major drivers was a shift in the collaboration with Unity Hospital. Prior to the merger of Unity Health with RGH to form

RRH, URMC sent many of its inpatients to Unity, which had a neurorehabilitation-focused inpatient unit. As a result, URMC had a very small department, containing three to four full-time clinical faculty and a few secondary faculty whose primary appointments and major responsibilities were in Orthopaedics. The lack of full-time faculty was particularly problematic for the PMR residency, which relied heavily on voluntary teaching faculty from Unity. With the establishment of RRH, it became clear that URMC would no longer be able to rely on Unity for acute inpatient rehabilitation, particularly for patients with brain injuries. At the same time, there was increasing demand for inpatient rehabilitation services at SMH. These factors drove URMC to develop a more robust program, which included the opening of an acute inpatient rehabilitation service line revolving around brain injury neurorehabilitation.

In 2018, Rajeev K. Patel, MD, a highly respected faculty member in Orthopaedics, was given the task of restructuring PMR. Patel received his MD from the Northeastern Ohio Universities Colleges of Medicine and Pharmacy. He completed a residency in PMR at Baylor College of Medicine's Institute for Rehabilitation and Research and a fellowship in interventional spine from the Penn Spine Center at the University of Pennsylvania. He joined the faculty of URMC's division of Spinal Surgery in 2000, eventually becoming chief of a newly created division of Non-Operative/Interventional Spine and director of the Interventional Spine fellowship program. In anticipation of being selected as chair of PMR, Patel developed an ambitious ten-year strategic plan aimed at creating a nationally prominent department that excelled in URMC's tripartite missions.

Figure 60.2. Rajeev Patel

Patel's strategic plan noted that the vast majority of employment opportunities for graduating PMR residents were in the ambulatory setting, with a focus on diagnostic and therapeutic procedures, whereas the vast majority of US PMR training programs had remained focused on acute inpatient rehabilitation. This misalignment between training and employment presented an opportunity for URMC. Patel reasoned that the creation of a robust outpatient practice consisting of faculty with primary appointments in PMR would galvanize the residency by creating a clinical and educational experience that would be second to none and unique to the University of Rochester. With the support of Orthopaedics Chair Paul Rubery, the four physiatrists housed within Orthopaedics transitioned their primary faculty appointments to PMR. In addition, Patel shifted from the recruitment of generalists to that of fellowship-trained subspecialists from premier training programs to lead divisions and service lines. Particular emphasis was placed on recruiting faculty with fellowship training in brain injury and spinal cord injury rehabilitation medicine.

Since 2018, the number of full-time faculty has grown from four to thirty-two, and the department has become a destination for graduating URMC residents. PMR now has six divisions: acute inpatient rehabilitation medicine; interventional spine and pain; the electrodiagnostic laboratory; sports and musculoskeletal medicine; outpatient neuro-physical medicine and rehabilitation; and education. PMR faculty practice has expanded from three to fifteen regional locations as outpatient faculty visit volume has increased from less than 1,000 in 2017 to over 35,000 in 2025. In keeping with this growth, departmental physical and occupational therapy staff has grown from fifty-four to eight-seven, and visit volume has increased from approximately 96,000 to 178,000.

PMR has been at the forefront of departmental collaborations, beginning with the University of Rochester Spine Center, a multidisciplinary integrated practice unit shared with Orthopaedics. The interventional spine program, a component of the Spine Center, is the signature clinical, education, and research program of PMR. This program has grown markedly with the opening of new state-of-the-art procedure suites at the Saunders Center for Orthopaedics and Physical Performance. The Spine Center has served as a model for the development of institutional musculoskeletal service lines in large joint arthritis, musculoskeletal medicine, and sports injury management, all of which are now supported by a unified access center to promote patient access and interface. PMR faculty recruits with subspecialty training in brain injury, spinal cord injury, and the medically complex have greatly expanded the scope of the acute floor faculty consult service at SMH and have optimized patient outcomes, length of stay, hospital flow, and patient placement.

An important addition to PMR was the University of Rochester Neurorestorative Institute (URNI). Its director, Bradford Berk, MD, transitioned his primary appointment to PMR, where he also serves as associate chair for Research. Central to the strategic plan and the growth of the URNI was the development of the inpatient neurorehabilitation unit. A major goal of the URNI is to develop a clinical trials program where patients with neurologic impairments (e.g. brain injury, spinal cord injury, stroke) have access to novel medical, technological, and procedural interventions. It is envisioned that the URNI will be the engine of neurorehabilitation research in PMR.

The restructuring and growth of PMR have resulted in a complete turnaround of the residency program, which has grown from three to six slots per year and attracts students from the top medical schools. Over the past three ACGME surveys, faculty and residents have given the program the highest possible score for overall evaluation of the department and residency, and the residency now exceeds the national mean in every measured domain. In addition, graduating residents are consistently matching into the top fellowship programs in the US.

In 2021, PMR developed an interventional spine and musculoskeletal medicine fellowship and recently recruited its first graduate to the faculty. With continued clinical program growth at SMH and at the Saunders Center for Orthopaedics and Physical Performance, PMR hopes to develop fellowship training programs in brain injury rehabilitation medicine, spinal cord injury rehabilitation medicine, cancer rehabilitation medicine, pediatric rehabilitation medicine, pain management, and sports medicine. The availability of such fellowships will be important in attracting the best residents to the University.

PMR also plays an important role in medical education, particularly in the Foundations of Biopsychosocial Practice course, where PMR faculty instruct students in performing histories and physical examinations on impaired and disabled patients. In addition, an increasing number of students from SMD and other prominent US medical schools are doing rotations in the department, a clear sign of the increasing reputation of the PMR residency program.

PMR is well on track to achieve the goals it established for 2028: to be a thriving, clinically outstanding, academically rigorous, and continually expanding department that is a destination for the best and brightest specialists, subspecialists, fellows, residents, and rotating medical students.

N. Cardiovascular Diseases

Cardiovascular diseases has been a long-standing program of excellence at URMC and a key component of its strategic plans. Although not yet a fully integrated service line, there has been a history of collaboration involving the Cardiology division in DOM, the Pediatric Cardiology division in Pediatrics, and the Cardiac Surgery and Vascular Surgery divisions in Surgery. This collaboration has intensified during the past twenty-five years and has led to the establishment of several clinical programs that have achieved regional and national prominence. The 21st century has seen several groundbreaking research programs that have made the University a leader in clinical, translational, and basic cardiology. This section will chronicle the major cardiovascular programs at URMC. The Vascular Surgery program is discussed within the chapter on Surgery.

Chapter 61

DIVISION OF CARDIOLOGY (DEPARTMENT OF MEDICINE)

Cardiology has a storied history at the University. Under the leadership of Paul N. Yu, MD, from 1957–82, Cardiology became a national leader in electrocardiography and exercise stress testing, and in utilizing cardiac catheterization to study the pulmonary circulation and ventricular function. Its national presence was further enhanced by the research programs of Arthur J. Moss, MD, and Jules Cohen, MD, who were recruited in the 1960s by William B. Hood, Jr., MD, who succeeded Yu as division chief in 1982. The 1980s and 1990s were characterized by growth in nuclear imaging (led by Ronald G. Schwartz, MD), cardiac ultrasound (Karl Q. Schwarz, MD), clinical electrophysiology (James P. Daubert, MD, followed in 2008 by David T. Huang, MD), and cardiac catheterization (Frederick S. Ling, MD).

In 1998, Bradford C. Berk, MD, PhD, was recruited as chief of Cardiology and Paul N. Yu Professor in Cardiology. At that time, the full-time faculty was quite small, largely consisting of the clinical section heads, and most of the patients were managed by private cardiologists. Berk oversaw the development of faculty-run academic cardiology services, including an ambulatory cardiology program at Clinton Crossings (led by James P. Eichelberger, MD, and subsequently by John D. Bisognano, MD, PhD), a "closed" cardiac care unit (Joseph M. Delahanty, MD), and a new heart failure/transplant program (Leway Chen, MD, MPH). The cardiac catheterization and electrophysiology laboratories were expanded and moved into the site of the old ED. To ensure adequate inpatient coverage, Berk developed a partnership with University Cardiovascular Associates (UCVA), a private group overseen by Maurice E. Varon, MD, and consisting predominantly of URMC-trained cardiologists. Key to centralization of cardiology services was also the development of a uniform compensation plan and an enhanced centralized billing system. Berk also began the process of developing a full-time cardiology service at HH, beginning with the appointment of Thomas A. Rocco, MD, as chief. Like at SMH, inpatient coverage was initially supported by physicians from UCVA, as well as from Rochester Cardiopulmonary Group (RCPG). Berk also markedly expanded the basic research program, which ultimately became the Aab Cardiovascular Research Institute (CVRI), and fostered Arthur Moss's clinical research program.

Mark B. Taubman, MD, was recruited in 2003 to be chief of Cardiology and Paul N. Yu Professor in Cardiology, succeeding Berk, who had become chair of DOM. Taubman continued the expansion of the clinical and research programs, joining Berk to develop and co-direct the Aab CVRI. He oversaw the completion of a full-time faculty service at HH and began expanding the regional presence by acquiring Finger Lakes Cardiology, a long-standing and highly regarded four-physician practice, headed by M. James Doling, MD, that served Canandaigua, Clifton Springs, and Penn Yan. Over the years, the group expanded and now is partnering with cardiologists in URMC's Geneva affiliate to coordinate cardiovascular care in the Finger Lakes. By the time Taubman stepped down as chief in 2008 to chair the DOM, the full-time faculty had grown to thirty-five.

Taubman was followed in 2008 by Charles J. Lowenstein, MD, a nationally prominent vascular biologist who was recruited from Johns Hopkins to lead the Cardiology division and direct the Aab CVRI. Lowenstein continued the expansion of clinical cardiology services and partnered with Surgery to create the Heart and Vascular Institute, enhancing collaboration across the cardiovascular service line. Of particular import was the development of the region's first transcatheter aortic valve replacement (TAVR) program. Taubman, Delehanty, and Lowenstein oversaw the acquisition in 2015 of RCPG, a group of twelve cardiologists, led by Eduardo A. Arazoza, MD, that had served the Rochester region for four decades. Over time, RCPG has become fully integrated into the division, with members taking leadership roles in many areas.

Figure 61.1.
Charles Lowenstein

Lowenstein, who returned to Johns Hopkins in 2020 as its chief of Cardiology, was followed as chief by Spencer Z. Rosero, MD. Rosero received his MD from SUNY Downstate Medical College, completed his residency in internal medicine and fellowship in cardiology at URMC, and then joined the cardiology faculty as an electrophysiologist in 2000. Rosero also has a keen interest in high-tech biosensors and invented an implantable wireless device that contains living cells that provide both sensing and processing of the body's own biological signals. Under his leadership, the division has continued to expand and to integrate cardiovascular services throughout UR Medicine.

Figure 61.2.
Spencer Rosero

The 21st century has seen marked changes in the diagnosis and treatment of cardiovascular disease. Of note has been the growth of electrophysiology services, related to the mapping and catheter ablation of arrhythmias, particularly atrial fibrillation, the implantation of defibrillators, and the use of increasingly sophisticated pacemakers. As discussed below, the electrophysiology program also served as the home for the MADIT studies and will act as hub for three recently awarded PCORI grants. This has led to substantial growth in the electrophysiology section, which now includes nine faculty and three electrophysiology fellows. In fiscal year 2025, the electrophysiology team implanted over 1,345 cardiac rhythm management devices (defibrillators, pacemakers, and cardiac resynchronization devices) and performed over 870 arrhythmia ablations.

There have also been significant advances in cardiac imaging, including the use of CT and MRI to image the heart and vasculature. The heart failure/transplant program was developed at the turn of the century and has become one of the busiest in the northeast. The cardiac catheterization laboratory, which now has a faculty of seven and two interventional fellows, has also grown to accommodate TAVR, transplant-related cardiac biopsies, and other transcatheter therapies.

The division has established several subspecialty programs of national distinction, such as its multisystem sarcoidosis clinic, recently recognized as a World Association of Sarcoidosis and Other Granulomatous Disorders Center of Excellence; the left atrial appendage occlusion program, serving patients with atrial fibrillation throughout upstate NY; and the hypertrophic cardiomyopathy (HCM) clinic, an integrated center of excellence staffed by cardiologists, cardiac surgeons, cardiac radiologist expert nurses, APPs, ultrasonographers, and genetic counselors. The involvement of pediatric cardiologists ensures lifelong continuity of care for affected individuals and their families.

As of 2025, Cardiology had a staff of over 1,300, including a faculty of seventy-eight cardiologists and 130 APPs. In fiscal year 2025, the division cared for approximately 130,000 patients in its ambulatory clinics, including 28,204 new patients, in more than twenty sites throughout UR Medicine. The three-year fellowship in cardiovascular diseases now accepts six residents per year. This highly regarded program was directed for many years by Richard M. Pomerantz, MD, who also served as director of clinical cardiology services for Berk and Taubman. Currently under the leadership of Burr W. Hall, MD, a cardiac electrophysiologist, the fellowship has trained many of the cardiologists practicing in western NY. In 2022, the division was chosen by the American College of Cardiology to pilot a "2 + 2 CVD to EP" program, in which fellows can complete a cardiovascular disease and electrophysiology fellowship in four years.

Chapter 62

DIVISION OF CARDIAC SURGERY (DEPARTMENT OF SURGERY)

Adult cardiac surgery at SMH began in 1951, when Earle Mahoney, MD, performed a closed mitral commissurotomy, subsequently adding pericardiectomies and tricuspid valve commissurotomies. In 1957, Seymour Schwartz, MD, and James DeWeese, MD, introduced the heart-lung machine to SMH, allowing for the repair of atrial septal defects and other congenital diseases. The program expanded markedly with the introduction of prosthetic valves in 1964, and then again in 1969, when DeWeese performed the first coronary artery bypass at SMH. That same year saw the establishment of a residency in thoracic and cardiac surgery. In 1974, Cardiothoracic (CT) Surgery became a separate division of Surgery, with DeWeese as its first chief; by that time the number of procedures had grown to more than 300.

George ("Jeff") L. Hicks, MD, received his MD, his residency in general surgery, and his fellowship in CT surgery at URMC, before joining the faculty in 1981. Hicks became surgical director of the ICU (opened in 1986), introduced the use of the internal mammary artery for coronary artery bypass, and helped refine cardioplegia. In 1991, Hicks became chief of the CT Surgery division. The following year, he recruited William Risher, MD, who was one of the first to use femoral artery stents and helped establish the division as a leader in aneurysm surgery.

Figure 62.1. Jeff Hicks

In 2004, CT Surgery was split into two divisions: Thoracic-Foregut Surgery and Cardiac Surgery, with Hicks remaining as chief of Cardiac Surgery. His term was marked by enhanced collaboration with Cardiology, enabling the University to develop two of its signature programs: heart failure/ transplantation and TAVR. Two key recruitments during Hick's tenure were H. Todd Massey, MD, who in 1999 helped establish the heart transplant program, and Peter Knight, MD, who joined the program in 2002. Knight received his MD from New York Medical College and completed a fellowship in CT surgery at URMC. Before moving to URMC, he had been at RGH, where he established a reputation as an outstanding cardiac surgeon and continued to build that reputation at the University.

Figure 62.2. Peter Knight

Some of Hicks's greatest contributions to the University and the national landscape involved residency training. As president of the Thoracic Surgery Directors Association (TSDA) and a member of the American Board of Thoracic Surgery, Hicks helped lead the development and piloting of a new paradigm in which graduating medical students entered an integrated six-year cardiothoracic residency, rather than beginning as general surgical residents for three years followed by an additional three years of cardiothoracic training. Hicks was also a leader in the use of simulation training for CT surgery. In 2008, he and Richard Feins, MD, the head of thoracic surgery at University of North Carolina, developed the first "Boot Camp," bringing thirty-two residents and thirty faculty to Chapel Hill, North Carolina, for two-and-a-half days of rigorous simulator training in the basics of CT surgery under the auspices of the TSDA. Since then, the Boot Camp has provided simulation education for 350 residents and a similar number of faculty from every program in the country.

In 2016, Hicks stepped down as division chief and was succeeded by Sunil Prasad, MD. Prasad received his MD at the University of Illinois and trained in cardiothoracic surgery at the Washington University School of Medicine. He was an expert in the use of extracorporeal membrane oxygenation (ECMO) to oxygenate blood in patients with severe cardiopulmonary failure and shock. He helped pioneer "walking ECMO," which allowed patients to get out of bed and walk with a portable device, reducing complications and improving outcomes. Under Prasad's direction, the University became the upstate referral center and a national leader in the use of ECMO for cardiogenic shock and other high-complexity patients.

With Prasad's departure, Knight became division chief. To accommodate URMC's growth as a major referral center, Knight continued to expand faculty and staff. The division now has a total of ten faculty divided into three areas: congenital cardiac surgery, adult acquired heart disease, and critical care. Knight also oversaw the opening of a twenty-two-bed Cardiovascular ICU staffed by more than ninety personnel and featuring round-the-clock cardiac intensivist coverage. The division has remained at the leading edge of cardiovascular medicine by adopting or pioneering less invasive therapies, and by performing the most highly complex, state-of-the-art, quaternary surgical therapies. The number of surgical procedures now stands at over 1,000.

Chapter 63

PEDIATRIC CARDIAC SURGERY

One of the great examples of collaboration among university-based medical centers has been the development of the regional pediatric cardiac surgery program. The pediatric cardiac surgery program currently provides care for over four million NY State residents, is the second-largest program in the state, and has a referral area greater than 40,000 square miles. The roots of the pediatric cardiac surgery program originated in 1949, when Earle Mahoney ligated a patent ductus arteriosus at SMH. At that time, pediatric cardiac surgery was rarely performed in the US due to diagnostic limitations, safety concerns using anesthesia, and limited technology. In 1955, the use of cardiopulmonary bypass allowed for repair of intra-cardiac defects. During the following eighteen years, URMC's general and adult cardiac surgeons periodically performed cardiac surgery on children.

Upon Mahoney's retirement in 1973, Scott Stewart, MD, was recruited as Rochester's first formally trained pediatric cardiac surgeon. Stewart developed a comprehensive team of pediatric cardiologists, anesthesiologists, nurses, and support staff, which began operating on "blue babies" and grew to a yearly volume of forty to ninety pediatric cardiac surgeries. However, further growth was limited due to competition with neighboring centers in Syracuse and Buffalo. Neonates and infants requiring the most complex cardiac surgery were often transferred to higher-volume centers, such as those in NY City, Cleveland, or Boston.

George Alfieris, MD, was a former URMC general surgery resident and cardiac surgery fellow who completed a pediatric cardiac surgery fellowship at Seattle Children's Hospital and was performing adult and congenital cardiac surgery at Upstate Medical Center in Syracuse. With an understanding that collaboration, not competition, was required to build a strong program, Alfieris proposed to Jeff Hicks to serve as the pediatric cardiac surgeon for Upstate Medical Center and URMC. In 1999, Alfieris began a bi-institutional collaboration, also involving pediatric cardiologists, that allowed him to provide pediatric cardiac surgical services to both cities.

After the departure of its pediatric cardiac surgeon, the Buffalo pediatric cardiology group joined the regionalization program in 2001, unifying the

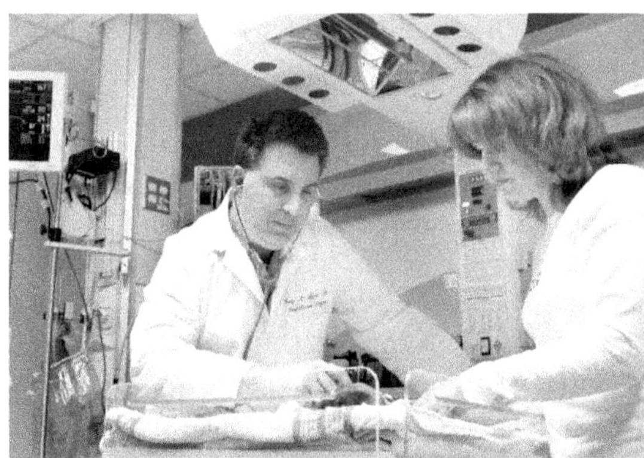

Figure 63.1. George Alfieris cares for a tiny patient in the ICU.

three cities. Due to the increased volume and experience, neonates with critical congenital heart disease requiring an operation during the first several days of life were no longer transferred out of the region. Over the following decade, SMH built a pediatric cardiac ICU, established an in-house Ronald McDonald house, allowing parents to reside in the hospital while their newborns were being treated, and initiated continuous ICU coverage by pediatric intensivists. As a result, URMC became the primary center for complex surgery for the regional program.

The regional collaboration enabled pediatric cardiologists to establish a network of outreach clinics that worked in concert to better care for children within the region. Currently, a baby born and stabilized in Syracuse or Buffalo can be discussed with all three pediatric cardiology groups using telemedicine links to determine a surgical plan. The baby can be transferred to Rochester for surgery and following discharge home can receive local follow-up care by the referring pediatric cardiologist. This bolsters, rather than degrades, local care, improves continuity, and provides a financial model that can support each referral center.

Due to the regionalization, the number of surgical cases at URMC has increased to about 350 annually, leading to markedly improved surgical results. Given the increased case volume, a second pediatric cardiac surgeon was hired in 2006, and URMC was able to attract subspecialty clinicians, including pediatric cardiac OR and ICU nurses, pediatric cardiac perfusionists, and pediatric cardiac anesthesiologists. A sixteen-bed pediatric cardiac care center was opened in the new GCH. The increased volume also led to the development of new graduate medical education programs at URMC, including fellowships for pediatric cardiac intensivists and pediatric cardiac surgery.

Over the past ten years, Cardiac Surgery has been the recipient of three endowed professorships. In 2015, Knight became the inaugural Marjorie B.

Morris Professor in Cardiac Surgery, an endowment gift that was inspired by his "expertise and compassion" in treating Marjorie B. Morris, a Clifton Springs resident. That same year, Alfieris became the inaugural Tansukh, Sarla, and Rajesh Ganatra Distinguished Professorship in Pediatric Cardiac Surgery, inspired by the congenital heart disease surgeries that Rajesh Ganatra received at SMH. In 2017, Prasad became the inaugural Dr. Jude S. Sauer Family Distinguished Professor in Cardiac Surgery. Sauer was an undergraduate, a medical student, and a surgical resident at the University of Rochester. He is the founder, president and CEO of LSI SOLUTIONS®, a surgical research and manufacturing company providing innovation for minimally invasive surgery. His wife, Eva Sauer, MD, is secretary and treasurer of LSI. The professorship is now held by Knight.

Chapter 64

HEART FAILURE/TRANSPLANTATION

Two landmark programs stand out as examples of the high level of collaboration between Cardiology and Cardiac Surgery: heart failure/transplantation and TAVR. In 1991, Jeff Hicks began to sow the seeds for the development of a heart transplant program at the University. Bradford Berk was equally enthusiastic about developing a program in heart failure and transplantation (in fact, his decision to come to the University was contingent on administrative support for such a program). In 1999, Leway Chen, MD, was recruited from University of Washington in Seattle to establish a heart failure/transplant program and H. Todd Massey, MD, was recruited from Duke University to become the first heart transplant surgeon. Chen and Massey developed a multidisciplinary team that included faculty from infectious diseases, nephrology, psychiatry, cardiac anesthesia, and cardiac pathology.

Figure 64.1. Leway Chen

Figure 64.2. Todd Massey

The first patient was listed for transplant on January 26, 2001 and the first transplant occurred on February 7, 2001. A dedicated advanced heart failure unit opened in August 2001 and was shortly followed by implantation of a variety of ventricular assist devices. Rochester quickly became a national leader in the implantation of left ventricular assist devices (LVADs), first as a mechanism for tiding people over until they could receive a transplant, but subsequently as destination therapy, enabling patients to return home and to work while using the device. An LVAD database was initiated at the University in 2011 and is now one of the largest in the country. To date, the program has implanted nearly 1,000 LVADs in dischargeable patients and currently follows 274 LVAD patients.

The 300th transplant was performed on June 6, 2022. For many years, the program averaged about ten transplants per year. However, in recent years the program has grown considerably: in 2023, forty transplants were performed. In keeping with the growth in transplant/VAD volumes and the substantial increase in heart failure in the US, the program has grown markedly and now boasts eight cardiologists, including Jeffrey D. Alexis, MD, who has been a mainstay of the program for over twenty years, and two surgeons. The program has also expanded its outreach efforts, with clinics established throughout the region.

Chapter 65

TRANSCATHETER AORTIC VALVE REPLACEMENT (TAVR)

A new era in the treatment of valvular heart disease began in 2011, when the FDA approved TAVR for the treatment of aortic stenosis. In response, cardiac surgery (Jeff Hicks) and interventional cardiology (Frederick S. Ling, MD) developed a multidisciplinary valve clinic, which included specialists in cardiac imaging and anesthesiology. Ling received his MD from NYU, did his residency in internal medicine at Beth Israel Deaconess Medical Center, Boston, and his cardiology and interventional cardiology fellowships at Yale. He was recruited to URMC in 1993 and appointed director of the cardiac catheterization laboratory in 1998.

Figure 65.1. Fred Ling

Initially, TAVR was only approved for the few patients assessed as high risk for surgical replacement of the aortic valve. To ensure that there would be sufficient volume to allow URMC to be included in the first group of US centers to be approved for TAVR, Hicks and Ling established a collaboration with RGH and Thomas P. Stuver, MD, of RCPG. With the success of TAVR for high-risk patients, Ling and Knight (who followed Hicks as surgical director of the TAVR program) led research efforts at URMC on using TAVR in patients at intermediate and low risks for surgery, helping to pave the way for FDA approval for these indications. In 2020, URMC became one of the first centers accredited by the American College of Cardiology for its TAVR program.

TAVR has become the dominant therapy for most patients with aortic stenosis, as well as the preferred therapy for surgically implanted aortic valves that have degenerated. Most patients undergo TAVR through a transfemoral percutaneous approach under moderate sedation, require only an overnight hospital stay, and resume all normal activities within a week or two. Cardiac surgery has also evolved, with Knight establishing URMC as an expert center in minimally invasive valve replacement for patients who are either very young or less suited for TAVR.

The success of TAVR and minimally invasive aortic valve surgery has led to a push for the development of less invasive therapies for a wide range of heart diseases. This has resulted in the development of the structural heart disease program, which now includes less invasive therapies for the mitral and tricuspid valves, such as transcatheter edge-to-edge repair, and is exploring transcatheter approaches to replace other valves.

Chapter 66

CARDIOVASCULAR RESEARCH AND THE AAB CARDIOVASCULAR RESEARCH INSTITUTE

Over the past twenty-five years, URMC has emerged as a major center for basic cardiovascular research with the development of the Aab CVRI. At the same time, clinical research in cardiology has been dominated by the internationally acclaimed work of Arthur Moss, MD, working with colleagues Wojciech Zareba, MD, PhD, Jean-Phillippe Couderc, PhD, MBA, and Ilan Goldenberg, MD.

During a career spanning six decades, Arthur J. Moss, MD, made some of the most significant advances in the prevention and treatment of sudden cardiac death. Moss received his BA from Yale University and his MD from Harvard Medical School. After an internship at MGH, he came to URMC for a residency in internal medicine and a fellowship in cardiology. Moss joined the faculty at URMC in 1966 and stayed for the rest of his career, ultimately becoming the Bradford C. Berk, MD, PhD, Distinguished Professor in Cardiology.

Figure 66.1. Arthur Moss

A visit in 1970 by a patient in her 30s who would suddenly fall unconscious while bowling sparked Moss's interest in Long QT Syndrome (LQTS). Moss devised the first effective surgical treatment for the disorder, and in 1979 established the International LQTS Registry, one of the first rare disease registries in the world. The registry, funded by the NIH, allowed Moss and colleagues to identify risk factors that enabled early diagnosis of LQTS. It also proved invaluable in developing treatment options that reduced life-threatening arrhythmias by more than eighty percent and for the discovery of multiple genes associated with the disorder.

Beginning in the 1990s, Moss led the MADIT (Multicenter Automatic Defibrillator Implantation Trial) series of clinical trials, which showed that the implantable cardioverter defibrillator (ICD) significantly reduced the risk of sudden death in specific groups of patients post-myocardial infarction. These findings changed medical guidelines worldwide and led to the use of

ICD therapy in hundreds of thousands of patients. In 2009, Moss completed the MADIT-CRT trial, which established that the addition of cardiac resynchronization therapy to ICD implantation prevented the progression of heart failure in patients living with moderate to severe heart failure. URMC has remained the hub for subsequent MADIT trials.

Moss was founding director of URMC's heart research follow-up program (HRFP), a worldwide hub of international studies on medical interventions for sudden death, cardiac arrhythmias, heart attack, and heart failure. He published more than 750 scientific papers, including a 1962 article—his first of many in the *New England Journal of Medicine*—highlighting the first three published cases of cardiopulmonary resuscitation (CPR), which included external chest massage followed by external defibrillation. Moss received the Eastman Medal in 2012, the University's highest honor. In 2008, he received the Glorney-Raisbeck Award in Cardiology, the highest honor of the NY Academy of Medicine. The Heart Rhythm Society bestowed its top honor, the Distinguished Scientist Award, to Moss in 2011, and its Pioneer in Cardiac Pacing and EP Award to Moss in 2017. In 2017, Moss received the James B. Herrick Award at the American Heart Association's scientific sessions, given annually to a physician whose scientific achievements have contributed profoundly to the advancement and practice of clinical cardiology. Moss died in 2018 at the age of eighty-six.

Clinical Cardiovascular Research Center (CRCC)

Following Moss's death, Ilan Goldenberg, MD, was recruited to serve as the director of a new CRCC, which consolidated Moss's HRFP and the clinical research within Cardiology. Goldenberg received his MD from the Sackler School of Medicine in Israel and trained as an internal medicine resident and cardiology fellow at the Chaim Sheba Medical Center, Tel Aviv University, Israel. He came to URMC in 2004 as a postdoctoral fellow in Moss's program and remained on the cardiology faculty until 2011, when he returned to Israel to serve as director of Cardiology at Chaim Sheba Medical Center and director of the Israeli Center for Cardiovascular Trials. In Rochester, Goldenberg became an expert in arrhythmias and sudden death, working with Moss and Wojciech Zareba on the MADIT trials. In Israel, Goldenberg continued to collaborate with the HRFP and expanded his research focus to include advanced therapies for heart failure, atrial fibrillation, and secondary prevention. He has served as PI on more than 100 federal and industry-supported international clinical

Figure 66.2.
Ilan Goldenberg

trials and registries with an overall budget of more than $80 million, generating over 600 publications.

Figure 66.3. Wojciech Zareba

Wojciech Zareba, MD, PhD, the inaugural David Mortara Endowed Professor in Cardiology, has been a mainstay of the HRFP and of cardiovascular research since 1991, when he came to URMC for a postdoctoral fellowship with Moss. In 2003, Zareba took the lead in establishing the North American ARVC (arrhythmogenic right ventricular cardiomyopathy) registry, together with investigators at the University of Arizona and the University of Cincinnati. The program has enrolled over 1,000 probands, has established diagnostic criteria that are used worldwide, and has helped to identify thirty-nine genes associated with ARVC. In 2018, Zareba served as PI on the first randomized pilot trial testing the antiarrhythmic agent flecainide in ARVC patients with high risk of sudden death. He has also served as PI on the International LQTS Registry, the MADIT trials, and on the NIH-funded RAID trial, which examined the effect of Ranolazine on ventricular arrhythmias and death in high-risk patients with ICDs. Zareba has authored more than 600 publications and over thirty book chapters focused predominantly on sudden death, risk stratification, QT prolongation, device therapy, heart failure, and ECG-related cardiac safety biomarkers.

Figure 66.4. Jean-Phillippe Couderc

Another key figure in the CCRC is Jean-Phillippe Couderc, PhD, MBA, a biomedical engineer who came to URMC from France in 1997 as a postdoctoral fellow with Moss and Zareba and remained as faculty in Cardiology, where he became assistant director of the HRFP. In 2002, he received an MBA from the Simon School of Business. Couderc is an international leader in quantitative electrocardiography. Among his accomplishments is the development of novel software that provides more accurate and reliable methods to analyze data from electrocardiograms and other types of heart monitors to better determine whether a drug is cardiotoxic. This software was critical to the development of iCardiac Technologies, Inc., a Rochester-based company for which Couderc served for over a decade as chief technology officer. Over the years, iCardiac has introduced several breakthrough innovations, including high-precision QT and early precision QT methodologies, which have had a major impact on how patients are monitored during clinical trials or when receiving potentially cardiotoxic therapies.

In 2024, the CCRC was the recipient of three large awards from PCORI. Headed by Goldenberg and Zareba, the $27 million "Comparative Clinical Effectiveness of Implantable Cardioverter Defibrillator Versus Non-Implantable Cardioverter Defibrillator Therapy in Contemporary Heart Failure Patients With Low Predicted Arrhythmic Risk" study stems from the MADIT trials and seeks to determine whether, in the context of better medications being available to manage heart failure, patients with a relatively low risk of sudden cardiac death will do equally well when treated with medicine with or without implanting an ICD.

Headed by Goldenberg and Mehmet K. Aktas, MD, a cardiac electrophysiologist, the $27 million "Comparative Effectiveness of Carvedilol versus Metoprolol Succinate in Patients With Heart Failure With an Implantable Cardioverter Defibrillator" is the first large-scale study comparing the two most widely prescribed beta-blockers for the treatment of heart failure in patients with an ICD. Funded by a $17 million award, the third study examines the value of a repeat ablation following a failed initial ablation for atrial fibrillation. Leading the study are Goldenberg, Zareba, and Jonathan S. Steinberg, MD, adjunct professor of Medicine (Cardiology) at URMC and former chief of Cardiology and director of the Arrhythmia Institute at St. Luke's-Roosevelt Hospital Center, NY.

Aab Cardiovascular Research Institute (CVRI)

One of Bradford Berk's mandates upon becoming chief of Cardiology was to develop a nationally prominent basic research program in cardiovascular diseases, one of the six priority areas outlined in CEO Jay Stein's strategic plan. Berk began recruiting his former research fellows and collaborators to space in the KMRB. With Berk's accession to chair of DOM and Taubman's arrival as chief of Cardiology, the recruitment expanded and the Aab CVRI was born, supported by a generous gift from Rick Aab. Initially, all investigators moved into the newly opened MRBX, but as the program grew, it moved in 2007 into its own building in Henrietta. At its peak, the Aab CVRI consisted of twenty-five faculty, fifteen of whom had extramurally funded laboratories, with studies focusing on thromboembolism, laminar flow and shear-stress, novel genetic factors, atherosclerosis, and cardiomyopathy.

The move to the Henrietta facility anticipated continued growth of the cardiovascular research program. However, with the flattening of the NIH budget and the "Great Recession" of 2007–9, additional recruitment was curtailed. Accordingly, the Aab CVRI moved back to newly renovated space in KMRX, renamed the Del Monte Research Building. Upon Lowenstein's departure, Craig Morrell, DVM, PhD, who was recruited by Lowenstein, became the director of the Aab CVRI. Morrell received his DVM from Tufts University School of Veterinary Medicine and then completed a comparative pathology fellowship at Johns Hopkins, where he also earned a PhD in Lowenstein's laboratory, investigating the molecular mechanisms of nitric oxide inhibition of platelet degranulation. Morrell's nationally recognized research program focuses on how platelets regulate the immune response in vascular and inflammatory disease processes. The reader is referred to the CVRI website for a description of its current research programs. A few of the most long-standing programs are summarized below.

Figure 66.5. Craig Morrell

Chen Yan, PhD, who received her PhD in Berk's laboratory at the University of Washington, came to URMC shortly after Berk's arrival. Her well-funded research program focuses on the regulation and function of cyclic nucleotide phosphodiesterases (PDE). In particular, she has been instrumental in determining the regulation and function of individual PDE isozymes in hypertension, atherosclerosis, heart failure, and cardiovascular inflammatory diseases. Zheng-Gen Jin, PhD, who was also recruited to URMC upon Berk's arrival, has established a well-funded program focused on the molecular regulation of vascular endothelial function. Over the years his laboratory has identified key molecules and signaling pathways that respond to laminar flow and help protect from the development of atherosclerosis. Jun-ichi Abe, MD, PhD, recruited by Berk in 1998 from the University of

Figure 66.6. Left to right: Valentina Kutyifa, Alex Nakonechynl, Zheng-Gen Jin, Eric M. Small, Wojciech Zareba, Bradford C. Berk, Craig N. Morrell, Kim Martinod, Douglas Anderson, Chen Yan, Spencer Rosero, Jinjiang Pang, Peng Yao

Tokyo, developed a nationally recognized program focused on elucidating mechanisms of signal transduction, particularly those involving extracellular signal regulated kinase 5 (ERK5), in the cardiovascular system. Abe left URMC in 2014 to join the department of Cardiology at the University of Texas M. D. Anderson Cancer Center.

Eric M. Small, PhD, was recruited in 2011 by Lowenstein from the University of Texas, Southwestern Medical Center, where he had been a postdoctoral fellow in the laboratory of Eric Olson, PhD. Small's research program focuses on how disruption of cardiac gene expression programs in heart disease contributes to cellular pathophysiology and the decline in cardiac function. Of particular interest are the role of cardiac fibroblast plasticity in the development of cardiac fibrosis and the role of epicardium-derived progenitor cell mobilization in mediating cardiac repair.

Douglas M. Anderson, PhD, and Peng Yao, PhD, were recruited to the Aab CVRI in 2016 as part of URMC's focus on RNA Biology. Anderson studies the role of RNA-binding proteins and long noncoding RNAs as novel regulators of muscle development. His laboratory has recently found that many long noncoding RNAs encode small micropeptides that play important roles in regulating intracellular signaling. Yao's laboratory is studying the pathophysiological function and molecular mechanism of new noncoding RNAs and RNA binding proteins and their role in gene regulation of the cardiac system.

In 2023, in keeping with URMC's theme of creating multidisciplinary centers of excellence, the CCRC and Aab CVRI were merged into one entity, with Goldenberg and Morrell serving as directors. The new entity resides within DOM and is designed to better integrate the clinical and basic sciences, and maximize the translation of research from bench to bedside.

O. Environment, Drug Discovery, and Public Health

Environmental Medicine and Drug Targets and Medicine were among the programs of excellence identified in 2015 as part of CEO Mark Taubman's research strategic plan. Like the departments of Radiation Oncology and Biochemistry and Biophysics, discussed earlier, the departments of Environmental Medicine and Pharmacology and Physiology share roots in the Manhattan Project and the toxicology programs that were borne from it. The focus of the department of Public Health Sciences has increasingly aligned with those of the department of Environmental Medicine and plans are underway to merge the two. Therefore, it will also be discussed in this section.

Chapter 67

DEPARTMENT OF ENVIRONMENTAL MEDICINE

In keeping with its biopsychosocial roots, the University of Rochester was one of the first institutions to recognize the central role of environmental factors as drivers of disease, and has been leading national efforts in environmental health and toxicology for over fifty years. These efforts started in the 1940s, as part of the Atomic Energy project (see chapter 45), leading to the establishment of the department of Radiation Biology at the end of World War II. In 1966, Harold C. Hodge, PhD, the chair of the department of Pharmacology and the co-founder and first president of the Society of Toxicology, formally established the toxicology training program in collaboration with William F. Neuman, PhD, and Aser Rothstein, PhD, co-chairs of the department of Radiation Biology. Thomas W. Clarkson, PhD, served as the program's first director. In 1970, the University of became the first in the US to award a toxicology PhD.

In the 1970s, Clarkson was contacted by the University of Baghdad to help with what proved to be the largest mass organic mercury poisoning in history. This tragic event fueled international interest in the effects of environmental exposure on health. This included growing recognition of the effects of leaded paint and leaded gasoline on children's neurodevelopment. Research from the University of Rochester was instrumental in the CDC releasing a statement in 2012 that no level of lead is safe for children and led to the development of the first-in-the-nation city policies on lead paint remediation, including the abatement of lead-containing paint on porches.

Also in the 1970s, URMC faculty founded one of the first NIH-funded Programs of Excellence in Environmental Health Sciences, initially led by Clarkson. This was followed by an Environmental Protection Agency-funded Center of Excellence on air pollution, led by Günter Oberdörster, DVM, PhD. These multidisciplinary collaborative efforts, among others, catalyzed the University's national leadership in environmental medicine and set the stage for the establishment in 1992 of a new department of Environmental Medicine (DEM), chaired by Clarkson.

Figure 67.1. Deborah Cory-Slechta

Deborah A. Cory-Slechta, PhD, served as chair of DEM and director of the Environmental Health Sciences Center from 1998–2001. From 2000–2, she also served as dean for Research at SMD. Cory-Slechta received a PhD in Psychology and Pharmacology from the University of Minnesota and was a Junior Staff Fellow of the National Center for Toxicological Research. After completing a postdoctoral fellowship in behavioral toxicology and pharmacology at the University of Rochester, she joined the DEM faculty in 1984. In 2003, she left to become director of the Environmental and Occupational Health Sciences Institute of Rutgers University. In 2007, Cory-Slechta returned to the DEM, serving as interim chair from 2016–17. She also served in leadership roles for several of the University's graduate programs and received a Women's Health and the Environment over the Entire Lifespan grant from the NIH designed to create development and mentoring programs for junior faculty. Her research career has focused on the impact of lead exposures in children, including groundbreaking studies showing the contribution of environmental agents to neurodegenerative diseases and the impacts of air pollution on the brain. In 2018, she received a University of Rochester Lifetime Achievement Award in Graduate Education.

Figure 67.2. Tom Gasiewicz

Thomas A. Gasiewicz, PhD, was named chair of DEM and director of the Environmental Health Sciences Center in 2001. A native of Buffalo, NY, Gasiewicz received a PhD in Toxicology from the University of Rochester and subsequently completed a postdoctoral fellowship at Vanderbilt University. He returned to Rochester as a faculty member in 1980. From 1991–9, he served as director of the Toxicology Training Program and was among the inaugural faculty when the department was formed in 1992. He remained chair until 2015, when an illness caused him to take unplanned leave; he retired in 2018. Throughout his time on the faculty, Gasiewicz maintained an active and well-funded research program focusing on molecular mechanisms by which halogenated small molecules lead to cancer, particularly hematopoietic malignancies. He also actively studied the "flip side" of this issue, studying how natural polyphenols in green tea act as chemo preventative agents, protecting from cancer.

Beverly Paige Lawrence, PhD, Wright Family Research Professor in Environmental Medicine and Professor of Microbiology & Immunology, was appointed chair of DEM and director of the Environmental Health Sciences Center in 2017. Lawrence received her PhD in Biochemistry, Molecular, and

Figure 67.3. Paige Lawrence

Cell Biology from Cornell University. After a postdoctoral fellowship at Oregon State University, she joined the faculty at Washington State University, before being recruited to the University of Rochester in 2006. In 2023, Lawrence became the inaugural director of the new University of Rochester Institute for Human Health and the Environment. Her research focuses on determining how environmental signals influence the immune system, uncovering how early life exposures shape the way the immune system develops and functions later in life and across generations. Lawrence has served on numerous review panels and advisory committees for governmental agencies and nongovernmental organizations. She is deputy editor of *Environmental Health Perspectives* and an Associate Editor for *Toxicological Sciences.* Throughout her career, Lawrence has been actively engaged in learning about, developing, and using new strategies to improve recruitment, retention, mentoring, and career advancement, and fostering a culture of mutual respect, ally-ship, and advocating for others.

In 1999, DEM had sixteen primary faculty who held $6.5 million in total funding (approximately $400,000 per faculty). Only three faculty members were women, and none identified as non-white. Due to successful recruitment and mentoring, the department is substantially more diverse and far better funded. New recruitments, in addition to Paige Lawrence, included Irfan Rahman, PhD (2004), Katrina Korfmacher, PhD (2005), Matthew D. Rand, PhD (2012), Cristina Demian, MD, MPH (2013), Martha Susiarjo, PhD (2015), Marissa E. Sobolewski Terry, PhD (2018), Hae-Ryung Park, PhD (2022), and Souvarish Sarkar, PhD (2023). Sadly, three faculty members died, including Nazzareno "Ned" Ballatori, PhD, Victor Laties, PhD, and Bernard Weiss, PhD.

In addition to these, in 2014 the department also welcomed Jacqueline "Jacky" Williams, PhD, a University of Rochester faculty member since 1990. Williams, who had previously been in Radiation Oncology, was internationally recognized for her work on mechanisms that underlie the initiation and progression of tissue effects resulting from clinical or accidental exposure to radiation, including the types of radiation experienced by astronauts. At the time, Williams was the PI on a $15 million, five-year NIH award "Centers for Medical Countermeasures Against Radiation," which evaluates known drugs and experimental agents' ability to ward off systemic radiation injury that affects the lungs, brain, skin, and bone marrow.

Currently, the department has fourteen primary faculty, eighteen secondary faculty, and four adjunct faculty. Current primary faculty are seventy-seven percent women, and thirty percent identify as not white.

Primary faculty currently holds $18.5 million in grants and contracts, or approximately $1.32 million per faculty member. DEM faculty are very active teaching and mentoring in numerous graduate programs, including the MSTP, Toxicology, Translational Biomedical Sciences, Neurosciences, and Microbiology, Immunology & Virology. The Toxicology program is an interdepartmental training program for doctoral students and fellows and is administered by the department. DEM faculty also teach undergraduate courses, primarily in the Environmental Health major and in-course offerings in Public Health Sciences, such as *Environmental Health and Justice* and *Environmental Health Policy*. Katrina Korfmacher developed and teaches two separate courses in the medical humanities, both of which engage medical students in environmental health and environmental medicine. Marissa Sobolewski Terry designed and taught the first graduate-level course at URMC that weaves social justice directly into the curriculum.

DEM is a crucial nexus of leading-edge research, education, and community engagement, and the administrative home to several interdepartmental educational, research, and clinical programs. These are described below.

The National Institute of Environmental Health Sciences (NIEHS)-supported Environmental Health Sciences Center (EHSC) P30 grant has been funded since 1975. This Center has catalyzed new growth, new discoveries, and new technologies at URMC for almost fifty years. The EHSC currently has fifty-two members from sixteen departments in SMD, the SON, and the Colleges of Arts and Science, and Engineering. The Center's team science has led to cutting-edge research discoveries, including a recently identified maternally imprinted gene, the role of air pollution in neurodevelopmental and neurodegenerative disease, and influence of environmental exposures on vaccines. The EHSC has garnered over $100 million in extramural research funding and initiated URMC's Genomics and Flow Cytometry cores. EHSC's leading-edge Community Engagement Core was a critical driver of Rochester's local lead poisoning-prevention system, which has resulted in lead poisoning rates declining 2.4 times faster than elsewhere in NY state.

The Toxicology program (directors Alison Elder, PhD, and Matthew Rand, PhD) remains one of the most prestigious in the country. To date, this multidisciplinary, multidepartmental program, which has thirty-five faculty mentors, has awarded approximately 210 PhDs in Toxicology and trained over 150 postdoctoral fellows. Program alumni hold leadership positions in academia, governmental agencies and the private sector. There are currently twenty-four graduate students enrolled. The success of the program is in part due to excellent leadership and well-planned succession, that has enabled it to maintain a continuous NIH T32 training grant support for over forty-five years, one of the largest at URMC (twelve slots).

The Finger Lakes Occupational Health Services Clinic, led by Cristina Demian, serves a nine-county area in the Finger Lakes Region and responds to a serious and unmet need for clinical resources to address occupational diseases through prevention, diagnosis, and treatment. This unique clinic, supported at its inception by a NY State grant, opened in 1987 under the direction of Mark Utell, MD (Pulmonary and Critical Care Medicine and Environmental Medicine). It provides approximately 1,500 patient visits each year, including approximately 400 new patients.

The Life Sciences Learning Center (LSLC) is a unique hands-on science inquiry center for middle and high school students and teachers in Rochester, the Finger Lakes Region, and Western NY. Led by innovative educator Dina G. Markowitz, PhD, the LSLC provides an interactive hands-on learning environment aligned with NYS science education standards; develops, tests, and disseminates instructional programs and materials to make the latest science accessible to teachers and students; trains educators for laboratory-based teaching in the life sciences and to be a trusted resource for teachers who are developing new curricula. LSLC offers a variety of programming that includes laboratory investigation programs, professional development workshops for science teachers, and summer science camps. Funded by Markowitz's Science Education Partnership Award, the LSLC is creating a community-based course for parents and children to be offered at eight area YMCAs. The focus is "Medicines and Me," which explores concepts such as appropriate use of medicines, and increasing understanding of clinical trials and translational research.

The Western New York Center for Research on Flavored Tobacco Products (CRoFT), funded by a five-year $19 million U54 grant from the NCI, partners Roswell Park Cancer Institute with URMC (Irfan Rahman, URMC site PI). The goal of CRoFT is to inform the tobacco regulatory agencies regarding products, thereby protecting the public from the adverse health effects of toxicants and irritants. Among the accomplishments of the URMC component of CRoFT have been: pinpointing toxicity of key flavoring chemicals that led to regulation of fruit flavors by NY State in 2020 and nationwide in 2022; identifying biomarkers of exposures related to use of e-cigarette products; establishing toxicity parameters and indices of respiratory symptoms that are used by regulatory researchers; informing treatment strategies for acute illness associated with use of electronic delivery products; and raising awareness of social injustices and health inequities due to targeting of products at susceptible populations.

DEM has been at the forefront in responding to growing public concern about the health effects of microplastics. A 2019 EHSC pilot project awarded to James McGrath, PhD, William R. Kenan, Jr. Professor of Biomedical Engineering, explored the application of silicon nanomembranes developed in his laboratory to characterize microplastics in the City of Rochester's water supply system. McGrath also established the Microplastics Working Group of Western New York, which served as a learning collaborative for EHSC researchers and other researchers in the region. A collaboration between the University of Rochester and RIT has led to a new $7.3 million P01 grant from the NIEHS and the NSF "Centers for Oceans and Human Health Program" in 2023, with Katrina Korfmacher serving as PI. This proposal supports the Lake Ontario Center for MicroPlastics and Human Health in a Changing Environment (LOMP). Over the next five years, LOMP will support innovative integrated research on the environmental and human health effects of microplastics in the Great Lakes.

The "Cellular Senescence Network (SenNet) Program was established by the NIH to identify and characterize senescent cells throughout the body under various states of health and across the lifespan. The TriState SenNet Tissue Mapping Center (University of Pittsburgh, Carnegie Mellon University, The Ohio State University, and the University of Rochester) is analyzing human lung and heart tissue to create high-resolution maps of senescent cell populations. The University of Rochester team led by Irfan Rahman, Gloria Pryhuber, MD (Pediatrics), Vera Gorbunova, PhD (Biology), and Dongmei Li, PhD (Public Health Sciences) uses multi-modal, high-content approaches such as single-cell RNA and ATAC (Assay for Transposase-Accessible Chromatin) sequencing, proteomics, and spatial transcriptomics to define physiological drivers of senescence to understand the therapeutic potential of senolytic therapy.

Chapter 68

INSTITUTE FOR HUMAN HEALTH AND THE ENVIRONMENT

The environment is a major contributor to public health and a key driver of health disparities. In fact, zip-code supersedes genetic code as the major predictor of overall health, quality of life, and longevity. A deeper understanding of the molecular, cellular, and societal mechanisms that underpin associations between environmental factors and disease can transform public health and health care. Accordingly, Paige Lawrence convened a team of dedicated field drivers to develop the conceptual basis for a new institute and sought input from faculty, staff, and learners across the University of Rochester. The Institute for Human Health and the Environment (IHHE) was launched in 2023 to propel transformative research, education, career development, and community engagement to tackle the 21st century's most pressing health issues (climate change, environmental justice, the health impact of substances in air, water, and food) and to translate this knowledge into innovative approaches to address these issues. The Institute is structured

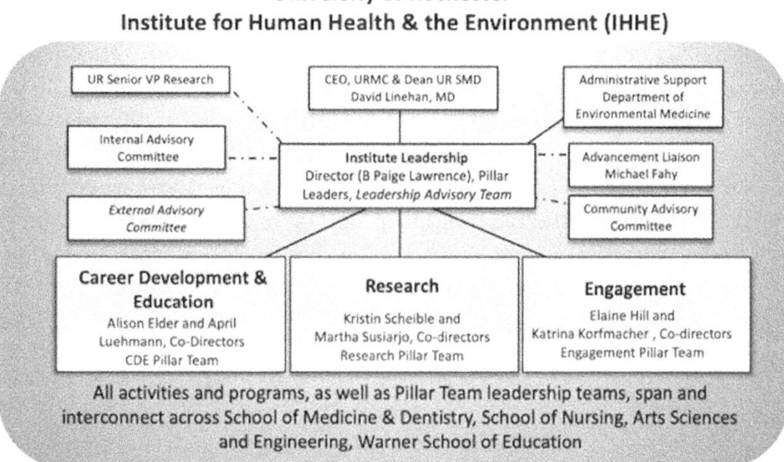

Figure 68.1. Structure of the IHHE

to foster collaboration, support a diverse and inclusive environment to recruit and retain highly talented individuals across the career continuum, and further elevate the University's international stature in solutions-oriented research to mitigate the impact of anthropogenic and environmental issues on health, reduce health disparities, and improve lives by preventing diseases.

The Research pillar supports transdisciplinary and collaborative research to discover how environmental factors influence health. This pillar fosters new projects that promote novel ideas and discoveries through pilot grants and collaboration-building workshops. These will ultimately lead to larger extramural grants, with a focus on cultivating multi-principal investigator, transdisciplinary projects.

The Career Development and Education pillar develops new pipeline programs that span across the educational spectrum from undergraduate to early-stage investigator. It also contributes to the educational and career continuum through programs that include K-12 education, integrating existing activities, and supporting applications for new training grants, education grants, and other innovative programs.

The Engagement pillar invests in multidirectional engagement with a diverse range of stakeholders to learn about, develop, implement, and evaluate scalable science-informed solutions to address community concerns and challenges. This pillar includes engagement with groups within and external to the University, including clinicians, government, public health professionals, educators, and diverse community-based groups in Rochester, the Finger Lakes region, and beyond.

In its first year, IHHE supported numerous new initiatives, including: new summer undergraduate research scholarships, a new partnership with the WCI on radon exposure, a student-driven and community-engaged project involving School 17, and a Research Workshop on "Housing, Health and Environmental Justice in the Rochester Region."

One of the foremost challenges of the future is understanding how the environment influences and shapes everyone's health and wellbeing. Moving forward, the IHHE will continue to provide a crucial nexus for these efforts by leading and coordinating multiple programs of excellence that connect and foster related research, education, and engagement throughout the University. Woven into the fabric of the IHHE is a major commitment to fostering community engagement, identifying issues, developing solutions, and disseminating new knowledge.

Chapter 69

DEPARTMENT OF PHARMACOLOGY AND PHYSIOLOGY

The department of Physiology traces its history to 1917, when Lewis P. Ross, a successful industrialist and philanthropist who served for more than twenty years on the University of Rochester Board of Trustees, bequeathed an endowment to fund a department of Physiology, originally called the department of Vital Economics, with John R. Murlin, MD, as chair. In 1924, Physiology was established as one of the original departments in SMD, with Wallace O. Fenn, PhD, as founding chair. Fenn, the first Lewis Pratt Ross Professor, was a physiologist of international stature known for his pioneering work in muscle metabolism, and electrolyte, respiratory, and space and undersea physiology. Fenn chaired the department for thirty-five years and remained active until his death in 1971. He was succeeded in 1959 by William D. Lotspeich, MD, a renal physiologist, and in 1971 by Paul Horowicz, PhD, a renowned authority on muscle and membrane physiology. During his twenty-six-year tenure as chair, Horowicz assembled a world-class department at the forefront of ion channel research.

The department of Pharmacology was established in 1958, with Harold C. Hodge, PhD, as its first chair, a position he held until 1970. Hodge, who had received his MD from the University of Rochester, had been chosen to head the Manhattan Project's division of Pharmacology and Toxicology. As Pharmacology chair, Hodge played a key role in promoting the implementation of water fluoridation. He was succeeded by Louis Lasagna, MD, a clinical pharmacologist and member of the Institute of Medicine, who chaired the department—renamed Pharmacology and Toxicology—from 1970 to 1980. In 1983, the department again changed focus under the leadership of M. W. (Drag) Anders, DVM, PhD, who over the next twelve years created a nationally recognized basic research-oriented Pharmacology department. During this time, Anders recruited several outstanding faculty members, including Richard Borch, MD, PhD, Shey-Shing Sheu, PhD, A. W. (Bill) Tank, PhD, Charles Falany, PhD, Jean M. Bidlack, PhD, Alan Smrcka, PhD, and Robert S. Freeman, PhD.

Following Horowicz's death in 1996, the two departments merged into Pharmacology & Physiology (Pharm/Phys). At the time, Physiology was comprised primarily of researchers who studied ion channel physiology at the molecular and cellular level, and neuroscientists who took a more integrative approach. Most of the ion channel investigators chose to join the newly merged department, whereas most of the integrative neurobiologists joined Neurobiology and Anatomy (now Neurosciences). To help grow the new department, Anders recruited David I. Yule, PhD, Denise C. Hocking, PhD, and Robert T. Dirksen, PhD, each of whom established well-funded research programs. In 2016, Yule was awarded the Louis C. Lasagna Professorship in Experimental Therapeutics in acknowledgement of his research on intracellular calcium signaling in normal physiology, and in diseases such as Sjögren's syndrome.

Figure 69.1. William Tank

In 2001, A. W. (Bill) Tank succeeded Anders as Lewis Ross Professor and chair of Pharm/Phys. Tank received his PhD in biochemistry from Purdue University and completed a postdoctoral fellowship at the University of Colorado, where he remained as faculty before joining URMC in 1986. Tank's research program focused on the molecular mechanisms that control tyrosine hydroxylase expression and function in the nervous system. Under his leadership, the department further solidified its international reputation in ion channel biology, receptor pharmacology, and membrane signaling, which was enhanced by the recruitment of three junior faculty members—Paul J. Kammermeier, PhD, Angela Glading, PhD, and Gregory Tall, PhD.

Figure 69.2. Robert Dirksen

In 2015, Robert T. Dirksen, PhD, was appointed Lewis Pratt Ross Professor and chair of Pharm/Phys. Dirksen received his PhD from the University of Rochester and did a postdoctoral fellowship with Kurt G. Beam, PhD, at Colorado State University. Dirksen established a highly regarded research program focused on the role of intracellular calcium signaling on the pathophysiology of muscular dystrophy and heart disease, and served as president of the Society of General Physiologists. Dirksen also served as director of an interdepartmental course on ethics and professional integrity required for all students, postdoctoral fellows, and new faculty members who conduct research. Due in part to the retirement of several faculty members, in 2015 the department consisted of only eleven faculty members, predominantly full professors. Under Dirksen's leadership, the department has recruited ten faculty and is not only more balanced across faculty levels (five assistant professors, five associate professors, and six full professors) but is also among the most diverse and gender-balanced in the histories of the Physiology and Pharmacology departments.

Pharm/Phys oversees the training of approximately fifty graduate students in two PhD programs (Pharmacology and Physiology) and three MS programs (Pharmacology, Physiology, and Medical Pharmacology). Whereas traditional pharmacology programs tend to focus on mechanisms of drug action while traditional physiology programs tend to focus on the functions of organ systems and tissues, the SMD program combines the fundamentals of these fields with cutting-edge approaches to understand cellular signaling at the molecular level and to apply them to the physiological mechanisms of drugs and drug targets. The program has produced many outstanding graduates, such as Wolfhard Almers, PhD, who subsequently developed an international reputation for his studies of exocytosis and endocytosis, and was elected into the National Academy of Sciences.

In fall 2021, Pharm/Phys established a new MS in Medical Pharmacology. The program provides students with specialized academic training and professional development skills needed to build stronger, more competitive portfolios to enter medicine, dentistry, veterinary medicine, pharmaceutical sciences, or other health professions career paths. Early outcomes are excellent, with twenty-four of twenty-seven graduates having either gained entrance into US MD, DO, or DDS programs, currently applying for medical school, or currently working at URMC in an enhanced role.

Pharm/Phys manages approximately $11 million in extramural research funds, and has, over the past twenty-five years, received seven patents and two licensing agreements. The research programs center in three major areas under the theme of "New Drugs to Cure Disease." G-Protein Coupled Receptors (GPCRs) are the largest family of cell surface receptors in the human genome and the largest class of targets for human therapeutics. The department is focused on the molecular analysis of GPCR signaling mechanisms; studying GPCR-dependent signaling pathways in pathological states to identify novel therapeutic targets and approaches; and developing small molecule therapeutics targeting GPCR signaling for treatment of pain, autoimmune diseases, cancer, and heart failure. Alan Smrcka, recruited in 1994, developed an internationally recognized research program on GPCR signaling for which he was awarded the Louis C. Lasagna Professorship in Experimental Therapeutics. He moved to the University of Michigan in 2016.

Like GPCRs, ion channels (IC) are expressed in all cells, underlie a multitude of debilitating diseases, and are among the most targeted proteins in clinical therapeutics. The department is working to unravel the molecular details that determine IC function and the mechanisms by which IC defects lead to human disease, with an eye towards the development of novel drug interventions. The department is also studying cell adhesion molecules and processes to determine how extracellular matrix proteins signal the development and function of neurons and vascular beds, how adhesion molecule dysregulation contributes to disease processes, how communication between different cell types controls integrated tissue and organ function, and how integrated signaling can be used to identify new drug targets. Details of specific projects can be found on the department website. Several programs are highlighted in the following paragraphs.

In 2009, the University was awarded a prestigious Silvio O. Conte Center for Basic and Translational Mental Health Research, funded by the National Institutes of Mental Health and designed to improve the diagnosis and treatment of mental health disorders. Rochester served as the hub of a five-year, $10.5 million collaborative effort that linked more than fifty researchers from URMC, Brown University, Harvard Medical School, University of Pittsburgh, and University of Puerto Rico to focus on how deep brain stimulation affects people with obsessive-compulsive disorder (OCD), one of the largest projects ever undertaken to elucidate the cause and develop treatments of OCD. The Conte Center was renewed in 2015 ($10 million) and again in 2022 ($15.6 million), with Washington University added to the network. Over the course of the first two awards, the center identified a neural "OCD network" that underlies the disorder and is linked to behavioral inflexibility and persistent avoidance. The current award focuses on identifying new approaches to treating OCD by modulating the "OCD network" and enhancing behavioral flexibility. Susan N. Haber, Dean's Professor of Pharmacology & Physiology, has been the guiding light and PI of the University's Conte Center since its inception. Haber received her PhD in Neuro- & Bio-Behavioral Science from Stanford University and did postdoctoral fellowships at the University of Minnesota and MIT.

Figure 69.3. Susan Haber

Pharm/Phys and the department of Anesthesiology & Perioperative Medicine have had a long-standing collaboration that has positioned the University as an internationally recognized center of excellence in mitochondrial biology. The collaboration was initiated by Shey-Shing Sheu, whose research program focused on mitochondrial calcium, ATP, reactive oxygen species, and fission/fusion dynamics in regulating cardiac function. Sheu received a PhD from the University of Chicago, and came to the University of Rochester in 1983, where he stayed for twenty-seven years. Sheu served as SAD for Graduate Studies from 1997–2000, during which time he oversaw the restructuring of the graduate programs into ten interdepartmental research clusters. In 2001, with the support of Anders and Anesthesiology Chair James Robotham, MD, Sheu founded the University of Rochester Mitochondrial Research and Innovation Group. The initiative was greatly strengthened by subsequent faculty recruitments, including Paul Brookes, PhD, Yisang Yoon, PhD, Gail Johnson, PhD, Andrew Wojtovich, PhD, and most recently John Onukwufor, PhD. This multidisciplinary research group, which currently consists of fourteen faculty and over fifty members from ten departments and centers throughout the University, has a common goal of advancing understanding of the role of mitochondrial function in human disease.

A key addition to the department was the establishment in 1994 of the Paul Stark Professorship in Pharmacology. Paul Stark was a PhD graduate of the department who went on to lead the clinical team at Eli Lilly that developed Prozac. In endowing this "term" professorship, Stark wished to provide early career support for promising young investigators in neuropharmacology. The professorship has provided critical support to outstanding young neuropharmacologists in the department, including Freeman, Tank, Bidlack, Xia, and most recently MacLean.

A fitting conclusion to any chapter on Pharm/Phys is to acknowledge the contribution of Patricia Hinkle, PhD, emeritus professor of Physiology. Hinkle received her PhD in biochemistry from the University of California, Berkeley, and completed a postdoctoral fellowship in pharmacology at Harvard University. During her forty-two years as a faculty member, Hinkle enjoyed a distinguished career studying how peptide hormones signal to create cellular responses. Hinkle's group made numerous seminal contributions to our understanding of thyrotropin releasing hormone and adenocorticotropic hormone action in pituitary and adrenal cells. Winner of a 2000 Arthur Kornberg Research Award, she remarkably held her first NIH R01 award for thirty-seven consecutive years. She trained numerous undergraduates, graduate students, MD/PhD students (including Bradford Berk), and postdoctoral fellows, and in 1991 received the Alumni Award for Excellence in Graduate education.

Figure 69.4.
Patricia Hinkle

Chapter 70

DEPARTMENT OF PUBLIC HEALTH SCIENCES

The department of Community and Preventive Medicine was established in 1958 with Robert L. Berg, MD, as the inaugural chair. Under Berg's leadership, the department exhibited commitment to improving the health of the community through lead screening, opening store-front health clinics, and through other preventive interventions targeted at disadvantaged populations. The department also established a vigorous research program related to health services, and spearheaded comprehensive evaluations of managed care and health system programs in the region. In 1974, a two-year master's degree program in community health was initiated, the first of its kind established in a medical school department. In 1989, this program was restructured to encompass a broader scope and was transitioned to an MPH program. This was followed, in 1994, by the development of a PhD program in Health Services Research and Policy.

During the past twenty-five years the department has grown significantly under the leadership of three chairs. Thomas Pearson served as chair from 1997 until 2007. Pearson received his MD, MPH, and PhD in cardiovascular epidemiology from Johns Hopkins, where he also completed residencies in preventive medicine and internal medicine, and a fellowship in cardiology. Pearson developed an international reputation in the epidemiology and prevention of atherosclerotic cardiovascular disease, and during his tenure as chair led basic science studies, clinical investigations, and community-based projects focused particularly on coronary heart disease, stroke, and lipids. He was a major contributor to the American Heart Association's guidelines for prevention of heart disease and stroke, and was chosen to serve on its 2010 Dietary Guidelines Advisory Committee, whose recommendations were viewed as the cornerstone of American food policy.

Figure 70.1. Thomas Pearson

Pearson established four divisions within the department: Epidemiology, Health Services Research, Social & Behavioral Sciences, and Public Health

Practice, and recruited several of their directors, including Timothy Dye, PhD, Fisher, and Deborah Ossip, PhD. He re-established a residency in preventive medicine, expanded the graduate programs to include a PhD in epidemiology and MS degrees in Clinical Investigation and Clinical Translational Research, and supported numerous faculty and clinician scientists through career development awards and training grants. In 2005, under his direction, the University was awarded a CDC Prevention Research Center (National Center for Deaf Health Research). He also co-led URMC's application for the CTSA. In recognition of his achievements, Pearson was appointed SAD for clinical research. He left the University in 2013 to become executive VP for Research and Education at the University of Florida Health Sciences Center.

Susan Fisher, MS, PhD, succeeded Pearson as chair in 2007. Fisher received an MS in biostatistics from Georgetown University and a PhD in epidemiology from the University of Illinois-Chicago. Prior to becoming chair, she served as the director of the epidemiology division and director of the PhD Program. Fisher had extensive experience in developing and conducting multicenter clinical trials and large observational studies. Her tenure as chair was marked by substantial change and growth. The Social & Behavioral Sciences and Public Health Practice divisions were merged, the Health Services Research division was renamed to Health Policy and Outcomes Research, and the department moved into the new Saunders Research Building, bringing all divisions under one roof. The educational programs were expanded to take full advantage of the new CTSI, and the department took the lead in developing a new undergraduate public health program. She also shepherded a name change to Public Health Sciences (PHS) in 2012.

Figure 70.2. Susan Fisher

Ann Dozier, RN, PhD, became chair of PHS and Albert David Kaiser Chair of Public Health and Preventive Medicine in 2014. Dozier received her MS and PhD in nursing from the University of Rochester. Her research interests focus on program evaluation, community engagement, and implementation of evidence-based strategies, particularly in maternal child health. During her tenure as chair, the faculty has continued to grow in size (from fewer than fifteen in 2000 to now twenty-eight), diversity (eight from traditionally underrepresented groups and thirteen women, including seven with tenure), and research funding. Educational offerings have expanded to

Figure 70.3. Ann Dozier

include certificate programs, master's degrees in epidemiology and health services research, a shift to more evening, hybrid, and online classes, and the University's first completely online master's program (MPH). Of particular note, Edith Williams, PhD, was recruited from the University of South Carolina to serve as Dean's Associate Professor and inaugural director of the CTSI's Office of Health Equity Research.

PHS graduate programs are designed to actively prepare graduates for careers in public health, health services research, epidemiology, and clinical research. Graduates pursue careers in the private sector (e.g. Pharma), consulting firms (e.g. RAND Consulting, RTI Consulting), government (e.g. CDC, HRSA), or academia. The department oversees two PhD programs (Health Services Research & Policy and Epidemiology, each with approximately fifteen students) and four master's programs (Clinical Investigation, Epidemiology, Health Services Research and Policy, and MPH, each with approximately twenty new students per year). The MPH program has both online and online/on-campus hybrid formats.

PHS faculty are also actively involved with physician education, including the Mastering Medical Information course for first-year medical students and a Community Health Improvement course during which fourth-year students engage with a community organization for a unique month-long experience. The department bestows Distinction in Community Health honors at graduation to students who have sustained community involvement over all four years of medical school. The preventive medicine residency is a two-year program (with two to three residents per year) for MD graduates who have completed a year of general internship. The program has a variety of practicum experiences, including rotations in Passport Health, Clinical Quality Improvement, the Center for Community Health and Prevention, and, most recently, Lifestyle Medicine training through a collaboration with the Ardmore Institute of Health. The program also leads to an MS or MPH.

In 2008, the University established an undergraduate program in public health under the directorship of PHS faculty member Edwin van Wijngaarden, PhD. PHS faculty direct introductory courses (with yearly enrollments of 100 to 150) and additional electives for students in one of five public health majors. The department oversees a combined degree program for undergraduate applicants, and accelerated programs for other undergraduates whereby they can be granted one of the master's degrees. PHS also oversees five post-baccalaureate advanced certificate programs (each with four to five courses) for students and practitioners who seek to enhance their professional development.

Figure 70.4. Edwin van Wijngaarden

Research in PHS encompasses nine overlapping areas: behavioral interventions; big data; dissemination and implementation; environmental health; global health; health policy and outcomes; maternal child health; nutrition; and older adults. The department's research programs are highly collaborative across the University, with other US academic institutions, and with global partners. The department website offers details of the individual research programs. The following paragraphs highlight examples of the breadth and depth of research of these collaborative programs.

The department has had a long-standing focus on smoking cessation, dating back to the 1980s, when Deborah J. Ossip, PhD, a clinical psychologist, developed a well-funded smoking cessation research program focused on behavioral interventions. Ossip built a critical mass of faculty and trainees who studied the effects of smoking cessation interventions among older adults, adolescents, community college students, and in international environments such as the Dominican Republic. She co-led the seminal work establishing the efficacy of Quitlines, a telephone-based tobacco cessation service that provides free evidence-based treatment and has been established in all fifty states. This highly collaborative program, which has particularly close ties with Environmental Medicine, has continued to evolve, responding to emerging trends, such as behavior change-based cessation support and the development of Internet- and mobile-based interventions. The current program, now known as the Nicotine and Tobacco Research Core, has extended the same research approaches to vaping and other tobacco-related products. A key component is the Nicotine and Tobacco Treatment Collaborative, which involves the WCI, the Center for Community Health and Prevention, the Center for a Tobacco-Free Finger Lakes, and the New York State Quitline and Quitsite. It offers cessation treatment programs serving a twenty-seven-county area in upstate NY. The latter involves a strong collaboration with Environmental Medicine. The recent recruitment of AnaPaula Cupertino, PhD, has led to a new focus on smoking cessation research in Latinx populations.

Figure 70.5. Deborah Ossip

Another notable area of research has been long-term care. Under the leadership of Helena Temkin-Greener, PhD, MPH, who has had a long-standing involvement in the Centers for Medicare & Medicaid Services All-Inclusive Care for the Elderly (PACE) program, PHS has been a leader in research on assessments of nursing home quality. In 2012, Temkin-Greener, who served as

Figure 70.6. Helena Temkin-Greener

interim chair of PHS in 2012, received the state's first PCORI grant, entitled *Improving Palliative and End-of-Life Care in Nursing Homes.* With support from the NIH and Agency for Healthcare Research and Quality, and through collaborations with the Veteran's Administration, Temkin-Greener and other PHS faculty have built a comprehensive data infrastructure, PACE Data Analysis Center, pertaining to nursing home and assisted living residents, as well as community-living older adults, that has identified disparities in outcomes based on nursing home quality and resident characteristics (e.g. obesity, race) and conditions (dementia, suicidality). They also recently extended their work to include the impact of COVID-19 on nursing home residents.

A great example of the collaborative nature of PHS has been in the field of maternal child health. PHS involvement began in the mid-2000s with the Seychelles Child Development Study, an NIH-funded research collaboration developed between the University of Rochester, the Ministries of Health and Education in the Seychelles, and the University of Ulster in Northern Ireland. This study, which is approaching its fortieth year, has been examining the effects of pre- and postnatal mercury exposure and factors on child development in the Republic of Seychelles and the factors, such as diet, that may modulate these effects. Van Wijngaarden currently leads the study, which, in addition to PHS, involves investigators from Audiology, Biostatistics, Dentistry, Environmental Medicine, Medicine, Neurology, and Pediatrics.

Figure 70.7. Elaine Hill

Elaine Hill, PhD, Dean's Professor of PHS, was recruited from Cornell University in 2014. The first microeconomist in PHS, her research interests align with the Environmental Health Sciences Center, and focus on health and environmental economics, particularly as they relate to vulnerable populations, such as pregnant women, children, rural populations, and older adults. Hill's team has studied the impacts of fracking on childhood asthma, drinking water contamination, and mortality. Hill plays a key role in the WCI National Community Oncology Research Program, where she focuses on drug shortages in oncology care. She also has been involved in URMC efforts regarding opioids, focusing on the use of opioids during pregnancy and how the COVID-19 pandemic exacerbated the opioid crisis.

Since 2000, PHS faculty members have overseen data management for the NY State-funded Finger Lakes Region's Perinatal Programs (a collaboration with Ob/Gyn and Neonatology), working with all regional hospitals to assure compliance with and promote utilization of NY State's electronic birth registry data. Maternal child health work encompasses issues such as father engagement (Paula Amina Alio, PhD), postpartum weight gain

(Diana Fernandez, MD, MPH, PhD), and lactation and breastfeeding (Ann Dozier). David Rich, ScD, MPH, has demonstrated the contribution of air pollution to poor birth outcomes in Beijing, China, and Todd A. Jusko, PhD, utilizing cohorts in Slovakia and elsewhere, has demonstrated the impact of Per- and polyfluoroalkyl substances (PFAS) exposure on immune and neurodevelopment.

Part IV

EXTENDING THE BIOPSYCHOSOCIAL MODEL

The biopsychosocial model has been a defining feature of medical education at SMD for fifty years. The past twenty years have been characterized by an attempt to move this concept forward to encompass the entire URMC community to create an inclusive and welcoming environment. This includes identifying Medical Center-wide values (iCARE), creating a new academic department of Health Humanities and Bioethics dedicated to expanding the scope and reach of the biopsychosocial model through research and new educational offerings, establishing the Eastman Performing Arts Medicine Program, building a robust infrastructure to focus on engagement and enrichment, and creating a new Office of Wellbeing.

Chapter 71

DEPARTMENT OF HEALTH HUMANITIES AND BIOETHICS

The department of Health Humanities and Bioethics is the newest SMD department, having been established in 2021. Medical humanities developed as an academic discipline in the early 1970s to integrate non-science perspectives into medical training. At the time, medical educators were concerned about the erosion of the doctor–patient relationship, the effects of rising technologies, changes in health care delivery leading to a decrease in time with patients, and a de-emphasis on interpersonal bedside skills in the education of doctors.

SMD was among the first schools to create a formal division of Medical Humanities. Founded in 1984 by Dean Robert Joynt and Jules Cohen, MD, SAD for Medical Education, its goal was to solidify the presence of the humanities in the curriculum by applying the materials and methods of the humanities and arts to medicine and doctoring. Kathryn Montgomery, a PhD in English literature and author of a landmark book on the role of stories in medicine, *Doctor's Stories: The Narrative Structure of Medical Knowledge*, was the division's first director. A required *Medicine and Society* course was taught by division faculty and by humanities scholars and clinicians throughout the University. Jane Greenlaw, RN, JD, became the division's director in 1988 and expanded its mission to include the education of medical students, residents, and faculty; scholarship; and a clinical bioethics consultation service, directed initially by a philosopher, Jeffrey Spike, PhD, and subsequently by nephrologist Richard A. Demme, MD. Greenlaw also established a collaboration with research ethics, inviting Gary L. Chadwick, PharmD, MPH, the head of the University of Rochester Research Subjects Review Board, to join the division and collaborate with members of the ethics team.

In 1998, as part of SMD's new Double Helix Curriculum, the division's offerings were expanded to include a variety of eight-week courses during the first two years and electives in medical history, literature, gender, disability, social justice, reproductive justice, clinical ethics, complementary medicine, and independent creative and research projects during the final two years. Bioethics also expanded into undergraduate education and residency

Figure 71.1. Jane Greenlaw (third from left) is joined by current and former leaders in Health and Humanities.

teaching. Pathway Programs were developed in Deaf Health, Culture and Language; Latino Health, Culture, and Language; Medical Humanities and Arts; and Bioethics.

Following Greenlaw's retirement in 2012, Stephanie Brown Clark, an MD with a PhD in medical history and English literature, became the division director. Bernard L. Sussman, MD, and Marjorie Shaw, a JD, PhD (ethics education), who currently directs the Clinical Bioethics Program, developed undergraduate bioethics education in SMD and clinical bioethics education and service at SMH. Under Stephanie Brown Clark's leadership, a new Interdisciplinary MS in medical humanities was initiated. Courses also were made available to undergraduate seniors from the College of Arts, Sciences, and Engineering.

Figure 71.2. Stephanie Brown Clark

During the last quarter-century, the division has spearheaded several important initiatives. A Year Out Fellowship in medical humanities was created in partnership with the Medical Student Enrichment Program in 2001. In 2006, a new literary arts journal, *Turtlequill*, was developed under the auspices of the division. Renamed *Murmur* in 2015, the journal continues to publish works by medical students, graduate students, residents, fellows, faculty, and staff across the Medical Center.

In 2002, Brown Clark partnered with Susan Dodge-Peters Daiss, MA, MDiv, of the Memorial Art Gallery to develop a protocol using the visual arts to enhance skills of observation for medical students and other health care practitioners. They developed the "Five Question Protocol," which deconstructs the diagnostic process into essential steps and articulates a series of premises that reflect sound clinical practice: 1) Observation before interpretation; 2) Communication depends on accurate verbal descriptions; 3) Associations influence interpretations; 4) Inquiry leads to questions. Questions lead to information; and 5) Teams are wiser together. This highly popular program now serves more than 500 learners per year from the SON, SMD residency and fellowship programs, faculty, and staff at URMC, as well as other health care schools in Rochester.

In 2020, in response to the recommendation of an *ad hoc* committee comprising faculty from the Medical Center and River Campus, Dean Taubman established the Health Humanities and Bioethics (HHBE) department, with Brown Clark serving as acting chair. The rationale for creating the department was the need to re-envision the biopsychosocial approach in light of the many medical, technological, and social changes. This new vision would give greater attention to the community, cultural, societal, and environmental levels; integrate person-centered relationships with science and technologies beyond the care of patients and families; and extend the biopsychosocial values of care to include all members of the medical center community. As a department, HHBE would have greater involvement in system-wide strategic planning and would be charged with developing robust research and scholarship programs. Lainie Friedman Ross, MD, PhD, a pediatrician, philosopher, and one of the nation's leading bioethicists, was recruited in 2023 to be founding chair of HHBE and the director of the Paul M. Schyve, MD, Center for Bioethics (see below).

Figure 71.3. Lainie Ross

Ross received her MD from the University of Pennsylvania and her PhD in philosophy from Yale University, and then trained in pediatrics at the Children's Hospital of Philadelphia and the Morgan Stanley Children's Hospital of New York-Presbyterian. Prior to joining the University of Rochester, Ross spent twenty-eight years at the University of Chicago, where she was the Carolyn and Matthew Bucksbaum professor of Clinical Ethics, co-director of the Institute for Translational Medicine, and associate director of the MacLean Center for Clinical Medical Ethics. She is a Hastings Center Fellow, John Simon Guggenheim Memorial Foundation Fellow, and was elected to the National Academy of Medicine in 2023. Ross's research portfolio addresses ethical and policy issues in organ and tissue transplantation, pediatrics, genetics, research ethics, and health care disparities. Ross has published five single-authored or two-person-authored books and over 400 articles in the peer-reviewed literature, and has lectured nationally and internationally in four separate areas of scholarship.

HHBE currently contains thirteen primary faculty (seven of whom have been recruited since Ross's arrival), two senior associates, thirteen secondary faculty, and four emeritus faculty. One of the main goals of the new department is to embed health humanities and ethics across the University by: collaborating with other programs to conduct funded research; promoting summer research opportunities for students in SMD and in the College; developing new ethics pedagogical programs and expanding the master's program to more formally include ethics; and providing more ethics rounds in various units across SMH and GCH.

The Paul M. Schyve, MD, Center for Bioethics

Figure 71.4. Paul Schyve

Paul M. Schyve, MD, is a Rochester native who received his BA and MD from the University of Rochester, then remained for his residency in Psychiatry. Schyve credits his education at the University as playing an important formative role in his professional career and ascribes his interest in bioethics as being sparked by the teachings of John Romano. He became increasingly interested in the ethics of health care in 1986, when he joined The Joint Commission on the Accreditation of Healthcare Organizations, where he developed accreditation standards related to clinical, research, and organizational ethics, and became senior advisor for health care improvement before his retirement in 2016. In 2014, Schyve made a visionary gift to endow a new center for bioethics at the University, thus providing enduring support to the study and practice of bioethics in clinical care, the health delivery system, and life sciences research. The Schyve Center was originally run as a stand-alone center led by Timothy E. Quill, MD, the chief of Palliative Care. Subsequently, Quill was followed by Linda Chaudron, MD, SAD and URMC VP for Inclusion and Culture, and then Shaw, when it was incorporated into the new HHBE.

The Schyve Center has three central aims: advance bioethical training, education, and research; help professionals, patients, and families think through ethically complicated decisions they face; and enhance community understanding of bioethical issues. Among its achievements have been: 1) an annual Paul M. Schyve, MD, ethics conference at the University; 2) a partnership with the University of Rochester Humanities Center that explores a single health humanities theme from a multidisciplinary and interdisciplinary perspective; 3) a health care ethics leadership consortium that convenes ethics leadership from health care institutions across the region to understand the local bioethics consultation service environment, establish regional best bioethics practices, and support national efforts to elevate bioethics practice; and 4) the Reel Mind Film Festival, a collaboration with Psychiatry, that screens and discusses documentary films around the theme of recovery from mental illness.

HHBE Clinical Bioethics Programs

The SMH Ethics Consult Service, which currently has seven fellowship-trained and health care ethics-certified consultants and two fellows, assists patients, family members, and all members of the health care team to identify, analyze, and resolve ethical dilemmas and questions. Consultants discuss their cases with an interdisciplinary ethics team from Philosophy, Medicine, Chaplaincy, Nursing, and Social Work. Ethics consultants also provide regular educational rounds across the institution. In 2023, the service responded to approximately 270 consultations in inpatient and outpatient settings.

The Ethics Liaison program was initially created as the Nurses Liaison Program by Marianne Chiafery, DNP, as her doctoral capstone project in 2021. It is a nine-month educational program originally developed to help bedside nurses develop the knowledge and skills necessary to address moral distress, including emotional distress, work dissatisfaction, poor patient outcomes, and nurse turnover. The program, now directed by Michele Baker, DNP, RN, CNI, and Laine DiNoto, NP, two graduates of the Ethics Liaison program, expanded in 2023 to include APPs and other care providers. Two leadership structures were also created to support ethical competence through education, infrastructure, and policy development: a Professional Nursing Council Ethics Sub-council and an APP ethics officer.

HHBE Educational and Research Programs

HHBE oversees curricular threads in bioethics and in health humanities that are embedded throughout the four years of medical school. These threads emphasize the importance of the biopsychosocial approach to health, engage students in understanding their own personal values, aid in developing skills in critical reflection, and provide students with the opportunity to reflect on the relationships between the ethical and professional obligations of the medical profession and on their professional identity formation. The department offers a unified HHBE pathway that provides students with extra educational seminars, reflective assignments, and the opportunity to conduct summer research with faculty mentors in the department. All pathway students develop creative and scholarly projects that they can present at a symposium.

The department supports a MS in health humanities and bioethics for students in medicine, nursing, and other health care disciplines, as well as students in humanities and social sciences. The program includes experiential sessions at the Memorial Art Gallery and classroom discussions emphasizing key philosophical, historical, clinical, and cultural issues in Western medicine around "looking;" a research course directed towards materials and methods of the humanities, and theoretical and empirical bioethics; supervised independent study; and various electives in health humanities and bioethics allowing for a concentration in "Clinical and Translational Bioethics" or "Medicine, History and Culture."

The Advanced Certificate in clinical bioethics, established in 2024, is a multidisciplinary graduate credential administered by HHBE that prepares students to identify, analyze, and discuss the ethical considerations and/or conflicts that arise in the context of health care decision-making. The National Collaborative on Humanities and Ethics in Dentistry is a partnership between HHBE and EIOH, the University of Colorado's Center for Bioethics and Humanities and School of Dental Medicine, and the Center for Humanities and Ethics at the McGovern Medical School in Texas. Its goal is to understand the forces that led to the divide between dental and medical education, and to explore the potential of moving towards the reintegration of oral health and general medical care.

In 1934, George Washington Corner, MD, the first professor of anatomy at SMD, organized a medical history club to provide opportunities to attend lectures and enjoy lively discussions on topics in medical history given by speakers from all SMD departments and knowledgeable members of the community. The George Washington Corner Society for the History of Medicine, or "The Corner Society," is one of the oldest uninterrupted medical history clubs in the country and continues the tradition of bringing together stimulating speakers and groups of physicians, historians, students, and others with an interest in the history of medicine. A collaboration between the HHBE and the University's History department, the Society sponsors lectures at the Rochester Academy of Medicine, many of which are available online.

One of the goals of HHBE is to promote interdisciplinary scholarship and collaborative grant applications throughout the University, and to lead the way in designing and implementing ethically sound clinical and translational research. HHBE has already established a variety of research collaborations at the University and recruited five new faculty who will markedly enhance these efforts. HHBE is well positioned to become a department that is nationally recognized for its engagement and contributions to the advancement of ethical, just, and humanistic health care, and for education and training in health humanities and bioethics.

Chapter 72

ENGAGEMENT AND ENRICHMENT

Diversity and inclusion have been important themes at URMC over the past twenty-five years. In 2006, Dean Guzick named Vivian Lewis, MD, as the inaugural associate dean for Faculty Development for Women and Diversity. Lewis received her MD from Columbia University, did a residency in Ob/Gyn at the Mount Sinai Hospital, NY, and a reproductive endocrinology fellowship at UCSF. Prior to coming to Rochester, she was on the faculty of the University of Illinois at Chicago, where she focused on reproductive endocrinology and ran a multidisciplinary menopause clinic. At URMC, she rose to the rank of professor of Ob/Gyn, the only female African American full professor at the University from 2008–19. During Lewis's term, the associate dean position was part-time, and its focus was to increase the diversity of the SMD faculty by developing strategies aimed at recruitment, development, and retention.

Figure 72.1.
Vivian Lewis

In 2011, Lewis was appointed deputy to the University president and vice provost for Faculty Development and Diversity. Dean Taubman took the opportunity to restructure the SMD position, changing to SAD for Diversity, and expanding the responsibilities to encompass medical students, residents, graduate students, fellows, and postdoctoral fellows, in addition to faculty. This enabled SMD to take a more longitudinal approach, recognizing that by developing a more diverse population of students, residents, fellows, and postdoctoral fellows, it would provide a pipeline for creating a faculty that would better reflect the diversity of the patient population.

Linda H. Chaudron, MD (Psychiatry), was appointed as the inaugural SAD for Diversity. Chaudron received her MD from the University of Rochester and completed a residency in Psychiatry and a fellowship in Women's Health at the University of Wisconsin at Madison. Chaudron, whose research focused on postpartum and perinatal depression in women, had served as associate

Figure 72.2.
Linda Chaudron

chair of Psychiatry for clinical services and was also a member of Vivian Lewis's advisory committee. In 2015, Chaudron's position was further expanded with the creation of the URMC Office for Inclusion and Culture Development. This office was unique among academic medical centers, taking advantage of the integrated nature of URMC to allow Chaudron, as VP for Inclusion and Culture Development, to integrate all culture and diversity efforts at URMC, not just at SMD.

As SAD, Chaudron developed programs aimed at increasing support for women and underrepresented groups in academic medicine, including peer mentoring initiatives, promoting participation in national leadership programs such as ELAM (see below), and establishing the Junior Women Research Faculty Group. Chaudron initiated the Tana Grady-Weliky Lecture on Women and Diversity in Medicine, named in memory of the former SAD for education and focused on inclusion in academic medicine. She contributed to national diversity and health equity efforts, including work aligned with the AAMC's Community Health and Health Equity initiative. Her contributions were recognized with several honors, including the University of Rochester's Susan B. Anthony Lifetime Achievement Award and designation as a Distinguished Fellow of the American Psychiatric Association.

Figure 72.3. Adrienne Morgan

In July 2020, Adrienne Morgan, PhD, succeeded Chaudron as SAD and VP for Equity and Inclusion. Morgan received a master's degree in Cross-Disciplinary Professional Studies from RIT and a PhD in Higher Education from the Warner School of Education and Human Development. Her dissertation examined the lived experiences of US-born Black males attending predominantly white medical schools. For nearly twenty years, Morgan worked in SMD and served as director of the Center for Advocacy, Community Health, Education, and Diversity, where she strove to improve the recruitment and retention of students underrepresented in medicine by establishing affinity groups, pipeline programs, and visiting clerkships. She also linked SMD students to community engagement opportunities, establishing programs like the University of Rochester Well Medical Student-run Free Clinic, Street Outreach, and Rochester Young Scientist Club. In 2017, she was appointed assistant dean for Medical Education Diversity and Inclusion at SMD. Two years later, she was also appointed as associate VP in the University's Office of Equity and Inclusion. She currently serves as the Richard Feldman VP for Engagement and Enrichment, overseeing activities for the entire University.

As the COVID-19 pandemic unfolded, it became clear that Black and Latinx persons experienced significantly higher hospitalization and death rates than white persons, providing a tragic reminder of the health disparities borne for centuries by people of color. This followed closely on the heels of the "Black Lives Matter" movement, which spawned protests across the country in response to several high-profile killings. In response, in June 2020, CEO Mark Taubman convened an *ad hoc* committee, led by Morgan, to develop a comprehensive equity and anti-racism plan for URMC. For four months, the committee worked with students, residents, trainees, faculty members, and staff across the Medical Center, along with supportive groups and individuals from the Greater Rochester community, to gain their perspectives and ideas. The outcome of this collaborative effort was an Equity and Anti-Racism Action Plan (EARAP) designed to make every person in the organization feel welcome and supported.

The five-year plan had a series of goals that included detailed metrics and milestones that would be shared widely at the University and with community leaders: 1) Develop and sustain an infrastructure to support equity, diversity, and inclusion; 2) Enhance recruitment, retention, and promotion of diverse faculty, staff, and learners, including Black, Indigenous and People Of Color (BIPOC) and other underrepresented constituencies; 3) Cultivate a fair and just climate, culture, and community; 4) Enhance URMC's public presence through an equity, diversity, inclusion lens; 5) Engage and partner with the community to achieve racial justice by promoting equity in health and wellbeing. Each goal was divided into a series of objectives and identified personnel who were accountable for achieving them.

Since the adoption of the EARAP, Morgan and the multidisciplinary leadership team, bolstered by community input, have worked steadily to operationalize its goals and principles across the institution. Nearly five years into implementation, URMC has achieved some important milestones in advancing equity, diversity, and inclusion, while also confronting persistent challenges that underscore the ongoing nature of this work. Among these achievements have been the following:

Infrastructure and Policy Reform. URMC has created institutional mechanisms to support equity, including anti-racism training for senior leaders, a faculty professionalism committee, and restorative practices initiatives. Policies have been systematically reviewed and are being revised to ensure greater clarity, fairness, and accountability.

Education and Training. Anti-racism, unconscious bias, and restorative justice education has reached hundreds of faculty and staff members. Efforts to expand "Train-the-Trainer" models and certification for diversity officers are still in development.

Recruitment, Retention, and Advancement. Recruitment toolkits, updated job descriptions, and affinity networks have improved the hiring and support of BIPOC faculty, staff, and learners. Although career development programs and financial support initiatives have expanded, funding sustainability and internal leadership development remain important issues.

Campus Climate and Visibility. URMC has taken visible steps to foster a more inclusive culture, such as celebrating diverse cultural events, launching climate surveys, and curating spaces that reflect its diversity values. Public Safety leadership is more accountable and representative.

Community Engagement & Health Equity. Partnerships with local agencies, enhanced data systems, and targeted CME programs have positioned URMC as a regional leader in health equity, as has the development of the Office of Health Equity Research.

Office of Health Equity Research

Goal five of EARAP is to promote health equity research at the University of Rochester. In 2022, following a national search, Edith M. Williams, PhD, was recruited from the Medical University of South Carolina (MUSC) to be founding director of the Office of Health Equity Research (OHER) and Dean's Professor in Public Health Sciences and Medicine (Allergy, Immunology, and Rheumatology). The mission of the office is to create a learning health system, integrating community-engaged research to inform and improve equitable care. The office serves as a central resource to help all URMC departments develop health equity research projects, and encourage them to view research through a health equity lens.

Figure 72.4.
Edith Williams

OHER has contributed to the EARAP by building transdisciplinary research collaborations and establishing health equity research priorities within collaborative teams. A health equity research core investigator network and a searchable investigator database have been created; investigators have increased capacity to conduct health equity research and generate scholarship by providing technical support and pilot funding; and a health equity research course has been developed. Other activities of OHER include integrating health equity research with community needs and clinical practice by forming a Health Equity Youth Advisors board and advising departments in handling of newly available social determinants of health data in eRecord.

A Rochester native, Williams received her PhD in Epidemiology and Community Health at SUNY Buffalo, where she focused on systemic lupus erythematosus, an autoimmune disease that disproportionately impacts Black women. In South Carolina, she continued to expand her nationally recognized work on lupus and developed a pipeline program for students from historically Black colleges and universities to provide them with a path into MUSC's Public Health program. In 2023, Williams was named director of URMC's Center for Community Health & Prevention (CCHP), succeeding Nancy Bennett, MD, who founded the CCHP in 2006 (chapter 16). To help facilitate its mission, the OHER, which originated as part of the CTSI, was moved into the CCHP.

OHER is a key element in a broader infrastructure designed to promote health equity. This includes an interdisciplinary Health Equity Steering Committee, which sets overall strategy and direction, and conducts advocacy and engagement with community partners; an operational Health Equity Provider Task Force, which implements operational changes that improve access and cultural sensitivity; and a Health Equity Education Task Force. Using the Epic Health Disparities dashboard, clinicians and scientists capture accurate, de-identified, mineable, demographic, and social determinants data to reveal gaps in care and help inform specific priorities. In 2021, the URMC Board established a Health Equity Committee to provide a community touchstone for administrative and clinical leaders as they develop new ideas and set priorities for health equity. Like other board committees, it also serves to hold leadership accountable for progress in achieving the objectives of goal five of the EARAP.

Executive Leadership in Academic Medicine

Since its inception in 1995, the Hedwig van Ameringen Executive Leadership in Academic Medicine (ELAM) program, run by the Drexel University College of Medicine, has been one of the nation's most prestigious programs preparing qualified women leaders in academic medicine, dentistry, public health, and pharmacy on the national scale. The rigorous and highly selective one-year fellowship provides comprehensive coaching, networking, and mentoring focused on leadership development for women identified as having significant potential to assume executive leadership roles at academic health centers. As part of the program, fellows focus on a project that they wish to develop within their home institution. In its thirtieth year in 2025, the program has more than 1,600 alumni in high-level leadership positions (provosts, deans, chief officers, chairs, etc.) at 300 health institutions around the country. A recent expansion has been the Executive Leadership in Health Care (ELH) program, designed specifically for women looking to be leaders in health administration, as opposed to academia. ELAM has been an important component of the URMC diversity efforts for the past twenty years. Table 72.1 lists the URMC ELAM fellows and their projects.

Table 72.1

Year	Fellow	Role at Time	Project
2003–4	Vivian Lewis, MD	Professor of Obstetrics and Gynecology	Develop a sustainable research mentoring course at URMC
2004–5	Diane Hartmann, MD	SAD for Graduate Medical Education	Analysis of the Cost of Graduate Medical Education at URMC
2009–10	Susan Hyman, MD	Professor of Pediatrics	Feasibility of an Intellectual and Developmental Disabilities Research Center in Rochester
2010–11	Susan McDaniel, PhD	Associate Chair, Family Medicine	Physician Communication Coaching Pilot
2012–13	Yuhchyau Chen, MD, PhD	Chair, Radiation Oncology	Feasibility of Proton Therapy at URMC
2014–15	Linda Chaudron, MD	SAD for Diversity	Creating a URMC Office for Diversity and Inclusion
2015–16	Adrienne Bonham, MD	Associate Professor of Obstetrics and Gynecology	Integrated Practice Center for Pelvic Pain
2016–17	Annette Medina-Walpole, MD	Chief, Division of Geriatrics (department of Medicine)	Creation of the University of Rochester Aging Institute
2017–18	Karen Mustian, PhD, MPH	Co-Director, NCI Community Oncology Research Program	Strategic Plan for NCI Cancer Center Designation
2018–19	Antonia Kolokythas, DDS	Chair, Oral and Maxillofacial Surgery	Develop executive MBA Track During Residency
2019–20	B. Paige Lawrence, PhD	Chair, Environmental Medicine	Develop Peer-to-Peer Professionalism Program
2020–1	Colleen Fogarty, MD	Chair, Family Medicine	Anti-Racism Training in Academic Medicine
2021–2	Jennifer Harvey, MD	Chair, Imaging Sciences	Leadership Training Curriculum for Residents
2022–3	Flavia Nobay, MD	Associate Dean for Student Affairs	Longitudinal Cohort Program for Minoritized Students
2024–5	Jin Xiao, DDS	Associate Professor, Eastman Institute of Oral Health	[Project not yet available]
2025–6	Edith Williams, PhD	Professor, Public Health Sciences	[To be determined]

Chapter 73

PATIENT AND FAMILY CENTERED CARE AND THE ICARE VALUES

As noted above, a defining characteristic of the past twenty-five years has been the extension of the biopsychosocial model from a philosophy on how one approaches patient care taught chiefly to medical students to one that inculcated and operationalized a set of values for the whole institution. Leading the charge has been Jackie Beckerman, MPH.

In 2006, Beckerman, who received her MPH from the University of Rochester and has been at URMC since 1982, was made director of Patient Experience and asked to develop a strategy to improve patient satisfaction at URMC. She realized the need for a culture that engaged all employees, not just patients. At the time, the organization did not have defined values, so Beckerman convened a group that identified five guiding principles—Integrity, Compassion, Accountability, Respect, and Excellence—that would become known as the ICARE values. Initially her work centered on service training, patient satisfaction metrics, and the establishment of LEARN (Listen, Empathize, Apologize, Recover, Nurture), a service recovery model that remains a cornerstone of URMC practice. Momentum accelerated dramatically when CEO Brad Berk returned from his spinal cord injury with a deep commitment to building a culture grounded in Patient and Family Centered Care (PFCC) that was rooted in his own experience. PFCC and ICARE were launched together in 2011, signaling that patient- and family-centeredness was anchored in shared institutional values.

Figure 73.1. Jackie Beckerman

To ensure that PFCC received top priority, Berk placed the program under the auspices of Steve Goldstein, CEO of SMH and HH. Goldstein and Beckerman, who was named director of PFCC, built an extensive leadership structure spanning UR Medicine, with clear goals and metrics. To help assure faculty engagement, Jean Joseph, MD (Urology), was named medical director of PFCC. Joseph and Beckerman involved providers in ongoing dialogue that generated several lasting programs. Susan McDaniel, PhD, launched a provider coaching program to strengthen communication and help in building collegial relationships. Michael Privitera, MD, launched an early wellness initiative in response to concerns regarding provider burnout.

Beckerman and colleagues, with the help of consultants from Brand Integrity, spent over eighteen months engaging faculty and staff to articulate the non-negotiable behaviors that exemplified ICARE. Responses were remarkably consistent across the institution, leading to the adoption of a set of principles and behaviors for all URMC members, referred to as the *ICARE Commitment.* Acting on these principles, URMC began to experience tangible improvements: for example, as measured by a national survey, inpatient satisfaction rose steadily and remained strong for seven consecutive years.

A grassroots ICARE Guiding Coalition emerged, representing diverse departments across the institution. One of its earliest insights was the need for recognition programs that reinforced ICARE behaviors and kept values visible. The initial program, Strong Stars, recognized employees whose actions exemplified ICARE values. Built on appreciative inquiry, Strong Stars evolved into ICARE Stars, and eventually into UR Stars, now a university-wide recognition system. Each "star" nomination detailed the specific behavior and its impact, allowing others to learn from and be inspired by the action. At its peak, over 33,000 stars were awarded, with thirty-five percent nominated by patients and families. In 2013, the Show UR Stars program launched, awarding bronze, silver, and gold badges based on recognition levels. These badges, proudly displayed behind ID cards, became true "badges of honor." Monthly ICARE luncheons were also initiated, where as many as 150 recipients and their supervisors could share stories on how ICARE came alive in daily practice.

Because ICARE was introduced together with PFCC, it was seen primarily as a clinical initiative. With the support of CEO Mark Taubman, Beckerman established an ICARE Steering Committee consisting of clinicians, researchers, and educators throughout URMC to broaden ICARE's reach and revise the ICARE Commitment. In 2018, the committee identified the need to add inclusion as a sixth ICARE value, which had previously been embedded within Respect. By 2019, a refreshed IICARE Commitment and behaviors were introduced.

Another key element of PFCC and IICARE initiatives was the establishment of Patient and Family Advisory Councils (PFACs) designed to give patients and families a structured role in shaping care and in helping URMC uphold its core values. To ensure that a broad spectrum of patients and families were served, Beckerman and her team brought together groups with shared lived experiences, allowing for more focused dialogue. Currently, more than 100 Patient and Family Advisors participate across the PFAC network, representing most clinical specialties. Advisors also bring perspectives from communities including those who are deaf and hard of hearing, Black and African American, Latinx, LGBTQ+, and other communities. They ensure that everyone is represented and welcomed, and provide invaluable insights that shape improvements and enhance care. URMC's PFAC model has drawn regional and national attention, with invitations to present at the *New England Journal of Medicine Catalyst,* the Hospital Association of NY State, Press Ganey, and the Institute for Patient- and Family-Centered Care.

The unprecedented challenges of the COVID-19 pandemic led to national declines in patient experience scores. At URMC, the pandemic disrupted the culture that had been so carefully built, making experiences harder for patients, families, and staff alike. As URMC emerges from this era, it has become clear that the next chapter must balance patient- and family-centeredness with the wellbeing of staff and faculty. This challenge has been embraced by CEO David Linehan as ICARE Forward, a new initiative built on the vision "One Team, One Purpose" that celebrates the uniqueness of every individual and aims to ensure that each person feels respected, included, and valued.

Chapter 74

OFFICE OF WELLBEING

The remarkable growth within health care institutions over the past twenty-five years has been accompanied by increasing challenges related to feelings of burnout and healthy work–life balance. These issues were driven by increasing patient volumes in a setting of workforce shortages, increasing focus on quality and safety, and by substantial changes in reporting and documentation, exacerbated by the adoption of electronic medical records. Although issues related to wellness and burnout affect everyone involved in health care, the initial focus was on physicians, whose levels of burnout were reportedly close to fifty percent.

In 2015, Michael R. Privitera, MD, initiated the Medical Faculty and Wellness Program under the aegis of URMFG. Privitera, who had joined the Psychiatry faculty after completing his residency in psychiatry at URMC, had gained national recognition for his work on workplace violence, which culminated in *Workplace Violence in Mental and General Healthcare Settings* (edited by Michael Privitera; Jones & Bartlett Learning, 2010). The book won the 2012 Manford Guttmacher Award, given by the American Academy of Psychiatry and the Law.

Figure 74.1.
Michael Privitera

To address health system drivers of clinician burnout, Privitera convened a Wellness Strategic Plan Work Group (WSPWG) with representatives from most academic/clinical departments, advanced practice, clinical psychology, and pharmacy. The WSPWG was active in advancing measures to improve provider and employee engagement, mitigating occupational stressors, and understanding the needs of a diverse workforce. In 2018, URMC began formal assessment of wellbeing for clinicians using the Wellbeing Index (WBI), a nine-question (seven for residents and fellows) survey developed by the Mayo Clinic that assesses burnout and emotional distress. During the COVID-19 pandemic, the wellbeing program pivoted to focus on acute support of all health care team members, expanding access to critical incident support and providing dissemination of tools, strategies, and supportive messaging that could be adapted at the local level. In 2022, under the leadership of Jessica C. Shand, MD, MHS, a former resident in pediatrics at URMC and a faculty member in Pediatrics, WSPWG grew to include representatives from training programs, nursing practice, APPs, informatics, and quality/safety, and the WBI was expanded to non-clinical faculty, APPs, nurses, and pharmacy professionals.

Figure 74.2. Jessica Shand

In developing strategies to address wellness, the WSPWG was aided by several established programs at the University. The Employee Wellness Program was established by the SON in 2012 and includes a personal health assessment that uses biometric values and real-time coaching, an individualized wellness portal, and condition and lifestyle management. Well-U is a comprehensive program within the Office of Human Resources that incorporates physiological testing with a broad spectrum of mental health, exercise, lifestyle, dietary, and stress management services. These services come in the form of health screenings, individual and group coaching, and classes to manage conditions such as high cholesterol, aid in weight loss, reduce stress, and other needs. The Employee Assistance Program provides confidential evaluation, intervention, and treatments to help employees deal with challenging situations at home or at work. Behavioral Health Partners is a mental health resource for University of Rochester employees, non-Medicare eligible retirees, and adult dependents enrolled in a University Health Care Plan. Services include a range of therapies for mental health concerns such as anxiety, stress, and depression.

Figure 74.3. Craig Rooney

System-wide stresses on wellness were further fueled by the COVID-19 pandemic and the subsequent staff shortages, particularly within nursing. As individual wellness programs began to develop throughout the Medical Center, URMC administration established a new position of chief wellness officer (CWO), with oversight of all wellness initiatives throughout URMC. In 2024, S. Craig Rooney, PhD, who had served as director of psychological services and wellbeing at the University of Missouri's School of Medicine, was recruited to serve as URMC VP and inaugural CWO. Rooney earned his PhD in counseling psychology from the University of Missouri-Columbia and completed an internship in psychology at the University of Utah Counseling Center in Salt Lake City. Prior to joining URMC, Rooney developed a reputation for his work on health care worker wellbeing and related topics. In recognition of her efforts on behalf of wellness at URMC, Shand joined Rooney as the associate CWO.

Upon arrival, Rooney established the new Office of Wellbeing (OWB), using "wellbeing," rather than "wellness," to clarify the OWB's focus on organizational drivers of occupational distress rather than on individual wellness, and to highlight the concept of institutional accountability. An OWB website shares all wellbeing and wellness resources in one location and helps communicate URMC's commitment to wellbeing. The Wellbeing Strategic Plan Work Group meets monthly to review best practices in health care workplace wellbeing, interpret institutional metrics (e.g. WBI, engagement surveys), and to guide and implement wellbeing priorities and interventions. In January 2025, the office welcomed its inaugural cohort of thirteen "Wellbeing Fellows," whose responsibility is to create executive innovative projects and to take the lead in socializing wellbeing efforts throughout the institution. The fellows include clinical faculty, pharmacy, clinical nursing, APPs, nurse education, and chaplaincy. A pilot "wellbeing mini grant" program was established to provide funds for innovative projects to enhance occupational fulfillment, as well as quick-fix ideas that improve workplace and individual wellbeing. The first round of mini grants engendered approximately 120 applications.

The OWB partnered with the CMO and Medical Staff services to change credentialing questions to communicate to providers that receiving mental health services would not negatively impact the credentialing process. This garnered recognition as a Wellbeing First Champion from the Dr. Lorna Breen Heroes' Foundation, whose mission is to reduce the burnout of health care professionals and safeguard their wellbeing and job satisfaction. OWB efforts were further recognized by the National Academy of Medicine, who recently designated URMC as a Change Maker for its "commitment to institutionalizing wellbeing as a long-term value." The OWB looks to capitalize on its first-year programs to identify scalable wellbeing initiatives and drive wellbeing engagement, create a data intelligence strategy to measure wellbeing metrics that matter most, and organize a framework for efficiently ameliorating local wellbeing drivers of occupational distress.

Chapter 75

EASTMAN PERFORMING ARTS MEDICINE

Another example of the extension of the arts and humanities into the Medical Center and into patient care has been the Eastman Performing Arts Medicine (EPAM) program. As one of the few universities to house both a premier music school and medical center, the University of Rochester was uniquely positioned to develop a coordinated program that would lead the field of arts in health care. EPAM grew out of a series of meetings involving Jamal Rossi, the Joan and Martin Messinger Dean of the Eastman School of Music (ESM), and Donna Brink Fox, PhD, associate dean for academic and student affairs at ESM, Ralph Manchester, MD, a long-respected national leader in performing arts medicine, and SMD Dean Mark Taubman and URMFG CEO Michael Rotondo, both of whom had deep roots in music. It was launched publicly in 2019 and named as a University of Rochester Center in 2024.

Figure 75.1. Gaelen McCormick

Key to the success of the new program was the appointment of Gaelen McCormick as the inaugural program manager. McCormick received her Bachelor of Music from ESM, where she studied with James VanDemark, and her Master of Music from Carnegie Mellon University, where she studied with Jeffrey Turner. She was a member of the Rochester Philharmonic's double bass section from 1995–2017. After losing her hearing in 2017, she began a career shift into arts administration and nonprofit leadership. As a member of the Arts Leadership Program at ESM, she teaches career skills for use on- and off-stage. Her three-book series on double bass bow pedagogy, *Mastering the Bow,* is published by Carl Fischer. She has been, and continues to be, the driving force for the expansion of EPAM and its ultimate designation as a University Center.

EPAM's goal is to be an international leader in the field of arts in medicine, expand access to clinical services, drive high-impact discoveries in music and health through transdisciplinary research, and create vibrant, healthy musicians equipped with the skills to maintain their wellbeing as they enter the world stages. EPAM provides a framework for collaboration related to four pillars, discussed below.

Care for Injured Performing Artists

Figure 75.2. Ralph Manchester

Ralph Manchester received his MD from the University of Vermont College of Medicine. After completing his residency in internal medicine at URMC in 1983, he joined University Health Services, where he served as its leader for close to forty years, retiring in 2024. Manchester had a deep interest in treating injured musicians and developed one of the first performing arts medicine programs in the country. He was president of the national Performing Arts Medicine Association and for ten years served as the editor of the journal *Medical Problems of Performing Artists,* the first clinical medical journal devoted to the etiology, diagnosis, and treatment of medical and psychological disorders related to the performing arts.

EPAM provides expert clinical care to performing artists for chronic conditions, such as carpal tunnel syndrome, tendonitis and vocal fold nodules, as well as acute illnesses or sudden injuries. Built on the URMC Sports Medicine model, EPAM specialists work closely with performers to develop treatment plans, balancing the need for a quick return to performance schedules with the realities of tissue healing. The "injured musicians hotline" is maintained by the URMC call center and involves over twenty health care specialists. Specialist appointments are provided within forty-eight hours. EPAM has also developed a hearing conservation program, which educates students and faculty at ESM and Nazareth University about hearing damage and preventive measures, offers regular free hearing screenings, and is developing performing anxiety workshops to address performance-related psychological and behavioral issues.

Creative Arts Therapies

The music therapy program at GCH was established in 1997 and currently serves over 1,000 pediatric patients annually. The program, which was spearheaded by Olle J. Sahler, MD, of Pediatrics, uses music to complement the healing process by addressing physical, emotional, cognitive, or social needs of patients, while also improving their quality of life and sense of wellness. Services, provided by board-certified music therapists, are available on all inpatient units on weekdays. Music therapy is offered routinely on admission to patients on the hematology/oncology service or in the Child and Adolescent Eating Disorders program, but is available to all patients by physician referral. Most music therapy is provided one-on-one in the patient's room; parents and siblings are encouraged to participate when appropriate. The music therapy program has served as a clinical practicum and university-affiliated internship site for bachelors and master's level students in an accredited music therapy program.

Since 2017, the NICU offers music therapy services to premature infants and their families; the only such unit to do so in upstate NY. A dedicated NICU music therapist provides live music that is appropriate for premature infants' tolerance level based on evidence-based research. Live/Localized Singing employs the live human voice to promote growth and neurologic development, stabilize behavior states, deepen sleep, reduce physiological and behavioral lability, and provide auditory respite from noise-induced stress. Musical Entrainments involves live music paired with rocking, which is matched to the rhythm and speed of the infant's breathing and movements. Multimodal Neurologic Enhancement involves gradually layering auditory (singing/guitar), tactile (massage), visual (eye contact/lights), and vestibular (rocking) stimulation so that the infant tolerates the input without startling. Developmental Music Therapy promotes visual tracking, hand–eye coordination, and fine/gross motor skills using various small instruments and song books.

In recognition of the importance of peer socialization and the power of music to bring community together, EPAM also offer regularly scheduled music groups such as Wee Bee Jammin' for children up to six years old, School Age Rock for ages seven to twelve, and Teen Music Group for ages twelve and older. Activities include musical games, group songwriting, song discussion, group drumming, and music-based art creation. Beginning in 2022, EPAM began offering music therapy to adult populations. The department of Physical Medicine and Rehabilitation hired a full-time music therapist with neurologic music therapy training, and a part-time position was created to serve the Pluta Integrative Oncology Center, the eating disorders clinic, and the Strong Recovery outpatient program.

Arts Integration in Health Care Spaces

EPAM has enriched the health care environment by integrating music into virtually all health care spaces, including daily live music in the public spaces of SMH, WCI, and HH, as well as periodically at the Miner Library, the SON (Musical Mondays), and in Café 601. A major innovation has been the Music at the Bedside program, which uses iPads to provide live music in patient settings. By acting as facilitators, medical students get a patient experience that is non-clinical and helps them develop listening skills and establish an empathetic bedside manner. The program has also had a significant impact on ESM students, many of whom feel that the opportunity to give back to the community and make a difference in the lives of patients and staff through performing has given new meaning to their studies and their pursuit of a professional performance career. Through a partnership between the Sibley Music Library and the Information Systems division at URMC, recorded music was provided in all inpatient settings via the patient Get Well Network. In 2023, EPAM received a grant from the National Endowment for the Arts, enabling the sharing of live music to patients and staff via the hospital's TV system. The Memorial Art Gallery (MAG) has recently become involved. Using the Get Well Network, MAG artwork is combined with Eastman live recordings to create "slow viewing" experiences that are intended to be relaxing and soothing. A mindfulness program for clinical works, Mindful Art Pause, integrates MAG artworks, ESM recordings, poems, and ambient sounds built on the Mindfulness Based Stress Reduction framework.

Research on Music in Medicine

The unique resources at URMC, such as functional MRI, gait motion sensors, and neurologic research labs, provide an opportunity to drive discoveries at the heart of music and medicine. The Sound Health Working Group, established by Neurosciences Chair John Foxe and now led by O. J. Sahler, includes a diverse array of researchers and academics from the Del Monte Neuroscience Institute, the ESM, The Hochstein School, music therapy, Brain and Cognitive Sciences, and the University of Rochester Aging Institute. Among the research studies conducted to date are: 1) Music Therapy for Women Undergoing Radiation Therapy for Breast Cancer; 2) The Effect of Music Training on Concert Experiences for Hearing Impaired Persons; 3) Subjective and Objective Measures of Brass Playing Using Electromyography; 4) Interactive Group Drumming and "Chemo Brain;" 5) Targeting Autonomic Flexibility to Enhance Cognitive Training Outcomes in Older Adults with Mild Cognitive Impairment; and 6) The Effects of Live Lullaby Music on Intraventricular Hemorrhage in Low-Birth-Weight Infants on Mechanical Ventilation.

Recently, EPAM received a major donation to fund a faculty position dedicated to research in music and medicine; a national search is currently underway. To further integrate EPAM into the fabric of the Medical Center, plans are underway for it to reside within the department of Health Humanities and Bioethics.

Part V

MODERNIZING OPERATIONS TO SUPPORT GROWTH

Chapter 76

FINANCES

Over the past twenty-five years, the University of Rochester health care system has grown into the largest employer in upstate NY, with a workforce of more than 26,000 and a budget which has increased nearly tenfold to approximately $6.7 billion. This remarkable growth has been driven in part by the development of a financial model that maximizes leadership's ability to make strategic, mission-driven investments. As an integrated medical center, wholly owned by its university, URMC was ideally positioned to create a fully integrated financial model. First it was necessary to create a centralized financial infrastructure and strengthen and/or restructure the financial underpinnings of the hospital, medical faculty group (discussed later), and academic units. The Medical Center was fortunate in having the right financial leadership to help accomplish this.

Michael C. Goonan, CPA, received his BS in Accounting from St. John Fisher and then joined the Rochester office of the international public accounting firm, KPMG Peat Marwick, where he specialized in the health care field, with particular emphasis on financial management, reimbursement, prospective reporting, and third-party cost reporting. In 1984, he was recruited to SMH, one of his former clients, and in 1990 became its CFO.

Figure 76.1. Michael Goonan

Upon his arrival in Rochester in 1995, and as a first step in creating a system-wide integrated financial model, URMC CEO Jay Stein promoted Goonan to URMC VP and CFO, with oversight of the budgets of all of its entities. Over twenty years, Goonan worked with the CFOs of SMH and HH, SMD, URMFG, the SON, and EIOH to maximize finances, enabling URMC to greatly expand its clinical and research operations. Among others, this included the construction of three research buildings, GCH and WCI. He also played a key role in the affiliations with HH and FF Thompson. Notably, Goonan helped steer URMC through the difficult times of the 2008–9 "Great Recession." Since his retirement as URMC CFO, Goonan has worked tirelessly on behalf of GCH, where he has been a member and past chair of the GCH Board. He has also served as a member and vice chair of the St. John Fisher University Board of Trustees.

Figure 76.2. Len Shute

Leonard J. Shute joined SMH in 1991 as director of Financial Operations, and in 1995, with the ascendence of Goonan to URMC CFO, he was appointed senior director for Finance and CFO at SMH, and subsequently CFO of HH as well. Shute received his BS in accounting from St. John Fisher University. Prior to joining URMC, he had served as CFO for Rochester Area Hospitals' Corporation, and from 1982 to 1991 as VP for Institutional Affairs for Blue Cross/Blue Shield of the Rochester Area. With his knowledge of the Rochester health care and health insurance landscapes, Shute was able to work with SMH and HH leadership to create programs that maximized clinical margins and could support the growth of the health care system and its academic missions.

Figure 76.3. Adam Anolik

Adam Anolik, CPA, received his BA in accounting from Franklin and Marshall. Like Goonan, he began as an accountant at KPMG Peat Marwick. He went on to serve as CFO at St. Mary's Hospital and then VP of finance and internal services at Planned Parenthood. Anolik joined SMH in 1999, where he quickly progressed, and upon Shute's retirement in 2014 was appointed as CFO of SMH and HH. In 2017, he was promoted to URMC senior VP and CFO. As CFO, Anolik completed the integration of the URMC budget, which is now presented to the University as a single balance sheet that includes its clinical (SMH, URMFG, outpatient services) and academic units, as well as the affiliated hospitals. This integration was particularly important in tripling URMC's investment in its research mission—providing critical funds for achieving NCI designation for the WCI and becoming an Intellectual and Development Disabilities Research Center (IDDRC). Over the past eight years, Anolik has provided the financial oversight for the entire UR Medicine network, working with Steven Goldstein and the administration of each affiliated hospital to effect remarkable financial turnarounds. Perhaps most importantly, he guided URMC through the financially turbulent times of the COVID-19 pandemic. He also developed financial modeling critical to the feasibility of the Orthopaedics and Physical Performance Center and the new Strong Expansion Project.

In 2017, Carrie Fuller Spencer succeeded Anolik as CFO of SMH, and subsequently as CFO of HH. Fuller Spencer received a BS in Accounting from SUNY at Oswego. She joined the Medical Center in 2014 as director of SMH financial services, where she was responsible for the overall management and supervision of financial operations at the hospital. Prior to joining URMC, Fuller Spencer served as the CFO of Arc of Onondaga and was a manager in the accounting firm PricewaterhouseCoopers (PwC), specializing in higher education, health care and not-for-profit organizations. Like Anolik, she played a key role in creating the integrated URMC budget and in navigating the financial headwaters of the COVID-19 pandemic and the changing health care environment.

Figure 76.4. Carrie Fuller Spencer

Although he spent less than three years (2015–17) at URMC, David A. Kirshner played an important role in URMC finances, succeeding Goonan as URMC senior VP and CFO. Prior to joining URMC, Kirshner had served for fifteen years as Boston Children's senior VP for Finance, CFO, and treasurer, where he had helped engineer a financial turnaround. Prior to that, he was VP of Corporate and Business Development for Valence Health, a long-established provider of value-based care services and solutions for hospitals and health systems. During his tenure as URMC CFO, Kirshner took important steps towards creating a fully integrated budget, including the introduction of Generally Accepted Accounting Principles (GAAP). Kirshner was able to build upon the collaborative structure established by Goonan with the CFOs of the various URMC units to develop a more formally centralized structure. He also drove creation of the Academic Reserve Fund, investing Medical Center reserves in the University endowment to help support the academic missions.

During the past twenty-five years, SMD finances have been overseen by two individuals. William Passalacqua, MBA, began his career at the University of Rochester in 1977, serving as a cancer research technician and subsequently enrolling in The Simon Business School, where he received his MBA. Passalacqua served in many capacities during his forty-two years at the University of Rochester, including twelve as a budget officer for the University, giving him a broad perspective. In 1998, he was appointed SAD for Finance and Administration at SMD, where he oversaw the construction and occupation of the three research buildings (Kornberg, Del Monte and Saunders) and the renovation of Medical School space within the Medical Center. In addition to managing SMD's finances, he served many of the functions of chief operating officer,

Figure 76.5. Bill Passalacqua

including strategic planning, personnel issues, and disaster management. During his more than twenty years as SAD, he was known for his honesty and integrity, his ability to find win-win solutions, his patience and warmth, and his sense of humor.

Figure 76.6. Gerard Mikols

Passalacqua was succeeded in 2019 as SAD for Finance and Operations for SMD by Gerard Mikols, MBA. Mikols obtained his BS from the University of Illinois Urbana-Champaign and his MBA from the University of Chicago. He began his career at Price Waterhouse and then moved to the University of Chicago, where for over thirty-five years he served as executive administrator for the department of Medicine, director of Planning and Budget for the School of Medicine, and associate dean for Medical Education Administration and Simulation. During his tenure, Mikols implemented a funds flow approach for SMD that was a crucial step in establishing an integrated URMC budget model. Replacing a model in which funding from clinical operations (SMH and URMFG) and academic support were tracked separately in each department, the funds flow model provided far greater clarity, and created a more effective finance structure focused on cash, capital, and operating margin. This enabled a doubling in capital investments that enhanced the recruitment of research faculty, many of whom were critical for achieving NCI Designation for the WCI and the establishment of the IDDRC. He also reorganized SMD operations, creating the position of senior director for Operations, which better integrated services such as space planning, design and construction, Medical School facilities, and environmental health and safety. Mikols stepped down from his position at the end of 2024 but remains active at SMD.

Chapter 77

ADVANCEMENT

Philanthropy has always played an important role in funding key programs and initiatives at the Medical Center. As part of CEO Jay Stein's research strategic plan, URMC undertook two Campaigns for Discovery aimed at funding the new research buildings. The first (1998–2001), for the KMRB, resulted in $36.4 million, including $6.3 million of government support. The second (2001–3), for the second new research building, yielded $33.2 million, with the majority ($24 million) from NY State. The SMD Scholarships Campaign (2003–8) raised $20.3 million. The SON Future of Care Campaign (2001–7) raised $21 million for the construction of the new Loretta C. Ford Educational Wing and other activities. The GCH Campaign (1998–2003) raised $30.9 million, anchored by a $14 million naming gift by Tom Golisano, to establish the GCH. The WCC Building Campaign (2003–8) raised $42.7 million, including $6.7 million in government funds, to construct the WCC and to support its research programs. The HH Building Campaign raised $9.9 million for major renovations.

Joel Seligman's accession to the University presidency in 2005 came with a commitment to reinvigorate the advancement efforts, including initiation of the largest University-wide capital campaign. The advancement programs, which had resided separately in each school, were merged into a single entity under a senior VP. There was a marked increase in staffing, in part supported by funds from URMC, and in 2007 all advancement team members were co-localized at East River Road (named the Larry and Cindy Bloch Alumni and Advancement Center in 2014 in recognition of the couple's support of advancement programs).

The capital campaign, the *Meliora Challenge*, had its public launch in October 2011 and concluded in 2016. The campaign raised $1.368 billion, exceeding the $1.2 billion goal. The URMC component raised $696 million, exceeding its goal of $600 million with sixty-three percent in current use funds, eight percent in capital, and twenty-nine percent in endowment. This included fifty-nine new endowed professorships and 121 new endowed scholarships/fellowships. The campaign for a separate children's hospital, the GCH Building Campaign, initiated during the *Meliora Challenge*, raised an

Figure 77.1. Sherwood Deutsch

additional $64.1 million, again anchored by a gift from Tom Golisano. The enhanced philanthropy seen during the *Meliora Challenge* has been maintained and surpassed, leading to further growth of the URMC endowment (which grew from $633 million in 2006 to $1.388 billion in 2024), new professorships, and increased support of capital projects.

The URMC signature philanthropic event, the *Toast to Your Health* wine auction, was initiated by CEO Jay Stein in 2001 at the Winter Garden and included wine classes and wine tastings organized by Sherwood Deutsch and Michael Misch of Century Liquors & Wine. By 2004, the event had shifted to the Flaum Atrium and included a wine auction, featuring fine wines and wine-related lots. In 2007, it moved to the Wegmans Conference Center under the sponsorship of Wegmans, with Stency Wegman overseeing the design of the event. Subsequently, the event has usually been held at either the Wegmans Conference Center or the Wegmans Organic Orchard in Canandaigua. To date, *Toast to Your Health* has raised close to $18 million. It was recently listed by *Wine Spectator* as one of the top wine auctions in the country.

Throughout the year, URMC hosts a variety of fundraisers, including the GCH Gala, which raised over $2.7 million in 2024, the WCI Discovery Ball, which raised nearly $1 million in 2024, and the HH Gala, which raised over $370,000 in 2024. URMC is looking forward to the public launch of the University's next capital campaign, *For Ever Better: The Campaign for the University of Rochester*, led by President Sarah Mangelsdorf.

A key goal of philanthropic efforts has been the establishment of endowed professorships, which provide support to outstanding SMD faculty and have

Table 77.1. To date, the *Toast to Your Health* wine auction has raised nearly $18 million.

Year	Beneficiary	Revenue	Location
2004	Strong Memorial Hospital (SMH)	$84,465	Rochester Convention Center
2005	SMH	$163,863	Rochester Convention Center
2006	Wilmot Cancer Center (WCC) Campaign	$411,754	Wegmans Conference Center
2007	WCC – Triology Image-Guided Radiation Therapy System	$699,488	Wegmans Conference Center
2008	Golisano Children's Hospital (GCH) – Equip and staff van to provide community-wide asthma programs	$536,323	Wegmans Conference Center
2009	SMH – Beds for Kessler Family Burn/Trauma ICU	$676,586	Wegmans Conference Center
2010	Treatment and prevention for Alzheimer's Disease	$548,528	Wegmans Conference Center
2011	WCC – Linde Klein fund for Head and Neck Cancer Research	$829,535	Wegmans Conference Center
2012	GCH – Pediatric Surgery Fund	$850,000	Wegmans Conference Center
2013	Pilot projects for Heart and Vascular Research	$1,000,000	Wegmans Conference Center
2014	Stroke Research Fund in Neurology	£1,200,000	Wegmans Conference Center
2015	Wilmot Cancer Institute (WCI) – Blood Cancer Research Fund	$1,050,000	Wegmans Conference Center
2016	Not held.		
2017	Orthopaedic Research and CHAMPP Fund: Life in Motion	$1,300,000	Wegmans Organic Orchard
2018	Memory Care in Psychiatry & Neurology	$1,570,000	Wegmans Organic Orchard
2019	Treatment, surgery, and research for heart and vascular disease	$1,341,445	Wegmans Organic Orchard
2020	COVID-19 pandemic		
2021	COVID-19 pandemic		
2022	WCI	$1,551,872	The Lake House
2023	Orthopaedics and Physical Performance Center	$1,557,150	Wegmans Organic Orchard
2024	Flaum Eye Institute Gift Fund	$2,050,446	Wegmans Conference Center

often been crucial to the recruitment of outstanding physicians and scientists. During his administration, Dean Taubman set a goal of establishing one professorship every other month. Not only was the goal met during the capital campaign, but it has subsequently been maintained. Table 77.2 at the conclusion of this chapter lists all endowed professorships in SMD and the SON, with the current recipient and others who have held the professorship since 2000. Included at the end of the list are professorships that have been committed to but are not yet fully funded. Throughout the book, efforts have been made to acknowledge all recipients of endowed professorships.

The growth in URMC philanthropy owes much to the efforts of the many individuals that comprise Advancement. Andrew Deubler served as associate VP for Development, Medical Center Advancement from 1999 to 2007, during the transition from an independent advancement office to a subdivision of University Advancement. He was succeeded by Chad Gobel, who served as associate VP, Medical Center Advancement, 2008 to 2010; Frank Interlichia, who served as senior associate VP (SAVP), Medical Center Advancement from 2010 to 2016; and Kellie Anderson, who served as SAVP, Medical Center Advancement from 2017 until her untimely death following a prolonged battle with breast cancer in 2024. Michael Fahy was recently named SAVP, Medical Center Advancement. Mary Ann (Dever) King and Melissa L. Head also played substantial roles in their capacities as directors of Advancement for URMC Academic Programs. In addition, Scott Rasmussen, assistant VP for URMC Advancement, has worked for many years on behalf of GCH, as well as working with Tom Golisano to identify key Medical Center priorities for the philanthropist.

The Medical Center has been supported by thousands of donors from alumni and alumnae of the various educational and training programs, faculty and staff, and the Rochester community. Efforts have been made throughout the book to acknowledge those who have contributed major gifts. However, four individuals/families stand out for their long-standing and extraordinary contributions to the Medical Center.

B. Thomas Golisano

No other single philanthropist has shaped the health of the region's children and intellectually disabled more than B. Thomas Golisano. Golisano's giving to the University spans three decades, beginning in 1994. His major gifts date to 2002, when he committed $14 million to name the Golisano Children's Hospital (GCH). In 2011, he augmented that initial gift with a second, $20 million, gift that led the campaign to build the dedicated children's hospital. He has also supported outpatient pediatric services, including

$5 million in 2017 to help fund the construction of the University of Rochester Golisano Pediatric Behavioral Health and Wellness facility on the campus of the Al Sigl Center. Golisano's generosity has enabled the GCH to emerge as upstate's most comprehensive pediatric care facility.

Figure 77.2.
B. Thomas Golisano

Golisano's largest gift to the University came in 2024 with a historic $50 million gift to build the Golisano IDD Institute at URMC. Golisano's gift will significantly expand the University's distinctive strengths in the care of IDD patients, community outreach, and caregiver support programs.

The founder and former president and CEO of Paychex, Inc., a provider of processing systems for payroll and human resource management, Golisano has been listed three times among the Forbes top ten bosses in the US. Through his foundation, the entrepreneur, philanthropist, and civic leader has helped to drive the success of numerous start-up businesses, nonprofit organizations, and educational enterprises. His support of the URMC has been unmatched and transformative.

E. Philip Saunders

URMC's status as a premier, upstate academic health system bears the fingerprints of philanthropist E. Philip "Phil" Saunders and his wife Carole.

Figure 77.3.
E. Philip Saunders

A long-time benefactor of URMC, Saunders's first of many gifts was in 1972 to what is now the WCI. In 2011, Saunders provided $10 million to support the groundbreaking translational research on myotonic muscular dystrophy of Richard Moxley, MD, and Charles Thornton, MD. In recognition of this, the new home of the Clinical and Translational Science Institute was named the Saunders Research Building. He subsequently established the Saunders Family Distinguished Professorship in Neuromuscular Research, the E. Philip and Carole Saunders Professorship in Neuromuscular Research, and the Saunders Endowed Fellowship in Neuromuscular Research.

Distinguished by his extraordinary leadership skills, Saunders—along with fellow University Trustee Richard Aab—co-chaired the $650 million URMC fundraising campaign completed in June 2016. In 2017, he drove philanthropic efforts to establish the Ann and Carl Myers Cancer Center at Noyes Memorial Hospital. In 2024, the Saunders Foundation pledged $30 million to support orthopaedic research and clinical programs, faculty at SMD, and nursing students. In his honor, the new outpatient orthopaedics facility in Henrietta was named the Saunders Center for Orthopaedics and Physical Performance.

An entrepreneur known for his diverse business interests, Saunders was instrumental in reshaping the travel center industry as founder of Truck Stops of America and Travel Centers of America. A University Trustee Emeritus, who served on the board from 2015 to 2020, Saunders remains honorary chair of the Rochester Philanthropy Council. In 2015, in recognition of his exemplary service, the University awarded him its Eastman Medal.

Wegman Family Charitable Foundation

Dedicated to helping their community live healthier, better lives, the Wegman Family Charitable Foundation has significantly advanced health care and education through generous partnerships with the University of Rochester and across the greater Rochester area. Established in 1991 by Robert Wegman, Danny's father, the Wegman Family Charitable Foundation grew out of the highly successful family business, Wegmans Food Markets, which has become a grocery industry icon for innovation and service.

As generous hosts of the University of Rochester Medical Center's anchor fundraising event, *Toast to Your Health* Wine Auction, Danny and his family have contributed and raised millions of dollars for numerous departments and critical initiatives across the Medical Center. In 2013, the Wegman Family Charitable Foundation made a $7 million lead gift that supported the construction and programming of GCH, including its Child Life Program that supports the emotional and developmental needs of children and their families.

Figure 77.4. Danny Wegman is joined by daughters Nicole and Colleen.

In 2013, the Wegman Family Charitable Foundation's $10 million lead gift advanced the University's data science initiative, helping create an interdisciplinary data science hub that brings together health and biomedical science, among many other disciplines, with exceptional faculty and innovation in research and studies. Other areas across the University, especially the Eastman School of Music and the Warner School of Education, have greatly benefitted from the Wegman family's generosity.

In addition to being one of the University's major philanthropists, Danny has also played a key role in guiding the University as a member and chair of the Board of Trustees, and as a member of the Medical Center board. He also served as honorary chair of the Medical Center component of *The Meliora Challenge.*

Wilmot Family

For decades, James P. Wilmot and his family have channeled grief at the devastating loss of multiple family members to cancer into extraordinary leadership, advocacy, and generosity—support that has helped transform the Wilmot Cancer Institute (WCI), named in honor of James P. Wilmot in 2000, into the region's leading provider of cancer care and promising therapies.

James P. Wilmot was founder of Page Airways, a flight school, charter service, and plane supplier, and later Wilmorite, a commercial and industrial development firm that built all of the major shopping malls in the Rochester area. After his diagnosis with a brain tumor, family patriarch James established the James P. Wilmot Foundation to fund the Wilmot Fellowship Program and train physicians in cancer research. Today, it has yielded more than 100

Figure 77.5. Judy Wilmot Linehan, Bill Wilmot and Tom Wilmot

Wilmot Fellows who have trained at the University of Rochester and have gone on to pursue cancer research careers. The Wilmot Foundation, James's children, James, William, Thomas, and Judy, along with their spouses and children, and his extended family have collectively given tens of millions to the University to support cancer research and treatment.

Judy and Paul Linehan have been champions of the Discovery Ball fundraising gala. In addition, Judy co-chaired the comprehensive campaign that raised $42.5 million for the new Wilmot Cancer Center facility and for cancer research. In 2014, Bill and Marion Wilmot, Tom and Colleen Wilmot, and Judy and Paul Linehan, along with the James P. Wilmot Foundation, established the Wilmot Distinguished Professorship in Cancer Genomics, enabling the recruitment of Paula Vertino, PhD, a world leader in cancer epigenetics. University of Rochester Trustee Emeritus Thomas C. Wilmot Sr. was the honorary chair of the WCI's campaign in support of *The Meliora Challenge*. A third generation of Wilmots has continued chairing the Discovery Ball, including the 25th anniversary event chaired by Mary Wilmot, Patrick and Caroline Wilmot, Jamie and Michael Cesare, and James and Shannon Wilmot.

Table 77.2. Endowed Professorships have been a key strategy in recruiting and retaining top talent

Fund Established in Fiscal Year	Professorship	Previous Holders since 2000	Current Holder	Department
1929	Charles Ayrault Dewey Professorship of Medicine	Bradford C. Berk, MD, PhD; Mark B. Taubman, MD; Paul C. Levy, MD	Ruth M. O'Regan, MD	Medicine
1932	Lewis Pratt Ross Professorship of Pharmacology and Physiology	M. W. Anders, DVM, PhD; Arnold W. Tank, PhD	Robert T. Dirksen, PhD	Pharmacology & Physiology
1955	Albert David Kaiser Chair of Public Health and Preventive Medicine	Tom Pearson, MD, MPH, PhD	Ann M. Dozier, PhD	Public Health Sciences
1955	Frieda Robscheit-Robbins Professorship; Previously George Hoyt Whipple Distinguished Professor of Pathology	Chawnshang Chang, PhD	Christa L. Whitney-Miller, MD	Pathology & Laboratory Medicine
1966	Segal-Watson Professorship of Medicine	Vivek Kaul, MD	Mark A. Levstik, MD	Medicine—Gastroenterology
1966	Margaret and Cy Welcher Professorship in Dental Research	William H. Bowen, BDS, PhD; Robert G. Quivey, PhD	Thomas Diekwisch, DMD, PhD	Eastman Institute of Oral Health
1968/1995	Seymour I. Schwartz Professorship in Surgery	James V. Sitzmann, MD; Jeffrey H. Peters, MD; David C. Linehan, MD	Ryan C. Fields, MD	Surgery
1972	Samuel E. Durand Chair in Medicine	Richard I. Fisher, MD	Jonathan W. Friedberg, MD, MMSc	Medicine—Hematology/Oncology

(cont.)

Fund Established in Fiscal Year	Professorship	Previous Holders since 2000	Current Holder	Department
1972	Marie Curran Wilson and Joseph Chamberlain Wilson Professorship	This professorship currently supports a professorship with outstanding accomplishments in research. A Wilson Professorship may be established in any area of the University	David J. Topham, PhD	Microbiology & Immunology
1973	J. Lowell Orbison Distinguished Service Alumni Professorship	Thomas Clarkson PhD	Lynne E. Maquat, PhD	Biochemistry & Biophysics
1976	George L. Engel Professorship in Psychosocial Medicine	Robert Ader, PhD; Jan A. Moynihan, PhD	Steven M. Silverstein, PhD	Psychiatry
1979	James H. Sterner Chair in Dermatology		Alice P. Pentland, MD	Dermatology
1980	Donald and Mary Clark Professorship in Orthopaedics	J. Edward Puzas, PhD	Hani A. Awad, PhD	Orthopaedics
2017	Donald and Mary Clark Professorship in Orthopaedics	Established by splitting the proceeds from the original Clark Professorship	Alayna E. Loiselle, PhD	Orthopaedics

Fund Established in Fiscal Year	Professorship	Previous Holders since 2000	Current Holder	Department
1980	George Washington Goler Chair in Pediatrics	Richard E. Kreipe MD; Barbara L. Asselin, MD; James Palis MD; Clement Ren, MD, MBA; Gloria Pryhuber, MD; Mary T. Caserta, MD; O. J. Sahler, MD	Matthew D. McGraw, MD	Pediatrics
1981	Frank P. Smith Professorship of Neurosurgery	Webster H. Pilcher, MD, PhD; Maiken Nedergaard, MD, DMSc	Vacant	Neurosurgery
1983	Edward A. and Alma Vollertsen Rykenboer Chair in Neurophysiology	Robert "Berch" Griggs, MD; Steven A. Goldman, MD, PhD	Robert G. Holloway, MD, MPH	Neurology
1983	Winfield W. Scott Chair in Urology	Edward M. Messing, MD	Jean Joseph, MD, MBA, FACS	Urology
1986	Kilian J. and Caroline F. Schmitt Chair in Neuroscience	Gary D. Paige, MD, PhD	John J. Foxe, PhD	Neuroscience
1986	Louis C. Lasagna Professorship in Experimental Therapeutics	Ira Shoulson, MD; Alan Smrcka, PhD	David I. Yule, PhD	Pharmacology & Physiology
1991	Henry A. Thiede Professorship of Obstetrics and Gynecology	David Guzick, MD, PhD; James Woods, MD	Eva K. Pressman, MD	Obstetrics and Gynecology

(cont.)

Fund Established in Fiscal Year	Professorship	Previous Holders since 2000	Current Holder	Department
1991	Paul N. Yu Professorship in Cardiology	Bradford C. Berk, MD, PhD; Mark B. Taubman, MD; Charles Lowenstein, MD	Spencer Z. Rosero, MD	Medicine—Cardiology
1993 (S/B 1992)	John Romano Professorship	Eric D. Caine, MD	Hochang Benjamin Lee, MD	Psychiatry
1994	Dr. Raymond J. Mayewski Professorship		Marc N. Berliant, MD	Medicine—General Medicine
1994	Paul Stark Professorship in Pharmacology	Robert Freeman, PhD; A. W. "Bill" Tank, PhD; Jean M. Bidlack, PhD; Houhui "Hugh" Xia PhD	David M. MacLean, PhD	Pharmacology & Physiology
1995	Philip Rubin Professorship	Paul Okunieff, MD; Yuchayau Chen, MD, PhD	Louis S. Constine, MD	Radiation Oncology
1995	Marjorie Strong Wehle Professorship in Orthopaedics	Randy N. Rosier, MD, PhD; Regis O'Keefe, MD, PhD	Paul Rubery, MD	Orthopaedics
1996	Helen Aresty Fine and Irving Fine Distinguished Professorship in Neurology	Richard T. Moxley, MD	TBD	Neurology
1996	James R. Woods, Jr. Professor in Obstetrics and Gynecology	James R. Woods, MD; Eva K. Pressman, MD	Loralei L. Thornburg, MD	Obstetrics and Gynecology

Fund Established in Fiscal Year	Professorship	Previous Holders since 2000	Current Holder	Department
1997	Paul H. Fine Professorship in Medicine	William Hall, MD	Annette M. Medina-Walpole, MD, PhD	Medicine—Geriatrics
1997	Robert and Dorothy Markin Professorship		K. Hartmut Land, PhD	Biomedical Genetics
1999	Ralph W. Prince Professorship in Medicine	Paul C. Levy, MD; Wallace E. Johnson, MD	Stephen R. Judge, MD	Medicine—Primary Care
2001	Robert J. Joynt Professorship in Neurology	Karl Kieburtz, MD, MPH; Erika U. Augustine, MD	TBD	Neurology
2005	William L. Morgan, Jr. Professorship in Medicine	Donald R. Bordley, MD	Amy E. Blatt, MD	Medicine—Hospitalist
2006	Lindsey Distinguished Professorship for Pediatric Research	Frank Gigliotti, MD	Laurie A. Steiner, MD	Pediatrics
2008	Louis S. Wolk Distinguished Professorship in Medicine		Stephen R. Hammes, MD, PhD	Medicine—Endo-Metab Div
2008	William H. Eilinger Chair of Pediatrics	Nina Schor, MD, PhD; Patrick Brophy, MD	Jill S. Halterman, MD, MPH	Pediatrics
2009	Dr. Laurie Sands Distinguished Professorship of Families and Health		Susan H. McDaniel, PhD	Psychiatry
2009	Fields Endowed Professorship in Neurology	Rabi N. Tawil, MD (al-Rabi N. Tawil)	TBD	Neurology

(cont.)

Fund Established in Fiscal Year	Professorship	Previous Holders since 2000	Current Holder	Department
2010	William and Sheila Konar Endowed Professorship		Anton P. Porsteinsson, MD	Psychiatry
1993/2010	Haggerty-Friedman Professorship in Developmental/Behavioral Pediatric Research	Tristram Smith, PhD	Suzannah J. Iadarola, PhD	Pediatrics
2011	Richard T. Bell Endowed Professorship		Yuhchyau Chen, MD, PhD	Radiation Oncology
2011	Philip and Marilyn Wehrheim Professorship	Craig T. Jordan, PhD	Supriya G. Mohile, MD, MS	Medicine
2011	Denham S. Ward, MD, PhD Professorship	Michael P. Eaton, MD	Michael J. Scott, MB, ChB	Anesthesiology
2011	Saunders Family Distinguished Professorship in Neuromuscular Research		Charles A. Thornton, MD	Neurology
2011	E. Philip and Carole Saunders Professorship in Neuromuscular Research		David N. Herrmann, MBBCh	Neurology
2012 (Exec. Committee Resolution as of 7/1/11)	C. Jane Davis and C. Robert Davis Distinguished Professorship in Pulmonary Medicine	Patricia J. Sime, MD	M. Patricia Rivera, MD	Medicine—Pulmonary & Critical Care
2012	Richard and Margaret Burton Distinguished Professorship in Orthopaedics		Edward M. Schwarz, PhD	Orthopaedics

Fund Established in Fiscal Year	Professorship	Previous Holders since 2000	Current Holder	Department
2012	Dr. Elizabeth R. McAnarney Professorship in Pediatrics	Richard E. Kreipe, MD; Jill S. Halterman, MD, MPH	Lauren G. Solan, MD, MEd	Pediatrics
2012	John J. Kuiper Distinguished Professorship	David A. Bushinsky, MD; Thu H. Le, MD	TBD	Medicine—Nephrology
2012	Ernest and Thelma Del Monte Distinguished Professorship in Neuromedicine		Webster H. Pilcher, MD, PhD	Neurosurgery
2013	Georgia and Thomas Gosnell Distinguished Professorship in Palliative Care	Timothy E. Quill, MD	Robert K. Horowitz, MD	Medicine—Palliative Care
2013	Georgia and Thomas Gosnell Professorship in Quality and Safety	Robert J. Panzer, MD	Michael J. Apostolakos, MD	Medicine—Pulmonary & Critical Care
2013	Shohei Koide Professorship in Biochemistry and Biophysics		Jeffrey J. Hayes, PhD	Biochemistry & Biophysics
2013	Adeline Lutz—Steven S. T. Ching, MD, Distinguished Professorship in Ophthalmology	Steven S. T. Ching, MD, Adeline Lutz Distinguished Professorship in Ophthalmology	Alex V. Levin, MD, MHSc, FAAP, FAAO, FRCSC	Ophthalmology
2013	Joseph M. Lobozzo II Professorship	Walter Pegoli Jr., MD	Marjorie J. Arca, MD	Pediatric Surgery

(cont.)

Fund Established in Fiscal Year	Professorship	Previous Holders since 2000	Current Holder	Department
2011	Dr. Stephen I. Rosenfeld and Elise A. Rosenfeld Distinguished Professorship in Allergy and Clinical Immunology		R. John Looney, MD	Medicine—Allergy, Immunology & Rheumatology
2012	Frederick A. Horner, MD, Distinguished Professorship in Pediatric Neurology	Jonathan W. Mink, MD, PhD	Jamie Capal, MD	Pediatric Neurology
2014	Catherine E. Aquavella Distinguished Professorship in Ophthalmology		James V. Aquavella, MD (Honorary)	Ophthalmology
2014	Bradford C. Berk, MD, PhD, Distinguished Professorship	Arthur J. Moss, MD	TBD	Medicine—Cardiology
2014	Robert C. and Rosalyne H. Griggs Professorship in the Experimental Therapeutics of Neurological Disease		Emma Ciafaloni, MD, FAAN	Neurology
2014	Joan and Gary Morrow Endowed Distinguished Professor of Supportive Care in Cancer	Gary R. Morrow, PhD (Held as Benefactor Distinguished Professorship)	Michelle Janelsins-Benton, MPH, PhD	Surgery
2014	James V. Aquavella, MD, Professorship in Ophthalmology		Krystel R. Huxlin, PhD	Ophthalmology
2014	Northumberland Trust Professorship in Pediatrics		James T. Palis, MD	Pediatrics
2014	David M. Levy Professorship in Neurology	E. Ray Dorsey, MD, MBA	Jamie L. Adams, MD	Neurology

Fund Established in Fiscal Year	Professorship	Previous Holders since 2000	Current Holder	Department
2014	Wilmot Distinguished Professorship in Cancer Genomics		Paula M. Vertino, PhD	Biomedical Genetics
2014	Dr. C. McCollister Evarts Professorship in Orthopaedics	John Gorczyca, MD; P. Christopher Cook, MD	Susan M. McDowell, MD	Orthopaedics
2008	Founders' Distinguished Professorship of Pediatric Allergy		Kirsi M. Järvinen-Seppo, MD, PhD	Pediatric Allergy/ Immunology
2015	Wright Family Research Professorship		B. Paige Lawrence, PhD	Environmental Medicine
2015	Donald M. Foster, MD, Distinguished Professorship in Biostatistics		Robert L. Strawderman III, ScD	Biostatistics & Computational Biology
2015	Donald M. Foster, MD, Professorship in Biomedical Genetics		Douglas S. Portman, PhD	Biomedical Genetics
2015	Martha M. Freeman, MD, Professorship in Biomedical Genetics	Mark D. Noble, PhD	Margot Mayer-Pröschel, PhD	Biomedical Genetics
2015	Tansukh, Sarla, and Rajesh Ganatra Distinguished Professorship in Pediatric Cardiac Surgery		George Alfieris, MD	Cardiac Surgery (Pediatric)
2015	Albert and Phyllis Ritterson Professorship	Stephen Dewhurst, PhD	Jacques Robert, PhD	Microbiology & Immunology

(cont.)

Fund Established in Fiscal Year	Professorship	Previous Holders since 2000	Current Holder	Department
2015	Edward A. and Alma Vollertsen Rykenboer Professorship in Neurology	This was created by splitting the proceeds of the original Rykenboer Professorship (see above)	Gretchen L. Birbeck, MD, MPH, DTMH	Neurology
2015	Marjorie B. Morris Endowed Professorship in Cardiac Surgery	Peter A. Knight, MD	TBD	Surgery
2016	John and Ethel Heselden Professorship		Aram F. Hezel, MD	Medicine—Hematology/ Oncology
2016	William and Sheila Konar Family Professorship in Geriatrics, Palliative Medicine, and Person-Centered Care		Joseph A. Nicholas, MD, MPH	Medicine (Highland)
2016	Dr. Jude S. Sauer Family Distinguished Professorship in Cardiac Surgery	Sunil Prasad, MD	Peter A. Knight, MD	Cardiac Surgery
2016	Walter and Carmina Mary Parkes Family Distinguished Professorship		Steve N. Georas, MD	Medicine—Pulmonary & Critical Care
2017	Linde Klein Professorship in Head and Neck Cancer		TBD	Wilmot Cancer Institute
2014	Julius, Helen, and Robert Fine Distinguished Professor in Neurology for Dr. Kluger		Benzi M. Kluger, MD, MS	Neurology
2018	David Mortara Endowed Professorship in Cardiology		Wojciech Zareba, MD, PhD	Medicine—Cardiology
2018	SKAWA Foundation Professorship in Endocrinology and Metabolism		Laura M. Calvi, MD	Medicine—Endo-Metab Div

Fund Established in Fiscal Year	Professorship	Previous Holders since 2000	Current Holder	Department
2019	Ann Aresty Camhi Professorship in Neurology		Nimish A. Mohile, MD	Neurology
2019	Esther Aresty Granite Professorship in Neurology		Giovanni Schifitto, MD '94M (Res), '10S (MS)	Neurology
2019	Rhea and Raymond White Professorship in Pediatric Cardiology		George A. Porter, Jr., MD, PhD	Pediatric Cardiology
2019	Ruth A. Lawrence Professorship in Pediatrics		Karen M. Wilson, MD, MPH	Pediatrics
2019	Gilbert B. Forbes Professorship in Pediatrics		TBD	Pediatrics
2019	David H. Smith Professorship in Pediatrics		Thomas J. Mariani, PhD	Pediatrics
2019	Carol A. and Lowell A. Goldsmith Professorship in Dermatology		Lisa A. Beck, MD	Dermatology
2020	Gordon Family Professorship in Pediatrics		Jill M. Cholette, MD	Pediatric Cardiology
1995	Dr. Stanley M. Rogoff and Dr. Raymond Gramiak Professorship in Radiology		Jennifer A. Harvey, MD	Imaging Sciences
2020	Wynne Distinguished Professorship		Thomas G. O'Connor, PhD '89	Psychiatry

(cont.)

Fund Established in Fiscal Year	Professorship	Previous Holders since 2000	Current Holder	Department
2020	Dr. Mina M. Chung Professorship		Vikas Khetan, MBBS	Ophthalmology
2021	Lynne E. Maquat Distinguished Professorship		David H. Mathews, MD, PhD	Biochemistry & Biophysics
2021	Dr. Sidney H. and Barbara L. Sobel Professorship in Radiation Oncology		Brian Marples, PhD	Radiation Oncology
2021	Dr. Eric M. Dreyfuss Professorship		TBD	Pediatrics—Allergy & Immunology
2021	Purcell Family Distinguished Professorship		Dennis Z. Kuo, MD, MHS	Pediatrics
2022	Henry C. Buswell, MD, Professorships		TBD	Urology
2022	Susan P. and Edward M. Messing, MD, Professorship in Urology		TBD	Urology
2023	Agnes E. Griffith Distinguished Professorship in Pediatric Mobility		P. Christopher Cook, MD	Orthopaedics
2023	Mark and Maureen Davitt Distinguished Professorship in Child and Adolescent Psychiatry		Michael A. Scharf, MD	Psychiatry
2025	Mark and Lois Taubman Distinguished Professor of Health Humanities and Bioethics		Lainie Friedman Ross, MD, PhD	Health Humanities & Bioethics

Professorships committed but not yet ready for installation

Fund Established in Fiscal Year	Professorship	Previous Holders since 2000	Current Holder	Department
2004	Chair in Neuroscience/ Astrocyte Research			
2005	Ralph F. Józefowicz, MD, Chair in Neurologic Education			Neurology
2011	Distinguished Professorship in Colon & Rectal Surgery			Colorectal Surgery
2012	Dr. Paul and Beverly Yudkofsky Professorship in Pediatrics			Pediatrics
2013	James David Brodell, Sr., MD, and Ann Pearsall Brodell Professorship in Orthopaedic Surgery			Orthopaedics
2014	Northumberland Trust Professorship in Neuroscience			Neurosciences
2015	Lawrence N. Chessin, MD ’58 and Rita R. Chessin Professorship in Infectious Diseases			Medicine—Infectious Diseases
2016	Lyons/Offermann Professorship for Cancer Biology			Wilmot Cancer Institute
2017	Paul J. Mayer, MD ’69 and Elizabeth F. Mayer Endowed Distinguished Professorship in Medicine			Medicine

(cont.)

Fund Established in Fiscal Year	Professorship	Previous Holders since 2000	Current Holder	Department
2018	Louis A. Goldstein Distinguished Professorship in Spinal Surgery			Orthopaedics
2019	Gary S. and Barbara M. Berger Professorship in Innovative Education			School of Medicine and Dentistry
2020	Neil and Karen Jonasse Tucker Distinguished Professorship in Orthopaedic Research			Orthopaedics
2022	Kenneth and Joy Ouriel Family Professorship			Vascular Surgery
2022	Karl J. and Urai Marchenese Professorship in Ophthalmology			Ophthalmology
2022	Douglas E. and Colleen M. Rogers University Distinguished Professorship in the School of Medicine and Dentistry			School of Medicine and Dentistry
2022	Serletti Family Professorship			Plastic Surgery
2022	Distinguished Professorship (Anonymous)			
2024	Randy N. Rosier Professorship in Orthopaedic Oncology			Orthopaedics
2024	Michael A. Robertson Professorship in Molecular Orthopaedics			Orthopaedics

School of Nursing

Fund Established in Fiscal Year	Professorship	Previous Holders since 2000	Current Holder	Department
1990	Independence Foundation Chair in Nursing Education	Madeline H. Schmitt, PhD, RN; Margaret Kearney, PhD, RN	Lisa Kitko, PhD, RN, FAHA, FAAN	School of Nursing
1993	Jean E. Johnson Chair in Nursing Oncology		TBD	School of Nursing
1994	Loretta C. Ford Professorship in Primary Care Nursing	Harriet Kitzman, PhD, RN; Gail L. Ingersoll, EdD, RN	Ying Xue, DNSc, RN	School of Nursing
1998	Ruth Miller Brody and Bernard Brody Professorship	Karen F. Stein, PhD, RN, FAAN	Susan Groth, PhD, WHNP-BC, FAANP	School of Nursing
2004	Endowed Chair for Nursing Science		TBD	School of Nursing
2004	Chair for Innovation in Health Care		James McMahon, PhD	School of Nursing
2014	Carol Anne Brink Professorship		Committed, but not yet fully funded	School of Nursing

(cont.)

Fund Established in Fiscal Year	Professorship	Previous Holders since 2000	Current Holder	Department
2014	Independence Chair in Nursing and Palliative Care	Established from the growth of the Independence Foundation Chair in Nursing Education	Sally A. Norton, PhD, RN	School of Nursing
2024	Independence Foundation Chair in Cardiovascular Nursing	Established from the growth of the Independence Foundation Chair in Nursing Education	Salah Al-Zaiti, PhD, RN, CRNP, ANP-BC, FAHA	School of Nursing

Chapter 78

INFORMATION SYSTEMS DIVISION

One of the most remarkable transformations in the past twenty-five years at URMC has been in the adoption of information technology (IT). As in many academic medical centers, URMC's Information Systems division (ISD) had grown organically in individual departments and in the hospital. This resulted in the development of dozens of "legacy" systems all running on various platforms that often could not interact and were not suited to support the necessary clinical integration or the explosion in data science and research technology.

Leading the transformation was Jerry Powell, MBA. Powell, who received an MBA in economics and information science from SUNY Albany, began his career as a data analyst and programmer at the US Department of Transportation before joining the University of Rochester in 1977, where he built a career spanning nearly four decades, ultimately becoming director of ISD at SMH and, in 1996, URMC's inaugural chief information officer (CIO), a role he held until his retirement in 2016. Powell was joined by David A. Krusch, MD, a general surgeon who had joined the University of Rochester in 1989 and had begun working with IT in 1994. Krusch was named the inaugural chief medical information officer (CMIO) in 2001.

Figure 78.1.
Jerry Powell

Powell and Krusch led SMH's early adoption of computerized physician order entry (CPOE) and standardized clinical order sets. At the time, only five percent of institutions in the US had CPOE. Replacing handwritten and verbal orders with electronic entry significantly decreased medication errors, reduced unnecessary variation in care, and improved communication among clinical teams by reducing handoffs and adding transparency. The structured data generated by CPOE also enabled continuous quality improvement and research. It positioned URMC as an early leader in demonstrating how technology could enhance both the

Figure 78.2.
David Krusch

science and the delivery of medicine. Krusch also oversaw the implementation of Flowcast, the business solution from IDX, replacing outdated systems that handled patient accounting and registration, maintained patient demographic and health insurance information, and hospital and patient billing.

These early successes in health care IT, as well as others in Radiology, Pharmacy and Pathology, proved the value of digitizing specific workflows. They also highlighted a major limitation: data remained siloed within individual systems. Clinicians had to navigate multiple platforms to piece together a complete patient story, leading to inefficiencies and gaps in care. Accordingly, URMC CEO Bradford Berk commissioned Powell and Krusch, supported by an external consultant, Dawn DePerrior, to develop a strategic plan for health care IT at URMC. As this process was unfolding, the Health Information Technology for Economic and Clinical Health bill was enacted by Congress as part of the American Recovery and Reinvestment Act, which accelerated the adoption and meaningful use of health IT, particularly electronic health records (EHR)s. This prompted the strategic planning group to recommend the implementation of the Epic EHR, subsequently referred to as eRecord.

The eRecord inpatient implementation was the largest technology transformation project that SMH has ever undergone and required an extensive governance structure to support decision-making, define scope and modules, and ensure appropriate resources allocation. The SMH inpatient eRecord go-live occurred in March 2011. The training team, provider informatics, "superusers," and Epic staff provided at-the-elbow support immediately following go-live to assist users with real-time issues and questions. A large, twenty-four-hour command center was established to monitor system performance, troubleshoot issues, and coordinate support efforts. The implementation was deemed highly successful and was followed by a similar process and success at HH in June 2011. The eRecord rollout served as a model for introducing new technology on a system-wide scale that involved all patient-facing members of the Medical Center community.

eRecord Ambulatory went live in 2012 to continue the process of establishing a single patient record. In 2015, eRecord applications for OR, anesthesia, and cardiovascular were added, followed by patient access, revenue cycle, and imaging in 2018. As the UR Medicine network expanded, eRecord was introduced to regional affiliates, beginning in 2019 with FF Thompson, followed in 2020 by the nursing homes, and in 2022 by Noyes Memorial, St. James, and Jones Memorial Hospitals.

The IT transformation was not limited to the clinical enterprise. In 2008, the University of Rochester created the Health Sciences Center for Computational Innovation in partnership with IBM, who gifted a previous

Figure 78.3. The Epic "Go-Live" Command Center at Highland Hospital

generation of its Blue Gene supercomputer system, the Blue Gene/P. Within a short time, more than 500 scientists had used the high-performance computing system and the Center had helped attract $84 million in new funding, including the NIH-funded Respiratory Pathogens Research Center and the Center for Biodefense Immune Modeling. In 2012, the University became one of the first academic institutions in the nation to receive the next generation of IBM's supercomputers—the Blue Gene/Q, one of most powerful and efficient computer systems in the world. Two years later, a Center of Excellence in Data Science and Artificial Intelligence, dedicated to using data science methods and tools to support NY businesses and funded by Empire State Development's division of Science, Technology, and Innovation (NYSTAR), was established at the University. Supported by a $20 million donation from the Wegman Family Charitable Foundation, a 59,000 square-foot building—Wegmans Hall—was opened in 2017 to house the Goergen Institute for Data Science and Artificial Intelligence.

Upon Powell's retirement in 2016, Thomas L. Barnett, MBA, was recruited to be URMC's CIO and VP for URMC IT. Prior to joining URMC, he served as VP of the NorthShore University Health System in Evanston, Illinois, where he led the system's Digital Health Initiative, collaborating with Epic's product development team. During his time at URMC, Barnett focused on developing a more robust infrastructure that would promote further consolidation of IT across URMC's three missions. In 2018, he appointed James Forrester, MS, as URMC's first chief technology officer, and Lisa Nelson, PharmD, BCBS, as senior director of Clinical Applications, charging them with implementing a technology governance structure that would build on centralization of IT started with eRecord implementation to better align IT resources with URMC strategic plans. This was followed in 2019 with the appointment of Rosemary Ventura, DNP, RN-BC, who was recruited from NY-Presbyterian to serve as the first chief nursing information officer, and Orthopaedics professor Gregg Nicandri, MD, who succeeded David Krusch, MD, as the CMIO. Ventura and Nicandri served as liaisons between ISD and clinical operations to communicate needs, ongoing initiatives, and improvements throughout the enterprise, with a particular focus on developing solutions to improve eRecord, building on work initiated by Otolaryngology Chair Sean Newlands, who had served for nine months as interim CMIO.

Following Barnett's departure in 2020, Forrester was named associate VP of ISD, expanding his role as chief technology officer. Nelson was also named associate VP of ISD and URMC's chief applications officer. Working in tandem to lead a staff of more than 500 in ISD, Forrester and Nelson were instrumental in URMC's response to the COVID-19 pandemic, leveraging technology solutions to support a pivoting workforce, expanding the use of telehealth, and staying up to date with rapidly changing testing and patient care requirements.

Forrester received an MS in information technology from RIT. He joined URMC in 1993 and held numerous IT leadership positions with Neurology, Imaging Sciences, Cardiology, and ISD. He was named chief technology officer in 2018, responsible for URMC's technology roadmap, architecture,

Figure 78.4. Lisa Nelson and James Forrester

and service delivery, and for representing URMC in the University's Project and Portfolio Management Office, which oversees the IT portfolio.

Nelson, who received a PharmD from the Albany College of Pharmacy and Health Sciences, spent eleven years at Beth Israel Deaconess Medical Center before joining URMC's Pharmacy department in 2005. She moved into Pharmacy IT in 2009 and then Pharmacy Informatics in 2014. In 2018, Nelson was appointed to a senior leadership position in ISD, where she was responsible for the planning, development, and implementation of clinical applications throughout the health system, focusing particularly on the EHR, and she also oversaw ISD's Enterprise Training and Supply Chain Management groups.

Through strong technology governance and deep business partnerships, Forrester and Nelson have advanced an enterprise-wide technology program that emphasizes value through standardization, reliability, and innovation. In partnership with Nicandri and Ventura, they have strengthened the consistency of clinical applications across the health system, ensuring greater efficiency, interoperability, and improved user experience. Their close collaboration with University IT and the Medical Center research community has also advanced technology support for the research and academic missions. These accomplishments have been underpinned by a sustained focus on advancing the institution's information security posture, safeguarding sensitive data while maintaining the agility required to meet the evolving needs of health care, research, and education. At the same time, they have guided the growth of a robust data and analytics program—expanding the enterprise data platform, empowering departments with local analytic capabilities, and creating domain-specific analytics centers of excellence.

Chapter 79

CENTRALIZED ADMINISTRATIVE FUNCTIONS

CEO Jay Stein's ambitious strategic plan transformed URMC's research enterprise and initiated the integration of the Medical Center's academic and clinical components. The plan created new demands and immense opportunities for the organization's shared administrative functions, particularly in areas such as strategic and space planning, marketing, public relations and communications, web services, legal counsel, and government relations, which would need to grow in size and scope. To organize this, Stein promoted Peter Robinson to VP and COO of URMC, and subsequently of the Strong Health system. Robinson received an MA from the New School for Social Research and an MPH from Columbia University School of Public Health. He joined URMC in 1988 as the director of strategic planning and marketing, and in 1991 was named associate VP for Health Affairs.

Figure 79.1. Peter Robinson

Government Relations

A key element in the extraordinary growth of URMC over the past thirty years has been its ability to garner community and government support, including funding, for its major initiatives. Peter Robinson has been at the center of these efforts, ultimately named by President Joel Seligman in 2014 as VP for the first institution-wide Office of Government and Community Relations, managing federal, state, and community relations. Robinson led the University's legislative efforts locally, in Albany, and in Washington, DC, developing strong relationships with elected officials, special-interest groups, and community leaders. His efforts helped secure several hundreds of millions of dollars for the KMRB and Del Monte Biomedical Research buildings, the Saunders Research Building, the Goergen Institute for Data Science and Artificial Intelligence, and the Strong Expansion Project currently under construction. He was instrumental in garnering community support for

URMC's affiliation with HH and for its subsequent expansion projects. His advocacy work has been critical to receiving sustained federal funding for the University's Laboratory for Laser Energetics and played an important role in gaining the endorsement of the entire NY State Congressional delegation on behalf of WCI's application for NCI designation. Robinson's relationship with local, county, and state leaders was also pivotal in placing URMC at the hub of a successful western NY strategy during the COVID-19 pandemic.

Robinson also played a leadership role in developing entrepreneurial opportunities for the University. He led the University's affiliation with NextCorps, a state and federally designated business incubator focused on advancing next-generation optics, photonics, and imaging-enabled companies. He was founder of Excell Partners, the University's affiliated venture fund, which now has more than $75 million under management. Robinson was a catalyst for the creation of the Empire Discovery Institute, a nonprofit entity aimed at identifying promising drug candidates and moving them towards clinical trials. He was also a key contributor to URMC's systemwide partnership with the YMCA of Greater Rochester.

Figure 79.2. Joshua Farrelman

Many of the successes described above reflect a partnership between Robinson and Joshua Farrelman, who recently succeeded Robinson as VP of Government and Community Relations. Farrelman previously served as senior legislative assistant to US Representative Rosa L. DeLauro (D-CT), legislative assistant for Monroe County's late US Representative Louise M. Slaughter (D-NY), and assistant director for the American Library Association's Office of Government Relations. He joined the University in 2005 as assistant director of government and community relations, and two years later was named director. He was promoted to University associate VP upon the establishment of the Office of Government and Community Relations in 2014. In these roles, he worked closely with Robinson and senior leadership to lead advocacy efforts in support of the University's legislative strategies and priorities, serving as a main point of contact for legislators, and government and community officials. Farrelman was heavily involved in advancing community-focused projects and initiatives, such as the University partnership with East High School, the Rochester-Monroe Anti-Poverty Initiative, and the Finger Lakes Regional Economic Development Council, and was a leading advocate for the University joining the Empire AI consortium.

Strategic Planning

Upon his promotion in 1996, Robinson appointed strong deputies within strategic and space planning and marketing, restructuring them as independent, sister functions. Betty Oppenheimer, who had been instrumental in the crafting of the ambulatory expansion plan and Stein's strategic plan, was promoted to director of Strategic Planning. With a strong history in project and institutional planning, Oppenheimer began monitoring the Stein plan's implementation. She also worked with the SON leadership to produce a turnaround plan, helped organize the integration of the Eastman Dental Center with SMD to form the EIOH, and drafted strategic plans for URMC CEO Mac Evarts. Upon Oppenheimer's retirement, Sean Ossont, MBA, became associate VP for Strategic Planning. He, along with Katy Stevenson, was instrumental in developing strategic plans for both Berk and Taubman before leaving to form his own consulting business.

Space Planning

With plans that called for substantial growth in facilities, an institutional approach was needed to ensure the efficient and optimized use of the Medical Center's on- and off-campus square footage. Robinson named Mary Ockenden, MPA, as the inaugural director of Space Planning, making URMC among the first of its peers to establish Space Planning as a function distinct yet adjacent to Finance and Strategic Planning. For nearly thirty years, Ockenden would instill inclusive, data-driven decision-making around the use of space, and a collective appreciation for making the "highest and best use" of our facilities and equipment through a series of facilities masterplans.

Figure 79.3. Mary Ockenden

In addition to overseeing the completion of the Ambulatory Expansion project, Ockenden led planning for the construction of KMRB with adjacent education space—a project remarkably completed in just two years. The result was a building that through its very design fostered team science. In this process, URMC was among the first to apply productivity metrics to research space. Simultaneously, new problem-based learning rooms and classrooms were added to support Dean Hundert's new Double Helix Curriculum.

Over the last twenty-five years, Space Planning has driven hundreds of clinical capital projects/renovations as well, such as the WCI, the GCH, and the planning and construction for the current Strong Expansion Project—always reflecting patient needs, faculty efficiency, and changing standards of care.

Space Planning has also spearheaded numerous, major off-campus faculty offices and practices, as well as clinic space, to ease access and decompress the main Medical Center campus. Space Planning's original scope also included the oversight of the University's Real Estate function, which was expanding as more programs sought to relocate to leased or purchased properties. Over the last twenty-five years, on-campus square-footage has grown by 250 percent to 5.4 million square feet, and leased space has increased more than six-fold to 2 million square feet. Centralization led to smarter decisions as to whether to lease or purchase off-campus space, consistent approaches to lease negotiation, and choices that reflected the broader institutional interest.

Upon Ockenden's retirement from full-time in 2020, Amber Foster, EdD, a graduate of the Warner School of Education, was named senior director of Space Design, Operations Excellence, and Administrative Services. During her tenure, Foster will have overseen two of the largest expansions in URMC history—the UR Medicine Orthopaedics & Physical Performance Center and the Strong Expansion Project.

Human Resources (HR)

The transformation of URMC into a regional health system more than doubled the number of employees. In some years, more than 1,000 employees were added to the system. This put great pressure on HR, not only to oversee a huge increase in recruitment volume, but also to expand and modernize programs to address employee training, development, and wellbeing. At the turn of the century, HR was a University function, overseen by associate VP Charles Murphy. The growth in URMC's HR needs led Murphy to create the position of URMC chief HR officer (CHRO), dually reporting to him and the URMC CEO. In 2012, Jeffrey Stevens, the VP for the University of Massachusetts Memorial Healthcare in Worcester, was hired to serve as the inaugural URMC associate VP and CHRO. Stevens quickly established the HR Business Partner model, which integrated HR into the operations, finances, and strategy of URMC academic, research, and clinical departments. Stevens also introduced the Cornerstone electronic learning management system, which greatly improved workforce learning and compliance with in-service requirements.

Figure 79.4. Kathleen Gallucci

At the end of 2015, Stevens was succeeded by Kathleen Gallucci as URMC VP and CHRO. Gallucci previously held HR positions at Wegmans Food Markets, where she ultimately served as director of corporate human resources. She joined HH in 2004, serving as

CHRO and director of Lean process initiatives. In 2021, Gallucci became University VP and CHRO. Gretchen Baumer, a former HR business partner and associate director of URMC HR, was subsequently named director of HR Operations for the clinical enterprise.

During Gallucci's tenure, she has overseen the development of a URMC Compensation division, a URMC Office for Engagement and Employee Relations, and a centralized Talent Acquisition function to ease hiring and strengthen relationships with community workforce pipelines. Gallucci has overseen the creation of a five-year roadmap that includes deploying new IT systems to support new programs, policies, and benefits; a Career Pathways program to address chronic talent shortages in high-need areas and support career advancement for UR employees; a Career Path Modernization project that standardized job structures, titles, and payscales; and myURHR, which allows employees to report time, and access payroll, benefits, and recruiting information.

Marketing

Clare Heffernan was named director of Marketing in 1996. Throughout her tenure, Heffernan's focus was on growing referrals for SMH's clinical programs by developing and placing marketing collateral throughout the region. Upon the affiliation with HH, she developed the first system branding, using Strong Health as the moniker for the emerging health network. Heffernan was also the first to use paid advertising, partnering with Excellus Blue Cross/Blue Shield to promote a jointly owned, limited-panel insurance product, StrongCare. She left the position in 1999 and was succeeded as chief marketing officer by Suzanne Sawyer, a recruit from Penn State Geisinger Health System. Sawyer established typographic and usage consistency to improve the coherence of the brand. Working with Dean Goldsmith, she also developed a major branding campaign that touted Project Believe, URMC's pledge to improve community health.

Karl Withers, MBA, succeeded Sawyer in 2007 as chief marketing officer. As the health care network grew and more affiliations were established, both Strong Health and URMC had limited utility as a network brand. Withers conducted extensive constituent research, dug deep into the organization's history, and studied CEO Berk's strategic plan. The result was new branding whose authenticity emanated from the words of URMC's founders, "Medicine of the Highest Order." Speaking to the aspirations of its workforce and patients alike, the

Figure 79.5.
Karl Withers

positioning phrase was enthusiastically adopted throughout the organization. Simultaneously, the health system's name was changed to UR Medicine, touting its valued connection to the University across all affiliates. This powerful brand was cited by new affiliates as one of the reasons they chose to join UR Medicine. Although Marketing's focus on providers remains strong, the function has expanded to digital advertising and works closely with colleagues in Public Relations and Web Services to ensure consistent branding and grow reputation.

Public Relations and Communications

Stein's plan for new space and exciting new faculty recruitments created an unprecedented opportunity to refresh the story of URMC's regional and national role in academic medicine. The University became seen as the bright spot in a regional economy that was suffering reductions in Rochester's manufacturing employers. The spotlight shone both ways, leading to greater public appreciation but also a demand for transparency—particularly around outcomes, safety, cost, and employment issues.

In 1999, Teri D'Agostino was named director of Public Relations and Communications (PRC) and charged with reinvigorating URMC's relationships with local, regional, and national media. She took over for David Irwin, who transferred to build the function at HH. D'Agostino had joined the University the previous year after overseeing the communications functions at RRH (then known as ViaHealth). She would directly lead URMC's PRC function until 2015, when she became chief of staff for URMC CEO Mark Taubman.

Figure 79.6.
Teri D'Agostino

Moving away from a traditional structure with distinct media relations and publications teams, PRC writers were reassigned to cover specific departments, labs, and programs, with certain staff continuing to serve as editors of publications for faculty, staff, alumni, or donors. The move deepened trust with faculty and uncovered stories used to illustrate academic medicine's ability to bring cures and novel treatments as well as economic growth. The reorganization was aided by Christopher DiFrancesco, who handled corporate communications before leaving the University. However, he would return periodically to URMC, ultimately backfilling D'Agostino's role before being recruited to head communications at Columbia University's medical school.

As URMC grew and health care faced intensifying changes, it was clear that a parallel team was needed to manage internal and operational communications. Germaine Reinhardt, a former PRC leader who had moved to ISD to manage eRecord deployment communications, was coaxed back to PRC to build that function. She converted the intranet's home pages into a dynamic internal online newsroom from which information was pushed in real-time to URMC employees and faculty—with weekly news roundups that quickly became must-reads. A series of list-serves were painstakingly tailored for precision delivery of urgent and routine information. The intranet was the first leg of an emerging digital communications strategy that would grow to encompass a multitude of social media platforms.

Figure 79.7. Germaine Reinhardt

Following D'Agostino's move to the CEO's office, Reinhardt would ultimately be tapped to oversee the PRC function (which now includes Chip Partner leading the media relations function) as well as its sister departments Marketing and Web Services. Singular leadership helped build synergy among URMC's media, publications, digital, web, and advertising efforts.

Web Services

URMC's Web Services originated in the mid-1990s when Miner Library launched a website that was managed by its IT and library staff who generated content within a prototype developed by colleagues in Public Relations. Organized around content categories of news, education, research, and health care, the site, which was hosted on the Miner server, also included links to a few departments. The library managed the technology and staff assisted with content updates; the team included Jeanette Dauenhauer and Michael Hazard, who together have shaped web development and strategy for more than twenty-five years.

Within Marketing, Sharon Martinez, RN, MSN, was hired to develop a parallel Strong Health website. During Berk's term as CEO, the sites were merged into "Web Services" to blend both the programming/technology and marketing/content aspects of the sites under Martinez, reporting directly to Peter Robinson. Over the next decade, Martinez built out the applications development and ultimately formed a singular URMC website. She also worked with Richard Burton, MD, SAD for Academic Affairs, to deploy a new electronic CV platform that ensured consistent faculty profiles populated by trusted online sources, and vastly improved users' ability to connect with URMC faculty.

Martinez was succeeded by Simon School graduate Steven Brewster, MBA. During Brewster's tenure, the applications development team was moved to

ISD, allowing Web Services to concentrate on the outward-facing website. After Brewster transferred to a leadership role in ISD, Wade Holdracker became the associate VP of Web Services. Holdraker's team has undertaken an ambitious overhaul of the site to improve the experience of users by integrating with eRecord, location finding, scheduling, and adding a Chat feature. The group is also working with the University on a plan to merge all academic content onto a single platform for ease of sharing.

Office of Counsel

In keeping with his mandate to create a more centralized administration, Dean Robert Joynt charged University General Counsel Jeanine Arden-Ornt, JD, with developing a more business-focused approach in the URMC legal function. Historically, URMC's in-house counsel included a single attorney assisted by outside firms to manage clinical risk, regulatory matters, and malpractice. Given the growing complexity and opportunities of the integrated Medical Center and the prospect of a multi-institution health system, a team of in-house lawyers was needed. A graduate of Albany Law School, Arden-Ornt had joined the University in 1988 with experience in corporate and business law at Rochester- and Washington-based firms. She would prove to be a skilled recruiter, immediately hiring three new attorneys—two of whom would go on to lead the URMC Office. She was a key adviser to Stein and Robinson as they furthered the centralization process. By the time she left for a position at Case Western Reserve in 2004, several more legal experts had been added to the team.

Arden-Ornt was succeeded at the University by Susan Stewart, JD, a highly respected Rochester attorney, who established a dedicated URMC legal division as part of her portfolio, selecting Christine Burke, JD, to lead it. URMC's Office of Counsel would continue to report to the University GC through Stewart's tenure, then under Gail Norris, JD, and today to Donna Payne, JD.

Burke attended New York Law School before completing her JD at SUNY Buffalo. One of Arden-Ornt's original recruits, Burke would lead the URMC Office for thirteen years, developing strong partnerships with senior leadership and the Office of Compliance. Her team brought standardization around faculty and chair appointments, and coordinated myriad physician/organizational affiliations, management contracts, and acquisitions by, in part, developing a checklist for administrators. Thompson Health, St. James Hospital, and

Figure 79.8. Christine Burke

Jones Memorial Hospital were all acquired during this time; given her corporate experience, university counsel Norris proved invaluable in overseeing these negotiations with her URMC team. During Burke's tenure as general counsel and associate VP, the team would expand to include thirteen busy legal professionals handling corporate, health care, employment, risk management, real estate, contract, and intellectual property legal and regulatory issues.

Upon Burke's retirement in 2017, Aileen Shinaman, JD (also one of Ardent-Ornt's original recruits), was named associate VP and general counsel after a national search. A graduate of Albany Law School of Union University, Shinaman would guide the organization through dicey legal issues that arose during the COVID-19 pandemic, ensuring compliance with shifting pandemic funding rules, workforce vaccination issues, a surge in the use of telehealth, and questions about eligibility for payroll protection and loan forgiveness. At the same time, her team managed continued network growth as Strong West was established, and Finger Lakes Health joined the list of affiliates. She managed a rise in the risk of data breaches and cyberattacks, challenges to 340B financing, and compliance with price transparency regulations. Shinaman integrated the legal work among UR Medicine organizations, improving value across the network. She left in 2023 for a position as senior VP and general counsel at the Medical College of Wisconsin.

Figure 79.9. Aileen Shinaman

Following Shinaman's departure, Carla Gazes, JD, an attorney with more than twenty years of academic medical center experience, was named deputy general counsel for health sciences and chief counsel to URMC. She came to Rochester from the University of Chicago Medical Center. Gazes holds a bachelor's degree from Northwestern University and is a graduate of Loyola University Chicago School of Law, where she also earned a certificate in health law. She has additional certifications in both financial accounting and mediation.

Medical Center Board

The Medical Center Board has played an important role in the transformation of the health system. It was initially delegated by the University Board of Trustees (BOT) to provide NY State-mandated governance responsibilities over SMH and the Eastman Dental Center (now part of EIOH), establishing policy, assuring quality patient care, and providing for institutional management and planning. However, in keeping with the development and growth of the clinical health care network, interdependence with the educational and research missions, and the establishment of an integrated URMC budget, the Board's role was expanded by the BOT to include assisting in the oversight and direction of the Medical Center as a whole. Comprised of local business leaders and health organizations, the Board has enhanced relations with the community and provided feedback and support for community-facing Medical Center projects. The Board has played a particularly prominent role in the shaping and oversight of the Medical Center quality and safety initiatives. Its depth of local knowledge has been crucial in helping to identify the best sites for clinical expansion, and its financial expertise has been invaluable in integrating the Medical Center budget.

The Board has nine standing committees: Executive, Advancement, Audit and Risk Assessment, Compliance and Compensation, Facilities, Finance, Health Equity, Nominations and Board Practices, and Quality of Care. Members are appointed by the BOT upon the recommendation of the Medical Center Board and include five members of the BOT. *Ex officio* voting members include the University and Medical Center leadership; two chairs of SMD clinical departments; and a community-based SMD physician. For much of the past twenty-five years, Peter Robinson has served as the liaison between URMC leadership and the Board, overseeing Board agendas and expanding its scope. Table 79.1 lists the Board chairs (note that the term was increased to three years in 2015 by CEO Mark Taubman to provide greater continuity in light of the increasing Board role).

Table 79.1. URMC Board Chairs, 1999–2026

Board Chair	**Chair Term**
Robert H. Gutkin	1999–2001
Roger B. Friedlander	2001–4
Robert H. Hurlbut	2005–6
Thomas S. Richards	2007–8
Ronald I. Zarrella	2009–10
Robert N. Latella	2011–12
George W. Hamlin, IV	2013–14
Susan R. Holliday	2015–17
Thomas S. Richards	2018–20
Diana R. Kurty	2021–3
Anne Francis, MD	2024–6

Part VI

CONFRONTING THE COVID-19 PANDEMIC

In 2020, URMC was confronted with an unprecedented challenge brought on by the COVID-19 pandemic. Its quick response to the challenge was extraordinary and placed the Medical Center in the forefront of shaping NY State policies regarding COVID-19. The ability to act quickly and in a coordinated fashion was due in part to the integration and centralization of URMC and to the development of a broad health care system, hallmarks of the past twenty-five years. This chapter therefore serves as a fitting culmination to the changes in URMC that have been chronicled in this book.

In late February 2020, as the NY City experience with COVID-19 escalated, email was sent by URMC administration to all clinicians containing basic information about COVID-19, outlining policies for triage, diagnosis, isolation of suspected COVID-19 patients, and providing guidance on safety procedures for treating them. An intranet portal, housing all information about COVID-19, went live on March 1.

On March 9, the Medical Center convened the COVID-19 Emergency Operations Center (EOC) to coordinate the many teams that had been preparing for a potential outbreak in Rochester. The EOC was led by SMH COO Kathy Parrinello and SMH CMO Mike Apostolakos, MD, and included leadership from all UR Medicine facilities, home care, and clinical departments, as well as representatives from employee health, supply chain, infection prevention, department of public safety, operations, nursing, communications, information technology, and informaticists. A process was put in place by Apostolakos and Robert M. Mayo, MD, the CMO of RHH, to assure that there would be uniform policies in Rochester for issues such as visitation rules, masking, use of personal protective equipment (PPE), etc.

Paul Graman, MD (Infectious Diseases), clinical director of infectious diseases at SMH, was also named to the leadership team. Graman, who received his MD and completed his fellowship in infectious diseases at URMC, was among NY State's leading epidemiologists and had led a Rochester-wide collaboration to reduce *C. difficile* infections. For more than two years, EOC meetings occurred daily, and then decreased in frequency until the EOC was disbanded in 2023.

Figure 80.1.
Paul Graman

The first confirmed case of COVID-19 in Rochester was identified on March 11. This led to the initiation of a daily countywide group, hosted by Monroe County Executive Adam Bello and including Michael D. Mendoza, MD, MPH, the Commissioner of Public Health for Monroe County. Among the early topics of discussion was preparing the region for the potential of a large-scale infection that could overwhelm hospital capacity, and addressing requests by the state to send equipment to NY City, where hospitals' capacities were overwhelmed.

On March 16, the URMC microbiology/virology laboratory, led by Dwight J. Hardy, PhD, began to run COVID-19 testing. The ability of URMC to quickly ramp up testing played a critical role in the region's response to managing the pandemic and was facilitated by the recent expansion of Pathology and Laboratory Medicine and move to the Bailey Road facility. It also involved extensive efforts by faculty and technical staff to keep up with a constantly changing landscape of types of tests and testing requirements.

On March 19, the EOC made the unprecedented decision to reduce patient volumes by postponing all non-essential surgeries, procedures, and imaging. This preceded the NY State mandate, which required similar reductions for all health systems until early May and established stringent inpatient occupancy requirements to assure bed availability for COVID-19 patients. On March 30, the EOC adopted universal masking in all UR Medicine facilities, again prior to any regulatory mandates, and required ambulatory sites provide social distancing in waiting rooms and electronic screening for symptoms.

The EOC also recommended that the faculty switch to video visits for appropriate ambulatory patients. Coincidentally, the eConsult program had been launched in January 2020 as part of URMC's "Digital First" strategic plan. URMC was able to quickly ramp up consults, going from a few consults on March 16 to approximately 4,000 consults on March 24 and approximately 6,000 in April. The digital health expertise of GCH physician-in-chief Patrick Brophy, MD, helped ensure that comprehensive pediatric services were available and that children throughout the Finger Lakes were able to maintain their routine immunizations and wellness visits when many other health systems struggled.

The EIOH was one of the only providers in NY State open for emergency dental services during the COVID-19 pandemic and treated patients from forty-eight counties. EIOH's teledentistry program became one of the most important tools for triaging and managing dental patients in a safe and timely fashion.

Within two days of the announced state of emergency, Human Resources established a Child Care Center in the SON, which remained active until July 2021. A second site on the University campus developed in partnership with the YMCA remained open until spring 2022. HR also took the lead in providing staffing continuity and safety, developing a formal Remote Work Policy that allowed for hybrid or fully remote roles. It also established the Office for Out-of-State Employment to manage compliance for remote employees across thirty-five states. URMC also initiated weekly video sessions to keep the community up to date with issues related to disease incidence and prevalence, treatment and isolation protocols, testing, vaccinations, etc. AHP played a particularly important role in this process, helping to establish standard procedures for ambulatory facilities and facilitating the distribution of PPE from the Medical Center to practices throughout the community.

With PPE in short supply at the onset of the pandemic, hospitalists took over bedside evaluations for some specialties (e.g. neurology, cardiology) and performed some nursing skills to minimize donning, doffing, and potential exposures. Hospitalists led multiple innovations, including COVID-only teams, processes for vaccinating inpatients, positioning non-intubated patients, caring for patients on medium-flow oxygen in ICU step-down units, and caring for geriatric COVID-recovered patients. A medical admitting officer team was initiated to remove the burden from Emergency Medicine of having to spend time determining appropriate inpatient teams for complex patients.

URMC teams were quick to innovate to help keep staff safe. The pharmacy produced extra hand-sanitizer, URell; a mechanism was developed to resterilize N95 respirators which were in scarce supply; and the orthotics and prosthetics team of the Orthopaedics department manufactured face shields. The Shared Service Center warehousing capabilities enabled the Pharmacy to compile a list of approximately 120 critical drugs that were then stockpiled at the Cold Storage Core to assure greater than six months of inventory. Unlike many of its peer organizations, URMC never ran out critical drugs.

Because oral health providers work near the patient's nose and mouth, dentists felt especially vulnerable. In May, EIOH led a global discussion with experts from five countries and seven universities on COVID-19 safety measures and research opportunities. Yanfang Ren, DDS, PhD, MPH, and his team published two highly publicized papers providing an evidence-based assessment of the risk for dental health care professionals. Because COVID-19 was transmissible via airborne particles, adequate ventilation was determined to be critical for patient and provider safety. Ren developed a widely used protocol to help dentists and other providers easily determine the ventilation rate, measured in air change per hour for any room in any clinical situation.

Particularly striking was the development by the Health Lab of "Dr. Chat Bot," an automated, online tool that asked several questions related to symptoms and health to help determine whether it was safe to report to work. Dr. Chat Bot was extended to the entire University of Rochester and subsequently as a ROC COVID screening tool that was launched in thirteen counties in the Finger Lakes region. The Health Lab also helped develop a patient monitoring system used by UR Home Care and the PCN to treat COVID-19 patients at home.

Because of the stay-at-home order issued by NY State Governor Cuomo and diligent social distancing in the Rochester area, the first wave of hospitalized COVID patients in Rochester was not overwhelming. Together with the pause in elective surgeries, SMH census dropped to the lowest levels experienced since the late 1990s. This enabled URMC to send a clinical team to Northwell Health on Long Island to help with their enormous COVID-19 patient surge. It also enabled URMC to be the first center approved by NY State to reinstitute elective surgery.

A high point in the University's response to COVID-19 was its approach to safety in the UR Medicine skilled nursing facilities. This included the early use of PPE, universal masking, strict limits on visitation, and the utilization of Dr. Chat Bot to screen everyone who might have contact with patients. This aggressive stance was in sharp contrast to many other such facilities. As a result, during the first wave of the pandemic, UR Medicine skilled nursing facilities experienced no COVID-19 outbreaks, in contrast to the widely criticized epidemics that led to large numbers of fatalities in many nursing homes throughout the state.

In contrast to the spring of 2020, the second wave of COVID-19 in the following fall and winter was accompanied by a huge increase in hospitalizations, with a peak daily census of 260 COVID-19 patients at SMH. The daily total census surged to over 900 patients, requiring teams to reconfigure much of the clinical spaces. HH experienced a similar increase in COVID-19 patients, with total occupancy routinely exceeding the number of licensed beds. At SMH, a separate post-surgery ICU was created in the post-anesthesia room, so that other ICU beds could be used to handle the large number of COVID-19 patients. At one point one of the campus surgical centers was closed, so that staff could be redeployed to the hospital campus—a dramatic example of the best in teamwork across the UR Medicine network.

On December 15, the COVID-19 vaccine became available. URMC was designated by NY State as the coordinator of the Finger Lakes COVID-19 Vaccine Hub and Task Force, led by Nancy Bennett, MD. URMC Employee Health organized numerous vaccination clinics for health care workers, and the ambulatory and primary care teams worked valiantly in following all the rigorous state requirements regarding the order in which the public could be vaccinated.

A third COVID-19 wave occurred in the fall of 2021 and winter of 2022. By the second wave, URMC affiliates at FF Thompson and Noyes Memorial Hospital had ramped up their capabilities of handling all but the sickest COVID-19 patients. This enabled UR Medicine to balance COVID-19 hospitalization across the system, enabling SMH to maintain its inpatient and outpatient surgical services. In contrast, other systems were required by the state to reduce their elective procedures. By April 2023, SMH had cared for over 8,500 hospitalized patients with COVID-19. By year three of the pandemic, the virus had lost virulence. Although rates of infectivity were still quite high, patients with the virus often could be managed in the community on isolation, and because those hospitalized did not have the same degree of complications experienced in the pandemic's early years, most did not require ICU care.

The COVID-19 pandemic had a profound effect on URMC's educational programs. In keeping with the stay-at-home approach to limiting disease spread, all in-person classes were suspended throughout the University and the faculty quickly pivoted to providing online education, which remained in place for over a year. However, the Medical Center had special challenges for clinical programs that required direct patient contact and for graduate students working predominantly in research laboratories.

The AAMC instituted weekly meetings for medical school deans to develop a uniform response to the education of medical students. Initially, it was recommended that students not participate in activities involving direct patient contact. This was in part due to the scarcity of PPE, which needed to be prioritized to those in the front lines of patient care. It also appeared prudent to get a better understanding of how best to protect caregivers from contracting COVID-19 before exposing medical students. However, understanding how to deal with a pandemic was felt to be an important part of the educational experience. Because most medical students had far more credit hours than required for graduation, the NY State Department of Health allowed fourth-year students to graduate early. This enabled some SMD graduates to volunteer their services to hospitals in NY City. By June, medical students were able to resume their clinical rotations and to participate in small problem-based learning groups using PPE and appropriate distancing. Unlike the medical students, residents and fellows continued their clinical activities. Like with clinical staff, the early and rigorous use of PPE, masking, and Dr. Chat Bot proved highly successful in limiting the number of house staff contracting COVID-19 from patients.

Another great challenge for URMC lay in securing its research programs. Stephen Dewhurst, PhD, SMD vice dean for research, convened a group that established policies for conducting research during the initial wave of COVID-19. Laboratory personnel were initially reduced to the bare minimum necessary to complete experiments that were already in process, to maintain important stocks of cells and other biologicals, and to maintain animal colonies. Graduate student classes were conducted online, but most graduate students remained at home and did not participate in bench research. Fortunately, students and other laboratory personnel were allowed back into the laboratory by June.

Clinical research programs faced other challenges. In general, new protocols were deferred to keep participants away from health care facilities and to limit exposure of researchers to people who might have COVID-19. Also, COVID-19 infections might significantly interfere with the interpretation of results. Those protocols that were already ongoing were maintained for participants already enrolled in the study, unless they could be safely deferred. In addition, trials involving potentially life-saving treatments were maintained. Nevertheless, there was a marked reduction in clinical trials for more than a year, in part due to the reluctance of people to spend time in health care facilities.

Although the research programs generally were able to get back to normal operations by the middle of the summer of 2020, many programs did experience significant disruption, including the availability of supplies and reagents. Accordingly, the University decided to extend the tenure clock for one year for those who requested it. In addition, SMD extended academic appointments for those whose work was significantly affected by the pandemic.

Despite these challenges, URMC played a major role in COVID-19-related research. In fact, URMC's COVID-19 website had so many hits that URMC was invited by Google to be one of the institutions to respond to questions related to COVID-19 research and biology. URMC researchers were at the forefront in efforts to understand the COVID-19 virus and the durability of immune response to coronavirus infection, and to develop new therapies and vaccines. The Vaccine and Treatment Evaluation Unit, directed by Angela Branche, MD, one of ten NIH-funded sites focused on the development of vaccines and treatments for respiratory viruses, was actively involved in COVID-19 research, helping to conduct natural history, therapeutic, and vaccine studies. URMC was a site for phase 3 clinical trials for coronavirus vaccines being developed by Pfizer/BioNTech and AstraZeneca/University of Oxford.

URMC researchers were also involved in studying the anti-viral drug remdesivir and in evaluating several other potential coronavirus therapies, including convalescent plasma, monoclonal antibodies, and immunosuppressive drugs. Christopher Palma, MD, ScM (Allergy, Immunology, and Rheumatology), currently the medical director for the URMC Clinical Research Center and the director of Research Services for CTSI, served as director for the COVID Interventional Trials Working Group, which coordinated many of these efforts. Researchers in Pediatrics led trials for multiple pediatric COVID vaccines, and a study published in 2021 about the

COVID mRNA vaccine's interaction with breast milk was one of the top-ten most-cited articles of the year in *JAMA Pediatrics.*

PHS played an important role in community engagement during the COVID-19 pandemic. Convened by Anne Dozier, several faculty, along with experts from UR Medicine, RRH, the Monroe County Department of Health and Common Ground Health (CGH, a local health planning agency), conducted iterative modeling to project the impact of pandemic-related hospitalizations. With the University of Rochester Health Lab and CGH, PHS co-led a Mother Cabrini Foundation-funded text-message-based symptom surveillance tracker across the county. PHS also joined with the Center for Community Health and Prevention, the CTSI, and CGH to address COVID-19 vaccine hesitancy in rural communities, supported by funding from the CDC.

With the suspension of most outpatient services and the reduction in inpatient census to accommodate potential COVID-19 patients, URMC faced huge financial challenges, with losses averaging $25 million per week. The River Campus also faced substantial challenges related to the suspension of classes and programs, the shift to online learning, and the lack of students on campus. This ultimately led to furloughing approximately 4,000 staff at the University; fortunately, most were brought back by the end of the summer. At URMC, a faculty group led by Neurology chair Robert Holloway was convened to make recommendations on potential salary reductions (senior leadership at URMC and the University had taken twenty percent pay cuts at the beginning of May). The group recommended a reduction in salary beginning in the new academic year, July 1, 2020. However, approximately 200 faculty offered to begin the reductions in May to help handle the immediate losses. Ultimately, the University made recommendations that included salary reductions and benefit reductions for faculty and higher-paid staff.

Although URMC experienced losses in FY2020, the rapid clinical turnaround in outpatient procedures and inpatient volumes, coupled with federal funds from the Coronavirus Aid, Relief, and Economic Security (CARES) Act, enabled URMC to return to solid financial footing. With that, the University was able to end salary reductions by the beginning of 2021 and even restore part of the benefit reductions.

Part VII

EPILOGUE

Figure 81.1.
David C. Linehan

As we close the chapter on a century of excellence, discovery, training, and service, we pause to reflect on the remarkable progress and growth of our health system and academic medical center over the past twenty-five years. Since our seventy-fifth anniversary, our academic medical center has evolved in unimaginable ways. We endured many challenges, each testing our resolve and commitment to our missions. Our mission remains clear. Our patients need the expert care we provide, the workforce that we train, and the impactful research that improves health outcomes.

In the last twenty-five years we have grown from a two-hospital partnership between SMH and HH to a comprehensive health system with eight hospitals and over 250 sites of service where we provide expert health care for Greater Rochester, the Southern Tier, the Finger Lakes, and beyond. We have completed several major capital projects such as the WCC, the GCH, and the Saunders Center for Orthopaedics and Physical Performance, to name a few. We are so excited about the Strong Expansion Project currently under construction, which will include a tripling of our ED capacity and a state-of-the-art inpatient tower that will enhance our specialty care with expanded, private, and modern rooms for our patients. This represents the largest capital project in the history of the University of Rochester.

We not only met but advanced our missions through the past twenty-five years and through challenging times, including a global health crisis, transitions in care delivery in the digital age, workforce burnout, and the need to reaffirm the public trust in the role that an academic health system plays in advancing medicine. We engaged our community partners in innovative ways to improve health outcomes for all patients.

Each challenge has strengthened our resolve and inspired impactful change. As we reflect on these years, we carry forward not only the lessons learned but the unwavering commitment to the mission and values that are both the bedrock of our success and a springboard to our future.

As we look towards the next twenty-five, fifty, even 100 years, the future is bright and we are well equipped to lead the way! We recognize that the future of medicine will not be defined by any one discipline, technology, or institution—but by our ability to adapt, to listen, to create high-performing, interdisciplinary teams, and to continue to lead with a shared purpose anchored by our core values. As scientists, caregivers, teachers, learners, innovators, health care workers, community members, and advocates together, we will not only respond to the future—we will shape it.

We are one team with one purpose, to help each other and humanity do better, feel better, and live better, and to *be ever better* for the people who entrust us with their lives. So, let's not spend too much time congratulating ourselves on the last 100 years of remarkable accomplishments. There is much hard work ahead, and each one of us here today plays a crucial role in optimizing health and alleviating suffering for all the patients that we serve. I am so thankful for all of the dedicated and inspired team members who are with me on this amazing journey. While all of the expanded facilities and capital improvements are wonderful, it is the *people* whose time and talents have shaped the last century and who will lead us into the next century of *Boundless Possibility*.

Meliora!

David C. Linehan
CEO University of Rochester Medical Center
Dean of the School of Medicine and Dentistry
Senior VP for Health Affairs

Part VIII

NOTES ON CONTRIBUTORS

Mark B. Taubman, MD, is a vascular biologist and cardiologist who was recruited to the University of Rochester Medical Center in 2003 to be chief of Cardiology and to establish the Aab Cardiovascular Research Institute. He subsequently served as chair of the Department of Medicine and for fourteen years as dean of the School of Medicine and Dentistry. During his last nine years as dean, he also served as CEO of the Medical Center. In 2024, he became Emeritus dean and CEO.

Leo Brideau is a hospital administrator with more than fifty years' experience. He is a former CEO of Strong Memorial Hospital, as well as a former Regional CEO for Ascension Health, the nation's largest health system. He currently serves as an advisor to University of Rochester Medical Center leadership.

Teri D'Agostino led Communications functions in Rochester health systems for nearly forty years. In 2015, she was named Chief of Staff for University of Rochester Medical Center CEO and School of Medicine and Dentistry Dean Mark Taubman, a position she held till her retirement in 2023.

INDEX

Page numbers in *italics* indicate figures; page numbers in **bold** indicate tables.

www.ingramcontent.com/pod-product-compliance
Lightning Source LLC
LaVergne TN
LVHW010552100826
845148LV00014B/2692

* 9 7 8 1 6 4 8 2 5 1 7 4 0 *